Beating the Dharma Drum: India Writings II

THE COMPLETE WORKS OF SANGHARAKSHITA include all his previously published work, as well as talks, seminars, and writings published here for the first time. The collection represents the definitive edition of his life's work as Buddhist writer and teacher. For further details, including the contents of each volume, please turn to the 'Guide' on pp. 737–45.

FOUNDATION

1 A Survey of Buddhism / The Buddha's Noble Eightfold Path
2 The Three Jewels I
3 The Three Jewels II
4 The Bodhisattva Ideal
5 The Purpose and Practice of Buddhist Meditation
6 The Essential Sangharakshita

INDIA

7 Crossing the Stream: India Writings I
8 Beating the Dharma Drum: India Writings II
9 Dr Ambedkar and the Revival of Buddhism I
10 Dr Ambedkar and the Revival of Buddhism II

THE WEST

11 A New Buddhist Movement I
12 A New Buddhist Movement II
13 Eastern and Western Traditions

COMMENTARY

MEMOIRS

POETRY AND THE ARTS

COMPLETE WORKS 8 **INDIA**

Sangharakshita

Beating the Dharma Drum: India Writings II

EDITED BY VIDYADEVI

w

Windhorse Publications
38 Newmarket Road
Cambridge CB5 8DT

info@windhorsepublications.com
www.windhorsepublications.com

First published in 2023.

Cover design by Dhammarati
Cover images: Front: Sangharakshita in India, 1967. Courtesy of Urgyen Sangharakshita Trust
Back flap: Sangharakshita and Dhardo Rimpoche, 1967. Courtesy of Urgyen Sangharakshita Trust

Typesetting and layout by Tarajyoti
Printed by Bell & Bain Ltd, Glasgow

British Library Cataloguing in Publication Data:
A catalogue record for this book is available from the British Library.

ISBN 978-1-915342-03-4 (paperback)
ISBN 978-1-915342-02-7 (hardback)

CONTENTS

FOREWORD

by Kalyanaprabha

The Buddha's Enlightenment 2,500 years ago is, for Buddhists, the pivotal point in human history. Sitting alone under the bodhi tree on that full-moon night, after years of struggle, his mind became free of all obscuring clouds so that he could see life to its uttermost core, see the nature of existence itself, see the nature of mind itself. Though the experience transcended all possible ways of speaking about it, in due course he tried to indicate something of its nature to those with whom he came into contact, speaking of it in terms of freedom, in terms of understanding, in terms of bliss, in terms of great love. In dependence upon this event, all Buddhist history unfolds. It begins with the Buddha and continues with the Dharma, his communication of his understanding and his explanation of the path leading to its realization. Those who were drawn to him and to his teaching and took it for their own became the Sangha. There were *bhikṣus* and *bhikṣuṇīs*, that is to say men and women who went forth from the home life into homelessness, as well as laymen and laywomen.

By the time his life ended under the *sāl* trees of Kusinārā, the Buddha had become known all over north-east India and beyond. The movement he had started quickly grew. As time rolled on there emerged great heroes who took the Buddha's teaching to distant lands, and for many centuries it flourished and spread so that according to different estimates at one time up to a quarter or even a third of the world's human population was Buddhist. But while the immense force of the Buddha's

Enlightenment conditioned events in one direction, hostile forces incessantly pulled in the contrary one. The forces of greed and hatred and delusion undermined the living spirit of the Buddha's message, bringing formalism and laziness into monasteries, letting superstition undermine the laity. In India external hostile forces in the form of Hindu assimilation and Muslim invasion were major factors in virtually wiping out the entire tradition from the land of its birth.

By the nineteenth century, Buddhism as a living tradition had long been extinct in most of India. But everywhere there were reminders of its long life, and of its decay. The ancient places where Buddhists had once gathered to meditate were deserted or had been taken over by Hindus for rituals inimical to Buddhism, even for animal sacrifice. The holy sites where, in the third century BCE, King Aśoka had proudly erected his pillars to mark where the Blessed One had been born and where he had preached his first sermon, had long been left to rack and ruin. And the Maha Bodhi temple – the temple of the Great Awakening built at the *vajrāsana*, the place where the sun of wisdom rose in the Blessed One's mind, and to which for century after century pilgrims had flocked from all corners of the Buddhist world – was barren of Buddhist activity. Hindu Brahmin priests had moved in. They left the great temple to decay and Buddhist images that had once been the objects of devotion now lay scattered here and there around the temple, exposed to the onslaught of sun, wind, and rain. A Hindu mahant[1] claimed the place as his own.

All things change. The Indian subcontinent came under British colonial rule and that meeting of East and West, though brought about by greed for wealth and power, was also the occasion of some good, for it was the British interest in archaeology and philology – brilliant minds that were able to decipher ancient scripts – that led to the rediscovery of India's ancient Buddhist tradition. Could that discovery reignite the living flame of the Dharma in the land of its birth? The first great attempt, the first name associated with the revival of Buddhism in India, is that of Anagarika Dharmapala, and it is with his story that this volume of Sangharakshita's *Complete Works* begins.

ANAGARIKA DHARMAPALA

It was after the rainy season in 1952 when, as a young *bhikṣu* living in the eastern Himalayas, Sangharakshita accepted an invitation to write a 'Biographical Sketch' of Anagarika Dharmapala for the Maha Bodhi Society's *Diamond Jubilee Souvenir*, Dharmapala having been the Society's founder. For a few weeks Sangharakshita took up residence at the Maha Bodhi Society's headquarters in Calcutta and, drawing on some twenty volumes of diaries, an unpublished biography, and the reminiscences of the *anagārika*'s disciple and successor, Devapriya Valisinha, soon found himself completely immersed in his subject. He 'lived, thought, and felt Dharmapala' – as if he actually witnessed each episode in his life as it occurred. When, after three weeks, he laid down his pen, he felt a profound sense of bereavement, as if he had lost a friend.[2] Nearly thirty years later, in a preface for a new edition of the 'Sketch',[3] he described how it had been written *con amore* – with love, with devotion or, as is meant by the musical direction, tenderly.

It is as if he found in the *anagārika* a kindred spirit. The intensity of Dharmapala's aspirations, his indefatigable – indeed extraordinary – energies dedicated to spreading the Dharma, were paralleled by Sangharakshita's own, as were some of Dharmapala's personal qualities: his loyalty to his friends and supporters, his willingness to speak out, to stand alone, to bear disappointment and betrayal. And again, Dharmapala's outlook as a Buddhist was universal. Like Sangharakshita, he related to Buddhists of all schools and in fact was part of the historic mission that for the first time connected the Theravādin Buddhists of South-east Asia with the Mahāyāna Buddhists of Japan (see pp. 29ff.). Some of Dharmapala's qualities would later find expression in Sangharakshita's life too. Dharmapala, moved to respond to the poverty created by the Hindu caste system which he observed first-hand, travelled from village to village in a bullock cart to speak to the village people about the Buddha's teachings – as would Sangharakshita. To bring the Dharma to the hearts and minds of people in the West, Dharmapala travelled all around the globe – as, too, would Sangharakshita.

Such lives are rare indeed. Perhaps for the modern reader, in an age that does not like to 'look up', but prefers to dwell on weaknesses and faults, the challenge is how to relate to the story of a life expressive of such single-minded energy and dedication. Perhaps the idealism of the youthful Sangharakshita, writing out of his deeply-felt resonance with Dharmapala, can draw us in.

A biographer has the task of placing his subject in context and this meant explaining the circumstances of colonial Ceylon into which

Dharmapala was born. Less attention has been drawn to the effects of European colonialism on freedom of religious practice than to the extremes of brutality that accompanied the kind of colonialism Joseph Conrad wrote about in *The Heart of Darkness*. Some of what we encounter in the 'Sketch' may be shocking; as indeed Sangharakshita's attacks on the excesses of Christian missionaries and politicians in Asia elsewhere in this volume may take some readers aback. A little further on in this foreword, I attempt to give an explanation of his position and why he may have written in this vein.

Dharmapala's earlier life is interwoven with the history of the Theosophical Society in India and Ceylon (nowadays Sri Lanka), but most central to his life was the battle for Buddhist control of the Maha Bodhi temple at Bodh Gaya. On his first visit to Bodh Gaya, aged 29, he 'at last stood face to face with his destiny'. Seeing the neglected state of Buddhism's most holy site, and the desecration of Buddhist images, he took a great vow to protect the place. The violence, intrigues, and intransigency of the Hindu party led by the mahant give a sense of the implacable forces with which Buddhism in India has had to contend.

One of the discoveries Sangharakshita made through reading Dharmapala's diaries was that, as well as being a tireless activist on behalf of Buddhism, with the support of his great patroness, Mary E. Foster (about whose significance for Dharmapala there is a short article in this volume), the *anagārika* also had a vivid inner life and was drawn to meditation. In the Ceylon of those days the practice had largely been forgotten but eventually he learned to meditate and kept up a daily practice throughout his life. He also read and reflected deeply on the Dharma, as his sixty-five 'Immortal Sayings', also presented in this volume, vividly demonstrate. These were put together by Sangharakshita and published in a tiny booklet by the Maha Bodhi Society in the Buddha Jayanti year of 1957 to commemorate the *anagārika*'s ninety-third birth anniversary. When, in September of that same year, Sangharakshita came to write an editorial to mark the *anagārika*'s birthday, he called the piece 'A Modern Bodhisattva'. The bodhisattva ideal, he said, was not just 'a beautiful dream', as one Christian writer had remarked, but a living reality. Dharmapala's life illustrated the practice of all ten of the *pāramitās*, or transcending virtues, to which a bodhisattva is dedicated. At that time, Sangharakshita had just completed his *A Survey of Buddhism*, in which he declared that 'the bodhisattva ideal is the perfectly ripened fruit of the whole vast tree of Buddhism'.[4] In his short article *Dharmapala: The Spiritual Dimension*, first published in India in 1992, he cites the beautiful words from the *Ratnagotravibhāga* which epitomize the life of the bodhisattva, and which the life of Dharmapala seems to exemplify:

> Like a fire his mind constantly blazes up into good works for others;
> At the same time he always remains merged in the calm of the trances and formless attainments.

Dharmapala, the great *dharmadūta*, or messenger of the Dharma, appears on the Triratna 'Refuge Tree' as a figure of inspiration, devotion, and respect. His birthday is celebrated not only by the Maha Bodhi Society, but also by the Indian wing of the movement Sangharakshita went on to found (now the Triratna Bauddha Mahasangha). Perhaps more people in Triratna outside of India will come to mark his birthday, celebrating and taking inspiration from his life.

HIMAVANTAVASI: IN THE LIGHT OF THE DHAMMA

It was in the year following the composition of the 'Biographical Sketch' that Sangharakshita took up his pen to write again for the Maha Bodhi Society, this time for its monthly journal, the *Maha Bodhi*. He wrote under a pseudonym, 'Himavantavasi', which means 'Dweller in the Snowy Mountains', a name suggested by his friend, Ananda Kausalyayan. Himavantavasi was a Buddhist hermit living in the Himalayas who had little direct contact with the outside world, but did get to know, especially through various magazines and journals that miraculously found their way to his retreat, what was going on in the Buddhist world, and sometimes in the wider world too. A series of pieces, with the title 'In the Light of the Dhamma', record his responses to what he heard, from the hypocrisy of established religion to Buddhist films, from the mispronunciation of Pāli to the Buddha image in contemporary art. We find Sangharakshita wielding the sword of his intellectual acuity, challenging harmful views and stupidity, seeking always to bring a Dharmic perspective, and writing with a refreshing wit that at times seems reminiscent of eighteenth-century *literati*. Nor does Himavantavasi fail to rejoice when there is some development in the Buddhist world that deserves recognition and salute. This includes a moment of poignancy for the contemporary reader in 2022: U Nu, Prime Minister of Burma, is saluted for the tolerance shown to Muslims in his country.[5] Sangharakshita's wide reading in Western philosophy and literature is reflected in pieces that refer to Schopenhauer, Amiel, Rolland, and Gide.

As Sangharakshita later recalled, 'Though the views to which I gave expression were very much my own, the manner in which I gave expression to them was not, in the sense that it was not quite the manner in which I would have expressed them had I been writing under my own name.'[6] Himavantavasi was able to say things that Sangharakshita could not – especially the Sangharakshita who, in January 1954, became the editor of the *Maha Bodhi* journal. Sangharakshita once told me that there had been *bhikṣus* – to whom he must have revealed the identity of Himavantavasi – who told him that privately they agreed with what he wrote, but confessed they would never have dared say it publicly and were glad that he did. Himavantavasi's contributions continued until the end of 1955, after which the hermit seems to have gone into permanent retreat.

BEATING THE DRUM

> To set rolling the wheel of Dhamma
> I go to the city of Kāsi.
> In a world become blind,
> I beat the drum of the Deathless[7]

> Go ye, O Bhikkhus, and wander forth for the gain of the many, the welfare of the many, in compassion for the world, for the good, for the gain, for the welfare of gods and men. Proclaim, O Bhikkhus, the doctrine glorious. Preach ye a life of holiness, perfect and pure.[8]

The Editor and the Maha Bodhi Society's Governing Body

When Devapriya Valisinha, General Secretary of the Maha Bodhi Society and editor of its journal, wrote to Sangharakshita in the later months of 1953 asking him to relieve him of the burden of editing the *Maha Bodhi*,

Sangharakshita naturally understood that he was being asked to take on the editorial chair. Although in theory there was an editorial board, Valisinha explained that its members left the work to him and showed little or no interest in the journal's production, though they sometimes liked to criticize it. At a meeting of the Society's Governing Body in January 1954, when the new editor was already in Calcutta taking on the work of bringing out the journal, Valisinha therefore proposed that Sangharakshita should be officially appointed editor of the Society's monthly publication. His proposal met with fierce opposition from the (majority) Hindu members of the Governing Body and it was only with difficulty that the General Secretary persuaded that band of devotees of 'International Buddhist Brotherhood' to accept Sangharakshita onto the editorial board at all.

It might seem ironic that the Governing Body of the Society founded by Dharmapala, who had fought so long and so hard against Hindu intransigence at Bodh Gaya, should be dominated by caste Hindus, and even stranger that a Buddhist monk willing to take on the editorial responsibilities of the Society's Buddhist journal should be the object of this intense anti-Buddhist feeling. The reason the Hindu members of the Maha Bodhi Society's Governing Body opposed Sangharakshita's appointment as editor was that they regarded him as anti-Hindu. They regarded him as anti-Hindu because he had spoken out publicly against the caste system. He had even had something published in the *Maha Bodhi* that in their eyes proved his anti-Hindu position. This was a review of a new translation of the great sixteenth-century Indian poet Tulsidas's *Rāmacaritamānasa*. Though conceding there were passages of great artistic merit, the reviewer wrote that as a whole the work was 'sadly marred by sectarian bias, devotional extravagance carried almost to the point of frenzy, and social orthodoxy in its more repulsive form'.[9] This last referred to the brahmin poet's recommendation that a brahmin was to be worshipped, even though he possessed all the vices, whilst a low-caste Shudra was to be despised, however virtuous he might be.

In a speech at the International Congress of the World Fellowship of Faiths held at Calcutta University that same month (January 1954), Sangharakshita made it clear that Buddhism rejected the idea of God, a statement that deeply upset a Hindu dignitary who was present and cannot have endeared him to the Maha Bodhi Society governors, had any of them come to hear of it. For Hindus, Buddhism was simply a branch of the parent tree that was Hinduism. The Buddha was not an Enlightened human being but an avatar of the god Vishnu. Hinduism, in fact, encompassed Buddhism. This was not, of course, the Buddhist view – and nor was it the view of all Hindus. Considering the fate of the Buddhist tradition in his native country, it is said that Swami Vivekananda, founder of the Ramakrishna Mission, put it like this: 'Hinduism killed Buddhism with a loving embrace.' No wonder Sangharakshita insisted on making the distinctive tenets of Buddhism clear. For Dharmapala, too, 'the only refuge for him who aspires to true perfection is the Buddha alone'. How was it, then, that Dharmapala had allowed members of the Governing Body of his Maha Bodhi Society to include Hindus? This is a question that deserves more thorough treatment. Suffice it to say that while Dharmapala clearly distinguished between Hinduism and Buddhism, his own lofty ideals sought to bring men together in the spirit of brotherhood and he was inclined to trust rather than otherwise. Sangharakshita, however, saw the deep divisions that were created in an organization when those who held office within it did not share its fundamental ideals. When he came to set up his own spiritual movement, he was adamant that those who held positions of responsibility should be committed Buddhists.

The same anomaly existed with regard to the Society's president. For nearly forty years the president had been a Bengali brahmin. Sir Ashutosh Mookerjee had been the first. The third and most recent holder of this office was his son, Syama Prasad Mookerjee, who was not only a Hindu but president of a right-wing Hindu political party. In his first meeting with Sangharakshita, Dr Ambedkar's first utterance was: 'Why does your Maha Bodhi Society have a Bengali Brahmin for its president?'[10] Ambedkar was not the only one to question this. The sudden and unexpected death of Syama Prasad Mookerjee had the usually diffident Devapriya Valisinha resorting to a little cunning to ensure a change took place. The president of the Maha Bodhi Society was elected to office by the Governing Body. The dozen or so *bhikṣus* supported by the Society were *ipso facto* members of that Body, but they lived far away from Calcutta and could not afford to travel to meetings to vote, the other governors having refused to allow them travel expenses. With the election pending, Devapriya Valisinha wrote to them apprising them of the situation and offering to pay their travel expenses out of his own pocket if they would come to the meeting and cast their vote. His strategy was successful: a Buddhist president, the Maharajkumar of Sikkim, was voted in as fourth president. The Hindu members of the Society, shocked and dismayed, accused the Buddhists of narrow-mindedness, bigotry, and sectarianism.

Sixty years later, such sentiments were still being expressed. In an on-line article published by the *Times of India* on 28 September 2008 entitled, 'Now Hindus Can't Head the Maha Bodhi Society' we read the following:

> KOLKATA: Buddha wasn't born as Buddhist? Sorry, even he can't be the president of the Mahabodhi Society of India. Following changes in its rules enforced here on Saturday only born-Buddhists are eligible.... These amendments will change the constitution of Mahabodhi which had Ashutosh Mukherjee, Manmatha Nath Mookerjee and Shyama Prasad Mukherjee as presidents between 1911 and 1953.

What Dharmapala would have said about this new policy it is hard to guess. While it apparently ensures Buddhist governance, it excludes all those who, rather than being 'born Buddhist', make a spiritual commitment to the Three Jewels in this lifetime. And of course it allows those who are only nominally Buddhist to take office. To be born into a Buddhist family does *not* make one a Buddhist in the true sense. Once again one scents beneath the outwardly religious sentiment the rank whiff of politics.

It is, then, not surprising that when they met in January 1954, the Maha Bodhi Society's Governing Body refused to allow Sangharakshita to take up the editorial chair but insisted that he only be allowed to squeeze onto an editorial settee, which officially, at least, would be shared with the rest of the editorial board.[11] It is for this reason that although he produced every volume of the *Maha Bodhi* journal for more than a decade, he is never credited with being more than an ordinary member of the editorial board. To do almost all the work but not to receive the credit due is a confrontation with the worldly winds which only spiritual practice can turn to advantage. Sangharakshita, I imagine, was well aware of that.

Collecting the Editorials

Sangharakshita composed nearly one hundred editorials over the years in which he was editor of the *Maha Bodhi* (1954–1964). Some of them were written originally for his magazine *Stepping-Stones* and appear elsewhere in the *Complete Works* (see *Crossing the Stream* in vol. 7). Most of the rest were gathered in a book on which Sangharakshita and I collaborated in 2012: *Beating the Drum*. My task was to write explanatory notes and an introduction drawing on interviews with Sangharakshita, as well as conducting a little research of my own. We met each week in his quiet flat located above the library at Madhyamaloka in Birmingham, then his UK headquarters. Sangharakshita's eyesight being seriously compromised, I would read to him the notes I had composed based on our conversations and ask for further information about people and things mentioned in the texts. The notes and the relevant parts of the introduction are included in this volume, the latter woven into this foreword or presented as Appendix 1, and to make this volume as complete as possible, editorials that we decided not to include in *Beating the Drum*, and don't appear elsewhere in the *Complete Works*, have been added here.

The Fundamental Message

The young Buddhist monk who took on editing the Maha Bodhi Society's journal was a deeply inspired man. His inspiration came from within, although sometimes its expression was sparked off by what he experienced from without. Inspiration was the hallmark of his life, its presiding genius, one might say, and it sustained itself even in the most trying of conditions. It first burst into blossom in the summer of 1942 when, at the age of 16, he read the *Diamond Sutra* for the first time. Of that experience he later wrote,

> Though this book epitomizes a teaching of such rarefied sublimity that even *arahants*, saints who have attained individual Nirvāṇa,[12] are said to become confused and afraid when they hear it for the first time, I at once joyfully embraced it with an unqualified acceptance and assent.[13]

I believe it was this joyful and unqualified acceptance of the Dharma that was the source of his inspiration.

In his editorials for the *Maha Bodhi* he writes on the most diverse themes: from the significance of the Buddha in the cosmic order to the extending of *maitrī* to animals, from the menace of horror comics to the importance of cultivating an inner life. The sweep of his gaze covers not just the Indian subcontinent but America, Africa, Burma, Vietnam.... The diversity is striking, but as one turns the pages and takes in the whole range of subject matter there seems to be a steady, unwavering heartbeat through it all: confidence in the Dharma, the steady insight that it is the Dharma that is so urgently needed in the world. It is needed by individuals, it is needed by organizations, and it is needed by nation states. If people can just get that message, if they can learn to see from that view point (he seems to be saying), the rest will naturally follow.

Against the Spirit of Our Times

Confidence in the truth of a particular way of seeing things goes against the spirit of the times,[14] or at least against the spirit of more liberal circles in the West. We have learned the importance of multi-cultural tolerance in the sense of living well alongside others of different custom and belief – a tolerance that Buddhists naturally support – but one can easily find oneself sliding down the boggy slope of relativism to that dank place where no view is deemed better than any other, where to hold that one view is superior to another – to advocate a hierarchy of values at all – is dismissed as intolerance. In his editorials, Sangharakshita demonstrates the nature of Buddhist tolerance, and he writes about it directly in 'Controversy'. Buddhist tolerance means to maintain a friendly, courteous, and open attitude towards another person *and* it means to speak up and speak out on attitudes and views, because views are an ethical matter. Perhaps Buddhism more than any other religion or philosophy has clarified the ethical dimension of views. Views not in line with Reality, views based on ignorance and delusion, lead to suffering. It is not hard to find obvious and dramatic examples of this: the view of Aryan racial supremacy that underpinned the Nazi holocaust; the Hindu view that one's worth as a human being depends upon the assignment of caste at birth; or the view that God created Nature for man, which has encouraged the irresponsible and greedy devouring of the earth's finite resources. Views may be held on ever more subtle levels and still contribute to bringing about suffering to oneself and others. A Buddhist therefore has a duty not only to maintain an attitude of *maitrī* or friendliness but also to speak up without compromise, to clarify views that do not accord with the Dharma, which means views that do not accord with the natural laws of reality – laws as inherent to existence on their own level as the law of gravity. It is these laws that the Buddha discovered and pointed out: the law that actions have consequences; the law that all things are impermanent, that there is nothing whatever fixed and finite in the whole of phenomenal existence; the law that all things arise in dependence on conditions and that there is a 'spiral' kind of conditionality which makes the human consciousness capable of an infinite development.

Buddhist Tolerance

That Buddhists very often do not speak up and speak out may have something to do with a false idea about the nature of tolerance, or even a false idea about what it means to be a Buddhist. Aren't Buddhists supposed to be nice, peace-loving people who don't do anyone any harm? Of course, Buddhists do not want to do anyone any harm, but speaking up and speaking out, though it may ruffle feathers or even upset people, may bring about the good. In the *Abhayarājakumāra Sutta* the Buddha explains that he knows the time when he should say what is true, correct, and beneficial, even though it may be unwelcome and disagreeable to others.[15]

It seems to have been second nature to Sangharakshita to speak out when he saw the Dharma being travestied or distorted and when he saw the grave effects of wrong views and the suffering to which they lead. We see it over and over again in the course of the editorials. He addresses the attitudes of parents and the state to children's reading of horror comics, and the wrong attitude of religious organizations that interpret success in terms of numbers, valuing quantity over quality. As he puts it in a terse little aphorism, 'the worship of quantity is the worship of Mammon'.

Perhaps many Buddhists fail to speak up and speak out not through a false idea about the nature of tolerance, but because they are themselves not clear about the Dharma. Sangharakshita understood the Dharma from an early age with a penetration that went beyond the merely intellectual, and was endowed with an exceptionally fine intelligence which he put at the Dharma's service and which made him perhaps uniquely able as editor of the *Maha Bodhi* to tackle views and attitudes inimical to the Dharma with a logic and clarity that is highly invigorating or – if it is one's own views that are being exposed – no doubt highly humiliating, perhaps even devastating. (Humiliation of the right kind is not deemed a bad thing in Buddhism.) We see this faculty coming into play as he exposes Hindu attempts to assimilate – even devour – Buddhism. See, for example, 'Bodh Gaya' about Vinoba Bhave's plan to establish a Samanvaya Mandir at the place of the Buddha's Enlightenment.

The Unity of Buddhism

Sangharakshita did not, of course, share the universalist outlook of the many Hindus he met, who included members of the Governing Body and editorial board of the Buddhist journal of which he was editor. For him the Buddha and only the Buddha was the true refuge, since it was the Buddha's discovery of the universal law that is the Dharma that was the real Refuge for humanity. It was this discovery which, Sangharakshita averred, underpinned all of Buddhism. He felt deeply the need for unity in the Buddhist world if the Dharma was to have anything like the effect in modern times of which he knew it was capable. 'Only a united Buddhism', he writes in his editorial in January 1956, 'will be able to contribute to the building of a united world.' For him, to be a Buddhist was to identify with the whole Buddhist world. In his persona as editor of the leading English-language Buddhist journal of the time, he took the opportunity to praise, to encourage, to question, and to criticize (as, for example, his comments addressed to the organizers of the Sixth Buddhist Council held in Burma in 'Unity is Strength'). He even sometimes pokes a little gentle fun. Indeed, one might say that he seems to have practised the four great virtues of the Good Friend in relation to the Buddhist world at large. Indeed, one might say that he acted as a spiritual friend in relation to the Buddhist world at large.

Christianity

But what about his attacks on Christianity? Do they not occasionally show a savagery unbecoming of a Buddhist monk and overstepping the bounds of Buddhist tolerance as defined above? Each reader must, of course, make up their own mind on this matter. My own understanding of Sangharakshita's attitude towards Christianity as expressed in some of these editorials is informed by (1) what I know of his cultural background, (2) the climate of Christian missionary work in Asian countries (which may be unknown to today's Westerners), and (3) what I understand about the nature of Buddhist tolerance.

(1) Through his extensive reading, Sangharakshita was steeped in the history of human civilization. For him 'Christianity' did not mean just his personal and very positive experience of the Boys' Brigade in Tooting or the friendly vicar with whom he stayed in Barnstaple as an evacuee. It meant just as vividly the history of the Church of Rome with its greed, its power, and its inhuman cruelty. The history of the Church of Rome is at times synonymous with the history of the greatest influences in Europe.[16] And then there were his philosophical and spiritual sensibilities, to which the whole structure of orthodox Christianity was repugnant. This is strong language indeed – and yet language which finds a resonance in me. Not long after I had started to practise Buddhist meditation, I found images of the bleeding head of Christ rising again and again before my eyes. From the age of 5, I attended a Roman Catholic school. There was a benign and kindly atmosphere, but on the wall at the front of every classroom hung a crucifix, that is, a cross to which was nailed the body of a dying man. There is something quite dreadful about an image of a tortured human being set up before small children for them to worship. I remember wishing that Jesus would get down off his cross, and I wondered why he had died for me; I wished he had not done so. The explanation that Christ's crucifixion is the atonement for original sin is to me repugnant. One cannot underestimate the effect that orthodox Christianity has had on the psyche of Western nations nor how radical is the Buddha's teaching for those who come from a Christianized culture.

(2) Beginning with Dharmapala's childhood, going on to Sangharakshita's accounts of experiences in Kalimpong, and looking at the 1956 report by the Buddhist Committee set up by the All Ceylon

Buddhist Congress to enquire into the state of Buddhism in Ceylon, we find that Christian missionary activity in Asia seems often to have shared the colonial ambitions that were apparent elsewhere. The Committee of Inquiry states that in Ceylon, for centuries a Buddhist country, the law imposed by the colonial conquerors created a situation in which the Christians enjoyed a 'fully autonomous status of a type that no religious body has anywhere else in the world except in the Vatican ... the Buddhist, Hindu, and Muslim religions having a subordinate state'. The colonial attitude is expressed in these words of Lord Acton: 'The pioneer of civilization has to get rid of the religion of India, to enable him to introduce a better culture, and the pioneer of Christianity has to get rid of the Indian culture before he can establish his religion.'[17] In *Facing Mount Kanchenjunga* Sangharakshita reports in some detail the activities and attitudes of the Christian missionaries in Kalimpong, including a tactic which he dubs 'conversion through pregnancy'.[18] Needless to say, he spoke out against the matter, writing to English-language daily newspapers, and he became known in some circles in the Himalayan township as 'The Enemy of the Church'.[19]

(3) Sangharakshita may have been the enemy of the church but he was *not* the enemy of individual Christians, as he makes clear in his memoirs. Though he may have disagreed with their doctrine, denounced their tactics, and upset them simply by being a Buddhist monk at all, he was very ready to enter into friendly relations with his Christian neighbours. His interactions with some local Catholic brothers, for instance, were curtailed not by Sangharakshita but by the Monsignor who forbade the brothers to have anything more to do with him.[20] The picture of local missionaries averting their eyes and clutching their Bibles more tightly when they passed him by is one of the enduring images from Sangharakshita's tales of life in Kalimpong.

Sangharakshita spoke out against bigotry and error wherever he perceived it, whether it came from Hindu, Christian, or Buddhist quarters. He spoke out against communism and against materialism in the strongest terms. We find all this in these editorials. For him the truth lay in the Buddha's teaching and only the Buddha's teaching, a sentiment expressed very beautifully in his poem 'Taking Refuge in the Buddha', whose every stanza ends with the line, 'My place is at Thy Feet'.[21]

The Climate in Which He Spoke Out

There is to me something quite astonishing about the clarity of vision with which Sangharakshita spoke and wrote at this time. He was operating in a mainly Hindu country, where fellow Europeans for the most part followed a religion that he had rejected, and where Buddhism had been on the decline towards virtual extinction for centuries. For him the Maha Bodhi Society headquarters represented 'a tiny island of Buddhism in the midst of the vast ocean of Hinduism'[22] but even that tiny island the ever-swelling tide of Hinduism was constantly threatening to overwhelm.

Sangharakshita arrived on the scene at a critical juncture. Buddhism, after centuries of decline, was in the ascendancy. On the political front, India had, after two hundred years, thrown off British colonial rule and established itself as an independent democracy. The new leaders were sympathetic to Buddhism, valuing it as part of the Indian national cultural heritage. It is noteworthy that the Indian flag that was agreed upon shortly before Independence (by a committee headed by Rajendra Prasad and including Dr Ambedkar and the poetess Sarojini Naidu) had as its motif not the *charkha* or spinning wheel favoured by Gandhi but the *dharmacakra* of the Buddhist king Aśoka. The seal of the Indian government depicts the lions of Aśoka.

In Ceylon, a new, post-colonial government was also promoting Buddhism and Buddhist values. Burma, too, had recently acquired a Buddhist prime minister. Nepal had made moves towards democracy, making it easier for Buddhists to practise their religion. In India, the work of Dharmapala to establish the Maha Bodhi Society meant there was at least one known and functioning Buddhist organization (also operative in a number of other countries, Eastern and Western.) The Theosophical Society, though in decline in terms of numbers, had many centres where lectures could be given to people sympathetic to Buddhism. In the north of India, among Tibetans arriving from the Land of Snows could be found a still spiritually vital Buddhism. It was at this crucial time that the 2,500th anniversary of the Buddha Jayanti was approaching, the anniversary of the Buddha's *parinirvāṇa* or final passing away, which the entire Buddhist world was poised to celebrate. Sangharakshita, reading the signs, felt that a revival of Buddhism in India and beyond was possible: 'According to a widespread tradition', he writes in his editorial for January 1956, 'with the coming Vaiśākha Pūrṇimā the Buddhist *śāsana*,[23] like a great banyan tree that has been decaying for centuries, will put forth fresh green shoots and flourish more vigorously than ever'.

But he did not think it would happen of its own accord. If the Buddhist *śāsana* was to flourish once more it would need tremendous effort to make it happen. With characteristic vigour he issued a call to the whole Buddhist world:

> Let every Buddhist who truly loves the teaching therefore resolve that, during the coming year, he will in one way or another disseminate the Doctrine; in traditional Buddhist language, that he will beat the drum, sound the conch-shell, and blow the trumpet of the Good Law, if necessary until his arms ache and his lungs feel as though they were about to burst. Let him strain every nerve, put forth every ounce of strength, for the accomplishment of the Great Work.

It goes without saying that he himself was prepared to follow his own exhortation. 1956–7 truly was a remarkable year. 'Ring in the New' is the title of the editorial for the special Vaiśākha number for the Buddha Jayanti. 'The Tide Turns', he announces in October, seeing in the forthcoming conversion of Dr Ambedkar the beginnings of a new era for Buddhism in India, while the last editorial of the year reflects on an 'Annus Mirabilis'.

Inner and Outer

In 1958 we notice a different emphasis, perhaps more inward. We read about 'The Necessity of Loneliness', and there are meditations on a flame and on water, and reflections on the aesthetics of the Buddha image. In 1959 and 1960 we again find the call to Dharma workers to come forward, arising especially out of Sangharakshita's strong awareness of the need of the newly converted Ambedkarite Buddhists for teaching and guidance. We are reminded of the scope of his vision when, in 'Buddhism and the "Dark" Continent' he asks, what about Africa? Who is taking the Dharma there? In another piece he uses the memorable image of a lens that can concentrate the sun's rays as an illustration for a Dharma training institution that would be able to set the whole of Asia ablaze with the Buddha's teaching. Particular Buddhist countries become the subject of the editor's pen in the later years: 'A Disturbing Dispute' in Korea and, towards the end of his editorship, the terrible events unfolding in Vietnam.

Taking the editorials as a whole, one is struck by how effortlessly Sangharakshita seems to move from concern with outer things to the concern with the inner life. His own experience is that the first arises from the second, so he insists over and over again that inner preparation, especially the practice of meditation and reflection, is the necessary condition for outward activity. Though it is meant for the benefit of ordinary people, his vision is, one might say, a purely spiritual one. A purely spiritual vision is, I believe, extremely rare.

The Editor's Voice

When Sangharakshita began his work for the *Maha Bodhi* he was 28 years old and still a junior *bhikṣu*. This did not deter him from taking a most authoritative stance as editor of the world's leading Buddhist monthly. A look at his very first editorial, 'Ancient Buddhist Site in Danger', illustrates this. He begins with a paragraph about the endangered site in which he demonstrates his command of Buddhist history. Then he spells out the issue: that a place of great significance to Buddhists is to be flooded by an irrigation scheme. Having expressed sympathy with the need for irrigation schemes, he takes the Andhra state government to task for its lack of awareness of the significance of the site it is about to submerge and upbraids the government that 'no attempt has been made to consult the Maha Bodhi Society'! In this way he identifies the Maha Bodhi as speaking for Buddhism in India.

But the editor's voice has many timbres. There is the reflective voice. There is the voice of the preceptor urging greater attention to the precepts. There is the lover of philosophy and literature celebrating great men like Schopenhauer and Tagore. And there is the sweet voice of the poet for the evocation of sentiments that are better expressed in verse – to me one of the most attractive aspects of Sangharakshita's style. The words of Shelley, Milton, Tennyson, and Kipling seem to burst onto the pages of the *Maha Bodhi*, transporting one to another world. They are complemented by the poetic utterance of the editor himself who cannot help sometimes breaking into metaphorical song, gladdening the heart of this reader at least. So in his evocation of 'Meditation Upon Water' he urges the Buddhist practitioner 'to prevent the waves of passion rising, however hard the winds of adversity may blow, however loud the thunder roars'. Sometimes metaphor expresses a more sombre mood. In 'Unity is Strength' he warns against 'making in the dyke of the Dharma a breach through which the rushing mighty waters of materialism may one day roll with full force and fury'.

There is another, quite different voice that speaks through the editorials from time to time. It is the sterner, more challenging voice of the reformist, seeking to remind both the monks and the laypeople of the Buddhist world of their duties, reminding them to keep up the standards that commitment to the Buddha's teaching demands. The editor does not hesitate to lay bare shoddy practices. He questions motives for giving, one of the foremost practices of the Buddhist laity (see 'Vaiśākha Dāna'). He exposes the shortcomings of monks. For example, when one might expect monks to be vegetarian or at the very least to be content with what they are given, they bring fish to eat at an important event when none is provided by their host. He exposes the degeneration of the monastic sangha in Ceylon that led to an unfortunate involvement in politics and a misuse of funds. Most deeply felt of all, he highlights the need of the wider world to hear the Dharma and the apparent indifference of *bhikṣus* to their duty to teach it. (See, for example, 'Spreading the Dharma', 'Implementation', and 'Buddhism and the "Dark" Continent'.) One gets the impression that Sangharakshita's awareness of the need for reform grew stronger and stronger, or at least his sense of urgency, perhaps even frustration, when he could see how formalism, laziness, and superstitious belief were choking the life of Buddhism in Eastern countries. It was as if the Buddhism he encountered was so lacking in vitality that it was hardly a suitable vehicle for propagating the living spirit of the Buddha's teaching, when the world was indeed on fire, a fire which the cooling waters of the Dharma might quench. Decades earlier, Dharmapala had gone so far as to speak of the 'lifeless corpse' of the Buddhism he had found in countries that were supposed to be Buddhist. Eventually Sangharakshita, in two articles published in the *Maha Bodhi* in October 1961 and March–April 1962, issued a great challenge to the existing Buddhist world, first to the *bhikṣus*:

'Wanted: A New Kind of *Bhikkhu*', and then to the laity: 'Wanted: A New Kind of *Upāsaka*'.

What are we to take away from these editorials? Each reader will, of course, gather their own harvest. When I first read them I found myself stirred – even shaken – by the intensity of the vision that they express, the devotion and dedication to the Buddha and his teaching, and by the deeply felt concern for the people, animals, organizations, and nations that together inhabit this planet. One thing is clear. Though meditation and reflection are indispensable, to be a Buddhist is not to have a quiet life. To be a Buddhist means to act. To be a Buddhist means to speak up and to speak out. To be a Buddhist means, in whatever way one can, to the best of one's ability, to participate in the beating of the Dharma drum.

BOOK REVIEWS

This volume was originally envisaged simply as a collection of Sangharakshita's writings for the *Maha Bodhi* which included his book reviews – for, as well as writing editorials, and some longer articles,[24] Sangharakshita contributed many book reviews, a genre in which he continued to write for many years. However, as the *Complete Works* project grew – more writings were discovered, and Sangharakshita wrote new articles during the last years of his life, coinciding with the first years of the project – space had to be found for what turned out to be a larger than expected group of writings: the book reviews. Indeed, even as this volume was nearing completion, seven further reviews, written for the *Aryan Path,* were found. Most of the early reviews *were* written for the *Maha Bodhi*, and these, together with the *Aryan Path* reviews, would clearly be part of a volume of 'India writings'. The others, however, were written and published much later, not in India, but in the West. The editor's solution to the problem was to make a virtue of necessity and gather the reviews into one harvest, giving readers the satisfaction and pleasure of finding them all in one place and more or less in chronological order.

These include: (1) Reviews published in the *Maha Bodhi* journal (1953–1962), (2) reviews published in the *Aryan Path* (1952–1963), (3) *Alternative Traditions*, a collection of reviews from 1974 to 1980 first published in *Golden Drum*, the FWBO's newsletter, and brought out in book form by Windhorse Publications in 1986 with a preface by the author, (4) a further review from *Golden Drum* (1986), (5) reviews from *A Moseley Miscellany* (Ibis Publications 2015), including eight that were originally published in *The Times Higher Education Supplement* (1998–2002) and one that appeared in the *Western Buddhist Review* in 1997.

Maha Bodhi Book Reviews

For the 2012 Ibis publication, *Anagarika Dharmapala: a Biographical Sketch and Other Maha Bodhi Writings*, Sangharakshita asked me to choose just fifteen of the longer reviews for inclusion. This I did, and it was only in recent times that I discovered that one of those reviews, that of Eugen Herrigel's *Zen in the Art of Archery,* was not in fact written by Sangharakshita at all but by Adrienne Bennett, as an erratum in the following *Maha Bodhi* issue makes clear. This is why that review does not appear in this volume.

The *Maha Bodhi* reviews are striking from a number of points of view. Taken as a whole, they are an expression of Sangharakshita *at work*: at work for the revival of Buddhism in India, for its rejuvenation in the East, and for spreading the Dharma throughout the world, especially in the West. Thus his approach is partly pragmatic. By writing a review in the foremost English-language Buddhist monthly, books and periodicals and even pamphlets on Buddhism or related topics could become more widely known; or if already known, shortcomings, especially weaknesses of doctrine, could be exposed, and virtues extolled. Sangharakshita's approach to writing reviews is interesting, even exemplary. It was generally his habit to clearly describe the content, to take issue with any glaring mistakes of doctrine and weaknesses in presentation, to give warm appreciation and praise where praise was due, and sometimes to comment on the physical appearance of the publication.

The concerns of the time are naturally reflected both in the choice of books reviewed and in the reviews themselves. It is no coincidence that the Buddha Jayanti year 1956–7 yielded an especially large crop. Sangharakshita himself felt that a tide was turning for the progress of Buddhism in India and beyond (see his editorial 'The Tide Turns'), and there was a great flurry of interest in publications about Buddhism. When these were written by Hindu scholars, there was an imperative to beat the Dharma Drum, to make clear the Buddha's fundamental doctrine of *anātman* (Pāli *anattā*) – not because this particular doctrine needs emphasizing in every circumstance but because in Hindu India the tendency to absorb Buddhism into its fold as a kind of Hinduism came with a repudiation of the *anātman* doctrine. In a review of *Buddhism in Kashmir and Ladakh*, Sangharakshita highlights the authors' view that 'the Buddha attained to godhead'. Reviewing the introduction to the *Companion Encyclopedia of Asian Philosophy* he takes issue with the rendering of *anattā* as 'no consciousness', declaring it to be 'patently absurd', an opinion he reiterated when he reviewed a new edition of the book many years later. Misrepresentations of Buddhism by Westerners get equally short shrift. To Mr Gabb, author of *The Goose is Out* and follower of Zen Buddhism, he roundly declares, 'The goose is *not* out'! explaining that 'it would appear that the essence of [the author's] thought is much closer to the Vedānta than to Buddhism'. Here is Sangharakshita at work in the garden of views, attempting to identify and remove the weeds of *micchā-diṭṭhis* (mistaken views) that can so easily overcome and choke the beautiful flowers of the Buddha's Dharma.

The celebratory Buddha Jayanti year was characterized by a growing interest in the *whole* of Buddhism, not just particular schools, an interest deeply shared by Sangharakshita. While he appreciates publications addressing this theme, he also notes in his review of *2,500 Years of Buddhism* that 'no attempt has been made to penetrate into the spirit of the Dharma' and 'there is hardly anything that might pass as an attempt to define the nature of Buddhism'. His own *A Survey of Buddhism*, published in the same year, tried not only to do both but also to discover the transcendental unity underlying all Buddhist schools.[25]

The *Maha Bodhi* reviews reflect awareness of more local (i.e. Indian) issues. For instance, there is a strong indictment of the Indian caste system in a book written by fellow member of the *Maha Bodhi* editorial board, Bhikkhu Dhammaratana – a book which went through a further five editions and is worth reading. Another feature is Sangharakshita's awareness of the contributions made by the lives of Great Men (Great Women not represented) such as the Bengali poet Rabindranath Tagore, Sadhu T. L. Vaswani the singer-saint of Sind, and the Chinese teacher and reformer, Taixu. Naturally there are reviews of new translations of Buddhist scriptures, including the Avalokiteśvara chapter of the

Saddharma Puṇḍarīka Sūtra, and a commentary on the *Maṅgala Sutta*. Then there is his interest in and appreciation of art and its value for spiritual life – on which note the collection of *Maha Bodhi* reviews concludes.

Aryan Path Reviews

Sangharakshita describes in his memoirs how he first came across this monthly magazine in 1947, with what pleasure he read it, and how, after his arrival in Kalimpong, he came to submit his own articles, poems, and book reviews.[26] It was a publication of the Theosophically-based India Institute of Culture in Bangalore, edited first by B. P. Wadia (to whom Sangharakshita dedicated his *A Survey of Buddhism*), and later by his wife, Sophia Wadia. It was under the auspices of the Institute that Sangharakshita gave, in July 1954, the four lectures that became the basis for his *Survey*. The seven reviews cover an eleven-year period and chart a discernible development, the young Sangharakshita gaining in confidence to speak out, and, as noted in the *Maha Bodhi* reviews, not only to give praise where praise is due, but to point out shortcomings and distortions of the Buddha's message. We also discover who are the authors he most admires, and why.

Alternative Traditions

This important collection of reviews, together with an article on William Blake, is introduced by a preface in which Sangharakshita explains where the reviews were originally published and how he came to place them in a particular order. They are, in fact, an exploration of Eastern and Western traditions.[27] Through the medium of the review, he explores some crucial themes including the religio-nationalism in twentieth-century Sri Lanka that allowed a Buddhist monk to assassinate the prime minister; and the failure of D. H. Lawrence – despite his vision of Rananim – to create a viable spiritual community. Zen and Tibetan Buddhism are well represented, and there is a look at the fate of the Cathars. The 1986 publication had an eye-catching image on the front cover. It was, as its artist, Dharmachari Aloka, told me, a 'loose' copy of a – possibly Dutch – medieval wood block depicting a man tied to a stake while two men with flaming brands, one of whom looks out at the reader, are about to light a pile of wood beneath. A review from *Golden Drum* that was not included in *Alternative Traditions* was of Martin Willson's book *Rebirth and the Western Buddhist.* Shortly before he died, Sangharakshita returned to this important theme in his article 'Rebirth Revisited'.[28]

Reviews from *A Moseley Miscellany*

A Moseley Miscellany: Prose and Verse 1997–2012), launched at a celebration of Sangharakshita's ninetieth birthday, consisted of poetry, reveries and reminiscences, and reflections on his personal ancestry. (These appear in *Complete Works*, vol. 26 under the title 'Madhyamaloka Reflections'). There were also nine book reviews, which are included here. The longest and most important of them is the first, originally published in the *Western Buddhist Review* under the title *Buddhism Without Beliefs?*, a review of a book by Stephen Batchelor which had the same title minus the question mark. Sangharakshita deals with Batchelor's promotion of agnostic, 'non-religious' 'Buddhism' by agreeing at times and vigorously disagreeing at others. Using the tool of logical reasoning in relation to Batchelor's assumptions, the review comes to a surprising conclusion.

The other eight reviews, much shorter in length, were written for the *Times Higher Education Supplement* in the years 1997–2002. Of these, the longest and perhaps most interesting is the review of the scholar Richard Gombrich's *How Buddhism Began*, which the reviewer describes 'as readable an introduction to a difficult and thorny subject as we are likely to find'.

CONCLUSION

Sangharakshita once said to me that people tended to speak of his adult life as if it were in two parts, first his life in India and then his life in the West. But, he said, to him it was a single flow, a single stream. He did indeed make the great move from the East to the West, from India to England – but then he just carried on doing what he had been doing before. By this I took him to mean that he carried on doing all he could to spread the Dharma. This was the master-current of his life and in a sense it had begun even before he left England for India in 1944 (see his first published articles in *Early Writings*, *Complete Works*, vol. 7). It began to take on more consistent and concrete form once he had settled in the Himalayan town of Kalimpong, heeding his teacher's injunction to 'stay here and work for the good of Buddhism'. One of the chief ways he had at his disposal – apart from lecture tours – was to write. He continued to write throughout his life, his last essays having been completed just a couple of weeks before his death.

In this volume we find Sangharakshita as writer, teacher, and Buddhist practitioner communicating not only on a tremendously wide variety of topics, but also on many different levels, both mundane and spiritual or transcendental. May it give you, the reader, the stimulation, interest, and encouragement to practise the Dharma and to pass it on that was, in the end, Sangharakshita's greatest wish.

Kalyanaprabha
Great Malvern
Worcestershire
30 July 2022

PART I

ANAGARIKA DHARMAPALA

ANAGARIKA DHARMAPALA:

A Biographical Sketch

PREFACE TO THE 1980 EDITION

Anagarika Dharmapala was the greatest 'Buddhist missionary' of our times and, next to Dr B. R. Ambedkar, the man most responsible for the revival of Buddhism in modern India. The *Biographical Sketch* that forms the central portion of this book was written in Calcutta in 1952. I wrote it at the request of the late Shri Devapriya Valisinha, General Secretary of the Maha Bodhi Society of India and a personal disciple of the *anagārika*, for inclusion in the Society's *Diamond Jubilee Souvenir*. Subsequently the Society brought it out in separate book form, as did the Buddhist Publication Society, Kandy. For the last few years it has been out of print. I am grateful to Anagarika Lokamitra for bringing out this new edition of the work under the auspices of the Trailokya Bauddha Maha Sangha, Sahayaka Gana, Pune (FWBO Poona). He has enhanced the value of the publication by including in it other writings of mine relating to the 'Lion of Lanka' as well as a collection of Dharmapala's 'Inspired Sayings' which I made many years ago in the course of my work as editor of the *Maha Bodhi* journal.

When I agreed to write my *Biographical Sketch* I knew very little about Anagarika Dharmapala. As I immersed myself in the materials placed at my disposal by Shri Valisinha, including volumes of the *anagārika*'s personal diaries, I not only became aware of the towering moral and spiritual grandeur of the man but was also greatly inspired by the picture of utter devotion to the work of spreading the Dharma that his whole life presented. The Sketch was therefore written very much *con amore* – as were all my other articles on Dharmapala. Such was the enthusiasm with which I wrote it, in fact, that it took me only three weeks to complete the work. Now, twenty-eight years later, I can only hope that it will be as inspiring for the present generation of Buddhists and friends of Buddhism to read as it was for me to write. In a letter to Mrs Mary Foster, the principal supporter of his work, Dharmapala wrote, 'Wealthy Buddhists are all dead. Self-sacrificing Bhikkhus are rare. India will again supply young heroes to preach the doctrine of Ahimsa, Karuna and Maitri – wearing the Yellow robe.' Whether wearing the white robes of the *upāsaka* or the yellow robes of the *bhikkhu* and *anagārika*, there is a greater need for such young heroes than ever before. May this book inspire them to come forward in their hundreds and their thousands.

Sangharakshita
Padmaloka
Surlingham
Nr Norwich
Norfolk (England)
24 June 1980

INTRODUCTION

The prospects for Sinhalese Buddhism in the 1860s were dark indeed. Successive waves of Portuguese, Dutch, and British invasion had swept away much of the traditional culture of the country. Missionaries had descended upon the copper-coloured island like a cloud of locusts; Christian schools of every conceivable denomination had been opened, where Buddhist boys and girls were crammed with Bible texts and taught to be ashamed of their religion, their culture, their language, their race, and their colour. The attitude of the missionaries is expressed with unabashed directness in one of the verses of a famous hymn by the well-known Anglican Bishop Heber, a hymn which is still sung, though with less conviction than in the days when it first made its appearance, in churches all over England:

> What though the spicy breezes
> Blow soft o'er Ceylon's isle,
> Where every prospect pleases,
> And only man is vile;
> In vain with lavish kindness
> The gifts of God are strown,
> The heathen in his blindness
> Bows down to wood and stone.[29]

Throughout the territories under Dutch occupation Buddhists had been compelled to declare themselves as Christians, and during the period of British rule this law was enforced for seventy years, being abrogated only in 1884, when on behalf of the Buddhists of Ceylon Colonel Olcott made representations to the Secretary of State for the Colonies in London. Children born of Buddhist parents had to be taken for registration to a church, where some Biblical name would be bestowed on them, with the result that most Sinhalese bore either an English Christian name and a Portuguese surname, if they were Catholic 'converts', or an English Christian name and a Sinhalese surname if they were Anglicans. The majority of them were ashamed or afraid to declare themselves Buddhists, and only in the villages of the interior did the Dharma of the Blessed One retain some vestige of its former power and popularity, though even here it was not free from the attacks of the thousands of catechists who, for twenty rupees a month, were prepared to go about slandering and insulting the religion of their fathers. Members of the sangha, with a few noble exceptions, were intellectually and spiritually moribund, monastic discipline was lax, the practice of meditation had been neglected and then forgotten, and even to those who truly loved the Buddha, the Dharma, and the Sangha, it must sometimes have seemed that, after reigning for more than twenty glorious centuries over the hearts and minds of the Sinhala race, they were doomed to be 'cast as rubbish to the void' and swept into the blue waters of the Arabian Sea by the triumphant legions of militant Christianity.[30] But this was not to be. Low though the fortunes of the Dharma had sunk, the great beam of the national karma was beginning to right itself, and gigantic forces were being set in motion which in the future would lift them to a position high even as their present one was low.

BEGINNINGS OF A GREAT SINHALESE PATRIOT

Among the few well-to-do families which through all vicissitudes stood firmly and fearlessly on the side of their ancestral faith was the Hewavitarne family of Matara in South Ceylon.[31] Hewavitarne Dingiri Appuhamy, the first member of this family with whom we are concerned, belonged to the large and respected *govigama* or cultivator class. He had two sons, both of whom exhibited the same devotion to the Dharma as their father. One of them became a *bhikṣu* known as Hittatiye Atthadassi

Thera and occupied the incumbency of Hittatiya Raja Mahavihara. His teacher, Mirisse Revata Thera, was fourth in pupillary succession from the Sangharaja Saranankara, the greatest name in eighteenth century Ceylon Buddhism. The other son, Don Carolis Hewavitarne, migrated to Colombo, established there a furniture manufacturing business in the Pettah area, and married the daughter of a Colombo businessman, Andris Perera Dharmagunawardene, who had donated a piece of land at Maligakanda, erected on it the first Pirivena or Buddhist monastic college in Ceylon, and brought a monk from the remote village of Hikkaduwa to be its principal.[32] Since then the names of the Vidyodaya Pirivena and Hikkaduwa Siri Sumangala Maha Nayaka Thera have passed, inseparably united, into the history of world Buddhism. Through the halls of this great institution of Buddhist learning, unrivalled throughout the length and breadth of Ceylon, have passed monks from Burma, Siam, India, Japan, and China, and the memory of the great Buddhist scholar, mathematician, and expert in comparative religion who for so many decades guided its destinies is revered wherever the Dharma taught in the Pāli scriptures is known.

Both Don Carolis and his young wife Mallika ardently desired a son, and when they knew that a child would be born to them their joy was great indeed. But although they both desired a son, the reasons for which they desired him were by no means the same. Mudaliyar Hewavitarne thought of a successor in the family business, while his wife dreamed of a *bhikṣu* who would guide the erring footsteps of the Sinhala people back to the Noble Eightfold Path from which they had so long been led astray. Every morning before sunrise the young bride, who was not yet out of her teens, would gather a trayful of sweet-smelling five-petalled temple flowers and offer them, together with coconut-oil lamps and incense, at the feet of the Buddha image in the family shrine, praying to the *devas* that she might bear a son who would rekindle the lamp of the Dharma in a darkened land. Every evening, too, she would lie prostrate in supplication before the silent image, which was a wooden replica of one of the great stone Buddhas of Anuradhapura, the ancient city whose very name wakes in every Sinhala heart an unutterably deep nostalgia for the temporal and spiritual glories of long ago. Who knows what subtle spiritual emanations from the liberated minds of old passed through that image and penetrated the receptive mind of the Sinhala maiden, steeping the lotus of her aspiration in the dews of kindliness and peace, and purifying her heart and mind until they were a fit receptacle for the Great Being who was to accomplish what even in her wildest dreams she had scarcely dared to hope for. As her time drew near, *bhikṣus* were invited to the house, and on the full-moon nights of three successive months the air was filled with the vibrations of the sacred Pāli texts, as from dusk to dawn they chanted from the holy books. Then, on the night of 17 September in the Pettah district of Colombo, where the national religion and culture had fallen to the lowest pitch of degeneration, there came, as though to strike the evil at its very heart, the birth of Dharmapala, like a vivid flash of lightning from a black and stormy sky.

Young David Hewavitarne, as he was named, grew up in an atmosphere of traditional Sinhala piety. Every day, morning and evening, he would kneel in the shrine with his father and mother, take refuge in the Buddha, the Dharma, and the Sangha, promise to observe the five precepts and chant the verses of worship with which millions of people have for five-and-twenty centuries expressed their gratitude to, and adoration of, him who showed humanity for the first time the way to Nirvāṇa. Nor was the practical application of the Dharma forgotten, for sweetly and reasonably his mother would point out to him any infringement of the precepts, and gently chide him into the careful observance of them all. It is a commonplace of educational psychology that the influences to which a child is subjected during its earliest years more or less determine the whole course of its subsequent development, and the biography of Dharmapala provides us with no exception to this rule. His deep and spontaneous devotion to the Buddha, his instinctive observance of the plain and simple rules of the Dharma through the complexities and temptations of modern life, his ardent love of all that was pure and good, as well as his unsparing condemnation of whatever was unclean and evil, were undoubtedly the efflorescence of seeds which had been planted in the fertile soil of his young heart by his mother's loving advice and his father's austere example. The spectacle of a life such as his, so fruitful in good for the whole of humanity, should be sufficient to convince anyone who might doubt the advisability of bringing up Buddhist children in a traditional atmosphere, and imparting to them from their earliest years both instruction and training in the sublime Dharma. Without that early religious training young David Hewavitarne might have grown up to wear top hat and trousers, speaking English to his family and Sinhalese to the servants, like thousands of his contemporaries, and Dharmapala, the Lion of Lanka, might never have been born – and the greatness of the difference which such a calamity would have made to India, Buddhism, and the world, it is now impossible for us to gauge. It should never be forgotten that piety of the old Sinhala type was the plinth and foundation of Dharmapala's whole character. Though well versed in his religion, he was not a scholar; though he wrote inexhaustibly, it is not as a writer that he will be remembered. For more than forty years he worked and organized and agitated unceasingly, but not even here is the secret of his character to be discovered. Fundamentally he was a Sinhala passionately devoted to his religion as only a Sinhala, after centuries of civil oppression and religious persecution, could at that time have been. With him religion was not an intellectual conviction but an instinct. He lived and moved and had his being in Southern Buddhism, and after centuries of stagnation it lived and moved and had its being again in him. Here lies the secret of his appeal to the Sinhala people. He was not a detached scholar looking down at their simple but profound piety from the outside, as it were, but flesh of their flesh, spirit of their spirit, feeling as they felt and behaving as they believed. In him all that was good in the national character was raised to a higher degree than they had dreamed was possible in modern times, and seeing him they saw and recognized themselves not only as they had been of old but as they yet might be again.

The child of Mallika Hewavitarne's dreams was now five years old, and the time had come when the already ardently devout current of his temperament was to be impinged upon by influences that would give to it a definite direction, and obstacles that would serve only to increase its natural impetuosity and inherent momentum. His first contact with the world that lay outside the charmed circle of family life, where the influence of the Dharma permeated everything like a sweet and subtle perfume, came when he was sent to a girls' school where the majority of pupils were Burghers, that is to say, of mixed Dutch and Sinhala descent. It is necessary to observe at this crucial point, where for the first time the innate genius of David Hewavitarne came in contact with forces intrinsically hostile to all that he loved and believed in, that throughout the whole of his long life his character remained wonderfully integrated and harmonious. Whether confronted with a problem of personal conduct or business ethics, whether faced by the customs of his own beloved island or the bewilderingly unfamiliar civilizations of the West and the Far East, he stood firm and unshaken, seeing and judging all things in the clear light of the Dharma, and doing straightforwardly and without fear or hesitation that which he knew was good and right. The suggestion that he might win a lawsuit by judicious bribery was scornfully rejected, with the characteristic comment that though the winning of the Bodh Gaya case was dearer to his heart than anything in the world he would rather lose it than resort to such detestable methods. When he saw the Niagara Falls, with their thousands of tons of water thundering down every minute, he merely remarked that it was the most impressive illustration of the transitoriness of human personality that he had ever seen. So long and deeply had he meditated upon the truths of the Dharma that they had become part of his character, so that to think, speak, and act in accordance with them was natural to him. But in spite of its inherent nobility, perhaps even because of it, such a character must sooner or later come into conflict with the cowardly conventions and mean hypocrisies of the world, so that it is perhaps inevitable that the life of a man like Dharmapala should be one unceasing battle against injustice, untruth, and unrighteousness in every conceivable form.

Naturally, the conflict did not begin until several years after the period with which we are now concerned, but it is interesting to note that even at this time questions rose to his lips which his mother could not always answer, and which his father thought better repressed by the exercise of paternal authority. Although he never experienced any diminution of his affection for the religious traditions of his family, he could not help becoming aware that those traditions were by no means universally accepted, nor refrain from trying to find some explanation for this difference. Gradually his childish mind came to understand that the world was divided into Buddhists like his mother and father who loved the Dharma, and Christians like his schoolteachers who hated it and were seeking to destroy it; but already he knew on which side of the gulf which lay between the two parties he stood and for whom it was his duty to do battle. But in these early years he gave no indication of the attitude he was insensibly adopting, and even when, at the age of six, he joined the Pettah Catholic School (later St Mary's School), and was one day asked to kneel down and kiss the ring of the visiting

Bishop Hilarion Silani, he obediently did so, probably without fully understanding the significance of the act.

The next school which David Hewavitarne attended was a Sinhalese private school, where he remained for two years, leaving at the age of ten. 'The first lesson was taught', writes Bhikkhu Devamitta Dhammapala, 'according to the old Sinhalese custom of offering betel to his teacher and making obeisance to him.'[33] He also writes of the teacher that he was a strict disciplinarian who impressed upon his pupil's tender mind the necessity of keeping everything clean and using plenty of water to keep the body physically pure. The lesson appears to have been well learned, for till the end of his life Dharmapala was almost fanatically particular about the cleanliness and tidiness of the objects of his personal use and of his surroundings. In the Sinhalese school he had to go through all the Sinhala books which were taught in the temples of Ceylon, with the result that he obtained a thorough grounding in the language and literature of his native land. On leaving the Sinhalese private school he was admitted to the lowest form of St Benedict's Institute, where among his teachers were Brothers August, Daniel, Joshua, and Cassion, several of whom he knew personally during the two years which he spent at the school. Every half hour the class had to repeat a short prayer in praise of the Virgin Mary, and on Thursdays the boy had to attend a special class conducted by a Brother as he was a Buddhist. On feast days he used to decorate the college chapel with sweet-smelling blossoms culled from the flowering trees of his father's garden, the family by this time having moved from Pettah to a new house in Kotahena, then a place of green paddy fields and graceful palms. It was only to be expected that one day a reverend father should ask the lad why he should not become a Catholic, and in later years Dharmapala himself commented that it was strange that, at a time when the power of Catholicism was so strong in Colombo, he did not become one. He moreover made the illuminating remark that the influence of his parents and grandparents was largely responsible for keeping him within the Buddhist fold. This contains a reference not only to his participation in the ritual of daily worship, his regular visits to the Kotahena Temple in the company of his mother, or the *Jātaka* stories which he read aloud in the cool of the evening, for there was another religious experience which engraved upon his mind an impression perhaps deeper than that left by any of these. In his ninth year he was initiated into the *brahmacarya* vow by his father at the temple, and advised to be contented with whatever he got to eat, and to sleep but little. The impression left by this experience was permanent, and in later years the *anagārika* or 'homeless one', as he then called himself, was accustomed to satisfy his hunger with whatever food he received, and to sleep only two or three hours at night. It behoves us to remember, in this connection, that in spite of his devastatingly energetic career of practical activities and achievements, Dharmapala's temperament had a pronouncedly ascetic side which was no less characteristic of the man as a whole. He loved solitude, meditation, and study, and if these do not occupy a more prominent position in his biography the fact is due not to his own lack of inclination for them, but to the circumstances of the times in which he lived, when the task of rousing the Buddhist world from its centuries-long slumber was the one which made the most imperative demand upon the resources of his genius. In May 1876 he was asked by the school authorities to leave St Benedict's, and although we are not informed of the circumstances that led to this request, it is not difficult, in view of the subsequent events of his career, to make a fairly accurate guess at what they were. Even as a cub the Lion of Lanka had sharp claws.

The next two years of young Hewavitarne's life were passed in the aggressively missionary atmosphere of the Christian Boarding School, an Anglican (CMS) institution situated at Kotte, a place six or seven miles from Colombo. Here he was daily forced to attend service at 6:30 a.m. in the church, where the Rev. R. T. Dowbiggin would recite the prayers and read a text from the Bible. Religious instruction by no means ended here, however. In class he had to recite some verses from Genesis or Matthew, and lurid light is shed on the intensive missionary methods of the day by the fact that he had hardly entered his teens when he knew *by heart* Exodus, Numbers, Deuteronomy, Joshua, all four gospels, and the Acts of the Apostles. The boarding master of the school was fond of liquor, and used to take delight in shooting the small birds that alighted on the trees. These revolting practices were against the teaching of mindfulness and compassion that he had learned in his own home, and the boy, already beginning to think independently, could not reconcile himself to such barbarous behaviour. An incident which occurred at this period must have made his sensitive mind more keenly aware than ever of the gulf that lay between Christian missionary fanaticism on the one hand and Buddhist wisdom and tolerance on the other, and surely added fresh fuel to the already smouldering fires of revolt. One Sunday he was quietly reading a pamphlet on the four noble truths when the same master came up to him and, true to missionary tradition, demanded the offending work from him and had it flung out of the room. Another incident that happened at this time gives us a valuable glimpse of a trait strikingly characteristic of Dharmapala during his whole life. A classmate died, and the teacher invited the students to gather round the dead body and join in the prayers that were to be offered. As David Hewavitarne looked first at the uneasy faces about him, and then at the corpse that lay so still on the bed, there came to him in a blinding flash of illumination the thought that prayer is born of fear, and at once his whole being revolted against the idea of being afraid of anything. In this dramatic manner he achieved that complete freedom from fear which was ever one of his most striking qualities, and entered into that dauntless courage which is one of the surest signs of spiritual mastery. Curiously enough, by continual reading of the Bible, Hewavitarne had acquired a fondness for the sonorous cadences of the Authorized Version, and even neglected his class studies in order to indulge his passion for the rhythmic beauty of its Jacobean diction. He did not read uncritically, however, and even at that early age his nimble wits were able to formulate questions that perplexed and irritated his teachers. The climax of criticisms was reached when he drew a picture of a monkey and wrote underneath it 'Jesus Christ', for which piece of juvenile impudence he was threatened with expulsion from the school. Of course, according to Buddhist teaching it was wrong of him to have offended Christian sentiment in this way, but we must remember that it was hardly possible for a boy of his age, intellectually undeveloped as he was, to express his opinions in any other manner. Even in his later writings we find page after page of vigorous anti-Christian invective which appears strangely un-Buddhistic, until we remember how utterly unscrupulous, cunning, and implacable the forces of missionary fanaticism then were, and how terrible was the ignorant hatred with which they assailed and sought to destroy the Dharma. When the young biblical critic eventually did leave school, it was not because the authorities found his presence embarrassing, but because the food he had to eat was, as he informs us himself, 'horrible', so that his father had to remove him when he saw how lean the youth had become. Then followed two months' rest at home after which, in

September 1878, he attended St Thomas's Collegiate school, an Anglican institution in North Colombo.

It was not long before his uncompromising championship of his ancestral Dharma brought him into conflict with the rigid discipline of the school. Warden Miller, the head of the institution, was a pedagogue of the old type, firmly believing and unflinchingly practising the maxim 'Spare the rod and spoil the child'. The students of St Thomas's were certainly neither spared nor spoiled, and so great was the awe in which the stern disciplinarian was held that the sound of his step in the corridor was enough to send a shiver of terrified anticipation through a hundred youthful hearts. Great must have been the astonishment of this dreadful figure when, one fine May morning, a slim young Sinhala appeared before him in his study, and after explaining that the day was sacred to the birth, Enlightenment, and death of the Buddha, whom he revered as the founder of his religion, boldly asked for permission to spend the day at home in worship and other religious observances. Recovering from his astonishment, Warden Miller explained in his strongest tones that the day was not a school holiday, and that as the head of an Anglican public school he did not feel justified in granting a holiday merely for the observance of a Buddhist festival. Whereupon David Hewavitarne picked up his umbrella and his books, and without another word walked out of school for the day. Next morning the young rebel received not only a wrathful reprimand for his insubordination, but also a few of Warden Miller's best cane-strokes on the seat of his trousers. This painful and humiliating experience did not, however, prevent him from repeating the escapade on the two remaining Wesak days which occurred during his career at St Thomas's and on both occasions the same punishment was meted out to him as before. His fellow students did not know whether to be amused at his impudence or to admire his courage, and Christian friends confided to him that they would not willingly have risked one of Warden Miller's thrashings for the doubtful privilege of observing Christmas Day. But the mantle of destiny had already fallen upon his youthful shoulders, and even in his middle teens he must have been aware of the gulf of difference that lay between his own burning enthusiasm for the Dharma and the dreamy adolescent indifference of his fellows. Not that this feeling of difference isolated him from his companions, or prevented him from making a number of friends. On the contrary, the circle of his friendship was always wide, and at a time when caste differences were keenly felt, even in Buddhist Lanka, it included boys of every class and community. He loved to relate how the Buddha had admitted even a scavenger, that most despised member of orthodox Hindu society, into the noble brotherhood of the sangha, and how in accordance with his teaching even Brahmin Buddhist converts had to bow their heads in worship at his feet.[34] His friendships were not, however, of that sentimental kind so common in public schools. He made friends chiefly in order to have the pleasure of arguing with them, and he argued in order to taste the still sweeter pleasure of polemical victory. For the spirit of controversy was already rampant in him, and it is said that at this period he was unhappy if he could not disagree for the day. The favourite objects of his attack were, of course, the dogmas of orthodox Christianity, and many were the occasions on which he gleefully confused and bewildered the minds of his opponents. To a Kandyan Buddhist schoolfellow who, weakly succumbing to the persuasions of the missionaries, had said that he supposed there must be a First Cause, the budding debater posed the question, 'Did God make a First Cause?' 'God is the First Cause,' glibly replied his friend. 'Then who made God?' came the next question. The Kandyan, now thoroughly out of his depth, stammered that he supposed God must have made himself. This was the opportunity for which Dharmapala had been eagerly waiting. 'Then God must be a Buddhist,' he retorted triumphantly. 'Every Buddhist is a result of his past karma. Besides, every man makes himself. Every man is a potential God. But even man, who was his own first cause, did not create the world. Gods and men can create themselves, but they can't create others.' On the following Sunday the Kandyan went to Sunday School armed with a question from Dharmapala. 'If "Thou shalt not kill" is a commandment, why did the Crusades ever take place, sir?' The Sinhala padre, whose mind had probably not been troubled by such a question before, replied rather naively that they had been inspired from heaven. When the answer was carried back to Dharmapala, who no longer attended Sunday School, he was ready with his usual unanswerable objection. 'Every war is an inspiration for Christians. Why should God inspire people to break his own commandments?' The first rumblings of that great thunder of denunciation against sham religion and false philosophy which was to burst in later years from his lips were already beginning to make themselves heard, and it is an ironical fact that the biblical knowledge that he was to use with such deadly effect was fostered and developed by the missionaries themselves, who could never have imagined that they were thereby placing in the hands of their pupil the instruments of their own discomfiture. When the Sinhala padre who took his religious class, attracted by the boy's intelligence and no doubt mindful of the desirability of inducing such a promising lad to become a convert, promised him a watch if he topped his class in religious knowledge, young Hewavitarne promptly studied hard and carried off the coveted prize. But if it was the Christian missionaries themselves who placed the weapons of debate in the hands of the youthful fighter, it was a Buddhist monk who first taught him how to use them.

THE PANADURA CONTROVERSY

Every day on his way to and from St Thomas's Dharmapala used to pass the Kotahena Temple, the incumbent of which was Migettuwatte Gunananda, the greatest orator and debater of Ceylon in modern times. On Saturday evenings, during the seventies and early eighties of the last [i.e. nineteenth] century, the place would be thronged with devotees, for on those days the great preacher, his forefinger raised as though to emphasize every word he uttered, his yellow robe flung back dramatically over his brown shoulder as if to leave his arms free for battle, and his black eyes flashing with the fire of denunciation, would launch one of those devastating attacks on Christianity, the noise of which would echo, during the following week, from one end of the island to the other. Now it was the doctrine of creation on which he trained the batteries of Buddhist reason, now the belief in a permanent individual soul, until one by one the crumbling bastions of Christian dogmatic theology were reduced to a heap of smoking rubble. These lectures, which were the first visible sign of Buddhist reaction against centuries of Christian domination, aroused wild enthusiasm on the one hand and excited violent indignation on the other. Determined to silence so formidable an antagonist once and for all, the Christians organized in 1873 a huge public meeting at Panadura, a place near Colombo, and Gunananda was challenged to meet in open debate the most able among their controversialists. Alone but undaunted, he faced the united forces of Christian orthodoxy, and so impressive was his eloquence, so powerful his reasoning, that the Panadura Controversy, which was intended to bring discredit to the Buddhists, sounded instead the death knell of Christian influence in Ceylon, so that never again did Catholic or Protestant dogmatism venture to cross swords with Buddhist wisdom.

COLONEL OLCOTT AND MADAME BLAVATSKY

The repercussions of this historic debate were felt more widely than even Gunananda could have thought possible, and great must have been his surprise and delight when, a few years later, he received a letter from an American colonel and a Russian lady of noble birth expressing satisfaction at his victory, and acquainting him with the formation of the Theosophical Society at New York in 1875. With the letter came two bulky volumes entitled *Isis Unveiled*. Gunananda immediately entered into regular correspondence with the two foreign sympathizers, and started translating their letters and extracts from *Isis Unveiled* into Sinhalese. These translations circulated all over the island, and before long the names of H. S. Olcott and H. P. Blavatsky were repeated with wonder and delight in every Buddhist home. David Hewavitarne, who had become not only a frequent visitor to the temple but also a great favourite of its incumbent, was among those whose hearts leapt with joy to hear of this unexpected aid, and in 1879 he had the satisfaction of hearing from his master's lips the news that the founders of the Theosophical Society had arrived in Bombay and that they would shortly be coming to Ceylon to help in the revival of Buddhism. He also saw the first number of *The Theosophist*, a copy of which had been sent to Migettuwatte, and he tells us himself that it was from this time, when he was 14 years old, that his interest in theosophy dated. His enthusiasm for the newly founded movement was still further increased by the lectures which the great preacher had started giving on Colonel Olcott, Madame Blavatsky, and the Theosophical Society, and when, in May 1880, the two founders at last arrived in Ceylon from India, his excitement was shared by every Buddhist heart in the island and the two visitors were received amidst scenes of religious fervour such as had not been witnessed within living memory. After centuries of Christian persecution and oppression the Buddhists of Ceylon could hardly believe that this dignified American colonel, with his patriarchal grey beard, lofty forehead, aquiline nose, and shrewd blue eyes, and this unwieldy Russian woman, with her beringed fingers, puffy cheeks, and dreamily hypnotic gaze – members, to them, of the ruling white race – had actually come to Ceylon not to attack the Dharma, as thousands of Christian missionaries had done, but to defend and support it; that they had come neither as enemies nor conquerors but simply as friends and brothers. However, when, on that memorable 21 May, the Buddhist devotees flocked in their thousands from the surrounding villages to Galle, and saw the strange pair on their knees in front of the High Priest and actually heard them repeat the familiar words of the Three Refuges and Five Precepts, as no other westerners had ever done before, all their suspicions were allayed, and it seemed as though their wildest dreams had come true. The tide had turned at last and Gunananda felt that all his labour had not been in vain.

This is not the place for an analysis of the characters of Colonel Olcott and Madame Blavatsky, nor for an examination of the motives with which they came to Ceylon, and space does not permit us to unravel the tangled skein of theosophical history even prior to the events with which we are now concerned. To what extent the founders were followers of the Dharma as that term is understood in the monasteries of Ceylon, and with what mental reservations they publicly embraced Buddhism at Galle, are matters which, though in themselves interesting and important subjects of inquiry, could make no material difference to the course of the narrative now being unfolded. We are concerned not so much with psychology as with history, and it is not only a fact but also an extremely important fact that the conversion of Madame Blavatsky and Colonel Olcott to Buddhism marked the beginning of a new epoch in the annals of Ceylon Buddhism. If at the Panadura Controversy, Christian fanaticism suffered its first serious repulse, by the ceremony at Galle, Buddhism scored its first positive victory, and that this victory was won for Buddhism by the founders of the Theosophical Society, is impossible for any fair-minded person to deny. At any rate, boundless was the gratitude of the Sinhala Buddhists to the two converts, through whose instrumentality the power of the Dharma had been so abundantly demonstrated, and their triumphal tour from South Ceylon up to Colombo was the occasion for a series of outbreaks of popular enthusiasm. On their arrival at the capital in June young Hewavitarne, his eyes bright with expectation and his heart thumping wildly at the prospect of seeing the idols whom he had until then been worshipping from afar, walked all the way from St Thomas's to the place where Colonel Olcott was to deliver his first lecture. At the close of the meeting, when everybody had left, his uncle and father remained behind, and with them the 14-year-old boy. His uncle had already become a great favourite with Madame Blavatsky, and more than half a century later, only a few months before his death, Dharmapala wrote that he still remembered the delight he felt when, along with them, he shook hands with the founders as they said goodbye. He adds that he was intuitively drawn to Madame Blavatsky, though he never suspected that she would later carry him off to Adyar in the face of the protests of his whole family, together with those of the High Priest Sumangala and Colonel Olcott himself. However, that day was still four years ahead, and in the meantime the youthful enthusiast continued to attend St Thomas's. In spite of his strictness Warden Miller liked the rebellious Sinhala boy for his truthfulness and one day told him, with rare candour, 'We don't come to Ceylon to teach you English, but we come to Ceylon to convert you.' Hewavitarne replied that he could not believe in the Old Testament although he liked the New. In March 1863 the Catholic riots took place, when a Buddhist procession, which was passing by St Lucia's Church in Kotahena to Migettuwatte Gunananda's temple, was brutally assaulted by a Catholic mob, and Dharmapala's indignant father refused to allow him to study any longer in a Christian school, even though he had not yet matriculated. On his departure from the school Warden Miller gave him an excellent certificate.

The next few months were spent eagerly devouring books in the Pettah Library, of which he was a member. The range of his interests was always remarkably wide, and we are told that at this period of adolescent intellectual ferment his favourite subjects of study were ethics, philosophy, psychology, biography, and history. Poetry he loved passionately, especially that of Keats and Shelley, whose 'Queen Mab' had been his favourite poem ever since he had chanced to find it in a volume of poetry in his uncle's library. 'I never ceased,' he says, 'to love its lyric indignation against the tyrannies and injustices that man heaps on himself and its passion for individual freedom.' Shelley's poetry, the bulk of which was composed under the blue skies of sunny Italy, has a particularly exhilarating effect when read in the tropics on a starry night, when the palms sway to and fro in the moonlight, and the scent of the temple-flowers drifts intolerably sweet from the trees outside, particularly when the reader is in his late teens, and perhaps it would not be too fanciful to trace in the noble accomplishments of Dharmapala's maturity the lingering influence of the poet of *Prometheus Unbound*. At any rate, he felt a strange sense of kinship with one who as a schoolboy had rebelled against the rigid dogmas of orthodox Christianity, and he wondered if Shelley and Keats had been reborn in the *deva* world or on earth, and whether it would be possible to trace them in their present reincarnations and convert them to Buddhism. Such are the dreams of youth, always aspiring after the impossible, ever enamoured of the unknown. Dharmapala admits in his 'Reminiscences' that from boyhood he was inclined towards the mystic, ascetic life, and that he was on the lookout for news about *arhants* and the science of *abhijñā*, or supernormal knowledge, even though, as he relates, the *bhikṣus* of Ceylon were sceptical about the possibility of realizing arhantship, believing that the age of *arhants* was past and that the realization of Nirvāṇa by psychic training was no longer possible. But his thirst for direct spiritual experience, his craving for personal contact with beings of supernormal spiritual development, was by no means quenched by the worldly scepticism of the official custodians of the Dharma, and it was with a thrill of joy that he read A. P. Sinnett's *The Occult World*.[35]

THE THEOSOPHICAL SOCIETY

Dharmapala decided to join the Himalayan School of Adepts, the necessary qualifications for which had been described in an article entitled 'Chelas and Lay Chelas' which he had read in the pages of *The Theosophist* only a month before, and accordingly wrote to the 'Unknown Brother' in November 1883 a letter intimating his desire to join the Order, and enclosed it in another letter to Madame Blavatsky at her Adyar address. Three months later, in January 1884, Colonel Olcott returned to Ceylon at the request of the Colombo theosophists in order to institute legal proceedings against the Catholics for their murderous and unprovoked attack on a peaceful Buddhist procession, and Dharmapala lost no time in meeting him and expressing his desire to join the Theosophical Society. The Colonel replied that the boy's letter had been received, and that he was prepared to admit him, even though he was under age. The ceremony of initiation accordingly took place in the temporary headquarters of the Theosophical Society in Maliban Street, two other Sinhala Buddhists being initiated at the same time, his grandfather, who was then president of the Society, paying the initiation fee of ten rupees. The young aspirant began to feel that his dreams of a higher life were beginning to come true, and as his thirst for occult knowledge increased it was inevitable that he should be drawn by the powerful magnetic influence of Madame Blavatsky, who had accompanied Colonel Olcott to Ceylon. Holding the boy spellbound with her hypnotic stare, she would speak to him in deep, guttural tones of the mysterious Brotherhood of Adepts who from their remote Himalayan vastnesses directed the destinies of the Theosophical Society, of the Master K. H. and of the Master M., playing with a master hand upon his youthful sensibilities until Dharmapala would feel himself being swept away on a current of uncontrollable enthusiasm. Wholehearted devotion to the feet of the unseen Masters, whom he of course understood to be followers of the Lord Buddha, and a fervent aspiration to dedicate himself to their service, now became the ruling passion of his life, and when Madame Blavatsky quoted to him the message that the Master K. H. had sent to A. P. Sinnett, 'The only refuge for him who aspires to true perfection is the Buddha alone', it awoke in his heart reverberations that were to last from that day until the hour of his death. How deep was the impression made upon him by these pregnant words is best measured by the fact that nearly half a century later he was still writing them at the head of every alternate page in his diary, sometimes in a firm bold hand, sometimes in letters made shaky and almost illegible by acute physical suffering. At the time with which we are dealing Dharmapala was completely under the influence of the Russian seeress, so that when she conveyed to him a personal message from the same Master, asking him to accompany her to Adyar and continue to be her disciple there, he embraced with eagerness the opportunity of qualifying himself still further for direct contact with the members of the Adept Brotherhood. Mudaliyar Hewavitarne agreed that he should go to Adyar in December, and all arrangements were made to leave Colombo. Colonel Olcott and Franz Hartmann arrived from Madras to escort the party, which in addition to Madame Blavatsky now included Mr and Mrs Oakley Cooper and Rev. C. W. Leadbeater from London. On the morning of the day fixed for their departure, however, the boy's father told him that he had had an unlucky dream in the night and that he should therefore not go. Of course, the young disciple of the Masters protested vigorously against this unexpected frustration of his cherished desires, saying that as he was being taken to Adyar by Colonel Olcott nothing would happen to him. His fears not set at rest by this reply, the Mudaliyar took his son to see his grandfather, who was also opposed to the Adyar journey. All three of them then entered a carriage and went to see the High Priest Sumangala who, to Dharmapala's dismay, also added his voice to the chorus of opposition. The boy gave vent to his grief, asking them why they should interfere with his karma, whereupon the High Priest deputed his assistant, Bhikṣu Amaramoli, to go with the party to Colonel Olcott and finally settle the matter in consultation with him. They all went, and Colonel Olcott positively declined to take him against the wishes of his family and the advice of the High Priest. At this point, when Dharmapala had sunk into the depths of despair, Madame Blavatsky rushed upon the scene, dramatically declaring that there was no cause for fear in going to Adyar, as she herself would be responsible for his safe return, but that if he was not allowed to go he would surely die.

Frightened by this prediction, Mudaliyar Hewavitarne committed his son to Madame Blavatsky's care, and exhorted him to lead the life of a bodhisattva. The Mudaliyar's fears were of course the outcome of paternal love and solicitude for his first-born. Besides, he had given him an English education with the intention of qualifying him to carry on and develop the family business, so that it must have been a sore disappointment for him to see how decidedly his son's mind was turning away from material interests, how innocent he was of all worldly ambition. But he was not only an affectionate, albeit stern, father, but also a pious Buddhist, and reflecting that David's departure was in the interests of the Dharma reconciled himself to the inevitable.

ADYAR AND RETURN TO CEYLON

Dharmapala had gone to Adyar with the intention of studying occultism, and there is no doubt that Madame Blavatsky could have been of considerable assistance to him in pursuing his studies in that recondite field. But curiously enough, instead of encouraging his enthusiasm for the occult, she turned his interests in a quite different direction. Calling him to her room one day, she made him sit by her and told him that he need not take up the study of occultism, but that he should study Pāli, where all that was needed could be found, and that he should work for the good of humanity, after which she gave him her blessings. Years later Dharmapala wrote in his 'Reminiscences' that there and then he decided that henceforth his life should be devoted to the good of humanity, and the history of Buddhism during the last sixty years is the witness of how faithfully he observed his youthful vow. He also writes that 'In those days the theosophic atmosphere was saturated with the aroma of the devotion of the Himalayan Masters to the Lord Buddha as is seen in the articles in *The Theosophist* of the Adepts showing their devotion to the Buddha Gautama,' and it could not have been without regret that after staying for only a short while at Adyar, he returned to Colombo, where he began faithfully carrying out his pledge. Meanwhile, the missionaries of Madras, rightly fearing that the presence of Colonel Olcott and Madame Blavatsky was prejudicial to the spread of Christianity in India, had been conducting a series of savage attacks on Madame Blavatsky, impugning her character and alleging that her psychic powers were not genuine but fraudulent. A couple called the Coulombs, whom she had discharged from her service, were bribed to furnish fabricated evidence, the husband (a carpenter) faking trap-doors etc. in a cupboard to prove trickery, the wife forging letters purporting to come from Madame Blavatsky herself. These letters the missionaries purchased and printed in their magazine. Shortly afterwards, the Society for Psychical Research published the report of an agent named Hodgson whom they had sent to India to investigate the phenomena which had been produced at A. P. Sinnett's Simla house in 1880, and who had based his findings on the evidence of the Coulombs, ignoring the fact that neither of them were present when the most important phenomena occurred, and deliberately suppressing the verdict of an expert graphologist, to whom he had submitted parts of letters attributed to a Master and some writing said to be by Madame Blavatsky, that 'Madame Blavatsky was not the writer of the letters attributed to the Master'. These two blows, coming as they did in quick succession, created a panic in the theosophical camp, and fearing legal entanglements and difficulties with the Government neither Colonel Olcott nor the Council would permit her to bring an action for libel, even though evidence against the Coulombs had been obtained, and in spite of the fact that the attacks were based on forged letters. Despite her protests Madame Blavatsky was hurried away from Adyar, and once away from the headquarters excuses were easily found to prevent her from returning. The steamer that took her back to Europe called at Colombo and Dharmapala went on board to say goodbye. It was their last meeting, but so deep was the impression she had succeeded in making upon the youth's plastic mind that for the remainder of his life he cherished her memory with affection and gratitude, firmly believing her to have been the innocent victim of a foul conspiracy. In his eyes she was a Buddhist, and the agent of Masters who were also Buddhists, and after her death it was with increasing concern and indignation that he saw the organization she had founded, and which had, as she once wrote, her 'magnetic fluid', turning under the leadership of Mrs Besant away from Buddhism first to Brahmanism and thereafter to a succession of pseudo-religious mummeries each wilder, more extravagant, and further removed from Madame Blavatsky's teachings than the last. It was the *anagārika*'s suggestion that Alice Leighton Cleather wrote her well-known book *H. P. Blavatsky, Her Life and Work for Humanity*, which was published in book form in 1922 after appearing as a series of articles in the *Maha Bodhi*, and perhaps we shall not be guilty of serious error if we assume that Dharmapala's mature views on the subject were in substantial agreement with those expressed in this work.[36]

LEAVING HOME AS A BRAHMACĀRĪ

At the time of which we are writing, when he was in his twentieth year, he believed, with the majority of Sinhala Buddhists, that the interests of Buddhism and the interests of the Theosophical Society were identical. In these circumstances it was but natural that when, a few months after Madame Blavatsky's departure, he wrote to his father a letter asking for permission to leave home and lead a *brahmacārī* life as he wished to devote all his time to the welfare of the *śāsana*, he should also request permission to stay at the Theosophical headquarters, on the grounds that the Society was working for the good of Buddhism. His father at first demurred, asking who would look after the younger members of the family if the eldest son left home. Firm in his determination, Dharmapala replied that each one had his own karma to protect him, and in the end the Mudaliyar had to agree to the arrangement. His mother, too, gave her blessings, saying that had it not been for his two younger brothers, who still required her care, she would have joined him in the new life he was about to adopt. The young man was now free to go forth from his home to the life of homelessness, free to dedicate his life to the service of humanity, and with characteristic enthusiasm he at once plunged into the work of the Theosophical Society. In a tribute which appeared shortly after his death an admirer has painted a vivid portrait of the *anagārika*'s life at this period:

> Nothing was too small or too big for him. He would clean his own room, make his own bed, attend to office work, write all the letters and take them to the post himself, not as a matter of virtue but as a part of his daily routine. He would interpret for one, he would prepare a programme for another, he would translate a lecture for someone else, he would write original articles for the newspaper, he would discuss the policy of the paper with the Editor and would correct proofs for him, and he would interview those who visited the office. He wrote to people all over Ceylon inviting them to visit the Head Office and to contribute their good will towards the progress of the cause. All were alike to him, whether one was old or young or a school boy, learned or ignorant, rich or poor did not matter; he instinctively knew what each was able to contribute towards the common good. He spent well nigh fifteen to sixteen hours a day in intensive work. He had a pleasant manner, cheerful at all times: his written and spoken words were eloquent and their sincerity went to the hearts of all those who met him. This bundle of energy and good will continued his useful career at the Buddhist Headquarters for nearly five years. He helped in the foundation of schools, and in Buddhist propaganda. He attracted men to the new organization till the Colombo Buddhist Theosophical Society became a power in the land.

This description might have been written at almost any time during the fifty subsequent years of Dharmapala's career, for his tireless energy in doing good, his unflagging zeal for the propagation of the Dharma, increased rather than diminished with the passing of years, so that we might fittingly apply to him the verse:

> *Appamatto pamattesu suttesu bahujāgaro*
> *abalassaṃ va sīghasso hitvā yāti sumedhaso.*

> Mindful among the unmindful, wide awake among the sleeping, the man of good understanding forges ahead like a swift horse outdistancing a feeble hack.[37]

TOURING CEYLON

In February 1886 Colonel Olcott and C. W. Leadbeater arrived in Colombo to collect money for the Buddhist Educational Fund. Dharmapala was then employed as a junior clerk in the Education Department, and his meals used to be sent daily from home to the Theosophical headquarters where he stayed. Colonel Olcott had planned to tour the whole island, and for this purpose he needed the services of an interpreter. When no one to accompany him could be found he declared that he would be merely wasting his time if no Buddhist was willing to go with him on his tour. Dharmapala promptly offered his services, and applied to the Director of Education for three months' leave. Previous to this he had appeared in the Clerical Examination, pledging to himself, however, that if he passed he would not join government service, but instead dedicate his whole life to the service of humanity. The trio set off from Colombo in the colonel's two-storeyed travelling cart, Olcott and Leadbeater sleeping at night in the upper storey, while Dharmapala occupied the lower berth. For two months they travelled up and down the country, thus inaugurating that long series of historic missionary drives which was eventually to make the bearded colonel and his youthful companion familiar figures in the Sinhala countryside, and which was to surround them before the end of the decade with a halo of almost legendary fame. The tour of 1886 occupies an important place in Dharmapala's development.

Besides bringing him in touch with the hopes and fears, the virtues and failings, of thousands of his fellow-countrymen, it also gave him a glimpse, through the commanding and active personality of Colonel Olcott, of the practical efficiency of the Western races. As interpreter he stood between two worlds, and it was not merely words but ideas which he had to translate. Circumstances made him the common denominator between ancient wisdom and modern knowledge, between the traditions of an old but decayed people and the innovating vitality of a people newly born, and the constant need of passing rapidly from one pole of understanding to the other gave his mind an elasticity and nimbleness of movement of great value to the development of his character. Before long he was not only functioning as the mouthpiece of Colonel Olcott's or Mr Leadbeater's ideas, but forcefully speaking out his own independent opinions on the various socio-religious problems of his day, many of which came under his clear-sighted scrutiny as he passed through the villages of the interior. He saw that many un-Buddhistic foreign customs had crept into the life of the people, and with youthful enthusiasm he extolled the glories of ancient and bewailed the degeneracy of modern Lanka. He fulminated against the habit of eating beef, railed against the use of foreign names and foreign dress, and to the huge delight of his listeners led them in smashing the head-combs which the Sinhalas had adopted from the Malays.[38] He saw how wide and deep was the influence of the Christian missions, how it had eaten into the vitals of the people and was corroding all that was noblest in the national character. He saw, too, how the villagers' faith in and observance of the Dharma were slowly crumbling before the attacks of the missionaries and their hirelings, and it was with all the eloquence of which he was capable that he interpreted Colonel Olcott's magnificent vindications of Buddhism and his impassioned appeals for its revival throughout the length and breadth of the land. Contact with the people who ploughed the fields and planted the paddy not only gave him a first-hand knowledge of his country's problems, but also prevented him from developing any of the bookish humours of a scholar. The peasants that assembled to hear the white Buddhist speak were mostly illiterate, and in order to make Olcott's message intelligible to them his interpreter had to draw upon all his resources of wit and repartee, humour and homely illustration. Not that he ever made them feel he was talking down to them. He spoke as one of themselves, as a Buddhist and as a son of Ceylon, and as such they accepted the young preacher and took him to their hearts. When Colonel Olcott left Ceylon for Madras, Dharmapala and Leadbeater carried on the lecturing tour alone. They were still in the villages of the interior when a letter arrived from the Colonial Secretary informing Dharmapala that he had passed the examination and had been appointed to a better post. Now completely absorbed in Buddhist work, the erstwhile junior clerk felt that the time had come to turn his back upon government service forever, so without delay he replied saying that he was going to work for his religion and requested the Colonial Secretary to accept his resignation. After their return to

Colombo his father advised him to accept the post and hand over his earnings to the Theosophical Society for Buddhist work. He also took him to call on the Colonial Secretary, who asked him to withdraw his resignation; but despite their persuasions Dharmapala was not to be shaken in his resolve, and in the end he was delighted to see that the last tie binding him to a worldly career had been broken. Henceforth he was free to devote himself single-mindedly to the work for which his own aspirations and the blessings of his teachers had already consecrated him.

HE BECOMES 'ANAGARIKA DHARMAPALA'

From this time onwards it becomes more and more difficult to do even a semblance of justice to the many-sided activities of the greatest Buddhist missionary in modern times. During the years 1885–1889 he devoted himself wholeheartedly to the affairs of the Buddhist Theosophical Society, and with the financial support of his grandfather and the cooperation of C. P. Goonewardane, Williams Abrew, Don Carolis, and others, the organization prospered. At Colonel Olcott's request Leadbeater prepared a shorter version of his *Buddhist Catechism*, the first part being translated into Sinhalese by Dharmapala with the help of Sumangala Nayaka Maha Thera, the second by two teachers of the Buddhist English School, James Perera and Wimalasuriya. Both parts were published at the Buddhist Press which Colonel Olcott and Dharmapala had established with the money obtained by issuing debentures. Resolving that this press should become the property of the Buddhist Theosophical Society, Dharmapala requested his grandfather, who owned more shares than anybody else, to present them to the Society, and once he had agreed to do so it was not difficult to persuade the other shareholders to follow his generous example. After liquidating the debts of the *Sandaresa*, their Sinhalese weekly, and establishing it on a firm foundation, Dharmapala decided that it was high time the Buddhists of Ceylon had an English weekly as well. Thirty friends contributed ten rupees each, and with the sum thus raised English type was obtained from Madras, and in December 1888 *The Buddhist* was issued under Leadbeater's editorship as a supplement to the *Sandaresa*. The Sinhalese organ gave publicity to the rural and urban branches of the Ceylon Theosophical Society, reported the progress of the educational fund, and appealed for the opening of more Buddhist schools to counteract Christian propaganda, while its English counterpart concentrated on more technical expositions of the Dharma in relation to Western science and psychology. The latter not only enjoyed a wide circulation among the English-educated upper classes of Ceylon but also circulated in Europe, America, India, Japan, and Australia, thus encircling the earth with the Word of the Buddha, and preparing the way for its more famous successor, the *Maha Bodhi*. Parallel to his journalistic ventures Dharmapala carried on his preaching activities among the people, touring indefatigably from village to village in Colonel Olcott's bullock cart, giving lectures, distributing Buddhist literature, and collecting funds for the educational work already inaugurated by the Theosophical Society. Meanwhile Leadbeater had started a number of Buddhist Sunday Schools in different parts of Colombo, besides establishing an English school (later Ananda College, one of the most celebrated schools in Ceylon) for the benefit of a few personal pupils, among whom was his young favourite Jinarajadasa, afterwards famous as the fourth president of the Theosophical Society at Adyar. It was during this period of intense activity that Don David Hewavitarne assumed the name of Dharmapala, or Guardian of the Law, under which he was subsequently to win the admiration and homage of Buddhists all over the world.

In spite of his preoccupations in Ceylon, Dharmapala was able to find time for a number of trips to Adyar. Under Colonel Olcott's active supervision the world headquarters of the theosophical movement had expanded at an amazing rate, but with the advent of T. Subba Row the influence of Madame Blavatsky had declined, the Buddha had lost ground to Śaṅkara, and after seeing that the occult room had been dismantled Dharmapala felt that the Masters had left the place.

JAPAN

In 1887 Dharmapala read an article on Japan in an issue of the *Fortnightly Review*, and a desire to visit the Land of the Rising Sun at once took possession of his mind. Two years later, in 1889, it was fulfilled. The Buddhists of Japan, hearing of Colonel Olcott's splendid services to the Dharma in Ceylon, were eager that he should visit their country as well, and therefore sent him a cordial invitation. The emissary to whom was entrusted the responsibility of escorting the colonel to Japan arrived in Colombo in December 1888, and after being entertained there by Dharmapala was so pleased with the selfless young Buddhist worker that he extended the invitation to him also. Colonel Olcott, seeing in the visit an opportunity of linking the Mahāyāna Buddhism of Japan with the Theravāda Buddhism of Ceylon, decided to accept the invitation, and urged his young friend, who had accompanied the emissary Noguchi to Adyar, to go with him. Back went Dharmapala to Colombo, and booked passages on the *S. S. Djeninah*, a French liner. Olcott arrived soon afterwards, and on 17 January 1889, the day before their departure, the Buddhists of Ceylon held a farewell function in their honour at the Theosophical Society hall. After delivering a splendid discourse, in the course of which he invoked the blessings of the *devas* and the Triple Gem on the mission, Sumangala Nayaka Maha Thera handed over to Colonel Olcott a Sanskrit letter of good wishes addressed to the chief high priests of Japan. This historic letter, the first official communication that had passed for centuries between a Southern Buddhist dignitary and the heads of one of the most important branches of the Northern Buddhist sangha, expressed the renewed hope that the Buddhists of Asia would unite for the good of the whole Eastern world. With the precious document in their charge, Olcott, Dharmapala, and the poet Noguchi left the shores of Ceylon, and after calling at Singapore, Saigon, Hong Kong, and Shanghai (where Dharmapala began to suffer from the intense cold, and saw snow for the first time in his life), the party arrived at Kobe, where the chief high priests of the seven leading sects of Japanese Buddhism had assembled on the jetty to receive them. Colonel Olcott had to respond alone to the warm welcome which they were accorded, as Dharmapala was too ill to do more than sit on the deck and watch the proceedings. But to the young Sinhala's delight and gratification all seven high priests insisted on coming onto the deck and paying their respects to him as the representative of the Buddhists of Ceylon. The visitors were then conducted to the Tendai sect temple in Kobe. Above the main gate the Buddhist flag fluttered in an icy wind, bearing huge Japanese characters which Noguchi translated as 'Welcome to Dai Nippon'. Inside the temple they found an enormous audience of Japanese youths waiting to hear a message from the West, which the imagination of Far Eastern Buddhists has always associated with the holy land of India. After Colonel Olcott had spoken in his usual impressive manner, Dharmapala addressed them emphasizing the cultural and religious unity of Japan and Ceylon, and pointing out that the present meeting was the first recorded contact in history between Sinhala and Japanese Buddhists. He concluded by saying that they were proud of Japan, eulogizing her as 'a sovereign star in a continent of servitude', words which not unnaturally drew loud and prolonged applause from his auditors. Almost immediately after their reception at Kobe, Colonel Olcott and Dharmapala left for Kyoto, where they witnessed the celebrations that attended the promulgation of the New Japanese Constitution of 1889. Not long afterwards a convention of chief high priests was held in the Chiongin Temple, and Colonel Olcott addressed them on his mission. Dharmapala, who was now suffering from rheumatic fever, had to attend the convention in an invalid's chair, but in spite of physical suffering, great was his elation when Colonel Olcott read Sumangala Nayaka Thera's Sanskrit letter of goodwill to the Buddhists of Japan, a Japanese translation of which was presented to each high priest. The bearded American theosophist and the slim, ascetic young Sinhala Buddhist realized that they were playing the leading roles in one of the most important scenes in the great drama of modern Buddhist revival, marking as it did the first official contact that had taken place between the sundered branches of the Buddhist world for nearly a thousand years. But when the curtain had fallen on this historic scene Dharmapala was forced to enter the Government Hospital at Kyoto for treatment, while Colonel Olcott embarked upon his triumphal tour of Buddhist Japan. But if in the colonel's case Mohammed went to meet the mountain, in Dharmapala's the mountain came to meet Mohammed. Doctors, priests, students, teachers, writers, philosophers, and businessmen poured in an endless stream to his bedside, so that by the time he was ready to leave the hospital, Dharmapala had not only added to his knowledge about Japan but also become an enthusiastic admirer of the Japanese. He was enthusiastic too about the ancient Buddhist city of Kyoto, where he saw the Daibutsu, the great image of Amitābha which is the biggest bronze statue in the world, and a temple which, when illuminated at night, glittered resplendently with five hundred golden figures of the Buddha. A few days before his departure from Japan, the officers and students of the Bungakurio, the Japanese Military Academy, several of whom had attended him during his illness with the utmost devotion, invited him to witness a huge military parade which was to be held in his honour. Five hundred students participated in the parade, which was followed by athletic sports. The five-coloured Buddhist flag fluttered above the gathering, and the grounds were decorated with five hundred lanterns. The representative of the chief high priest, together with other officers of the Hongan-ji sect, attended the function, and deeply moved though he had been by the boundless hospitality accorded him Dharmapala could not help feeling the incongruity of this union between Buddhism and militarism, even as he had previously been shocked by the way in which the majority of the Japanese clergy combined their religious duties with family life.

During the remainder of Dharmapala's visit bouts of illness alternated with brief periods of lecturing and sightseeing, and eventually he was forced to leave the country sooner than he wished. A farewell address was given to the chief high priests of the Japanese Buddhist sects, who handed over to Colonel Olcott a reply to Sumangala Nayaka Thera's Sanskrit letter of goodwill. This letter reciprocated the high priest's fraternal greetings, expressed the hope that in future the two great divisions of the Buddhist world might know each other more intimately, and described with satisfaction the wonderful success which had attended the mission. All Kyoto was decorated for the occasion, and in the evening, at a meeting attended by the governor and other high officials, Colonel Olcott spoke on India and Ceylon and Dharmapala poured out his love and gratitude to Japan in a highly emotional speech which was wildly applauded. After bidding the Colonel an affectionate and tearful farewell at Osaka, Dharmapala embarked for Ceylon, while Olcott, who had already delivered forty-five lectures all over the country, left for Kinsui Province to deliver ten more. The captain of the *Caledonia*, the ship for which Dharmapala had exchanged the *Natal* at Shanghai, was a friend of Madame Blavatsky, and it was therefore natural that he should soon be on friendly terms with his Sinhala passenger. He extolled Madame Blavatsky to the skies, declaring that she was a 'miracle of nature', and Dharmapala of course agreed enthusiastically with these eulogies of his beloved teacher. But when the captain confided that Olcott was jealous of her, and that he had engineered her departure from India, his young listener, ever faithful to his friends, hotly repudiated the suggestion, saying that if they had been jealous of each other the Masters would never have committed the destinies of the Theosophical Society to their joint care. After that they hardly spoke to each other again, and Dharmapala made friends with an

Italian with whom he played chess, and a Frenchman who prophesied war in Europe. His loyal, affectionate, and grateful nature could never bear in silence an attack upon a friend, and at this period especially devotion to the Colonel was one of the major passions of his life. A few years later, when serious charges were made against Swami Vivekananda in Calcutta, it was Dharmapala who spoke publicly in his defence with such vigour that he was at once restored to popular favour. To him a friend in need was a friend indeed, and great was his disappointment, therefore, when in the course of his career he discovered that people whom he had defended, helped, and trusted were slandering him behind his back and secretly plotting to frustrate his plans. Ever frank, honest, open, and outspoken himself, Dharmapala heartily detested every form of trickery, subterfuge, and intrigue. Boldly and uncompromisingly he stated his objectives; fearlessly and wholeheartedly he strove to realize them. In a world where diplomacy in politics, cheating in business, misrepresentation of facts in journalism, and deceitfulness in all the relations of life, have become the order of the day, straightforwardness such as this does not always make for material success, but as a sign of absolute integrity of character it is one of the hallmarks of spiritual greatness, and as such must ever command our admiration and respect. Whatever Dharmapala did was noble and upright, and it was therefore done, not in the obscurity of shadows, but in the full blaze of the all-revealing light of day.

BACK IN CEYLON

Colonel Olcott returned from his mission to Japan, where his activities had inaugurated a major revival of Buddhism, in the middle of June 1889, accompanied by three Japanese priests who intended to study Pāli and the Theravāda traditions of Ceylon. A meeting of welcome was held in the Theosophical Society headquarters, which were gay with Buddhist flags and Japanese lanterns, and Colonel Olcott told a crowded audience of the success of his mission and paid warm tribute to the work of his young Sinhala colleague. Receptions over, he and Dharmapala plunged once more into the work of the Buddhist Theosophical Society, travelling together by train and bullock cart from one end of the country to the other. Day after day for more than a year they collected funds, opened schools, and addressed meetings.

Whenever Olcott was called on theosophical business to India or Europe Dharmapala carried on the work either single-handed or in cooperation with one or another of the European theosophists who had started coming to Ceylon to help in the revival of Buddhism. On one such occasion, when he was touring with Dr Daly in the hill country near Kandy, he discovered at the Hanguranketa village temple a palm-leaf book on meditation, and requested the incumbent of the temple, Bhikṣu Ratanapala, to get it transcribed for him. Many years later the same work was published by the Pāli Text Society, and translated by F. L. Woodward as *The Manual of a Mystic*. In the course of his travels Dharmapala came across a number of such books, but in spite of all his enquiries he never succeeded in finding even a single person, whether monk or layman, who could instruct him in the actual meditational practices that they described. Being from boyhood of strongly mystical temperament, as we have already pointed out, it was impossible for him to rest satisfied with a merely theoretical knowledge of the subject, and in spite of all difficulties, after making a careful study of the *Satipaṭṭhāna Sutta* and the *Visuddhimagga*, he embarked upon the regular practice of meditation, rising each day before dawn for the purpose.[39] The personal diaries that he kept for more than forty years abound in references not only to the practice of yoga, but to his unremitting efforts to achieve absolute mental purity and his ceaseless cultivation of goodwill to all sentient beings, and bear eloquent testimony to the fact that beneath the dynamic activity of the selfless worker for Buddhism there lay the serenity and mindfulness of the yogi. At the Adyar theosophical headquarters, whither he had gone to attend the annual convention of 1890, he joined the Esoteric Section of the Theosophical Society, and received some practical instructions on meditation from an old Burmese gentleman who had come with the deputation sent to Colonel Olcott by the Buddhists of Rangoon, who had already collected a lakh of rupees for the propagation of Buddhism in foreign lands, inviting him to come to Burma and assist them in their work.

PILGRIMAGE IN INDIA

Colonel Olcott left for Burma with the deputation, while Dharmapala, who had been spending most of his time in study and meditation, decided to visit the Buddhist holy places in northern India, and invited the

Japanese priest Kozen Gunaratana, who had accompanied him to Adyar from Colombo, to go with him. He agreed, and they left on 12 January, arriving at Bombay, where they spent a couple of days sightseeing, on 14 January, and at Benares on 18 January. Hearing from his host of a yogini known as Maji (Reverend Mother) who lived in a cave on the banks of the Ganges, Dharmapala at once went to see her, and after what he describes as a pleasant chat she presented him, at his request, with a rosary. The next day, 20 January, Babu Upendranath Basu drove them over to Sarnath where the Lord Buddha had preached his first sermon nearly five-and-twenty centuries before, and after describing the ruined appearance of the place Dharmapala remarks in his diary for the day, 'What a pity that no Buddhists are occupying the place to preserve them [the stupa and carvings] from the hand of vandals.'

FIRST VISIT TO BODH GAYA

Yet it was not at Sarnath, but at Bodh Gaya, which they reached on 22 January 1891, that Dharmapala Hewavitarne, then in his twenty-ninth year, received the inspiration that was to change not only his own life but the whole course of modern Buddhist history. The crucial moment of his career had come. At last he stood face to face with his destiny. The happenings of that most decisive day in his whole life, when for a moment the fate of Buddhism in modern India, with all the incalculable consequences thereof, hung trembling in the balance, is best described in the words of his own diary:

> 22 January. After taking breakfast we went in the company of Durga Babu and Dr Chatterjee to Buddha Gaya – the most sacred spot to the Buddhists. After driving 6 miles [from Gaya] we arrived at the holy spot. Within a mile you could see lying scattered here and there broken statues etc. of our blessed Lord. At the entrance to the mahant's temple on both sides of the portico there are statues of our Lord in the attitude of meditation and expounding the Law. How elevating! The sacred Vihara – the Lord sitting on his throne and the great solemnity which pervades all round makes the heart of the pious devotee weep. How delightful! As soon as I touched with my forehead the Vajrasana a sudden impulse came to my mind. It prompted me to stop here and take

> care of this sacred spot – so sacred that nothing in the world is equal to this place where Prince Sakya Sinha gained Enlightenment under the bodhi tree.... When the sudden impulse came to me I asked Kozen priest whether he would join me, and he joyously assented and more than this he had been thinking the same thing. We both solemnly promised that we would stop here until some Buddhist priests came to take charge of the place.

It is characteristic of Dharmapala that when he made this momentous decision the question of the ownership of the temple never even occurred to him. He saw that the most sacred spot in the Buddhist world was being shamefully neglected, its sculptures carted away, the image desecrated, and he assumed that as a Buddhist he had not only the duty but also the right to stay there and protect the holy place. Nor did the government officials whom he met give him, as yet, any cause to think otherwise. The keys of the Burmese Rest House, built twenty years before by King Mindon of Burma, were given to him, and as soon as he had settled down there he started writing the first of those thousands of letters which he was afterwards to write in the interests of the Bodh Gaya temple. He wrote to scores of people in Ceylon, Burma, and India describing the appalling condition of the sacred spot, and pleading for the revival of Buddhism and the re-establishment of the sangha there. He also wrote long articles in Sinhalese and English respectively to the *Sandaresa* and the *Buddhist*. For some time he received no replies, and great was his agony of spirit when he began to think that his appeal had gone unheeded, and that the Buddhist world, still sunk in the torpor of centuries, was indifferent to the fate of the Maha Bodhi temple. Shortage of money began to add to his difficulties, for he had brought with him enough to provide the necessities of a few days only, but with his determination strengthened rather than weakened by the difficulties he was undergoing he resolved to die of starvation rather than quit the sacred place. In spite of mundane anxieties the atmosphere of the moonlit nights, when the imposing structure of the temple stood in bold relief against the starry sky, played upon his spiritual sensibilities to such an extent that one day he writes in his diary:

> 17 February ... This night at 12 for the first time in my life I experienced that peace which passeth all understanding. How

> peaceful it was. The life of our Lord is a lofty and elevating subject for meditation. The Four Truths and the Noble Eightfold Path alone can make the devoted pupil of Nature happy.

At last the letters for which he had been waiting with such eagerness, and the money which he so badly needed, began to arrive, and Dharmapala no longer felt that he was alone with his enthusiasm in an indifferent world. Not until he met Mr G. A. Grierson, the Collector of Gaya, did he begin to glimpse the enormous obstacles, the deeply entrenched vested interests, that blocked his path. Hitherto he had been led to suppose by the minor officials with whom he had discussed the matter, that the Maha Bodhi temple was government property, and that there would be no difficulty in transferring it from the management of the Hindu mahant to the custody of its legitimate proprietors, the Buddhists. But now, to his astonishment, Mr Grierson informed him that the temple, together with its revenues, belonged to the mahant, adding that with the help of the government it might be possible for the Buddhists to buy it from him. Having by this time spent more than six weeks in Bodh Gaya, Dharmapala at once left for Calcutta, intending to raise funds in Burma for the purchase of the temple. In Calcutta, then not only the political but also the intellectual metropolis of India, he stayed at the house of a Bengali theosophist, Babu Neel Comal Mookerjee, who became a lifelong friend of the *anagārika* and a loyal supporter of his mission. Together they visited various places of interest in the city, including the Indian Museum and the Royal Asiatic Society of Bengal, where, to his great delight, Dharmapala made the acquaintance of Sarat Chandra Das, famous for his travels in Tibet, and for his knowledge of the language and religious literature of that country. He also won the friendship of Narendra Nath Sen, the editor of the *Indian Mirror*, a theosophist whose eloquent pen was for many years ready to plead for the revival of Buddhism in India. From Calcutta Dharmapala sailed for Rangoon, where he spent most of his stay with Moung Hpo Mhyin, a theosophist and a student of Buddhist yoga, who encouraged him in his plans for the restoration of Bodh Gaya to Buddhist hands, and promised to help financially. Other Burmans also became interested in the scheme, and although unable to raise the funds for which he had hoped, Dharmapala was by no means disappointed with the success of his mission. He noted that the Burmese were better versed in the subtleties of their religion than were his own countrymen, and that in Burma the practice of meditation had not been allowed to die out as in Ceylon. He sailed for Colombo via Adyar with high hopes, determined to found a society for the reclamation of Bodh Gaya. On his arrival at Madras he heard of the unexpected death of Madame Blavatsky. He wrote in his diary:

> The loss is irreparable. Humanity will feel the loss. The spiritual world lost its dearest well-wisher, guide and teacher in her. Who will take her place? I little expected that she would die so soon. The E. S. must be carried on if the T. S. is to live and do good; but who will be the agent between the world and the Masters?[40]

ESTABLISHMENT OF THE MAHA BODHI SOCIETY

The Bodh Gaya Maha Bodhi Society was founded in Colombo on 31 May 1891. The Ven. Hikkaduwe Sumangala Nayaka Maha Thera presided over the inaugural meeting, at which Dharmapala related how the impulse to restore the sacred shrine to Buddhist hands had come to him as he knelt beneath the ancient spreading branches of the bodhi tree. After the high priest had spoken in support of the scheme the office-bearers of the newly-born Society were elected, with Ven. Sumangala as president, Colonel Olcott as director, Weerasekera and Dharmapala as secretaries, W. de Abrew as treasurer, and Pandit Batuwantudave and twelve others as members of the committee. The formation of one more society did not attract much attention in those days of widespread Buddhist revival, and Dharmapala not only experienced difficulties in rousing the interest of the laity, but also in finding monks willing to accompany him to Bodh Gaya. But by this time he was used to difficulties. Determined that on the full-moon day of the month of Āsādha, when the Buddha preached his first sermon, members of the sangha should once more be in residence in Bodh Gaya, he appealed first to the Siamese, then to the Burmese sect, and in the end succeeded in obtaining four monks: Dunuwila Chandajoti, Matale Sumangala, Anuradhapura Pemananda, and Galle Sudassana. On 10 July the party set out on its historic mission, reaching Calcutta on 15 July and arriving at their destination a few days later. In the evening of the day following that of their arrival, the full moon rose bright and glorious in the blue sky, and Dharmapala notes with satisfaction in his diary that after seven centuries the Buddhist flag had been hoisted at Bodh Gaya:

> Ah, how beautifully it flutters in the moonlight breeze! May the mission be a success! I hope and sincerely trust that the priests may be a light to the people and they will lead a life of purity and show the people of India the intrinsic merits of our holy religion. On 22 January last I pledged that I will work on to make this sacred spot to be cared for by our own Bhikshus and I am glad that after seven months of hard work I have succeeded in establishing a Buddhist Mission.

Sanguine words! Having installed the four monks in the Burmese Rest House, Dharmapala opened negotiations with the mahant for the purchase of a piece of land, and at this point begins the story of his unequal struggle with the second wealthiest landlord in the whole province of Bihar, a struggle in which we hardly know whether to be more astonished at the invincible determination displayed on one side, or at the incredible baseness and brutality on the other. The intervention of the Government, and the ambiguous nature of its policy in the matter, only served to 'make confusion worse confounded', and it is impossible for us even to outline all the vicissitudes of Dharmapala's single-handed struggle to secure for the Buddhists a foothold in their own most holy shrine. First the mahant promised a piece of land, then he denied that he had promised it, and in the end agreed to give a much smaller piece. Hereupon Mr Grierson entered the scene, first ordering registration of the deed to be postponed, and then suggesting that a different plot of land should be selected. Annoyed at Grierson's interference, the mahant told Dharmapala to return to Ceylon and come back and discuss the matter later. After shuttling for some time between the two parties Dharmapala succeeded in appeasing the mahant and persuading him to part with the plot indicated by the Collector. But this time the size of his original offer was reduced by half, and Dharmapala had to interview his notary no less than seven times before the deed was considered to be in order. Weary of all these vacillations, which were only a foretaste of what was yet to come, Dharmapala decided to organize an International Buddhist Conference, and after his return from a brief visit to Ceylon, the conference had its memorable sitting at Bodh Gaya on 31 October 1891, on the eve of the Lt Governor of Bengal's visit to the holy spot. Representatives from Ceylon, China, Japan, and Chittagong attended, and the Japanese delegates informed the conference that the Buddhists of their country would be willing to purchase the temple from the mahant, in consequence of which it was resolved that a deputation should wait on him with a proposal to the effect. It was further resolved to call for subscriptions from all Buddhist countries for the construction of a Buddhist monastery, to establish Buddhist propaganda, and to undertake the translation of Buddhist texts into the Indian vernaculars. Ever an enthusiastic admirer of Japan, Dharmapala had hoisted the Japanese flag beneath the bodhi tree side by side with the Buddhist flag, and it is more than likely that when the Lt Governor and his party visited the place the sight of it not only reminded him of the Russo-Japanese problem, but also suggested to his mind the possibility of the Japanese using Bodh Gaya as spearhead of their ambitions not only in India but throughout the whole of Asia. At any rate he refused to meet the Buddhist delegation, and sent Dharmapala a message through Mr Grierson to the effect that the temple belonged to the mahant, and that the Government could not accede to the Buddhist request that it should intervene and restore Bodh Gaya to their control.

MAHA BODHI JOURNAL

On 25 October Dharmapala gave his first public lecture in India, at the Albert Hall, Calcutta, under the presidency of Narendra Nath Sen, his subject being 'Buddhism in its Relation to Hinduism'. At the beginning of 1892 the office of the Maha Bodhi Society was shifted to Calcutta, where the Bengali intelligentsia looked with sympathy upon the object for which it had been founded, and in the month of May Dharmapala started the *Maha Bodhi* journal in order to facilitate the interchange of news between Buddhist countries. The first issue of the magazine, which has now been published uninterruptedly for more than sixty years,[41] consisted of eight closely printed quarto pages, and bore as its motto the Buddha's great exhortation to his first sixty disciples,

> Go ye, O Bhikkhus, and wander forth for the gain of the many, the welfare of the many, in compassion for the world, for the good, for

> the gain, for the welfare of gods and men. Proclaim, O Bhikkhus, the doctrine glorious. Preach ye a life of holiness, perfect and pure.[42]

The journal was edited by Dharmapala, and his two articles on 'A United Buddhist World' and 'The Mahāyāna School of Buddhism' were the first of the hundreds of articles which he was subsequently to write for its pages. It is interesting to find him controverting Sir Monier-Williams' opinion that the Southern School of Buddhism belongs to the Hīnayāna, maintaining instead that 'the Buddhism of Ceylon belongs to the oldest school of the Mahāyāna', and asserting that only 'the eighteen schismatic schools, offshoots of the Theravāda school, because they taught the incomplete doctrines, were included in the Hīnayāna'. Besides an article by Colonel Olcott entitled 'The Sweet Spirit of Buddhism', the magazine contained historical notes by Dharmapala, correspondence, news of Buddhist activities in Japan and Burma, and a reproduction of a significant article from the *Indian Mirror*, which contains the statement 'India dates her misfortunes since the day of the disappearance of Buddhism', and indicates the extent to which educated Indian opinion was in agreement with Dharmapala's views. Translations from the Buddhist scriptures and papers on Buddhist philosophy, as well as articles on Buddhism by writers both oriental and occidental, were included in subsequent issues, and before many months had passed the journal had attained a fairly wide circulation not only in Asia but in Europe and America as well. Progress was by no means either smooth or easy, however; funds were often lacking and frequently the Society's sole worker had to choose between buying stamps for posting the journal and food for his evening meal. But the sacrifice was made joyfully, with the reflection that since there was no self there was no sacrifice either. In those days Dharmapala used to spend the night with the Mookerjee family at Baniapukur Road rising at two or three o'clock in the morning for meditation. Then he would read the Buddhist scriptures, together with the works of Max Müller, Sir Edwin Arnold, and Sir William Hunter. During the day he would attend the office which the Maha Bodhi Society and the Theosophical Society shared at 2 Creek Row, devoting himself to the editing and managing of the journal, and engaging in a voluminous correspondence, frequently writing twenty or thirty letters with his own hand in the course of a single day. With unflagging zeal and tireless energy he worked for the cause to which he had dedicated his life, appealing for funds to Buddhists all over the world, arranging weekly public meetings, and labouring to interest every person he met in the redemption of the Maha Bodhi temple from the sacrilegious hands of those to whom it was nothing but a source of income. In spite of his activities in Calcutta and at Bodh Gaya, Dharmapala found time to attend the Annual Conventions at Adyar, as well as to establish relations with the Himalayan Buddhists of Darjeeling, to whom he presented some relics of the Buddha, a few leaves from the bodhi tree, and a Buddhist flag. After the relics had been taken in a colourful procession through the crowded streets of the town to the residence of Raja Tondub Pulger, where a number of Tibetan and Sikkimese dignitaries, both lay and ecclesiastical, had assembled, Dharmapala gave a speech on the ancient decline and modern revival of Buddhism, and appealed to the Buddhists of Tibet to support the work of the Maha Bodhi Society. Some months after this historic function, when Sinhala and Tibetan Buddhists met once again after centuries of separation, Colonel Olcott arrived in Calcutta, and it was decided that he, Dharmapala, and Mr Edge, a European theosophist from Darjeeling, should visit Bodh Gaya. On their arrival at Gaya Station on 4 February 1893 they were met by Ven. Chandajoti, who excitedly informed them that on the evening of the previous Friday the mahant's men had made a murderous assault on the two monks and their servants, at the Burmese Rest House, while they were peacefully engaged in reading the Vinaya and religious conversation. Bhikṣu Sumangala, who is described as a particularly quiet and inoffensive monk, was so badly beaten about the head with sticks that he had to be removed to hospital, and when the horrified party visited the Rest House the bloodstains were still visible upon the floor. The news of this cowardly and unprovoked attack created a sensation, and meetings of protest were held not only in India but in several Buddhist countries as well. Colonel Olcott at once interviewed the mahant, who stubbornly refused either to sell or lease the land on any terms, or to allow the Buddhists to erect a rest house for pilgrims. Dharmapala was insistent that the assailants should be detected and punished, and the well-known Gaya pleader Nanda Kishore Lall was therefore retained as counsel for the Maha Bodhi Society. In these circumstances began a connection which soon transcended the usual relation of lawyer and client, and developed into a strong mutual affection which was terminated only by death. The sole redeeming feature of the whole sordid business was the exemplary behaviour of the injured monk, who had not only made no attempt to defend himself from the vicious blows of his attackers, but who actually sent to the police, while still in hospital, an application stating that neither he nor his fellow monks could be witnesses to the case under issue and thus cause their assailants to be punished. It is said that the District Superintendent of Police roared with laughter when he read this, remarking, 'I always thought these Indian priests made a living out of religion. These Buddhist priests from Ceylon actually practise it.' The mahant in his palace merely chuckled.

A few weeks later Dharmapala was informed by Nanda Kishore Lall that the mahant's lease on the land had expired, and that he had renewed his application for a permanent lease. With his usual optimism, Dharmapala was confident that it would now be easy for the Maha Bodhi Society to acquire the place, and that the Buddhists of the world would willingly combine to subscribe the *lakh* of rupees which, he was informed, would be required to make the purchase. He rushed back to Calcutta, and at once wrote appeals for help to every quarter. Chandajoti was dispatched to Akyab, while Colonel Olcott sailed on the same mission to Rangoon where he found the city in the throes of a business depression and was compelled to return empty-handed. After a month devoted to office work, lectures on Buddhism in the public squares, theosophical meetings, correspondence, study, and meditation conversations on yoga with his friend Nirodanath Mookerjee, and exhortations to Nirodanath's son Naranath, a boy of 16 or 17 of whom he had become extremely fond, Dharmapala left for Burma on 13 May, and three days later reached Rangoon, where he found his old friend Moung Hpo Mhyin and a number of other gentlemen waiting at the jetty to receive him. Another month went by in a whirlwind round of visits to wealthy Buddhists in Rangoon, Mandalay, and Moulmein, and although the required sum was not actually collected, the necessary promises were made, and Dharmapala returned to Calcutta feeling that his mission had not been wholly unsuccessful. After extricating the Society's work from the confusion into which it had fallen during his absence, he entrained for Gaya, where he found that events were fast taking a new turn. Nanda Kishore told him that the Maha Bodhi temple was really situated in the village of Maha Bodhi, and not in the village of Mastipur Taradi as the mahant's people claimed. Again Dharmapala's hopes rose high, but when they called upon the Collector, Mr McPherson, explained the situation to him, and mentioned Sir Edwin Arnold's recent article about Bodh Gaya in the London *Daily Telegraph*, he merely remarked that everything should be done as quietly as possible and that it would be better to postpone negotiations until after Dharmapala's return from Chicago. The circle of the young Buddhist missionary's activities was becoming wider still, embracing not only India and Ceylon, not only Asia, but the whole world, and although the fate of the Maha Bodhi temple remained unsettled, the course of events was compelling Dharmapala to direct his steps elsewhere, and the time had come for him to carry the message of his compassionate Master across the seas to races to whom it was as yet unknown.

THE WORLD'S PARLIAMENT OF RELIGIONS IN CHICAGO

The World's Parliament of Religions which was held in Chicago in 1893 was one of the most important and characteristic events of the late nineteenth century. Fifty years earlier the influence of Christian dogma and popular ignorance even of the existence of the great oriental religions would have rendered such a gathering an impossibility. As it was, the organizers of the Parliament were accused by a missionary in China of 'coquetting with false religions' and 'planning treason against Christ'. Fifty years later, political unrest and widespread indifference to religion would either have made the venture abortive or reduced it to little more than an anthropological curiosity. In the closing decade of the nineteenth century, however, the time was ripe for the presentation of the diverse religions of the world from a common platform not by scholars but by men who actually followed them, and when the special committee appointed for the purpose by the president of the Columbian Exposition circulated their plans the idea of a World's Parliament of Religions met with general acceptance. The chairman of the committee, Dr J. R. Burrows, who had received copies of the *Maha Bodhi*, entered into correspondence with Dharmapala, and in the end invited him to Chicago as the representative of the Southern Buddhist Church. With his usual modesty, Dharmapala doubted his ability to expound the Dharma before such a distinguished gathering, but his friends were insistent that he should go, one of them declaring that far more important than any amount of scholarship was the living conviction of the truth of the Buddha's word. Such a conviction was the breath of Dharmapala's life. After much consideration he decided to accept the invitation, reflecting that it would enable him to visit Japan and China in the interests of the Society without putting any additional strain on its resources. Only Colonel Olcott was against the trip, roundly declaring that with so much work to be done in India it was a waste of time. However, Dharmapala was by this time accustomed to deciding things for himself, and in the end the Colonel's opposition collapsed and he promised to write to Mrs Besant, who was also attending the Parliament, asking her to keep an eye on his young colleague.

After entrusting the journal to Sarat Chandra Das, Dharmapala left Calcutta at the beginning of July, and on the evening of the day of his arrival in Colombo was presented with a purse by the Ceylon Theosophical Society. Sumangala Nayaka Thera invoked the blessings of the *devas* on his mission, and on behalf of the Buddhists of Ceylon gave him a mandate to Dr Burrows. On 20 July his parents, relatives, and friends, together with a number of Buddhists and theosophists, came on board the *Britannia* to bid the young adventurer farewell. His mother kissed him on the face, and his father, who had generously provided him with new clothes and money for the trip, kissed his hand. At last the ship weighed anchor, and as the sun set in red and golden splendour over the palm-fringed shores of Ceylon, Dharmapala was left alone with his Buddha relic and image, and the twenty thousand copies of the five precepts which he had had printed for free distribution. The journey to England passed quietly enough in the usual round of study, meditation, and voluminous correspondence, together with occasional sightseeing at Aden, Port Said, and Brindisi, and conversation with some of the passengers on board, to whom he distributed his leaflets. At Gibraltar he saw some fine silk handkerchiefs impressed with the picture of the Rock, and felt that he would like to see the Buddhist flag and the five precepts printed on silk handkerchiefs in the same way.

FIRST VISIT TO ENGLAND

On 11 August Dharmapala saw England for the first time, afterwards writing in his diary,

> The first sight of English foliage made me think of England with a feeling of affection. I have seen beautiful scenery, but I was simply delighted at this first glimpse.

A telegram arrived from Sir Edwin Arnold, author of *The Light of Asia,* whom Dharmapala reverenced as his 'English Guru', and his heart was warmed as he read the words, 'Welcome to England, etc.' Upon reaching Gravesend the following day Dharmapala was delighted to find Sir Edwin himself waiting at the Albert Docks to receive him. With the poet were several theosophists, including Leadbeater and his young favourite Jinarajadasa, whom he had kidnapped and carried off to England. It was arranged that Dharmapala should stay with Sir Edwin Arnold, with whom he called on the Secretary of State for India, Lord Kimberley, who promised that the letter Sir Edwin had already written him about the Maha Bodhi temple should be forwarded to the Viceroy. Leadbeater took him to see Mrs Besant, introduced him to the leading British theosophists, showed him the sights of London, took him out to lunch and dinner, and was in fact so unfailingly kind and lavishly hospitable that a mind less innocent of intrigue than Dharmapala's would have immediately understood that the theosophists, who had no doubt been warned by Colonel Olcott that the young founder of the Maha Bodhi Society had begun to be impatient of their control, were doing their best to entice him back into the fold. Leadbeater even told Dharmapala that he had received money from the Master to be spent on his account. Visits to Dr Rhys Davids, the great Pāli scholar, the British Museum, and theosophical groups, filled the days until the time of their departure. With him on board the *City of Paris* were the theosophists Chakravarti and Miss Müller, and of course Mrs Besant, who had already told him in London that for the sake of the Masters and the Cause she must take care of him, and who now declared that before her death Madame Blavatsky had actually said the same thing! Naturally, Dharmapala was impressed by these statements, and wrote in his diary that Mrs Besant was like a mother to him. On 2 September the party arrived at New York, where more theosophists were waiting to welcome them, and on 6 September they reached Chicago.

Dharmapala was one of the most popular speakers at the Parliament, and his addresses and lectures were considered to be important contributions to its proceedings. Apart from a sermon on 'The Pure Life' which he delivered at the Unitarian Church, his first public appearance was at the close of the crowded first session of the Parliament when, surrounded by representatives of the world's religions, many of them attired in brilliant national costumes and gorgeous ecclesiastical vestments, he brought to the four thousand people who had assembled in the Hall of Columbus to hear him

> the good wishes of four-hundred-and-seventy-five millions of Buddhists, the blessings and peace of the religious founder of that system which has prevailed so many centuries in Asia, which has made Asia mild, and which is today, in its twenty-fourth century of existence, the prevailing religion of those countries.

The impression that he made on the assembly is preserved in a letter published at the time:

> With his black, curly locks thrown back from his broad brow, his keen, clear eye fixed upon the audience, his long brown fingers emphasizing the utterances of his vibrant voice, he looked the very image of a propagandist, and one trembled to know that such a figure stood at the head of the movement to consolidate all the disciples of Buddha and to spread 'the light of Asia' throughout the civilized world.[43]

During the week that followed, Dharmapala made the acquaintance of a number of the delegates, among whom were several Japanese Buddhists, spoke two or three times a day on Buddhism and theosophy, and attended the protracted and crowded meetings of the Parliament, remarking with disgust after one long and tiring session, 'All papers full of Theology and Anthropomorphism but pure life naught.' Needless to say, his own paper on 'The World's Debt to Buddha' which he read on 18 September, with the centuries-old image of the Buddha on a table beside him, contained no trace of either theology or anthropomorphism, although quite a lot of it was devoted to the pure life. The paper was moreover innocent of oratorical effects, and showed none of the dazzling intellectual brilliance exhibited by other contributors, the modest young speaker doubtless feeling that after having endured for five-and-twenty centuries his venerable religion could make its way in the world without the adventitious aid of rhetoric and paradox. What he therefore laid before the Parliament was a plain statement of Buddhist principles, supported by numerous citations from the scriptures, without any plan or artistic arrangement, but simply classified under various sub-headings. Dharmapala, 'the servant of the Lord Buddha' as he loved to call himself, was not eager to make a splendid speech, being content if he could function as the humble mouthpiece of the voice of Truth. This very lack of artifice was not without its attractions, apparently, for Mr C. T. Strauss of New York, a life-long student of philosophy and comparative religion, was so impressed by what he heard that he expressed his desire to become a Buddhist, and at what the newspapers described as 'a simple, yet impressive' ceremony held under the auspices of the Theosophical Society of Chicago, he received the five precepts from Dharmapala, becoming not only the first person to be admitted to the Buddhist fold on American soil, but also the devoted friend of his preceptor, and a staunch supporter of the Maha Bodhi Society. The closing days of the Parliament were for Dharmapala full of strenuous activity. So striking was the impression made by the young preacher from Ceylon that whereas his colleague Vivekananda was compared with the noble but passionate Othello, Dharmapala was compared with no less a person than Jesus Christ. We are not told that any of the Christian delegates were paid this handsome compliment. So popular had he become, moreover, by his amiable disposition and evident spirituality that, in the words of a contemporary newspaper report, 'The mere announcement that he would lecture in the Athenaeum building on Buddhism and theosophy was sufficient to attract an audience too large for the hall.' By the time the final session of the Parliament had ended, and Dharmapala had spoken his last words to the great gathering, the conviction had formed itself in his mind that he could disseminate the Dharma in America, and he decided that after two years he would return and establish Buddhism. The concluding words of his farewell address are an apt summary of the message that he so earnestly sought to deliver to the peoples of the West, and of which he was himself the living embodiment:

> Learn to think without prejudice, love all beings for love's sake, express your convictions fearlessly, lead a life of purity, and the sunlight of truth will illuminate you. If theology and dogma stand in your way in the search of truth, put them aside. Be earnest and work out your salvation with diligence and the fruits of holiness will be yours.

HONOLULU: MEETING WITH MRS MARY E. FOSTER

The Parliament of Religions closed on 27 September, and after delivering a number of lectures at Oakland and San Francisco, on 10 October Dharmapala left the shores of America for India by way of Japan and China. At Honolulu Dr Marques and two lady theosophists came on board to see him, bringing with them gifts of brilliant South Sea flowers and fruits, all of which he distributed among the passengers. One of the visitors, a stout, middle-aged woman of about 50, confessed that she suffered from violent outbursts of temper which were a source of misery to herself and her relations, and asked Dharmapala how they could be controlled. As a student of Buddhist yoga, Dharmapala was able to give her the help for which she had sought in vain elsewhere, and by following his few simple words of advice she was eventually able to overcome her failing altogether. The name of the hot-tempered lady was Mrs Mary E. Foster, a descendent on her mother's side of King Kamehameha the Great of Hawaii, and although their meeting lasted for only a few minutes, so deep was the impression made by Dharmapala's words upon her mind that she became in later years the most munificent of his supporters, her donations totalling in the end almost one million rupees. Temples, monasteries, schools, hospitals, and numerous other institutions were through her generosity established in India and Ceylon, so that today her name is ranked with the names of Anāthapiṇḍika and Viśākhā as one of the greatest benefactors of Buddhism that have ever lived, and will be remembered by millions of grateful Buddhists as long as that of Dharmapala himself.[44]

JAPAN – SIAM – INDIA

On the morning of the last day of October Dharmapala disembarked at Yokohama, and by evening he was in Tokyo, where Noguchi, Horiuchi, and about one hundred young priests had assembled at the station to receive him. During the four years that had passed since his first visit to Japan, Dharmapala had not only increased enormously in spiritual and intellectual stature, but he had also discovered the work he had been born to do, and it was of this great work, the deliverance of the Bodh Gaya temple from the bondage of sacrilegious hands, that he spoke to the Japanese people, endeavouring through public lecture and private conversation to inflame their hearts with the burning enthusiasm of his own. That they were capable of enthusiasm, devotion, and supreme self-sacrifice, he knew. Had not the old pilgrim-priest, who had visited Bodh Gaya on foot, out of excess of devotion fallen down senseless before the Buddha-image of the Gupta period which he had brought with him from Ceylon via Chicago? Yet in spite of the interest shown by high priests of various sects and the Japanese nobility his endeavours met with no tangible success, and when a meeting of priests at the Seisho-ji Temple informed him that after two years it might be possible to raise twenty thousand yen, which was a ridiculously small sum for such a huge country, Dharmapala realized that he was wasting his time in Japan. Disputes between the priests over the custody of the Gupta image, and intrigues to monopolize the manufacture and sale of clay models of the sacred object, had moreover embittered his stay, so feeling that his presence was more urgently required in India he left Japan on 5 December, having spent six weeks there, and at once began to think of calling on the Buddhist Kingdom of Siam [Thailand] for assistance. At Shanghai Dharmapala wrote a message to the Chinese Buddhists, and with the help of Dr Timothy Richards, a Christian missionary who afterwards published an English translation of Aśvaghoṣa's *Awakening of Faith*, he addressed the priests of the temple at Mount Emei, and presented them with a bodhi tree leaf and some other relics. In Siam he was able to achieve no more concrete success than in Japan. Despite the interest and enthusiasm shown by several members of the royal family, and the sympathy of the Foreign Minister, Prince Devawongse, most people seemed apathetic in religious matters and indifferent to the propagation of the Dharma, and he noted in his diary, 'The true spirit of Buddhism has fled and only a lifeless corpse is to be seen in Buddhist countries of the Southern School.' After three busy weeks in Siam he left Bangkok for Singapore, arriving two weeks later in Colombo, having been not only the first native of Ceylon to travel round the world, but what was infinitely more important, the first Buddhist missionary of modern times to girdle the globe with the message of the Master. A royal reception awaited him. The crowds that had assembled at the jetty rent the air with thunderous shouts of 'Sadhu!' as the long-absent hero again set foot on his native soil, and he was taken in a magnificent procession, with elephants, drummers, and yellow-robed monks, to the Vidyodaya Pirivena Maligakanda where his venerable preceptor, Sumangala Nayaka Maha Thera, received him with blessings. But the time that he could spend in Ceylon was short, for the work in India called him, and after lecturing in Colombo, Kandy, Kalutara, and other places on his Chicago experiences and the Bodh Gaya restoration scheme he left for Madras. At Adyar he met Colonel Olcott, who told him that W. Q. Judge, the leader of the American theosophists, was to be impeached by a committee for fabricating messages alleged to have come from the Masters. Dharmapala's hopes that harmony would prevail were doomed to disappointment, for the secession of Judge and his followers was the first of a series of schisms that eventually broke up the theosophical movement into a number of warring groups, and reduced the Adyar headquarters to a platform for the antics of Mrs Besant and her followers. The last day of March saw the wanderer in the arms of his friends in Calcutta, where the Bengalis flocked to him for news of Swami Vivekananda, and his diary tersely records, 'I told them of his heroic work and the great sensation he is creating in America.' Unlike certain other religious leaders, Dharmapala was free from petty feelings of competition and rivalry, and was ever ready not only to recognize but even to direct attention to the merits of other workers in the same field. On 11 April he arrived at Gaya, bringing with him for installation in the upper chamber of the Maha Bodhi temple a beautiful seven-hundred-year-old Japanese image which was to be for many years the storm-centre of the battle for Bodh Gaya.

After Mr McPherson, the Collector of Gaya, had advised him to win over Hindu opinion to his side, Dharmapala visited Benares, the citadel of orthodoxy, and consulted the Brahmin pandits there. But implacable as ever in their hatred of Buddhism, they were emphatic that since the Buddha was an incarnation of the Hindu god Vishnu, the Bodh Gaya temple was a Hindu shrine and that the Buddhists therefore had no right to it. The mahant was of course of the same opinion, and objected to the installation of the Japanese image on the grounds that its presence would be a desecration. He moreover threatened that if Dharmapala attempted to bring the image to Bodh Gaya five thousand men would be lying in wait to kill him and that he was prepared to spend one hundred thousand rupees for the purpose. It was not until a year later, however, after Dharmapala had spent some months in Ceylon for the collection of funds, that the great clash between spiritual right and legal wrong finally came. Dharmapala writes in his diary for 25 February 1895:

> At 2 in the morning I woke up and sat in meditation for a little time and then my mind suggested, as it did yesterday, under the bodhi tree, to take the Japanese image to the Maha Bodhi temple. I woke up the priests and then asked them to sit in contemplation for a time. Then it was decided that we should take the image early morning from Gaya to Buddha Gaya. In silence I vowed 7 times giving up my life for the Buddha's sake. Before dawn we packed the image and by 7 were off to Buddha Gaya. On our way we met two Mohammedan gentlemen driving towards Buddha Gaya. Soon after our arrival at Buddha Gaya the boxes containing the image were taken upstairs to the Maha Bodhi temple and by a strange coincidence these two gentlemen were present and were witnessing the placing of the image. My friend Bepin Babu was also present and when we were going to light candles the mahant's *gosains* and the Mohammedan Muktiar came up and threatening me asked me to remove the image. Oh, it was painful indeed. Buddhists are not allowed to worship in their own temple. Great excitement. The mahant rushed off to Gaya and in the evening the Collector Mr D. J. McPherson came to investigate the case. Several witnesses were examined and when he was leaving the place the Collector said a great desecration had been committed in the temple. He ordered the Inspector to take care of our party. We stayed in the Burmese Rest House by the temple.

Dharmapala does not mention that the *gosains* (Hindu 'monks'), who were heavily armed with clubs and sticks, numbered forty or fifty, that he himself was grossly insulted, and that the ancient Japanese image was flung head foremost into the courtyard below. News of the outrage immediately flashed round the Buddhist world, and on all sides expressions of indignation were heard. Proceedings were instituted on the advice of Mr McPherson, who in his capacity of Magistrate of Gaya found the miscreants guilty and sentenced them to one month's simple imprisonment and a fine of one hundred rupees apiece, finding in his judgment that the temple had been continuously used by the Buddhists as a place of worship, whereas no Hindu, including the mahant and his disciples, ever worshipped there, and that there was nothing to show that the mahant was ever the proprietor of the temple. This judgment was upheld by the District Court, to which the mahant's minions appealed, but set aside by the judges of the High Court, both of whom were distinctly hostile to Dharmapala. They patronizingly conceded that although in the possession of the mahant the place had never been converted from a Buddhist into a Hindu temple, and observed that there was no previous instance of any disturbance between the Buddhist worshippers and the Hindu mahants or their subordinates in regard to their respective rights. As though to add insult to injury, the Government of India ordered Dharmapala to remove the Japanese image from the Burmese Rest House, but in view of the popular resentment roused in Burma and Ceylon by this high-handed action the order was eventually rescinded. In 1897 the mahant returned to the attack, making representations through the British Indian Association, a powerful organization of big landowners, for the removal of the image on the grounds that its presence 'near the Bodh Gaya temple which had been held, it was stated, to be a Hindu temple by the High Court, was deemed objectionable by the Hindus'. The Government did not accede to this request, however, stating that it could not admit any claim to treat the temple as a purely Hindu shrine, while at the same time it had no desire to interfere with the mahant's position. For the next few years the image remained in the Burmese Rest House, worshipped and cared for by the gentle Sumangala, while Dharmapala was scattering broadcast the seed of the Dharma in foreign fields.

SECOND VISIT TO AMERICA

With the advent of Dharmapala in 1891, the founding of the *Maha Bodhi* journal in 1892, and the Bodh Gaya temple case of 1895–6, the cultured Bengali public was becoming more and more sympathetic towards Buddhism, with the result that on 26 May 1896 the Buddha's birthday was celebrated in Calcutta under the presidency of Narendra Nath Sen.

It was the first organized celebration of its kind to be held in India for hundreds of years, and when, a few weeks later, Dharmapala left for America at the invitation of Dr Paul Carus, founder of the American Maha Bodhi Society, he must have felt that although the Maha Bodhi temple was still in alien hands his work had not been wholly without fruit. In London he dined with Sir Edwin Arnold, renewed acquaintance with Prof. Rhys Davids, visited the venerable orientalist Max Müller at Oxford University, and lectured in the Theosophical Society and at Hyde Park. During the year he spent in America he was no less busy, visiting among other places New York, Chicago, San Francisco, the Grand Rapids, Manistee, Freeport, Guelph in Canada, Cincinnati, Duluth, St Cloud, Fargo, Minneapolis, Genesis, Davenport, Iowa City, and Des Moines. Everywhere he went, he proclaimed the unadulterated Dharma of the Lord Buddha, popularized the scriptures of Buddhism, expounded the subtleties of Buddhist psychology and yoga, and exposed the commercialized pseudo-oriental mysticisms by which America was then deluged. Above all, he exhorted his listeners to lead 'the life of holiness, perfect and pure'. He wrote in his diary,

> Slaves of passion, controlled by the lower senses, wallowing in sensuality, these so-called Christians live in killing each other, hating each other, swindling each other, introducing liquor and vice where they hadn't existed. Themselves slaves of passion they enslave others to themselves and their vices.

For Dharmapala himself the trip to America was by no means without temptations. Several American women attempted to seduce the handsome young ascetic, but all their efforts to soil the radiant purity of his character failed, and instead of the words of endearment for which they had hoped, they heard from his unsullied lips only the Word of the Buddha. The American theosophists were at this time divided into two camps, one maintaining that on the death of Madame Blavatsky, W. Q. Judge had become the agent of the Masters, the other holding that Annie Besant had been so chosen, and both parties added to his vexations by trying to use him for their own ends. But shortly before his departure from India, Colonel Olcott had resigned the office of director and chief adviser of the Maha Bodhi Society, so that Dharmapala's link with official theosophy was now weaker than it had ever been, and although for him 'H. P. B.' had no successor he refused to be drawn into the controversy. He concentrated his energies instead on Buddhist work, and in May 1897 had the satisfaction of conducting the first Vaiśākha celebration ever to be held in the United States. About four hundred people attended the service, which was held in a room that had been temporarily transformed into a Buddhist shrine. As thirty-seven candles, symbolizing the thirty-seven principles of wisdom,[45] blazed on the steps of the altar before the Buddha image, the *anagārika* gave an address on Buddhism and chanted the *Maṅgala Sutta* from an old palm-leaf book. In spite of his multifarious religious activities in America he did not forget the suffering masses of Bengal, and found time to collect funds for the Maha Bodhi Famine Relief work. His energy was in fact inexhaustible, and even after a year of strenuous missionary labours in America he could write:

> I hope to leave the US in November for London and via Paris, Berlin, Rome I shall go to Ceylon, meet my dear mother and father, travel all round the island proclaiming the holy life and call upon all priests to practise samadhi and then go to Darjeeling via Calcutta and Kapilavastu and then find the way to Tibet in search of the Holy Masters. There make my way to Pekin if possible, there to Japan and return to America. Death is nothing. I have died a million times and will die a million times. I will do this great work and save the world from the evils of ignorance, selfishness and passion.

PARIS – LONDON – ROME – CEYLON

In Paris, Dharmapala attended the Congress of Orientalists, and on 14 September 1897 held a Buddhist Peace Celebration at the Musée Guimet. After a short sojourn in London, where the theosophists, finding that he was now completely free from their leading-strings, were unanimous in their opinion that he was 'conceited', he proceeded, via Zurich and Florence, to Rome. 'The centre of Roman Catholic superstition. Immense wealth', he remarks about St Peter's in his diary. A cardinal who lived 'in gorgeous and princely style' promised him an audience with the Pope, but when Dharmapala, who could no more conceal his intentions than the sun its light, let it be known that he intended to speak to the Holy Father about the drunkenness which

European civilization had introduced into Ceylon, and that he wanted a letter asking the Catholics to live in peace and amity with the Buddhists, the horrified ecclesiastic not only cancelled the audience but refused to see Dharmapala again. Back in Ceylon, the solitary fighter found that a clique in the Theosophical Society was against the Maha Bodhi Society, and feeling that Buddhism and Annie Besant's neo-Brahmanism were incompatible he suggested to Colonel Olcott that the word 'theosophical' should be dropped from the name of the Ceylon Buddhist Theosophical Society. Enraged at what he considered an impertinence, the Colonel did his best to check Dharmapala's activities in Ceylon, and his erstwhile pupil regretfully came to the conclusion that the older man was jealous of his success, and that in his anxiety to remain in power at Adyar he was willing to allow Annie Besant and her followers to drive the Buddha and his Dharma from the place. Not until several years later, however, did he resign from the Society, and when, after Olcott's death, Annie Besant became president, he was unsparing in his condemnation of the vagaries into which she and Leadbeater led the movement.

The whole of 1898 was spent working in Ceylon. Once again the *anagārika*, now a popular hero in the eyes of his countrymen, travelled by bullock cart from village to village until he had covered the whole island. Once again his ardent championship of the national religion and culture produced a wave of enthusiasm which swept from one end of the country to the other. Feeling that in spite of all its advantages the Western university system of education was without ethical value, and that it failed to develop the mind's infinite potentialities, he persuaded his father to buy a plot of land near Colombo, and planned to start there the Ceylon Ethico-Psychological College. Worship, meditation, and study of comparative religion were to be included in the curriculum. Another institution known as the Sanghamitta Convent, for training Buddhist sisters in social work, was also started, and the Countess Canavarro, an American convert to Buddhism who had accompanied the *anagārika* to Ceylon, was placed in charge of the convent and of the orphanages and schools attached to it.

TOURING INDIA

With so much to be done in his native land, Dharmapala did not return to India until the beginning of 1899, and after spending two months in Calcutta he went on an extended tour of North India. Bankipore, Bodh Gaya, Gaya, Benares, Cawnpore, Meerut, Aligarh, Delhi, Agra, Saharanpur, Amritsar, Ludhiana, Amballa City, Amballa, Muttra, Brindavan, Thaneswar, Lahore, Rawalpindi, Peshawar, Nowshera, Abbotabad, Hassan Abdul, Mardan, and the Yusufsai Valley were the places included in his itinerary. A contemporary account of the tour, which lasted for four months, and in the course of which he travelled more than fifteen hundred miles, says:

> He travelled as a pilgrim, not caring at all for comforts, mixing with the sannyasis, ascetics, Hindu pilgrims, and with passengers of the third and intermediate classes, eating at times the poorest food, sleeping at times in places where the poor sleep and gaining an insight into the characteristics of the poor classes, who are suffering from intense ignorance, superstition and poverty.

How keenly his compassionate heart felt the sufferings of the masses with whom he mixed may be judged by the following extract from an open letter which he wrote from Saharanpur:

> Open your eyes and see, listen to the cries of distress of the 141 millions of people and let their tears cool your dry hearts. Don't imagine that 'Providence' will take care of you, for the 'Almighty' does not calculate time by your watches. 'A thousand years is one hour' for him, and it is foolish for you to wait with folded hands. Wake up, my brothers, for life in this world is short. Give up your dreamy philosophies and sensualizing ceremonies. Millions are daily suffering the pangs of hunger, drinking the water that animals in the forest would not drink, sleeping and living in houses, inhaling poison day after day. There is wealth in India enough to feed all. But the abominations of caste, creed and sect are making the millions suffer.

His missionary labours for the year were by no means ended, however, for on his return to Calcutta from the Punjab he received an invitation to South India, where he not only lectured on Buddhism but also emphasized the need of educating the masses and removing the disabilities of the 'Untouchable' community. With the founding of a branch of the Maha

Bodhi Society in Madras the Banner of the Dharma was firmly planted in the South, where differences of caste and sect were perhaps more strongly felt than in any other part of the country. The early months of 1900 saw the indefatigable missionary in Siam and Ceylon after which he again visited Burma, this time to raise funds for the erection of a rest house at Bodh Gaya, the District Board having undertaken to do the work provided the Buddhists would meet the cost.

THIRD VISIT TO AMERICA

From 1902 till early 1904 Dharmapala was again in the United States, where the campaign inaugurated during his second visit to that country was continued with unabated vigour. As before, he was eager not only to teach but also to learn, and visits to laboratories and technical institutes alternated with lectures on the Dharma and exhortations to lead a life of purity. At Boston he wished to attend one of the classes which Prof. William James, the celebrated psychologist, was holding at Harvard University. The yellow dress that he had adopted after his return from the Parliament of Religions made him a conspicuous figure in the hall, and as soon as Prof. James saw him he motioned him to the front. 'Take my chair', he said, 'and I shall sit with my students. You are better equipped to lecture on psychology than I am.' After Dharmapala had given a short account of Buddhist doctrines the great psychologist turned to his pupils and remarked, 'This is the psychology everybody will be studying twenty-five years from now.' Time may not have fulfilled the professor's prediction to the letter, but it is beyond dispute that to Anagarika Dharmapala belongs much of the credit for making the existence of Buddhist psychology more widely known in Western countries.

MRS FOSTER'S HELP – ENGLAND – INDUSTRIAL SCHOOL IN SARNATH

Numerous visits to leading educational institutions had convinced Dharmapala that the East needed the technology of the West no less than the West needed the psychology of the East, and he therefore wrote to Mrs Foster asking her help in the establishment of an Industrial School at Sarnath. She promptly sent him a cheque for five hundred dollars, following it up a year later with another for three thousand.

Thanks to these generous contributions he was able to engage the services of an American expert, and to dispatch, before his departure from the country, the necessary agricultural implements from Chicago to Calcutta. Arriving in Liverpool after a rough passage across the Atlantic, this preacher who took the world for his parish proceeded to London, where he not only met old friends like Sir Edwin Arnold, now totally blind, but also made new ones like Prince Peter Kropotkin, the famous anarchist, by whom he was introduced to Lady Welby, Mr Thyndman, Mrs Cobden Unwin, Prof. Patrick Geddes, and a number of other socialist and radical intellectuals. As though his energy and curiosity were still unexhausted, he took a boat from Harwich to Holland, where he visited elementary schools and industries in Bussum, Copenhagen, Askov Vigin, and Amsterdam, thence returning to London. Another excursion took him to Genoa, Paris, and Turin, after which he at last boarded the steamer for Colombo. Once again his native land saw him for a few weeks only. Hurrying back to India, he at once began to put into operation his long-cherished plans for industrial, agricultural, and manual education. The Industrial School at Sarnath was opened, and Mr Veggars, the American expert, installed as director. But the theosophists of Benares displayed open hostility to the scheme, and upon the Commissioner desiring the removal of Mr Veggars the project upon which the *anagārika* had lavished much time and energy, and which would have been a source of manifold blessings to the local people, had to be abandoned. Arrangements for instruction in the vernacular were continued, however, and some years later took shape first as a high school and then as a college.

BACK IN CEYLON – 'SINHALA BAUDDHAYA'

In November 1904 the *anagārika* went to Ceylon at the request of the Lanka Maha Bodhi Society to conduct a campaign in the general interest of the Buddhists of the island. Once again he travelled by bullock cart from village to village, lecturing this time not only on religion but on the various projects for technical education which then engrossed his attention as well. Impressed by the astonishingly rapid industrial progress made by the Japanese, he persuaded his father to organize a fund of sixty thousand rupees for sending Sinhala students to Japan in order to learn weaving and other arts and crafts. The first weaving school was established in Ceylon in 1906 and soon developed into a large and flourishing institution. In the same year the *anagārika* sustained a heavy blow in the loss of his father, the good Mudaliyar, who since 1891 had given unstinted financial support to his son's efforts to resuscitate the Dharma. When the sad news was communicated to Mrs Foster the warm-hearted lady wrote to Dharmapala asking him to regard her as his foster-mother, and at once embarked upon that series of benefactions without which the *anagārika*'s work could hardly have achieved such ample proportions. For six years she sent an annual donation of three thousand rupees, most of which was spent by Dharmapala on the establishment of Buddhist schools, a printing press, and a vernacular weekly called the *Sinhala Bauddhaya* which he started to counteract the un-Buddhistic tendencies of the Theosophical Society.

LOSS OF BODH GAYA LAW CASE

In 1906 the great legal battle between the Anagarika Dharmapala and the mahant entered its final phase, and for four years the whole Buddhist world watched the sordid proceedings drag on to a conclusion as shameful to the Government of India and orthodox Hinduism as it was bitter, humiliating, and outrageous to the feelings of the Buddhists. The offensive was of course taken by the mahant, who at the instigation of the Commissioner of Patna filed a suit against Sumangala Thera, who all these years had been taking care of the image, and Dharmapala, for a declaration that he was the sole owner of the Burmese Rest House, and for the ejectment of the defendants and the removal of the image. The Government of India was also made a party to the suit inasmuch as it had refused to order the removal of the image in 1896. 'The sub-judge who decided the suit,' says a Maha Bodhi publication, 'in the first instance held that the Rest House had been built by the mahant for convenience of the Burmese Buddhists who had been allowed to stop in it, that the defendants were not entitled to make it their permanent abode and to place the Image in it and ordered their ejectment with the Image'. Dharmapala not unnaturally appealed against this infamous decision to the High Court, which varied the decree of the sub-judge, holding that inasmuch as the building had been intended for the use of Buddhists in general the defendants were not entitled to make it their permanent abode or to install any image there. They found that the Rest House had been erected with money at least part of which had been donated by the Burmese. The mahant's position was found to be that he held possession of the building and had the control and superintendence of it subject to the right to use it in the customary manner, if any such right be shown to have existed; but no decision was given on this question of right as in this suit it did not arise. Two decades of struggle to regain the lost rights of the Buddhists thus ended in total failure, and the sinister collaboration between political and religious imperialism at last succeeded in depriving the followers of the Buddha of any foothold in their own most sacred shrine. One stands aghast at the enormity of the wrong done by a powerful government to the largest religious community on earth; one beholds with amazement the brazen impudence with which a mercenary Hindu mahant is permitted to pollute and desecrate the holy of holies of the Buddhist world. Nor is the position at present very much better, even though nearly fifty years have passed since Dharmapala was ejected from the Rest House, and even though an independent government has meanwhile arisen bearing on its enfranchized brow the symbols of Buddhist India. Bodh Gaya languishes in the hands of a predominantly Hindu managing committee, and the Buddhists continue to be deprived of all effective control over their own most sacred shrine.

WORK FOR NATIONAL REVIVAL IN CEYLON

With the Maha Bodhi Rest House as the sole concrete result of twenty years of selfless labour for the holy spot, Dharmapala left Bodh Gaya for Ceylon, where he spent the greater part of 1911 and 1912 striving to infuse some of his own boundless vitality into the sluggish veins of his countrymen. He was now at the height of his powers, and as though unable to exhaust himself by incessant travel and lecturing, he poured out his ideas for the regeneration of the nation in a series of articles entitled 'Things That Should be Known' which he contributed to the *Sinhala Bauddhaya*. Of these articles it has been said,

> They became the basis of a propaganda which was confined to no single question. They scintillated with wit and wisdom and called men and women to a more truthful and courageous life. These articles led to a reawakening of the national spirit among the Sinhalese.

With characteristic bluntness he attacked the shortcomings of the clergy, the majority of whom were corrupt and indolent, and soon the fires of controversy were ablaze. The class of unworthy *bhikṣus* found a champion in a member of the Buddhist Theosophical Society, who criticized the *anagārika* personally in the *Sandaresa*, the journal for whose improvement the great Buddhist missionary had as a young man done so much. Religion was in Dharmapala's eyes not separate from life but most intimately connected with every part of it. To his comprehensive vision religious revival, moral uplift, and economic development were aspects of one great progressive movement which should include in its scope every department of individual and social life. He therefore inveighed against the Sinhala people not only for surrendering their religious and cultural individuality to the Christians but also for giving up their economic independence to the Hambayas, a class of immigrant Indian Muslim traders who had practically monopolized the retail business of the coast and the interior. The revival which he inaugurated therefore had not only religious, but also political and economic consequences, for the Muslims, dismayed by the reawakened commercial spirit of the Buddhists, began resorting to methods of intimidation and coercion which eventually led to disaster.

VISIT TO MRS FOSTER – WORLD WAR – CEYLON RIOTS

Having once again galvanized his fellow-countrymen into activity, Anagarika Dharmapala in 1913 left Ceylon for Honolulu in order to thank Mrs Foster personally for the magnificent support which for so many years she had given the Maha Bodhi Society, due to which it had been possible to purchase a building in Calcutta and to increase the usefulness of the Society in numerous other ways. The good lady, now well stricken with years, was so pleased to see the *anagārika* that before his departure she gave him sixty thousand rupees with which to found in Colombo a charitable hospital in memory of her father. The Foster Robinson Hospital, open to all in need of medical treatment, was started immediately after Dharmapala's return in a large house which he had inherited from his father. At public request the treatment given in the hospital was in accordance with indigenous Sinhala medical science. On the way back to Ceylon the *anagārika* called at Japan, and although shadowed by two detectives boldly criticized the shortcomings of British administration in India at a number of meetings. In Seoul, the capital of Korea, he addressed a distinguished gathering which included the ex-empress, and presented to the Korean sangha a relic of the Buddha. After travelling in Manchuria and China, the *anagārika* visited Shanghai and Singapore, and having seen the ruins of Borobudur in Java returned to Ceylon at the end of the year. In 1914 war broke out in Europe, and in the middle of the following year the increasing arrogance of the Hambayas, whose aggressions culminated in an attack on a Buddhist procession in Kandy, and the murder of a Sinhala youth under the indifferent eyes of the police, precipitated the Muslim-Buddhist Riots. Excited crowds streamed from the surrounding villages into Kandy to protect the Temple of the Sacred Tooth from violence, and immediately the disturbances spread to other parts of the island. Alarmed by what they interpreted as a revolt against British rule, the authorities proclaimed martial law on 2 June, and for three months the innocent Sinhala Buddhists were ground beneath an iron heel as ruthless as any which marched to the battlefields of distant Europe. Influential persons were arrested without a scrap of evidence against them, public servants were dismissed, and civilians tried by court martials after the cessation of the riots, and while the ordinary Courts of Justice were uninterruptedly sitting. Had Dharmapala not had the good fortune to be in India at the time he would certainly have been arrested and shot, as his frequent visits to Japan and his efforts to gain the Bodh Gaya temple had already made him an object of suspicion. Determined to wreak vengeance on the Hewavitarne family, the authorities arrested the *anagārika*'s younger brother Edmund, tried him by court martial for treason, found him guilty, and sentenced him to penal servitude for life. He contracted typhoid fever owing to the insanitary condition of the jail in which he was confined, and before the end of the year he was dead.

INTERNMENT IN CALCUTTA – DHARMARAJIKA VIHARA (1920)

Dharmapala himself was not allowed to escape punishment altogether, being interned for five years in Calcutta at the request of the Government of Ceylon. This long period of confinement within the limits of a city was naturally irksome to one who all his life had been accustomed to the freedom of three continents, and the volcanic energy which continued to explode in the pages of the *Maha Bodhi* must have found such a narrowing of its activities almost unendurable. These years were by no means devoid of solid achievement, however, and with the erection of the Sri Dharmarajika Caitya Vihara, which had been made possible chiefly by donations from Mrs Foster and the *anagārika* himself, his long-cherished ambition of building a vihara in Calcutta was at last fulfilled. At an impressive and colourful ceremony at Government House towards the end of 1920, Lord Ronaldshay presented a sacred body-relic of the Buddha, which had been discovered in a crystal casket during excavations at Bhattiprolu Stupa in Madras Presidency, for enshrinement in the vihara, and it was with deep emotion that the now ageing *anagārika* descended the carpeted grand staircase bearing in his hand the golden casket which contained the sacred object and bore it through the reverential crowds to the open phaeton in which it was to be drawn in procession by six horses through the streets of Calcutta. Lord Ronaldshay also presided over the consecration ceremony of the vihara, which was witnessed by a large and distinguished gathering, and in the course of an eloquent speech paid splendid tribute to the Buddha and his teaching, concluding with the hope that 'this ceremony in which we have taken part today may prove symbolical of a return once more to that peace which is the most treasured offspring of the gentle and lofty teaching which Gautama Buddha bequeathed to men two thousand five hundred years ago'.

ILLNESS

In spite of these triumphs, Anagarika Dharmapala was not permitted to return to Ceylon until 1922, by which time his health had completely broken down, the combined effects of the privations he had endured as a young man and the lack of sufficient exercise from which he had recently suffered being responsible for attacks of sciatica, beriberi, palpitation of the heart, and anaemia, which troubled him for the rest of his life. Physical suffering was not able, however, to prevent him from reviving the *Sinhala Bauddhaya*, which had been suppressed during the riots of 1915, nor from attempting to increase the usefulness of the various institutions that he had organized some years before. In 1919 and 1923 Mrs Foster had continued her apparently inexhaustible benefactions with donations of fifty thousand and one hundred thousand dollars respectively, the major portion of which was carefully invested by the *anagārika* so as to ensure a regular income out of which to maintain in perpetuity the various institutions and activities of the Maha Bodhi Society. By 1925 the condition of his health had become a matter for serious concern, and at the beginning of the year he had to go for treatment to a sanatorium near Zurich in Switzerland, where an operation for sciatica in both legs was successfully performed. Even while his body was lying on the sickbed, his mind was busy formulating plans for what was to be his last great missionary venture – the founding of the British Maha Bodhi Society and the establishment of a vihara in London. Though he had suffered much at the hands of the British Government in Ceylon and India, he had no hatred for the English people. Knowing that hatred ceases not by hatred but only by love, and that force could be overcome only by patience, in return for the injuries which he had received at their hands he wished to give the people of England the most precious gift he had, the gift of the Dharma. Such a gesture is typical of Dharmapala. Frequently deceived and swindled by those whom he had trusted, betrayed by those whom he had helped, he entertained no desire for retaliation, but like the great broad earth patiently endured and suffered all.

MISSION WORK IN LONDON

Arriving in London in August 1925, the *anagārika* commenced activities by giving lectures and talks under the auspices of the Buddhist Lodge of the Theosophical Society (now the Buddhist Society, London), the first of these meetings being attended by the three existing English Buddhist organizations, as well as by members of the United Lodge of Theosophists and the Blavatsky Association. Convinced that the association he planned to start should function in its own premises, he sailed for San Francisco to appeal for help to Mrs Foster, who agreed to give not only a substantial initial contribution but also a regular monthly grant. Returning to England at the beginning of 1926 after a severe illness, he took up residence at 52 Lancaster Gate, where he was interviewed by Francis Yeats-Brown, well known as the author of *The Lives of a Bengal Lancer*, who a few weeks before had heard him lecture in the New York Town Hall on 'The Message of Buddha'. Yeats-Brown incorporated his impressions of the transatlantic lecture and a report on the proposed Buddhist mission in London into an article which he published in the *Spectator* of 30 January entitled 'A Buddhist in Bayswater'. This article gives a good picture of the *anagārika* at this period of his life, when he was more than 60 years of age. 'Certainly he looked delicate', wrote the Bengal Lancer, 'but he seemed to hold an inner light within him, a latent fire of purpose.' After summarizing the New York lecture he describes its effect upon those who heard it:

> Not a move or cough from the audience. Not a tremble in those lips that thundered the denunciations of Isaiah against our spiritual sloth nor any hint of exhaustion in that frail frame. Here was a man with a message. He delivered it erect, composed, master of himself and his hearers, with the art of an orator and the dignity of a priest to whom the world is nothing. When he sat down there was a dead silence, followed by a burst of applause.

A report of his interview with the *anagārika* follows, after which Yeats-Brown concludes:

> The Anagarika Dharmapala will create few eddies in the spiritual life of this country for his teaching is too alien to our mental habits. But he should be heard by those interested in Eastern faiths for as a teacher he is as authentic as he is eloquent.

In May the *anagārika* spoke at the Vaiśākha meeting held by the London Buddhist organizations at Holborn Town Hall, and in July he purchased a house in Ealing which he called Foster House, in honour of his patroness. Meetings were held on Sunday afternoons and evenings, and a number of distinguished speakers were always ready to address the audience. At the end of the year Dharmapala left England to raise funds in Ceylon for the London Mission, and to visit India in connection with the great temple, afterwards known as the Mulagandhakuti Vihara, that he was building in Sarnath for the enshrinement of a sacred relic of the Lord Buddha which had been offered by the Government of India. Before leaving England he had started a monthly journal, *The British Buddhist*, the first number of which was written entirely by himself. His expectations of aid from Ceylon and Burma were as usual disappointed, but he returned to London before the middle of 1927 with funds sufficient for the purchase of a house in Gloucester Road, Regent's Park, which was to be used for the mission work prior to the construction of the stately vihara of his dreams. In November of the same year he succumbed to an attack of bronchitis, and years of overwork began to take their final toll on his frail body. Leaving the London mission in the hands of his nephew, Dayananda Hewavitarne, he returned to Ceylon with his health irreparably broken. The physical suffering which he now had to endure did not cause him to forget the work for which he could no longer labour personally, and in June he dispatched three Sinhala *bhikṣus*, Pandits Parawahera Vajiragnana, Hegoda Nandasara, and Dehigaspe Pannasara to keep burning in England the Lamp of the Sublime Law. They were accompanied by the *anagārika*'s personal disciple Devapriya Valisinha, a young student of Ceylon who since 1917 had been gradually taking over from his master the heavy responsibility of maintaining the Society's institutions and activities in India. During the two years in which the party propagated the Dharma in England, Mr Valisinha attended to the management of the mission, helped the *bhikṣus* to form classes for the study of Pāli, Buddhism, and meditation, and by his amiable disposition endeared himself to all with whom he came in contact. On his return to India in 1930 he resumed his secretarial duties, after the ordination of the *anagārika* succeeding him as General Secretary of the Society, and becoming, on his death, the inheritor of his unfulfilled ambitions and the chief instrument for the perpetuation of the work and ideals to which he had dedicated his life.[46]

BACK IN CEYLON (1927)

After his return to Ceylon, Anagarika Dharmapala began the painful entry upon the last stages of his heroic career. For three years he was confined to bed with stomach trouble and heart disease, and his sufferings were acute. In June and August 1929, and in February 1930, his life was despaired of, and when the heart disease finally left him Dr Frank Gunasekera, his physician, was astonished at the seeming miracle and declared that it was not so much the effect of medical treatment as of the *anagārika*'s will-power, of his strong determination to see the consummation of the last of his prodigious labours, the opening of the Mulagandhakuti Vihara at Sarnath. But life had still a few more blows in store for the aged warrior before she would permit him to quit the field. In 1929 his only surviving brother, Dr C. A. Hewavitarne, who had for many years been of inestimable help to him in all his undertakings, met a tragic death in a railway accident, and Dharmapala felt as though his right hand had been cut off. Then in January 1931 he received belated news of Mrs Foster's death in Honolulu on 22 December 1930 at the advanced age of eighty-six years and three months, and although he must have known that her days would soon be numbered, so sudden was the shock that it almost brought about a relapse of his heart disease. In great agony of spirit he recalled her unparalleled benefactions to the Buddhist cause, and wondered who would support the London mission now that she was gone. The future seemed dark. There was still so much to be done, and those who would carry on his life-work were still few in number, and young in years and experience. Even while he had been lying on his sickbed, when more than once it had seemed that the messengers of death had drawn near and warned him to make ready for the journey, certain of his fellow countrymen had not suffered him to lie in peace, but had launched shafts of spiteful criticism against the stricken giant whom they had never before dared to face, finding fault with the life which they were too selfish to follow, and picking holes in the work which they had never lifted a finger to help. Only the sympathy of the poor and oppressed, who when he was nigh to death prayed in their thousands that the *devas* might restore him to health, comforted him in the midst of his afflictions. The teachers, friends, and colleagues of his youth and maturity had all departed, and he knew that he must soon follow whither they had gone. Of all he had loved only his aged mother now remained, having outlived three sons and two daughters and having now to behold her first-born, who had so wonderfully fulfilled the pious dreams of her youth, stricken down by mortal sickness in the midst of his gigantic labours.

SARNATH – LOWER ORDINATION (1931)

By March 1931 the *anagārika* had recovered sufficiently to be borne in a chair onto the steamer which would take him to Calcutta. With a last great gesture of renunciation he had disencumbered himself of worldly goods, creating from the Mary Foster Fund and his own handsome patrimony the Anagarika Dharmapala Trust, which was to be administered by five trustees for the furtherance of the objects to which he had dedicated his life. As a free man, therefore, he watched for the last time the palm-fringed shores of his native land disappear over the horizon, and steadfastly set his face towards the holy land wherein for so many years he had laboured, and the sacred site at which was to be enacted the closing scene of his career. He arrived in holy Isipatana, Sarnath, from Calcutta at the end of the month, and although his doctors had ordered him to take a complete rest he at once began to take an active interest in the society's affairs. His body was infirm, but his thought flashed out with all its old brilliance and grandeur, and his voice could still thunder denunciation or ring out in reproof. He paid special attention to the training of the ten young *sāmaṇeras* whom he had sent from the Foster Seminary in Kandy to Santiniketan, Rabindranath Tagore's beautiful rural academy, and who were now completing their studies in Sarnath. Knowing that the future of Buddhism in India depended to a great extent on their endeavours, he was continually exhorting them to lead lives of purity and self-sacrifice. One of the *sāmaṇeras* was particularly attentive to the *anagārika*'s needs, and with unflagging devotion was ready to serve him at any hour of the day or night. This zealous attendant is now known as Ven. M. Sangharatana Thera, who has for many years occupied the responsible position of secretary at Sarnath. Himself unwearied in his efforts to diffuse the Light of the Dharma among the Indian masses, he is never tired of talking about the *anagārika*'s wonderful energy and exhorting people to follow his glorious example.[47] Another project that occupied Dharmapala's thoughts at this time was the creation of an international Buddhist Institute, whereto he saw in his mind's eye students flocking in their thousands from every corner of the Buddhist world. Busy as he was with mundane schemes of this kind, his eagle mind soared often upon the trackless paths of higher spiritual experience, and on 13 July he took the *pabbajjā* or lower ordination from Ven. Boruggamuwe Rewata Thera, receiving the monastic name of Sri Devamitta Dhammapala. In August he was strong enough to spend a month in Calcutta and deliver there a public lecture, and at the end of the year he had the satisfaction of seeing the opening ceremony of the Mulagandhakuti Vihara set as it were a crown upon his labours. The celebrations lasted for three days, during which there were accommodated in Sarnath nearly one thousand visitors, more than half of whom had arrived from overseas. In the afternoon of 11 November, when the sun shone from a clear blue winter sky on the yellow robes of the *bhikṣus* and the brilliant silks of the assembled devotees, a golden casket containing Sacred Relics of the Lord Buddha was presented by the Director General of Archaeology to the Maha Bodhi Society on behalf of the Government of India. Amidst great jubilation the Sacred Relics were placed on the back of an elephant and taken in a colourful procession which circumambulated the vihara thrice. In his address at the opening ceremony of the vihara Ven. Dharmapala recalled his first visit to Sarnath in January 1891 when, he said, it was 'in the occupation of low-class hog breeders'. The vast audience was silent while he recounted some of the difficulties he had faced, and it was with a thrill of triumph in his voice that the old warrior, who had been wheeled to the pandal in an invalid chair, declared, 'After an exile of eight-hundred years the Buddhists have returned to their own dear holy Isipatana. It is the wish of the Maha Bodhi Society,' he said in conclusion, 'to give to the people of India without distinction of caste and creed the compassionate doctrine of the *sammā-sambuddha*. I trust that you would come forward to disseminate the *āryadharma* of the Tathāgata throughout India.'

HIGHER ORDINATION (1933)

Dharmapala knew that his days were numbered, and that the work which he had so nobly begun would have to be continued by younger and stronger hands. In April and December of 1932 he was again seriously ill, and wishing to die as a full member of the holy order he received the *upasampadā* or higher ordination on 16 January 1933. More than a dozen leading monks arrived from Ceylon to perform the historic ceremony, which took place in a *sīmā* specially consecrated for the occasion. Though he had been suffering from a variety of complaints, particularly from heart disease, he appeared so active and energetic, so radiantly happy, that none could have suspected that he was in reality a chronic invalid. After his initiation he spoke as though he had shed forever all worries, cares, and anxieties, writing in his diary that he felt like one of the Ābhassara gods, that live only on joy. His spiritual happiness seemed to inspire him with fresh energy for the sacred cause which he had for so many years espoused, and he not only published the first number of the *Sarnath Bulletin* but even spoke of setting up his headquarters at Gaya and conducting a final campaign for the recovery of the Maha Bodhi temple.

It was the last flaring up of the candle of his life before its extinction. In the middle of April he caught a chill, and fever developed. As his condition became more and more serious his disciple Devapriya Valisinha was summoned from Calcutta, and his physician Dr Nandy arrived soon after. A few days later his nephew Raja Hewavitarne came from Ceylon, and the six *sāmaṇeras* who had been dispatched to Bodh Gaya returned to the bedside of their beloved leader. Ven. Dharmapala, now in the grip of excruciating pain, had no wish to live any longer. Many times he refused to take medicine, saying that it was a useless expenditure on his decrepit body. 'Leave the money for Buddhist work', he would tell Mr Valisinha, pouring the mixture into the spittoon. As his sufferings increased he again and again repeated, 'Let me die soon; let me be born again; I can no longer prolong my agony. I would like to be reborn twenty-five times to spread Lord Buddha's Dharma.' This was not the cry of a coward, but of a warrior whose weapons have been broken in battle and who calls for a new suit of armour so that he may carry on the fight. Towards the end of his life, when the vigorous mind felt keenly the body's decrepitude, he made a solemn asseveration that he would take birth in a Brahmin family of Benares and in a new body continue the battle for Bodh Gaya. With all the strength at his command he *willed* that it should so come to pass and today his intimate followers believe that before long he will return to direct the movement to which he had vowed to dedicate himself life after life. Even while he was lying on his deathbed, however, his enemies did not scruple to direct a blow at his defenceless head. The leader of a certain Buddhist group in Ceylon, eager for notoriety, concluded a secret agreement with the mahant which would have ruined Ven. Dharmapala's labours. Subsequent protests from the Ceylon Buddhist public prevented this agreement from being put into operation, but when he heard of the treachery his grief and indignation were terrible to behold. 'It was the greatest shock of his life,' writes Devapriya Valisinha, 'and I can vividly recollect his pain and anguish.... Alas! He never recovered from the shock. How could he forget such treachery even on his sickbed?' He exhorted those about him to carry on the great work of his life, and never rest until Bodh Gaya was restored to Buddhist hands. Thereafter he showed no desire for food, which had to be injected into him against his will. On 27 April he suddenly demanded pen and paper, and despite his semiconscious condition with great difficulty scribbled something. One line was illegible, but the other read, 'Doctor Nandy, I am tired of injection: I may pass away.' His eyes were now closed.

The following morning he was almost unconscious, and made no sound except to mutter 'Devapriya' once. At twelve o'clock his temperature began to rise, and in spite of the physician's efforts, by two o'clock it had risen to 104.6. With anguish in their hearts, those who stood round his bedside realized that the hour which was to release him from his sufferings had come. The bhikkhus and *sāmaṇeras* were summoned and requested to chant *paritrāṇa*, and as they recited the age-old verses of the sacred texts, the Great Being's consciousness, radiant with a lifetime of wisdom, energy, and love, relaxed its hold on the worn-out body and flashed into new realms of service, leaving upon the face of the corpse it had forsaken, a serene smile of happiness and content.

MRS MARY E. FOSTER:

'Queen of the Empire of Righteousness'

The truism that effects of colossal magnitude proceed often from causes seemingly insignificant has been elaborated in a number of well-known stories and sayings, the most famous of which is Pascal's remark that had Cleopatra's nose been half an inch shorter the history of the world would have been different.[48] This seeming lack of correspondence between cause and effect is observable not only in matters temporal but in affairs spiritual as well, and has been explained on the assumption that, as the proverbial straw suffices to break the camel's back, so the addition of one more factor to a whole latent complex of conditions is sometimes enough to bring the whole cause into operation. A man may lose his temper, for instance, not because his friend said something particularly provoking, but because the remark came at an unfortunate psychological moment, when the irritations of the day had exhausted his patience and left him in a morbidly sensitive mood. In the Buddhist scriptures we again and again read how a few words of wisdom were sufficient to work a tremendous revolution in a man's life. Aśvajit recites to Śāriputra, then a wandering ascetic, a single verse of the Master's teaching, and the latter forthwith achieves the First Stage of Holiness.[49] When the Buddha smilingly offers him a golden flower Mahākāśyapa becomes Enlightened, even though the Lord utters not a single word.[50] The explanation of such phenomena, when a result so significant is achieved by means apparently so trivial, lies partly in the concentrated spiritual energy that lay behind what was said or done, and partly in the disciple's own state of preparedness and receptivity. That such incidents belong not merely to the dead past of pious legend but to the living present as well is demonstrated by the story of what happened when Anagarika Dharmapala, the founder of the Maha Bodhi Society of India, and the greatest Buddhist missionary of modern times, first met Mrs Mary E. Foster, who was afterwards to become the wish-fulfilling tree in the garden of the *anagārika*'s dreams of Buddhist revival in India and Ceylon.

They met in Honolulu, the capital of that group of islands each one of which may be described as a precious stone set not in a silver but a turquoise sea, and which was, at least before the advent of modern materialistic civilization, so full of beauty and happiness that one would have thought that Indra's heaven had descended with its inhabitants upon the blue waters of the Pacific Ocean. Over this island paradise there ruled, more than a century and a half ago, King Kamehameha the Great of Hawaii, who not only knit the scattered islands into one kingdom but also strove to stem the rising tide of Western influences which, he felt, would sweep away the happiness and innocence of his people. From this great monarch Mary Elizabeth Mikahala Foster was on her mother's side descended, though apart from this fact little is known of the details of her biography except that the names of her parents were James and Rebecca Robinson, that she was born on 21 September 1844, and that she married T. R. Foster, a wealthy banker of North America. The paths of this descendant of Hawaiian royalty and the scion of an aristocratic Sinhala family did not cross until 18 October 1893, when Mrs Foster was in her forty-ninth year and the *anagārika* in his twenty-ninth. He was on his way back to Ceylon via Japan after having scored a tremendous success at the World's Parliament of Religions in Chicago, and surely could never have dreamed of the far-reaching consequences of the chance meeting which took place on the *S. S. Oceanic*. The entry he made in his diary for the day deserves to be quoted in full:

> 18 October – Meditated. Relic in hand. My life will be spent for the good of others. I will preach Buddha's saving Law. Went ashore. I engaged a cab for $2 to take me to all interesting sites and the driver charged me $2 more for taking 2 of the Japanese whom I met halfway. The Hawaii women are unwieldy masses of flesh, they eat pork and poi. The queen is deposed and the

> Government provisional. I went to see the Palace which is now converted into an Executive Office. The Kamehameha school is nice. The principal Mr Richards was very courteous. Dr Cr Marques and two lady theosophists came to see me on board and they brought flowers and fruits which I distributed among passengers. Slight touch of headache.

One of the ladies referred to in the last sentence but one was, of course, Mrs Foster, and the fact that Dharmapala does not mention either her name or their brief conversation indicates how little importance he then attached to the interview. Only from his later reminiscences do we learn that Mrs Foster confessed to having an indomitable temper which she was powerless to control, and that she asked him how she could overcome such a troublesome defect. As one who practised Buddhist yoga Dharmapala was well qualified to advise her, and the remedy which he proposed was as simple as it was effective. He asked her to cultivate will power and to repeat the formula, 'I will be good, I will control the rising anger.' Once again, this time in the full blaze of modern history, do we find words apparently simple bringing about a mighty psychological effect. Not only did Mrs Foster eventually succeed in conquering her recalcitrant temper, but so deeply was she impressed by the spiritual qualities of the *anagārika* that, in later years, with implicit faith she entrusted to him for his work sums which before her death had reached a grand total of not less than one million rupees.

This flood of generosity, which helped bring to such rich fruition the field of the *anagārika*'s labours, did not commence to flow forth in its fullness until many years after the momentous meeting in Honolulu. In the meantime Mrs Foster was sending small annual donations to Dharmapala, of whose movements and activities she was kept informed through the pages of the *Maha Bodhi*. Not until August 1902, when he was in Los Angeles, California, and thought of starting an agricultural school in Sarnath, did an impulse come to him to write to Mrs Foster a letter explaining his schemes for alleviating the miseries of the illiterate people of Northern India and soliciting her help. The kind-hearted lady's response came promptly. She sent a donation of $500, following it up a year later with a further contribution of $3,000 for the same purpose. Thereafter she began helping his work with a generosity which would have done credit to Viśākha, and when, in 1906, the *anagārika* wrote informing her that his father, who had for so many years supported his work, was dead, she at once replied saying that he should in future regard her as his foster-mother. As his foster-mother he therefore regarded her, and as the foster-mother of the *anagārika* and his work she therefore acted from that time onwards until the day of her death. From 1902 till 1913 she contributed 3,000 rupees a year to the Maha Bodhi Society, the greater part of which was utilized for the purchase of a printing press and for the maintenance of the society's educational work in Ceylon. In 1913 the *anagārika* made a special trip to Hawaii in order to thank her for the unstinted support which she was giving to his efforts for the revival of the Dharma, and so pleased was his benefactress with the visit that before his departure she gave him 60,000 rupees for an institution named the Foster Robinson Free Hospital to be opened in Colombo in memory of her late father. Thereafter her benefactions were unparalleled, and it is hardly to be wondered at that the *anagārika*, who had appealed in vain to the wealthy Buddhists of Ceylon, Burma, Siam, and Japan, should behold with amazement the princely donations which poured in from the tiny Pacific island, or that in the fullness of his gratitude he should bestow upon his patroness the title 'Queen of the Empire of Righteousness'. His ardently grateful nature could not help believing that she had been born to assist his work, and that the subtle threads of destiny had knit the lives of a daughter of Hawaii and a son of Sri Lanka together for the sublime work of propagating the Dharma. Anagarika Dharmapala was always the first to admit that if he was the father whose fiery will had engendered the Maha Bodhi movement, Mrs Foster was the mother who fed and sustained it with the milk of her charity, and that it could no more have come to maturity without one 'parent' than without the other.

It is not possible to give a detailed account of Mrs Foster's contributions to the Maha Bodhi Society. Mention may be made, however, of the fact that it was with her help that the Society was at last able to acquire a building of its own in Calcutta. It was she, again, who contributed the greater part of the cost of erecting the Sri Dharmarajika Vihara, the magnificent edifice wherein the *anagārika*'s long-cherished dream of establishing a Buddhist temple in Calcutta was finally fulfilled. The Buddhist movement in India is no less indebted to her for the part she played in the construction of the Mulagandhakuti Vihara at Sarnath, for the generous Hawaiian lady's name heads the list of donors whose contributions rendered possible the erection of this mighty monument of modern Buddhist revival, through whose majestic portals thousands of people flock every year from every corner of the world to pay their homage to the Lord of Sarnath. In 1918 and 1923 respectively her munificence culminated in gifts of $50,000 and $100,000, which sums were carefully invested by the *anagārika* so as to ensure the continuance of his work. The letter which followed the second of these donations deserves to be quoted in full, since it reveals that the spirit in which Mrs Foster gave her donations was no less remarkable than the size of the amount given:

> Chicago III. 21 May 1923
>
> My Dear Brother,
> Your letter of 12 April reached me in Chicago to-day. I left San Francisco on 12 May to visit my sister living in this town and your letter was forwarded to me. I note what you state in regard to self-denial on your part. The money sent you is for you to use for your comfort as well as for the work you are accomplishing. I am grateful to you for all you have done for me. Please grant me this one wish. Do take care of yourself and take enjoyment and make enjoyment by being with your mother more often. Live for your work, that is by taking good care of your health, and give yourself more comforts. Have pleasant quarters such as you should have, in which to receive your friends. Take the money for it, for you deserve it and I insist, take good care of yourself for my sake.
> I thank you for the itemized accounts of the good work you have accomplished with the money sent you. How often the thought comes to me how wonderfully your work has grown. You must have given yourself very little rest to accomplish such good results. Words cannot express my gratitude, and how fortunate indeed it has been to me to have met a man so unselfish. As I said in the beginning, 'We will work together and the honour must be as much mine as yours.'
>
> May it please the Great All that we may meet again.
> Me ke Aloha Nui, Your Sister, Mary E. Foster
> Please give my Aloha Nui to your mother.

When Mrs Foster's gifts were made in such a gracious manner as this, and when the good lady had in fact asked him to regard her as his foster-mother, it is hardly surprising that whenever the *anagārika* was most desperately in need of help he should turn not to the rich but indifferent Buddhists of Asia but to the warm-hearted old Hawaiian lady whose generosity had helped give to his ideals 'a local habitation and a name'.[51] When he was in London in 1926, therefore, and saw the necessity of the British Maha Bodhi Society operating in premises of its own, he had no hesitation in ploughing across the Atlantic and travelling all the way to San Francisco, where Mrs Foster was then staying, in order to seek his patroness's help. With rare humility the old lady, then eighty-one years of age, said, 'I have money. I want to do good, but I don't know how best to do it. So I entrust my ideals to you to achieve by your work.' Before Dharmapala left San Francisco Mrs Foster had promised a substantial initial contribution and a subsequent monthly contribution of 900 rupees for the London Mission. On the eve of the *anagārika*'s departure she asked him to recite some Pāli verses, and he chanted a famous passage from the *Mahāvagga* of the Vinaya Piṭaka, an English translation of which appears at the head of the *Maha Bodhi*, where Mrs Foster had often seen it and been inspired by the compelling words:

> Go ye, O Bhikkhus, and wander forth for the gain of the many, for the welfare of the many, in compassion for the world, for the good, for the gain, for the welfare of gods and men. Proclaim, O Bhikkhus, the Doctrine glorious, preach ye a life of holiness, perfect and pure.[52]

Appropriately enough, he also recited Maung Tin's English translation of some well-known verses 'On Anger' from the *Visuddhimagga* of Buddhaghosa, for it was Mrs Foster's short temper which had been the means of bringing them together:

> If in his sphere thy foe lays pain on thee,
> Why dost thou wish to suffer in thy mind
> Outside his sphere? Thou canst give up thy kith
> And kin who have done thee great services,
> With tearful face. Why canst thou not forsake
> Thine anger-foe that has done thee much harm?

Thou playst with anger that uprooteth precepts
That thou hast kept. Is there a fool like thee?
Thou waxeth wroth because someone has done
Thee harm. Then couldst thou do unto thyself
The self-same thing? Someone wishing to rouse
Thy anger does thee some unpleasant thing.
Fulfillest thou his joy by waxing wroth?
Angry, thou mayest cause him harm or not.
But on thyself thou now inflictest pain
That comes of anger. If thy enemies
Pursue the unprofitable path of wrath,
Why dost thou imitate their angry deeds?
Cut off that hate by which thy foe has done
Thee harm. Why frettest thou where no occasion is?
Because at every moment states break up,
Those aggregates which caused thee harm have ceased.
With which of these art thou in anger now?
When on someone a man inflicteth pain,
No one gets pain beside the sufferer.
Thou art thyself the cause of pain. Then why
Wouldst thou get angry with another man?[53]

This was the last meeting that took place between Anagarika Dharmapala and Mrs Mary Elizabeth Foster, to whose joint efforts the revival of Buddhism in the land of its birth in general, and the Maha Bodhi Society in particular, owe so much. It is worthy of comment that although they worked together for more than thirty years, Mrs Foster and the *anagārika* met only thrice. The understanding which existed between them was, however, complete. If the founder of the Maha Bodhi Society was the ideal worker for Buddhism its patroness was the ideal donor. People who contribute a few rupees sometimes clamour for accounts and almost think that they have bought the organization they have condescended to help. Mrs Foster gave hundreds of thousands, but not once did she enquire what had been done with the money. Her confidence in the *anagārika* was absolute and with humility as deep as her generosity was wide she entrusted to him for his Buddhist and humanitarian work a considerable portion of her fortune. It is hardly to be wondered at that on his side the *anagārika* entertained sentiments of boundless gratitude to his benefactress, or that even before her death he had directed that her birthday should be celebrated at all centres of the Maha Bodhi Society, a practice which continues unbroken down to the present day.

Mrs Foster passed away in Honolulu on 19 December 1930, but the news of her death did not reach the *anagārika* until several weeks later. He was then confined to bed at the Maligakanda Seminary in Ceylon, having only recently succeeded in shaking off the heart disease by which he had for so long been troubled. It was then his custom to rise in the early hours of the morning long before dawn with crimson fingers had drawn back the curtains of the night, and sit and meditate and invoke the blessings of the *devas*, the shining ones, on all who were helping him in his work, particularly on his mother and Mrs Foster. In his diary for 14 January 1931 he writes:

> Got up at 2 a.m. For the first time I have to omit the gracious name of Mrs Mary Foster as she had passed away on the 22nd ultimo. She was my foster mother and 'Mascot'. She brought luck to me. She was phenomenally generous and now *the romantic career of unparalleled generosity* has ended. Her benefactions were manifold.

In the Mrs Mary E. Foster Memorial Number of the *Maha Bodhi* journal Dharmapala paid a moving tribute to the Viśākha of modern Buddhist revival, who even in death had not forgotten the sacred cause which she had so long espoused, leaving $50,000 for the maintenance of the foster schools and hospitals of Ceylon and India. After recounting the difficulties which, in the course of his life-work, he had had to face, the *anagārika* concludes with these words:

> Single-handed I persevered but no help could be got from the Buddhists of Burma, Siam, and other countries. Thanks to the unparalleled generosity of Mrs Mary Foster, the Buddhists have now a beautiful dominating shrine with a hundred feet tower. No Sinhalese Buddhist, no Siamese, no Japanese, no Chinese, no Tibetan came forward to co-operate with me. But from distant Honolulu help came from Mrs Foster to revive the *śāsana* in India and establish anew the *śāsana* in England. There is none to take

> her place in the Buddhist world. Wealthy Buddhists are all dead. Self-sacrificing Bhikkhus are rare. India will again supply young heroes to preach the doctrine of Ahimsa, Karuna, and Maitri – wearing the yellow robe. I have worked for India since 1891, and now I am an invalid with only one wish in my heart: to die on the holy ground where stands the Mulagandhakuti Vihara.

It was not long before the *anagārika*'s wish was fulfilled. Two years later he, too, passed away, leaving behind him a name with which that of Mrs Mary Elizabeth Foster of Honolulu, 'Queen of the Empire of Righteousness', will be forever linked in the grateful memory of millions of Buddhists, to whom the founder and patroness of the Maha Bodhi Society shine forth as examples of a noble collaboration that is perhaps without parallel not only in the history of Buddhism but in the annals of mankind.

IMMORTAL SAYINGS OF ANAGARIKA DHARMAPALA

1. Without effort progressive development is impossible. Buddha built his religion on the foundations of energetic effort and vigilant activity.
2. Buddhism is a religion of strenuous endeavour. Its mission is to enlighten each human being to cleanse himself from psychical impurities of covetousness, anger, pride, stubbornness, conceit, malice, envy, etc.
3. The uncontaminated mind is radiant. The contaminations are later accretions.
4. The development of consciousness, strengthening the memory, avoiding recollections of associations tinged with sensual desires, resolute effort to generate thoughts of kindness, and renunciation are necessary to realize Nirvāṇa.
5. Anger makes man a demon; fear is caused by ignorance, and ignorance is the cause of all physical and mental suffering.
6. The glory of the Buddha depends not on his own royal birth, but in the supreme wisdom that he obtained by self conquest and his infinite love.
7. Avoid the path of injustice. To please friends, relations, one should never do an unjust act. Never do anything in anger and malice, and show no fear and do no cowardly act, and avoid doing things foolishly.

8. Activity in doing good is the law of progress. Delay and neglect produce suffering and misery.
9. Nothing should be done without thought. Sitting, standing, walking, lying down, every movement of each limb should be associated with consciousness.
10. One should never dogmatize; but always analyse.
11. Inasmuch as all good deeds proceed from the elements of renunciation, one should always strive to avoid sensuous pleasures, that are correlated with sin and lust.
12. Sleep should be regulated. There should be a union between sleep and wakefulness.
13. Exert to realize the unconditioned, infinite eternal happiness of Nirvāṇa, in full consciousness in this life, on this earth.
14. Freedom is Wisdom's highest gift, depending on perfect *brahmacarya*.
15. The past is infinite. It has no known beginning. With an infinite past, with the future before you, which you make for good or for evil, with the present under your control, your destiny is in your hands.
16. The Buddha is the embodiment of the Dhamma. The elements that go to make up the personality of the Buddha are identical with the principles that he enunciated. By thought, words and deeds the Buddha does not differentiate from absolute truth.
17. Renunciation of sense pleasure may cause a temporary painfulness, but it has its reward in the realization of the infinite bliss of Nirvāṇa.
18. Nirvāṇa simply means freedom from ignorance, freedom from anger, freedom from lustful desires. It is a consummation worth striving for. Renunciation therefore from all sense pleasure and from all evil is Nirvāṇa.
19. Pessimism has no place in the dynamic doctrine of the Lord Buddha. The wise man is a potential god. His powers are infinite; but they must be brought into existence by effort. The way to become a god is to practise the Noble Eightfold Path.
20. It was given the lion-hearted Prince of the Śākyas to proclaim the religion of truth (Dhamma) breaking the barriers, of caste, creed, race, and territory. Territorialism was vanquished by the sunlight

of truth. An imperial religion was for the first time proclaimed by the Buddha as King of Righteousness, whose territory extended to the uttermost limits of the Earth.

21. A progressive evolution with a definite ideal, its realization here and now, making life cheerful, energetic, serene, worth living for the sake of doing good for the welfare of others, this the Tathāgata proclaimed.
22. The innocent bliss is born of perfect purity without attachment to the things of the world, where no question of the '*ahaṃkāra* and *mamaṃkāra*' arises in the mind, free from covetousness, free from ill will, hatred, anger, and free from foolish superstitions born of fear and delusions.[54]
23. Here is the religion of consciousness, of perfect recollection, of presence of mind, of fearlessness, of freedom, of activity, of loving compassion and of immortality.
24. A cooperative commonwealth working for the welfare of the many and for the happiness of the many is the kind of institution that civilized humanity needs.
25. The doctrine that Buddha taught was an analytical ethico-psychology based on the principles of evolution and causality.
26. There is no permanency but change. From the minutest atom to the highest heaven everything is becoming. It comes into being, stays for a time and passes away, like the volume of water in the flowing stream.
27. It is here that all philanthropic projects are accomplished, it is here that meritorious work is done. It is here human kindness and self-sacrifice are appreciated. It is here that man can transcend the gods and save suffering humanity.
28. Morality is the most solid foundation that is needed to build up a lasting society. The Lord Buddha again and again emphasized that the Āryan religion shall only last so long as the disciples would strictly follow the path of purifying morality. When morality disappears society degenerates.
29. The sensual-minded people fond of sense pleasures yearn to be born in the regions of the gods, but the follower of Wisdom looks with loathsome disgust on the pleasures of the senses, whether human or divine.

30. Effort is what the Buddha wished that people should make. Effort is all in all. Effort is the basis of karma. Even the effort to think is karma.
31. No truth can come out of the man who is not absolutely free to express his highest convictions. Absolute freedom is a needed factor when we are in search of truth.
32. Neither the existence of an eternal hell nor of an eternal heaven is acknowledged in Buddhism. Each individual being has to suffer according to the evil karma he has done, it may be for a *kalpa*, but at the end, cessation of suffering is the law.
33. Buddhism is a kind of spiritual athleticism. It teaches you the way to develop your spiritual muscles and to strengthen your spiritual tendons. If another does your work where is the glory of your effort?
34. The passionate sensualist could never comprehend what Nirvāṇa is. Where there is anger there is no Nirvāṇa. Where there is no anger there is Nirvāṇa. Where there is covetousness, there is no Nirvāṇa. Where there is no covetousness there is Nirvāṇa. Where there is ignorance, there is no Nirvāṇa. Where there is no ignorance, no ego desires of 'this is mine, this is I', there is Nirvāṇa. Absence of evil, development of good, and purification of the heart are what constitute Nirvāṇa.
35. The desire to destroy all evil desires should be ever active in the mind. When all ego desires are abandoned Nirvāṇa reveals itself to the mind.
36. Absolute peace amidst the clanging of a million bells is only possible when the Nirvāṇa consciousness unfolds itself.
37. Greater than Nirvāṇa is compassionate activity for the uplifting of the ignorant world leading them to enlightened happiness.
38. Instead of making an effort to cleanse the heart from sin, ignorant man seeks to gain happiness by outward purification.
39. The Blessed One was the embodiment of strenuousness. He adopted as the motto of his religion the two words *appamāda* and *viriya* (non-delay and diligent activity).
40. If only the *bhikkhus* would stir themselves and follow the Holy Master, Buddhism would not be then called a religion of pessimism.

41. The foundations of the Āryan doctrine were laid not on asceticism, neither on sense perceptions. It is the doctrine founded on joyous cheerfulness, radiant mentality, strenuousness, aesthetic calm, analytical investigation of truth, contentment, and supreme wisdom.
42. Power and pride degenerate man into a demon. The way to truth is one, the way to power is another. All civilizations that were founded on mere materialism have ceased to exist.
43. This doctrine of mine and thine is the chief source of all human suffering, enhanced by covetous desire, egotistic pride, and the lack of insight to recognize truth in the right way.
44. Without *dhyāna* there is no way to acquire the wisdom of Nirvāṇa, and without the acquisition of *prajñā* there is no realizing of *dhyāna*.
45. As long as the people of ancient India remained true to the wisdom teachings of the Blessed One there was happiness in the land.
46. The *attā* doctrine is injurious to the progressive development of the individual. It makes man arrogant and develops his conceit. Biologically, psychologically, superpsychically, sociologically, and morally the ethic is destructive to progress and expansion.
47. It is in lonely retreats that spiritual visions always come to the ascetically inclined. Investigate into the history of each religious founder regarding his early religious experiences, and the fact will be revealed that he was a mystic, given to fasting, away from the crowd, and desiring for spiritual unfolding.
48. The Buddha laid great emphasis on the moral progress of the individual. The householder without morality is like a ship without a rudder. When a man is morally conscious of his own progress, he is able to transcend the knowledge of gods.
49. Mere morality is insufficient to realize the wisdom of Nirvāṇa. Nirvāṇa is all wisdom, and only by the strenuousness of earnest effort in the Middle Path can the *brahmacārī* obtain the realization of Nirvāṇa.
50. When the Brahmin shall change his haughty spirit and look on the other people with compassion, and work for the elevation of the masses, then will India again take the supreme place which she, in ancient times, occupied.

51. We are selfish, and our luxurious lives are the cause of our forgetfulness of our duty to our fellow man.
52. One individual, like the Buddha, gives happiness to countless millions of human beings, and they in their turn give others happiness.
53. The blood of innocent animals slaughtered by man through false religious convictions if measured would make an ocean.
54. The real understanding of Buddhism is an attainment that has to be obtained by gradual spiritual progress; it cannot be obtained by mere reason, nor can it be destroyed by criticism; not because it is a matter of faith but because to those who have tasted its flavour, there is no other flavour that can replace it.
55. Parents, teachers, spiritual and secular, should be examples of the highest virtue, so that they will be able to influence the future generations.
56. The more the teachers show the spirit of self-sacrifice, associated with the spirit of compassion, like the mother that takes every care of herself for the love of her unborn child, still in the womb, the better it will be for the development of the future generations.
57. If the householder does not see in the spiritual teacher virtue, why should he pay him homage? He must be an example of self abnegation, cultivating the higher life, to receive the homage of the householder.
58. The religion of the Buddha was intended for all castes. He made no distinction between the Brahmin and the Shudra. To all he gave the ambrosia of the eternal Dhamma.
59. There is no World-Teacher that loved India more than the Lord Buddha. Millions of times he renounced the eternal peace and bliss of Nirvāṇa for the love of humanity.
60. The exclusive teachings of the Brahmins can never help cosmopolitan India. If there is any religion that can bring about the consummation of the cherished desires of Indian patriots, it is Buddhism.
61. The essential principle that the Lord Buddha emphasized is ceaseless activity – activity in destroying evil, activity in generating good thoughts, good words, good deeds – thereby achieving the peace and happiness of Nirvāṇa.

62. Every good act done with an unselfish motive and without the association of the ego consciousness is helpful to realize the Nirvāṇa ideal.
63. To save the world from ignorance by means of wisdom and love was the object of the Buddha.
64. The earth, season after season, gives fruits; the sky gives rain, the cow gives milk, and the beggar who visits the door of the householder gets his dole. Charity is the law of life.
65. Those who wish to get at truth should not be contented with the myths and theories of the mystics and ascetics. They should be daring, courageous, and full of intense earnestness.

DHARMAPALA:
The Spiritual Dimension

Anagarika Dharmapala is best known to the Buddhist world as the founder of the Maha Bodhi Society, the resuscitator of Bodh Gaya, and the fearless proclaimer of the Dharma in three continents. In the course of the fifty years from 1883 to 1933 he built temples and viharas, established schools, hospitals, and rest houses, opened Buddhist centres, organized the celebration of Buddhist festivals, sponsored international Buddhist conferences, reclaimed sites connected with the life of the Buddha, revived Pāli studies in India, promoted traditional Sinhalese arts and crafts, encouraged technical education, founded and edited journals, printed and distributed Buddhist literature, wrote articles, lectured on Buddhism, politics, and social reform, corresponded with friends and sympathizers throughout the world, and did a hundred other things in pursuit of his declared objective of working – through Buddhism – for the good of humanity.

So much did he in fact do that one might be forgiven for thinking that he was no more than a Buddhist activist, of the type that was later to become only too common, and that he had allowed himself to become absorbed in external activities at the expense of his inner life. Such was my own impression, at least, until the year 1952, when the late Devapriya Valisinha, the chief lieutenant and principal disciple of the *anagārika*'s later years and his successor as General Secretary of the Maha Bodhi Society of India, invited me to contribute a biographical sketch of his guru to the Society's *Diamond Jubilee Souvenir*. This sketch I wrote at the Society's Calcutta headquarters, where I had the opportunity of examining some of the bulky quarto volumes of the Dharmapala Diaries – diaries the *anagārika* had kept for about forty years. At the head of every alternate page he had, I found, written 'The only refuge for him who aspires to true perfection is the Buddha alone'. These were the words – originally a message from the Master K. H. to A. P. Sinnett – which Madame Blavatsky had quoted to him in 1884, when he was only 20 years old and still Don David Hewavitarne, and they had, it seems, remained permanently inscribed on his heart. This is highly significant. Going for Refuge to the Buddha (and to the Dharma and the Sangha) is the central and definitive act of the Buddhist life, and the fact that Dharmapala should have gone on writing out the words quoted by Madame Blavatsky in the way he did showed that for him Going for Refuge was not a formality to be observed on special occasions but something that had to be personally experienced – or at least called to mind – every single day. It showed that for him being a Buddhist was not something that one could take for granted. Being a Buddhist represented a commitment that had to be constantly renewed. Moreover, the Master's message spoke of the Buddha alone being the only refuge *for him who aspires to true perfection*. True perfection was ethical and spiritual, and ethical and spiritual perfection was synonymous with *bodhi* or Enlightenment. Since the Buddha was the embodiment of Enlightenment it followed that the act of Going for Refuge to the Buddha and the aspiration to true perfection were inseparable. It is therefore not surprising that throughout his life Dharmapala should not only have observed the basic ethical precepts of Buddhism but also have striven unremittingly for complete purity of body, speech, and mind. Nor was that all. The Buddha *alone* was the *only* refuge for the aspirant to true perfection. Though he was a man of broad religious sympathies, having joined the Theosophical Society at an early age (he remained a theosophist, though not a member of any theosophical organization, to the end of his life), Dharmapala was by no means a woolly-minded universalist for whom all religious teachers were equally enlightened and all religious teachings equally true. For him the Buddha was the *supremely* Enlightened One and his teaching the way to Enlightenment *par excellence*.

On examining the diaries I also found that Dharmapala's day began at two or three o'clock in the morning and that it began with meditation.

He had always been interested in meditation, and admits in his unfinished 'Reminiscences of My Early Life' that from boyhood he was inclined towards the mystic, ascetic life, and that he was on the lookout for news about *arhants* and the science of *abhijñā*, or supernormal knowledge, even though, as he relates, the *bhikṣus* of Ceylon were sceptical about the possibility of realizing arhantship, believing that the age of *arhants* was past and that the realization of Nirvāṇa by psychic training was no longer possible. These mystic and ascetic tendencies were strengthened by his contact with the teachings of theosophy, especially its teachings about the Masters, and by the fact that in the course of his travels on behalf of the Buddhist Theosophical Society – travels which took him to every corner of the island – he came across a number of palm-leaf books on meditation, one of which he had transcribed. But though he came across books on meditation he was unable to find anyone, whether monk or layman, who actually meditated or who could instruct him in the practices the books described. The nearest he came to finding such a person was when a monk told him that his late guru had practised meditation – and had gone mad! Some time in 1889 or 1890, therefore, when he had sought in vain for a teacher for several years, Dharmapala started practising meditation without the benefit of a personal teacher after making a careful study of the *Satipaṭṭhāna Sutta* or 'Discourse on the Foundations of Mindfulness', and the relevant sections of the *Visuddhimagga*. Having thus made a start he continued, and for the next forty years meditation formed an integral part of his day, as the pages of the Dharmapala Diaries abundantly testify. Shortly after embarking on the practice of meditation, however, he travelled to Adyar for the Theosophical Society's Annual Convention of 1890 and there, besides joining the Esoteric Section of the Society, had the good fortune to meet a Burmese Buddhist layman from whom he received some practical instructions on meditation. This friendly mentor appears to have been Moung Hpo Myhin, with whom Dharmapala stayed when he visited Rangoon the following year on his way back from Japan and who proved to be a staunch supporter of his work. Another significant contact, in view of Dharmapala's confessed inclination towards the mystic, ascetic life, was a female yogi known simply as Maji or Reverend Mother. Dharmapala heard of her at Benares, which he visited shortly after the convention, and at once went to see her in her cave on the banks of the Ganges. They had a pleasant chat, he reports, and at his request she presented him with a rosary. What use he made of the rosary we do not know. Perhaps he recited on it the epithets of the Buddha as enumerated in the *iti'pi so* formula – a traditional Theravāda practice.[55] We do not, in fact, know much about the methods of meditation practised by Dharmapala at this stage of his career or just how extensive was his experience of higher states of consciousness, though a diary entry for 17 February 1891 speaks of his experiencing, for the first time in his life, 'the peace which passeth all understanding'. What we do know is that *mettā bhāvanā* eventually became the sheet anchor of his spiritual life and that not a day passed without his consciously directing thoughts of loving-kindness to parents, benefactors, and friends and, indeed, to all living beings.

Meditation must be well grounded in ethics. It is hardly possible for one to develop skilful concentration of mind when the mind is disturbed by those unskilful states of lust, hatred, and so on which are the effect, even as they are also the cause, of unethical behaviour. As the Buddha repeatedly reminded his followers in the course of the last few months of his life: 'Great becomes the fruit, great the advantage, of meditation (*samādhi*) when it is set round with ethical behaviour (*sīla*); great becomes the fruit, great the advantage, of understanding (*paññā*) when it is set round with meditation'.[56] In Dharmapala's case meditation was certainly well set round with ethical behaviour, even as understanding was well set round with meditation, and for him, therefore, the fruit and advantage of both meditation and understanding can be assumed to have 'become great'. The importance of leading 'the life of holiness, perfect and pure', formed, in fact, one of the major themes of his lectures and addresses in East and West alike. His first lecture – actually a sermon – in the United States, immediately before the World's Parliament of Religions, was on 'The Pure Life', and after a long and tiring session of the Parliament he characteristically remarked, 'All papers full of Theology and Anthropomorphism but pure life naught.' Not that Dharmapala saw purity of life solely in terms of its bearing on meditation. Purity of life, or ethical behaviour, was as necessary to the householder as to the monk, to society as to the individual. 'The Buddha laid great emphasis on the moral progress of the individual,' he wrote in the *Maha Bodhi* journal. 'The householder without morality is like a ship without a rudder.' Similarly, 'Morality is the most solid foundation that is needed to build up a lasting society.

The Lord Buddha again and again emphasized that the Aryan religion shall only last so long as the disciples would strictly follow the path of purifying morality. When morality disappears society degenerates.' In the course of his travels in the West, especially, he could not but observe how many rudderless ships there were adrift on the ocean of humanity and the extent to which society had therefore degenerated. 'Slaves of passion,' he wrote in his diary during his second trip to the United States (1896–7), 'controlled by the lower senses, wallowing in sensuality, these so-called Christians live in killing each other, hating each other, swindling each other, introducing liquor and vice where they hadn't existed. Themselves slaves of passion they enslave others to themselves and their vices.'

Dharmapala himself, though of an ardent temperament, was far from being a slave of passion. At the age of eight, he tells us in his unfinished 'Reminiscences', he was initiated into the *brahmacarya* vow by his father at the local temple, and advised to be contented with what he got to eat, and to sleep but little. What form the initiation took, and whether the ceremony was performed by his father personally, or by the incumbent of the temple, we are not told, but the experience left a permanent impression. Besides being accustomed, in later years, to satisfy his hunger with whatever food he received, and to sleep for only two or three hours at night, Dharmapala continued to observe the *brahmacarya* vow and remained, despite all temptation, chaste in body, in speech, and – to the utmost of his ability – in mind, to the end of his days. His mature commitment to the life of chastity was signalized by his adoption of the title of *anagārika* or 'homeless one', an *anagārika* being one who, without being technically a monk, observes the precept of abstention from unchastity (as distinct from the precept of abstention from sexual misconduct) and whose life is wholly dedicated to the service of Buddhism. Prior to this he had signalized his rejection of foreign manners and customs, which were having a deleterious effect on the cultural and religious life of the nation, by dropping the Portuguese-Christian 'Don David' and assuming the name of Dharmapala, or 'Guardian of the Law'. It was therefore as Anagarika Dharmapala that he became known to the world and as Anagarika Dharmapala that he has his place in Buddhist history.

Being an *anagārika*, and observing as he did the *brahmacarya* vow, Dharmapala was free as he could never have been as a married householder. He was freer than even the monks, restricted as these then were by the requirements of the Vinaya. He was free to work for humanity, free to work for Buddhism, free to travel, free to speak his mind, free to sacrifice health, strength, and life itself for the sake of his ideals. He was also free to form friendships with men of all sorts and conditions in many different parts of the world. Dharmapala in fact had something of a gift for friendship. By nature warm-hearted and enthusiastic, he not only made friends easily but, once having made a friend, he remained loyal – even fiercely loyal – to the friendship through all vicissitudes. That he had this gift for friendship was fortunate, since the best part of his life was spent in a foreign land, working for a long-vanished faith, and struggling (in the matter of the Bodh Gaya temple case) against powerful vested interests, and had he not enjoyed the support of friends and well-wishers he would have encountered even more difficulties than he did. Some of his closest friends were to be found among the English-educated Bengalis of Calcutta, where from the beginning of 1892 Dharmapala made his homeless home and where he lived on terms of intimacy with men who were, or who subsequently became, prominent in the life of the great city, then the capital of India. In more than one instance the friendship continued through two, and even three, generations of the same family, being handed down from father to son like a precious heirloom.

Dharmapala's gift for friendship was naturally strengthened by his practice of *mettā bhāvanā*, in the course of which he sought to develop thoughts of loving-kindness towards all living beings, not excluding animals. As a boy he was revolted by the fact that one of the masters at the Christian school he attended took delight in shooting birds. It is therefore not surprising that he should have been a lifelong vegetarian (as was his disciple Sri Devapriya Valisinha), being particularly opposed to the eating of beef. A photograph taken on one of his preaching tours in Ceylon (now Sri Lanka), and reproduced in the Maha Bodhi Society of India's *Diamond Jubilee Souvenir*, shows him leaning out of the window of a small omnibus on the side of which are emblazoned, in large Sinhalese characters, the words 'Don't eat beef'.

Thus there was a definitely spiritual dimension to Dharmapala's life, and it was because of this spiritual dimension, as exemplified by his recognition that the Buddha alone was the only refuge, his aspiration to ethical and spiritual perfection, his inclination to the mystic, ascetic life, his devotion to meditation, his observance of the *brahmacarya* vow, his adoption of the homeless life, his gift for friendship, and his vegetarianism, that enabled him to found the Maha Bodhi Society, to resuscitate Bodh Gaya, and to proclaim the Dharma, as well as to engage in numerous other activities. All these activities were, in fact, the outward and visible expression of an intense inner life. His illustrious Hindu colleague at the World's Parliament of Religions, Swami Vivekananda, defined the ideal man as he who, in the midst of the greatest silence and solitude, finds the intensest activity, and in the midst of the intensest activity finds the silence and solitude of the desert. By this definition Anagarika Dharmapala was an ideal man or, in Buddhist terms, a bodhisattva – the kind of being of whom the *Ratnagotravibhāga* declares:

> Like a fire his mind constantly blazes up into good works for others.
>
> At the same time he always remains merged in the calm of the trances and formless attainments.[57]

It was the life of a bodhisattva that his father exhorted him to lead when he entrusted him, in his twentieth year, to the care of Madame Blavatsky, and it was accordingly the life of a bodhisattva – a life dedicated to the highest good of humanity – that he endeavoured to lead for the next forty years. Consequently it would not be too much to describe Anagarika Dharmapala as 'a modern bodhisattva', as I did in an editorial I wrote for the September 1957 issue of the *Maha Bodhi*. In that article I considered his practice of the bodhisattva ideal in terms of his cultivation of the ten perfections (*daśa pāramitā*) of Theravāda tradition, from giving (*dāna*) to equanimity (*upekṣā*), concluding: 'As we remember his ninety-third birth anniversary … we recall his practice of the bodhisattva ideal and are grateful for the fact that even in these dark days we have before our eyes the inspiring example of a modern bodhisattva to follow.' Thirty-six years later I see no reason to revise that judgement, and on the occasion of the one hundredth anniversary of the Society he founded salute the memory of the great *anagārika* with renewed appreciation.

ANAGARIKA DHARMAPALA AND MRS MARY E. FOSTER

Sometimes, wandering through the forest solitude, or walking in the broad open spaces of a city park, we see before us a great banyan tree which for sheer massiveness of trunk, thickness and length of bough, and abundance of foliage, far surpasses all its brethren. Approaching, we pass into an

> ample shade,
> Cloistered with columned dropping stems, and roofed
> With vaults of glistening green
>
> (from Edwin Arnold's *Light of Asia*)

and rest for a few moments in the coolness and the shadow. As we gaze up at the tangle of interlacing branches, through which the sun sends only a feeble and misty ray, the thought suddenly strikes us 'and this great tree, which flings its shade over almost half an acre of ground, sprang from a tiny seed no bigger than a pea!'

The same kind of thought flashes across our minds when, travelling from one part of India to another, there unrolls before our eyes scene after scene of the vast panorama of modern Buddhist revival and renaissance. *Here* we see a new vihara under construction, *there* an exhibition of Buddhist art; in *this* place a yellow-robed monk is preaching the Dharma to a crowd of eager listeners, in *that* the traffic is being halted so that an image of the Buddha, which is being taken in procession by milling thousands of devotees with all the traditional pomp and ceremony, may have room to pass. Yet only sixty years ago the name of the Buddha was almost unknown in India. In the whole length and breadth of the land there could be found hardly an active Buddhist centre. How did the change take place? What was its cause?

In January 1891, a young man of 25 came to India from Ceylon on pilgrimage. With him was a Japanese friend. On 22 January the pair arrived at Bodh Gaya, where the Blessed One attained Enlightenment. Let us relate what happened at the sacred place in the young man's own words, transcribed from his diary.

> 22 January: After taking breakfast we went in the company of Durga Babu and Dr Chatterjee to Bodhgaya – the most sacred of all sacred spots to the Buddhists. After driving 6 miles (from Gaya) we arrived at the holy spot. Within a mile you could see lying scattered here and there broken statues etc. of our blessed Lord. At the entrance to the mahant's temple on both sides of the portico there are statues of our Lord in the attitude of meditation and expounding the Law. How elevating! The sacred Vihara – the Lord sitting on his throne and the great solemnity which pervades all round makes the heart of the pious devotee weep. How delightful! As soon as I touched with my forehead the Vajrasana a sudden impulse came to my mind. It prompted me to stop here and take care of this sacred spot – so sacred that nothing in the world is equal to this place where Prince Sakya Sinha gained Enlightenment under the bodhi tree…

This was the seed of Buddhist revival in India. How tiny! How insignificant! An unknown young man, of delicate constitution and emotional temperament, comes to Bodh Gaya on pilgrimage with a friend, on the spur of the moment he makes a resolution to care for the Vajrāsana and, lo and behold! out of that boyish resolution is born not only the Maha Bodhi Society of India, with all that it has been able to accomplish for the revival of the Dharma in the land of its birth, but also a worldwide movement for the dissemination of the Sublime Doctrine of the Buddha. Is the phenomenon not even more astonishing than the emergence of the mighty banyan from a tiny pea-sized seed?

Sitting in the shade of the banyan it is fitting that we should remember the tiny seed from which it sprang, and enjoying as we now do some of the first fruits of Buddhist revival and renaissance in India, it is but proper that we should recall with gratitude the one who planted them. Gratitude is one of the Buddhist virtues. We are grateful to the Lord Buddha for having revealed to us the Path to Enlightenment. We are grateful to all the eminent Buddhist saints and sages who have contributed to our understanding of the Dharma. We are grateful, too, to that young pilgrim from Ceylon – Anagarika Dharmapala, the founder of our Society – to whom we owe the rebirth of Buddhism in India and its propagation not only in Ceylon and Burma, China and Japan, but also in many Western lands. We remember him more, perhaps, this month than at any other time of the year, for it was on 17 September 1864 that he was born in the Pettah district of Colombo, Ceylon.

The story of his life has been told more than once in these pages and need not be repeated on this occasion. More than the details of his biography do we need to recall his inspiring example. Two outstanding characteristics distinguish the life of Anagarika Dharmapala: *vīrya* or energy, and *sati* or mindfulness – both essential Buddhist qualities. His energy has been vividly described by one who knew him intimately in his early days, when he was still working at the headquarters of the Colombo Buddhist Theosophical Society:

> Nothing was too small or too big for him. He would clean his own room, make his own bed, attend to office work, write all the letters and take them to the post himself, not as a matter of virtue but as part of his daily routine. He would interpret for one, he would prepare a programme for another, he would translate a lecture for someone else, he would write original articles for the newspaper. He would discuss the policy with the Editor and would correct proofs for him, and he would interview those who visited the office. He wrote to people all over Ceylon inviting them to contribute their good will towards the progress of the cause. All were alike to him, whether one was old or young or a schoolboy, learned or ignorant, rich or poor did not matter; he instinctively knew what each was able to contribute towards the common good. He spent well nigh fifteen to sixteen hours a day in intensive work. He had a pleasant manner, cheerful at all times; his written and spoken words were eloquent and their sincerity went to the hearts of all those who met him.

So much work for a single cause cannot be accomplished unless one bears that cause constantly in mind. It would hardly be an exaggeration to say that for more than forty years of his life Anagarika Dharmapala had no other thought than the revival of the Dharma. Concentration of thought leads to concentration of energy. He was totally indifferent to his own comfort and convenience. He cared nothing for fame or popularity. His life was in the fullest sense a dedicated life.

But even a man like Dharmapala could not make bricks without straw. For the maintenance of his numerous activities connected with the establishment and propagation of the Dharma in half a dozen countries he needed funds, and funds are a thing which enthusiastic young men with ideals usually find it very difficult to get. The leader of a Buddhist group in the West once remarked that he sometimes felt as though there was an organized conspiracy in the world to prevent money from being used for good purposes. Fortunately for Dharmapala, on his return from the Chicago World's Parliament of Religions at the end of 1893, he had met Mrs Mary E. Foster, descendant of King Kamehameha the Great of Hawaii. In the course of the next four decades this large-hearted lady gave the *anagārika* a series of donations which eventually reached the magnificent total of one million rupees. Without Mrs Foster's help the *anagārika* could hardly have accomplished the work which has given him his place in history. We therefore remember her generosity with no less gratitude than we recall the noble endeavour of the hero she so nobly helped. As her birthday falls on 21 September we remember this month not only Anagarika Dharmapala but his benefactress and 'foster mother' Mrs Mary E. Foster. As she said to him at the beginning of their long and wonderful collaboration, 'we will work together and the honour must be as much mine as yours'. They have won much more than honour. They have won immortal renown.

September 1955

A MODERN BODHISATTVA

A Roman Catholic writer once taunted Buddhism with the remark that the bodhisattva ideal was very beautiful, but it was a beautiful dream. No historical person, according to him, had ever practised it, and indeed he seemed to think it impracticable. Evidently he knew nothing of the life of the late Ven. Anagarika Dharmapala, the founder of our Society, who not only had a firm faith in this loftiest of all spiritual ideals, but, as some of us are beginning to realize, was himself a bodhisattva – one whose every thought, word, and deed was dedicated to the highest good of his fellow men.

A bodhisattva, as all serious students of the Dharma are aware, is required to practise the ten perfections *(daśa pāramitā)*. With a few variations of minor importance these are the same for all schools of Buddhism, but since Ven. Dharmapala followed the list in its Theravādin formulation it is in terms of this version that we shall consider his practice of the Bodhisattva ideal.[58]

1. *Dāna* or giving. This, according to Buddhist tradition, is threefold: *vastu-dāna,* the giving of material things; *śikṣā-dāna,* or the gift of education, and *Dharma-dāna,* or the gift of the Dharma. All three kinds of giving are fully exemplified in the life of the Anagarika Dharmapala. The allowance which, in his younger days, he received from his father, was spent on Society work. His handsome patrimony went into the Dharmapala Trust, out of which numerous Buddhist undertakings are still being financed. He grudged spending money on himself. As a young man he went without food so that he could buy stamps and dispatch this

journal to the subscribers. Even when, old and famous, he lay dying at Sarnath, he told his chief disciple, Sri Devapriya Valisinha, not to waste money on medicines but to use it for Buddhist work. Whatever he had he gave to the movement. Through the educational institutions that he founded, and which the Society still conducts in his memory, he gave the gift of education. Last but not least, through his lectures and articles, and through the Society which he founded, he gave back to India – in fact he gave to practically the whole world – the infinitely precious gift of the Dharma of Lord Buddha. For his practice of *dāna* alone, Dharmapala might be regarded as a bodhisattva.

2. *Sīla* or morality. Dharmapala's life was one of spotless purity. Despite the temptations that never fail to beset those who are trying to tread the spiritual path, he all his life faithfully observed the five precepts of not taking life, not taking what was not given, not misbehaving sexually, not telling lies, and not taking intoxicants. Even at the risk of giving offence to people – and offence was frequently given – he was uncompromising in his adherence to ethical principles. From beginning to end his life was a blaze of purity in which all things evil and unclean were consumed.

3. *Nekkhamma* or renunciation. Coming as he did from a wealthy and respected family of Colombo, David Hewavitarne (as he was then called) had every opportunity of enjoying worldly pleasure and prosperity to the utmost. He could have followed in his father's footsteps and become a distinguished businessman. Or he could have stayed in the civil service (which he was made to join after leaving school) and risen to a position of power and influence. He could have become a doctor like one of his brothers, or a lawyer. If he liked he could have remained all his life in seclusion studying the books in which he took so much delight. But he gave them all up. At the age of 18 he made his great decision and turned his back upon worldly life. Henceforward he was the *anagārika*, the homeless one, with no other thought than to benefit humanity through propagating the Dharma. Like his Master, the Buddha, he gave up wealth for poverty, luxury for hardship, ease for grinding hard work. Towards the end of his life he, as it were, set a seal upon his life of renunciation by formally joining the *bhikkhu* sangha to which he had so long belonged in spirit.

4. *Paññā* or wisdom. As a lifelong student of the Dharma and as one who regularly practised meditation, Anagarika Dharmapala was able to develop that keen insight into the fundamentals of the Dharma, and that ability to apply them to any given situation, which is so striking a feature of his life and writings. In a humorous mood, he used to tell his friends that during his first voyage to America he kept a copy of the Bible and a copy of the *Visuddhimagga* in his trunk. When he reached his destination, he was astonished to find the Bible in shreds but the *Visuddhimagga* quite intact. The story illustrates his attitude towards error. He was fearless in his condemnation. Neither would he tolerate the least misrepresentation of Buddhism. Once, in the Mulagandhakuti Vihara, a very distinguished citizen of Benares was, as some people are very apt to do, holding forth on what the Buddha 'really' taught. Dharmapala, who was present, waved his hand in the air and shouted to the man to sit down. Which, discomfited, he did.

5. *Viriya* or energy. Though he practised all the ten *pāramitās* to some degree it was *viriya pāramitā*, the perfection of energy, that we particularly associate with the memory of Anagarika Dharmapala. From morning to night he was indefatigable. Not a moment was wasted. Even when he was old, and worn out by his unequalled exertions, he would take no rest. Disease might cripple his body but could not weaken his mind. He was 'a hero in the fight' if ever there was one. But a spiritual hero, who fought only for the right, and who in fighting was of indomitable courage.

6. *Khantī* or forbearance. Though intolerant of opposition to his work, and ready to resent any slight upon the Buddha or his teaching, Ven. Dharmapala was indifferent to personal attacks. He frequently forgave and helped those who had slandered him and striven to do him injury. Unfortunately, some of those whom he forgave and helped turned against him again. In the story of his life there is more than one instance of bitter ingratitude which must have smitten his noble heart. But like the great broad earth he bore it all.

7. *Sacca* or truthfulness. This *pāramitā* is really covered by the fourth precept. Probably it is reckoned as a separate *pāramitā* in order to emphasize its extreme importance. Like George Washington, Dharmapala

could not tell a lie: however great the offence it might give, he spoke the truth. Even for the sake of his work he would not deviate a hairsbreadth from truthfulness.

8. *Adhiṭṭhāna* or resolution. Without unshakeable resolution Anagarika Dharmapala could never have achieved the success which ultimately crowned his work. In fact, that work itself grew out of the resolution which, as a young man of 28, he made on 22 January at Bodh Gaya, that he would dedicate his life to the reclamation of that most sacred spot in the whole Buddhist world. The history of the Maha Bodhi Society which he subsequently founded, and the great revival of Buddhism which we see going on in India today, are the living witnesses to how true the *anagārika* was to that youthful resolution. Like a thread of gold running through crystal beads it shines through all the activities of his career.

9. *Mettā* or loving-kindness. Anagarika Dharmapala was a lifelong devotee of meditation. Every day he would rise early, long before daybreak, and follow the time-honoured Buddhist practice of radiating *mettā* first towards parents, teachers, and benefactors, then friends and fellow workers, little by little widening the circle of loving kindness until it embraced not only all human beings, regardless of creed and nationality, but gods and animals too. In particular he sent out his *mettā* to his great patroness, Mrs Mary E. Foster, whom he met only thrice, whose munificent donations were the mainstay of his work. Those who saw only the sometimes harsh exterior of the man could not imagine that his whole being vibrated with intense love for humanity. The sufferings of the Indian masses, especially of the so-called Untouchables – many of whom, thanks to the guidance of their great leader the late Dr B. R. Ambedkar, have now rallied round the banner of Buddhism – appalled him. He longed to uplift them. Surely his great heart would be comforted if he could see them now with radiant faces taking refuge in the Buddha, the Dharma, and the Sangha!

10. *Upekkhā* or Equanimity. It was probably this *pāramitā* which Ven. Dharmapala found it hardest to practise – for we should be failing in our duty not only to Buddhism but to our founder himself if we attempted to conceal or gloss over any little weakness. He was not perfect. But he was on the path of perfection.

As we remember his ninety-third birth anniversary on the 17th of this month, and as we remember at the same time his generous patroness, Mrs Mary E. Foster, whose birthday falls on the 21st, we recall his practice of the bodhisattva ideal and are grateful for the fact that even in these dark days we have before our eyes the inspiring example of a modern bodhisattva to follow.

September 1957

THE ANNIVERSARIES OF ANAGARIKA DHARMAPALA AND MRS MARY E. FOSTER

The date of 17 September is memorable for the Buddhist world as on that day is celebrated the birth in 1864 of a baby who was destined to rouse the followers of the Dhamma from the apathy into which they had fallen during the last century and to light a candle whose flame has since been growing steadily, bearing witness to the life of a man who can only be called 'great' whether with reference to his work, his character, or his being.

But a flame cannot spread or even maintain itself without fuel on which to feed, and this date is doubly worthy of remembrance in that it also marks the anniversary of the person who fed the flame. In the world today little can be accomplished without money and few personalities are so self-sufficient that they pursue their activities without a single word of encouragement from others. Mrs Mary E. Foster it was who fed the fuel to the flame which Anagarika Dharmapala had lighted so that it continued to leap upwards and gain in strength as it was fanned by the breezes of adversity. She also gave her moral support, and her birthday, being separated by only a few days from that of the man she cherished and assisted in every way in her power, is remembered with his, for without her he would never have been able to accomplish all he did.

The product of typical English schooling received in his native island of Ceylon, Dharmapala showed early that he could not be compelled by persuasion or fear of punishment to conform to standards with which he did not agree. He evolved his own convictions at an early age, not uninfluenced by the pious Buddhist upbringing given him by his parents, with whom he performed the puja daily, and while at school he was taught the Christian religion and took part in the routine Christian observances.

Before he had left school he came under the influence of that famous person Madame Blavatsky and her partner Colonel Olcott. He felt then that in such secret knowledge as she professed to impart and powers that she claimed to have, there was an opportunity for him to advance in his search for truth and for spiritual experience beyond that which either worship of the Buddha or of the Christ had, as yet, been able to give him. He joined the Theosophical Society that they had lately formed, his own grandfather standing sponsor for him.

A mysteriously inspired message was the match that set the spark alight:

> The only refuge for him who aspires to true perfection is in the Buddha alone.

From that moment Buddhism as a religion and way of life held him and eventually even replaced his occult aspirations. But while still working for the Theosophical Society, he began to pay attention to the state of his own land, where the Buddhist religion had sunk so far from anything resembling what the Founder had taught that it seemed as if, ere long, it would die out altogether and fade into the religion inculcated by Christian missionaries or be beaten into a form of Hinduism.

The Theosophical Society, with Colonel Olcott and Mr Leadbeater at its head, worked also to resuscitate Buddhism, and at this period Dharmapala identified the interests of the two systems and toured with the two men in missionary zeal. And as he toured he observed that his own people had not only strayed from their hereditary faith but also from their own national customs and were adopting the language, dress, and habits of the West.

In 1887 he toured Japan by invitation, and during the tour he and Olcott took part in functions that were designed to try to unite the branches of Buddhism that had for so long diverged from the main tree. But Dharmapala was ill, and Olcott left him in hospital in Kyoto with rheumatic fever, to which hospital, therefore, there came a ceaseless flow of Buddhists of all professions, who had heard of the unflagging zeal of this young Sinhalese on behalf of the revival of their religion.

But of all his travels and of all the places he visited, none excelled in importance or portent than Bodh Gaya, which was to be the arena for a titanic struggle between the zealot who wished to rescue that holy of holies from the unworthy Hindu who held it, despite the fact that it had no connection whatever with the beliefs or history of the Hindu religion and was to Buddhists what Nazareth was to Christians or Mecca to Muslims.

The struggle has been well recounted elsewhere (see pp. 36 et seq. above) and suffice it here to say that it showed the tenacity and courage of this remarkable man, courage that was not only moral but physical as well, for his opponents did not stop short of violence to prevent the transference of the decaying temple to its rightful owners. The fact that he showed all the characteristics of the bulldog which, once it has its teeth firmly fixed in something will not let go again for blows or cajolery, is responsible for the opportunity every Buddhist now has to make pilgrimage to Bodh Gaya, worship in the temple in his traditional manner, and contemplate under the bodhi tree, at least once in a lifetime.

But the struggle that was protracted for thirty years left its mark upon the man physically. By the time a foothold in Bodh Gaya was won he was a sick man, though his life was by no means nearing its end. He continued to work unceasingly, touring America to try to raise an interest in Buddhism. London, Rome, and many other places saw this strange Eastern figure in flowing robes with long hair and flashing eyes which were of abnormal depth and seemed to penetrate the person on whom they were fixed, who spoke with such wholehearted conviction that he must have moved many by the sincerity of his passion.

During this period, too, he founded the Maha Bodhi Society and published the first of its journals. He had also started a journal in England entitled *The British Buddhist* and, having by now severed connections with the Theosophical Society, which had sadly degenerated after Madame Blavatsky's death, he interested himself to such an extent in the economic situation of his own Ceylon and the progress of his people there, that he founded schools and colleges and introduced modern machinery and methods and imported persons who could teach them to the Sinhalese.

He died in 1933, after receiving his higher ordination a few months before, for he wished to be a full member of the Holy Order after a lifetime of devotion which had left no opportunity for doing so before. For this devotion, for his clear-sightedness and singleness of purpose and courage and determination, we honour his anniversary this day and could do no better than be inspired by his example to follow it even if we cannot attain to his stature. It is only by the lives of her few great men that the world is vindicated and humanity justified.

September 1958

ANAGARIKA DHARMAPALA'S ACHIEVEMENT

Much has been written about Anagarika Dharmapala, and the main events of his career have often been reviewed in these columns. Now that twenty-eight years have passed since his death perhaps it is time for us to take a broader view and try to ascertain the place of his achievement in Buddhist history. In this connection five considerations are of outstanding importance.

Firstly, his life and work represent, so far as the Buddhist world is concerned, the first reactions of the age-old spiritual traditions of the East against the industrial civilization of the modern West. This civilization, if it can truly be called such, was mainly imposed by force, the trader, the Christian missionary, and the political adventurer each playing a part. In some places, such as Ceylon, where Dharmapala was born, the indigenous religion and culture had been crushed for centuries and when Portuguese ferocity, Dutch brutality, and British indifference had done their worst precious few traces of them were left. Against conditions such as these Dharmapala protested with the whole force of his being and at every level of existence. Even in the schoolroom he rebelled against Christianity. He was vehemently patriotic. Year in and year out he urged his fellow countrymen to give up vicious foreign habits such as that of drink. But his reaction was positive, not merely negative. He also stood above all for the revival of Buddhism.

Secondly, he stood not merely for the revival of Buddhism in Ceylon, where it had been weakened for centuries, but for its renaissance in India, where it had been dead for a millennium. This was indeed an astounding idea, and one which could have occurred only to a man of exceptional spiritual vision and outstanding courage. To revive in the land of its birth a religion that had been dead there for a thousand years! 'The impracticable dream of a young idealist!' scoffed his contemporaries. But undeterred Dharmapala set to work, fought vigorously to rescue Bodh Gaya, reclaimed the sacred places, established centres, and kept up a continuous stream of propaganda with the result that before his death he was able to plant, and see beginning to sprout, the seed that is now fast growing into a noble tree.

Thirdly, Dharmapala sought to focus on the renaissance of Buddhism in India, and particularly on the legally complicated but morally simple question of the Maha Bodhi temple at Bodh Gaya, the attention of the entire Buddhist world. In other words, he tried to foster a sense of common purpose – and as a corollary thereof to formulate a plan of united action – among all followers of the Buddha. Thus he was the father of the various movements which, since his passing away, have insisted on the oneness of the Buddhist world and sought to promote mutual understanding, harmony, and cooperation between its various parts.

Fourthly, Dharmapala's interests and activities were not limited to the Buddhist countries of Asia and to India but overspread the whole Earth. As far as we know, he was the first who, in his own words, girdled the globe with the message of the Master. His historic appearance at the World's Parliament of Religions, Chicago, in 1893 is described elsewhere in this issue. He traversed the greater part of Europe and the USA preaching the Dharma. The journal he started found, and continues to find, its way to every continent. He was the first Buddhist missionary ever to take the whole world for his parish.

Fifthly, the missionary was for the longest and most active part of his career not a monk but a layman – technically an *anagārika*, one who, without receiving monastic ordination, devoted himself to the life of a celibate full-time worker for Buddhism. This marks another innovation. Since the inception of the *śāsana* the chief custodians of the Dharma, the missionaries and the teachers, had with hardly any exception been monks. Dharmapala's advent and example mark the beginning of a new tendency, not indeed to minimize in any way the role of the sangha, but rather to encourage an increased participation in active Buddhist work by the laity.

These five considerations by no means do justice to an exceptionally many-sided career of one of the most remarkable Buddhist personalities of recent times. But as we remember him on his birth anniversary this month they may help us to appreciate the magnitude of his achievement and also to understand its place in Buddhist history.

September 1961

PART II

MAHA BODHI WRITINGS

IN THE LIGHT OF THE DHAMMA

by Himavantavasi

WOLVES OR LAMBS?

A few weeks before Vaiśākha Pūrṇimā Dr Kailash Nath Katju, the Home Minister, made a statement in the Council of States (repeating it later in Parliament) which must have come as an unpleasant shock to the thousands of Christian missionaries working in this country. Everyone in India, he declared, was free to propagate his religion, but the Government did not want people from outside to come and do that. The discussion that followed this bold statement revealed that while it had been made clear to all foreign missionaries that if they were engaged in social welfare work, medical work, and education, they were welcome, if they indulged in proselytization it would be undesirable. 'If they come here for evangelical work', said Dr Katju, 'the sooner they stop it the better.'

A storm of missionary protest followed this declaration, and the air of injured innocence assumed by some Christians would have been amusing if the questions in both Houses that gave rise to the Home Minister's statement had related to less serious charges. Interference in politics, making invidious comparisons with the previous regime, and bribing members of some backward communities to become Christians, were among the 'altruistic' activities which missionaries had been found carrying on. Any cultured Indian who has been educated in a Christian institution, or who has lived in a town infested by missionaries, could make any number of additions to this already formidable list.

The situation is worst in the hills, and in areas inhabited by tribal peoples, and it is inevitable that after more pressing problems have been attended to the Government would take up this matter also for consideration. The missionaries have already started raising chauvinistic cries of 'harassment' and 'persecution' but with such recent experience of 'Christian' methods not only in India, but in almost all countries of Asia, and while the Catholics of Colombia are burning, drowning, and torturing to death the Protestant minority in that republic, the Government and people of India will not be deceived when missionary wolves try to pass themselves off as Christian lambs. The terrible words of Christ are a sufficient sentence on these 'followers' of his: 'By their fruits ye shall know them.'[59] Indeed, the Hindu and Buddhist peoples of Asia have known those bitter fruits to their cost, and would prefer not to know them any more.

September 1953

BUDDHISM AND ASTROLOGY[60]

Does Buddhism encourage astrology? We had thought that the Buddha himself had answered this question with an emphatic negative.[61] But apparently we were mistaken. The Buddha Day Number of a periodical which rather plumes itself on its strict orthodoxy carries as its leading article a contribution by a learned Burmese monk (the possessor, it seems, of six names and titles, totalling no less than thirty-eight syllables) which conveys the impression that the Vaiśākha Pūrṇimā is an auspicious day not for spiritual but for astrological reasons. To us this view seems diametrically opposed to the spirit of Buddhism. Surely the Buddha did not, as the article maintains, elect to be born, attain Enlightenment, and die, on Vaiśākha Pūrṇimā Day, simply because certain supposedly favourable constellations were visible; for this would have made him a slave of the very superstitions that he condemned. Even supposing that all three events actually did occur on the same day, as Theravāda tradition believes, surely it is they which make the thrice-sacred day auspicious, and not vice versa. The Buddha might conceivably have become Enlightened on any other day, and then that day would have been, for Buddhists, the most auspicious of the year. Auspiciousness does not depend on planetary conjunctions, but on the presence of *alobha, adveṣa*, and *amoha* in the mind.[62] We feel sure that the publishers of this Buddha Day Number – which in all other respects is a very fine production – did not intend to create the misleading impression that Buddhism looks with approval on astrology, and we hope they will not mind us drawing attention to the matter. Many *bhikṣus* seem to have a penchant for astrological studies. But are such studies in keeping with the spirit of the Dharma? Are they in accordance with the Vinaya? These are questions which every Buddhist must honestly ask himself. If the answer is in the negative then, for a Buddhist at least, astrology must go.

September 1953

THE DEMONIACAL IN THE FAR EAST

For the last four years the Istituto Italiano per il Medio ed Estremo Oriente has been publishing an excellent quarterly magazine, *East and West*. Articles on Buddhist subjects appear frequently in its pages, and are often beautifully illustrated. Of very special interest in the current issue (April 1953) is a striking article by Prof. Giuseppe Tucci on 'The Demoniacal in the Far East', which combines scholarship, sympathetic insight, and imaginative expression in a manner rarely met with.[63] Those who have been puzzled by the 'demoniacal' forms so often met with in Tibetan Buddhist art will find in this essay an illuminating explanation of their significance. Says Prof. Tucci:

> In Asia the demoniacal does not stand for the absolute opposite of the divine; it is not the will necessarily intent on evil. Rather it is the possibility of infinite creation, contradictory, indistinct, shapeless, measureless; or else primordial fears, an inexorable impulsive will to live, as at the origins of the Universe.

September 1953

THE DEMONIACAL IN SPAIN

In 'heathen' lands missionary wolves try to bleat like Christian lambs. At home, however, they are not ashamed to show themselves in their true colours. A few weeks ago (according to *Time* magazine) Cardinal Segura of Spain expressed his annoyance with General Franco's government for allowing limited religious toleration of non-Catholics. In a pastoral letter His Eminence wrote: 'It caused one real pain to see the tolerance shown towards non-Catholic sects among us and the indifference of the Catholics towards this question.' Himavantavasi feels that comment would be superfluous.

September 1953

IS ABHIDHAMMA NECESSARY TO THE ATTAINMENT OF NIRVĀṆA?

Enthusiasm for his favourite study may sometimes betray even a Buddhist, who should be a model of impartiality and objectivity, into gross exaggerations of its value and importance. An instance of such misguided enthusiasm is supplied by a writer in one of the recent numbers of a Buddhist periodical, who declares that 'Only by the study of Abhidhamma will [a man] be freed from the state of a blind worldling (*andha puthujjana*) and become first, a well-intentioned worldling (*kalyāṇa puthujjana*).' Earlier in his article the writer had gone so far as to suggest that a person is the follower of the Buddha to the extent that he is 'crowned by a knowledge of the Abhidhamma', whatever that may mean.

While fully recognizing the greatness of the ethico-psychological system of the Abhidhamma, which is undoubtedly one of the supreme achievements of human intellect, we cannot agree with the author of this article when he makes study of the Abhidhamma an indispensable part of the spiritual life. His dogmatic assertion is all the more amazing inasmuch as it appears in a Buddhist paper which, only a few months ago, published a brief biography of a modern Burmese *arahant* who, it was explicitly stated, had attained Nirvāṇa by the practice of *ānāpānasati* alone, being ignorant not only of the Abhidhamma Piṭaka but even of the Sutta Piṭaka. Indeed, if we were to press the matter still further, we might enquire how the Buddha and his immediate disciples were able to attain Enlightenment, considering that the Abhidhamma Piṭaka was not in existence in their time. By all means let us encourage the study of Abhidhamma to the fullest possible extent, but let us be under no illusions as to its true value and importance. Spiritual progress is not achieved by the study of books, even books of Abhidhamma, but by meditation and insight.

Bhadanta Narada Thera represents the more orthodox, and more balanced, view of the value of Abhidhamma when he writes:

> Did not the sorrow-afflicted Patacara realize Nibbana by watching the water that washed her feet? Did not child-like Kisa Gotami, who lost her only child, attain Saintship by reflecting on a lamp that was extinguished? Did not Cula Panthaka, who could not even memorize a verse for four months, attain Arahatship? Did not Upatissa, later Venerable Sariputta, realize Nibbana on the mere hearing of half a stanza relating to cause and effect? A fallen withered leaf was alone sufficient for some thinkers to attain Pacceka Buddhahood. Was [it] not mindfulness of breathing (Anapanasati) that acted as the basis for the Bodhisatta to attain Buddhahood?[64]

Yes, according to the Pāli scriptures all these great men and women attained Nirvāṇa without knowledge of Abhidhamma. Himavantavasi wonders how near to arahantship is the learned and reverend gentleman who sang such a paean in praise of the third Piṭaka.

September 1953

PRONUNCIATION OF PĀLI: *A Suggestion for the Sixth Buddhist Council*

A few weeks ago, Himavantavasi attended a Buddhist function at which a visiting Burmese *mahāthera* took the trouble of reciting a long *sutta* which he knew by heart. Unfortunately, his exertions were useless, as his pronunciation of the Pāli was so incorrect that only a word or two here and there could be made out. At present the Union Government of Burma is spending huge sums of money in preparation for the Sixth Great Buddhist Council which is scheduled to be held in Rangoon next year. An excellent monthly bulletin, the *Sangāyanā*, is being published in English so as to acquaint the world with the progress of these preparations. It appears that prominent among the proceedings of the Council will be a recital of the entire text of the Tipiṭaka, and it is understood that teams of *bhikkhus* have already started committing portions of the sacred books to memory.

This is all very commendable, but one cannot help wondering with what sort of pronunciation the Buddha-Word will be recited. Frankly, Burmese pronunciation leaves much to be desired, and it would be a thousand pities if, at the Sixth Great Council, which is being convened from all parts of the Theravāda world, the recitation of the Tipiṭaka was unintelligible to monks from India, Ceylon, Siam, and other lands.

Apart from this inconvenience, there is the much more serious question of corruptions having been introduced into the written and printed versions of the Buddha's teaching through errors of pronunciation that have been perpetrated through the centuries. An editorial in the first issue of the *Sangāyanā* (May 1953) rightly says:

> If the alphabets be wrong, the words would be wrong; if the words be wrong, the construction of phrases and sentences would be wrong; if the construction be wrong, the scriptures would be wrong; if the scriptures be wrong, the interpretations would be wrong; if the interpretations be wrong, the methods of practice would be wrong; and with wrong methods of Insight practice, one can never expect even to approach the portals of Emancipation.

But what if even the alphabets be wrong to begin with? It is a well-known fact that there are several letters of the Pāli alphabet, such as 'a' and 'ch', which even the most learned Burmese monks habitually mispronounce. Himavantavasi suggests that the Union Government of Burma should take action before it is too late, and either send their Burmese reciters to Ceylon, where the pronunciation of Pāli is perfect, in order that they can master the Pāli sounds in time, or else invite a team of Sinhalese monks to Burma to coach them in the correct pronunciation. Such a procedure would furnish an outstanding example of that unity which the Sixth Buddhist Council is being convened to promote.

November 1953

WHY BUDDHISM DISAPPEARED FROM INDIA

The problem of the reason why Buddhism, after flourishing so long and gloriously in the land of its birth, should have so catastrophically decayed and disappeared from the Indian scene, is one which has exercised better brains than Himavantavasi's. Pandit Jawaharlal Nehru relates in his *Autobiography* the story of the eagerness of a leading French intellectual to find an answer to this oft-debated question, and regretfully confesses that he was unable to provide him with one.

The latest attempt to solve a problem that has perplexed the minds of many other thoughtful students of Indian religious history has been made by the veteran Buddhist scholar Dr Nalinaksha Dutt, whose brilliant article on 'Why Buddhism Disappeared from India' is published in the September issue of the Bulletin of the Ramakrishna Mission Institute of Culture, Calcutta, under whose auspices it was originally delivered as a lecture.[65]

Though we feel that Dr Dutt has underestimated the part played by the active hostility of the Brahmin community towards Buddhism, it cannot but be admitted that the learned author has, with remarkable scholarly acumen and philosophic insight, laid bare the principal causes which led to the disappearance of Buddhism from the soil of India.

These causes, five in number, are according to Dr Dutt, loss of royal patronage, lack of a well-knit lay community, the worship of gods and goddesses, the appearance of the Tantric cult, and absorption by Brahmanism.

A wise man should not commit the same mistake twice, and we feel that Dr Dutt's analysis of this complex religio-historical phenomenon is of value not only to the student of history, but even more especially to all those who are concerned with the propagation of Buddhism in India and abroad. A correct understanding of why Buddhism disappeared from India is indispensable to a knowledge of how it can most easily be brought back.

In a modern secular state no religion can expect official patronage (Burma alone provides today a noble exception to this rule), and the first cause of the decline of Buddhism, though historically a fact, has little relevance to modern conditions. The second cause, however – lack of a well-knit lay community – is, we feel, not only the most important of all from an historical point of view, but also of the most vital interest to the *dharmadūtas* of the present day.

Dr Dutt's findings under this heading appear to us conclusive. He says of Buddhism,

> Its religious literature did not make any provision for its lay followers to perform the common ceremonies of birth, initiation, marriage or death and allowed them to continue to observe the code of rituals which they were already observing.... For the purpose of propagation this had a favourable effect in foreign

> lands, where people were left undisturbed in the observance of their old customs, but in India the effect was quite different. Brahmanism and the Brahmanic community were inseparable and this feature was taken up by the Jainas; but the Buddhists never took the lay society seriously and gave their sole attention to the education and spiritual uplift of the recluses.... It was this liberal attitude to the lay believers that cost Buddhism its life in India.

Hard words indeed, but the truth is not always palatable, and we would do well to swallow the bitter dose that Dr Dutt offers us and have the intelligence to profit by an understanding of past mistakes.

With regard to the worship of gods and goddesses, Dr Dutt shows with his usual wealth of historical citation that it was the introduction of this practice in later Buddhism which, by narrowing the gulf between Buddhism and Brahmanism, was to a great extent responsible for the disappearance of Buddhism from India.

The fourth cause, that of the appearance of the Tantric cult, is, in our opinion, much less important. Though a wrong understanding of the doctrine that the highest bliss could be attained by union with Tārā, who was represented by a female recluse, undoubtedly did lead to abuses, such abuses were found in the Hindu Tantric cults also, and far from causing the disappearance of Hinduism from India, helped it to flourish down to the present day.

Lastly, the author has dealt with absorption by Brahmanism, which all scholars have recognized as one of the most important factors in the causation of Buddhist decline. The use of the word absorption is apt to be misleading, though. It does not connote an actual assimilation of Buddhism in the form in which it was taught by the Buddha himself, but only an incorporation into the body of Brahminical belief of a version of Buddhism travestied and caricatured almost beyond recognition. The acceptance of the Buddha as the ninth incarnation of the god Vishnu, to which Dr Dutt refers, is a well-known example of this process. To transform the Buddha, who had clearly said that he was an Enlightened human being, into one of the incarnations of a being whose existence he had strongly denied, is not assimilation but misinterpretation. We feel that Dr Dutt has not sufficiently emphasized the point that misinterpretations of this kind were part of a deliberate – and ultimately successful – attempt by the Brahmins to oust Buddhism from India. That this attempt was motivated by sectarian hostility, and fear of the loss of social privileges, it is unnecessary for us to point out to our readers.

Despite such minor defects, Dr Nalinaksha Dutt's account of the disappearance of Buddhism from India is of immense interest and value to all engaged in the propagation of the Dhamma, and the distinguished author deserves to be congratulated for having placed so much information at their disposal. We strongly advise Buddhist magazines to reprint this important article so that the home truths it contains may have the widest possible circulation.

November 1953

WELCOME, *WESTERN BUDDHIST*!

From the heart of the snow-crowned Himalayas Himavantavasi salutes with joy the appearance of a new star of the first magnitude on the Buddhist literary horizon. The *Western Buddhist*, a quarterly magazine published by the Western Buddhist Order (founded last year by the Ven. Robert Stuart Clifton),[66] made its first appearance this summer under the editorship of the Rev. Jack Austin, registrar of the Order. Prophesying is a proverbially risky business, as Mr H. G. Wells discovered to his cost,[67] but Himavantavasi does not mind wagering his begging-bowl that the seed that has been planted by the publication of this journal will germinate and develop into a mighty tree which will one day overshadow the whole Western world.

Unpretentious in appearance, the *Western Buddhist* contains a dozen neatly cyclostyled pages of well-arranged matter, besides several lovely drawings by the wife of the editor. Particularly attractive is the bright saffron cover with its lighted candle set in an ornate candlestick, a spray of roses, and the lotus-flower emblem of the Order, an explanation of which is promised us in the next issue.

Among the contents, mention may be made of the Superior-General's forthright article 'Beyond Immediacy'. Ven. Clifton does not pull his punches (if readers will pardon such an un-Buddhistic metaphor) and the article is a brief but invigorating piece of writing. 'Few appear to realize that today is the future that was not faced yesterday' is a warning we should all do well to ponder.

Prominent among those who sent greetings for this first issue is Prince Patriarch Kocho Otani, of Higashi Hongwanji. In view of the suggestions that have been made in certain quarters that Ven. Clifton is not a genuine Shin priest, it is interesting to note that the Prince Patriarch writes, 'Higashi Hongwanji is pleased to have the closest fellowship with the Western Buddhist Order, and to recognize it as a legitimately established Order with correct Dharma succession.'

The news section of the journal contains an astonishing array of information about Buddhist activities in Europe and America. Most Buddhist periodicals find their way to Himavantavasi's mountain retreat, but he must honestly confess that none of them presents such an integrated picture of Buddhism in the West.

The notes on Buddhist publications are helpful, and the two poems of a much higher standard than one usually finds in Buddhist magazines, some of which effusions are painful reading indeed.

Once again Himavantavasi salutes the *Western Buddhist* and invokes the blessings of the Triple Gem on the editor and his associates for the fruition of their noble work.

A word to wealthy *dāyakas* of the East: the *Western Buddhist* has no fixed rates of subscription, but it does accept *dāna*. Now *where* did you put that cheque book?

November 1953

BUDDHIST TOLERANCE IN BURMA

While the Roman Catholic primate of Spain was lamenting even the limited religious toleration shown to non-Catholics in that country, the Buddhist Prime Minister of Burma was taking special steps to ensure that the Muslim minority in 'the Land of Yellow Robes' was not molested during the Bakri Eid festival, even though the celebrations would involve the slaughter of cows, a practice thoroughly repugnant to the sentiments of the Buddhist majority.

In a broadcast to the nation a few days before Eid, U Nu made it clear that, as a Buddhist, he was averse to the killing of any living thing, and that this aversion had made him a vegetarian.[68] But reminding his listeners that not all the peoples of the Union were against taking life, and that not all of them believed the taking of life to be evil, or were inclined to become vegetarians, the Burmese premier emphasized his allegiance to the democratic principle that minority rights are to be respected, and that even though the Buddhist majority might loathe the slaughter of cattle it would be impossible to withhold from the Muslims licences for the slaughter of cows at the time of Eid.

He appealed to the leaders of the sangha and to the laity to exercise restraint, and Himavantavasi learns with satisfaction that as a result of this truly Buddhist broadcast, and as a result of the measures taken by the Union Government of Burma in collaboration with Buddhist and other organizations, the Muslims of Burma celebrated Eid on 21 August without a single untoward incident taking place.

The moral is obvious. In a Buddhist state such as Burma the rights of religious minorities are not only fully respected, but steps are taken to enable them to observe even customs that directly violate important Buddhist precepts. Whenever there is any talk of making Buddhism the state religion of Ceylon the Roman Catholics of that country are loud in their denunciations of what they call an undemocratic proposal. Protestants generally remain silent. Having taken a look at Catholic Spain on the one hand and Buddhist Burma on the other they probably understand only too well under which regime it would be less dangerous for a good Protestant to live.

December 1953

TO FILM OR NOT TO FILM

For several months the Buddhist periodicals of Ceylon were inundated by articles and correspondence on the much-debated topic of eggs. 'To eat or not to eat' was the question of the day. But now a new controversy fills up their columns: 'to film or not to film' the life of the Buddha. Himavantavasi feels that the principles involved in the controversy are of such fundamental importance that it would be almost an impertinence for a mere columnist to touch upon them, especially when a Buddhist paper of Colombo crams nearly the whole of its latest issue with protests, diatribes, and denunciations on the subject.

One thing he notices, however, and feels constrained to mention. The party in favour of Buddhist films adduces the argument that the film is a form of art, that art appeals to the emotions, and that as the masses are influenced more easily through their emotions than through reason, the making of Buddhist films is desirable. The argument is eminently rational, as indeed is the pro-film party's whole approach to the problem. The anti-film group, on the other hand, though it maintains that Buddhism is a religion of reason, endeavours to rouse the readers of its paper to action by an undisguised appeal to their religious feelings (not to say prejudices).

Himavantavasi is left wondering which is more paradoxical, a reasoned argument in support of the place of emotion in our spiritual life, or an emotional appeal on behalf of the supremacy of reason. There seems to be little doubt which is more truly Buddhist.

December 1953

ĀNĀPĀNASATI IN MOUNT ATHOS

One of the most fascinating branches of comparative religion is the study of the ways in which religions have influenced each other. Much as orthodox Christians may dislike it, the fact cannot be denied that 'light comes from the East', and that the stream of influence has flowed from East to West more often than from West to East.

Another interesting and hitherto unknown instance of Indian, probably Buddhist, influence on Christianity, was revealed recently in the July number of *East and West* (Rome). In a short article on 'Hesychasm and Yoga' the Italian scholar Ranieri Gnoli describes some of the meditation practices of the Hesychasts, a group of contemplatives whose methods of attaining mental tranquillity and ecstasy were introduced into Mount Athos from the Christian monasteries of Asia by Gregory the Sinaite at the beginning of the fourteenth century.

Prominent among the practices of the Hesychasts is what the author describes as the syntonization of the rhythm of respiration with the mental repetition of the prayer, 'Lord Jesus Christ, Son of God, have mercy on us'. As a result of these and other practices the Hesychasts perceive what they believe to be the ineffable light seen by the apostles on Mount Tabor during the transfiguration of Christ, and experience a feeling of inner peace and bliss.

The resemblance to the Buddhist practice of *ānāpānasati*, or mindfulness of breathing, is obvious. The perception of light is a phenomenon frequently produced by Buddhist methods of concentration, but in Buddhism it is explained not mythologically but scientifically.

Though the author of this interesting article is aware of the parallelism between the practices of the Hesychasts and those recommended by

Indian Yoga he admits that he is inclined to rule out the possibility of Eastern influence, remarking that he believes the relation to be exclusively a phenomenological one, and that the explanation is to be found not so much in history as in the mind of man.

Himavantavasi does not feel quite satisfied with this solution of the problem, and suggests that Buddhist scholars should take up the whole subject afresh and endeavour to disentangle the threads of influence which connect Buddhism not only with Hesychasm but with other heterodox movements within the Christian Church.

December 1953

THE CULT OF DEATH

Modern scientific investigations result, every now and then, in curious confirmations of Buddhist teaching. An instance of this is provided by the facts adduced in 'The Cult of Death', an article by Peter Weston that appears in the December number of the *Literary Guide*. After referring to what Freud terms the Death Instinct, the author turns to the religious side of the question, remarking,

> The history of religious persecutions shows that many 'martyrs' did not meet their fate with stoical fortitude, or from prudential considerations of eternal rewards, but in a frenzied demand for destruction.

This demand for destruction manifested itself in Japan between the wars in the form of a suicide epidemic when, as Mr Weston says, 'hundreds of people hurled themselves into the volcano of Mihara-Yama'. In ten months no less than 143 people had died by suicide in this way.

Buddhist psychology distinguishes between three kinds of craving: *kāma-taṇhā*, or craving for sensual pleasure; *bhava-taṇhā*, or craving for existence; and *vibhava-taṇhā*, craving for non-existence.[69] All three forms of craving the follower of the Buddha is expected to renounce. Writers on Buddhism have sometimes been puzzled by the third of these species of thirst or craving, and have even questioned whether it was possible for a human being to desire not to exist. Recent discoveries in the field of psychology would seem to indicate that such a desire is a fact of human nature at least under certain conditions. A study of the

Buddhist conception of *vibhava-taṇhā* in relation to the modern cult of death might lead to interesting results.

January 1954

VEDANTIC BUDDHISM – NOT OF THE BUDDHA

Who has not been at some time or other delighted to find his own ideas expressed, with incomparably greater power and beauty, by some admired speaker or writer? On such occasions our belief in the correctness of those ideas becomes stronger, for their truth now stands, not on the flimsy basis of our own belief, but on the unshakeable foundation of a universally respected authority.

Our pleasure in discovering such confirmations and parallels is quite innocent. It becomes harmful only when we have so little confidence in ourselves that we start imagining correspondences of thought where none in fact exist simply in order to create in our minds a feeling of security. When we begin misinterpreting the thoughts of a great religious teacher merely to lend the authority of his name to our own conceits then the habit becomes positively vicious.

The name of the Buddha is, unfortunately, often misused in this way. People who have not studied his teaching, either in the original language or in some reliable translation, are only too ready to invoke the name of the Buddha and his Dharma in support of their own vague fancies. Some of them even go so far as to manufacture imaginary 'sayings' of the Buddha, and to place in the mouth of the Master words which are found in no Buddhist scripture, and which are even diametrically opposite in meaning to his recorded teachings.

An instance of this kind of misrepresentation came to our notice recently. On opening the Fall Issue of the Vedānta quarterly *Message of the East*, which is issued by the Ananda-Ashrama, La Crescenta, California, USA, Himavantavasi was astonished to find the following apocryphal 'saying' attributed to the Buddha: 'The Buddha teaches a complete surrender of self, but he does not teach a surrender to those powers that are evil.' It is not without significance that the source of this 'quotation' is not mentioned. The words are simply attributed to 'Gautama Buddha'.

One's breath is almost taken away by the unabashed impudence with which the Buddha's teachings have been travestied. He never spoke of 'a complete surrender of self': the idea and the expression are alike foreign to his doctrine. Neither did he ever make the dangerously ambiguous statement that he did not teach 'a surrender to those powers which are evil'. Such language smacks far more strongly of pseudo-Christian justification of war than of any Buddhist teaching.

Himavantavasi challenges the editor of *Message of the East* to supply him with: (1) The name of the discourse wherein the Buddha made the statement here attributed to him; (2) the original language of the book in which the statement is found, whether Pāli, Sanskrit, Chinese, or Tibetan; (3) the name of the English translator of this 'saying' together with the title, and date and place of publication, of the book in which it is contained. Himavantavasi promises to inform his readers if this challenge has been answered, and if so, whether satisfactorily or not, in the March issue of this journal.[70]

January 1954

FROM A 'SINCERE EUROPEAN BUDDHIST'

Himavantavasi's postbag contained some interesting letters last month. One of them was from 'a Sincere European Buddhist' (name and address supplied), who writes, 'It was indeed refreshing to read your enlightened comments in the September issue of the Maha Bodhi journal'.[71] The comments referred to were on the topics 'Is Abhidhamma Necessary to the Attainment of Nirvāṇa?' and 'Pronunciation of Pāli: A Suggestion for the Sixth Buddhist Council'. Our Sincere European Buddhist friend proceeds to make some comments of his own, and offers a few suggestions which, Himavantavasi feels, are deserving of careful consideration by all Buddhists. We reproduce the remainder of the letter in full for the benefit of readers who are not afraid of taking up the Buddha's own challenge that his words should be tested as the goldsmith tries the gold on the touchstone.[72] Our correspondent writes:

> Most adult Buddhists and all serious students of Buddhism are aware of such traditional stories as that in which Lord Buddha is said to have taught Abhidhamma to his departed mother in Tuṣita heaven and returned to earth to expound it to mankind; and that the Tipiṭaka was rehearsed at the First Council held a few months after the Parinibbāna. But it seems deplorable that in these

scientific times Buddhist children in Buddhist countries are taught to regard these legends as facts; such, indeed, is the case in Ceylon and perhaps, too, in Burma. Under such circumstances as these, westerners ignorant of Buddhism cannot be blamed for finding in Buddhism as many exasperating appendages as they had also done – to the disgust of many of them! – in Christianity. To imagine that the Lord Buddha, or any one man, could have been the author of the contents of all the three Piṭakas (or of those portions of them that are attributed to him by tradition), in spite of the fact that they exhibit a development and natural process of elaboration (historical, doctrinal, etymological, etc.) that must have covered at least three centuries – is as incongruous as the Christian legend that the world and all that is in it was made by a creator-god in six days.

There is in existence a copious library of scholastic research into the chronology of the Pāli canon, contributed over the last half-century by the finest scholars of Buddhism of both the East and West (of Ceylon, Bengal, Burma, Japan, America, UK, France, Germany – to mention some). Does not the approaching Sixth Council offer an admirable opportunity for the best brains of the Buddhist world to face this vitally important subject in a rational and scientific manner, and work out an acceptable detailed chronology of our Three Piṭakas?

But alas! a suggestion of this sort coming from a mere individual such as myself would probably go unheeded in view of the notorious prejudice in favour of these legends that still exists with some Theravādins. But if *you* could see your way to making the suggestion in the columns of the *Maha Bodhi* – i.e. the premier and eldest mouthpiece of our Buddhist world – providing, of course, that you agree as to its importance – it might bear fruit.

At the same time I should have liked to have made so bold as to offer two other suggestions for the Council's agenda: (1) that a uniform system of referencing the Pāli canonical quotations be introduced, of (a) Book, (b) Vagga, (c) Sutta, (d) verse. At present, confusion in European language translations not infrequently arises because there are two or three different systems of reference: (i) and (ii) are incomplete variations of the above (a), (b), (c), (d); (iii) that of readers of the editions of the Pali Text Society of London, who simply give the volume number and page number (which is of course meaningless to those without the volume in question). I should like to suggest how useful it would be to the cause of Buddhism – particularly in the spreading of the Dharma – if the Council were to issue a detailed Index of the Canon – such as that made in the 1930s by the Buddhist Lodge, London (but for some time out of print) – by way of being a Standard of References.

(2) That the Council agree upon a chronology of dates for our Buddhist era. Here again, the scholars and research workers of Buddhism have found that the current Theravādin system that makes the present year 2497 is incorrect. One of the best expositions of this as an error is that found in W. Geiger's introduction to his translation (into English) of the *Mahāvaṃsa*. A new edition of this translation was actually published by the Ceylon Government Information Department, Colombo (in 1950); but, in spite of this, and together with the fact that Geiger's findings have been ably supported by Wickramasinghe and other eminent Sinhalese savants, no one in Ceylon has (to my knowledge) attempted to rectify the error by reverting to the correct dates – i.e. those based on 563BC as being the birth date of Gotama. Moreover, the dating of our Buddha *sāsana* should surely commence from the most momentous event of the *sāsana*, namely: the Setting in Motion of the Wheel of the Dharma, i.e. at the full moon of Asalha (June-July) in 528BC. With this as zero year, we have now reached the year 2482.

Kindly consider these humble suggestions (and quote any part of them that you feel able to), offered by a Sincere European Buddhist.[73]

February 1954

THE BUDDHA IN CONTEMPORARY ART

Not long ago Himavantavasi happened to be sitting in a Buddhist monastery that shall be nameless. By chance his eye wandered over a number of Buddhist pictures that hung on the wall opposite. One of these gave him quite a shock. Though apparently intended to represent the Lord Buddha in meditation under the bodhi tree it seemed much more like a picture of a contemporary Hindu ascetic. To begin with, the Master was shown seated, not on a heap of *kuśa* grass, but on an antelope skin. Round his neck hung several strings of *rudrākṣa* beads, such as are worn by worshippers of Shiva; while at his side was a water pot *(kamaṇḍalu)* of the type used by orthodox Hindu sannyasins. Himavantavasi stared at the picture almost expecting to see a 'sacred thread' on the body of the Master; but fortunately the artist had not gone so far as that.

We mention this incident to draw attention to the fact that artists who have no knowledge of Buddhist traditions are nowadays often commissioned to illustrate events in the life of the Buddha. The results are sometimes even more deplorable than the example we have described. Many artists, even those living in Buddhist lands, appear never to have observed how a *bhikkhu* wears his robe, or carries his bowl. Most of them appear ignorant of the rules that govern a *bhikkhu*'s life.

Now that Buddhism is becoming popular, not to say fashionable, among the Indian elite, the manufacturers of those little ivory curios which tourists are cajoled into buying as examples of 'ancient Indian art' have thought it a good idea to add the image of the Buddha to the Vishnus and Ganeshas, the elephants and the dancing girls, with which their stalls are filled. Such examples of this kind of craftsmanship as we have seen are extremely crude and clumsy, and compare most unfavourably with specimens of traditional Buddhist art executed by Buddhist artists. In every image of the Buddha the hands of the Lord are shown in a particular *mudrā*. The non-Buddhist manufacturers of ivory figurines for the tourist market are quite ignorant of this fact, with the result that the Buddha is represented as making some vague gesture which has no significance whatever to a Buddhist mind.

In order to ensure that the figure of the Tathāgata is depicted in accordance with Buddhist traditions Himavantavasi makes the following suggestions:

1. Institutions under Buddhist management should be established for the study of ancient Buddhist art and for the production of images and religious pictures of a purely traditional kind;

2. Buddhists should refrain from buying images and pictures which represent the Buddha in an untraditional attitude;

3. Buddhists organizations should send protests to the manufacturers of images, and the printers of pictures, calendars, etc., that depict the Buddha in an objectionable manner and should endeavour to get such pseudo-Buddhist works of art withdrawn from circulation.

Most important of all, the Buddhist countries of Asia should conserve and develop the precious heritage of art which has been handed down to them as part of the priceless legacy of Buddhist culture.

March 1954

'WITH *METTĀ*'

A few days ago Himavantavasi received a copy of the latest issue of a certain fortnightly paper published in Ceylon. During the three years of its existence this paper has won a deservedly high reputation for two things: firstly, for the fervour and eloquence with which it advocates the practice of *mettā* towards all beings; and secondly, for the vigour and virulence with which it attacks, abuses, and libels anyone who ventures to differ from its dogmatic views in even the slightest particular. After reading this latest issue, which contains an unusually violent radiation of *mettā*, we were reminded of the following incident.

A friend of ours decided to take up the practice of *mettā bhāvanā*. As soon as he awoke in the morning he sat up on his bed and started cultivating thoughts of love, first towards himself, then towards his servant (he had no relations), then the neighbours, and finally towards all sentient beings. One day the servant, bringing in his master's early morning cup of tea, happened to trip over the edge of the carpet. The cup fell from his hands with a crash. The noise of the breaking crockery roused our friend from his meditations, and his face became livid with rage at the unwonted interruption of his practice. Leaping from his bed, he seized a heavy walking stick that stood in the corner and began belabouring the poor servant unmercifully. 'You rascal!' he bellowed, 'You scoundrel! You rogue! You fool! You blithering idiot! What do you mean by interrupting me in that way? *Can't you see that I'm radiating mettā?*'[74]

March 1954

A STRANGE EXPERIENCE

A few days ago Himavantavasi found himself standing at the side of a great highway. All around him were dense crowds of men, women, and children in holiday attire. The trees were festooned with flags and coloured electric bulbs, while a noise of drums and trumpets could be heard on all sides. Every now and then the people pressed forward impatiently, as if they were expecting someone. All heads were turned in the same direction, and Himavantavasi, too, though he did not know what all the fuss was about, turned his head with the rest and watched to see what would happen. The heat was stifling, and the air thick with an odour of coconut oil from hundreds of thousands of heads. Every minute the crowd grew denser, and Himavantavasi began to think that before long he would be crushed to death. He tried to ask the people around him what all the excitement was about, and for whom or for what they were waiting so eagerly, but none of them took any notice of him.

At last there was a great roar from the crowd, a flourish of trumpets not very far away, and the men, women, and children about Himavantavasi dropped as one man to their knees and buried their foreheads in the dust, leaving him standing and looking over their prostrate backs. Along the road gleamed a wide expanse of crimson carpet embroidered in gold thread and fringed with pearls, over which there slowly came the most wonderful procession Himavantavasi had ever seen.

First walked a portly gentleman with heavy features and a military air. He wore a magnificent green silk lungi. What attracted Himavantavasi's eyes still more, however, was the resplendent object that he carried before him with the utmost reverence in both hands. This was a triple fan. Made of gorgeous peacock feathers, with a handle of solid gold, and richly encrusted with rubies almost as big as pigeons' eggs, it was a fitting emblem of the rank and power of the dignitary who walked behind.

He was thin and bald-headed, with a tight mouth and piercing eyes, and was dressed in monastic robes of the richest yellow silk. Over his head was a canopy of cloth-of-gold, sprinkled with diamonds, and supported at the corners by rods of gold which were borne by personages who appeared to be ministers of state. Perfumes were wafted around from censers swung by pretty boys dressed in garments of white silk.

As the procession drew almost abreast of the spot, Himavantavasi was suddenly pulled down onto his knees by one of his neighbours, who asked in a shocked whisper, 'What do you mean by standing up in front of His Holiness? Do you want to get us all sent to jail for the rest of our lives?'

Himavantavasi just had a glimpse of a disciple, also clad in yellow silk, walking behind His Holiness with a begging-bowl of some pale metal, and of a vast concourse of silk-robed figures, flashing jewels, and tossing plumes, before the magnificent spectacle was shut out from sight by the sleek heads in front.

'What is that bowl made of?' he asked the neighbour who had pulled him down. 'Is it gold?' The man gave him a curious look. 'Don't you know that His Holiness is a strict observer of Vinaya rules? He cannot touch gold or silver. Everything he uses has to be made of platinum.'

'But *who* is this Holiness?' asked Himavantavasi, almost bursting with curiosity, 'And what is the meaning of the procession? Where are all these people going?' For the men, women, and children all around had risen from their knees, and were streaming off in the wake of the procession, which had now passed by.

'I see you are a stranger here,' said Himavantavasi's new friend. 'You can think yourself very lucky that you have had the opportunity of seeing His Infallibility the World Head of Buddhism on his way to attend an act of *mettā*. All these people are going to see the fun too. It is a great day for us.'

'What is an act of *mettā*?' asked Himavantavasi, now thoroughly bewildered by all these strange events.

'Probably you haven't heard about it. Yesterday some heretical Buddhists from the Himalayas came here. They refuse to admit that ours is the only true form of Buddhism. So today they are being burned at the stake in the presence of His Infallibility and his court.'

When he heard these dreadful words Himavantavasi broke into a cold sweat. 'Burnt at the stake?' he whispered. 'Could they really do anything so horrible, so utterly against the teachings of the Buddha?'

'Be careful what you say!' said his friend sharply, with a scared glance over his shoulder, 'One of the O.P. may hear you.'

'O.P? What's that?' asked poor Himavantavasi, thinking that he had surely gone mad.

'Why, the Orthodoxy Police, of course.'

Alas! It was too late. A burly gentleman standing nearby slowly moved over to where the pair were talking and laid a heavy hand on Himavantavasi's shoulder. Himavantavasi stood rooted to the spot, frozen with terror. He opened his mouth to let out a scream and – woke up. It was only a dream! He had fallen asleep while reading a copy of the *Buddhist World*.[75]

April 1954

BUDDHISM IN THE WEST

How interest in Buddhism is spreading in Christian countries, despite the fact that there is no organized propaganda of the Dhamma in non-Buddhist lands, is illustrated by a letter from a Scandinavian artist, now in India with his wife, to one of Himavantavasi's elder brothers in the sangha. The following extract, simple in expression and obviously sincere in feeling, will perhaps be of some interest to readers of this column.

> My wife and I are from Sweden in Scandinavia. Since a long time ago, we have been interested in Buddhism. Therefore, we tried to live a pure life and to follow the eight rules as far as it is possible during life as a human being. Naturally, it became our greatest wish to come to Asia and to get personal contact with a religion, or better a philosophy, we respected so much. Therefore, since several years ago, we carefully prepared for a journey to this part of the world.
>
> In our country, as in all European countries, the Christian church has a kind of religious monopoly and Christian missionaries, coming back from different parts of the world, have by books and teachings done much to give a bad and wrong impression of religions other than Christianity. And nobody has said or written anything against them. In our time, when all traditions become broken, the tradition of the Christian church has also lost its power, and materialism has followed religious feeling; but since – in the common opinion – all religions other than the Christian are paganism, and the Christian church, after people's own experience, cannot help them, most people are in the most important questions of life helpless like in a moonless night.
>
> At last, we were able to come to Asia and to come in personal contact with Buddhists and Buddhism. It is our hope to be of some help to a Buddhist missionary in Europe.

May–June 1954

A MAMMOTH MEETING

Last Vaiśākha Day Himavantavasi was present at a public meeting organized by a certain Buddhist association. The meeting was attended by about a hundred persons, Buddhist and non-Buddhist, songs were sung by a group of small girls, four or five speakers addressed the audience on the teachings of the Lord Buddha and the significance of the thrice-sacred day, and in its modest way the function was quite a success. Imagine, therefore, Himavantavasi's astonishment when, a few weeks later, he read in various Buddhist journals a report, signed by the secretary of the association concerned, describing the function as a 'mammoth meeting'. Now 'mammoth' is a pretty strong adjective, and when one hears about a 'mammoth meeting' he generally imagines milling crowds of people tens of thousands strong, certainly not a little gathering of one hundred.

The reason for such exaggerations is not far to seek. In the modern world far more importance is attached to quantity than quality, and even members of Buddhist organizations, even members of the sangha, are not exempt from the frailty of thinking that the more people attend a meeting the more 'successful' it is, whatever this ambiguous word may mean. When a meeting is really mammoth, not much harm is done in describing it as such, apart from the harmfulness of strengthening an already existent preference for a purely quantitative evaluation of things. But when a tiny gathering in an insignificant town is described as a mammoth meeting the person responsible for such an overstatement has evidently gone to such extremes in his worship of mere number, and considers it to be of such overwhelming importance, that he is prepared to sacrifice to it even his regard for truth. Himavantavasi hopes that writers of reports of Vaiśākha functions this year will stick to the facts, and not try to impress people by exaggerating the success of the celebrations which they have helped to organize. The Buddha certainly is not honoured by such deviations from truthfulness.

May–June 1954

A VAIŚĀKHA BOUQUET

Himavantavasi was filled with joy to see the really splendid array of Vaiśākha numbers which the English Buddhist journals of Ceylon, Burma, India, England, America, and Australia have brought out this year. Literary and artistic standards were higher than ever, and it really seemed that the editors and their associates had spared no pains to make their own particular contributions to the success of the Vaiśākha celebrations as perfect as possible.

First to reach Himavantavasi's mountain abode was *The Bosat*. Though the smallest of the magazines, it is by no means the least valuable, as a glance at the contents will show. We were sorry to notice, though, that some of the contributors had sent old articles instead of new ones. The article on Buddhism and Sinhala Culture (p. 47), for instance, had already appeared in the April issue of the *Maha Bodhi*, when our editors corrected the writer's confusion of Sophocles the dramatic poet with Socrates the philosopher, which mistake, however, the editors of the *Bosat* have overlooked. Surely our Buddhist writers could contribute new articles in honour of Vaiśākha Pūrṇimā! In any case, it is time the deplorable practice of sending *one* article to *all* Buddhist magazines for publication was discontinued. Readers become tired of seeing the same contribution over and over again.

Another really splendid Vaiśākha number from Ceylon is that brought out by *The Buddhist*, organ of the Young Men's Buddhist Association. Nearly a hundred pages of matter, on art paper, with numerous illustrations, is in these days no mean achievement. The standard of the articles, too, is high, though some of the poetry leaves more than a little to be desired. To Himavantavasi one of the best and most interesting articles is 'Some Popular Misconceptions' by H. A. C. Wickremeratna. The author relates an amusing incident that occurred when, last year, he went on pilgrimage to Kusinara with a number of ladies. These pious souls, it seems, really thought that the colossal *parinirvāṇa* image of the Buddha represented the true size of the Master, and not even a decisive quotation from the scriptures could shake their conviction. It is also good to find the author protesting against the legend which makes the Buddha exhibit, on his deathbed, special solicitude for Ceylon. Another article worth reading is 'A Message for the Buddha Jayanti' by Ceylon's ambassador to the USA, His Excellency R. S. S. Gunawardene. One is happy to note that Ceylon has at least one Buddhist ambassador who seems to care for his religion. 'My travels throughout Italy and Europe', he writes, 'only confirmed my belief that there existed in the Christianized countries of the West a tremendous interest in Buddhism.'

Himavantavasi had not seen the *Middle Way*, journal of the Buddhist Society, London, for many months; so that when, a few weeks ago, he happened to see half a dozen back numbers at the house of a friend, he was agreeably surprised to see the high standard to which it had attained. The May issue fully maintains this high standard. Among the contributors are D. T. Suzuki, Edward Conze (whose series of articles on love and compassion every Buddhist should read and ponder), Christmas Humphreys, Terence Gray, Francis Story, and G. F. Allen (Y Siri Nyana). An interesting editorial note says:

> It is a sign of the sudden and remarkable expansion of interest in the Dhamma that never before in thirty years of this journal have so many books of such importance reached us for review in a single issue.

Eight pages of reviews have therefore been added to this Vaiśākha number and greatly enhance its interest and value.

The Vaiśākha number of the American *Golden Lotus* contains the usual thoughtful articles, together with a fair percentage of material of rather dubious authenticity which, many Buddhists will feel, has little or nothing to do with the Dharma. 'The Buddha's memory', says the editorial, 'cannot die while there is still a full moon in the month Vaiśākha, in the springtime of each year.'

Crossing the Pacific we return to Ceylon once more – our Vaiśākha numbers having girdled the globe – in time to express our appreciation of the *Ceylon Daily News Vesak Annual*. Of all Vaiśākha publications this year, this is easily the most artistic. The cover, in full colour, depicts 'Vesak Orchids which bloom during the time of Vesak, and lotus flowers adorning the feet of the Avukana Buddha Statue in Ceylon which is one of the best and largest sculptures in the world'. Prominent among the other art features are 'Sasa Jātaka', a three-colour plate by Ceylon's internationally famous artist George Keyt, and photographs of the eight principal places of worship in Thailand so entrancingly beautiful that the moment he saw them Himavantavasi wanted to leave his mountain retreat for the wats and other shrines of this delightful Buddhist land. The articles in this *Annual*, though not of the same quality as the illustrations, are nevertheless worth reading.

Himavantavasi feels that the editors of all these Buddhist magazines may congratulate themselves on having done a fine job this year and after giving themselves a pat on the back may settle down in their editorial armchairs for a good rest until – the next issue.

July 1954

Himavantavasi has at last received a reply to his challenge to the editors of the Vedānta quarterly *Message of the East* to reveal the source of the 'quotation' published in their pages which represents the Buddha as saying that he 'teaches a complete surrender of self, but he does not teach a surrender to those powers that are evil'. It is not so much a reply as an explanation, and comes not from the editors of the quarterly – who have kept very quiet – but from one who is evidently a careful student of Buddhism. We reproduce the letter in full:

> Dear Himavantavasi, Permit me to swell your mailbag some more. In a recent issue of *Maha Bodhi* you called attention to some remarks attributed to Buddha, published in a Vedānta journal issued in La Crescenta, Calif., USA. Just in case the editors of that periodical do not reply to your request for verification of their source, allow me to furnish it to you. It is taken from Paul Carus, *The Gospel of Buddha*, 15th printing, (my edition) page 127, printed in quotes in such a manner as to cause a casual student to assume that they are the direct words of the Teacher.[76] Your perusal of page 127 will be very interesting to a person of a penetrating intellect such as you possess. Now, in the back of the book, page 237, the good Doctor lists his sources. Verses 1–14 and 31–5 are from the *Mahāvagga*, while verses 15–30 are given as 'Explanatory Additions'. As from whom these additional explanations emanated, you will have no trouble in discerning since they betray the shortcomings inherent in the Christian Theological system. This attaches no blame to the noted philosopher and scholar of Buddhism whose good faith and well meaning intentions are above comment. It does however accentuate the responsibility of those who would interpret the words of greater Minds accurately, both as to source and original meaning. This could be an excellent opportunity for you to stress this whole business in your widely read columns.
>
> Use this letter in any way you deem advisable; I realize that all things are transient, and that it will eventually end up in the wastebasket to be 'ground over in the workshop of nature'.

Sincerely,
(Sd.) James W. Thompson.

No; even though all things are transient your letter is far too valuable to go into the wastepaper basket, Mr Thompson, and Himavantavasi is glad to accept your timely suggestion that 'this whole business' should be stressed in our columns. (Are they really widely read, though?) It is indeed a deplorable fact that so many people, even professed students of Buddhism, continue to derive their knowledge of Dharma from second- and third-hand sources. We emphasize once again the necessity of turning, not to what others, however eminent in scholarship, have said about 'Buddhism', but to what the Buddha himself has said about the Dharma-Vinaya. Those who cannot read the original Pāli and Sanskrit texts, or their versions in Chinese and Tibetan, should at least read translations into modern languages which have been made by competent scholars. Dr Carus's Explanatory Additions, though well meant, have, we fear, proved a stumbling block and a stone of offence on more than one occasion. Only a few days ago Himavantavasi read in an old Buddhist magazine a report of a Buddhist celebration 'somewhere in India' at which a dialogue purporting to be between the Buddha and General Sīha was read as part of the proceedings. In this dialogue the Buddha is represented as saying that he is not against war provided that it is waged for a righteous cause![77] Source? These same 'Explanatory Additions'.[78] So once again we point the moral and adorn the tale: Don't rely on second- and third-hand information; go direct to the sources; read the Buddha-Word in the original language or in a good translation. Eschew books which are merely about Buddhism, except, of course, the small group of really reliable presentations of which Dr Conze's *Buddhism* is such an outstanding example.

Nor should it be thought that only non-Buddhists studying Buddhism are likely to be tripped up by wrong views. What of those 'Buddhists' who habitually attack, abuse, and vilify other so-called 'heretical' forms of Buddhism without having studied them? Is their conduct not even more reprehensible than that of those who, more or less unconsciously, misrepresent Buddhism in the way in which the editors of *Message of the East* have done? Is it not they who are detrimental to the interests of the Dhamma?

August 1954

Buddhists believe dying well is almost as important as living well. The controversy which has recently arisen in England on the subject of whether or not a patient should be warned of approaching death should therefore be of interest to all students of the Dhamma. Writing in *The Inquirer* for 17 July, Dr R. W. Wilde reports that

> The Roman Catholic bishop of Leeds, addressing recently two hundred Catholic nurses, denounced the conspiracy of silence that seemed, he said, to be growing in hospital circles – the policy of not telling a patient that he was in danger of death. Catholic nurses should, he said, never be parties to this policy, but should tell a patient frankly (whether Roman Catholic or not) if he were likely to die, so that he could prepare himself properly and in good time for the most important event in life – death.

Dr Wilde does not ignore the conflict of loyalties which such a declaration is bound to precipitate. He is aware that the conflict is made more serious, and becomes a genuine moral problem, precisely because there is so much to be said on both sides of the question. Like many Unitarians, he is almost painfully conscious of the limitations of human judgements, and anxious to do justice to the elements of truth lying behind each of these radically divergent views. His almost wistful sympathy for the forthrightness and positive character of the Catholic bishop's declaration does not cause him to forget that 'in Roman Catholic theology a man may be in danger of the eternal fires of hell if he dies unbaptized or unshriven'. Neither does his appreciation of the fact that the current medical viewpoint – that 'to tell a man he is on the way to death may be the surest way to bring about such a consummation' has been arrived at 'after long experience and pondering' make him overlook the fact that for all Christians, as for all Buddhists, there is beyond holy living such a thing as holy dying. The psychological astuteness which he brings to the consideration of the whole problem is shown by the following comment: 'Possibly, too, there is a subconscious fear on the part of the medical fraternity that, should they frankly tell a patient he is destined for early death, they will raise problems, in the shape of deep human needs and cravings on the part of the patient, that they themselves, simply as medical men, will not be able to answer or supply.' Unfortunately, Himavantavasi does not have at his disposal a large enough slice of the *Maha Bodhi* journal to enable him to reproduce Dr Wilde's thoughtful discussion of this important moral problem. The writer concludes, however, with an observation which seems to lean to the Catholic rather than to the strictly medical viewpoint:

> I am inclined to think that truth is, on the whole, better even than well-intentioned pretence and a realistic facing of the facts, more helpful than an uncomfortable avoidance of actuality.

There are not many points of agreement between Buddhism and Roman Catholicism, but this does seem to be one of them. Buddhism leans even more decidedly towards the view expressed by the Catholic bishop of Leeds than does Dr Wilde. 'A realistic facing of the facts' is perhaps more characteristic of Buddhism than any other religion, certainly than any form of Christianity. But though Buddhism may agree with Catholicism on the advisability of telling a patient that he is in danger of death, its reasons for so doing are quite different. Unlike Christianity, Buddhism believes in 'rebirth' (*punarbhava*, literally 'again becoming'), and it considers conscious preparation for death to be necessary, not because a man is about to stand before the Throne of Judgement – much less still because he can ward off the pains of hell by the timely administration of this or that sacrament – but because the state of the mind at the moment of death is one of the factors which determine the nature of the succeeding rebirth. A quiet and peaceful atmosphere in the room in which the great change is about to take place, joyful recollection of good deeds performed, constant remembrance of the Buddha and his Teaching, the sight of members of the holy order, the sangha, and the hearing of the sacred texts, are far more important, as preparations for death, than sprinkling with water or anointing with oil. One of the most solemn duties that a Buddhist can perform is ensuring that the environment in which a friend or relation passes away is conducive to the cultivation of states of mind which will help rather than hinder the departing pilgrim in his journey to another life.

Catholic practices with regard to death are inspired by hope of an eternal heaven of bliss and fear of an everlasting hell of torment and suffering. Their purpose is to create in the dying person a false sense of security. Dying in the arms of the Church, repentant of past sins and reconciled with his creator, he feels, regardless of the purity or impurity of his life, that he is sure of escaping hell, and that, after a brief sojourn in 'the milder shades of Purgatory', heaven will be his eternally.

Buddhist mindfulness in the face of death is based upon clear and scientifically exact knowledge of what happens after the consciousness 'leaves' the body. It is free from hope and fear alike, for it knows that the consequences of action are inescapable, and that although a man may flee into the clefts of the mountains, or hide himself in the depths of the sea, there is no place on earth where the results of his evil deeds will not find him out.[79] Mindfulness will come naturally at the hour of death if it has been cultivated during life. There are no deathbed conversions in Buddhism, in the sense of a complete wiping out, even by tears of genuine repentance, of the consequences of past evil deeds. The state of the mind at death is undoubtedly one of the conditions determining the nature of the next rebirth, but it is only one condition among several others, the most important of which is the total result of the actions of the present life. Holy living is the surest means to holy dying, and holy living and holy dying together the surest means to happy rebirth.

November 1954

THE NEW YEAR

If Himavantavasi's memory serves him aright, it was in September 1953 that he was first given the opportunity of bringing into the Light of the Dhamma the odd facts and stray fancies that happened to cross his path in the Himalayan retreat from which he generally writes this column. By January 1954 he did not feel quite well enough acquainted with his readers – in fact, at that time he hardly knew if he *had* any readers – to wish them a happy new year. But now things are different. He has penned his monthly paragraphs more than a dozen times; he has seen with astonishment his mailbag growing from month to month; he has blushed to see his modest little contributions to this distinguished journal quoted, commented upon, made subject of controversy, and even translated into foreign languages. At the beginning of 1955 Himavantavasi therefore feels that he knows his readers very well. So to all of them – to the throwers of bricks no less than the bestowers of bouquets; to the writers of anonymous articles and virulently abusive letters signed 'Yours with *mettā*' as well as to those who wrote with sympathy and appreciation; to the gentleman who called him Devadatta and the friend who said that 'In the Light of the Dhamma' was the best thing in the journal – to all of them, to all of *you*, a happy new year from Himavantavasi's mountain abode! Be your letters grave or gay, sweet or sour, filled with praises or packed with abuse, he will be as happy to hear from you in the new year as he was in the old.

January 1955

THE OLD, OLD STORY

One would have thought that with the publication in recent times of so many Buddhist texts and their translations there could be no excuse, even among the most bigoted Brahminical circles, for persisting in that mistaken attitude towards Buddhism about which Rev. U Dhammaratana wrote a fine and vigorous article in our November issue.[80] Judge how great, therefore, was Himavantavasi's astonishment when, in a glossy transatlantic publication which came his way a few days ago, he found Indian writers going out of their way to spread in America the same poisonous ideas that have already been circulated in India. Admittedly the book in question is not about Buddhism. It is about Hinduism. But surely it was possible to do justice to Hinduism without doing injustice to Buddhism. Or perhaps it was not. *The Religion of the Hindus* is a book of more than 400 pages, has been edited by a well-known American scholar, and comprises seven sections written by seven scholars of whom the editor says:

> They have lived all their lives in India, and are known for their competence as scholars and their devotion to Hinduism. Each writer has been conscious of friends and colleagues looking over his shoulder as he wrote, checking him as to accuracy in citing facts, caution in generalizations, and justice to his religious faith.

Whether the same virtues are exhibited with regard to Buddhism the reader may judge for himself from the following passages. The writers do not seem to have remembered that Buddhist friends and colleagues also might look over their shoulder!

Speaking of the medieval mystical poets of South India, Prof. D. S. Sarma gives us this beautiful example of scholarly generalization.

> Beside their flaming devotion to God, their utter humility and self-surrender, and the joyousness of their religious experience, the atheistic creeds of Buddhism and Jainism shrank into cold and repulsive systems of self-torture. (p. 37)

Himavantavasi wonders if the author had ever heard of the *Bodhicaryāvatāra* of Śāntideva. Whether one prefers the path of devotion or the path of knowledge is of course a personal matter; but there is no excuse whatever for describing Buddhism as a system of self-torture. Something even worse than ignorance is at work here.

The longest reference to the Buddha in the whole book is the passage from the distinguished pen of Prof. Jitendra Nath Banerjee:

> Buddha, the founder of a religious order which is heterodox from the Brahminical Hindu point of view, is given a place in the ten incarnations [of Vishnu]. In the *Purāṇas* Vishnu is said to have been born as 'the Deluder' in the Sakya race in order to delude demons with false doctrines and thus work for their undoing. They accepted his teachings, gave us Vedic rites and practices, and as a consequence were defeated by the gods. This is a peculiar way of acknowledging the greatness and sanctity of the heretical teacher and decrying the doctrines attributed to him. (p. 57)

A very peculiar way indeed! Especially when we find Prof. Sarma waxing eloquent over what he calls the religious hospitality of Hinduism, declaring that 'In its hospitable mansions there is room for all sorts and conditions of men' (p. 5). The Buddha and Buddhism seem to be the unwelcome guests! Moreover, are not the words 'the founder of a religious order' rather a minimizing description of the one who discovered the path that is followed by a third of the human race?

When he first perused this book – which by the way is designed, according to the editor, to be useful for all people interested in a better understanding between East and West – he was at a loss to understand how these could be the best things that seven learned Hindu writers, with 400 pages at their disposal, could find to say about one whom the prime minister of this country habitually describes as the greatest son of India. Could it be ignorance? Hardly. Or religious prejudice? One hopes not. Deliberate misinterpretation? One hardly dare think so. Then what was the reason?

While he was racking his brains in this way, Himavantavasi idly turned over the first few pages of the book and his eye happened to travel down the list of contributors. Sarma, Banerjee, Chatterjee.... In a flash he understood. All seven contributors were Brahmins!

January 1955

EXPERIMENTS WITH HUMILITY[81]

Himavantavasi does not usually read newspapers, but a few days ago an elder brother in the sangha who is more assiduous in his devotions to this popular modern demigod handed him a copy of the Republic Day supplement of a well-known Calcutta daily, and requested him to read therein a certain article. This article, which was entitled 'Land Through Love – Bhoodan', had been reprinted from a prominent English monthly, and dealt with the life and mission of Acharya Vinoba Bhave.[82] Some of Himavantavasi's readers may remember that this gentleman's name has already been mentioned in the *Maha Bodhi*. Only last May, our editors, in their Vaiśākha number editorial 'Buddha Gaya', drew the attention of the Buddhist public to the fact that he was planning to make Bodh Gaya, the holiest spot on earth, 'assume further importance' by building there a Mandir of his own; that after equating the teaching of the Lord Buddha with *ahiṃsā* he had declared that it 'could never have a solid basis without the foundation of the Vedānta'; and that, finally, after announcing on 17 April 'God has initiated me into Bhoodan Yajna and he has guided me throughout' he asserted on 18 April 'I was inspired in my Bhoodan work in Bodh Gaya by Lord Buddha.' Sri Bhave now goes a step further than this. According to Hallam Tennyson, the writer of the article referred to, he no longer claims to be inspired by the Buddha; instead, he says, 'People call this an age of sin and degradation. Yet how can that be? The Buddha is supposed to have lived in a time freer of sin than our own. Yet someone as great as he had to pay a heap of gold for a small parcel of land, while I, a mere humble devotee of God, have [been] entrusted with millions of acres as free gifts.' Sri Bhave very conveniently forgets that the Buddha never himself bought a single acre of land; he accepted, on behalf of the sangha, what was bought and offered to him by devoted lay people. However, it suits the purpose of Sri Bhave, who of course is a great lover of Truth (don't forget the capital!) that the Buddha should have to pay a *heap* of gold for a *small* parcel of land, for then it is possible to point out, with the greatest humility of course, how *he*, on the contrary, gets *millions* of acres *free*. The Buddha, as Sri Bhave so kindly tells us, was a great man. Does it not follow, then, that the High Priest of 'Bhoodan Yajna', having done even more than the Buddha (according to him) was able to do, is even greater? How adroitly criticism is disarmed by those few modest words about a humble devotee of God! Himavantavasi cannot help wondering what fresh light Sri Bhave will throw on Buddhism next.

March 1955

BUDDHISM IN ENGLAND – NEW VERSION

One of our contemporaries reports a speaker at a London Buddhist meeting as saying, 'Mistakes are very important to a Buddhist, because from them we learn.' Obviously, then, we should make as many mistakes as possible in order to learn as much as possible. One who has broken all the five precepts must have learned quite a lot, Himavantavasi should think.

March 1955

AMIEL, SCHOPENHAUER, AND BUDDHISM

Full many a gem of purest ray serene
The dark, unfathomed caves of ocean bear;
Full many a flower is born to blush unseen
And waste its sweetness on the desert air.[83]

Himavantavasi has found that these lines of Gray are very well known in India, and often quoted. They can be used with good effect in a number of different contexts. For instance, with regard to writers. Some writers, like comets, begin with a great blaze of light but quickly dwindle into a trail of insignificant sparks: famous during life, they are forgotten within a few years of their death. With others the reverse is the case. Blushing unseen while living, the sweetness of their perfume, still lingering in the air, is appreciated only long after the blossom exhaling it had withered and dropped from the stalk.

Such was Henri-Frederic Amiel.[84] Born in Geneva in 1821, he lived virtually unknown until his death fifty-three years later, having published, besides a slim volume of poems, only a few magazine articles and reviews. Yet with the posthumous publication, in 1882 and 1884 respectively, of the two volumes of his *Journal Intime*, he at once stepped into the front rank of European letters, where he has remained ever since. For combined beauty of style and intensity of psycho-spiritual interest, Amiel must be classed with Augustine and Pascal, with Milarepa and Śāntideva – though perhaps, so far as psychological complexity and *perplexity* are concerned, he is more akin to the former than to the latter pair. At any rate, it is a singularly fascinating personality that stands revealed in the sometimes bright, sometimes gloomy, and sometimes mysteriously crepuscular pages of the *Journal Intime*; his ideas, like those of Sir Thomas Browne, pass to and fro in his mind like fishes moving about in the dim depths of some weed-haunted pool.[85]

Browsing through the pages of the *Journal* a few days ago, Himavantavasi came across a few references to Buddhism, via Schopenhauer, which, though not revealing a very accurate knowledge of the Dhamma, may yet be of interest to his readers inasmuch as they demonstrate how powerfully the Buddha's teaching was impinging on thoughtful European minds even as many as eighty years ago.[86]

> *16 August 1869* – I have been thinking over Schopenhauer. It has struck me and almost terrified me to see how well I represent Schopenhauer's typical man, for whom 'happiness is a chimera and suffering a reality,' for whom 'the individual life is a misfortune, from which impersonal contemplation is the only enfranchisement.' etc. But the principle that life is an evil and annihilation a good lies at the root of the system, and this axiom I have never dared to enunciate in any general way, although I have admitted it here and there in individual cases. What I still like in the misanthrope of Frankfurt, is his antipathy to current prejudice, to European hobbies, to Western hypocrisies, to the successes of the day. Schopenhauer is a man of powerful mind, who has put away from him all illusions, who professes Buddhism in the full flow of modern Germany, and absolute detachment of mind in the very midst of the nineteenth-century orgy....

29 August 1869. – Schopenhauer preaches impersonality, objectivity, pure contemplation, the negation of will, calmness and disinterestedness, an aesthetic study of the world, detachment from life, the renunciation of all desire, solitary meditation, disdain of the crowd, and indifference to all that the vulgar covet....

30 August 1869. – Still some chapters of Schopenhauer. Schopenhauer believes in the unchangeableness of innate tendencies in the individual, and in the invariability of the primitive disposition. He refuses to believe in the new man, in any real progress towards perfection, or in any positive improvement in a human being. Only the appearances are refined; there is no change below the surface. Perhaps he confuses temperament, character, and individuality? I incline to think that individuality is fatal and primitive, that temperament reaches far back, but is alterable, and that character is more recent and susceptible of voluntary or involuntary modifications. Individuality is a matter of psychology, temperament, a matter of sensation or aesthetics; character alone is a matter of morals. Liberty and the use of it count for nothing in the first two elements of our being; character is an historical fruit, and the result of a man's biography. – For Schopenhauer, character is identified with temperament just as will with passion....

Later – One has merely to turn over the *Lichtstrahlen* of Herder[87] to feel the difference between him and Schopenhauer.The latter is full of marked features and of observations which stand out from the page and leave a clear and vivid impression. Herder is much less of a writer; his ideas are entangled in his style, and he has no brilliant condensations, no jewels, no crystals. While he proceeds by streams and sheets of thought which have no definite or individual outline, Schopenhauer breaks the current of his speculation with islands, striking, original, and picturesque, which engrave themselves in the memory....

What is the faculty which gives relief, brilliancy, and incisiveness to thought? Imagination. Under its influence expression becomes concentrated, coloured and strengthened, and by the power it has of individualizing all it touches, it gives life and permanence to the material on which it works. A writer of

> genius changes sand into glass and glass into crystal, ore into iron and iron into steel; he marks with his own stamp every idea he gets hold of. He borrows much from the common stock, and gives back nothing; but even his robberies are willingly reckoned to him as private property. He has, as it were, *carte blanche*, and public opinion allows him to take what he will.
>
> *31 August 1869*. – I have finished Schopenhauer. My mind has been a tumult of opposing systems – Stoicism, Quietism, Buddhism, Christianity. Shall I never be at peace with myself? If impersonality is a good, why am I not consistent in the pursuit of it? And if it is a temptation, why return to it, after having judged and conquered it?...

The European mind continues to be a 'tumult of opposing systems'. Stoicism and Quietism have dropped out of the picture, and more aggressive ideologies have taken their place. The influence of Christianity is unmistakably on the decline. That of Buddhism, though still limited to a narrow circle, is definitely increasing. Perhaps it will one day bring to the West the sense of spiritual certainty and that feeling of peace with oneself – the only real basis for peace with one's neighbour – for which Amiel longed.

April 1955

A HOT-HOUSE RELIGION?

A new item in the February issue of the journal informs us that the proposed London Buddhist Temple will contain 'a bodhi tree which will be maintained within a hot-house'. Why not put the *bhikkhus* into the hot-house too? It would then be possible for them to remain dressed exactly as they are in the subtropical countries of South-east Asia, thus ensuring the strict maintenance of Vinaya rules. Better still (Himavantavasi thinks), put the whole temple under glass and give it central heating, like certain sections of the Regent's Park Zoo. Pure Buddhism would then be really established in the West!

April 1955

ENLIGHTENED BUDDHISTS

From his mountain retreat Himavantavasi watches with keen interest the spread of Buddhism in different parts of the world. Only a few days ago he happened to be reading an account written by a certain Buddhist preacher of his tour in a number of non-Buddhist countries. The tour seemed to have been quite successful, and the writer was evidently more than satisfied with the results of his efforts. What surprised Himavantavasi, however, was the number of 'enlightened Buddhists' that the preacher had met in the course of his travels. In one place he writes of some 'enlightened Buddhists' meeting him at the airport, and in another of 'enlightened Buddhists' attending his lectures. Himavantavasi started wondering where all these *arahants* had sprung from. If even non-Buddhist countries could produce such a rich crop of enlightened beings what was the use of preaching the Dhamma there? At length, however, it dawned on him that the venerable writer was using the word 'enlightened' in quite a different sense than the one it usually bears in a Buddhist context; in fact, to him it was simply a synonym for 'intelligent' or 'intellectual'. The confusion is by no means without significance. For some people, even for some *bhikkhus*, it seems, the Enlightenment attained by the Buddha is not so very different from the 'enlightenment' preached by Voltaire, Diderot, D'Alembert, and the rest of the eighteenth-century encyclopaedists. If we adopt this point of view then the attainment of Enlightenment will not be such a difficult matter as some of us had supposed.

May 1955

'NOT PEACE BUT A SWORD'

Himavantavasi could not help smiling – rather grimly – when, upon opening his newspaper a few days ago, he saw that in his Easter Message the Pope had called upon the statesmen of the world to ensure peace. According to the proverb, you can't teach an old dog new tricks. The Catholic Church is a very old dog. During the nineteen centuries of its existence it has probably been responsible for more war, bloodshed, murder, looting, torturing to death, arson, rape, destruction of property and burning at the stake than any other religious body in the whole world. And now it hypocritically cries for peace! But who was it that solemnly invoked divine blessing upon the troops and tanks and machine-guns, to say nothing of the poison gas, with which Mussolini conquered innocent and helpless Abyssinia while the world looked on and did nothing? Why, the Roman Catholic church, in the person of the predecessor of the present occupant of St Peter's chair! And should an H-bomb or some other such product of Christian civilization happen to fall on some 'godless' state we are quite sure it would fall with the heartiest blessings of the present pontiff. 'The end justifies the means,' says the Church. In order to enlarge the Kingdom of Christ (which in effect means the political and economic influence of the Church) any crime is not only permissible but even praiseworthy. Truly did Christ say 'I come to bring not peace but a sword.'[88]

May 1955

A PARADOX

Himavantavasi knows that even Buddhist magazines have to pay printers' bills, and that it is therefore necessary to tap sources of income apart from the donations of the charitable. Advertisements are the obvious solution to the problem. But advertisements *for what*? 'There lies the rub,' as Hamlet says. Advertising is the gentle art of creating and stimulating desire for unnecessary things, that is to say, for luxury goods. The necessities of life require no advertisements, for we shall have to buy them anyway. But is it not paradoxical that magazines published ultimately for the sake of contributing, however slightly, to the elimination of worldly desires, should through the advertisements they accept be a means of inflaming them?

Such were the reflections induced in Himavantavasi by the perusal of the Vesak number of a certain Buddhist magazine. Casually opening it a few days after its arrival, he found on page 51 an earnest Buddhist writer declaring, apropos of Ceylon, 'The village preaching halls are deserted and the motley crowds throng the cinema halls which spring overnight like poisonous mushrooms in the countryside.' But on page 50, right beside this declaration, a full-page advertisement announced 'Here are the brilliant new Vauxhalls! New colour schemes! New de-luxe interiors! New styling! New value!' Worse, however, was to come. Turning to other pages, Himavantavasi was astonished to find that the same 'poisonous mushrooms' against which the earnest Buddhist writer had declaimed so fiercely had to their credit no less than three advertisements, the last of which consisted of an enormous question mark with the caption 'This space should remind you of the good smashers given you by Cinemas Ltd.' Other advertisements were for various types of insurance, for radios, for refrigerators, and for at least a dozen different makes of motor car. In one of these artistic masterpieces, which was printed in full colour (pictures of the Buddha were all in black-and-white!), a young lady whose appearance was certainly not conducive to the keeping of the third precept gaily informed Himavantavasi that 'a Frigidaire in the tropics is not luxury!' Underneath was shown an open Frigidaire plentifully stocked with milk, fruits, puddings, pies, tinned stuffs, pickles, preserves, and joints of meat, while coyly hiding behind the milk were two green glass bottles of what looked to Himavantavasi suspiciously like beer.

Obviously, the advertisement policy of some of our magazines needs revision.

July 1955

'TALKING SHOPS'?

Parliaments are sometimes called 'talking shops'. It seems that the Buddhist conferences of which we have become so fond lately are talking shops too! Writing in the Spring issue of the *Young East* about the Third Conference of the World Fellowship of Buddhists, held in Burma towards the end of last year, W. P. Woodard says,

> I had supposed that there would be considerably more attention to devotional practices, including periods of meditation. My friends in asking about the conference almost invariably bring up this suggestion. The relatively small place given to devotions was indeed a surprise. Am I merely betraying my occidental and Christian background in saying that worldwide Buddhism as a vital force will never come into existence until there is a spiritual basis, more concrete than mere acceptance of a common faith? Is there not a need for a common litany with sacred texts and hymns to bring emotions to a focus?

No, Mr Woodard, Himavantavasi does not think that you are betraying any bias. Buddhists, in fact, by excluding devotional practices from the programme of their conferences, show a bias that is distinctly non-Buddhist and non-oriental. The suggestion that we need 'a spiritual basis more concrete than mere acceptance of a common faith' puts a finger on one of the weakest points in the modern Buddhist movement of revival. Himavantavasi recommends it to the very serious consideration of his readers.

July 1955

BOUQUETS

Himavantavasi continues to be agreeably astonished by the constantly improving quality and increasing quantity of the various Buddhist periodicals which find their way to his mountain retreat. Gone are the days (gone for ever, let us hope!) when shoddy format, shabby production, shockingly bad proof-reading, and a general appearance of negligence and neglect could be tolerated on the grounds that a Buddhist magazine was not expected to be a commercial proposition anyway. Almost without exception, our journals have taken on a 'new look' during the last year or two. The London Buddhist Society's *Middle Way*, the Buddha Sāsana Council of Burma's *Light of the Dhamma*, and Philadelphia's independent, though theosophically inclined, *Golden Lotus*, are now more than ever models of careful and conscientious editing. The first two have, of course, the obvious advantage (from the editor's, if not from the reader's, point of view) of being quarterlies. But this fact is far from explaining the recent remarkable all-round raising of standards. Even the World Fellowship of Buddhists' little eight-page monthly, now only in its fourth year of publication, is already beginning to look like a really professional piece of work, while the *Western Buddhist*, which Himavantavasi had the pleasure of introducing to his readers in November 1953, is already beginning to fulfil the optimistic predictions which he made – somewhat rash, it seemed at the time on that occasion. Improvement is visible not only in the appearance but also in the contents of our journals. Gone, too, are the days when a little mild bleating about *ahiṃsā* passed for an article on Buddhism. This is as it should be: wisdom without faith and faith without wisdom are equally dangerous. Himavantavasi has, in fact, no complaint at all to make against our periodicals, except that the 'poetry' which most of them publish is still dreadful.

August 1955

TAILPIECE

In case, as Himavantavasi suspects, he has not yet succeeded in filling up two pages of the journal, he proposes to share with his readers the following quotations from the great French writers André Gide and Romain Rolland:[89]

> I am amazed to the point of ecstasy at the world's wealth.
>
> Life brings me its freshness as an ineffable gift.
>
> Every moment renews my vision.
>
> The smallest moment of life is stronger than death and cancels it. Death is no more than permission granted to other modes of life to exist, so that everything may be ceaselessly renewed.
>
> The ploughshare of sorrow, breaking the heart, opens up new sources of life. The land again bursts into flower. A new soul is born.
>
> Without sacrifice there is no resurrection. Nothing grows and blooms, save by giving. All you try to save in yourself wastes and perishes. All things ripen for the giving's sake and in the giving are consummated.
>
> The possible and the future are one. The possible is striving to come into being; and all that can be will be, if man helps.
>
> You who are to come after me, take the hope, the heritage, the joy, of those who have gone before. Let your happiness be to increase that of others. Work and strive, and accept no evil that you might change.
>
> Happiness is the perfume of the soul, the harmony that dwells, singing, in the depth of the heart. The most beautiful of all the music of the soul is kindness.

Let your life be a heroic symphony, wherein the very discords clash and mingle, and grow into a serene whole.

August 1955

MISSION TO MARS

Scientific discoveries are still able to trouble theological waters.

Himavantavasi could not help smiling when, a few days ago, he read an account of the controversy provoked in Roman Catholic circles by recent scientific announcements that other parts of the universe might be inhabited. If they are, argue the theologians, the inhabitants must either be in a state of grace, or a state of sin. In the latter case, can they or can they not be redeemed by Christ? Some say yes, others no.

Whatever the answer may be, Himavantavasi feels pretty certain that if interplanetary transport ever does become a reality, among the first batch of space-travellers to land on Mars will be an emissary of the Vatican. Dr Billy Graham would no doubt be not far behind.[90] What a disappointment it would be if the Martians greeted them not with *Ave Marias* and *Hallelujahs* but with *Namo Buddhāya!*

Himavantavasi's readers will probably join him in smiling at the fanatical proselytizing zeal of the Christian, especially the Catholic, Church. But let them reflect that if Mars, even, is threatened with invasion, how great is the danger that looms over their own easily accessible Buddhist homelands here on Earth!

December 1955

A MODERN BODHISATTVA

While Himavantavasi is on the subject of the Catholic Church, it occurs to him that, in a recently published essay on Buddhism, a theologian belonging to this body asserts that the bodhisattva ideal is a mere product of the imagination, and has never been realized in actual life. Stories of the bodhisattva sacrificing his life and limbs, and offering his blood for others are, he declares, a beautiful dream, but they are only a dream.

Himavantavasi only hopes that this friend of Buddhism had the good fortune to read the story, published last month in the Ceylon newspapers, of a young Buddhist monk who had written to the Governor of Ceylon offering to take the place on the scaffold of a condemned murderer – a Christian. The condemned man had apparently announced that, if so fortunate as to obtain a reprieve, he intended to become a Buddhist. No reprieve came. So the monk came forward and offered his own life. Said the monk: 'Thanks to my good karma, I have had the opportunity of studying the Dhamma and entering the sangha. This man has had no such opportunity. That he should also be able to study and practise the Doctrine is more important than that I should continue to live. Let me die therefore instead of him.'

The action of this young monk speaks louder than any words of Himavantavasi's.

August 1955

SIGNS OF THE TIMES – BUDDHIST VERSION

It has been said that there are lies, damned lies, and statistics. All the same, Himavantavasi was both surprised and pleased to learn the other day that Buddhism now ranks as one of the six major US religious groups. For what they are worth, the figures are as follows: Protestant, 57,124,142; Roman Catholic, 32,403,332; Jewish, 5,500,000; Eastern Orthodox, 2,024,210; Old Catholic and Polish National Catholic, 367,918; Buddhist, 63,000.

According to Buddhist sources in the US, however, the number of Buddhists there is in fact treble that given in the statistics. Living as they do in a land where every form of religious quackery flourishes, and where superstition and exploitation thrive in the name of 'the Eastern Wisdom', many American followers of the Enlightened One are, not unnaturally, reluctant to declare themselves Buddhists publicly.

To Himavantavasi it is a saddening thought that the number of Buddhists in the US and in India should be about the same.

August 1955

BEATING THE DRUM:

Maha Bodhi Editorials

1950

SECRET WORSHIP

Massed are the glowing blossoms
  In fragrance at Thy feet –
The crimson, spiky-petalled
  Dahlias, surpassing sweet
    White temple flowers four-petalled,
    Geraniums lemon-scented,
    With full-blown, dawn-pink roses
  Which here in beauty meet.

The dragon-breeding incense
  Wreathes upward dimly white;
The place is softly golden
  With many a votive light;
    While sound of voices chanting
    In praise of the Awakened;
    His Doctrine and Disciples,
  Steals sweetly through the night.

I linger till the incense
  Has drifted from the room;
Till, one by one, the golden lights,

Are swallowed by the gloom;
Until in the deserted,
Darkened, silent chamber,
The flowers are left distilling
Invisible perfume.

And then, unseen by any,
With awe and loving dread.
With rhythmic breath for incense
And hymns for blossoms red,
Before my Lord and Master,
Before my wild heart's Tamer,
Before my Path-Revealer
I bow with reverent head.

October 1950

1954

ANCIENT BUDDHIST SITE IN DANGER

Nagarjunikonda, in the newly created Andhra State, is one of the largest and most important Buddhist sites in South India.[91] Not only does it cover an extensive area but it is also extremely rich in ancient Buddhist remains. A number of monasteries, stupas, and images have so far been excavated, though a great deal of archaeological work will have to be done before all the treasures which the area contains are brought to light. For the Mahāyāna Buddhists of China, Japan, and Tibet, Nagarjunikonda possesses a special sanctity inasmuch as the patriarch Nāgārjuna, founder of the Madhyamaka school of Buddhist philosophy, resided at the place for many years.[92]

It has now come to the notice of the Society that the whole of this area, with its shrines and sanctuaries, and its two thousand years of religious and cultural traditions, is to be totally submerged under an irrigation scheme which, we understand, is to be put into operation by the Andhra State Government. While fully sympathizing with the condition of the people of this locality, for whose benefit the scheme is to be carried out, we are frankly astonished to find that no cognizance whatsoever seems to have been taken, by the authorities concerned, of the religious and cultural importance of Nagarjunikonda, the very existence of which they are apparently ready to wipe out with a single stroke of the draughtsman's pen. No attempt has been made to consult the

Maha Bodhi Society, which learned of this grave threat to an invaluable Buddhist monument only by an accident, or to ascertain the feelings of hundreds of millions of Asian Buddhists to whom Nagarjunikonda is a place of great sanctity. This complete disregard of Buddhist sentiment will surely come as a great shock to the followers of the Lord Buddha in Ceylon, Burma, Siam, Cambodia, Tibet, Nepal, Korea, China, Japan, and Mongolia, to whom India is the Holy Land, the birthplace of Buddhism, and who are eager to maintain relations of friendship with those who are the lineal descendants of the disciples of the Master. Such an action as the Andhra Government appears to contemplate will surely do little to improve those relations.

We understand that a protest against the destruction of so many ancient Buddhist monuments has already been made by the Archaeological Department of the Government of India, and that a resolution condemning the vandalism has been adopted by the Indian Historians' Congress which met last month at Waltair.[93] While adding our own protest to those already made, we hope that Buddhist organizations all over the world will unite to take immediate and vigorous action to save the shrines of Nagarjunikonda from being 'cast as rubbish to the void'.[94] Resolutions of protest should be forwarded to the Prime Minister of India, Pandit Jawaharlal Nehru.[95]

VAIŚĀKHA PŪRṆIMĀ AS A PUBLIC HOLIDAY

Vaiśākha Pūrṇimā, the thrice sacred anniversary of the birth, Enlightenment, and passing away of the Lord Buddha, is the holiest day in the Buddhist calendar.[96] Though complete unanimity does not as yet prevail among the Buddhists of the world regarding the precise date of these great events – not a very surprising fact, when we remember the vast size of the areas where Buddhism flourishes, and the number of centuries during which there was no contact between the Buddhist countries – there is a growing feeling that the full-moon day of Vaiśākha should be observed by all Buddhists, regardless of sect and nationality, as the anniversary of the three most important happenings in the Buddha's life. The Theravādin countries of Ceylon, Burma, Siam, and Cambodia have always recognized this day, and Buddhist organizations in China and Japan, as well as those of Europe and America, have now begun to follow suit.

In India, too, the thrice-sacred day has for more than sixty years been celebrated at all centres of the Maha Bodhi Society, and in recent times celebrations have been held by many other organizations as well. As yet, however, in spite of repeated representations, the Government of India has not thought fit to honour the memory of India's greatest son by declaring the Vaiśākha Pūrṇimā a public holiday. Last year, as a result of a demand voiced in the Sanchi Cultural Conference, the Central Government did declare the Vaiśākha Pūrṇimā a government holiday; but this simply means that offices of the Central Government (not of the states governments) will be closed for the day. Members of the public will have no opportunity of honouring the memory of the Buddha.

With a view to rectifying this state of affairs at least in West Bengal, where more Buddhists live than in any other part of India, a delegation from the Maha Bodhi Society waited upon the Chief Minister, Dr B. C. Roy, on 23 December 1953, with the request that he be pleased to declare Vaiśākha Pūrṇimā as a public holiday. The delegation was led by Sri Keshub Chandra Gupta, one of the Vice-Presidents of the Society, and consisted of Ven. Bhikkhu Silabhadra, Ven. N. Jinaratana Thera, Dr Arabinda Barua, Sri D. Valisinha, Dr M. R. Soft, and Sri J. C. Ghosh. Replying to the representations of the delegation, Dr Roy said that he was not in favour of increasing the number of public holidays, and that he had already reduced the number of days allotted to the Durga Puja. In fact, the Chief Minister added, he was in favour of having only Sunday as a holiday. If he received an order from the Central Government, he would have to obey it, but until then he had no intention of declaring Vaiśākha Pūrṇimā as a public holiday.

This blunt and unsympathetic reply came as a rude shock to the members of the delegation. While appreciating the impossibility of increasing the number of public holidays, we feel that they might easily be redistributed so as to satisfy the demands of the Buddhists. The number of public holidays allotted to Christian festivals is quite out of proportion to the religious and cultural importance of Christianity in India. Republic Day on 26 January and Independence Day on 15 August could surely be combined into a single national day as observed by most other civilized countries. What shocks us most in Dr Roy's statement is the fact that while he has no objection to having fifty-two public holidays in the year for Sunday (a Christian holy day which was introduced by a foreign government, and which has no connection whatever with

Indian traditions) he is definitely unwilling to allow even one public holiday in the year in honour of the Buddha, who occupies in the annals of Indian religion and culture a place second to none. We trust that maturer consideration will convince Dr Roy of the advisability of declaring the Vaiśākha Pūrṇimā as a public holiday throughout West Bengal. Meanwhile, the spectacle of such indifference in high places to the things that have made India truly great and glorious astonishes us. We fear that it is a relic of foreign influence which does not augur well for the future of the country.

January 1954

BUDDHISM AND THE PARLIAMENT OF RELIGIONS

Though gatherings of the representatives of different religions were held in ancient times in most Asian countries, especially India – generally under the patronage of powerful kings interested in the political unification of their domains – the idea of a Parliament of Religions, or Fellowship of Faiths, which would assemble on one platform the endless diversity of religious belief, was conceived only recently. The Parliament of Religions held in Chicago in 1893, at which Southern Buddhism was represented by the founder of the Maha Bodhi Society, Ven. Anagarika Dharmapala, may be mentioned as the first of a long and illustrious line of such assemblies, the most recent of which was held in the Senate Hall of Calcutta University only last month.

Such assemblies have done immense good not only by promoting friendship between people of admittedly divergent views, but also by stimulating the attempt to formulate a common creed or confession of faith equally acceptable to the followers of all religions. In Western countries, where the fierce bigotry of Christianity long reigned supreme, the influence that they have exercised has indeed been wholly salutary. Colonel Ingersoll, the famous Agnostic lecturer, once told Swami Vivekananda that had he attempted to preach Vedānta in America a few years earlier he would have been burned alive.[97] That a representative of any of the great religions of the East no longer runs such a risk in the United States (Colonel Ingersoll's remark still holds good of certain Roman Catholic countries) is to a large extent due to the increased knowledge and understanding of 'heathen' religions which the holding of Parliaments of Religions has helped to disseminate.

In all human activities, however, there is a tendency to go to extremes, and though Semitic exclusiveness is now the prerogative only of the mentally backward and spiritually enslaved section of mankind, some of the promoters of movements aiming at inter-religious fellowship seem to have slipped almost unawares into a no less extreme and one-sided *inclusiveness*. Examples of this tendency came to our notice not only in connection with the International Congress of World Fellowship of Faiths held in Calcutta during the last week of January but also at a Fraternity of Faiths meeting organized by the Sadharan Brahmo Samaj in the same city a few days earlier.[98] With regard to the first, it was stated that the aim of the Congress was 'to draw together in common bond of fellowship people of all denominations, races, and countries and to comprehend the whole human race as one and that all religions are but different manifestations of the Supreme Reality'. With the first part of this pronouncement we have no quarrel, but with the second part of it no informed Buddhist could possibly agree. The expression 'the Supreme Reality' evidently has a theistic connotation, whereas Buddhism is notoriously atheistic. A similar theistic bias was exhibited by Dr H. C. Mookerjee, M.A., Ph.D., D.Litt., Governor of West Bengal,[99] who in the course of his inaugural address at the First Session of the Congress, speaking of Kabir, Nanak, Dadu and Babalal etc.,[100] said, 'All these great saints brought the masses of the people round *to the central creed – the religion of Man in relation to his Maker, not his sect*.' Such a formulation of the central creed of religion completely excludes the Buddhists, who can hardly be expected to meet the followers of other religions on a 'platform' which contradicts one of the most vital points of Buddhist doctrine. How would Christians and Muslims react if they were invited to meet on a 'common platform' of 'No God and No Soul'?

A Christian speaker at the Fraternity of Faiths meeting went a step further than Dr Mookerjee, asserting that all religions believed in the Fatherhood of God and the Brotherhood of Man, and that apart from the former belief the latter was unthinkable. The Buddhist speaker who followed him had to contradict this statement, declaring that though Buddhism denied the very existence of God its followers have exemplified the spirit of Brotherhood more fully than the adherents of other religions. At the beginning of the speech from which we have already quoted Dr Mookerjee said, 'Christianity, whose doctrine is love, broke out in a fury of persecution and vengeance even within its own fold. Likewise, Islam, preaching the mercy of God, brandished almost a merciless sword against non-Islamic religions and peoples. Hinduism in India expelled Buddhism and developed into a domineering doctrine.' It is significant that His Excellency could find no similar charge to lay at the atheistic door of the fourth great world religion, Buddhism.

How determined is the attempt which is being made in some quarters to force Buddhism into a doctrinal framework thoroughly repugnant to it was nakedly apparent in the presidential address delivered by the Shankaracharya of Puri at the first session of the Congress.[101] The Buddhist representative's emphatic assertion that Buddhism rejected the idea of God, and exhorted man to depend for deliverance upon himself alone, had apparently upset His Holiness, who spent nearly an hour attempting to prove that Buddhists, even though they professed not to believe in God, really did believe in him, and that atheists and theists were bound for the same goal.

It is time that Buddhists stopped allowing people of other religions to tell them what they 'really' believe. Buddhists do *not* believe in God, neither do they believe that all religious doctrines are true. If the organizers of Parliaments of Religions and Fraternities of Faiths make such beliefs their 'common platform' then it is obvious that such a platform is not broad enough to accommodate the followers of atheistic religions. Buddhists should be courageous enough to refuse to participate in any inter-religious meeting that endeavours to drag down the Dhamma of the Enlightened One into the morass of theistic superstition.[102]

February 1954

CONTROVERSY

One of the facts by which even the most casual reader of the Pāli scriptures cannot fail to be impressed is the singular urbanity with which the Buddha engaged in discussion with the rival teachers of his time, the unwearied patience with which he answered the questions and solved the difficulties of the *samaṇas* and *brāhmaṇas* who came to see him,[103] and the amazing tact and understanding with which he dealt with the more obtuse among his own disciples. However serious and important the subject under discussion, however greatly his doctrine differed from that of his interlocutor, the Buddha, while firmly adhering to his own position, invariably maintained a serene and dignified demeanour. However angry his opponent might become, he remained calmly smiling; in the face of abuse his affability was unshaken; in victory he was not elated, and defeat he never knew. The Buddha was indeed the ideal controversialist, willing to listen to points of view different from his own, courteous in rejoinder, pleasant and sweet of speech, of unrivalled clarity in the exposition of his own views, he provides not only to all Buddhists but to every person who engages in religious controversy a perfect model of thoroughly civilized behaviour.

That the refined qualities displayed by the Buddha in debate were not universal in India, even among his own disciples, is shown by a stock passage which is often repeated in the Pāli scriptures, wherein quite a different manner of conducting religious controversies is described. The Buddha's term for such undignified debates is 'wordy warfare' (*viggāhika*) and this is the description he gives of how a wager of wordy warfare speaks:

> You know not about this Norm-Discipline. I do know about this Norm-Discipline. How could you know about it? You have fallen on wrong views. I have come by right views. You speak last what should come first, and first what should come last. I am speaking to the point: you are not. What you have thought out so long is quite upset. Your view is confuted. Go, explain yourself. You are shown up. Clear yourself if you can![104]

Needless to say, this description of wordy warfare is repeated so many times in the Pāli scriptures with the object of showing how a follower of the Buddha should *not* speak when engaged in religious controversy.

One of Addison's essays in the celebrated *Spectator* is on 'Methods of Disputing'.[105] After mentioning the 'catechetical method of arguing' introduced by Socrates, and 'the great variety of little weapons, called syllogisms' invented by Aristotle, he goes on to mention

> the *Argumentum Basilinum* (others write it *Bacilinum* or *Baculinum*), which is pretty well express'd in our *English* word *Club-law*. When they were not able to confute their Antagonist, they knock'd him down.

This species of argument was apparently held in high esteem in the universities of medieval Europe, and is not unknown in certain countries even today. After making mention of 'the logic of kings' (i.e. war), and of arguing by poll and by wager, Addison gives a lively description of what he terms 'arguing by torture'. The whole passage deserves to be quoted at length, but we have room for the first part only.

> But the most notable way of managing a Controversy is that which we may call *Arguing by Torture*. This is a Method of Reasoning which has been made use of with the poor Refugees, and which was so fashionable in our Country during the Reign of Queen *Mary*, that, in a Passage of an Author quoted by Monsieur *Bayle*,[106] it is said the Price of Wood was raised in *England* by reason of the Executions that were made in *Smithfield*. These Disputants convince their Adversaries with a *Sorites*, commonly called a Pile of Faggots. The Rack is also a kind of Syllogism which has been used with good Effect, and has made Multitudes of Converts.

Those who read last year the reports of the treatment meted out to Protestant minorities in certain South American 'republics' will know that the method of arguing by torture is as popular in the Roman Catholic Church today as it was in Mary Tudor's time. Unfortunately, however, the lack of understanding shown by most European states prevents the Church from making as extensive a use of this kind of argument as it would like to do.

> There is another way of Reasoning which seldom fails, tho' it be of a quite different Nature to that I have last mentioned: I mean, convincing a Man by ready Money, or, as it is ordinarily called, bribing a Man to an Opinion. This method has often proved successful when all others have been made use of to no purpose. A Man who is furnished with Arguments from the Mint will convince his Antagonist much sooner than one who draws them from Reason and Philosophy. Gold is a wonderful Clearer of the Understanding: it dissipates every Doubt and Scruple in an Instant, accommodates itself to the meanest Capacities, silences the Loud and Clamorous, and brings over the most Obstinate and Inflexible.

This method of arguing is extremely well known in all Asian countries, where it has been widely used by Christian missionaries of every denomination. The method has various subsidiary forms, such as arguing by education, arguing by employment, and arguing by medical treatment. The expansion of Christianity in India, Ceylon, China, Japan, and other Asian countries undoubtedly owes more to these irrefutable arguments for the truth of the Christian religion than to all other reasonings in the whole armoury of Christian theology.

Though Buddhists have long been familiar with the Socratic and Aristotelian modes of disputing, the various Christian methods of arguing described by Addison have been quite unfamiliar to them. Partly as a result of the Buddha's personal example, and partly as a result of his teaching on the subject of right speech, the third stage of the Noble Eightfold Path, controversies between Buddhist and Buddhist, or between Buddhist and non-Buddhist, have generally been conducted with dignity and restraint. There is no record that Buddhists have at any time endeavoured to prove the truth of the doctrine of *anātman* by resorting to the *Argumentum Basilinum*, or that they have sought to demonstrate the superiority of Buddhist compassion over Christian love by means of 'arguing by torture'. Though Buddhism has spread widely in many Western lands, it has convinced people, not by ready money, but by the purity and excellence of its doctrines.

With such a tradition behind them it is not surprising that even in modern times an exchange of views between Buddhists of different schools is marked by good humour, mutual respect, and an attempt to understand the opposite point of view. Controversial articles published in magazines, however vigorously the views of the author are expressed, seldom overstep the limits of decency. To every rule, however, there is an exception; in every flock there is at least one black sheep; and we now have to direct our attention to a certain fortnightly paper published in Colombo which has thought fit to ignore the example and teaching of the Buddha with regard to the right way of engaging in religious controversy.[107] This paper has discovered a mode of disputing unknown to Addison, which we may call 'arguing by abuse'. Whoever disagrees with its narrow, dogmatic, and intolerant views is at once attacked in the vilest and most virulent language imaginable. 'Heretic', 'pseudo-Buddhist', and 'Devadatta' are among the milder epithets with which it favours anyone whose ideas do not coincide in every particular with its own. The leading Buddhist layman of Ceylon,[108] who has done more for the revival of Buddhism than any other Sinhalese since Anagarika Dharmapala (who, by the way, had to face similar attacks even on his deathbed), is assailed with accusations so wild and abuse so gross that one wonders how the paper concerned can venture to describe itself as Buddhist. Of course it is not difficult for ill-nature to disguise itself as zeal for religion, or dogmatism to pose as '*saddhā*'. In fact, the paper's official description of its mud-slinging policy is 'radiating *mettā*'. To quote once more from Addison:

> Ill-nature is another dreadful imitator of zeal. Many a good man may have a natural rancour and malice in his heart, which has been in some measure quelled and subdued by religion; but if it finds any pretence of breaking out, which does not seem inconsistent to him with the duties of a Christian [or a Buddhist], it throws off all restraint, and rages in its full fury. Zeal is therefore a great ease to a malicious man, by making him believe he does God [or the Dhamma] service, whilst he is gratifying the bent of a perverse revengeful temper.[109]

As might have been expected, the journalistic vipers who discharge their venom in the pages of the paper under review generally prefer to do so from behind the slimy stones of anonymity and pseudonymity. Rarely, if ever, do they come out into the open and sign their names to their attacks. Though they are loud in their protestations of orthodoxy (whenever we read them we are reminded of the old adage that orthodoxy is my doxy, and heterodoxy is your doxy), they do not appear to have understood the Buddha's teaching on the subject of right speech. The language of their paper is a deplorable lapse from Buddhist traditions of courtesy in discussion; in fact, it appears to be a remarkably faithful version of the 'wordy warfare' described by the Buddha in the passage quoted above. We sincerely hope that this paper will in future express its views in a more truly Buddhist manner, and that at least a modicum of the *mettā* of which it speaks so often and so loudly will find its way into the controversies for which it appears to have so great a predilection. Meanwhile, we recommend to the editor and his associates a careful consideration of the following passage on 'The Ariyan Speech':

They who talk angrily, full of wrath and proud,
Carp at each other's failings when they meet,
And take delight in blame and finding fault,
And in their rival's fall. But Ariyans
Will never follow practices like these.
If there be one, a wise man, fain of speech,
He knows the proper time, and speech concerned
With righteousness and practice of right talk.
Thus speaks a sage, not angry, well restrained,
With humble mind, not laying down the law,
Not curious; but wisely speaks fair speech,
Welcomes the kindly word, rejects the cruel,
Knows no resentment, does not carp at faults,
Does not retort nor crush his rival down,
Nor from the issue speak. O true it is
That Ariyans' words alike instruct and please!
Thus Ariyans speak, such is the Ariyan talk;
And knowing this the wise should humbly speak.[110]

March 1954

VAIŚĀKHA DĀNA

Vaiśākha Pūrṇimā, the thrice-sacred anniversary of the birth, Enlightenment, and death of Gautama the Buddha, is fast approaching. In every Buddhist land preparations are already being made to celebrate the great day in a befitting manner. Committees are being formed, programmes drawn up, and funds collected, in order that the most important festival of the Buddhist calendar shall be celebrated with all the pageantry and devotional fervour traditionally associated with it. Though the spirit is one, the manner of the celebration will naturally vary from country to country. Here it will be celebrated with processions of gorgeously caparisoned elephants; there, with processions of figures fantastically masked and enormous paper dragons. In one place the chant of adoration to the Blessed One will arise beneath dull grey skies; in another, beneath a heaven of cloudless blue.

But in all Buddhist lands, beneath skies of whatever hue the thrice-sacred day may be celebrated, there will be at least one feature of the celebration which will not vary from country to country, but which will be found, in more or less the same form, in all of them: the giving of *dāna*. To the Theravādin Buddhists of Ceylon, Burma, Siam, and Cambodia, the making of gifts at a suitable time and place, to the proper person, and in the right spirit, is a practice which must precede entrance into the three stages of *śīla*, *samādhi*, and *prajñā* into which the Noble Eightfold Path leading to Nirvāṇa is divided. To the Mahāyāna Buddhists of China, Japan, Tibet, Mongolia, Nepal, Bhutan, and Sikkim, universal charity without thought of the deservingness of the recipient and without expectation of reward is the first of the six *pāramitās* of *dāna*, *śīla*, *kṣānti*, *vīrya*, *dhyāna*, and *prajñā*, which are to be practised by the bodhisattva.

> I have devoted and abandoned my frame to all creatures. Much more my outward possessions: any being who shall require it for any purpose, it being recognised for a good, I will give hand, foot, eye, flesh, blood, marrow, limbs great and small – my head itself to such as ask for them; not to mention outward things: wealth, corn, gold, silver, gems, ornaments, horses, elephants, chariots, cars, villages, towns, markets, peoples, kingdoms, capital cities, menservants, maidservants, messengers, sons, daughters and retinue. Whoever shall want it to him will I give so it be for his good. Without regret, and without grudging, without waiting for merit to mature, I will abandon them, without respect of persons, to show them kindness, out of compassion and pity, to be theirs to possess, so that these beings, well entreated by me as by one who has attained wisdom, may learn to know the law.[111]

Thus, in the *Śikṣā-Samuccaya* of Śāntideva, is the bodhisattva exhorted to think.

Though one may justly doubt whether the modern practice of *dāna*, the perfection of giving, is comparable to the ancient one, it is beyond question that during the days preceding Vaiśākha Pūrṇimā the hardest hearts will soften, the tightest purse-strings unloosen, and a great wave of generosity roll from one side to the other of every truly Buddhist land. Beggars in the streets, the sick on their beds of pain in hospitals, animals, children and old people, the poor, and, last but by no means least, the members of the sangha, the noble order of disciples, will all be 'fields of merit' wherein the skilful giver will plant seeds which may bear for him, one day, the highest fruit of all, the fruit of immortality.

Will our readers forgive us if we show for a moment the darker side of this bright picture, and point out imperfections in our manner of giving, and suggest one or two new fields for the casting of the seed of our liberality? It must be plainly stated that in all Buddhist countries in the name of *dāna* money is being simply wasted. In Ceylon *bhikkhus* are frequently brought by car from viharas far from the abode of the *dāyaka* and served with rich food in such abundance that they become sick and unable to perform their duties.[112] In Tibet enormous sums of money are spent each year – it used to be a third of the entire government revenue – on burning butter-lamps before thousands of images. Chinese Buddhists sometimes ruin themselves by indulging in costly funeral rites. In Burma millions of rupees are spent annually on building new shrines and gilding old ones, not because there is any real need to do so but simply for the glorification of the giver. Let our meaning not be mistaken. There is nothing wrong in any of the traditional forms of giving to which we have referred; they are in themselves in the highest degree praiseworthy; but in modern times they have become liable to corruption and abuse, and much of the money which is spent on them could be utilized in far better ways.[113]

We are not introducing a note of humanitarianism into the symphony of Buddhism. *Dāna* is given, ultimately, for the advancement of the Dharma, for the *spiritual* good of humanity, and for the material only insofar as it subserves the spiritual. None of the traditional forms of giving should be discontinued, but money which is now being wasted in the name of *dāna* should be devoted, instead, to the propagation of the teachings of the Buddha. The dissemination of the message of the Master far and wide, as an indispensable preliminary to the actual practice of the Doctrine, is the great need of the hour. There are three fields for this dissemination, and for all of them, particularly for the last, regular *dāna* is urgently required.

Firstly, there is the *dāyaka*'s own land. Let him, if he has not already done so, join and support some Buddhist association, or subscribe to a Buddhist magazine. Let him, if his means permit, print at least one book or pamphlet on the Sublime Dharma. Most of all, let him remember that *dāna* is not of money only, but of time and energy, of health and strength, and even of life itself. Blessed is he who can wear out his body in the service of the Dharma!

Secondly, there is India, the Holy Land of Buddhism, wherein the three great events that we celebrate on the Vaiśākha Pūrṇimā took place. The Buddhist movement in India is still struggling for its existence. The workers are few, the funds scanty, the difficulties which have to be faced many and great. Pilgrims to the four great shrines come and go,[114] but few of them think of the desperate plight of Buddhism in the land of its birth, and fewer still leave anything behind to help carry forward the movement of revival which Anagarika Dharmapala launched more than sixty years ago and which his successors are still striving to carry on. *Bhikṣus* who visit India say, when they are asked to stay and preach the Dharma, 'Why should we? We are very comfortable in our own country.' This is not the spirit which spread Buddhism all over Asia. Let those lazy ones who cling to the comforts of their well-furnished viharas remember that if the *bhikṣus* of India had adopted such an attitude there would be today in their country no Buddhism, no viharas, and no daily *dāna* to fill the stomachs of indolent *bhikṣus*.

Thirdly, there are the whole continents of Europe, Africa, America, and Australasia, where indigenous Buddhist movements are in urgent need of a few drops of that flood of *dāna* which will be inundating so many lands during the forthcoming month. Pause a moment, my good *dāyaka*, before you give your subscription towards the twentieth re-gilding of some image or temple pinnacle, and reflect with shame that, while the Christians of Europe and America maintain thousands of missionaries in your country, you do not support even one *dharmadūta* in theirs. Stop a moment, venerable sir, before you lift to your lips the succulent morsels which are being offered to you during the month of Vaiśākha and ask yourself what you have done, and what you are now doing, for the propagation of the Dharma either at home or abroad.

Vaiśākha Pūrṇimā should be a day of heart-searching for all sincere Buddhists, and the month preceding it should, in the same way, be a time not for that ostentatious waste of money which nowadays so often passes as *dāna* but for truly wise and skilful giving.

EDUCATION WITHOUT A RELIGIOUS FOUNDATION

The condition under which the high school final examination of the Board of Secondary Education, West Bengal, has been abandoned is not only regrettable. What is of more concern to everybody is that the ugly incidents which have taken place prove beyond doubt that a section of young men in the schools of Calcutta has become a positive menace to society and that it is for the Government of West Bengal to deal with the situation in an effective manner.

In our view, the moral degradation of the students is solely due to their not being given religious and moral instruction in schools. Without religion and without morality, left to themselves entirely without guidance either by parents or teachers, they are being rapidly brutalized. The Board of Secondary Education made enough new rules, effected many changes in the syllabus of studies, and otherwise kept themselves busy in their office to justify their existence. But the wholesale moral degradation of the students failed to attract their attention and they seem to be supremely indifferent to it. Things have not improved a bit but rather deteriorated, since Calcutta University was compelled to hand over the matriculation stage of education to the newly-formed Board, a thoroughly inefficient body. We think the Board should be abolished and the matriculation examination reintroduced and re-transferred to the University.

April 1954

BODH GAYA

On 17 May Buddhists all over the world will recall the birth, Enlightenment, and death of Gautama the Buddha. But inasmuch as to be born and to die is the lot of every being, whereas the attainment of Enlightenment is an event rare as the flowering of the *uḍumbara* tree,[115] it is to the Enlightenment, to that deepest spiritual experience whereby mortal man achieved immortal Buddhahood, rather than to the physical accidents of birth and death, that our thoughts turn on the thrice-sacred Vaiśākha Pūrṇimā Day. It is to Bodh Gaya, to the diamond throne beneath the bodhi tree, rather than to the garden at Lumbini or the quiet grove at Kusinara, that the main stream of our devotion flows. As we sit, morning and evening, and meditate on the Buddha's Enlightenment, there dawns upon our inner eye a vision of the stately spire of the Maha Bodhi temple as it rises above the tops of the surrounding trees. We see the great bodhi tree, lineal descendant of the one beneath whose branches the young Indian ascetic sat, five-and-twenty centuries ago, resolving that though the blood should dry up in his veins, and his body crumble to dust, he would not stir from his seat until Enlightenment had been attained. For an instant we have, as it were, a glimpse of a figure sitting radiant and victorious in the rays of the early morning sun, and hear the songs of praise which were echoed by the *deva* hosts from the earth even to the highest heaven. Then the centuries roll like clouds across our mind's eye, and when they have passed we find ourselves back in the twenty-fifth century. The eye of faith, which opens so rarely, has closed, and the eye of flesh sees Bodh Gaya as it is today – a hot, dusty, and dilapidated place where, after more than sixty years of agitation, the Buddhists of India still have less than half a share in the management of their own holiest shrine – to them the most sacred spot in the universe – and the millions of Buddhists in Ceylon, Burma, Siam, Cambodia, China, Japan, Tibet, and Nepal no share at all.

Hence there must be a touch of sadness in our remembrance of the Buddha's Enlightenment. Though conditions at the sacred shrine have in many ways improved considerably since the Government of Bihar passed an Act which provided for the setting up of a managing committee, the fact that this body is so constituted as to have a permanent non-Buddhist majority, is a state of affairs perhaps even more humiliating to the Buddhists than was their previous total exclusion from the management of the affairs of the temple. Surely none but Buddhists would have had the forbearance to acquiesce in such a thoroughly inequitable arrangement! However, they did so acquiesce, in the hope that they would eventually be able to obtain by peaceful means recognition of the justice of their claim that the management of the world's most sacred Buddhist shrine should be in the hands of Buddhists. Now that the Chief Justice of Burma, who recently came to India on pilgrimage, has submitted a report on the temple to the Union Government of Burma, it is to be hoped that the movement for full restoration of the temple to Buddhist hands which was started by Ven. Anagarika Dharmapala, founder of the Maha Bodhi Society, and which has unfortunately slackened off during the last few years, may increase in momentum until a long outstanding injustice to the whole Buddhist world is removed and the Maha Bodhi temple at last made over to the followers of the Enlightened One.[116]

Meanwhile, we have to bring to the notice of our readers yet another threat to Buddhist interests in Bodh Gaya. At a village eight miles from the sacred spot there took place, from 18 to 20 April, the sixth Sarvodaya

Conference.[117] The conference was presided over by Acharya Vinoba Bhave,[118] the veteran follower of Mahatma Gandhi, whose movement for the voluntary donation of land (Bhoodan Yajna) has recently attracted the attention and enthusiastic support of a large section of both public and press. Six hundred delegates from various parts of the country attended, and Dr S. Radhakrishnan, vice-president of India,[119] and Pandit Jawaharlal Nehru, the prime minister, were also present and addressed the conference. On the social, economic, and political aspects of the Sarvodaya movement we have no comment to make. What most gravely concerns all Buddhists, however, is the announcement made by Sri Bhave at the morning session of the conference, an announcement that has already produced effects which may well be detrimental not only to the interests of Buddhists but also, here in India at least, to Buddhism itself. Sri Bhave announced his intention to establish at Bodh Gaya a Samanvaya Mandir, or centre for religious, cultural, and racial synthesis. The way in which this announcement was hailed (under banner headlines, of course) by one newspaper gives a clear indication of the kind of mental attitude which could lead to the conception of such a project. 'Buddha Gaya', we are informed, 'is shortly to assume further importance in the eyes of the world.' The attainment of Enlightenment was not, apparently, sufficient to give the place that full importance which it will now gain by having a Samanvaya Mandir built there by Sri Bhave. Could blasphemous impertinence go further than this? It is as though one should think to increase the importance of the Himalayas by building a sandcastle upon their lower slopes.

Not only is the importance of Bodh Gaya to be enhanced, but the teachings of the Buddha are, apparently, to be improved upon.

> Vedānta and *ahiṃsā* (teachings of Lord Buddha) were interlinked, one could not fully develop without the other. Particularly *ahiṃsā*, non-violence, could never have solid basis without the foundation of Vedānta.[120]

Thus runs the newspaper report of Sri Bhave's speech. Here we find him playing the good old game, so popular among certain people, of belittling Buddhism, with all its elaborate ethics, intricate psychology, and profound metaphysical conceptions, by reducing it to a single negative ethical precept which occupies in the whole system a place analogous to that of a single leaf on a gigantic tree. Having reduced it is this way, they complain of the deficiencies of Buddhism, and declare that it needs to be supplemented by some outside teaching. Holding as he does such a low opinion of Buddhism, we need not be surprised that Sri Bhave continues his speech with the assertion '*Satya* (truth) was revealed in all its glory only in Vedānta'. Naturally, one would not expect a system which teaches only *ahiṃsā* to reveal the truth in all its glory! The result is that we are to have at Bodh Gaya a centre for the synthesis of Buddhism and Vedānta.

How completely removed is Sri Bhave's line of thought (if such confusion of views can be represented by a line at all) is still further revealed by the fact that on 17 April he declared 'God has initiated me in Bhoodan Yajna and he has guided me throughout', while on the 18th he asserted 'I was inspired in my Bhoodan work in Bodh Gaya by Lord Buddha'. Either the speaker equates the Buddha with God (a fantastic idea) or one of the statements is simply false. To try to enlist the prestige of a great name in support of some ephemeral movement is a trick which modern people, especially politicians, are fond of playing. We have been told that the Buddha was an agnostic, a rationalist, a social reformer, a democrat, a socialist, and even a communist. Now we are told 'Lord Buddha's teachings were in fact the teachings of Sarvodaya'.

Let the Buddhist world know fully the facts to which we have referred, and let them understand the significance of those facts. At a spot only two hundred yards from the diamond throne of the Buddha an institution is to be established for the propagation of ideas that are not only different from but even hostile to the teachings of Buddhism. This institution is being established by a person who, doubtless in all sincerity, believes himself to be inspired by God, a being whose very existence was emphatically denied by the Buddha. The ideological background of the institution is the notion that since the Buddha taught nothing but *ahiṃsā* his teachings are inadequate, and need to be supplemented by the teachings of Vedānta which, we are explicitly told, alone reveals truth in its fullness. That Sri Bhave's ideas are not without powerful backing is evinced by the fact that the digging of the well which will mark the centre of the Sarvodaya Mandir was inaugurated by the President of the Indian Republic, Dr Rajendra Prasad,[121] while the prime minister, Pandit Jawaharlal Nehru, made a donation toward the cost of sinking the well. The mahant of the Shaivite Monastery at Bodh Gaya,[122] whose predecessors opposed by all means, fair and foul, the transfer of the Maha Bodhi temple to Buddhist hands, has donated five *bighas* of land to the institution – a circumstance which must surely arouse the worst suspicions of any Buddhist who has even the slightest knowledge of events in Bodh Gaya during the last sixty years.

We wonder what would be the reaction of the Muslim world if a movement that denied the existence of Allah, and asserted that the teachings of Mohammed were in serious need of supplementation, should attempt to establish in the shadow of the Kaaba an institution for the dissemination of ideas which were opposed to the doctrines of the Koran. Or what would be the Catholic reaction if Sri Bhave, after declaring that Christ was not the Son of God, that his teachings were defective, and that truth in its fullness could be found only in the Vedānta, should try to found in St Peter's Square an institution for the synthesis of Christianity and Vedānta? Possession, we are told, is nine tenths of the law, and the fact that Māra has been in possession of the diamond throne for so many centuries, and has only recently been made to shift a few inches in his seat, seems to have made the Buddhist world reluctant to insist upon their right and their duty to care for the sacred place. But the challenge now made to the very existence of Bodh Gaya as a centre for the dissemination of pure Buddhist religion and culture cannot be allowed to go unanswered. What answer will the Buddhist world make? And when?[123]

May–June 1954

UNITY IS STRENGTH

The Dharma taught by the Lord Buddha is in its essence *sanātana*, eternal, being based not on mythology or unverifiable dogma, but on truths which can be tested and verified in their own experience by all who are prepared to dedicate their lives to the attempt. But though the Dharma remains the same age after age, the framework of events within which it finds its temporal manifestation is inevitably subject to change, so that in almost every generation the Dharma has to face and solve, albeit in the same unchanging spirit, the fresh problems which press upon it from all corners of the contemporary world.

The problem of our age and generation is the collapse, in many parts of the world, of what we may term the traditional way of life. People no longer care for religion (by which we mean the active recognition of an order of values higher than those pertaining to the body and the lower mind). They are either hostile to it or merely indifferent. A wave of overt or covert materialism has engulfed many people in many lands, in the East no less than in the West, and threatens to roll on claiming fresh victims.

In circumstances such as these Buddhism has to rally all its forces if the Dharma of the Enlightened One, too, is not to be overwhelmed and swept away with the flotsam and jetsam of other traditions. Unity, as Aesop pointed out in his fable of the quarrelsome brothers and the bundle of sticks, is strength,[124] and if the Buddhist world wishes to resist the onrushing tides of materialism, whether dialectically naked or clad in a decent garment of pseudo-idealism, it must be prepared to stand together. We do not mean that genuine differences of doctrine as between one school of Buddhism and another should be minimized or ignored. What we mean is that the fundamental spiritual basis of all schools of Buddhism, namely the four noble truths *(catvāri āryasatyāni)*, dependent origination (*pratītya-samutpāda*), and the three characteristics (*tri-lakṣaṇa*) of suffering (*duḥkha*), impermanence (*anitya*), and non-ego (*anātman*) should be recognized as of far greater significance than secondary doctrinal differences, to say nothing of mere differences in social customs and 'ecclesiastical millinery'. We should cease inquiring about the colour of robes and the cut of hair, and look instead at the heart and at the life. External things do not make one a Buddhist any more than they make one a Brahmin. Those who emphasize superficial differences at the expense of fundamental unity are weakening the whole Buddhist movement. Unwittingly they are making in the dyke of the Dharma a breach through which the rushing mighty waters of materialism may one day roll with full force and fury. Be the crack in the wall of our unity ever so small, we must hasten to seal it up before it widens beyond hope of repair.

Two such cracks we have observed recently, one in the March issue of the *Sangāyanā Monthly Bulletin*, the other in the *Sangāyanā Souvenir* published by the Union of Burma Buddha Sāsana Council in commemoration of the inauguration on Vaiśākha Pūrṇimā this year of what they term the Sixth Great Buddhist Council.[125] On page 3 of the former issue of this publication we read that a certain 'fervent Mahayanist, was converted to pristine Buddhism'. We are not concerned to contest the claim that Theravāda Buddhism on the whole represents an earlier tradition than the Mahāyāna, or to deny the possibility of a follower of the Buddha transferring his allegiance from one school to the other with perfectly valid reasons for so doing. The word 'conversion', however, is generally understood to connote not a change from one branch of a religion to another branch, but from one religion to another, and what pains and surprises us in the above quotation is its adroit insinuation that Mahāyānists are not Buddhists at all. Even when the word 'conversion' is used by Christians, for instance by Roman Catholics and Seventh Day Adventists, to describe the coming over of a follower of another Christian sect to their own denomination, it carries the unpleasant suggestion that members of the sect to which the 'convert' formerly belonged are doomed to eternal perdition (or, as the Adventists believe, to eventual total combustion, which they consider a very charitable view). As far as we know, neither of these views is entertained by Buddhists, even in Burma, and the use of the word 'conversion' in this connection was, to say the least of it, extremely unfortunate. We should not be astonished to learn that the writer of the report in question was a westerner who has not yet succeeded in ridding himself of Christian concepts.

Turning to the *Sangāyanā Souvenir*, we find that the first article of this otherwise wholly admirable production is headed 'Another Page of Buddhist History. Five countries preserve the Buddha-Dhamma against the Materialists'. According to this article (we hope no scholar in Buddhism ever reads it) the five Buddhist Councils of Theravāda tradition were held to combat five successive waves of materialism. With the first, third, fourth, and fifth councils we are not concerned. What we should like to point out, however, is that, according to reliable scholars, the Second Council was held to refute ten points put forward by the monks of Vaiśālī. These monks, on being excluded from the Council, formed themselves into a school (*ācariyavāda*) known as the Mahāsāṃghikas. It was among the Mahāsāṃghikas that the Mahāyāna movement arose. We can now understand that the writer of the article (anonymous, of course, as such articles usually are, not even the name of the editor or editors appearing anywhere in the magazine) is trying to suggest in his section on the Second Great Council that Mahāyānists are materialists, and that the previous five councils are only so many attempts at combating the contemporary equivalent of Communism – a reading of history which seems as crude as that of the Marxists themselves.

Combining the two extracts to which reference has been made, and rendering fully explicit what they dared only to suggest, we are confronted by the extraordinary statement that Mahāyānists are not Buddhists, and that Mahāyāna Buddhism, which in its Vijñānavāda and Śūnyavāda forms elaborated the most highly idealistic and uncompromisingly spiritual philosophies known to mankind, is – materialism. Could even Christian ignorance and bigotry have gone further than that? Such, apparently, being the view of those responsible for the production of the *Sangāyanā*, we were hardly surprised to learn that at the Sixth Great Buddhist Council Mahāyāna priests (they must never be called monks) were not treated with much ceremony. In fact they were seated not with the Theravādin *bhikkhus* but with the laity. We are quite aware that for purely technical reasons it would not have been possible to seat 'priests' who were not conversant with Pāli together with those whose sacred duty it was to recite the Pāli texts. But surely the members of the Mahāyāna sangha (who, by the way, treated their Theravādin brethren with such wonderful hospitality during the second session of the World Fellowship of Buddhists held in Japan in 1952) could have been seated separately from the laity, and the danger of a grievous misunderstanding with the whole Mahāyāna world thereby avoided. To invite guests and then to insult them would be regarded as a sin by even the most ignorant Buddhist layman, and that so august a body as a Buddhist Council should have been guilty of so deplorable a lapse not only from the spirit of Buddhism but even from ordinary good manners is a matter for the greatest astonishment.

It should not be thought that we are unaware of the importance of the work of textual revision that is being done by the Sixth Great Buddhist Council, or that we have anything save unbounded respect and admiration for U Nu and other members of the Union Government of Burma, thanks to whose devotion the whole grand enterprise has been planned and executed. Our only motive in making the above remarks – though doubtless others will be attributed to us by interested persons – was regret that the perfect accomplishment of so magnificent an undertaking should be prejudiced in even the smallest degree. Those who are seeking to combat, by means of Buddhism, materialism in all its forms, are no doubt doing humanity in general and the Buddhist world in particular a great service. But let them remember that unity is strength, and that by decrying and condemning fellow Buddhists they are only cutting the branch on which they themselves are sitting, thus running the risk of falling headlong into that abyss of materialism from which they are now so anxious to save others.

July 1954

WORLD FELLOWSHIP OF BUDDHISTS

We are happy to learn that the third conference of the World Fellowship of Buddhists is scheduled to open in Rangoon on 3 December, and that part of its proceedings have been planned to coincide with the second session of the Chattha Sanghayana or Sixth Council, which commenced its historic work on the full-moon day of Vaiśākha this year. Burma is indeed fortunate in being within the short space of a few months the venue for two gatherings of such outstanding importance, interest, and significance for the whole Buddhist world.

The following facts about the origins and objects of the World Fellowship of Buddhists may be recalled. At its twenty-eighth annual session, held in December 1947, the All Ceylon Buddhist Congress, one of the most active and influential organizations in the whole island, decided to convene a World Buddhist Congress in Sri Lanka in 1950. The congress was to be called for the purpose of bringing closer together the Buddhists of the world, of exchanging news and views about the conditions of Buddhism, and of discussing ways and means for the adoption of the Buddhist way of life. The first session of the World Fellowship of Buddhists was accordingly held in Kandy and Colombo from 25 May to 6 June 2494 (1950 CE) with conspicuous success, and is now part of Buddhist history. The constitution which was adopted at the conclusion of the proceedings declares that the aims and objects of the newly-founded organization should be: (1) to promote among the members strict observance of the teachings of the Buddha; (2) to secure unity, solidarity, and brotherhood among Buddhists; (3) to propagate the sublime doctrine of the Buddha; (4) to organize and carry on activities in the field of social, educational, cultural, and other humanitarian services; and (5) to work for securing peace and harmony amongst men and happiness for all beings and to collaborate with other organizations working for the same ends.

These aims and objects are obviously in essence identical with those of the Maha Bodhi Society of India, and we have therefore always followed the progress of the World Fellowship of Buddhists with keen interest and strong sympathy. As a matter of fact, the idea of holding such a gathering originated with our revered founder, Ven. Anagarika Dharmapala, who as long ago as 1891, only a few months after the Society's inception, organized at Bodh Gaya an international Buddhist conference. Naturally, the conference was held on a very small scale, and in the midst of his tremendous labours for the revival of Buddhism in India the *anagārika* was never able to spare the time necessary for the full development of the idea. In his article on 'The Maha Bodhi Society, its History and Influence', contributed to our *Diamond Jubilee Souvenir*, Dr Nalinaksha Dutt writes:

> The conference was held, though on a small scale, on 31 October 1891, and it was attended among others by Y. Ato, C. Tokuzawa and Kozen Guneratne of Japan, Bhikṣu Sumangala of Ceylon, Lama To-Chiya, of the Yung-ho-kung temple in China, and Krishna Chandra Chaudhury and Girish Chandra Dewan, of Chittagong Hill Tracts.

We feel sure that the promoters of the World Fellowship of Buddhists will be proud and happy to find it anticipated in idea, even though not in execution, by the illustrious protagonist of Buddhist revival in India, Ceylon, and other Asian lands.

The tentative general programme that has been drawn up for the Third Conference of the WFB is of great interest. The opening proceedings will take place in the Maha Pasana Guha, the same great cave wherein was inaugurated the Sixth Council. Thereafter delegates and friends will be conducted on a tour of Mandalay, Amarapura, Sagaing (a famous meditation centre), Myinggyan, Pagan, Pegu, and other places of historic and religious interest. We are sure that those who are so fortunate as to visit these sacred sites, which contain so many relics of the glory and grandeur of Buddhism in past ages, will find the tour of no less interest than that which followed the second session of the Fellowship when, having concluded their deliberations in Tokyo, the delegates were taken by train, omnibus, and motor cars to visit the ancient temples and shrines of Japan. We invoke on the third session of the World Fellowship of Buddhists the blessings of the Triple Gem, and, with the conviction that its proceedings will advance the propagation of the Dharma and materially contribute to the unity and solidarity of the entire Buddhist world, cordially wish it every possible success.

November 1954

THE FUNCTIONS OF A BUDDHIST JOURNAL

At the end of another year of publication, with which we complete the sixty-second volume of our journal, it may be thought not out of place to recall the function of Buddhist periodical literature within the wider and more complex economy of the propagation of the Dharma. This function is broadly threefold: (1) To reflect the unchanging light of Truth in the mirror of contemporary attitudes and aspirations; (2) to furnish news of Buddhist activities; and (3) to foster a sense of community between both individual Buddhists and Buddhist groups in different parts of the globe to whom no direct means of contact are open. We shall take up for consideration each of these in turn.

1. A magazine is not just a miniature book, and the function of the former is different from, though still akin to, that of the latter. From standard scholarly works on the Dharma, to say nothing of the Buddhist canonical literature, we expect a breadth and amplitude of treatment, an attention to detail, and a copiousness of documentation, for which there would be but little scope in any Buddhist magazine that was not intended solely for the delectation of specialists. Magazine articles have of necessity either to deal in outline, which in practice generally means superficiality, with a wide range of subject matter, or in detail, with a range much more restricted – in which case there is the danger of the reader failing to see the wood for the trees. Articles on Buddhism have to follow a middle way between both extremes. They must be comprehensive without being vague, and deal with details without losing sight of fundamental issues. Apart from straightforward expositions of this or that particular doctrine, Buddhist periodicals may naturally be expected to contain presentations of different aspects of Buddhism in relation to specific modern problems, interests, and needs. They should also make room for the most recent interpretations of traditional ideas which, though possessing a certain contemporary interest, are nevertheless not of sufficient importance to warrant their being dealt with in a whole book. Provisional or specimen translations of Buddhist

texts should also find a place. Apart from the question of the nature of such contributions themselves, however, there is the related question of the budding Buddhist writer. By encouraging those with literary gifts to devote their talents to the service of the Dharma, Buddhist magazines make an indirect contribution to the enrichment of the more permanent forms of Buddhist literature.

Such a practice also promotes the study of the Dharma, for he who writes even a little must needs read much in order to be, or at least appear to be, wiser than his readers. The ideal Buddhist magazine should be a clearing house for the latest ideas about the teaching of the Buddha, and in its columns they should be as it were sifted and winnowed before being allowed to find a place among the permanently acceptable interpretations of the Dharma.

2. We are all cogs in the mighty revolving wheel of the Law; but we are intelligent cogs, and we are able to perform our own humble function all the more efficiently if we know what the other cogs are doing. One who regularly receives information about Buddhist activities in lands far removed from his own is not only inspired by the magnificent spectacle of the mighty forward movement of the whole Buddhist world, but also enabled to appreciate his own small part in that movement, in consequence of which his determination is strengthened and the torch of his enthusiasm kept brightly burning. The circulation of such information renders possible concerted and coordinated action for the advancement, consolidation, and defence of the Dharma between widely separated organizations and groups.

3. Unity is more important that uniformity, and allegiance to an ideal of greater value than formal membership of a society. Between the readers of a magazine, especially a Buddhist magazine, there exists a bond which is nonetheless strong for depending upon something much deeper and more indefinable than the mere payment of an annual subscription, important and necessary from the material point of view though such a transaction may be. Buddhism is on the whole rather an unorganized religion. It has no official head, no universally accepted hierarchy, very few powerful instruments of propaganda, and hardly any trained workers. Many are the individual Buddhists, and Buddhist groups, especially in western lands, whose only direct contact with the rest of

the Buddhist world is the eagerly awaited little magazine which comes to them through the post each month. As they remove the wrapper and turn over its pages their sense of being isolated in the midst of a hostile, or at least alien, religious environment, suddenly leaves them; they feel like a child who has just been gathered to his mother's breast; a sensation of warmth and kinship possesses them; they feel that they 'belong'.

Such are the functions which a Buddhist journal exists to perform. In its own special way it seeks to bring about the same glorious consummation towards which more ambitious agencies are making their own still more important contributions. By indicating the functions of a periodical devoted to the service of the Dharma we have at the same time reminded ourselves, at the end of this our sixty-second year of publication, of the noble purpose with which our own journal was founded and to which it will be our endeavour to be faithful in the coming year.

December 1954

1955

GOOD RESOLUTIONS

In many countries it is the custom for people to make, at the beginning of a new year, certain rules and regulations for their own proper guidance during the coming twelve months. These good resolutions, as such promises to oneself are generally called, are of various kinds. Some are positive, others negative. The resolution to give up smoking is a very popular one: there are people who make it every year. Resolutions to stop drinking, to give up gambling, to eschew late hours, and other forms of 'that unrest that men miscall delight', are very frequently made.[126] Then there are the more positive resolutions. To get up early in the morning, to read an improving book every month, to take exercise regularly, to greet everybody with a smile – these are only a few of the things that in a moment of strength or weakness people bind themselves to do for the remaining three hundred and sixty-four days of the year.

Alas! How soon those good resolutions are broken, those solemn promises forgotten. Human nature is strong as a giant in resolution, feeble as a new-born babe when it comes to execution. Did we promise to give up smoking? We suddenly discover that it is an indispensable aid of concentration. To get up early? But it makes us feel tired during the evening, and in the end time is lost rather than saved. As for all the other good resolutions, well, gambling isn't really bad if you are careful to lose no more than you can really afford, and even the Buddha (thus Māra disguised as reason whispers) was not against drinking, provided that it was done in moderation. Reading improving books is less useful to humanity than reading newspapers; exercise might strain the heart; the people whom you tried to greet with a cheery smile might think you an imbecile. However barren it may be of good deeds, the human mind somehow manages to spawn excuses like a herring. One by one, for this reason or that, our good resolutions are broken, and the month of January, through no fault of its own, is generally strewn with the pitiful wreckage of such broken promises.

Why, then, do people take the trouble of making resolutions which from past experience they well know will be broken before the month is out? When a smooth white sheet of paper lies immaculate before you, it is difficult to resist the temptation to scribble on it, even though you have nothing particular to write. If instead of one such sheet there are three hundred and sixty-five the temptation becomes irresistible. The new year is like a writing pad. Why not scribble on the first sheet something quite fresh and original? But however excellent the precept inscribed on that first white leaf may be, and however beautifully written, the impression is not transmitted to the sheets below; for the carbon paper of will power is either not there or, if there, is of such poor quality that the copies it makes are too faint to be read.

Yet though most people undoubtedly do break by the tenth day of the month all the resolutions they made on the first, there are nevertheless a few earnest souls who make their good resolutions seriously and keep them loyally: 'Mongst millions faithless faithful only *they*.'[127] Obviously the practice itself cannot be blamed simply because people fail to carry it out. Its utility would remain unimpaired, even though nobody followed it. Those, however, who do keep their good resolutions find in them a source of strength. Human nature is weak. Often we cannot develop our virtues without enlisting the cooperation of our vices. Pride is generally more powerful than its brother bad qualities, especially in the virtuous. One of the best ways of shaking off a bad habit or forming a good one is by making it a matter of pride to succeed. Hence the good resolution. We have given our word, pledged our faith, if only to ourself, and shall we be false and untrue? Perhaps we have told our friends. How can we make ourselves a laughing stock to them? In this way Māra himself is tricked into fighting with the armies of righteousness.

The five precepts taken by pious Buddhists on new- and full-moon days and other solemn occasions can be regarded as so many good resolutions, not only because they are frequently broken, but also because they are promises rather than commandments – promises made to ourselves, not to the Buddha, much less still to any god. These five precepts the Buddhist has in any case to observe all the year round. If he wishes to make good resolutions for the new year he will therefore have to find some work of supererogation, some virtue or vice not covered by the precepts, and resolve to cultivate or to abstain from that.

We suggest that the best resolution for any Buddhist to make for the new year is the resolution to help propagate more widely the glorious Dharma, to share with others less fortunate than himself the Light of Truth. This was the good resolution made by Aśoka after the Kalinga war when, sickened by the sight of all the innocent blood shed in those disastrous campaigns, he turned in intense anguish of spirit from conquest by force of arms to *dharma-vijaya*, conquest by means of righteousness.[128] How faithfully and how ardently he kept his good resolution, and how pre-eminent a place among the monarchs of the world his idealism gave him, is now one of the commonplaces of history and need not be repeated here. It was the same good resolution that our noble founder, Anagarika Dharmapala, made when still a boy, vowing that he would girdle the globe with the Message of the Master. That, too, is a matter of history. Let every Buddhist who truly loves the teaching therefore resolve that, during the coming year, he will in one way or another disseminate the Doctrine; in traditional Buddhist language, that he will beat the drum, sound the conch-shell, and blow the trumpet of the Good Law, if necessary until his arms ache and his lungs feel as though they were about to burst. Let him strain every nerve, put forth every ounce of strength, for the accomplishment of the Great Work.

But good resolutions, if they are to be carried out, must be precise, not vague. Let the devout and determined Buddhist therefore resolve that during the coming year he will take up some particular work *of real utility* for the propagation of the Dharma. Printing a book or pamphlet, constructing a vihara, subscribing to a Buddhist journal, giving *dāna* to the sangha on certain stated days, attending the temple regularly, sending a *dharmadūta bhikṣu* to non-Buddhist lands, keeping up correspondence with foreign Buddhist friends, especially those in western countries, despatching images and Sacred Relics to places where they are needed, organizing the proper celebration of holy days, arranging lectures on the Dharma … the list is endless. Let the Buddhist maker of good resolutions choose whichever work appeals to him most, let him go to his own private shrine (which every Buddhist home should have), or to the nearest temple; let him light lamp or candle, offer flowers and incense; and with hands reverently folded and with bowed head, let him promise – to himself – in front of the Enlightened One, maker of the greatest good resolution of all, the resolution to attain Enlightenment for the sake of all sentient beings: 'During the coming year I will do this good work for the propagation of the Dharma, that the *śāsana* may shine more gloriously, that the Triple Gem may be revered throughout the world, and for the happiness, profit, and welfare of all living creatures.' Thus should a follower of the Blessed One, his heart full of *mettā* (though he will not advertise the fact), make his good resolutions for the new year.

January 1955

LUMBINI

> There are these four places, Ānanda, which the believing clansman should look upon with emotion. What four?
>
> Saying 'Here was the Tathāgata born,' Ānanda, should the believing clansman look upon the birthplace of the Tathāgata.
>
> Saying, 'Here did the Tathāgata reach supreme Enlightenment,' Ānanda, should the believing clansman look upon the place (of the bodhi tree).
>
> Saying, 'Here did the Tathāgata set rolling the unsurpassed wheel of the Dharma,' Ānanda, should the believing clansman look upon the place.
>
> Saying, 'Here did the Tathāgata pass away with that utter passing away which leaves no remnant for rebirth,' Ānanda, should the believing clansman look upon this place.'[129]

Such are the clear and unmistakable terms in which the Blessed One, shortly before his *mahāparinirvāṇa*, addresses Ānanda, his faithful servitor and personal attendant, on the subject of the four sacred places of Buddhism. For many centuries, especially those immediately succeeding the reign of Emperor Aśoka, the Master's injunction was faithfully obeyed, and the magnificent buildings, some with 'roofs bright with a million tiles of gold'[130] which the munificence of kings and merchant princes raised at all four sites, each with its contingent of permanently resident monks, bore witness to the depth and sincerity of the emotion which stirred the hearts of pilgrims from all parts of the Buddhist world.

Then came the fire and sword of invading vandalism, and darkness descended upon India. When, centuries later, the curtain of history is again raised, the scene that confronts our eyes is a sad one indeed. The sites of the sacred places are almost unknown; their monuments are in ruins; three out of four of them have been overgrown by jungle, and wild beasts crouch among the crumbling stones of the deserted sanctuaries.

The first real step towards the renovation of the four sacred places was taken by Ven. Anagarika Dharmapala. How, in the face of obstacles seemingly insuperable, he succeeded in restoring Bodh Gaya, the place of the Lord's Enlightenment, and Sarnath, where he preached his first sermon, to a semblance at least of their former grandeur, so that pilgrims might once more flock thither from all corners of the earth, is a story too well known to all readers of this journal to be repeated here. Kusinara, where the Lord attained *mahāparinirvāṇa*, was not forgotten either; thanks to the valiant efforts of the Burmese monk, Ven. Chandramani Mahasthavir, who has resided there for half a century, this sacred site too is again an active Buddhist centre.

Lumbini alone of the four sacred places remained in a condition unbefitting its unique spiritual significance and ancient glory. This was due chiefly to the fact that the former Government of Nepal, which was under strong Brahminical influence, conducted itself in an unsympathetic, at times hostile and aggressive manner towards Buddhism, indeed going so far as to prohibit the ordination of *bhikṣus* and the preaching of the Dharma. When the Maha Bodhi Society of India applied for permission to open a centre at Lumbini the request was curtly refused. With the recent inauguration of a democratic form of government in Nepal the situation has, however, changed, and the Buddhists of Nepal are now able to work for the regeneration of their religion not only with the sympathy, but often with the active support, of prominent members of the Government, many of whom see in the teachings of the Buddha the fundamental spiritual basis of their own political ideals. Special tribute should be paid to our sister organization, the Dharmodaya Sabha of Nepal, which since its inception in 1944 has striven by all possible means to disseminate a deeper understanding and more faithful observance of the Doctrine among the fellow countrymen of the Lord Buddha. It was in 1952, when the Maha Bodhi Society of India took the relics of Sāriputta and Moggallāna *arahants* to Nepal, that the Government of Nepal recognized at last the right of the Buddhists to the sacred place.[131] By its recent action in setting up a special Dharmodaya Lumbini Committee, of which His Majesty the King of Nepal is the patron, the present Government of Nepal has not only given clear indication of its own favourable attitude towards Buddhism; it has also recognized the importance of reviving Lumbini as an active Buddhist centre and made official acknowledgement of the valuable services rendered to the religious and cultural uplift of the country by the Dharmodaya Sabha.

Even apart from its importance as the birthplace of the Lord, Lumbini is particularly suited to be the venue of an international Buddhist movement. Situated as it is only three miles from the Indo-Nepalese border, whatever activities are conducted in this place – once the site of splendid religious edifices, but where now, alas! only the shattered Aśoka column, standing solitary amid the debris, proclaims to the world 'Here the Blessed One was born' – will be bound to exercise an influence not only in Nepal but over the whole of northern India too.

That the renovation of Lumbini is becoming a matter of increasing concern to Buddhists of all nationalities and schools is evinced by the following resolution, adopted at the third session of the World Fellowship of Buddhists held in Rangoon last November:

> Resolved that as Lumbini Park, the Birthplace of the Enlightened One, is one of the *samvejanīyaṭṭhānas* (places of deep religious significance to all Buddhists), and as it is now in need of restoration and proper maintenance, and that as there should also be in the hallowed spot an image of the Lord Buddha, a Dharmasala, a monastery and an ordination hall, this Conference urges Buddhists throughout the world to help in the restoration of the Park and in the erection of the necessary buildings.

We strongly support this important resolution, and hope that before many years have passed its modest recommendations will have been not only accepted but carried out. The condition of a religion, whether one of prosperity or decay, can almost be judged by the material condition of the birthplace of its founder. If that spot, in one way the most sacred of all, is neglected by those who profess to revere it, then there is nothing which may not be neglected. Now that so many of the obstacles piled up by interested parties have been removed, the united efforts of the Buddhists of the world, who are numerically the largest religious body in existence, should be able to effect the restoration of Lumbini. If they cannot do even this for the sake of the Dharma, then it is doubtful if they can do anything. But with this great work accomplished, and with a renascent Lumbini as a starting point, who can predict the extent or the magnitude of the work which it may then be possible for us to accomplish.

February 1955

THE INDIVIDUAL EFFORT

As the president of the London Buddhist Society, Mr Christmas Humphreys,[132] reminded his audience at the Society's thirtieth anniversary celebrations a few months ago, 'the race is won by one and one' and never, as Kipling went on to say, by two and two – or, for the matter of that, by any possible numerical combination.[133]

The reminder is timely. Sacrificing the end to the means, like failing to see the wood for the trees, is a very common human error. Preoccupied as we are with associations, committees, resolutions, celebrations, appeals, funds, accounts, and the rest of the organizational impedimenta and paraphernalia, only too easily do we forget that these are not ends in themselves but only means to an end. Not that organizations can always be dispensed with; but their chief value resides, as Mr Humphreys suggested, in 'the stimulus given to individual effort' by collective work on study and meditation.

We would do well to ponder these words. One receives and reads so many Buddhist journals. In each there are detailed reports of so many different Buddhist activities, some of them being conducted on a very large scale and at the cost of large sums of money. Mankind worships quantity; we are easily impressed by size and number. If we read on one page of the 'Notes and News' section of the journal that a certain

Buddhist function was attended by fifty people and on another page that some other function was attended by five hundred people, we at once assume that the second meeting was ten times more successful than the first. A Christian missionary, questioned as to why he had spent forty years preaching the Gospel in India when, in so many nominally Christian lands the majority of people now had very little faith in it, replied that there was more need for missionary work in India than in Canada (his own country) because the number of churches there was so much smaller! We need not smile at his simplicity, for can we deny that we ourselves often think of our own work of propagating the Dharma in exactly the same way? We too sometimes worship quantity; and the worship of quantity is the worship of Mammon.

The question we should ask ourselves at the termination of every Buddhist undertaking, on however grand or however humble a scale it might have been conducted, is simply this: What was the effect upon the hearts and minds of those participating in it? Did it give any of them a deeper comprehension of the Dharma? Was it a means of helping some struggling soul in his progress along the Path to Peace? However large the number of people associated with it, however distinguished the patronage under which it is held, and however widely publicized its aims and objects, if it has not been able to exert a genuinely spiritualizing influence on at least one person, then from the strictly Buddhist point of view it has been a waste of time, energy, and money. Buddhism being concerned primarily with the 'individual', the success or failure of any Buddhist activity is to be judged solely in terms of its moral and spiritual effect on the life and conduct of the individual.

Here in India we are not likely to commit the mistake of thinking our movement for the revival of Buddhism important on account of its mere size. Rather are we liable to fall into the opposite error of assuming that because, with few centres and even fewer trained full-time workers at our disposal, we are able to reach only a fractional percentage of the vast population of the country, our work is therefore comparatively insignificant and unimportant. Today the number of people professing Buddhism in the land of its birth is indeed very small, the number of students possessing anything like an adequate understanding of the Dharma even smaller; but we venture to think that the extent of their cultural and religious influence bears no relation at all to the place – almost the lowest of all – in the table of vital statistics.[134]

More, perhaps, than any other traditional teaching does Buddhism worship quality rather than quantity. As Mr Humphreys did not fail to point out, 'There is in Buddhism no baptism or signing of books, no counting of heads', so that we need not be astonished to learn that nobody knows exactly how many English Buddhists there are. The orthodox Buddhist attitude towards mere number is nowhere more clearly, emphatically, and categorically enunciated than in the *Sahassa Vagga*, or Chapter of the Thousands, of the *Dhammapada*, from which we select the following verses:

> Though a speech consists of a thousand words, if these be lacking in sense, better a single word full of meaning, on hearing which one is at peace.
>
> Though one should in battle conquer a thousand men a thousand times, he who conquers himself has the more glorious victory.
>
> If month after month for a hundred years a man should sacrifice (in charity) a thousand pieces of money, if he should pay honour even for a moment to one well grounded (in true knowledge), better is such honour paid than the sacrifices of a hundred years.
>
> It were better to live one single day in the development of a good life and meditation than to live for a hundred years corrupt and of a wandering mind.
>
> Though one should live for a hundred years taking no note of the origin and cessation of that which is component, better to live one single day regardful of such origin and cessation.
>
> Though one should live for a hundred years without visualizing the Deathless State, it were better to live a single day in the realization of the Deathless State.[135]

Group activities may be all very well in their own way, and very praiseworthy, but our participation in them should never cause us to forget the great truth that in the long run it is the individual effort that really counts.

March 1955

As the Vaiśākha Pūrṇimā – the anniversary of the birth, Enlightenment, and death of the Lord Buddha – again draws near, our thoughts naturally turn not only to the *sambodhi* but to the steps by which the *sambodhi* was attained. We remember not only the Buddha but the bodhisattva; and remembering the bodhisattva we inevitably call to mind the various stages through which he has to pass, and the great transcendental virtues he is required to practise.

These virtues, known as *pāramitās*, are enumerated in different ways by different Buddhist texts. The most popular and widely known version, however, is that in which they are given as *dāna*, *śīla*, *kṣānti*, *vīrya*, *samādhi*, and *prajñā*. Recollection of these six *pāramitās*, meditation upon their significance, and determination to practise them during the coming year, is the best and most suitable way in which the individual Buddhist can prepare himself for the forthcoming Vaiśākha celebrations.

Dāna, or giving, is the first of the six great virtues. It is the most efficacious antidote to greed. Normally we want to cling on to our possessions, our acquirements, our virtues, our own personalities. But *dāna* says, 'Give them all up. Nothing really belongs to you. Death will come along one day and take from you by force that to which you are so deeply attached. Learn to renounce during your life and you will be happy in the hour of death.' *Dāna* is traditionally explained as threefold: first there is the giving of material things; secondly, the giving of education; and thirdly, most important of all, the giving of the Doctrine, Dharma *dāna*. But these by no means exhaust the possibilities of giving. One can sacrifice time and energy no less than money. Another point. *Dāna*, as we tried to point out in these columns a year ago, is something more than mere expenditure; we must not only give but give wisely and skilfully as well. We must give in such a way that the Dharma of the Lord Buddha is really advanced either directly or indirectly; and we must be careful that the act of giving does not enhance the ego-sense of the giver.

Śīla, or morality, is the indispensable foundation of the whole spiritual life. Without it, the cultivation, by means of meditation, of the higher stages of consciousness, and the development of liberating insight, are alike impossible. The strict observance of the five precepts of not taking life, not taking that which is not given, not committing adultery, not telling lies or indulging in other forms of wrong speech, and not partaking of intoxicating liquors, is the ethical minimum required of all Buddhists. Falling below it, we forfeit the right to describe ourselves as followers of the Blessed One.

Kṣānti or patience is much more than forbearance in the face of abuse or ill-treatment. Neither is it merely stoical endurance of suffering. The Buddha declared that even though one was being sawn in two with a two-handled saw by robbers who were highwaymen, if he indulged in even the slightest thought of resentment against his tormentors he was not his disciple.[136] Patience is a form of love. But love in Buddhism is not the feeling of attachment that one has to personalities. It arises out of the perception of the impersonality of existence. The true disciple of the Buddha does not feel resentment against 'others', whatever they may do to him, because he knows that, in the ultimate analysis, 'others' do not exist. Patience means fundamentally the acceptance of the egolessness and impersonality of all phenomena.

The fourth *pāramitā* strikes a more active note. *Vīrya* means energy, Enlightenment is not to be attained without effort. Since Enlightenment takes place in the mind it is primarily in the mind that energy is to be put forth. *Vīrya* is accordingly described as the effort to eradicate arisen unwholesome states of mind, to check the arising of unarisen unwholesome states, to develop unarisen wholesome states, and to maintain arisen wholesome states.[137] By 'wholesome' and 'unwholesome' are meant states of mind which are respectively free and not free from the taint of greed, anger, and ignorance.

Samādhi or meditation is the heart of Buddhism. Alas! it is nowadays much neglected; but without it there can be no real understanding or practice of the Dharma. Essentially it consists of the wholesome one-pointed fixation of the mind on a single object. Not a very difficult thing to do, the reader may think; but the very fact that he thinks it easy shows that he has never seriously tried to practise it. Meditation should be an integral part of the life of every Buddhist. At least a few minutes of each day should be set apart for quiet recollection, for concentration on the chosen object of meditation, and for development of insight. According to Buddhist tradition, for the practice of meditation a teacher is indispensable. For the pitfalls are many, and only one who has himself trodden the path will be able to point out just where they lie and how they may best be avoided.[138]

Sixth and last of the great transcendental virtues is *prajñā*, wisdom. Other religions may, to a certain limited extent, participate in the other five *pāramitās*, but *prajñā* is the glory of Buddhism alone. Fundamentally it consists in the realization of the miserable, transitory, and unsubstantial nature of all phenomena. This realization, when attained in its fullness, is equivalent to Nirvāṇa. It is the *sambodhi* won by the Lord five-and-twenty centuries ago, the winning of which we shall be celebrating in a month's time. As we have already pointed out, the best way in which we can prepare ourselves for this great event is by the practice of the six perfections by which Enlightenment was attained. Let us, as Vaiśākha draws near, resolve that we, too, one day, will attain Enlightenment for the sake of all sentient beings.[139]

April 1955

THE REIGN OF LAW

More emphatically than any other religion does Buddhism teach the universality of law – not, indeed, of law in the materialist-mechanical sense of the term, but in an ethico-spiritual sense as well. The law which governs the universe, in accordance with which the possibility of perfection inherent in man gradually unfolds itself, may be compared not to the law that controls the movements of a clock but rather to that which watches over the development of a flower.

The advent of a Buddha, though from a merely human point of view so miraculously rare an event, nevertheless takes place, like all other events in the universe, strictly in accordance with law. According to the scriptures, there is not merely one Buddha but an infinite number of Buddhas, some belonging to the past, some to the present, and some to the future. The present *kalpa* is known as the *bhadra kalpa*, or Auspicious Aeon, because it is to be blessed with the advent of five Buddhas, four of whom have already appeared, the latest being Gautama Buddha, and one of whom – Maitreya Buddha – is yet to come.

What is the reason for the advent of a Buddha? He makes his appearance at a time when mankind has forgotten the Way to Nirvāṇa, and the whole meaning and purpose of his advent lies in the rediscovery and reproclamation of that Way. It is a grievous mistake, therefore, to treat the Buddha merely as a liberated and Enlightened being, since this would be to overlook his supremely important cosmic function.[140]

The *devas* rejoiced at the birth of the Lord and the whole Buddhist world continues to rejoice on the anniversary of that great event, not simply because one more being destined to Enlightenment had come into the world, but because the Way to Nirvāṇa, after having been lost for centuries, was about to be thrown open once again for the benefit of all mankind, and the *sanātana* Dharma again preached for the welfare and happiness of gods and men.

Since the Buddha is essentially the rediscoverer of the Path, it necessarily follows that the Path could not have been known to any of his contemporaries or immediate predecessors. Hence there can be no grounds for claiming that his teaching was simply a rehash of Upanishadic speculations or of some other theories already current. What the Buddha has handed down to us is the Dharma taught by his predecessors the Buddhas of old, and this Dharma was not known on the earth, as far as the present historical period is concerned, before the advent of Gautama the Buddha. The Dharma is therefore unique.

Unless we have a clear understanding of these ideas we shall miss the whole meaning and purpose of the Vaiśākha celebrations. Essentially we celebrate the rediscovery of the Path, the reappearance on earth of the eternal truth, the Dharma. Of that truth Gautama the Buddha is not only the discoverer but the living embodiment; for he has discovered it by realizing it in his own Enlightened personality. He is thus not only teacher but exemplar; not only the preacher of the truth but the truth itself in human form.

Not that the truth has taken up the abode in a human body, as claimed by certain other traditions, but that a man, by his own human efforts, has attained to the level of truth. That attainment, the various Buddhist scriptures declare as though with one voice, can be ours too, if we will but faithfully follow the Path first trodden by the Lord: that is another thing that we ought to remember on Vaiśākha Day. In the spiritual life nothing depends upon fate or chance, or upon the arbitrary grace of a theistic divinity. Rather does everything depend upon our own efforts, working in accordance with the universal spiritual law. For the law reigns supreme.[141]

May 1955

Conversion, in the sense of an outward and visible sign of an inward and visible change,[142] is an inevitable concomitant of Buddhist revival in India.[143] Several hundred people, during the last few years, have publicly taken refuge in the Buddha, the Dharma, and the Sangha, and it seems that in the decades to come there are to be thousands, perhaps tens of thousands, more. In these circumstances it becomes necessary to raise the question of motive. Buddhism has ever attached more importance to quality than to quantity, and hence, despite its widespread popularity, it has ever been a teaching for the thinking few rather than for the unthinking many. Are those who become 'converted' – we would be glad if this ugly word, with its unpleasantly Christian associations, could have been avoided – to Buddhism actuated by the right motives? Or is there a debasing admixture of ulterior interests? These are questions to which, in the best interests of the Buddhist movement itself, we must now direct our attention.

First of all it is necessary to arrive at a clear understanding of what a Buddhist really is, for only when this preliminary question has been settled will it be possible to determine the precise nature of the proper motives for becoming a Buddhist.

What, then, is a Buddhist? The traditional answer to this question is singularly unambiguous. A Buddhist is one who takes refuge in the Buddha, the Dharma, and the Sangha, and who undertakes to do his best to observe the five precepts of morality. Let us see in a little more detail what exactly is the significance of such a procedure.

To take refuge in the Buddha means privately to accept and publicly to profess him as being so far as the present world-period is concerned the first to attain the transcendental state of Nirvāṇa and the first to proclaim to gods and men the Way leading to its attainment. Taking refuge in the Buddha consequently means taking refuge in him exclusively, without the possibility of resorting to other teachers, much less still of continuing to cherish a belief in the theistic God or in any of his alleged incarnations. Teachers adhering to pre-Buddhist traditions cannot be Enlightened and hence should not be followed.[144] Of those belonging to post-Buddhist traditions it may be said that either they are Enlightened or they are not. If they are Enlightened (though we should not be understood as asserting that Enlightened non-Buddhists do exist) their Enlightenment must be derived either directly or indirectly from

Buddhist sources, and inasmuch as it is better to entrust the vessel of our faith to the mighty river rather than to the insignificant tributary stream it is more to our advantage to take refuge in the Buddha than in those who have in effect themselves taken refuge in him. If the teachers referred to should happen to be unenlightened, as from the orthodox Buddhist point of view they all must be, then of course it is foolish and meaningless to talk of going for refuge to them. While we have every respect for those who in all sincerity regard the founders of other religions, to say nothing of a multitude of minor non-Buddhist religious teachers and prophets, as being no less Enlightened than the Buddha, we are unable to regard them as Buddhists. None take refuge in the Buddha save those who take refuge in him alone.[145]

Similarly, to take refuge in the Dharma, the truth discovered by the Buddha and by him proclaimed to the world, means to accept it as the one and only means of attaining Nirvāṇa. Must a Buddhist, then, reject other teachings? Inasmuch as they contradict the tenets of Buddhism, yes. One who accepts the Dharma taught by the Lord Buddha cannot possibly subscribe to erroneous doctrines such as those which posit a creator God, or an eternal unchanging soul or self, or which maintain the efficacy of certain external acts to procure salvation.[146] As for doctrines which happen to coincide with this or that aspect of the Buddha's teaching, the Buddhist is of course free to accept them. In fact, he regards them as being part of the Dharma itself.

Taking refuge in the Sangha means resorting for spiritual guidance to those who, by virtue of their ordination, training, and personal attainments are qualified to help others along the arduous road to spiritual perfection. It means providing such persons with the necessities of life, so that they may devote themselves to the duties of their vocation untroubled by worldly cares, as well as showing them proper respect. It means not resorting to and not supporting religious teachers whose views are not in harmony with the sublime doctrine of the Buddha. A Buddhist who gives a donation to a Christian mission, for example, or who directly or indirectly supports any of its activities, is no better than a traitor to his religion, and does not deserve the name of a Buddhist. Buddhism has ever been famed for its tolerance, but tolerance does not mean condoning untruth and error, much less still assisting in their dissemination.

We are now in a position to make an answer to the question 'Who is a Buddhist?' He is one who takes refuge in the Buddha, the Dharma, and the Sangha *in the manner described above* and who moreover makes a serious and sincere attempt to observe the five precepts of not injuring living beings, not taking what is not given, abstention from sexual misconduct, from false speech, and from the use of intoxicants.[147]

Becoming a Buddhist, or being converted to Buddhism, means to take the Three Refuges not in some arbitrary sense of one's own but in the orthodox and traditional sense of which an outline has been given. The only right motive for becoming a Buddhist is the conviction that the Buddha alone is the Discoverer and Revealer of the Way to Nirvāṇa, that the Dharma alone is the Means to Enlightenment, and that the members of the sangha alone are the custodians of the Truth.[148]

To believe that the Buddha was primarily a social reformer is not to take refuge in him. Consequently the conviction that Buddhism is a means of obtaining social justice is not an adequate reason for becoming a Buddhist, and the hope that through Buddhism social iniquities and economic inequalities will be removed is certainly not the right motive for conversion to Buddhism. One occasionally meets people who profess to have embraced Buddhism but who, when interrogated, admit that they believe celibacy to be antisocial, meditation a waste of time, and Nirvāṇa a myth. One would think, to hear them, that the Buddha had spent the whole of his life preaching the *Vasala Sutta*.[149]

No doubt the social teaching of Buddhism constitutes an interesting and, on the mundane level, quite important application of the Buddha's ethical principles; but their place is at the circumference, not in the centre, of Buddhism, and the Dharma would not be a whit the less complete and perfect without them.

Glad we are to see in India, the birthplace of Buddhism, a revival of the Dharma, and most heartily do we welcome those who, from the trials and anxieties of life, take refuge in the Blessed One, in his Doctrine and his Order. But we should be failing in our duty towards Buddhism if ever we allowed ourselves to forget that quality is more important than quantity, or if we omitted to emphasize, on every possible occasion, the great truth that however numerous the factors bringing about one's 'conversion' to Buddhism may be, the thought of material profit or mundane advantage should have no place amongst them. One becomes a Buddhist for reasons which pertain ultimately to the transcendental order.

June 1955

The spectacle of one man fighting single-handed against tremendous odds is always an inspiring one. It becomes more inspiring still when he fights not for any personal gain or selfish advantage but for the sake of truth and righteousness. When he fights on behalf of those who are unable to defend themselves he is more than a hero: he is a saint.

When, eight years ago, Dr Frederic Wertham launched, in the United States of America, his campaign against horror comics he thought that he was fighting merely an obnoxious and pernicious form of literature. He was soon driven to realize that he was fighting big business with powerful supporters, vast resources, and capital amounting to tens of millions of dollars – all built up from, and fed by, little boys' and girls' pennies and 'candy money'.

The book in which, a few months ago, the results of his investigations were made public, is aptly entitled *Seduction of the Innocent*.[150] Containing as it does startling and revolting revelations about matters of urgent concern to every moral human being it has attracted widespread attention, and drawn much comment. Here we are concerned only with the ethical, or rather unethical, influence of horror comics, and feel that in this connection we cannot do better than quote the vigorous and authoritative words of the *Times Literary Supplement*. In a front page article entitled 'Marihuana in the Nursery' this paper makes, among others, the following points:

> The term 'horror comics' is not only a misnomer but a euphemism. The worst aspect of their effect is not that they horrify the children but that after a certain number of doses they fail to horrify them any more. The children get used to them; they become hardened and brutalized. A fitting name for these publications might be 'primers in crime' because they teach children how to commit crimes, not in six easy lessons but in hundreds of easy lessons a week. The permanent occupation with crime and violence, from murder, blackmail, rape, and hold-up down to a simple stealing and picking pockets, cannot fail to make its effect on those who are soaked in this kind of reading. Anything that a child occupies himself with for a few hours a day, for year after year, cannot fail to act as a character-forming influence. The endless cavalcade of

> these gangsters, gunmen, and corpses could not but cause grave harm even if crime and criminals were condemned. But they are, in fact, glorified. In all these stories the killer, the man with the whip and the gun, is the glamorous hero and his girls – the 'hellcats' or 'gun-molls' – are the true heroines, while the police are treated with contempt and the victims are 'suckers'. The philosophy radiating from these pages, invading a child's mind and hammered into its brain, is expressed in such 'balloons' as 'I ain't goin' to be ... all my life at a little job. I'm gonna get in the big dough the easy way....' Or 'Since when do we worry about killin' people?' Or even 'It's wrong not to kill. The victim may tell.' Force and violence are romanticized and, to quote Dr Wertham, 'trust, loyalty, confidence, solidarity, sympathy, charity, compassion are ridiculed.'

Passion, however, is taken seriously. To quote again from *The Times:*

> It is enough to glance through half a dozen crime comics to see that, in addition to other reprehensible features, they are thinly disguised pornography. Half-naked women, vamps, alluring blondes – their secondary sex characteristics over-emphasized – populate these pages. The meaning of sex and violence has become identical. The girl is to be won in a fight or by show of violence and she, in turn, reserves her favours for the 'tough guys', the brutes and the killers. Gentleness, consideration, and sympathy have nothing to do with love; the notion of love is lumped together with those of fear, murder, and robbery. Girls are to be used for one single purpose and rape is a frequent method of winning them.

Horror comics moreover encourage racial prejudice:

> Negroes, Jews, Asiatics, and all foreigners are always portrayed as inferior, contemptible, or ridiculous people. Race hatred is fostered and the idea of American superiority encouraged by crude and subtle means.... Lynching is also approved and in one comic book mob justice is extolled in these words: 'The story ... proves that fearless people banded together will always see that justice triumphs.'

Sadism, among other horrors, also finds a place in this type of literature:

> The Nazi concentration camps are recalled with nostalgic longing: 'I like to remember the past!... It was wonderful!' says the young wife of a former S. S. guard. In other pictures, recalling the wonderful past, she exclaims 'Hit him Franz! Make him bleed more! Hit him!' And 'I like to remember the prisoners suffering, the beatings and the blood.' At this point sadism, Fascism, race-hatred, sham-patriotism, and criminality merge on the lowest horror-comics level.... The fact that 98 per cent of American children and adolescents read these comics, and about 75 per cent read nothing else, deserves more than a passing thought.

More than a passing thought indeed, not only in the West but in the East! Partly as a result of Dr Wertham's courageous campaign a bill officially known as the Children and Young People (Harmful Publications) Bill has now become law in Britain. India has followed suit with similar legislation. (In the USA we are told, Dr Wertham's fight is 'far from won', and *ninety million* comic books – apart from the strips – continue to be published *every month*.) But what about the Buddhist countries of Asia? A hundred years ago China struggled against the forcible importation of opium. We are now faced by something more pernicious than opium. Opium poisons the body; but horror comics poison the mind. In his talk with the stage-manager, Talapuṭa, the Buddha has made quite clear the terrible fate that will overtake those who stimulate and exacerbate the lust, hatred, and delusion already existing in the minds of other beings.[151] This episode from the Tipiṭaka has been used as a handle against the production of Buddhist films. We might much more fittingly quote it against those who make money out of the horror comics industry, whether in the capacity of writers, artists, printers, publishers, distributors, or agents. Indifferent and irresponsible parents, who make no attempt to check the menace even in their own homes, are hardly less guilty than those who line their pockets with the proceeds of this wholesale psychological debauching.

Literature is capable of exerting a tremendous influence for good. Hence the publication of literature on the Dharma: editions of canonical texts, translations into modern languages, expositions of Buddhism, etc. as well as periodicals of every kind. Such publications are now sponsored by the governments of several Buddhist lands. But what is the use of seeking to irrigate the field of human life with the pure and pellucid waters of the Dharma while at the same time allowing them to be inundated by the sewage of Christian civilization? No doubt the situation in the Buddhist lands of Asia is by no means so grave as it was in the United Kingdom until recently – certainly a thousand times less grave than it is in the USA itself even now. But even a small dose of poison is sufficient to kill a man, whether physically or morally. If we enforce quarantine in our ports to keep out smallpox and cholera, how much more vigilantly should we guard against the entry of the moral leprosy of the horror comics.

We therefore suggest that in the interests of the moral need and spiritual welfare of their respective nations and of the whole world, the governments of Ceylon, Burma, Siam, Cambodia, Laos, Japan, and Korea be pleased to follow the example of the United Kingdom and India, and make the import or sale of this 'distillation of viciousness', as Dr Wertham calls it, an offence punishable by very heavy penalties. In a Buddhist land there can be no place for this type of literature. The *Jātaka* stories have fascinated hundreds of generations of Buddhist boys and girls. Presented properly, they would fascinate, instruct, and uplift them still.

July 1955

PŪJĀ CA PŪJANĪYĀNAṂ[152]

The recent publication of *The Central Philosophy of Buddhism* by T. R. V. Murti, who succeeded Dr Krishnan as Spalding Professor of Eastern Religions and Ethics at Oxford, is undoubtedly an event of outstanding importance in the world of Buddhist scholarship. Just now, however, we are concerned not with a theoretical evaluation of this work but with an appraisal of one at least of its practical implications.

The central philosophy of Buddhism is, according to Dr Murti – and the evidence he adduces in support of his contention is weighty indeed – the Śūnyavāda or Madhyamakavāda. Of this school, which he regards as being of absolutely pivotal importance in the development of Indian philosophy, the author says that it 'seems to have been perfected at one stroke by the genius of its founder – Nāgārjuna'. Does it not stand to reason, therefore, that next to the Buddha himself Nāgārjuna is the most important figure not only in Buddhist but even in Indian philosophy?

Once this is admitted, the duty of perpetuating and honouring his memory is inevitably incumbent upon all those who have the good of Indian culture in general, and Buddhist culture in particular, at heart. Yet, as we warned our readers as long ago as January 1954, under the proposed scheme for the irrigation of the area, Nagarjunikonda in the newly created Andhra State, where the sage spent many years of his life, is threatened with total submersion, with the consequent irrecoverable loss of priceless archaeological remains.[153]

Despite protests from the Maha Bodhi Society and other religious and cultural organizations the Andhra Government has not yet seen fit to modify its scheme to the extent of making it possible for this sacred site to be preserved intact for posterity. What lover of culture but would protest, and protest with all his might, if the Taj Mahal or the Ajanta caves were threatened with a similar calamity! Yet Nagarjunikonda is of no less value to humanity. Legends tell us that Nāgārjuna retrieved the *Prajñāpāramitā sūtras*, the scriptures of Perfect Wisdom, from the depths of a lake. It would be a pity indeed if we were to put the clock back and allow the treasures of Nagarjunikonda to be sunk fathoms deep beneath the waters of a dam! The Old, it seems, is ever at war with the New, and Value with mere Utility.

But if India is to retain her ancient and honourable position in the comity of nations it can only be by remaining true to her spiritual traditions and by continuing to cherish her cultural heritage.

Fortunately for Nagarjunikonda and similar sites the more cultured members of the community are thoroughly alive to these considerations. Among them is Mr P. R. Ramachandra Rao, a notice of whose stirring appeal to 'Save Nagarjunikonda', made in the course of a lecture on 'Andhra Art' delivered in Arundelpet under the auspices of the United States Reading Room, appeared in our Vaiśākha number.

We have great pleasure in presenting the text of this eloquent appeal as our leading article this month. To his convincing and forceful reasonings we have nothing to add. We can only hope that they will not pass unheeded by those in whose hands rests the responsibility of either saving or destroying a site which deserves preservation not only for its intrinsic aesthetic value but also by reason of its intimate association with one of the profoundest and most influential thinkers the world has ever known.

The Buddha has declared
That Being and non-Being should both be rejected.
Neither as Being nor as non-Being
Nirvāṇa therefore is conceived.[154]

August 1955

UNTIE THE BOAT!

Once upon a time there was a wise man who lived in a small hut not far from the bank of a river. Every morning and every evening he used to go to the river and bathe, after which he would return to his hut and perform his devotions. One day, just as he was about to step down into the water, which was neither very wide nor very deep, he noticed near the opposite bank a man in a boat. Strange to relate, though the man was gripping the oars tightly and rowing vigorously, the boat was making no progress at all, but remained exactly where it was. Seeing that the wise man was looking at him the man in the boat turned his head. His face was red as the proverbial beetroot and streaming with perspiration. 'Hi, you!' he shouted across the river to the wise man, 'There's something wrong with this boat. It won't move.' The wise man smiled. 'Why don't you unfasten the rope that ties it to the shore?' he replied.

This anecdote, which some of our readers might have heard before, illustrates a certain aspect of spiritual life which most of us are unwilling to consider. We sincerely do want to make progress. We strive hard to follow the Noble Eightfold Path. We read books on Dharma, go on pilgrimage, give donations, feed *bhikkhus*, build temples, practise meditation, even write articles and give lectures on Buddhism, but somehow, despite all our efforts, we make no progress at all. We just stay where we were. It is a very puzzling experience. Sometimes we feel rather aggrieved, as though the universe was playing tricks upon us, or as though the law of karma, after smoothly operating for so many centuries, had at last gone out of order and was no longer working properly. Then one day, after we have blamed the books we have read, blamed our spiritual teacher, blamed our environment, blamed the climate, perhaps even blamed Buddhism, we have a humiliating but wholly salutary experience. Someone seems to be smiling at us, and we hear a voice saying – perhaps in the secret recesses of our own heart, perhaps through the mouth of a friend – 'But why don't you untie the rope? Why don't you give up drinking? Or smoking? Or debauchery? Or your bad temper? These are the things that are holding you back.'

As with individual men and women, so with societies and states. Nations commit exactly the same mistakes as the people of whom they are made up, only they commit them on an infinitely larger scale. What is war but mass murder? How does peace between nations differ, except in extent, from the good will that exists between neighbours? An international conference, even at the topmost level, is based on the same principle as the chat over the back garden fence by means of which neighbours settle their differences instead of assaulting each other outside in the street. Similarly, the attempt made by an individual to follow the Noble Eightfold Path, and the efforts made by any state, whether Buddhist or non-Buddhist, to revive, consolidate, or propagate the Dharma, are in a very real sense analogous, and just as the individual may fail to make the progress he desires because he neglects to remove some very real hindrances to progress, so the state too may be unsuccessful, or only partially successful, in its work for Buddhism, because certain important factors in the national life are exerting their influence in the opposite direction.

The Path to Enlightenment is divided, as is well known, into three successive stages – *śīla* or morality, *samādhi* or meditation, and *prajñā* or transcendental wisdom. Leaving aside the second and third, which are comparatively advanced, let us take up morality, the first stage of the path, and see how certain factors in the national life of many Buddhist lands are hindering its universal practice. Unless these hindrances are removed the protection and propagation of Buddhism on a national scale becomes not only futile but even a mockery.

In our July editorial we spoke of the menace of the so-called horror comics, of their thoroughly corrupting influence on the minds of the millions who read them, and pleaded for their complete banishment from the soil of Buddhist Asia. But what about the menace of film, especially the normal(?) Hollywood product? The film is today probably the most powerful medium of mass propaganda in the world. Potentially it is a power for incalculable good. In reality it is a source of untold moral evil. Once a month, or two or three times a year, the young men and young women of India, Ceylon, Burma, Siam, and other Eastern lands may go to a temple or monastery, and listen half attentively as they are told not to kill, steal, commit adultery, tell lies, or drink intoxicants. The sermon usually makes very little impression upon them. Truth to tell, it is usually a long-winded droning out of dull and feeble platitudes. But at least once a week, perhaps twice or thrice a week, those same young people visit the local cinema. Instead of sitting on hard ground they recline in luxuriously cushioned seats. And what lesson does the cinema usually teach them? That to kill is manly and heroic; that to steal is the lawful prerogative of a handsome face and a superior intelligence; that sex is the most important thing in life, and the performance of the sexual act, whether inside or outside of marriage, the chief occupation and principal pleasure of man; that to tell lies is one of the normal ways of getting what one wants, and foul language a sign of superior culture; and that, finally, to drink intoxicants and smoke cigarettes is an integral part of the daily round. The lesson of the average contemporary film may be summed up in the phrases 'Have a good time,' and 'Enjoy yourself.' The lesson makes a very deep impression indeed. What with the warmth and darkness of the cinema, the lush music, and the panorama of seductive sights unfolded on the screen, the young people are thrilled, excited, stimulated.[155] Then we wonder why they are not good Buddhists, why they are not interested in Buddhism. And what does the state do? Does it ever think of stopping the profanity? No, it draws good dividends in the form of entertainment tax, and plans to publish a few little pamphlets on Buddhism, especially the five precepts!

Then there is the sale of liquor. More than one Indian province, and more than one Buddhist state, still derives a handsome revenue from this polluted source. Yet the teachings of Mahatma Gandhi, the Father of the Nation, and of the Buddha, are militant against this evil. Those who accept the Vedas can, of course, plead the example of the holy rishis as their excuse, but for those who accept the Tripiṭaka there exists no such loophole.

A Ministry of Health (Govt. of India) news item says the ban on the export of monkeys has been lifted as transport conditions have now improved. Under this apparently quite innocent piece of information lies concealed the hideous and revolting fact that the Indian monkeys are being transported not to zoos, not as pets, but to the laboratories of scientific institutions *for the purposes of vivisection*. We do not know what were the thoughts of the Health Ministry official concerned when he (or she) scribbled the signature that lifted the ban and condemned thousands of monkeys to a protracted and agonizing death. We feel sure that he (or she) had forgotten the noble words of Mahatma Gandhi, who said, 'Vivisection, in my opinion, is the blackest of all black crimes that man is at present committing.... We should be able to refuse to live, if the price of living be the torture of sentient beings.'[156] Fortunately for the descendants of Hanuman, they have found a champion in Sri C. Rajagopalachari, formerly Governor-General of India, who has published in a recent issue of the *Harijan* a pathetic and deeply moving poem on the monkeys' plight.[157] It is in fact one of the noblest cries of compassion that have ever come from the human heart, and shows that the writer is not only a deeply religious but even a saintly man.

Illustrations of our thesis could be multiplied indefinitely but these three must suffice. Of what use is it for any government to seek to propagate even the ABC of Buddhism when it is at the same time allowing the films, drink, cruelty to animals, and a hundred other factors, to exert therein incalculably more powerful influence in the opposite direction? Surely there would appear a smile on the face of Enlightenment to behold their efforts if only a voice would call out to them, 'Untie the boat!'

October 1955

IN THE NAME OF HUMANITY

In the October issue of the journal we referred in these pages to the Health Ministry's act in lifting the ban on the export of Indian monkeys to foreign countries for purposes of vivisection. Further information bearing on this painful topic has now been received from a humanitarian organization in Cologne, Germany, one of the places to which the unfortunate monkeys are being despatched.

This first-hand information makes it perfectly clear that the monkeys which the Ministry of Health allows to be exported from India are principally destined not for zoological gardens, but for the laboratory of the vivisectionist. Rhesus monkeys are in fact being exported in preference to other species because of their greater suitability as subjects of these cruel experiments: they can endure scientifically planned torture for a much longer period.

Attached to the copy of the letter which our friends in Germany have addressed to the authorities for the Prevention of Cruelty to Animals,

New Delhi, is an illustrated pamphlet in the German language in which the enormities now being perpetrated in the name of scientific research are exposed in all their hideousness. No one can look at these photographs of living monkeys, rabbits, and bats skewered on more than half a dozen foot-long needles without being smitten to the very heart. Revolting as these pictures are, we must confess that in the pages of other antivivisectionist publications we have seen even worse. Surely there is no hope for the spiritual progress of humanity, or for peace on Earth, so long as members of the human race are capable of inflicting sufferings so dreadful.

'Inaction in a deed of mercy', says *The Voice of the Silence*, 'becomes an action in a deadly sin.'[158] We appeal to the religious and humanitarian organizations of India, and of the Buddhist world, to use every means at their disposal of having the ban on the export of monkeys from this country reimposed. In the name of humanity let it not be said, to the everlasting shame of India, that in the days of Aśoka she sent out preachers of the message of *ahiṃsā*, but that in the middle of the twentieth century she exported helpless rhesus monkeys to the tables of the vivisectionist.

December 1955

1956

THE COMING YEAR

The year upon which, with the commencement of the sixty-fourth volume of the *Maha Bodhi*, we now enter, is without a doubt the most important and significant for Buddhism not only in the career of this journal but even in the history of modern times. On 24 May we shall be celebrating what is, according to the current chronology of the Southern Buddhist lands, the two-thousand-five-hundredth anniversary of the *mahāparinirvāṇa* of the Blessed One. The occasion is significant and important not for historical reasons merely. According to a widespread tradition, with the coming Vaiśākha Pūrṇimā the Buddhist *śāsana*, like a great banyan tree that has been decaying for centuries, will put forth fresh green shoots and flourish more vigorously than ever. An ancient Sinhalese poem represents Sumana, the deity of Sripada, the Mount of the Holy Footprint, as declaring that five-and-twenty centuries after the passing away of the Enlightened One, a king would arise in Lanka who would spread the Dharma over the whole earth.[159] The kings of Lanka are no more, but there is little doubt that not only the present government and people of Ceylon, but the governments and the people of all Buddhist lands, together with Buddhists and friends of Buddhism everywhere, will unite in making a supreme effort for the widest possible dissemination of the Dharma.

The magnitude of the preparations that are already being made in honour of the great anniversary, both here in India, the birthplace of

Buddhism, and in the sister lands of Asia, are themselves evidence of the revival which, to all appearances, we may with confidence expect. Coming events are casting not their shadows but their sunlight before. Other indications have not been wanting. During the last year, for example, the Western world has exhibited an unprecedented interest in Buddhism. Last May the American magazine *Life* devoted a whole issue to Buddhism and sold fifteen million copies. The first edition of E. A. Burtt's *The Teaching of the Compassionate Buddha*, a Mentor pocket book published only a few months ago, was exhausted within two weeks; a new edition was rushed through the press, and hundreds of thousands of copies have been sold.[160] Obviously Buddhism is capable of meeting a very definite need, satisfying a spiritual hunger, not only in the East but in the West. Creeds based on blind faith in dogma and unquestioning submission to authority are either crumbling to pieces beneath the hammer blows of modern knowledge or petrifying into immobility and death. Buddhism, with its message of Enlightenment through balanced ethical living free from all one-sidedness, progressive mental training and meditation, and a compassionate understanding of existence as a whole, comes like a sudden path of vivid sunlit blue, appearing between a cloud-rift on a stormy day. Buddhism, with its blameless and stainless record, shows, as do not other teachings, the way leading from private trial and public turmoil to perfect peace of mind.[161] We will not say that Buddhism is the religion of the future; for not only is it much more than a religion, it is the Eternal Truth and Way, stripped of all accretions and disguises, practicable and reliable, at all times and in all climes, by all sorts and conditions of men.

Obviously, the Vaiśākha Pūrṇimā of 1956 will present the whole Buddhist world with a unique opportunity. It will also present us with a challenge. For opportunities, besides revealing our strength, also exhibit our weakness. The great weakness of the Buddhist world today is lack of unity. By unity we do not, of course, mean mere external uniformity, much less still simply a keeping up of friendly social relations. We mean by unity an effective recognition of the fact that despite differences of presentation and interpretation, both *yānas*[162] and all schools of Buddhism accept, teach, and follow that threefold path of morality, meditation, and wisdom, leading to Enlightenment, wherein consists the very essence of the Dharma of the Lord Buddha. The nearer we approach to actual practice of the essentials of the teaching the nearer we shall approach to each other. That 'unity is strength' is nonetheless true for being a truism. The nearer we approach to each other the more effectively shall we be able to take advantage of the opportunity, to meet the challenge that the coming anniversary represents. Only a united Buddhism will be able to fulfil the old prophecy that from this year the Dharma will begin to overspread the whole earth. Only a united Buddhism will be able to contribute to the building of a united world.[163]

January 1956

THE INNER PREPARATION

All truly spiritual movements proceed not from without within but from within without. The most striking illustration of this principle is to be found in Buddhism itself. As it exists today, the religion of the Śākyamuni is in numerical strength, area of distribution, and length of life – as well as in the richness of its contribution to the spiritual and cultural heritage of humanity – unsurpassed by any other tradition. Yet whence did this incomparably fertile and influential movement originate? What was its matrix? Five-and-twenty centuries ago a man sat under a peepul tree in the forests of north-eastern India and *meditated*. That was the origin of Buddhism. No organization; no propaganda; no making of speeches. Just a solitary figure sitting there all night under the wide-spreading branches, beneath the star-sprinkled canopy of the sky, and going deeper and deeper into the inmost reaches of his being until the Veil was suddenly rent and he saw for himself that imperishable Truth which stands unmoved behind the flux of phenomena and the perpetual round of births and deaths.

It is said that the branches of a tree are no higher than its roots are deep. Buddhism was able to spread so wide outwardly only because the sources of its inspiration lay so deep within. This fact carries with it an important lesson for us today. As our regular readers know, not only here in India, but all over the Buddhist world, and in some parts of the non-Buddhist world too, preparations for the forthcoming 2500th anniversary of the Lord Buddha's *mahāparinirvāṇa* have for some time been going on. As far as we are at present able to judge, the celebrations that will begin on the Vaiśākha Pūrṇimā will be the grandest with which the name of Buddhism has ever been associated.

But there is one question that all who are in any way connected with these epoch-making events have to ask themselves. What is the inner basis of these manifestations of zeal for the Buddhist cause? Is it a love of pomp and circumstance, of the parade and pageantry of religion? Is it merely faith? Or is it, again, merely an opportunistic taking advantage of a particular conjunction of circumstances of the historical order?

The tree of Buddhist revival can shoot high only if its roots are planted deep in the soil of our hearts. The modern Buddhist movement must be based not on faith, not on unreflecting enthusiasm, much less still on meaner motives, but on actual realization of the import of the Dharma.

To such a realization there is only one way: meditation. The Buddhist texts are unanimous that the truth can be discerned only by the mind which has been thoroughly purified by the systematic practice of meditation. Not to the intellect, not to the emotions, but only to the mind which is at equilibrium in *samādhi* do there arise these flashes of insight which destroy all wrong views, such as belief in a creator God and the reality of the ego-soul or *ātman*, and which eventually culminate in the attainment of that Āryan knowledge which constitutes the Path to Supreme Enlightenment.

Hence we urge upon all our readers the necessity of making during the coming months a special effort not only to study and propagate the Doctrine but to realize it through meditation. All Buddhist countries possess numerous centres where instruction in meditation is imparted by qualified guides. Both monks and laymen should take the fullest possible advantage of such facilities. Having obtained the precious boon of a human body, one should not fritter away its strength in idle enjoyment, but concentrate all energies on the attainment of the Goal. On an occasion so auspicious as the one we shall be celebrating shortly, we should make every effort to raise our consciousness to the highest possible level. For only if it proceeds from within without will the modern movement of Buddhist revival be truly successful. Without underrating the part played by external organization, it may be said without fear of contradiction that it is the inner preparation which is the more important. To that inner preparation, therefore, let us devote ourselves during the coming months, so that the coming Vaiśākha Pūrṇimā will be an anniversary not merely in the history of Buddhism but in our own spiritual life.[164]

February 1956

There is a story in the Tripiṭaka to the effect that a disciple of the Buddha, who before his conversion to Buddhism had been a Brahmin, one day approached the Blessed One with the request that he be pleased to allow his teaching to be rendered into Sanskrit verses. The Buddha's reply was emphatic and unambiguous. Addressing the assembled brethren, he declared: 'I permit, O monks, everyone to learn the Dhamma in his own language (*sakāya niruttiyā*)'.[165] To us at the present day these words may seem quite unremarkable. But when they were first uttered their import was revolutionary. That Sanskrit, the *deva-bhāṣā*, or language of the gods, should be dethroned and each and every local dialect allowed to take its place, was to the fossilized Brahmin mentality of the day an unthinkable sacrilege. Even now there are not wanting, in the citadels of brahminical orthodoxy, those who in all seriousness maintain that the gods actually do speak in Sanskrit and in no other tongue.

One of the results of the Buddha's unexampled freedom from religio-linguistic prejudice is that Buddhism can boast of a larger canonical literature in more languages than any other tradition. While Hinduism, Zoroastrianism, Judaism, Confucianism, Taoism, Christianity, and Islam is each based on a single book, or small collection of books, the scriptures of Buddhism constitute whole libraries. The Royal Siamese Edition of the Pāli Tipiṭaka comprises forty-five volumes; the Tibetan Kangyur and Tengyur number three hundred and thirty-seven huge tomes printed from wood blocks; the Chinese Tripiṭaka comprises more than sixteen hundred works which, in the standard edition, fill one hundred volumes of a thousand double-columned pages each. Then there is the Mongolian version of the Tibetan canon and a Japanese translation of the Chinese canon, both of which enjoy canonical authority in their own countries, as well as a mass of independent *sūtras* and *śāstras* which have survived in the original Sanskrit. It is therefore hardly surprising that we find Buddhism on the whole quite free from the bibliolatry which is so common a feature of almost all other religions. In truly orthodox Buddhism the Dharma is never confounded with its verbal expressions.

We have adverted to the Buddha's insistence that everyone should be permitted to learn the Dharma in his own language because it has a special significance for us in these days. During the current year, in which we celebrate the 2500th anniversary of the Lord Buddha's *mahāparinirvāṇa*, a number of organizations and institutions in various Buddhist lands will be making efforts for the wider dissemination of Buddhism in India, the original home of the Dharma. In the absence of trained personnel, whether members of the sangha or laymen, these efforts will, for the present, necessarily be largely confined to the distribution of Buddhist literature, either free or nominally priced.

So far, whatever literature has reached us here in India has been in English. For this there is still a great, indeed growing, demand. But if we are to reach the Indian masses, millions of whom are now for the first time in centuries becoming conscious that in Buddhism is a force that can elevate and enrich their lives as can no other teaching, and if we are to be true to the Buddha's own injunction, it is imperative that the whole of India be literally flooded with simple and attractively written books, pamphlets, and leaflets in Hindi, Bengali, Nepali, Marathi, Gujerati, Punjabi, Tamil, Telegu, Malayalam, and Kannada. The gift of the Dharma, as we need hardly remind our readers, excels all other gifts. But it must be made in a way which will really go home to the business and bosoms of those for whom that supreme gift is intended.[166] What better way of reaching a man's heart, what more admirable way of teaching him the mighty truths of Buddhism, than through the medium of his own mother tongue, with which are interwoven so many of his tenderest associations, his noblest hopes, his sublimest aspirations?

We therefore appeal to our friends in every corner of the Buddhist world to inaugurate, as part of their Jayanti programme, a movement to have as much Buddhist literature translated into as many Indian languages as possible. In India itself steps have already been taken in this direction, and some of the most important portions of the scriptures have been in print in Hindi, Bengali, and other languages for the past several years. But to produce in the fourteen major languages of India enough Buddhist literature to reach its 340,000,000 inhabitants is obviously far beyond the capacity of any single institution of any single country. Christians boast that the Bible is available in more than a thousand languages and dialects; usually it is distributed free. It should be a matter of shame to the entire Buddhist world that not even a small but justly celebrated text like the *Dhammapada* can be read in all the languages of India.

We suggest that every Buddhist country should finance Buddhist publications in as many Indian languages as possible. Ceylon, for instance, could easily undertake the publication of Buddhist texts in Tamil. Burma could be responsible for the production of Hindi Buddhist literature. And so on. In those countries where facilities for printing books in the Indian languages do not exist funds could be raised for the purpose and sent to India. Eventually it should be possible for organizations like the Union of Burma Buddha Sāsana Council, the Buddhist Council of Ceylon, the World Fellowship of Buddhists, and the Buddhist Association of Thailand to maintain their own publishing houses in India. Only when, in this way, streams of Buddhist literature inundate the thirsty soil of India will we have fulfilled the Buddha's exhortation not only to preach the Dharma but to preach it to every man in his own language.[167]

March 1956

BUDDHA JAYANTI AMONG THE BIRDS

In his Preface to the delightful book from which this month's excerpt from the scriptures has been taken,[168] J. Bacot observes:

> In Europe a wide gulf separates man from even the most advanced species of animals, and a poem about Buddhism among birds may well strike him as nothing more than a literary fantasy. In India, however, this gulf was never more than a very shallow depression which could apparently be crossed with little effort. Even today, in India, one can see animals, both domesticated and wild, living together with mankind in conditions of familiarity which the westerner finds unusual and at times even touching. The Buddhist concept of universality is not confined to man alone. It is a total universality which extends to all living creatures both above and below him, and it is this totality which is of the very essence of the doctrine.

This being so indisputably the Buddhist position, it is all the more a matter for astonishment that, as far as we know, arrangements for enabling our furred and feathered friends to participate in the forthcoming Buddha Jayanti are conspicuously absent from the various published programmes. Here in India, cows and other animals are, on certain festive occasions, garlanded with flowers and sumptuously fed

– a beautiful custom which exemplifies the universal brotherhood of all forms of life, both high and low. Why should not similar observances be associated with the sacred anniversary which we are about to celebrate? Buddhists are fond of advertising the fact that Buddhist *maitrī*, unlike Christian love, extends not only to members of the human race but to the animal creation as well. Why not demonstrate this in practice? Chinese Buddhists, we understand, often show special kindness to animals on important festival days, releasing, for example, captive birds and turtles. The ransomed turtles are often to be seen lying in the courtyards of Chinese temples, auspicious characters painted in red on their backs, patiently waiting to be set at liberty in the water. This is of course not the only way of showing kindness to animals. There are many other ways. We suggest here a few only, leaving the reader to discover others for himself.

One of the best ways of showing our *maitrī* towards animals is by not eating them. Though some Buddhists appear oblivious to the fact, it is hardly possible to eat animals without their first having been killed: beef and pork do not, unfortunately, grow on trees. We therefore suggest that a measure of vegetarianism would go a long way towards showing our *maitrī* for birds and beasts and also towards enabling them to participate in the Jayanti celebrations. Of course we know that in some Buddhist lands great hardship would be experienced in abstaining from meat for any length of time, and for this reason we have advocated only 'a measure' of vegetarianism. Slaughterhouses should at least be closed for the week in which the Vaiśākha Pūrṇimā Day falls, if not for a longer period – suitable compensation for loss of business being given to the butchers.

Buddhist pilgrims to India in particular would be well advised to abstain from fish and meat during the period of their pilgrimage. Whether rightly or wrongly, the average Indian is deeply shocked at the spectacle of Buddhists, especially monks, who even while on pilgrimage are unable to control their palate to the extent of forgoing even temporarily this particular article of diet. When the Sacred Relics of Sāriputta and Moggallāna *arahants* were enshrined at Sanchi in 1952[169] not only was the slaughter of animals for food strictly prohibited, but all the Muslim officers of the Bhopal State who participated in the function became vegetarian for the occasion out of respect for the Relics. Imagine, therefore, their astonishment, when the monks from a certain

Buddhist country, dissatisfied with the vegetarian fare provided, pulled out from beneath their robes large bottles of highly odiferous dried fish which they were carrying with them on their pilgrimage. True it is that, under certain stringent conditions the Lord Buddha has allowed even monks to partake of meat;[170] but he certainly would not have approved of wearers of the yellow robe being so inordinately fond of and chronically attached to flesh diet as to take the trouble of bringing it with them from their own country, thousands of miles away, so as to avoid having to go without their favourite dish even for a single day!

Should we wish to show our *maitrī* for birds and animals more positively than by a little occasional vegetarianism, then we could not do better than follow the Indian custom and feed them liberally. Not only our own pets and domestic animals but also the waifs and strays of the streets should share our bounty. To feed pigeons and other birds, as the Jains do in Bombay, or as even Christian Londoners do in Trafalgar Square, would be a delightful way of practising *maitrī* towards all living beings. Those fortunate enough to possess the necessary resources might ransom cows and other animals from the slaughterhouse and make arrangements for them to spend the remainder of their days in comfort free from the threat of violent, frequently painful death. Others might found animal hospitals, or homes for aged birds and beasts, in memory of the great occasion.

If the Buddha's Law could be preached among the birds, why should not Buddha Jayanti be celebrated not only among the birds but the animals too?

April 1956

RING IN THE NEW

Rabindranath Tagore, in a well-known poem, has given felicitous expression to the striking idea that certain prominent aspects of life, which generally seem in our eyes contradictory and therefore mutually exclusive, are in reality complementary, being as it were the obverse and reverse of a single coin. Most of our troubles, and nearly all our sorrows, are caused by the fact that we insist upon seeing one aspect of life only, usually that which immediately confronts us. Take, for example, one of the commonest facts of life, that of death. In reality birth and death are inseparable, the one following the other in uninterrupted succession. But we see only death, forgetting birth, and seeing only death we grieve.

According to the poet if we could see, too, the birth in which death will inevitably result – if we could see the other side of the coin – death would be a cause not for sorrow but for rejoicing.[171]

The moral is obvious. Every event, whatever its scope, duration, and dimension can be regarded from two points of view simultaneously. It can be regarded either as the end of an old or as the beginning of a new mode of existence.

This principle is particularly applicable to historical movements, in whose pages the lesson, since it is 'writ large', may be easily read. The Reformation in Europe, for instance, may be regarded as representing either the end of the Middle Ages or the beginning of the Modern Period, in other words either as a death or as a birth. To the Catholic historian it is the former, and therefore the cause of regret; to his Protestant counterpart the latter, and thus an occasion for congratulation. To the average Englishman – to take an example from more recent times – the year 1947 marks the end of British rule in India; to the Indian it means the beginning of a new era of independence. Thus, both of these great historic milestones – the Reformation and Indian independence – can be appraised from two points of view which, while apparently contradictory, are in reality complementary. No historical judgement can be considered complete which does not somehow include both. Here, as elsewhere, 'the truth is the whole'.[172]

So is it in the case of the 2500th anniversary of the *mahāparinirvāṇa* of the Lord Buddha, which we celebrate this month. We can regard it either as marking the end of a cycle of two and a half millenniums of spiritual achievement, cultural efflorescence, and geographical expansion, or as inaugurating a new cycle of one knows not how many thousands of years. The kind of emotions the occasion excites in us will be largely determined by which of these two viewpoints we adopt. If the former, our attitude will be retrospective, our mood reminiscent, with perhaps more than a touch of nostalgia for the vanished glories of long ago. If the latter, it will be prospective, reaching forward into the future, with an air of eagerness and expectation as of those who await the rising of the sun amid the setting stars.

It is perhaps inevitable that most of the contributions in this issue of the journal reflect the first rather than the second attitude: they deal more with the past of Buddhism than with its future. But the second is nevertheless no less valid than the first, and, in respect of its influence upon the Buddhist movement today, even healthier. We cannot always be brooding over the past – though with a history so long and glorious behind them it is hardly to be wondered at that followers of the Blessed One should yield sometimes to such a temptation. If we reflect on the past it should be chiefly with the intention of deriving inspiration for the future. Aśoka extended the frontiers of Buddhism: he did not fix them for all time to come. Hence the present anniversary does not mean that the Buddhist world with twenty-five centuries of achievement behind it, is now justified in resting still more comfortably upon its laurels. Rather does it mean that, enriched by twenty-five centuries of experience, it can now prepare itself for a concerted effort to make the limits of the Dharma coterminous only with the limits of the globe itself. For now, more than ever, does the world need the message of the Buddha, and in spreading that unique message of wisdom and compassion the followers of the Enlightened One will be performing their duty not only to the Dharma itself but to humanity. Let us, therefore, on this unprecedentedly solemn and auspicious occasion, vow to make so great an effort for the worldwide dissemination of the Dharma that when, after two and a half millenniums, we celebrate the five thousandth anniversary of the *mahāparinirvāṇa*, we shall do so in a world united by a common allegiance of the Buddha, the Dharma, and the Sangha.[173]

May 1956

THE FIFTH PRECEPT

In Tibet there is a well-known story to the effect that a monk who had offended a certain demon was compelled to atone for his fault by breaking any one of the five precepts. Thinking that the fifth precept, that of abstaining from intoxicants, was the least important, the unfortunate man agreed to drink several pots of wine. As a result, he became completely intoxicated, and while in this condition broke all the remaining precepts. Whether the story be true or not hardly matters: what matters is that it draws attention to the extreme importance of observing the fifth precept. The first step, the ABC, of Buddhism, is, as we all know, *śīla* or morality, and as our story illustrates the whole of our moral life, and perhaps the moral life of others too, can be completely wrecked by failure to abstain from intoxicants. It would hardly be going too far to say that a man who indulges in alcohol, certainly one who indulges regularly, has very little right to the sacred name of Buddhist. Similarly, a society which instead of condemning the drink habit tolerates it as a harmless manifestation of good fellowship, or a state which instead of prohibiting trade in drink encourages it as a source of revenue, are not truly Buddhist either. One cannot have one's cake and eat it too. One cannot spend one evening at the tavern and the next in the temple – at least not in the Buddhist temple – without grave moral inconsistency, not to say hypocrisy. Much less can one pose as a writer or speaker on Buddhism, or as a Buddhist representative or leader, when one's enthusiasm for the sacred cause is stimulated not by study and meditation but by the bottle.

More than once in the course of the last few months have we tried to remind the readers of these columns that the best way of celebrating the 2500th Buddha Jayanti is by actual practice of the teaching. That practice must begin with morality; and without abstention from intoxicants morality itself, as our story illustrates, rests on insecure foundations. It is a matter for sincere regret that in more than one ostensibly Buddhist land abstention from alcohol is not considered incumbent on a follower of the Dharma. We therefore suggest that in all those parts of the Buddhist world which have fallen under the influence of this evil habit a strong effort should be made, as the first step towards the better practice of the Dharma and the true celebration of the Buddha Jayanti year, to eradicate it once and for all. In this connection we cannot but commend the fine action of the present Government of Ceylon, which, as soon as it assumed office, banished intoxicants from all official functions.[174] May the whole Buddhist world be not behindhand in following this noble example.

June 1956

BUDDHA JAYANTI AND THE SECULAR STATE

In several places in the scriptures we are told that the Wheel of Dharma set rolling by the Buddha can be turned back neither by *śramaṇa* nor *brāhmaṇa*, nor yet by Māra together with Brahmā.[175] Whether the last two personages have ever seriously attempted to obstruct the progress of the Wheel of Dharma we have no intelligence; but *śramaṇas* and *brāhmaṇas* alike, both in ancient and in modern India, have at times made every effort to do so. Dialectical criticism, persecution, social ostracism, and a particularly subtle policy of destruction by assimilation, have in various historical periods all been resorted to. At present the small group of diehards who continue to cherish their traditional bitter hostility towards Buddhism on the whole favour indirect rather than direct methods of attack. Their latest cry is that by spending public money on the celebration of Buddha Jayanti the Government of India has violated that article of the constitution which makes provision for a secular state. The whole question really revolves about what we mean by the term 'secular'. This problem has been discussed in an exchange of correspondence between the vice-president of India, Dr S. Radhakrishnan, and a person known as Srimad Acharya Swami Neminath Maharaj. Ignoring Dr Naga Raja Sharma's hysterical outburst – inspired, it seems, by hatred of Buddhism and antipathy towards Dr Radhakrishnan of the most virulent type – in his foreword to this publication,[176] and leaving aside the question of the mutual relations between Buddhist and Hindu thought, we shall confine ourselves to elucidating the meaning that Dr Radhakrishnan and his colleagues in the Government of India attach to the word 'secular'.

Among the literal meanings of the term given by *Chamber's Twentieth Century Dictionary* the one which most concerns us here is 'pertaining to the present world, or to things not spiritual'. But since things sacred cannot be rigidly separated from things profane, least of all in a land like India, the question that therefore arises is that, granting that the peculiar concern of the state is with the present world, what attitude is it to take up towards the things of the spirit? Besides open hostility, which is out of the question, there are two attitudes only which it is possible for the state to adopt with reference to the various religions and religious organizations of the country: it can be either equally indifferent to or equally appreciative of all of them. People like Acharya Neminath are so horrified by the prospect of the Buddha Jayanti being celebrated under government auspices (in an unguarded moment he admits that to hear national leaders praising Buddhism as the best of religions causes him 'heart-burnings') that he is willing to insist on the negative definition of the word 'secular', thus depriving Hinduism too of all government support, rather than allow a particle of patronage to reach the hated Buddhists. 'Let the Government', he declares, 'solidly stand on the pedestal of a secular state and keep themselves absolutely away from all religious functions'.[177] This is cutting off one's own nose to spite somebody else's face with a vengeance!

Dr Radhakrishnan, however, having no such prejudice against Buddhism, not unnaturally adopts the more reasonable alternative. 'When we call ourselves a secular State', he writes in a vain attempt to make the Swami see reason, 'we do not mean by it that we are worshippers of comfort, security and worldly goods. We mean by it respect and appreciation of all faiths which have found a home in this country'.[178] Even the most orthodox Hindu cannot avoid paying lip tribute to the ideals of religious toleration and universalism, and Swami Neminath is therefore constrained to remark 'Buddhism is *one of the religions* and rather in my view, a Branch of Hinduism, and as such needs praise to the extent it deserves',[179] and further, 'I am not in the least against Buddhism or Buddha and we even claim him as an avatar of Vishnu (on pp. f, k and l he strenuously *denies* that the Buddha is an avatar of Vishnu!!), and as such we hold him in respect as a good son of this land'.

'To the extent that it deserves' – in these words, perhaps, lies the key to the whole difficulty. To Dr Radhakrishnan and his colleagues the Buddha is the greatest of the sons of India and Buddhism the central and most significant fact in the whole long history of Indian thought and culture. That Śaṅkara, Rāmānuja, and Madhvācārya 'criticized' Buddhism[180] – a point on which the Swami lays great emphasis, though he also declares that in the Buddha's preachings 'there is nothing new or novel except what is found common to all other religions' – is rightly dismissed by Dr Radhakrishnan as 'neither here nor there': every scholar knows that in order to criticize Buddhism Śaṅkara first grossly misrepresented it. In the eyes of Swami Neminath and others of his ilk Buddhism is so dangerous that its importance is to be minimized at all costs. Hence all the bitterness and self-confessed heart-burnings over the Buddha Jayanti celebrations and the strained interpretation of the word 'secular'. Unfortunately Swami Neminath and his party find themselves uncomfortably lodged on the horns of a dilemma: either Buddhism and Hinduism are the same, in which case they would have to give the same support to both religions; or they are different, in which case a choice between them has to be made and all pretence of universalism abandoned. To insist that Buddhism and Hinduism are in essence identical yet at the same time to fight Buddhism tooth and nail – an attitude very common in certain quarters – is both dishonest and illogical. We may not always fully agree with the views expressed by Dr Radhakrishnan concerning the mutual relations between the two great traditions but his attitude is at least consistent. That Buddha Jayanti should have been celebrated on such a grand scale and with so much popular enthusiasm all over India shows that the majority of Indians feel, with Dr Radhakrishnan, that India is a secular state in a positive rather than in a negative sense and that in spending money on the Jayanti the Government did no more than show a becoming sense of the position occupied by Buddhism in the history of Indian culture. The fact that the expenses for the purely religious celebrations were borne almost in their entirety by the non-Buddhist Indian public – the Government, as Dr Radhakrishnan points out, helping to finance only the cultural programmes – should give the Swami food for thought. Let him and his fellows heed the prime minister's noble and inspiring words to the Bombay Buddha Jayanti meeting and learn 'to get out of the clutches of blind superstitious faith, spurious worship, religious hatred and the evil of casteism'.

July 1956

THE ORIGIN OF BUDDHISM

The principle of conditionality, which is one of the fundamental principles of Buddhism, being of universal application, it is but natural that writers on Buddhism should endeavour to locate and define the conditions in dependence on which the Dharma itself, as a particular historical phenomenon, should have arisen in the world. 'What is the origin of Buddhism?' is a question which, in the course of the last hundred years, has agitated some of the best brains in Europe and Asia. In principle the question is a perfectly legitimate one, for as we have already indicated it is nothing but an application to the Dharma as a historical fact of one of the basic principles of the Dharma as metaphysical truth. But the legitimacy of the question is far from guaranteeing the correctness of the answer. In fact it can be said of practically all the non-Buddhist scholars in Buddhism who have attempted to grapple with this problem that 'despite their learning they have gone far astray'.[181] The reason for their failure to answer correctly the question they had posed themselves is very simple. All of them, consciously or unconsciously, laboured under the assumption – quite false from the Buddhist point of view – that the cause of a phenomenon is necessarily of an order inferior to that of the effect. In other words they fell victim to the pseudo-scientific fallacy that *the higher can be explained in terms of the lower*. Mind is an epiphenomenon of matter. Psychological processes can be reduced to chemical changes. Man is merely a risen ape. Similarly (they say) it is possible to give a full and final explanation of the origin of Buddhism in terms of the various teachings and traditions immediately preceding it in India.

This wrong application of the principle of conditionality has enabled persons of a certain type to assert, indeed to emphasize, in the course of speeches delivered and articles written in connection with the Buddha Jayanti celebrations, that Buddhism is 'merely' an offshoot or branch of Hinduism. Wrong views, as the Buddha pointed out, are symptomatic of wrong desires, and consequently it is not very difficult to detect the real motive underlying the assertion. As we had occasion to observe last month, in the eyes of some people Buddhism is so dangerous that its historical importance and spiritual significance must at all costs be minimized. If Buddhism is really 'the same' as Hinduism, as these champions of universalism and tolerance would have us believe, then its independent propagation is superfluous, and the entire movement of the revival of Buddhism in India falls to the ground, and what the prime minister habitually describes as 'blind superstitious faith, spurious worship, religious hatred and the evil of casteism' can reign unchallenged and unchecked. No doubt there are a few disinterested scholars who sincerely believe that the teaching of the Buddha is simply a restatement of Upanishadic idealism with an ethical emphasis, but with the advance of Buddhist studies on a truly scientific basis they are becoming rarer and rarer. The majority, or at any rate the more vociferous, advocates of the 'shoot and branch' theory of the origin of Buddhism are, however, influenced not by scholarly considerations but by prejudice against Buddhism. Needless to say, just as Procrustes could not fit strangers into his famous bed without either amputating their limbs if they were too tall or stretching them if they were too short, so Buddhism is not accommodated in Hinduism by these generous folk without serious mutilation.[182] Some in their folly go so far as to assert that the Buddha 'believed' in a personal God and an immortal soul *(ātman)*. Others that Buddhism is 'merely' (how often this word crops up in such discussions!) an ethical teaching with no metaphysics and no higher spiritual truth.

Nevertheless, there is a right application of the principle of conditionality to the problem of the origin of Buddhism. All branches of Buddhist tradition are agreed that the origin of the Dharma is to be sought for in no other place than the Buddha's Enlightenment. The Dharma is, in fact, simply the conceptual and verbal formulation of that supreme realization in such a way as to function as the means of its eventual attainment by others. If the origin of the Buddha's Enlightenment itself is looked for it is to be found, according to the same unanimous tradition, not in the austerities he practised under his Brahmin teachers – who, as we are explicitly told, had failed to realize the truth – but in his faithful practice of the ten *pāramitās* or perfections during the innumerable births through which he passed between his encounter as the ascetic Sumedha with the Buddha Dīpaṅkara and his final appearance as the son of Śuddhodana and Māyā.[183] The Dharma is unique because the Buddha's Enlightenment was – so far as the present world-period is concerned – unique, and his Enlightenment was unique because of the uniqueness of his career as a bodhisattva. Between this view, which represents the correct application of the principle of conditionality to the question of the origin of the Dharma as a particular historical phenomenon, and the wrong application made either by misinformed scholars or those unfriendly to Buddhism, there can be no compromise. Hence even in the face of opposition we are compelled to insist that the higher cannot be explained in terms of the lower, and that Buddhism is the product not of the social changes and philosophical upheavals of north-eastern India in the sixth century BCE but of that timeless wisdom which transcends the ages, being the same yesterday, today, and for ever, and which is realized by the purified mind of the Buddha and by him revealed to humanity.

August 1956

TWO GREAT LIVES

> Lives of great men all remind us
> We can make our lives sublime,
> And, departing, leave behind us
> Footprints in the sands of time.[184]

These noble lines by the poet Longfellow are particularly apt to come into our minds this month, for on 17 September we celebrate the birth anniversary of one to whom their application is so fitting that they might have been specially written for him – Anagarika Dharmapala. Some men there are, no doubt, who lead sublime lives – lives of humble virtue and obscure self-abnegation – without being able to leave even a single footprint on the sands of time: their names are 'writ in water'. Others, on the contrary, even though their lives are far from sublime, somehow succeed in leaving very large footprints indeed.

Anagarika Dharmapala was one of the rare souls to whom it is given to do both. None of those who knew him personally – hundreds of them are still alive today – ever doubted that the life he led was a sublime one, and the same impression is conveyed even by the bare facts of his career, as chronicled for instance in the Society's publication *Anagarika Dharmapala: A Biographical Sketch*.

Such an impression is in a sense perhaps only natural, for it is well known that the *anagārika*'s mission was inspired by the sublimest of all ideals – that of the self-sacrificing and compassionate bodhisattva. While it would be an exaggeration to claim that we may find exemplified in his biography all the ten perfections which are to be practised by those who aspire to Supreme Enlightenment for the sake of all sentient beings, it is no more than the truth that many of them are exemplified. Morality (*sīla*), renunciation (*nekkhamma*), energy (*viriya*), truthfulness (*sacca*), resolution (*adhiṭṭhāna*), and love (*mettā*) – to draw from the list in its Theravādin formulation – could all be illustrated again and again from his biography, and the practice of these six perfections is enough, surely, to set the stamp of sublimity on any life.

That the Anagarika Dharmapala left footprints on the sands of time is a fact of which we are particularly reminded in this, the 2500th Buddha Jayanti year, for it is the fruits of his tremendous labours that we are now enjoying. Though even without him and his work the historical importance of Buddhism would have received scholarly recognition in this country, especially after Independence, it is doubtful whether a movement of popular revival would ever have developed. But speculations are unprofitable, undeniably and indisputably. Anagarika Dharmapala is the man who put Buddhism back onto the map of India. As such he has a permanent place both in the history of Buddhism and the history of India. This is surely a 'footprint' large and deep enough to satisfy even the most captious of critics.

No remembrance of the *anagārika*'s birth anniversary would be complete without a corresponding commemoration of his friend and benefactress the inexhaustibly bountiful Mrs Mary E. Foster, whose own birth anniversary falls, by a remarkable coincidence, on 21 September. Though even without the backing of his 'foster mother', as she became after his father's death, the *anagārika*'s career would have exhibited the same moral grandeur, it is doubtful whether it would have been so rich in concrete material achievement. As we observed on a previous occasion, no man can make bricks without straw:[185] it was Mrs Foster's humble but indispensable function to provide the 'straw' for the bricks with which a large part of the edifice of Buddhist revival in India was built. Consequently we remember her whenever we remember her 'foster son', and with the same gratitude. She made her life sublime simply through giving (*dāna*), the first of the ten perfections. Hence she too has left 'footprints' – scarcely distinguishable from those of the *anagārika* himself.

As the first two lines of Longfellow's quatrain insist, the lives of great men – and great women – are a reminder that *we can make our lives sublime*. Remembrance is only a means to imitation. We should not merely commemorate the birth anniversaries of Anagarika Dharmapala and Mrs Mary E. Foster; we should find in the story of their lives the inspiration for our own. Now, more than ever, does the great work of Buddhist revival call, especially here in India, for the active cooperation of all Buddhists and friends of Buddhism. If we are unable ourselves to work actively for the propagation of the Dharma we should at least encourage and support individuals and organizations who do. Either Anagarika Dharmapala or Mrs Mary E. Foster should be our ideal. To the extent to which we succeed in following their inspiring example our own lives will become sublime and we too shall leave footprints on the sands of Buddhist history.

September 1956

THE TIDE TURNS

Ever since the inception of the Maha Bodhi Society more than sixty years ago we have been accustomed to regard our work for the revival of Buddhism in India as constituting a hopelessly minority movement. Though as the decades went by more and more people acquired knowledge of and developed sympathy for the Dharma of the All-Enlightened and All-Compassionate One, it was but rarely that some courageous soul came forward and declared himself to be not merely a sympathizer with Buddhism but a Buddhist.

Mighty unseen forces were, however, all the time at work behind the visible framework of events, and when, shortly after the glorious day on which our country achieved independence, the Sacred Relics of the *arahants* Sāriputta and Mahāmoggallāna were brought back from London to be re-enshrined at the site whence they had been removed a century earlier, all India rose as one man to welcome them.

Now comes the news that on 14th of this month, which by a strange coincidence is the Vijayadaśamī day, the day which, according to Hindu mythology, commemorates the victory of the forces of light over the powers of darkness, one of our great national leaders will be converted to Buddhism together with hundreds of thousands of his followers.[186]

Let none think that Dr B. R. Ambedkar has taken this momentous step hastily or without due consideration, or that he has embarked upon this truly revolutionary course without full consciousness of its socio-religious implications and its far-reaching historical significance. It is perhaps five-and-twenty years since Dr Ambedkar first declared that though he had been born a Hindu he did not intend to die a Hindu.[187] Twenty-five years back is a big enough slice of anybody's life, and a period of time sufficiently long for the pondering even so momentous a step as the changing of one's religion. Brahminical clamours to the contrary notwithstanding, Dr Ambedkar knows what he is doing, and his followers know what they are doing, too.

Not theoretical considerations merely but their own bitter experience of all the unspeakable cruelty, the soul-searing injustice and systematic relentless inhumanity through the ages has eventually convinced them that Hinduism is incapable of reformation and that the only course now open to them is to break away from it and embrace Buddhism.

Within the Buddhist fold they will find not only social emancipation but, what is even more important, a way of life conducive to the attainment both of happiness here and hereafter and that unshakeable deliverance of mind which is the gist of the Buddha's teaching. They will also find the hand of brotherhood stretched out to them from every side, not only welcoming but assisting and supporting them as they take their first step along the Noble Eightfold Path.

When, on the coming Vijayadaśamī day, the lion-hearted leader and his followers make that momentous step forward, a threefold shout of

'Sadhu!!!' will surely rise from every part of the Buddhist world and be taken up by the *devas* and other celestial beings and echoed from heaven to heaven until finally it reaches the foot of the Throne of Enlightenment; and those who labour in the heat of the day in the field of Buddhist revival in India, hearing that shout, will pause a moment in their work, and know, with joy in their hearts, that at last the tide has turned.[188]

October 1956

HIS HOLINESS THE DALAI LAMA

The Dalai Lama is coming to India! A few weeks ago, even, it would have seemed impossible that the most distinguished and celebrated religious leader in the entire Buddhist world should be coming to bless with his inspiring presence the culminating phases of the Government of India's 2500th Buddha Jayanti celebrations in New Delhi. Certain obstacles, we had been informed, stood in the way, and it would not be possible for His Holiness to leave Tibet. But now, thanks to the efforts of our beloved prime minister, obstacles have been swept aside, the impossible has happened, and at the end of this month His Holiness the Fourteenth Dalai Lama, the spiritual and temporal ruler of the 'Land of Snows', will pay his first visit to India.

The full significance of this truly epoch-making event will, we believe, emerge only gradually. For in the Dalai Lama we have not merely a recognized religious and political leader, however eminent, but a spiritual star of the first magnitude. Not only in Tibet, but in all the adjacent Himalayan regions such as Nepal, Sikkim, and Bhutan, in Mongolia, in a large part of China, in the border areas of India, and in parts of Russia, he is universally revered as the bodhisattva Avalokiteśvara in human form. How deep is the devotion with which Tibetan Buddhists look upon the Dalai Lama has been well brought out by Lobsang Phuntsok Lhalungpa in his chapter on 'Buddhism in Tibet' in the recently published book *The Path of the Buddha*:

> Tibetans and Mongolians alike look upon him as being anxious to protect them from external enemies and injustices and as being their living Buddha – the one who will help them realize the Buddha and the Bodhisattva ideals. He is honoured by all; all

> put their wholehearted faith in him and all love him more dearly than anything else. To the Tibetans the Dalai Lama is not just a ruler or a teacher but a father, guide, protector, and above all, the great Bodhisattva. His words act upon them like magic, while his personality is so holy, so serene, and so forceful that they are thrilled and deeply moved whenever they happen to be in his presence. For his sake they are prepared to make any sacrifice. He is the unifying force of the country and as such is unmatched by any other spiritual master.[189]

This being the case, it is only to be expected that the effects of the Dalai Lama's advent in India will not be confined to the political and cultural, nor even to the religious sphere, but will propagate themselves in all directions on the invisible spiritual planes as well. Indeed, we might hazard a surmise that the mere presence of His Holiness will do more to stimulate the revival of Buddhism in the land of its birth than any merely secular agency. Be that as it may, one thing is certain: that whether the Dalai Lama's visit is regarded as being of political and cultural or primarily of spiritual significance, or whether he is regarded as a great national and religious leader or as the incarnate bodhisattva appearing out of compassion in the world, the people of India – both Buddhists and non-Buddhists – will accord His Holiness a rousing welcome when he visits their country at the end of this month and will take him to their hearts.[190]

November 1956

ANNUS MIRABILIS – THE YEAR OF WONDERS

Sixty-five years have passed since Anagarika Dharmapala founded what was then known as the Bodh Gaya Maha Bodhi Society, thus inaugurating the great movement for the revival of Buddhism in the land of its birth. Searching the rolls of the Society's history, we find that almost every one of these five-and-sixty years is distinguished by some great achievement or other, some forward step by means of which we were brought a little nearer to our goal. But never, we feel, was any single year so filled with events of far-reaching significance, with what promise to be enduring solid achievements, as that which has just passed over our heads; never has the pace of our advance been so rapid; never before was it possible to do so much in so short a time.

Three events of 1956 stand out as being of very special importance and significance. First, of course, there was the inauguration, in May, of the celebrations held to commemorate the 2500th anniversary of the *parinirvāṇa* of the Lord Buddha. These celebrations, which were sponsored by the Government of India, reached their climax in New Delhi last month, and even now have by no means exhausted their momentum.[191] They will, in fact, continue until next May. Second, on 14 October the great Scheduled Caste leader, Dr B. R. Ambedkar, embraced Buddhism at Nagpur along with half a million followers.[192] Third, as though to bless all that had been accomplished this year, His Holiness the Dalai Lama and His Holiness the Panchen Lama arrived at the end of November in New Delhi, whence, after participating in the 2500th Buddha Jayanti celebrations, they have gone on pilgrimage to the holy places.[193] These events, together with a multitude of hardly less important associated events, have undoubtedly made a deep impression on the minds of at least the thinking section of the Indian public. Buddhism, they now realize, has become a factor to be reckoned with in Indian affairs. Indeed it is by no means devoid even of global significance. There are people in India who feel uncomfortable in the presence of such facts. Some of them have attempted to stem the rising tide of Buddhism. But their efforts have met with no success. Doubtless the historians of the future will aver that the year 1956 marks the real emergence of Buddhism as a spiritual, cultural, and social force in India. If that be so, this year may indeed be described as 'The Year of Wonders'.[194]

December 1956

1957

DR AMBEDKAR

The death of Dr Ambedkar, at the comparatively early age of 65, has come as a shock not only to his followers but to Buddhists all over the world. Less than eight weeks earlier, on 14 October, he had launched a major social and religious revolution by taking the Three Refuges and Five Precepts at Nagpur together with half a million of his supporters. On that historic occasion he spoke with all his accustomed fire and brilliance. Again, when he addressed the inaugural assembly of the World Fellowship of Buddhists at Kathmandu on 15 November, despite his obvious bodily weakness few who heard him could have thought that the end of one of the most colourful careers of modern times was so close at hand. After going on pilgrimage to the holy places Dr Ambedkar returned to his home in Delhi. On 5 December he finished writing the preface to his book on Buddhism, working far into the night. Next day, the servant who took him his early tea found him dead. His last waking thoughts must have been of the Buddha.

Born into an 'Untouchable' family of Maharashtra, Bhimrao Ambedkar experienced very early in life the soul-sickening cruelty and injustice of the socio-religious system under which he had had the misfortune to be born. Forced to drink foul water, refused food and drink for days together, thrown out of a public vehicle in which he had dared to seat his polluting carcase, stoned and beaten when he ventured to protest, humiliated at school, where he was relegated to a corner and where caste Hindu teachers refused to touch his copybooks: grim and terrible were the memories of Hinduism with which he grew up. Unlike his millions of oppressed brethren, however, he was not destined to suffer in silence. As he grew in years and experience, and as despite heart-breaking difficulties he gradually carved out for himself a place in the political life of the nation, he became more and more outspoken in his condemnation of the evils of caste. The harsh unpalatable truths he uttered naturally awakened the fierce resentment and implacable hatred of the champions of orthodoxy, who till the end of his days treated him as their sworn enemy. Tens of millions of Scheduled Caste people, however, hailed him as their leader and saviour. But not even at the height of his power, not even when as Government Minister of Law and Justice he drafted the Constitution and the Hindu Code Bill, did either his friends or his enemies realize how wide and how deep his influence extended. That became apparent only on 14 October and afterwards. A lifelong student of religions, Dr Ambedkar had step by step come to the conclusion that orthodoxy was incapable of reformation, and that the victims of age-old socio-religious oppression and exploitation in India could be freed from their disabilities only by embracing Buddhism. Towards this consummation he gradually bent more and more of his energies. Some, even among his own people, opposed him, feeling perhaps that no mere 'religion' could solve a problem of such tremendous complexity. But Dr Ambedkar's faith in Buddhism stood firm as a rock. With characteristic boldness, he declared that he was going to become a Buddhist even if nobody else became one. But when the time for taking the momentous step actually came, far from taking it alone he carried hundreds of thousands with him. All over India, wherever the name of Dr Ambedkar was honoured, people gathered in their thousands and in their tens of thousands to take Refuge in the Buddha, the Dharma and the Sangha.

Before the movement of mass conversion could reach its height Dr Ambedkar, worn out by the labours of a lifetime, died. Some there were who thought that with his death the movement would come to an end, or at least receive a serious setback. Never were prophets more false. The ashes of his funeral pyre were hardly cold before the movement gathered a momentum beyond the expectations even of the most wildly optimistic. Nay, even as all that was mortal of him was consigned to the flames the sacred chant '*Buddhaṃ saraṇaṃ gacchāmi*' rose spontaneously from the lips of the tens of thousands of mourners assembled there. Since then reports have come in of mass conversion ceremonies in Nagpur, Poona, Ahmedabad, Agra, and a score of other important centres. Great as Dr Ambedkar's influence was during life evidently it is greater still in death.

The disciplined courage and enthusiasm which Dr Ambedkar's followers have displayed since their great leader's demise should not cause us to think that the movement can be safely left to look after itself. Repetition of the Three Refuges and Five Precepts is not by itself sufficient to make one a Buddhist. One must put the Three Refuges and Five Precepts into practice in one's life. But practice proceeds from understanding, and understanding depends upon proper instruction. Unless the Buddhist countries come forward with at least a few hundred full-time *dharmadūta* workers, preferably *bhikkhus*, there is every danger that the movement so gloriously inaugurated by Dr Ambedkar will not be properly consolidated. Organizations which have no trained personnel to spare should at least contribute funds from the publication of books and pamphlets in Hindi, Marathi, and other languages. But under no circumstances should the Buddhist world fail to do its duty by those who are struggling towards the light of Buddhism after dwelling for centuries in darkness. There is no better way for any of us to honour the memory of Dr Ambedkar than by devoting ourselves to the continuation of his work.[195]

January 1957

THE STUDY OF BUDDHISM

Depth and breadth, extension and intension, are notoriously hard to combine, especially where religious movements are concerned. Even as a sheet of beaten gold becomes thinner and thinner as the area that it is made to cover expands, so does the understanding of spiritual truths tend to become more and more superficial as the number of people among whom they are disseminated increases. This fact has, unfortunately, received of late abundant confirmation and it is for this reason that we are pausing, in the midst of the rejoicings of the 2500th Buddha Jayanti year, to draw it to the very serious attention of our readers.

It is well known that during the last few years there has taken place in India a truly remarkable resurgence of interest in the Buddha and his

Dharma, a resurgence that has culminated in the nationwide celebrations we have recently witnessed. But it is not so well understood that despite processions and mass meetings, exhibitions and publications, lectures and films, the Indian public, for all its greatly enhanced awareness of Buddhism, is still not only very much in the dark about its basic teaching but even still under the influence of many a hoary prejudice and ancient misunderstanding.

This would not be a matter for such serious concern if the educated and cultured minority, by whose views the majority might be expected eventually to be won over, could be said to possess even a tolerably correct and adequate understanding of the fundamental principles of the Dharma. But this is very far from being the case. On the contrary, indeed, those who, stimulated by the greatly increased demand for Buddhist literature, engage themselves in the production of books and pamphlets on Buddhism, frequently are found not only purveying all the old misunderstandings and misinterpretations but also making the confusion worse confounded by introducing many new ones of their own.

What is the reason for this unfortunate and even dangerous state of affairs? Deliberate hostility towards Buddhism apart, the principal cause is, we believe, the fact that the writers concerned simply do not take the trouble of studying Buddhism before they begin writing about it. One can open many a book, ostensibly on Buddhism, containing page after page of the most sweeping, not to say wildest, generalizations about the Dharma, without coming across confirmatory quotation from a Buddhist text or a single reference to a Buddhist writer of repute. Quite a big book on 'Buddhism' can sometimes be spun out of a nodding acquaintance with *The Light of Asia*.[196]

If we were desirous of probing a little deeper, we might further question what the reason is for this strange neglect of the most elementary rules of research. It is, perhaps, twofold. On the one hand we have a riotously exuberant speculative imagination of which it could be said, as of Herbert Spencer, that its idea of a tragedy is a theory killed by a fact – a tragedy the writers with whom we are dealing would never permit to occur. On the other hand there is the strongly individualistic, not to say egoistic, urge of the writer to find an audience to whose admiring gaze he can exhibit the antics of his own darling brainchildren. With these two factors reinforcing each other all serious concern for a correct presentation of Buddhism is crushed out of existence. One group of writers, indeed, on the pretext of a comparative study, has not scrupled to preface to a vigorous defence of the religious and philosophical position of their own sect a ridiculously meagre and misleading account of Buddhism.

The only remedy for such intellectual dishonesty is a conscientious attempt to ascertain the true nature of Buddhism at least by means of a careful study of all the literary sources available in the languages known to the would-be writer. Besides the supplying of correct information, its immediate object, such a study would naturally clip the wings of the speculative imagination and impose a check on the urge to individualistic self-expression, thus further reducing the chances of misunderstanding and misinterpretation. It is therefore upon the importance of the study of Buddhism that we must now lay the strongest possible emphasis. Festivals and celebrations are all very well in their way, but without the proper study of Buddhism the practice of the Dharma, as well as its dissemination and revival, is in any true and effective sense out of the question.

February 1957

THE LESSON OF HISTORY

Canonical texts of all schools of Buddhism are unanimous that the Buddha's unique discovery under the bodhi tree at Bodh Gaya, by virtue of which Siddhartha became the Supremely Enlightened One, was that of the essentially conditioned and dependent nature of all phenomena. By applying this great principle to the problem of human suffering was he able to enunciate the second of the four noble truths, the truth that the origin of suffering is craving; by applying it to the problem of the cessation of that suffering was he able to enunciate the fourth noble truth, the truth that the cessation of suffering, the realization of Nirvāṇa, depends upon the following of the progressive scheme of ethical and spiritual self-culture outlined in the Noble Eightfold Path. Other applications are, of course, possible, for the principle of conditionality is universal. Whether we look at the so-called material universe without, or at the infinitely subtler mental world within, we find confronting us a vast network consisting of unimaginably complicated relations. Physics, chemistry, biology, psychology – all alike bear witness to the fact that nothing in the world is single, but that interdependence is necessary to existence, is existence itself. Interrelation is the law of life. Isolation is death.

Such being the case, it need not be a matter for astonishment to find the history of Buddhism itself exemplifying this principle. If there is any lesson to be learned from a study of the vicissitudes of fortune undergone by this great religion in the course of its five-and-twenty centuries of history it is this: that whenever there was free communication and regular friendly intercourse between the different parts of the Buddhist world the Dharma flourished, and that whenever individual Buddhist countries and communities, under compulsion of historical events or for other reasons, withdrew into isolation, the Dharma declined. The days of Aśoka were days of expansion. Not only all over India, but even in distant Ceylon, Egypt, Palestine, and Greece, was the impact of the Buddha's teaching felt. In the heyday of Nālandā, when scholars from a hundred lands thronged the portals of the great Buddhist university, the Buddhist world was bigger than it had ever been before or has ever been since. The Buddhist world is one world, and its various parts, like the limbs of a healthy body, cannot function except in unison.

Is it not good cause for rejoicing, therefore, that in this 2500th Buddha Jayanti year Buddhists are coming together as never before, and that they are meeting and mingling on the sacred soil of India, in the land where the Buddha lived and taught? Only sixty years ago pilgrims came by dozens. Now they are coming in their tens of thousands. In those days they found, at the end of their long journeys, little more than crumbling piles of brick and stone to remind them of the great events of the Master's career. In these days, thanks to the pioneer work of Anagarika Dharmapala and the interest more recently taken by the Government of India and the state governments concerned, they find splendid temples, spacious rest houses, and beautiful gardens. More important still they find that, like a great decayed trunk which at last puts forth the shoots of tender green, the Dharma, after centuries of virtual extinction, is again reviving in the land of its birth. Most important of all, by their coming they themselves help water those tender shoots and stimulate them to a sturdier and more vigorous growth. For as we have already insisted, interrelation is the law of life and wherever Buddhists come together, even if only temporarily, the conditions for the study, practice, and propagation of the Dharma become more favourable.

Let us, therefore, as the 2500th Buddha Jayanti year draws to its close, resolve to work for the strengthening of the ties that bind the different parts of the Buddhist world into the greatest cultural and spiritual fellowship that has ever been known, so that the Dharma, the essence of which is the teaching of universal conditionality, may flourish not only in India, not only in Asia, but throughout the world.

March 1957

THE SANGHA

'The continuity of the monastic organization has been the only constant factor in the history of Buddhism.'[197] This statement, made by one of the greatest Buddhist scholars of our day, deserves to be very seriously pondered by all who are concerned with, or interested in, the consolidation and expansion of the Dharma. Besides drawing our attention, in a most pointed way, to the vital importance of the part played by the sangha in the history of Buddhism in the past, it brings into sharper focus its present-day role.

Living as he did at a time prior to the use of writing for religious purposes, the Buddha had of necessity to create a special agency for the preservation of his teaching. This agency was the sangha. Critics who, without even being Buddhists, take it upon themselves to carp at the members of the monastic organization, accusing them of misinterpreting the Buddha's original gospel, would do well to remember that had it not been for the sangha the Dharma would have been very soon forgotten. All that survived would have been the caricature of the life and teaching of the Buddha such as we find here and there in Brahminical literature. For such reasons as these, no doubt, did a very eminent Mahāyāna monk from Tibet recently declare, 'Where there is no Sangha, there is no Dharma.'

Not only has the sangha to preserve the Dharma; it must interpret, practise, and propagate it as well. Through the ages it has been the monks who were responsible for the formulation of the various systems of Buddhist thought by means of which the Dharma was made more and more intelligible to an ever-increasing variety of people. It was the monks again who exemplified the Dharma in their lives. With more time at their disposal than the average layman, with a deeper understanding of the teaching and a more ardent resolve to practise it, it was they who produced the great saints and sages thanks to whose kindling breath the lamp of the Dharma burned brighter and brighter in a hundred lands. The monks it was, moreover, who, sometimes with the support and patronage of powerful kings and rich merchants, sometimes with only their own enthusiasm to sustain them, braved the desert and the sea to bring the greatest of all gifts, the gift of the Dharma, within the reach of their fellow men in distant lands. When we remember that the monks were in addition poets, writers, doctors, architects, engineers, and spiritual advisers, in fact the guides, philosophers, and friends of the entire community, it is small wonder that the laity should have come to reverence the sangha as the living embodiment of Buddhism, or that it should still extend to its humblest member a respect which arouses the astonishment of the non-Buddhist.

But there is another side to the picture. Privileges impose duties. With so much respect for the sangha, the Buddhist public has not unnaturally been highly intolerant of any failure on the part of members of the sangha to live up to the lofty ideals of their estate. Though this attitude has been productive, here and there in the Buddhist world, of a certain amount of hypocrisy, of a desire to keep up appearances rather than to keep the precepts, it may with confidence be said that even today, with all the disruptive forces of the modern world at work, the sangha has nothing to fear from a comparison with any similar body of men anywhere in the world,

One of the principal factors which have made, not only for the maintenance of the sangha in something like its original integrity, but even for the very continuity of the monastic organization, is the strictness, not to say rigidity, with which the rules governing the admission of new members were applied. Whether belonging to the Theravāda or to the Mahāyāna, in all Buddhist lands (with the exception of Japan, where the *upasampadā* has been virtually extinct since medieval times), the very highest importance is attached to proper ordination. The reason for this is to be found chiefly in the fact that, as already stated, the sangha is the custodian of the Dharma, so that it has to be on its guard not only against those who, without being properly ordained, represent themselves as *bhikṣus* and preach what may not be the true Dharma, but also against those who present themselves as candidates for ordination for purposes of infiltration and subversion. In Buddhist countries such as Ceylon and Tibet these dangers hardly exist. But in those lands where the Dharma is being newly preached, or where it is being revived, they are very real. The well-known story of the *bhikkhus* whom Aśoka found wearing sacred threads beneath their robes and performing *homa* ceremonies in the viharas, and whom he expelled from the sangha, has much more than a historical interest: it is a warning to us at the present day.

Both in India, where the Dharma is beginning to revive, and in the various western lands where for the last few decades it has been spreading, the sangha will have to insist more strongly than it has done heretofore upon the necessity for proper ordination in the strictest sense of the term. It should resolutely refuse to give either the lower or the higher ordination to those who are unable to rid themselves of the lingering vestiges of the theistic or ātmanistic ideologies in which they were born. After ordination pupils should remain with their teachers for a fixed minimum period: no *bhikkhu* should be allowed to ordain as *sāmaṇeras* pupils whom he is unable to teach and train. Moreover, the sangha should stoutly refuse to recognize as a *bhikkhu* one who has not been properly ordained in accordance with the Vinaya rules common to the Theravāda and to practically all the Mahāyāna schools. Especially in western countries, where owing to their remoteness from authentic Buddhist tradition the public is more easily beguiled by those who claim to be not merely *bhikkhus* but the *mahānāyaka theras* or high priests of some spurious 'order' or other, is it necessary for us to make perfectly clear what a member of the sangha is and what he is not. Only then will the continuity of the monastic organization, and with it the integrity of the Dharma, be ensured for the benefit of future ages even as the constant efforts of monks and laymen in the past have ensured them, with all their unspeakable blessings, for the benefit of our own generation.

April 1957

BUDDHA JAYANTI AS A PUBLIC HOLIDAY

The 2500th Buddha Jayanti year has ended. As those who have read these pages regularly will know, it has been a year of unprecedented expansion for Buddhism not only here in India but throughout the world. Plans that the small hands of devoted Buddhist workers had striven for decades to put into execution suddenly came to fruition.

Blocks and pillars that for years together they had vainly struggled to lift into their places in the great edifice of Buddhist revival were swung into position in an instant when the lever of government and public cooperation was applied. Dreams that we had cherished for nearly half a century came true almost overnight. For all this we are truly thankful, though, if truth be told, in honouring her greatest son India has done no more than honour herself as the matrix in which the seed of the Dharma was deposited, the chosen vessel into which the waters that would slake the thirst of humanity were first poured. But though much has been done much remains undone. The edifice of Buddhist revival, far from being finished, is still in its first building. Many a mighty block and pillar will have to be carved out of the living rock and hoisted into position before the pile stands foursquare and complete. Many a dream has yet to come true.

Among these unfulfilled dreams of ours is the declaration of the Buddha Jayanti Day, the thrice-sacred Vaiśākha Pūrṇimā, as a public holiday for the whole of India. Ever since its inception the Society has striven, practically year in and year out, for the addition of this most auspicious day to the roll of recognized public holidays. When, in 1947, this country gained independence, we felt quite confident that one of the first acts of free India would be to declare Buddha Jayanti day as a public holiday. But our hopes were dashed to the ground. The only concession that we were able to wring from the government was the recognition of Buddha Jayanti day as an official holiday, which meant that Central Government offices only would be closed. Even this meagre satisfaction was given only after it had been pointed out, in the course of the meeting held in connection with the re-enshrinement of the Sacred Relics of the *arahants* Sāriputta and Mahāmoggallāna at Sanchi in 1952, how anomalous it was for the birthdays of Jesus, who was born in Palestine, and of Mohammed, who was born in Arabia, to be observed as public holidays in India, while that of India's greatest son, the Lord Buddha, was not so observed.[198] The only redeeming feature of this otherwise black situation was the fact that some state governments did declare the Vaiśākha Pūrṇimā Day as a public holiday, and that the Centre itself was good enough to recognize the day as a holiday for the year 2500/1956 only.[199] There is a Zen Buddhist conundrum to the effect that the body of a cow can pass through a door but the tail cannot pass through. Having spent the magnificent sum of two crores of rupees on the 2500th Buddha Jayanti celebrations of the past year it would be strange indeed if the Government of India could not see its way to declare the Buddha Jayanti day a permanent public holiday. However, perhaps Shri Nehru, in whom the Buddhists have no greater friend in India, has even now decided to take a step which, we know, will give him no less pleasure than it will give us, and will very shortly declare Buddha Jayanti a public holiday henceforward. With such a hope in our hearts shall we be celebrating the thrice-auspicious occasion this year.[200]

May 1957

THAILAND CELEBRATES BUDDHA JAYANTI

It is a fact well known to all serious students of Buddhism that in the different Buddhist lands different systems of chronology have been preserved. Even regarding the date of the birth and the *mahāparinirvāṇa* of the Buddha there is no unanimity of opinion. Hence the various reckonings of the Buddhist era, which all followers of the Enlightened One agree began in the year of the *mahāparinirvāṇa*, do not coincide from one Buddhist country to another.

In these circumstances it speaks well of the fundamental unity of the Buddhist world that, setting aside all differences, the various countries and regions of which it is composed agreed to join together in celebrating the year which came to an end last month as the 2500th anniversary of the *mahāparinirvāṇa* of the Blessed One. On how grand a scale the anniversary celebrated were held, both in India and abroad, is well known to all readers of this journal.

Thailand, however, while fully participating in the international celebrations last year, decided that her own national celebrations should conform to the Thai Buddhist calendar, according to which the 2500th Buddha Jayanti year instead of *ending* on the last Vaiśākha Pūrṇimā *began* on that day. This decision of the Thai Buddhists is not without great advantages. Not only shall we be having another year of Buddha Jayanti celebrations, but Buddhist dignitaries and representatives of Buddhist organizations from all over the globe will be able, this year, to enjoy the hospitality and participate in the religious life of one of the most devoutly Buddhist nations in the world.

The enthusiasm generated by the celebrations now taking place in Thailand will inevitably have repercussions that will be felt here in India. Already, we understand, plans are being made for a vihara at Bodh Gaya, and there is no doubt that the Thai *bhikkhus*, with their reputation for strict discipline, will be able to contribute much to the revival of the Dharma in this country. To the Sangha, the Royal Government, and the people of Thailand we extend our cordial *mettā* on the auspicious occasion of the inauguration of their 2500th Buddha Jayanti celebrations, with the hope that before long they will be playing a leading part in the affairs of the whole Buddhist world.

June 1957

A GREAT INJUSTICE

One of the greatest events of the 2500th Buddha Jayanti year was undoubtedly the conversion to Buddhism of the late Dr B. R. Ambedkar together with hundreds of thousands of his followers. Certain interested parties have questioned the genuineness of a change of faith affecting such a vast number of people. But those who, under Dr Ambedkar's guidance, took the *triśaraṇa* and *pañca śīla* at Nagpur on 14 October last year did not change their convictions overnight.[201] For years Dr Ambedkar and a handful of devoted henchmen had been endeavouring to impress upon the minds and hearts of the 'Untouchables' the fact that only in Buddhism was there to be found a spiritual force strong enough to effect their all-round amelioration, and slowly but surely their efforts bore fruit. Even after the tragically sudden demise of the lion-hearted leader the great movement of mass conversion did not slacken off. Indeed it increased in momentum. This fact alone should be sufficient to convince even the most sceptical that we have to deal not with a 'political stunt', as some of them tried to make out at the beginning, but with the greatest spiritual upheaval that India has known in modern times.

But even spiritual upheavals take place within a specific socio-economic framework. The Neo-Buddhists, as they are now generally styled (the term meaning not those who follow a new form of Buddhism, but simply those who have newly become Buddhists) are drawn almost entirely from what are officially known as the Scheduled Castes, Scheduled Tribes, and Other Backward Classes, or in other words, from those people, numbering between seventy and eighty millions, whom the orthodox Hindus have for centuries despised and ill-treated as outcastes and untouchables.[202] Recognizing that on account of generations of systematic degradation and social persecution these Depressed Classes, as they were also called, stood in need of special consideration, the Indian Government granted them, though on a small scale, certain special political and educational facilities. Among these facilities were scholarships for deserving 'Untouchable' students. The Constitution envisaged their continuation for a period of ten years from the date of its promulgation.

Now, however, comes the news that the Government of India and the State Government of Bombay (the state in which the majority of Neo-Buddhists are to be found) have decreed that on becoming Buddhists the Neo-Buddhists shall automatically forfeit the facilities to which as members of the Scheduled Caste communities they were formerly entitled. When an 'Untouchable' renounces Hinduism he does, of course, cease to be an Untouchable at the same time that he ceases to be a Hindu, for from its very inception Buddhism has resolutely refused to countenance the inhumanity that, in the name of religion, degrades a fellow human being to a level lower than that of a beast. But change of religion is not necessarily synonymous with an immediate improvement of socio-economic conditions. By getting themselves converted to Buddhism the Scheduled Caste people have not automatically become rich, well educated, and respected. The vast majority of them continue to live as they have lived for centuries – in poverty, ignorance, and ignominy. The only difference is that while as Hindus they lived without hope, as Buddhists they live full of hope, for Buddhism tells them, not that they have been born Untouchables as a result of sins committed in past lives and that unquestioning submission to the insults of the caste Hindus is the only means of expiation, but that they are the masters of their own fate, the architects of their own destiny, and that by right effort every man can become the peer of the Buddha.

Since the socio-economic conditions of the Neo-Buddhists are the same as they were before their conversion it is difficult to understand why the Central Government and the State Government of Bombay should have discontinued even the meagre facilities that they were formerly enjoying. One would have thought that the government of a secular state would have welcomed the opportunity of continuing to help a socially and economically backward section of the community without having to place itself in the anomalous position of recognizing *de facto* those very caste distinctions which it does not recognize *de jure*. By discontinuing the scholarships and other educational concessions of such Scheduled Castes students as become Buddhists the Government of India and the State of Bombay have in fact discriminated against Buddhism in favour of Hinduism. They have indirectly encouraged untouchability. They have set a premium on social injustice and inequality.

We sincerely hope that the damage so far done is not irreparable and that saner counsels may in the end prevail. In celebrating the 2500th anniversary of the *parinirvāṇa* of the Lord Buddha the Government of India set an example to the whole world. It would be a thousand pities if the Buddha Jayanti celebrations should be followed up by an action which seems strangely like a deliberate attempt to discourage people from trying to put into practice the very principles those celebrations were intended to recall. Unless the educational concessions to which, as members of a still backward community, the Neo-Buddhists continue to be entitled are promptly restored to them, certain national leaders will find it hard to escape the charge of paying lip sympathy to Buddhism for purposes other than strictly religious.

Whether the Neo-Buddhists continue to enjoy the same social and economic concessions after conversion as they enjoyed before or whether they do not, of one thing all those concerned would do well to be assured: that the movement of mass conversion started by Dr Ambedkar cannot be checked or even halted. Surely it is not too much to expect that after treating the Untouchables with cruelty for centuries the majority community will now at least refrain from attempting, however vainly, to frustrate their efforts to achieve not merely a higher standard of living but a better standard of life. By helping the Neo-Buddhists at the present juncture the caste Hindus will be sowing the seeds of future friendship. By renewing their efforts to harm they will only enlarge the gulf of hatred and misunderstanding which is already alarmingly wide.

July 1957

BUDDHISM AND ADVERTISING

News comes to us that the Catholic Church in England has recently been advertising its particular brand of faith in the newspapers with such marked success that other Christian denominations, notably the Church of England and the Free Churches, have in self-defence been compelled to plan similar if less expensive campaigns. About the ethics of such a procedure public opinion in England seems to be divided. The Catholics have of course always maintained that 'the end justifies the means', but even those who would hesitate to subscribe to such a policy seem to feel that in an age of widespread indifference to religion no means of recapturing the imagination of the common man need be considered too unconventional: a man who is fighting for his life cannot afford to be choosy about weapons. Others, however, hold that religion advertised is religion profaned. In the scornful words of a well-known Free Religious journal, 'It is treating religion like packets of soap powder to be sold by high-powered salesmanship.'

The Catholic Church being not only an international but a highly centralized body, there is little doubt that its advertising campaign will one day spread East. With their lower standard of literacy, which of course means a smaller newspaper-reading public, the peoples of the Asian countries are less exposed to such a threat than are those of Europe and the Americas. Forewarned, however, is forearmed, and though the danger may not be immediate it would be well if the Buddhists considered what their own policy would be if the Catholic Church, or any other non-Buddhist religious body, started advertising on a large scale in the newspapers of a Buddhist land.

If the advertisements are offensive to Buddhist sentiment the government of the country concerned can always be moved to take action, but it is unlikely that the Catholic Church will make a tactical error of this sort. Its approach will be much more subtle and insidious. Editors who happen to be devout Buddhists will naturally refuse to allow the insertion of advertisements detrimental to Buddhist interests. But unfortunately in at least one Buddhist country Catholic-owned newspapers already constitute a serious problem. News of Buddhist interest is hardly ever reported in them, while Catholic events and personalities are given undue prominence. In the event of an advertising campaign planned to boost the Catholic faith such newspapers would play a vitally important role. It therefore behoves the Buddhists of the countries concerned to bestir themselves and take precautions before it is too late.

The best method of defence is attack. Before the Catholic Church has a chance to take possession of the field, let the Buddhists occupy it, or at least a portion of it. We do not mean that Buddhists should indulge in an undignified scramble for converts, as the various Christian denominations seem to be doing in England. But it cannot be denied that many people, including many 'born Buddhists', know so little about the Dhamma and about Buddhist activities largely because they have never been made to understand that it is possible to know more. Every year Buddhist organizations (to say nothing of commercial publishers) bring out hundreds of books on Buddhism. If the sales are so small, is it not due largely to lack of proper advertising? For the same reason, the issues of a Buddhist magazine circulate in hundreds instead of in tens of thousands. The least that the Buddhists of Asia can do, in view of the menace that may confront them before very long, is to plan a campaign to advertise Buddhist literature. The campaign need not be confined to Asia. The war should be carried right into the enemy camp, and advertisements for Buddhist books and magazines should find a place in the great newspapers and periodicals of the West. All this will cost money. But the response will be enormous. Will the Buddhist world be far-sighted enough to realize the importance of advertising?

August 1957

RIGHT MEDITATION

It is well known and universally recognized that meditation *(samādhi bhāvanā)* occupies a place of central importance in the Buddhist life. So much so, indeed, that one who fails to meditate for at least a few minutes every day is rightly regarded as being a Buddhist only in a very nominal sense indeed. As the second of three *śikṣās* – *śīla*, *samādhi*, and *prajñā* – which all schools of Buddhism recognize as constituting the three great successive states of the Path to Liberation, the vital importance of *samādhi bhāvanā* can be neither neglected nor ignored.[203] Surely it is not without significance that the best known and most characteristic representation of the Buddha depicts him in the posture of meditation!

With the worldwide revival of the Dharma that we have witnessed in the course of the present century, especially during the last decade, it is but natural that there should have been a revival of interest in this, the most ancient, authentic, and essential of all Buddhist spiritual practices. In more than one Buddhist land meditation centres have been opened and manuals published, while from those portions of the globe to which the Dharma has but newly spread – where it is spreading still – come enquiries which testify to an eagerness to experience that peace and illumination of heart and mind which meditation alone can give.

Less widely recognized, however, than the necessity for meditation, is the vital importance of an understanding of the distinction between *samyak-samādhi*, right meditation, and *mithyā-samādhi*, wrong meditation. The distinction is implied by the fact that *right* meditation, and not just any kind of meditation, has been made the eighth step of the Noble Eightfold Path. Wrong meditation is to be avoided no less sedulously than, for example, wrong speech and wrong action. Indeed, it is to be avoided with even greater care, for its consequences are frequently far more disastrous, including as they do not only, on the negative side, failure to develop *prajñā*, but on the positive side a wide variety of physical and mental disturbances.

In those Buddhist lands where knowledge of the correct practice of meditation has been transmitted, through an unbroken succession of teachers and pupils, from the earliest times to the present day, the student will in most cases be made familiar with the right methods, and guided in the right direction, from the very beginning. But students who live in virtual isolation, away from the main streams of Buddhist tradition, and even the English-educated in Buddhist lands, will naturally be exposed to the dangerous influences emanating from the growing body of literature which, generally under the name of yoga, professes to teach the secrets of meditation, but which in fact teaches something quite different from Buddhist *samādhi bhāvanā*. Some years ago a book was published on Tibetan yoga that was little more than a rehash of an English version of the *Yoga sūtras* of Patañjali with a little pseudo-Tibetan colouring added. The author had very obviously never been out of Europe. In a more recent book the author, who professes to have been born and brought up in a Buddhist country, describes how his 'third eye' was opened by means of a surgical operation![204]

In order to avoid being misled by works of this type certain obvious precautions should be taken. The Buddhist student of meditation should never have recourse to non-Buddhist teachers or teachings. If he does so he violates all Three Refuges and in effect ceases to be a Buddhist. Wherever possible he should place himself under the guidance of someone – either a monk or layman – who knows both the theory and the practice of Buddhist meditation. Failing this, he should carefully study the canonical and other authentic Buddhist literature on the subject and take up some simple practice – such as the *mettā bhāvanā* – which he feels will suit his temperament. He should remember that it is better to take one step in the right direction than a thousand in the wrong direction. He should not allow himself to fall prey to either impatience or despair. The Buddha has taught a path which leads *gradually* to perfection, and he may be sure that, under the law of karma, his solitary but sincere practice of right meditation will set up reactions that will eventually bring him into contact with a teacher who will be able to guide him even further up the steep and perilous slopes of that mountain upon whose topmost peak lies the sunshine of Supreme Enlightenment.

November 1957

BUDDHISM AND ANIMALS

The World Day for Animals, which was observed recently by religious and humanitarian organizations in a large number of countries, ought to have caused serious-minded Buddhists to reflect on the nature of the principle governing their relations with the furred, feathered, and scaled world.

Unlike Judaism, Christianity, and Islam, the Dharma of the Buddha makes no distinction between creatures who possess and creatures who do not possess 'immortal souls'. Theology and metaphysics apart, for the Buddhist it is enough that without exception *all sentient beings*, by the mere fact that they are sentient, feel pain no less keenly than he does. Moreover, explicitly denying as it does the false conception of an omniscient, omnipotent deity who has created the various animal species especially for the service of man, Buddhism does not countenance the ruthless exploitation and wanton destruction of animal life that has prevailed wherever the great monotheisms flourished. It is not without significance that whereas at the birth of Jesus the angels proclaimed to the shepherds of Bethlehem 'Peace on earth, good will towards *men*', the motto of Buddhism has ever been 'May *all* sentient beings be happy' (*sabbe sattā sukhī hontu*). Love, which involves a desire for the happiness of its object, is not really love (*mettā*) unless it is universal, unless it is not exclusive of anyone but all-inclusive. It is this universal love or *mettā* which governs the relations of a follower of the Buddha not only towards his fellow men but also towards animals.

Such being the case there is incumbent upon the thoughtful Buddhist not only the negative duty of refraining from causing pain to animals but also the positive duty of helping them and making them happy. He should not, therefore, kill for 'sport' or food, or wantonly inflict pain and suffering for the sake of 'amusement', as is done in the bullfights of Catholic Spain. He should not deal, whether directly or indirectly, in flesh or in animal products, or allow himself to profit in any way from such transactions. He should not attend circuses or visit zoos.[205] Above all, he should not indulge his appetite for a non-vegetarian diet on the specious plea that he is not individually responsible for the slaughter involved. Instead, emulating the noble example of the emperor Aśoka, who established hospitals and dispensaries for beasts and birds, he should do all that lies in his power to ameliorate the lot of domestic and draught animals, and to prevent the destruction of wild animal life. At the same time he should remember that kindness to animals does not compensate for cruelty to human beings, otherwise his practice of love will be no less one-sided and incomplete than that of the Christian. Cultivating universal love (*mettā*) as his first principle he should radiate it impartially towards *all* sentient beings. Says the Buddha in the *Dhammapada*:

> He who, seeking his own happiness, strikes with a stick beings who also long for happiness, will not find happiness after death.
>
> He who, seeking his own happiness, does not strike with a stick beings who also long for happiness, will find happiness after death.[206]

December 1957

1958

A NEW LOOK

This month, when a new year begins and when winter is about to enter upon its annual passage into spring, we naturally tend to reflect upon the passing of time and the transitoriness of human life. Everything changes. This, surely, is one of the fundamental tenets of Buddhism, exemplified not only in the years and the seasons but in all worldly phenomena.

Exemplified, too, in our journal. Since its humble beginnings in 1892 the *Maha Bodhi* has undergone numerous changes in format and vicissitudes of fortune. Sometimes it has looked fat and prosperous, and sometimes – as during the war years, when paper was rationed – it has presented a thin and famished appearance. Old contributors have passed away to be replaced by new ones. Editors have come and gone.

Yet in the midst of all these changes, which have now spanned six and a half decades, was there not something that, relatively speaking, remained unchanged? Surely the spirit of the journal, the ideal to which it was dedicated, did not change but, like the unwavering flame of a lamp uplifted in the gloom for the guidance of weary travellers, continued to shed light upon the Noble Eightfold Path of the Buddha, so that all who had eyes to see and feet with which to walk might tread it to the end – even to the matchless security of Nirvāṇa.

Hence as we not only set out on another year of service to our readers, but signalize it by a change of format, we ask them to remember that though the external appearance of the *Maha Bodhi* may change, its spirit remains unchanged. In this it does but resemble the doctrine itself which, despite external vicissitudes and internal developments innumerable, remains ever faithful to its mission of bringing nearer to Enlightenment all sentient beings. Even as the Dharma, though old, is yet eternally new, so the *Maha Bodhi*, we hope, is not only the oldest but at the same time the youngest of Buddhist magazines.

January 1958

THE NECESSITY OF LONELINESS

The *Khaggavisāṇa Sutta* of the *Sutta-Nipāta*, which exhorts the disciple to wander alone 'even as the horn of the rhinoceros is single', has been thought by some to uphold an individualistic, even an anti-social, ideal.[207] At the time of the Buddha, when food was plentiful and charity universally regarded as a virtue, it could have been argued that such an attitude was in essence escapist, and that it provided the weak and the irresponsible with an excuse for shirking the obligations of life. But the danger that we have to face in our day lies in the opposite direction; not in too easy an escape from society, but rather in the impossibility of finding any way of escape at all, does the difficulty now consist. Hence the extreme relevance of the teaching which we consider this month.

In all religious traditions and ascetic disciplines the value of solitude, of loneliness, of withdrawal from the crowd, is recognized. Out of solitude have come all great spiritual revelations. But it would seem that such reasons as have been advanced in explanation of this strange concomitance between solitude and religious, even aesthetic, inspiration, are either inadequate or misleading. Solitude, it is true, by shutting out distracting sense-stimuli, does help one to concentrate better. But that is not the whole story, for solitude really consists in physical isolation from other human beings, not necessarily in the absence of external disturbances. One can, for instance, be solitary even in the midst of a thunderstorm.

We think the profound import of solitude is not unconnected with the ideal, so important in Buddhism, which for the benefit of the ancient Greeks was summed up in two pregnant words: *Know Thyself*. It is natural, perhaps inevitable, that when in society we should behave as we are expected to behave, modifying our personality in accordance with that of the person with whom we are for the time being in contact. Ordinarily all that we know is ourselves as we appear to others, or think we appear to others, not ourselves as we really are. The series of personas or masks that we assume in our commerce with other personas constitutes our so-called 'personality'. Only when we are alone, in solitude, are the masks down, revealing not the relatively unchanging 'face', the soul or self *(ātman)*, but the void of utter impersonality – *anātman*. It is for this reason that most people fear to be alone, for they would be compelled not only to recognize their masks as masks but to realize that there was no visage beneath. Hence their need for God, who may in this context be defined as a supernatural personality posited to support and guarantee the reality of their natural personalities. True solitude, the solitude of which the Buddha speaks in the *Khaggavisāṇa Sutta*, consists in the absence of all contacts, all society, both human and divine. It is solitude *per se*.

Obviously, therefore, unless we can make in our lives adequate provision for solitude, at least periodically, it will be difficult for us to follow the exhortation to wander alone 'even as the horn of the rhinoceros is single', much less still to realize the profound import of the Dharma. The necessity of loneliness is one of the greatest things that urbanized and industrialized man of the twentieth century has to understand.

February 1958

DELAY AT BODH GAYA

One of the brightest features of the 2500th Buddha Jayanti Celebrations which took place from May 1956 to May 1957 was the great attention given by the Central and State Governments to the renovation and beautification of the various holy places. Ancient monuments were restored, parks and gardens laid out, and museums and rest houses erected so that the devotees who continue to stream in from a score of lands can now make their pilgrimage with far greater amenity than heretofore.

But at least in one sacred site, and that the most important of all, the work remains more or less incomplete. The pilgrim to Bodh Gaya will still find with mingled distress and amazement, that although a good deal of improvement has been done, the external appearance of the place is not yet commensurate with its unique importance in the history of mankind. The same unsightly collection of squalid huts continues to occupy the ground between the Maha Bodhi temple and the River Neranjana where a park should have been laid out, and improvised shops still disfigure the approach to the sacred edifice.

We are given to understand that a master plan for Bodh Gaya is being talked of. But it seems that what is needed at the moment is a master mind. Should the Government of Bihar, upon whose shoulders the heavy responsibility for the improvement of Bodh Gaya rests, be so fortunate to find one soon, he will have many problems to tackle. In addition to the two already mentioned there are such vitally important questions as the beautification of the temple building, repair of the old railing, erection of a boundary wall, laying out of the garden in the already acquired plot of land to the west of the temple, and many other items. Once the work is taken up in good earnest, the authorities may be assured, substantial contributions will be forthcoming from all parts of the Buddhist world. Hence there should be no further delay in taking up a matter of vital concern to hundreds of millions of Buddhists.[208]

March 1958

BUDDHISM AND PEACE

This month we shall be celebrating the 2502nd Buddha Jayanti. Though the celebrations will, no doubt, be on a rather more modest scale than those which marked the beginning and end of the 2500th Buddha Jayanti, they will certainly be conducted not only with solemn enthusiasm but with an awareness that, with the passage of years, Buddhism is more and more coming into its own; that the Dharma of the Enlightened One alone among the religious and spiritual traditions of mankind possesses both the strength to meet the challenge of aggressive materialism and the power to show to humanity the means of avoiding irremediable disaster.

Especially during the last few years, when the constant threat of atomic warfare has kept the whole human race trembling upon the verge of annihilation, has the astounding truth and relevance of the Buddha's message become more and more obvious to those who have eyes to see and ears to hear. Religions may prate of peace; but the Dharma of the Buddha alone can point to a record – a record covering twenty-five centuries – unstained by a single drop of blood.[209] Only the Dharma can claim that it has not preached now war and now peace, according to whether the one or the other was more expedient, but that from the very beginning it has upheld on principle the cause of universal peace and good will. That this should be so is hardly a matter for astonishment, for Buddhism is unique, not only in its exploration of the mind in all its amazing complexity, but also for its methods of systematic mental discipline and development. In no other teaching is the moral and spiritual life so firmly grounded on the facts of psychology.

Yet as the thoughtful Buddhist looks out on the contemporary scene he cannot help experiencing a painful sense of frustration. Here is a world so obviously in need of the Buddha's teaching, but no organized attempt is being made to bring that teaching to bear on the problems which at present beset not one race or one nation but humanity. At no point does Buddhism impinge with force on world events. It has not yet risen, it seems, to the position of a global influence. That this is so should be a matter of serious concern to all of us. As yet another Buddha Jayanti approaches let us resolve to celebrate it not merely with speeches and resolutions but by devoting serious thought to the question of how the Buddha's teaching of peace may be made effective in the troubled world of today. Tomorrow it may be too late.

May 1958

THE BUDDHA IMAGE

Among the priceless treasures which make up the glorious heritage of Buddhist art, it is the Buddha image, in all its sublime simplicity, that occupies the foremost place. More important still, in every Buddhist land it has become the focal point of all acts of devotion, public and private, individual and congregational, in this respect very largely superseding the more primitive stupa. Hence it becomes necessary for us to look more closely into the real nature of this main support of Buddhist piety.

The fact that we speak not of the *Siddhārtha rūpa* or *Gautama rūpa* but invariably of the Buddha *rūpa* is of the utmost significance. The image is not a naturalistic representation of the physical appearance of the great being who attained Enlightenment beneath the bodhi tree; on the contrary it is an attempt to convey the nature of Enlightenment. It is not a photograph but a symbol, and its significance is therefore not historical but metaphysical and transcendental. Not only the Buddha image but all other branches of Buddhist art, such as painting and architecture, possess this symbolical significance and value. They all aim not at satisfying historical curiosity or gratifying the aesthetic sense but at orienting our thoughts, feelings, and actions in the direction of Enlightenment.

Unfortunately, what passes as modern Buddhist art shows an increasingly pronounced tendency towards naturalistic representation of the most vulgar kind. Quite unconsciously, artists now take as their subject not the Buddha but Siddhārtha, with the result that the image or picture offered to the Buddhist public for worship is not a sublime symbol but a feeble portraiture. Indeed, to such an extent has the rot set in that very often paintings depicting 'the life of the Buddha' are not intended to fulfil any religious function at all. Small wonder, then, that instead of the noble types of the past we are confronted by sleek, smiling figures, very carefully executed as to drapery and fingernails, from which every trace of spiritual significance has been excluded.

What is now needed is a return to the canons of traditional Buddhist art. Not only the Buddhist artist but also the Buddhist public must become more deeply aware of the situation, for if they do not the forces of secularism will encroach still more aggressively and eventually destroy another vehicle of the Doctrine.[210]

June 1958

RAINY SEASON RETREAT

Rhythm is the law of life. Every living thing, from the amoeba to the elephant, passes through the same interrelated cycles of growth and decay, assimilation and excretion, movement and rest. Similar is the case with organizations and institutions which, though they are in themselves only metaphorically alive, nevertheless consist not of bricks and stones but of the living human beings who make up their membership, so that they may more properly be spoken of in terms of analogy with animate rather than with inanimate things.

In the life of the Buddhist sangha, for example, there has been since the earliest times a rhythm of expansion and contraction, of diffusion and consolidation, not unlike that of wakefulness and sleep in the life of the individual organism. For nine months of the year the *bhikṣu*, the fully ordained member of the sangha, is free to wander from place to place preaching the Dharma; but for three months he is obliged by the rules of the community to reside in one spot, being permitted to leave it, even for a single night, only under conditions of grave emergency.

The immediate occasion for the Buddha's forming of the rules of the rainy season retreat (*vassāvāsa*) was, as is well known, the complaint of certain members of the public of his time that, unlike wanderers of other religious orders, the followers of the Buddha travelled during the rainy season, thus causing damage to the young crops and harm to the swarming insect life. That the Buddha satisfied them by enacting the rules in question is a good example of his practical sagacity. But it should not be thought that the rainy season retreat is no more than a politic concession to the prejudices of an agricultural community. This is shown by the fact that, in countries such as Tibet, where quite different climactic conditions prevail, the retreat continues to be observed.

For the *bhikṣus*, the rainy season retreat is a period of intensive spiritual practice, study, and teaching, through which they experience a renewal of spiritual energy for their work during the remainder of the year. For the devout *upāsakas* and *upāsikās*, the men and women lay devotees, it is a time of more frequent attendance at temple and monastery, where, in discussion with the *bhikṣus*, they may increase their knowledge of the Dharma and resolve doubts.

This year the *vassāvāsa* begins on the Śrāvaṇa Pūrṇimā, 30 July, and ends on the Kārtika Pūrṇimā, 27 October. It is sincerely hoped that throughout the Buddhist world, which now embraces both East and West, the period will be utilized by monks and lay people alike for a profounder study and more energetic practice of the Dharma. By keeping up the age-old rhythm of the Buddhist life in this way we shall undoubtedly contribute to the vitality and longevity of the *śāsana* throughout the world.

August 1958

MEDITATION ON A FLAME

Formless yet having shape, expanding and contracting, yielding to the force of currents to avoid extinction, giving forth its own nature always; this is a flame. Potentially ever present in the world, actual only where it has been kindled by some external hand, it may be small and weak like that of a candle, liable to be blown out by a draught too strong for it, or immense and spreading, using all air currents merely to augment itself and against which they have no other power.

As with an actual flame, so with the flame of the spirit in man: it is always potential, not always actual, but in virtue of his human status it must be there waiting for the hand that strikes the match and kindles it into being. Starting at first weak and flickering, liable to extinction should the draughts which are the adversities and obstacles of life, prove too strong, it may yet learn to yield and alter itself, ever changing its shape, and so come in time to be able to use life's adversities to augment itself by conquering them, until the man, instead of railing against his hard lot, thanks all those who make life hard for him, because they offer him the means for his own development.

But there is one thing a flame needs to remain actual: it must be fed constantly from without itself. The fuel of man's spiritual flame is events, stimuli, without which he must become a fossil, a being dead while yet technically alive. When man loses his sense of wonder at and interest in the things and works of nature, he is dying – and how few retain their sense of wonder after childhood is past, for the cares of the world and the wrong sense of values attributed to things material, slowly but surely extinguish the flame, withdrawing its fuel until, with a last feeble flicker perhaps at something more than usually startling, it finally dies away – and what is left of the man? A body, an intellect, some emotions, but where is the spirit? It has returned to the potential state and only a match can reignite it.

This is the condition of the greater part of so-called humanity today, dead in life, with spirits potential only, lacking fuel and not responsive to the match that always hangs over them.

If too many flames flicker and die away, with what will the world be lighted?[211]

October 1958

MEDITATION UPON WATER

Whence comes the water that gives life to the Earth and without which man would die? Does it not come from the sea? And whence came the sea? We are told the sea was formed by the rising vapour from the ball of fire that was later to cool down until it gave birth to plants and animals and men. How many aeons this took is unknown, for the Earth must have been at a temperature inconceivable when it first swung into its orbit and encircled the sun. And many aeons must have passed ere it was sufficiently cooled for the water vapour to cease to rise and fall and rise again, and by then the deep crevasses and great basins were filled to form the oceans and the seas. And after that time, yet many more aeons have passed while the Earth has still been engaged in the conquest of her own past history, in the effort to stabilize herself and achieve an equability of temperature so that the winds, as they pass over the waters, may carry away just so much and no more of the vapours to drop them again in gentle showers upon the land.

But Nature is not yet completely subdued, for floods, typhoons, and tidal waves burst the bonds of her restraint and wreak havoc and destruction and again subside and all is calm.

And this pattern of Nature is reflected in Man. In childhood there is no self-restraint, passions burst forth and evaporate as quickly. Slowly, by external discipline first, self-discipline is learned and the adolescent knows when it is wiser and safer to restrain himself. But the adult, if he is to develop in spirit, must, as years bring wisdom, practise that self-discipline for its own sake, until he no longer emulates the oceans and the seas, showing now a sparkling calm, now a raging tempest, now a mild swell of irritation and again a calm, when the sun is shining and all is well. It is for him to prevent the waves of passion rising, however hard the winds of adversity may blow, however loud the thunder roars; to maintain that calm blue surface on which the sun sparkles and which makes all who see it feel the beauty and goodness of Nature, where savagery and violence have no place, and which bears up the craft that ride upon it safely to their havens.[212]

December 1958

1959

SPREADING THE DHARMA

Sabbadānaṃ dhammadānaṃ jināti says the Buddha in the *Dhammapada* – 'The gift of the Dharma excels all gifts.'[213] Nowadays, in an age of increased secularization even of religious ideals and practices, we tend only too often to think of *dāna,* giving, in more or less exclusively material terms. True charity, we think, consists in supplying the underprivileged with the necessities of life, with a standard of living worthy of a human being, with education and leisure. But the Buddha, while by no means discounting these inferior but still highly praiseworthy forms of *dāna,* insists that the highest and best of *dānas* is that of the Truth which he taught, for this is the means not of material and intellectual, but of spiritual life, without which humanity were in truth more dead than alive.

So it behoves all Buddhists, who strive to follow, however falteringly, in the footsteps of the Enlightened One, to remember that far better than any material donation is the gift of the Dharma. With the vast changes which, during the last few decades, have overtaken the Buddhist countries of Asia, have come ever greater and greater opportunities of disseminating the teaching which, like a precious family heirloom, they have for century after century faithfully transmitted to succeeding generations. Though still torn by strife and wracked by mutual suspicion, the world is now one to a greater degree than it ever was before. Astonishing increases in facility of transportation and communication have taken place. While we need not, like some of the more fanatical churches of the West, dream of sending missionaries to the moon, there is no doubt that here on Earth we are confronted by an opportunity for disseminating the Dharma such as Buddhism has not enjoyed since the days of Aśoka.

Of that opportunity it is our duty to take advantage. Only too often is the charge levelled against Buddhists, and especially against the members of the sangha, that they lack imagination, that great opportunities are being lost, perhaps for ever, through neglect, indifference, and laziness. Ensconced in his own small corner of the Buddhist world, only too many a Buddhist cares nothing for what is happening to the Buddhist movement in the world at large. If we think of the missionary activities of other religions, which we consider less developed than our own, we cannot but be filled with shame. A thin trickle of Buddhist monks has only just begun to reach India, Europe, and America. Africa, the Muslim Middle East, and Australasia, as well as Russia and South America, are untouched.[214] Surely the time has now come for us to bestir ourselves and, realizing that the gift of the truth is the greatest of all gifts, take upon ourselves more seriously than ever the task of spreading the Dharma.

January 1959

A GREAT RESPONSIBILITY

On 6 December tens of thousands of Buddhists all over India celebrated the second anniversary of the passing away of the great Buddhist leader Dr Ambedkar. At the time of his demise many thought that this tragic and unexpected event would result in the check, or at least the retardation, of the movement of mass conversion which he had so magnificently initiated only nearly two months earlier. Fears proved to be liars. During the last two years at least ten million people have, at a very conservative estimate, taken refuge in the Buddha, the Dharma, and the Sangha, and it may be confidently expected that by the beginning of 1961 the number will have risen to twenty-five million.

This phenomenal increase in the number of converts naturally has placed a tremendous strain on the resources of all Buddhist organizations working in the country. The strength of the few dozen *bhikkhus* available is being taxed to its utmost. The time has come when the

Buddhist countries of Asia – all of whom received the Dharma, directly or indirectly, from India – should realize their indebtedness and repay it with massive contributions towards the *dharmadūta* work which is being carried on among the new converts. Even more than funds, workers are needed. At present there is only one *bhikkhu* to every million new Buddhists. There should be at least one for every ten thousand. This means that one thousand *bhikkhus* are needed immediately. So far, we must admit, the response of the Buddhist countries to the needs of their Indian younger brothers in the Dharma has been most disappointing. However, it is still not too late, and we trust that during the current year both organizations and individuals will come forward with substantial assistance. Without proper guidance, it may be that the new Buddhists will, quite unintentionally, be borne in a direction quite contrary to that intended by Dr Ambedkar. Let the Buddhist world look to its great responsibility in this matter while there is yet time.

February 1959

MEDITATION UPON EARTH

Much of the grandeur of the world's landscape is made up of mountains; huge granite masses hurled up by the internal grumblings and outbursts of a planet not yet stable in itself. Solid, inert, they can only be worn a little away by the fury of the elements and those upon whose surface trees and vegetation grow suffer little even from this. They are fixed, immutable; but triflingly changed through centuries and even through aeons.

But all are not granite, and those of chalk and sandstone swiftly alter before the blasts of gales and driving rain. They are looser in composition, less dense, and change with the onslaughts that they suffer.

Then there are the deserts, fine sand, the finest of earthy particles, which remain arid and kill all those who wander in them, unless they have their own means of sustenance. Here and there an oasis may be descried, a spot which one can touch and perish not; and sometimes there is only the mirage.

The soil, the surface of mountains that have been worn away from repeated friction despite their intrinsic nature, is various; clay, sand, chalk, rich, poor, fertile, or barren, one can but try it and see what will grow in it.

And people, those who till the soil, who live on the fringe of the desert or who climb the mountains – do not they, too, resemble the earth in its varied aspects? Some there are – too many – who are hard as granite, untouched by finer things, impervious to the winds that blow, brushing off those who try to seek shelter on them; affected only more superficially by repeated friction; unfeeling, inert, rigid, unchanging; life after life they live for themselves alone and heed not the needs of others. The sandy ones there are who have no depth although their surfaces can be swept by the prevailing wind which can indeed raise a storm but, after it has died down, all is as it was before. Then there are those of clay who bog the purposes of others, by pessimism, ridicule, disapproval, and all negative emotions. But little grows in clay soil. The chalk can be seen from afar, shows up white and gleaming but, apart from its appearance, is no better than the sand – friable, easily broken up and re-formed again.

Then the soils of varying fertility resemble those of the human race with their differing levels of being and potentialities. The rich loam is the soil formed from the decay of vegetation; those who allow life to affect them and who learn from it. Absorbing their lessons into themselves and expanding themselves, fitting themselves for development and growth. And from them men – lesser men – gather fruits, the fruits of a life well used and not wasted.

March–April 1959

DIKSHA BHUMI

On 14 October 1956, the greatest religious revolution India has seen in modern times took place when the late Dr B. R. Ambedkar of revered memory was publicly initiated into Buddhism by the Ven. Chandramani Maha Sthavira along with half a million of his followers.[215] It is now a matter of history that the great movement of Buddhist revival thus inaugurated has since swept over the whole of central and western India, besides penetrating into many other parts of the great subcontinent, and despite the tragically sudden demise of the lion-hearted leader shortly after his conversion it continues to make tremendous progress.

It is only natural that, to those who received the light from Dr Ambedkar, as well as to fellow Buddhists all over the world, the Diksha Bhumi, or Initiation Ground, as the spot where the historic event took place is now universally known, should be regarded as a place of pilgrimage, 'with odours visited and annual flowers'.[216] Natural, too, is their desire that on that spot, hallowed by so many memories, should be erected not only a worthy memorial to Dr Ambedkar but also viharas and other institutions that would further the cause of Buddhism in India.

Since the land in question belongs to the Bombay State Government no difficulty was anticipated in connection with its acquisition. However, it is reported that despite vigorous pressing of their claim by the newly initiated Buddhists and other interested persons, the Bombay State Government refuses to grant more than the tiny plot on which stands an obelisk, erected shortly after the conversion ceremony, to mark the exact spot on which Dr Ambedkar stood when he accepted the Three Refuges and Five Precepts. The excuse given is that the land in question is required for an agricultural college.

That an agricultural college in Nagpur is a desideratum, even a necessity, may be freely admitted; but alternative plots no less suitable for the purpose are easily available. The religious sentiment that attaches to the Diksha Bhumi, on the other hand, cannot be transferred to any other piece of land, however convenient. We therefore earnestly hope that the Bombay State Government will graciously accede to the legitimate request of the Indian Buddhists by handing over to them the fifty or sixty acres of land which to them constitute the hub of the great wheel of revival of the Dharma set revolving by their intrepid leader.[217]

July 1959

IMPLEMENTATION

That the world needs Buddhism, that the message of peace and universal love preached by the Buddha alone can save mankind from impending catastrophe, is a view one nowadays finds adumbrated by the Buddhist press and platform times innumerable. In fact it has become a platitude. Even non-Buddhist speakers and writers have caught the contagion, and solemnly assure us that the Dharma of the Lord Buddha is the one panacea for all ills.

But what do these protestations and assurances mean? How much are they really worth? It needs but half an eye to see that those who, from the public platform, are loudest in their praise of the Buddhist ideals and most emphatic in their professions of loyalty to Buddhist principles, once they have stepped down from that platform only too often act, or unprotestingly allow others to act, in a manner that is the antithesis of all Buddhism stands for. Small wonder, then, that many have come to feel that the sacred name of the Dharma is being unspeakably profaned by those to whom it is little more than a convenient screen for individual and collective ambition and aggrandizement.

Yet such profanation does not diminish the world's need for the Dharma. It makes it greater still. Indeed, the very enormity of the offence constitutes a challenge to all those Buddhists and friends of Buddhism who do genuinely and deeply feel mankind's terrible and tragic need for the Buddha's message at this crisis in world history. To such it acts, or should act, not only as a challenge but as a stimulus, urging them to a more active and ardent advocacy of the unique and timeless truth, the universal relevancy, of the Dharma.

Only too often, it must be admitted, those upon whose shoulders rests the responsibility for preserving and disseminating the sublime Doctrine have failed in their duty. Lassitude, indifference, neglect, and procrastination have been allowed to retard the progress of the Buddhist movement in the modern world. Personal rivalries, sectarian differences, and lack of intelligence and imagination have also played their part.

There is now not a moment to be lost. Mankind does need Buddhism – and needs it more desperately than ever. Let the Buddhists of the world, already united through their common allegiance to the Triratna, unite in a vigorous movement for the worldwide *implementation* of the Buddha's teaching of selflessness and compassion before it is too late.

August 1959

WORDS AND MEANINGS

Every department of knowledge, every art and science, has its own peculiar vocabulary, its terminology as we generally say, and the learning of any subject consists in part of so well mastering that terminology that we are not only able to understand the significance of the terms when used but to employ them ourselves with aptness and precision. To attempt to study, much more so to discuss and write about, subjects that have attained a high degree of development without first acquainting ourselves with their special language, is likely to result in confusions and misunderstandings worse than complete ignorance.

This is particularly true in the domain of philosophy and religion, and above all in that of the Buddha-Dharma. Much unnecessary dust has been raised by people, not excluding experienced scholars, confidently writing and speaking about Buddhism without first ascertaining what its keywords are and what are their respective meanings. Buddhism was first preached in India. Naturally, in order to communicate its ideas it had to have recourse to such philosophical and religious terms as were then available. But the meanings it attached to them were not always the accepted meanings. This is evident to anyone who goes from the texts of the early Upanishads to those of the *Nikāyas*.[218] Yet those are not wanting, even now, who argue from an identity of words to an identity of meanings. 'The word *nirvāṇa* is found in both Buddhist and Hindu literature, therefore....' etc.

Yet it must be admitted that, in modern times, the Buddhists themselves are sometimes not over-careful in the use of their own terminology. This is particularly true of those who do not have the opportunity of regular contact with *bhikṣus*, from whom the laity in Buddhist lands usually acquire the correct use of Buddhist terms by a process of unconscious imitation. The word *parinirvāṇa*, for instance, is traditionally used only in referring to the final passing away of a *samyak-sambuddha*, a Fully Enlightened One. Yet some Indian Buddhists, we regret to say, are inadvertently making use of it in speaking of the deaths of persons who, however eminent they might have been, were certainly not Buddhas. Mistakes such as this make it obvious that if further misunderstanding and confusion are to be avoided we must in future insist upon a more intensive study of words and meanings in Buddhism and a stricter attention to the correct use of the traditional terminology.[219]

September 1959

THE BUDDHIST WORLD

That, owing to greatly increased facilities of transport and communication, the world has grown 'smaller' than it was in the days of our grandparents, is now a commonplace hardly worth repeating. What we do not realize, or realize much less clearly, is that the 'worlds' constituted by different human activities and interests have grown proportionately smaller too.

Take what we call the Buddhist world. Less than a hundred years ago each Buddhist land, though faithfully maintaining its own distinctive form of the Buddhist tradition, as it had been handed down for centuries, was content to remain in a state of total ignorance regarding alternative forms of the same tradition that were being followed elsewhere. The term 'Buddhist world', had it been current in those days, would have had a merely geographical significance.

Now the situation is greatly changed. It is no longer possible for Buddhists of one country or school to ignore the beliefs and customs of Buddhists belonging to other countries or schools. Apart from the fact that books on all the major aspects of the Buddhist tradition exist in most of the more widely known modern languages, increased facilities of communication have enabled thousands of Buddhists from different parts of the world to enjoy personal contacts of a kind which, in ancient days, were open only to the most heroic and adventurous.

Such contacts give rise to re-evaluations. It is becoming more and more widely realized that no one form of Buddhism, however venerable, can claim a monopoly of the Dharma; in each has been prescribed the essentials of the Teaching plus additions of local origin which, though not necessarily prejudicial to the integrity of the Dharma, are not indispensable to its practice either.

The time is now fast approaching when a Buddhist of Ceylon will have to be no less familiar with the Buddhism of Japan than with that of his own country, and vice versa. The Theravādin will have to study the Mahāyāna and the Mahāyānist the Theravāda. 'He knows not England who only England knows,' sings the poet.[220] Similarly he knows not Buddhism in all its wonderful breadth and amplitude who is acquainted with but a single aspect of the total tradition. Only by eschewing sectarianism and understanding and putting into practice this idea of unity will 'the Buddhist world' cease to be a mere geographical expression and become a living spiritual reality capable of giving light and guidance to the larger human world of which it is a part.

October 1959

WELL DONE!

More than once, in these columns, have we called the attention of our readers to the very great need for the dissemination, on the widest possible scale, of Buddhist literature attractive in format and authoritative in content.

For a long time it seemed as though our words had gone unheeded; but eventually there appeared, here and there, in the Buddhist world, signs which showed that others were not only thinking along similar lines but actually trying to implement our suggestions. The most important of these manifestations was the founding, in January last year, of the Buddhist Publication Society, Kandy,[221] whose report for the year 1958 has just been issued by the honorary secretary, the Ven. Nyanaponika Mahathera.[222]

The objects of the Society, as stated in the report, are refreshingly simple: to publish and supply free Buddhist literature to foreign countries. The main emphasis, we are told, is on the issue, primarily in English, of concise booklets and small tracts, though it is hoped some time in future to publish larger books on Buddhism. Two serial publications are issued regularly – the booklet series 'The Wheel' and the tracts 'Bodhi Leaves', several issues of both of which have been reviewed in the pages of this journal.

In the year under review there were issued no less than seven booklets and four tracts, surely a fine achievement for a small and recently founded organization with limited resources. The field of distribution covered 55 countries and literature was sent to 470 foreign addresses (now, in 1959, increased to 830), which included individual Buddhists, Buddhist associations, and friends of Buddhism. Though the Society started publishing with 1,000 copies of 'The Wheel' and 2,500 of 'Bodhi Leaves', the issues were later increased to 5,000 and 10,000 respectively. This to some extent was made possible by the generous subsidy sanctioned by the Ministry of Cultural Affairs, Government of Ceylon. The Report notes that the revival of Buddhism in India alone and the demands made by Buddhist associations there make a considerable increase of the Society's output imperative. Such an increase is entirely contingent upon the extent of the funds available for the purpose, and any special support in this direction, we are told, would be welcomed.

From the impressive list of helpers appearing at the end of the report it would seem that the venture is a cooperative one. We are told that the work of publishing, editing, distributing, accounting, and correspondence has all been a labour of love, no charge having been made on the finances of the Society. From the uniformly high standard of the publications it would appear to be a labour not only of love but of wisdom too.

Confronted by such a noble effort, one can only cry, in the traditional Buddhist manner, 'Well done!'

November 1959

THE SPIRIT IN WHICH WE WORK

Time, admittedly, is relative, and such things as dates and anniversaries are in the nature of a conceptual superimposition upon the timeless and spaceless Reality. Still, the ending of another year of Buddhist activity according to the international calendar may be considered as giving us an opportunity for appraisal.

More important than what has been done is the spirit in which it has been done. By the very nature of the human mind, things which are only a means to an end only too easily tend to become perverted into ends in themselves. We all realize the necessity of propagating the Dharma which the Buddha lived and taught. What we do not always realize quite so clearly is that our methods of propagating it must be in accordance with the spirit of the Dharma.

Perhaps it is better to live a 'worldly' life – earning one's livelihood and supporting a family – in a truly Buddhist spirit than to conduct so-called 'Buddhist' activities in a worldly, self-seeking spirit. Which, in any case, is more likely to impress and attract the non-Buddhist enquirer into Buddhism?

When even an ordinary life, lived in accordance with the Buddha's teaching, is a good advertisement for the Dharma, what must be the effect of religious work conducted by workers deeply imbued with that attitude of wisdom and compassion, energy and mindfulness, inculcated by the Enlightened One?

In the modern world organized religion is very much on the defensive. Everywhere people are less disposed than formerly to accord automatic respect to a man because he wears a special dress or makes certain professions. The homage of the spiritually uncommitted person has more and more to be actually won: it must never be taken for granted. Under such conditions the spirit in which we work for Buddhism, whether as members of the Society[223] or in any other capacity, assumes a more decisive importance than ever before.

December 1959

1960

BUDDHISM AND THE 'DARK' CONTINENT

One has only to pick up the daily newspaper to be reminded of the fact that, in the field of politics, nations and governments – especially the larger ones – tend more and more to think in global terms. In such fields as economics, health, and culture too, global thinking is no longer the exception but almost the rule. Religious organizations, especially the various Christian churches, have also been influenced by the current tendency, so that one sometimes finds even quite small denominations represented, so far as missionary activities are concerned, in a hundred or more countries.

The most backward of the great religions in this respect is Buddhism. Despite its long and glorious record of missionary endeavour in ancient days, it is still astonishingly inactive. Even numerically insignificant Christian bodies like the Seventh Day Adventists or Jehovah's Witnesses maintain far more workers in foreign lands than do all the Buddhists of the world put together. If we look at the globe continent by continent, we shall find that Buddhism is still effectively present only in Asia. Not more than two or three *bhikṣus* have ever visited Australasia; two or three, perhaps, are permanently stationed in Europe; while a few dozen Japanese priests between them have to cover the whole of the North and South Americas.

But it is in the case of Africa that our negligence becomes most glaringly apparent. Among the sixty-odd states – many of them scheduled for independence in the course of the year – and three hundred million people of the 'Dark Continent' there has been as yet not the slightest attempt at Buddhist missionary activity. Churches and mosques have been established there by the hundred, perhaps by the thousand, but not one Buddhist stupa or vihara lifts its gilded pinnacles to the blue African sky as though pointing out the way to Nirvāṇa; not one yellow robe is seen disappearing down the jungle paths or passing between the kraals; not one page of one Buddhist book has ever been translated into any one of the many hundreds of African tongues. Surely these are omissions for which the whole Buddhist world may well be deeply ashamed.

Yet even now it is not too late to repair the omission. Let the Buddhist countries of Asia hasten to open diplomatic relations with every African state that attains independence this year and in the coming years and let them appoint, in every embassy, cultural attachés who, like Aśoka's *dharmadūtas* of old, will be responsible for making arrangements for prominent *bhikṣus* from their respective countries to undertake extensive preaching tours. Non-governmental agencies can then take up the responsibility of establishing permanent Buddhist missions. In this way the Buddhist countries of Asia will not only make up for the time already lost but also pave the way for a day when a free and resurgent Africa will, thanks to the Buddha's teaching, be no longer the 'Dark Continent' but a 'Continent of Light'.[224]

January 1960

NEEDED: A LENS

The sun's rays, falling upon the earth, produce merely a pleasing sensation of warmth. The same rays, made to pass through a lens, not only give rise to an unbearable sensation of heat but eventually cause the object whereon they are focused to burst into flame.

In all walks of life, in all spheres of activity, it is not just the expenditure but also the unification and concentration of energies which produces results.

Our Buddhist activities, only too often, are comparable to isolated rays of sunshine. All proceed from the same ultimate source, all are beneficial in effect; but being divergent their total impact upon humanity as a whole, or upon the area or sphere of work with which they are specially concerned, is negligible.

What is needed is a lens.

These observations apply with special force to the steps now being taken by various organizations and individuals to instruct the hundreds of thousands of newly initiated Indian Buddhists in the essentials of the Dharma in which they have with such zeal and sincerity taken refuge. Even more forcibly do they apply to the arrangements that are having to be made for the instructing of the instructors.

What is needed is a central institution, situated preferably in one of the four great places of pilgrimage, which will provide for the moral, intellectual, and spiritual training of *śrāmaṇeras* and *bhikṣus* who, after an intensive course of say three years duration, will be able to fare 'from village to village and town to town' preaching the Dharma.[225]

If the now divergent sun-rays of our various activities could be focused through such a lens would not the whole of Asia soon be ablaze with the spirit of the Buddha's teaching?

February 1960

VAIŚĀKHA PŪRṆIMĀ

In religion, as in other departments of life, it is only too often the obvious that escapes attention. We descry what is afar off, but fail to notice what lies directly beneath our nose. Familiarity breeds, if not contempt, then at least indifference, and more often than not the real significance of an idea that we think we understand very well, or an occasion with which we believe ourselves to be perfectly acquainted, is entirely overlooked.

This month we celebrate the Vaiśākha Pūrṇimā. That is, we celebrate, principally, the anniversary of the Buddha's attainment of Supreme Enlightenment. But in many cases have we not celebrated it so often, over a period of so many years, that we no longer either clearly comprehend or sincerely feel the real significance of the thrice-sacred day? Some are busy organizing meetings. Others are putting up decorations, or participating in processions, or struggling through the crowds that throng the temples in an effort to light a candle and offer a few flowers before they are swept aside by the relentless pressure of the devotees. No one, apparently, has time to sit down quietly and reflect on the true meaning of the festival, much less still actually to emulate the Master in his quest for Enlightenment.

When such is the state of affairs on the Vaiśākha Pūrṇimā day itself, what is to be said of our attitude towards the Dharma during the remainder of the year? Even for the best of us, it is largely a matter of external, ostensibly Buddhist activities amidst the details of which we only too often forget the living principles that the Buddha enjoined us to practise. Even if we do not commit the mistake of seeking to propagate Buddhism by un-Buddhistic methods, we are oft-times more deeply concerned with matters of secondary importance than with fundamentals, more interested in moistening the twigs than in watering the root. Organizational activities do of course have their place, just as does the more spectacular and colourful side of the Vaiśākha festival, but even the most efficiently conducted organization, the most well planned function, or the most widespread missionary activities, are no substitute for the practice of the Dharma in one's own life. Buddhism will never be fostered or protected through the acquisition of political or economic power, though its external forms may indeed be perpetuated by such means. The existence of Buddhism depends above all on the sincerity with which we try to implement the Master's teaching in our individual and collective life.

These remarks apply with even more force to the monk than to the layman. Only too many *bhikkhus* think that they do their duty by being reasonably educated and comparatively interested in the maintenance of the institutional side of the religion which, after all, guarantees them their daily bread and butter with very little exertion on their part. The thought that they ought to devote themselves to the attainment of Enlightenment hardly crosses their mind from one year's end till the next. Even if it does, it is at once dismissed with the consoling thought that in these degenerate times arhantship is no longer attainable and that one does one's duty by piously hoping to be reborn in the days of Maitreya Buddha, when things will be much easier and when one can expect to become an Enlightened being if not automatically then at least with the minimum of personal effort.

Nowadays all religions are increasingly under pressure from the far-reaching changes that scientific methods have brought about and with difficulty maintain their ground. Though Buddhism is in many ways better equipped to resist this pressure than other teachings, being uncommitted to dogmas that conflict with scientific facts, it should not be supposed that it can therefore maintain itself in the modern world without further exertion on the part of those who profess to be its followers. Mankind needs the message of the Buddha perhaps even more urgently than in earlier centuries. Yet now, more so than previously, must that message be driven home by sheer force of personal example. Platitudes are not enough. Mere organizational activities fall short. What we need, not only on the Vaiśākha Pūrṇimā, but throughout the year, is a constant recollection of the fact that as Buddhists our goal is Enlightenment in the present life and a determined effort to advance each day a little nearer to its attainment.

May 1960

RELIGION VS GOD

A few years ago a courageous English woman psychologist, Margaret Knight, delivered over the BBC two talks on 'Morality Without Religion'. Her main point was that it was possible to lead a moral life without believing in dogmas such as those of a personal creator God and an incarnate divine saviour with which religion has been identified for centuries in Western countries. Despite their quiet, courteous, moderate tone, or perhaps because of it, the effect of the talks was devastating. Thousands of ordinary, decent English men and women suddenly realized, for the first time in their lives, that they did not really believe in Christianity. The orthodox reaction was one of extreme violence and ferocity. No epithet was too bad for Mrs Knight. When the clamour had died down, however, even churchmen were compelled to admit that she had focused attention on an important question.

Is it possible to be moral without believing in God? For centuries, in fact since its inception, the Christian church (or rather churches, for there are now about 700 of them, nearly all claiming to be the one true church) has taught that morality requires a supernatural sanction, that unless one believes that certain 'commandments' have been imposed upon humanity through the medium of revelation by an omniscient and omnipotent deity who will inflict punishment after death for any infringement one is likely to go around cutting people's throats and stealing their purses. These beliefs, together with others no less crude, Christianity of course shares with Judaism, Islam, and other theistic systems.

But is this assumption, basic to all these religions, really justified? If we look at the millions of people who have for centuries followed

Buddhism, Jainism, Taoism, and Confucianism, all of which are unambiguously non-theistic, we shall find that they exhibited in their lives no less goodness than their counterparts in other faiths who trembled before the wrath of an angry God. How, then, is it possible for any unprejudiced student of comparative religion to avoid the conclusion that religion, in the sense of belief in such a God, is not necessary to the leading of a moral life?

We may go even further. If we examine the bloodstained history of Christianity, so full of persecutions, religious wars, burnings at the stake, whippings, torture, and every kind of intolerance, all for the glory of God, and contrast it with the peaceful record of Buddhism, which in the course of twenty-five centuries has shed hardly a drop of blood in the name of its founder, we cannot help thinking that religion in the Christian sense is not only unnecessary to morality but positively detrimental to it, so that it is not only possible to have morality without religion, as Mrs Knight so clearly saw, but even desirable to do so.

Of course it is largely a question of the proper definition of terms. In the West religion traditionally means belief in God and his son Jesus Christ, who is conceived as the saviour of the human race, and for the purpose of her talks Mrs Knight not unnaturally took this definition for granted. But why should religion be defined so narrowly? Surely the time has come to recognize the fact that religion does not necessarily imply belief in God. So much should be conceded even from the standpoint of comparative religion. The Buddhist point of view is even more radical. Buddhism has affirmed from the beginning of its history that belief in God has nothing to do with religion; it is a survival from pre-scientific times which degrades rather than elevates man. As an early attempt to explain the origin of the universe the belief has a certain historic interest; but far from being any longer relevant to religious life God, from the standpoint of advanced thought, is no more than an exploded scientific hypothesis.

Buddhists should not feel afraid of emphasizing the non-theistic nature of Buddhism. If in the supposed interests of inter-religious harmony they attempt to gloss over this important fact they will be doing a disservice to the larger interests of humanity, to say nothing of betraying the truth. They should also beware of expositions of Buddhism that attempt to smuggle the word 'God' in through the back door, as it were, by giving it some fanciful interpretation of their own. As Buddhists we are definitely committed to the propagation of a non-theistic outlook. Morality stands, we aver, not on the shaky foundation of arbitrary and unverifiable dogmas, but on the sound and solid basis of psychological and spiritual laws. In the elucidation of these laws, and the inculcation of a way of life based thereon, consists the *raison d'être* of Buddhism.

June 1960

STOP THE ROT!

Even those who, like this journal, have no concern with politics, will have experienced a feeling of satisfaction on learning that a neighbouring Buddhist land had at last, after nine months of uncertainty, been able to give itself a government strong enough to ensure stability and progress for the next few years.[226] Our satisfaction is all the greater because the new government is headed by a woman.[227] The great democracies, as well as the communist countries of the world, all pay lip service to the ideal of equality of opportunity for men and women; but we have yet to see, in any of them, a woman at the helm of affairs. Even in India, in this respect more progressive than some other nations, women have as yet risen no higher in public life than an occasional ministership or governorship. It was left to Ceylon, a Buddhist country, to distinguish itself by electing the first woman prime minister in history. Not that this was wholly unexpected, for unlike other religions Buddhism throughout its long history has stood for the spiritual and social equality of the sexes. That a Buddhist land should have taken the lead in such a matter was therefore right and natural.[228]

Whether a man or a woman heads the Government of Ceylon, however, there are problems to be faced and solved. Regarding political and economic problems we can say no more than that they should be solved in the spirit of the Buddha-Dharma. But with politics and religion intertwined as closely as they so often are, there are problems which, though basically religious, those now holding political power in Ceylon will not be able to evade.

One of the most pressing of these relates to the participation of *bhikkhus* in politics. The assassination of the late Mr Bandaranaike highlighted, in dramatic and tragic fashion, the well-known fact that an unworthy section of the sangha had for a decade been playing an active role in politics, even to the extent of personally standing for election and conducting election campaigns for favoured political parties and groups. Herein certain misguided laymen were hardly less at fault than the *bhikkhus* themselves, for far from discouraging them they sought to utilize their undoubted influence over the Buddhist masses for political ends of their own. Owing to the sharpness of public reaction to the assassination of Mr Bandaranaike *bhikkhus* have now withdrawn from open participation in politics. But the possibility of their continuing to pull strings from behind the scenes remains. Some ecclesiastical establishments in Ceylon are wealthy, and it is known that some of the incumbents, who traditionally exercise untrammelled control over temple revenues, have made lavish contributions to the funds of different political parties. Resources which the piety of earlier generations of Ceylon Buddhists had destined for the upkeep and propagation of the *śāsana* were thus diverted from their rightful channels. As soon as it has settled down in office the new Government of Ceylon will undoubtedly have to consider the desirability of taking temple revenues out of the hands of the incumbents (who in any case as *bhikkhus* ought not to handle money) and setting up lay bodies legally responsible to the Government for the management of ecclesiastical properties and the proper application of their income. Such a move will certainly be resisted by those who, whether *bhikkhus* or laymen, have a vested interest in the continuance of the present system. On the other hand all those, whether in or out of the sangha, who realize that its true strength consists not in the possession of worldly goods, but in the moral and spiritual character of its members, will surely welcome it and give it their unstinted support and wholehearted cooperation. We hope that the prime minister, herself a devout Buddhist, will take action to stop the rot before it becomes too late.

August 1960

TWO ANNIVERSARIES

This month we celebrate two great anniversaries; the 100th death anniversary of Arthur Schopenhauer, the celebrated philosopher,[229] and the 96th birth anniversary of Anagarika Dharmapala, reviver of Buddhism in India and Ceylon and preacher of the Dharma in Western lands. The two events are not unconnected, any more than are the lives and works of the great thinker and the great organizer. They represent, in fact, two aspects of a single movement: the penetration of the utilitarianism not of the West alone but of the secularized society of the whole modern world by the lofty spiritual ideals of the traditional East, particularly those of Buddhism. It is well known that, as the first stanza of the *Dhammapada* teaches us, thought precedes deed. Consequently it is not surprising that the work of the thinker should have preceded that of the man of action. Schopenhauer was born in 1788, when dogmatic Christianity, despite the blows administered by the rationalists, still reigned supreme, and when oriental religions were dismissed as mere systems of idolatry. The Buddha was then hardly a name. The fact that, in the course of the nineteenth century, some of the most distinctive doctrines of Buddhism became familiar, in however imperfect a form, not merely to professional orientalists, but to the cultivated reading public all over Europe and America, is due very largely to the influence exerted by the writings of Schopenhauer. Thus it was that when, in the last decade of the century, the ardent young apostle of the Buddha rose to proclaim for the first time to an American audience the glorious message of his Master he could meet not with a shower of stones or worse, as would have happened half a century earlier, but with a profoundly respectful hearing. On the other hand it should not be forgotten that without the strenuous lifelong labours of Anagarika Dharmapala the tiny seeds planted by Schopenhauer, as well as by orientalists and theosophists, might never have been able to shoot and flower. This month, therefore, we rejoice to honour both the great thinker, Arthur Schopenhauer, and the great worker, Hewavitarne Dharmapala, for their complementary contributions to the deeper knowledge and wider practice of the Dharma in the modern world.

September 1960

A BOLD PROPOSAL

Students of modern history are well aware of the fact that the subjugation of Asian lands by the forces of Western imperialism was largely the work of the unholy triumvirate of the trader, the soldier, and the missionary. Who was first in the field depended upon local circumstance, but wherever one went the other two were sure to tread not far behind. Usually the whisky bottle and the bayonet led the way, while the Bible nobly followed. Even after the territorial conquest had been completed and political power consolidated, the alliance between the three forces continued, each being necessary to the safety of the other two: the missionary blessed the soldier and the trader, and taught his growing flock that they were the representatives of a superior culture sent by a merciful Providence to civilize the country, while the soldier protected the missionary and the trader supplied him with funds.

In this way a stranglehold was imposed not only on the political and economic, but even on the religious, cultural, and educational life of the conquered nation. With the firm conviction that Western education was the halfway house to conversion to Christianity, the missionary opened schools innumerable. These were supported largely out of government grants, which meant that the Hindu and Buddhist taxpayer had to bear the cost of the efforts made to induce them to change their faith. Students in missionary schools were deliberately and systematically denationalized; they were (and still are) taught to despise their own race, culture, and religion.[230]

It is hardly astonishing, therefore, that many an Asian land, after winning independence in the present century, should seek to remove not only the political and economic but also the educational stranglehold of their erstwhile masters on the national life. It is intolerable that the government and people of an independent Buddhist land, for instance, should continue to give financial support to an educational system which is thoroughly anti-national.

Against such a background must be viewed the Ceylon Government's bold proposal to nationalize all grant-aided denominational schools in the country. The denomination most seriously affected is the Roman Catholic Church, which with its monolithic organization and enormous resources can be expected to put up a tough, protracted, and wholly unscrupulous fight for what it regards as its rights. We sincerely trust, though, that despite all opposition the Ceylon Government will give immediate effect to its proposal and end forthwith the monstrous anomaly whereby the Buddhist public of Ceylon are obliged not only to acquiesce in the destruction of their own religion and culture but even to bear the cost of digging the grave.[231]

October 1960

One of the most permanently valuable features of the 2500th Buddha Jayanti celebrations held in India from 1956 to 1957 was the vigorous attempt made by both the Union and States Governments to improve and beautify the various sites connected with the life of the Buddha and the history of Buddhism. Even after the celebrations ended the good work, far from being discontinued, has in many cases not only been kept up but expanded. Among other famous sites, mention may be made of the Kanheri Caves, 45 miles out of Bombay in the State of Maharashtra, where an extensive National Park is being laid out which will surely add to the attractiveness of the place and swell further the number of tourists and pilgrims who visit it every year.

Unfortunately, the good intentions of those concerned are at times frustrated not only by the unimaginativeness of minor officialdom but also by the insensitiveness of certain members of the public. On visiting the Kanheri Caves recently a small party of Buddhist *bhikkhus* and *upāsakas* were astonished to find that the place had been temporarily turned into a set for the shooting of a film. Gone were the peace and quiet which they had expected to find there. Producers, directors, actors and actresses, extras, cameramen, and electricians, all quite oblivious to the hallowed associations of the spot, swarmed over the sunlit hillside. One cave, where formerly monks lived and meditated, had been transformed into a dressing-room, and before being shooed away by the shouts of some of the workers, who seemed to think they had no right to be there, they caught a glimpse of a well-known actor reclining in a barber's chair and receiving the attentions of the make-up man. Outside another cave, servants were clearing away the remains of a meal, in which more than twenty people appeared to have participated, flinging papers and other debris down the hillside to the next cave terrace. The *bhikkhus* and *upāsakas*, on entering the area, had been asked to leave their modest parcel of sandwiches outside on the grounds that, as a notice in fact informed them, the consumption of foodstuffs within the caves enclosure was prohibited! With similar disregard of the rules, three or four of the film company's employees were breaking off armfuls of flowering branches from the trees, even though, according to another notice, the plucking of flowers was prohibited too. Most surprising of all, it was learned on enquiry that the film being shot there had nothing whatever to do with Buddhism.

From the fact that uniformed guards were very much in evidence, especially in the area where the shooting was in progress, it could be inferred that the Kanheri Caves were being misused in this way with the knowledge, or at least the connivance, of the authorities concerned. The Archaeological Commissioner has, we believe, the power to permit film companies to make use of protected places and monuments for shooting purposes; but surely, in the case of religious sites which are still centres of pilgrimage for thousands of people, enquiries should first be made whether the film has any real connection with the traditions of the place: caves and shrines such as those of Kanheri are not lightly to be used as a background to sex or crime. In any case, there is no valid reason why rules that are strictly enforced with regard to the general public, including pilgrims, should be relaxed for the privileged members of the film industry. It would be worth enquiring, perhaps, whether the palms of those responsible for enforcing the by-laws pertaining to the place had been greased. Whatever be the explanation, the vandalism perpetrated at the Kanheri Caves is disgraceful, and we hope the Government of Maharashtra will take prompt and vigorous action to ensure that there is no repetition of the incident described.[232]

December 1960

1961

STAND STILL!

Buddhi, it has been well said, is that which makes one out of two; *manas*, that which makes two out of one. The former is the faculty of integration and unification, the latter that of diffusion and differentiation.

From *manas*, the differentiating principle, two modes of differentiation arise: one between phenomena as existent simultaneously, the other between phenomena as existent in succession. The first, considered objectively, is space; the second, time. Inasmuch as *manas* is the highest *operative* principle of human consciousness, our experience ordinarily takes place within the framework of these two categories.

Time is threefold: past, present, and future. If we analyse these three tenses, however, we shall discover an important difference between past and future time, on the one hand, and present time on the other. This difference may be briefly expressed by saying that whereas the present is perceived the past and the future are only conceived. In other words, past and future are never directly experienced; all we actually experience is the present. Past and future exist only as concepts.

The possibilities of human experience are immense. They range, as regards our relation to time, from a state of present-time experience unsullied by either conceptual constructions of past and future or the emotions based upon them, to a state so heavily overlaid with such constructions that present-time is hardly perceived at all.

Now it is obvious that experience of duration, of the passage of time, depends upon the concepts of time as past and time as yet to come: in the unalloyed perception of present-time there is no sense of duration. Hence to the extent that we can live spiritually in the present we are no longer conscious of the shortness of human life, or obsessed with a longing either for its prolongation or for personal immortality; for desire is possible only with regard to a past or a future, that is to say, a conceptual object, but not with regard to what is actually present and perceived.

Through the concepts of past and future, which constitute their common foundation, the sense of duration and desire are closely interconnected. We find, indeed, that an acceleration of the one results in an intensification of the other, and vice versa.

It is now possible to fly from India to England in eight hours. Within a few months, perhaps, human beings will be rocketed to the moon and back at enormous speeds. Even those who cannot afford a seat in a jet-propelled Boeing aircraft frequently travel long distances at speeds which their great-grandparents would have considered incredible.

What is the effect of this acceleration of the speed at which we can travel – indeed of the pace at which we now live – on the general human consciousness?

Physical speed and the sense of duration being intimately related, the more quickly we are able to do anything the less time there appears to be in which to do it. Conversely, the less time there appears to be in which to do a thing, the more quickly we desire to do it, whether the action concerned be that of travelling or anything else. Such is the vicious circle in which a rapidly increasing section of the human race now finds itself involved. In the expedience of time, there would seem to operate a principle analogous to the law of diminishing returns in economics, in accordance with which the more time-saving devices are placed at one's disposal the more pressed for time one becomes. Under such conditions the activities of twentieth-century humanity are increasingly characterized by a feverish haste which eventually results in physical exhaustion, nervous strain, and mental breakdown.

Aṅgulimāla the bandit, pursuing the Buddha along the jungle path with drawn sword, found himself in a similar predicament. However fast he ran he was unable to catch up with the Enlightened One, though the latter was walking at a slow, dignified pace. Eventually, exhausted by his efforts and terrified by the inexplicable phenomenon, he called to the Master to stand still. Back came the reply, 'I am already standing still (i.e. have attained Nirvāṇa); it is you who are running (i.e. round and round in *saṃsāra*, impelled by the force of ignorant desire).'[233]

The more desperately we try to catch up with the future the more it eludes our grasp. Like Aṅgulimāla, we have to listen to the exhortation of the Buddha – to the voice of our own immanent Buddhahood – and learn simply to 'stand still' at all levels of our being, both physical and mental. This can be done, initially, only by becoming aware that we are running. Awareness of speed, of duration, of the three tenses, eventually enables us to realize that past and future are concepts only. With this realization comes about a subsidence, a calming down and dying away, of all those emotions – desires and fears, anxieties and regrets – that are based on those concepts. We begin to live in the present in the true spiritual sense, and thus living in the present, unobsessed by the passage of time, find that we have time enough in which to do all things. Having reached such a state of awakened *prajñā*, we shall be able to board a jet-propelled Boeing, if circumstances so require, or even go for a weekend on the moon, with the same unruffled composure, the same freedom from all sense of haste, with which we walk at night in our garden among the fragrance of tranquil flowers.

January 1961

THE CENSUS

During the weeks beginning from 10 February a census will be taken of the entire population of India. The results of this immense undertaking, involving hundreds of thousands of enumerators, will naturally be awaited with great eagerness. Besides providing the Government of India with vital statistics indispensable to the proper planning of the nation's economy, the census results will furnish the sociologist with important data for study and evaluation. To the Buddhist, one of the most interesting features of the operation is the fact that it will provide him with a means of gauging the extent of the numerical increase in the strength of Buddhism that has taken place in the subcontinent during the last five years as the result of the movement of mass conversion to the Buddha-Dharma inaugurated by the late Dr B. R. Ambedkar of revered memory.

In order that we may know the exact number of Buddhists in India it is obviously of the utmost importance that each and every individual Buddhist takes all possible care to ensure that he or she is correctly enumerated. In so vast an undertaking a few genuine mistakes are, perhaps, inevitable, and no undue significance need be attached to them. Nevertheless it should not be forgotten that at the time of the last census, in 1951, many complaints were received by Buddhist organizations that Buddhists were in a number of cases enumerated as Hindus, sometimes even in spite of their vigorous protests.[234] This time, therefore, it behoves the Buddhists to be on their guard. In the case of illiterate persons, especially women, all entries made in the census forms regarding them, especially that concerning their religion, should be carefully checked by educated relatives or friends. If precautions are taken in this way, and if the Buddhists of India are fully and correctly enumerated, the result may well come as a surprise to all concerned.

February 1961

A DISTURBING DISPUTE

From Korea comes the news of a rather disturbing dispute. During the Japanese occupation of the country a number of Korean *bhikkhus* renounced the monastic vows, married, and began functioning as Japanese-style married priests. Though the sequence of events is not clear, it appears that they functioned as such from their own homes and other centres which they set up after leaving the sangha and that the remaining *bhikkhus*, who continued to observe their vows, remained for many years in peaceable occupation of the viharas and other sangha properties. Now, however, taking advantage of a shift of political power in Korea, the married priests are not only laying claim to the same rights and privileges as the celibate *bhikkhus*, including, apparently, the right to occupy the viharas together with their wives and families, but also attempting to gain possession of sangha property. In this attempt they are being backed up by forces inimical to Buddhism and it is reported that lawsuits have been filed against the *bhikkhus* seeking to evict them from the viharas.

Though naturally one should refrain from taking sides in any dispute until all the facts of the case are known, the celibate *bhikkhus* are evidently being made the victims of grave injustice. It is well known that any member of the sangha is free to leave it at any time he wishes. But it is axiomatic that on reverting to lay life he automatically ceases to enjoy the status of a *bhikkhu* or any of the rights and privileges annexed thereto. Even if out of ignorance or worse he forms a marital connection without formally giving up the robes, the fact that according to the common Vinaya tradition of all Buddhist countries such a connection constitutes a *pārājika* offence means that he automatically ceases to be a *bhikkhu*. There can be no question, therefore, of a married priest claiming the right to occupy a vihara or to share in the control and management of sangha property on the grounds that he was once a *bhikkhu* or on any other grounds.

This is not to say that the institution of married priests is not a good and useful one, or that such persons may not be men of exemplary life and worthy of all possible respect. But they are not *bhikkhus*, not members of the sangha in the ecclesiastical sense, and for them to lay claim to the same status as *bhikkhus* is an absurdity which runs counter to the entire Buddhist tradition. The celibate *bhikkhus* declare that if the decision of the courts goes against them they are willing to suffer persecution and martyrdom rather than vacate the viharas. While commending their courage and resolution we trust that matters will not go so far as that. All Korean Buddhists should clearly understand the difference between a married priest and a celibate *bhikkhu*, and if the law of the country fails to recognize the difference they should bring pressure to bear on the Government by constitutional means until it is amended.[235]

March 1961

VAIŚĀKHA PŪRṆIMĀ AND MEDITATION

This year, the Vaiśākha Pūrṇimā, the thrice-sacred anniversary of the Buddha's Enlightenment, falls earlier than usual, coming on 30 April. Early or late, however, in all Buddhist lands, as well as in those regions where the Dharma has only recently begun to make headway, it will be celebrated with a wide variety of traditional observances in the usual enthusiastic manner. Religious services will be conducted, processions taken out, meetings held, speeches delivered, alms distributed, firecrackers exploded, animals reprieved from slaughter, and so on. A spirit of jubilation will pervade the atmosphere; the stream of human kindliness will flow more lavishly and in greater abundance than on other less hallowed days of the year.

In the midst of all these rejoicings, however, it may be only too easily forgotten not only that we celebrate the Buddha's attainment of Supreme Enlightenment but, what is of no less importance, that his Supreme Enlightenment was attained not amidst the distraction of speeches but through the silent practice of meditation. If we honour the Buddha most when we most faithfully follow his example, as none who has carefully studied the records of his teaching can doubt, surely for a few minutes at least on the Vaiśākha Pūrṇimā Day, if not for an hour or more, we ought to withdraw from external celebrations, concentrate the mind, and try to fathom the significance of the teaching *within*.

What has been said with regard to our mode of celebrating the great day that commemorates the Buddha's Enlightenment in principle applies to our Buddhist activities throughout the year. These latter, we usually think, consist in the propagation of the Dharma through the medium of the spoken or written word, or even, at a lower level still, in the heaping up of brick and stone, steel and cement. What the Buddhist movement really needs, both in India and abroad, is a chain of meditation centres where those who are in real earnest, whether monks or lay folk, can be provided with facilities for assisting them to see the truth face to face.

Already, here and there, some effort in this direction has been and is being made. Most of the traditionally Buddhist countries have centres wherein are found the facilities of which we speak. The need is greatest and most urgent here in India, where after centuries of apparent extinction the Buddha's teaching is again reviving, and in those lands of the West where it has but recently struck root.

Those who, whether prompted by these words or of their own initiative, realize the true significance of the Vaiśākha Pūrṇimā festival, should not only strive to make it, in part at least, a day of meditation, but also to make Buddhism itself, even on the level of popular practice, more and more a religion of meditation.

May 1961

MORE VANDALISM

Readers may recollect that in the December 1960 issue of the journal attention was drawn, through these columns, to an act of vandalism perpetrated in the Kanheri Caves. Whether the Maharashtra Government has taken steps to ensure that there should be no repetition of the deplorable incident described we have as yet received no information. Meanwhile comes still more distressing news from another set of famous cave temples located in the same part of western India and within the jurisdiction of the same state government.

This time we have to draw attention to the unhappy state of affairs prevailing at the Karle Caves, situated about three miles east of Malavli on the Bombay–Poona railway line. When, a few weeks ago, a party of about three dozen pilgrims, including three monks, visited the spot, they found to their astonishment that a Hindu temple had been erected immediately in front of the carved and sculptured entrance of the main *caitya* cave, well known as the largest and most magnificent of its kind in India, with the result that the grandeur of the architectural ensemble has been seriously impaired. The function of the temple, a squat and ugly building painted in garish red and green and aluminium, was sufficiently obvious: Brahmin priests sat on the steps with outstretched palms demanding money from the pilgrims and other visitors who were constantly passing in and out. On enquiry, it transpired that the temple had been erected only two years previously. We are therefore to suppose, either that a cement building about fifteen feet square was erected within the protected area without the knowledge of those responsible for the care and maintenance of one of the best known and most important religious monuments of India, or that official sanction was given for its construction. In either case those responsible have been guilty not only of most serious dereliction of duty, but also of an act, whether of omission or of commission, most hurtful to the feelings of millions of Buddhists all over the world. Insult is added to injury when we learn that, though pujas go on merrily in the Hindu temple outside, followers of the Buddha are not officially permitted to offer so much as a flower within.

Bad as this is, it is not the worst. The pilgrim party was further informed, by the guards at the place, that the deity installed in the temple was a bloodthirsty goddess named Ekavira Devi, and that animals and fowls were regularly sacrificed to her, being slaughtered *within the protected area of the caves itself*. In proof of this statement, the party was taken to a small cave, only a few yards from the main *caitya* cave, and asked to look into the ancient well sunk at one side. Peering within, they were horrified to see a noisome collection of chickens' heads, black goatskins, and other offal from the sacrifices. Proceeding further in the same direction, they found another cave in which had been installed, immediately in front of the Buddha image, a large stone phallus which, judging from the amount of fresh vermilion with which it was smeared, was evidently an object of much popular devotion.

We have no comment to offer. The facts speak for themselves. Once again we appeal to the Government of Maharashtra to prompt and effective action.[236]

June 1961

A SERIOUS MATTER

From the very inception of Buddhism the sangha or monastic order has been the backbone of the religion and such, despite its backslidings, it continues to be still. Wheresoever the Dharma has spread the first concern of those responsible has been to establish an indigenous sangha, for unless this was done it was not considered that the *śāsana* had taken firm root in the native soil. However, the establishment of the sangha never meant simply putting droves of young men into yellow robes. No less important than the actual ceremony of ordination, sacred and significant as this undoubtedly is, was the proper preparation and training of the ordinands. Rules dealing with this subject are laid down in the Vinaya or code of monastic discipline. Unless the ordaining authority, technically called the *upajjhāya*, is both able and ready not only to confer ordination but also to shoulder the responsibility thereafter for teaching and training those who, by virtue of his having ordained them, have become his pupils, he has no moral right to confer either the higher or the lower ordination.

These observations are prompted by several unhappy incidents that have recently come to our notice. One concerns an Indian Buddhist who, on the very day of his arrival in a certain Buddhist country, was ordained as a *sāmaṇera* and then turned loose to fend for himself. Cases are not unknown of *sāmaṇeras* being quite ignorant of such elementary things as the ten precepts taken by them at the time of their ordination. Even worse, some such persons, through lack of training, not only behave in a manner that is a source of scandal to the public but also propagate views that are not those of Buddhism or even anti-Buddhist. Now that Buddhism is being revived in India, and candidates for ordination are beginning to come forward, all senior monks, whether in India or abroad, should fully realize the seriousness of the matter and refrain from giving ordination to persons whom they are unwilling or unable to train in the manner prescribed by tradition. Unless this is done we may have people in yellow robes but we shall not have a sangha.

August 1961

THE WORLD FELLOWSHIP OF BUDDHISTS

As even its critics concede, the Buddha's teaching appeals initially to the intelligence; it not only admits, but even demands, the unfettered exercise of the power of independent consideration, judgement, and decision. Alone among the religions of the world it has encouraged, instead of suppressing, freedom of thought, with the result that wherever it has spread there has been diffused among men a spirit of tolerance and good will. Because of these and allied characteristics Buddhism naturally addresses itself not to man *en masse* but to the individual thinking and reflecting human being; it is a stranger to appeals directed to the emotions or to the cruder and more primitive psychic forces wherefrom mass movements, whether religious or political or of any other kind, derive their impetus. Consequently it has never attached much importance to organizations and institutions: its aim has been the production of Enlightened individuals.

At the same time, however, it has not gone to the opposite extreme of anarchism. In keeping with its character as a teaching of the Middle Way it has avoided, on the one hand the extreme of subjecting the individual to the overwhelming pressures of a monolithic organization of the Roman Catholic type, and on the other the extreme of abandoning him entirely to his own devices. A Buddhist organization is therefore not something imagined to exist in its own right above and beyond the individuals who compose it but simply the means of their spiritually fruitful communication one with another.

These reflections are prompted by the fact that the Sixth Conference of the World Fellowship of Buddhists will meet next month in Phnom Penh, the capital of Cambodia. In view of the very nature of Buddhism it is impossible that the Fellowship, or any other Buddhist organization however widespread, should develop into a kind of super-body which would control its constituent and affiliated groups in a dictatorial manner and think, speak and act on their behalf. Yet surely more is expected of the WFB, after more than a decade of existence, than simply to assemble every two or three years for the purpose of sightseeing in the host country, listening to messages of greeting, and passing resolutions that it is powerless to implement.

No thinking person needs to be reminded that we live in critical, even dangerous, times, when the continued existence of the human race itself is at stake. In circumstances such as these it is imperative that the Buddhist point of view should be powerfully projected in the world and the pacific moral influence of the Buddha's teaching brought massively to bear on contemporary issues. This year's conference should give its most serious attention to the question. The WFB urgently needs a permanent headquarters, an efficient secretariat, and a really first-class journal; makeshift arrangements will no longer suffice. It must devise ways and means of bringing about a much closer understanding and more active cooperation between the Buddhists of the world than at present obtains. Unless such steps as these are taken without delay the WFB will never be a force to reckon with in the world of Buddhist affairs, much less still a vital factor in the much wider, more complex, and more dangerous world of the Cold War and the atom bomb.[237]

October 1961

A FRIEND OF BUDDHISM

The birth centenary of Rabindranath Tagore has been and still is being celebrated not in India alone but in many other parts of the world. This is indicative of the fact that he, like all truly great creative writers, while deeply and firmly rooted in the soil of his native tradition, was at the same time universal in outlook and appeal. Even when singing of the green paddy fields and broad slow rivers of his own 'Golden Bengal' he struck chords which reverberate in every heart sensitive to universal values. Whether it can be said of him that 'he was not of an age but for all time'[238] yet remains to be seen; but even now, less than two decades after his death, it is evident that he was not for one land only but for the whole world.

One aspect of Tagore's universality was his deep and abiding interest in those aspects of the cultural heritage of India that had been for centuries unknown, neglected, or overshadowed. Among the least known and most neglected was Buddhism, which, thanks to the energetic efforts of Anagarika Dharmapala, was beginning to attract the attention of the Bengali intelligentsia at about the same time that Tagore himself, then a promising young poet, was rising to fame. With his broad humanist outlook it was only natural that he should have felt drawn to Buddhism. From the life of the Buddha, the *Jātaka* stories, the legends of Buddhist history, and allied sources, he in fact derived not only poetic inspiration but material for the expression of his own advanced social and religious ideas. The poems and plays with Buddhistic themes which he wrote, all imbued with a deep reverence for the person of the Buddha, won for the Good Law a far wider audience than could have been obtained by purely religious means. Tagore therefore played an important part in the modern movement for the revival of Buddhism in India, and it is for this reason, as well as by way of tribute to his intrinsic greatness, that we are bringing out this special Tagore number of our journal.[239]

At the same time, it cannot be denied that Tagore was interested in Buddhism as a culture rather than as a religion and that he saw Buddhist culture as one aspect of Indian culture. It is doubtful whether he appreciated, or even understood, the distinctive spiritual emphasis of the Buddha-Dharma. Brought up as he had been in the liberal theism of the Brahmo Samaj[240] he, like so many others before and after him in India, found it difficult to fathom the profound metaphysical and spiritual significance of the Buddha's denial of a creator God and an unchanging immortal *ātman*. This is not to denigrate him or depreciate his achievement, but only to point out that he was a poet rather than a philosopher, and, as such, though a safe and indeed inspiring guide to the beauties of Buddhism, not so reliable an exponent of its doctrines.[241]

In personal character Tagore in many ways approximated to the Buddhist ethical ideal. Broad-minded and large-hearted, he scorned all that was narrow, petty, and intolerant. He was singularly free from superstition and prejudice. To him the whole human race constituted one family: hatred and discrimination based on differences of race, caste, and nationality he abhorred. He was a man of peace. Even his patriotism, in days of intense nationalist fervour, never degenerated into chauvinism, but remained indissolubly linked to higher values. The world will remember him not only as a great poet but as an even greater man. Buddhists will remember him as a true friend to Buddhism.

November–December 1961

1962

MORE VANDALISM IN MAHARASHTRA

Attention has already been drawn in these columns to the deplorable fact that the celebrated cave temples of Maharashtra are not being cared for by the authorities in a manner consonant with their high religious, artistic, and historical importance. The Kanheri Caves have been used for the shooting of profane films and a motley crowd of actors, technicians, and directors allowed to disfigure the sacred precincts in a shameful manner (see December 1960 issue). At Karle, also a protected monument nominally under the care of the Archaeological Department, a most inartistic Hindu temple has been constructed immediately before the entrance of the main *caitya* cave, the biggest of its kind in India; Brahmin priests ply a brisk trade, and animal sacrifices are regularly performed (see June 1961 issue). So far as we know, no steps have been taken by the authorities concerned even to enquire into the shocking state of affairs obtaining at Kanheri, Karle, and elsewhere, much less still to remedy it. Meanwhile comes information still more hurtful to Buddhist sentiment.

One of our correspondents, a foreign Buddhist student, happened to pay a visit to the Karle Caves on the occasion of Diwali, the Hindu Festival of Lights, last October. He writes:

On arrival one surprise awaited me which proves that at least the local authorities of the Archaeological Department are helping or perhaps even encouraging the pujas in that temple. For all the ten days of the 'festival' no entrance fee is charged for entering the premises as well as the caves! (Usually one has to pay 19NP.) This is, of course, a small matter in itself, but it is surely significant. I wonder whether on Buddhist festivals the same is done. Probably not; perhaps some enquiry about this should be made...

Before one middle-sized cave barbed wire had been drawn, so that it was extremely difficult to enter it. As I was told, this was done for the convenience of people who wanted to stay near the temple at night during the ten days. The question is: Who put this wire there and thus made the cave ugly? Perhaps the Archaeological Department?

But things were even worse than this. As you had written in your editorial, Buddhists are not even allowed to make offerings etc. in the main cave where the stupa is standing. Apparently, Hindus are entitled to, or, at any rate, do so. Just in front of the stupa there was placed a red-painted rectangular stone. The paint had been applied so liberally and the stone was so near to the stupa, that quite much of the red colour could be seen at the stupa itself, being sprinkled up to one foot high approximately. The stone measures 3 feet by 1 foot by 5 inches. On it were a few (old) flowers and similar things. I wonder how this is possible, though there were even some policemen on duty within the premises? The board with the description of the history of the Karle Caves standing before the stupa had been removed!

After having thus surveyed the whole place, I collected information about the puja next day by the help of others accompanying me.... So I was there in the morning of the next day (18th). Following picture was to be seen *inside the premises*. (Italics ours – Editors, the *Maha Bodhi*)

Exactly before the entrance of the main *caitya* cave (near to the temple, only about 3 or 4 feet away from the iron fencing) there was burning a mighty fire, nearly obstructing the whole way to the entrance. By the side of this were exploded some crackers and fireworks ignited. Between 1000 and 2000 people (I think nearly

> 2000) were standing around the temple in crowds or dancing nearby. Other people were sitting around cooking, eating, etc. Above all this there was loud and particularly horrifying music.
>
> Inside the cave not much had changed, except that there was to be found waste paper and skins of oranges and bananas on the ground. On the red stone there was burning some light. Occasionally even there some people were dancing as if mad.
>
> Into the Hindu temple lots of people were going, generally with goats or hens and cocks which were garlanded. Coming out of the temple, these poor animals were immediately dragged to the slaughterhouse, which I will describe now. A short distance from the premises (I don't think it was as much as 300 yards away) there was a piece of land surrounded by mats. Into this compound the goats, cocks, and hens were driven. After cutting the throats, the still living animals were thrown like sacks outside the compound where the owners picked them up. Seeing that, I felt terribly sick, but resolving to see the whole truth about this 'festival', I forced myself to go nearer to see how the animals are murdered. Looking inside, I was not very far from losing consciousness. Two men were incessantly cutting the throats of goats on a stone platform fully covered with blood. Within the time of my being there more than six of these poor animals must have been murdered! But I could stand it only for a very short time, most probably much less than a minute. Quickly I had to leave the place. As the killing was going on incessantly for more than an hour, I estimate that more than 300 goats must have been killed as well as a great number of fowl. As I was told, in April it will be even worse: at least 500 goats are generally slaughtered then, not to speak of hens and cocks.... I think some steps against this should be undertaken soon, if possible before next April, to prevent further murdering of animals there.

One of the most distressing features of the above account is that the desecration seems to be carried on with the regular connivance, if not the actual cooperation, of the authorities concerned, especially of the Archaeological Department. One is hardly surprised therefore, however deeply shocked, to learn that, as reported elsewhere in this issue, the Archaeological Department has itself been responsible for the doing of irreparable damage to two of the most celebrated wall paintings of the world-famous Ajanta Caves. With so many instances of this kind before us, and with no signs of any attempts being made to prevent their recurrence, we cannot help wondering how much further vandalism will be allowed to go, and how many more of the cave temples of Maharashtra will be desecrated and ravaged before the Central and States Governments bestir themselves and take belated action in the matter.

January 1962

STARS AND STUPIDITY

Error, it has been said, is coeval with truth. Certain wrong beliefs, being rooted in primitive emotions of desire and fear, are, like weeds, extremely tenacious of existence, and however often cut down spring up and flourish again as soon as the agency which kept them in check is removed. Beliefs and practices which the Buddha, twenty-five centuries ago, exposed as harmful and irrational still maintain a firm grip on the minds of millions of people in the very land sanctified by the dust of the Lord's feet and hallowed by his teaching.

According to the Hindu system of astrology (though not, it would seem, its Western and Far-Eastern counterparts) there is to be a conjunction of eight planets in the zodiacal signs of Cancer and Capricorn lasting for three days, from the 3rd to the 5th of this month. So inauspicious a conjunction, it is said, has not occurred since the time of the Mahabharata War, and global conflicts involving unprecedented loss of life, to say nothing of floods, fires, and earthquakes all over the world, are therefore confidently predicted for these days by the star-gazing fraternity. How a particular conjunction of planets comes to exert so malefic an influence on the course of human life, or indeed any influence at all, none of them has so far deigned to explain: presumably it is sufficient that such things are written in some old book, or form an article of faith with somebody's grandmother. It also appears to be forgotten that the Mahabharata War, far from being of world significance, was a petty inter-tribal conflict, lasting for a few days only, that occurred in a remote corner of north-western India and resulted in only a hundred or two casualties. Indeed, it seems to have been quite a leisurely affair, with intervals for long-winded and rather pointless philosophical debates.[242]

Having assured us that we are threatened by imminent destruction, the astrologers are kind enough to indicate a possible means of escape – a true combination of wisdom and compassion. *Yajñas* and *homas* must be performed;[243] clarified butter and other food-offerings must be burned in the sacred fire (it would be impious to give them to the hungry); the Vedas must be chanted; and, of course, as many brahmins as possible must be fed, clothed, and given liberal cash donations. For the last month and more, reports of a frantic round of propitiatory rituals all over the country have appeared daily in the newspapers. Incredible as it sounds, tens of millions of rupees are being lavished on these superstitious outbursts of extravagance which benefit nobody except astrologers, priests, and other social parasites. Even the vehement criticism of the prime minister, Shri Nehru, who in the course of a speech at Ludhiana on 21 January remarked that those who conducted *yajnas* were lacking in intelligence, has been powerless to dam the flood of expenditure. From the peasant to the prince, the coolie to the cabinet minister, a large portion of the Hindu public, whether educated or uneducated, has temporarily reverted to the mentality of the Cowdung Age.

Yet despite the extraordinary expenditure on *yajnas* and *homas* the fear of impending doom persists. Thousands of people have returned to their native places in order to die with their families. Others, afraid of being crushed beneath falling masonry, are camping out in the open air. Railway bookings have dropped by more than 60 per cent. Taxi drivers have announced that they refuse to ply on the fatal days, and even train and plane services, it seems, will be suspended. One is reminded of *Dhammapada* 188–9:

> Many people, tormented by fear, resort for refuge to hills, woods, groves, trees and shrines. This refuge is not secure; this is not supreme. Resorting to such a refuge one is not released from all sorrow.

Amidst the general hubbub, the few saner voices, like that of the prime minister, are barely audible. The Indian Buddhist community has, of course, remained unaffected by the rising tide of popular hysteria. Elsewhere, in at least one place, astrologers and sadhus who, by way of levying a voluntary contribution to the *yajñas*, had deprived some illiterate women of their gold ornaments, were roughly handled.

Cartoonists and columnists, for once provided with a really good target for ridicule, are making merry at the expense of the credulous public. Cases are even reported of brahmins being threatened with a beating if the catastrophes fail to take place as predicted.

Apart from the undesirability of any resort to violence, it is no use trimming the twigs and leaving the root intact. It is not so much astrology and its kindred 'low and lying arts', as the Buddha called them,[244] together with the whole racket of commercial ritualism, that needs to be exposed and destroyed as the system which makes such aberrations possible. The events of this month prove, if further proof were needed, that India still stands in need of a religion which is not incompatible with intelligence; it still needs Buddhism.

> He who seeks refuge in the Buddha, in the Dharma and the Sangha, he who sees with right knowledge the four noble truths, namely, suffering, the cause of suffering, the cessation of suffering and the Noble Eightfold Path which leads to the cessation of suffering – this indeed is the refuge secure; this is the refuge supreme. Seeking such a refuge one is released from all suffering.[245]

But how many people, one wonders, rising above desire and fear, will have the strength of mind to throw off the shackles of age-old superstitions and take refuge in the teaching of Enlightenment?

February 1962

THE FUTURE OF BUDDHISM

As with many other things that have centuries of history behind them, we are often more concerned with the glorious past of Buddhism than with its future. Is this altogether correct? Lessons are no doubt to be learned from the events of bygone days, but does this mean that we should be forever trying to go forward while looking backward?

Consideration of the future of Buddhism is all the more necessary today because there are many who are doing their best to ensure that it will have no future at all. In more than one part of the world Buddhism is menaced by militant materialism and dogmatic spiritualism, both unscrupulous, fanatical, and highly organized.[246] The stark fact must now be faced that if Māra is allowed to carry on his nefarious work unchecked Buddhism may soon cease to be a world religion.

At the same time, it cannot be denied that, in principle, Buddhism has a better chance of survival than any other faith, being more consonant with the modern spirit of free investigation and independent inquiry. It is, in fact, the only teaching which does no violence to the scientific conscience of contemporary humanity. In this sense it most certainly has not only a future but a bright one.

The danger lies in the Buddhist community, or any part of it, thinking that Buddhism, having existed for so many centuries, will automatically go on existing without much effort on the part of individual Buddhists or Buddhist organizations. Fortunately or unfortunately, this is no longer the case. The Buddhist way of life is now facing a tremendous challenge. The future of Buddhism will be determined by how that challenge is met.

From now onwards there must be three lines of vigorous concerted actions. (1) At home, that is to say in the Buddhist countries of Asia, the Dharma must be consolidated. (2) Ground which has been lost, as in India, China, and Tibet, must be regained. (3) In the non-Buddhist regions of the globe, especially in Europe, Africa, and the Americas, systematically organized *dharmadūta* activities must be launched without delay.

The future of Buddhism depends on every Buddhist.

March–April 1962

AN IMPORTANT FESTIVAL

The Buddhist year is marked by a number of festivals and celebrations. One of the most important of these is Kaṭhina. In the days of the Lord Buddha, and perhaps for several generations after his time, the monk's year was divided into two parts, one consisting of eight or nine months, during which he wandered from place to place preaching the Dharma, and one of three or four during which he remained stationary in one place. The second of these was known as the rains retreat (*vassāvāsa*). The conclusion of this period is marked by two observances, the first of which is the Pavāraṇā, a ceremony of mutual confession and satisfaction between the monks who have observed the retreat together. The second is the Kaṭhina.

Ostensibly, the Kaṭhina ceremony consists in the presentation to the monks, by the lay followers, of robes and other requisites without which they might find it 'difficult' (the literal meaning of the word *kaṭhina*) to go out and about preaching. In reality, however, it is very much more than this. Essentially it is an affirmation not only of the dependence of the monks on the laity for material support, but of the laity on the monks for spiritual instruction, and therefore of the unity and solidarity of the whole Buddhist community. Without the material support of the laity, the sangha either ceases to exist, or, what is perhaps worse, its members are compelled to resort to means of earning their livelihood that are incompatible with the dignity of the monastic life. Without instruction, the laity lapses into either secularism or superstition and in either case becomes indifferent to the well-being of the sangha. The Kaṭhina ceremony is one of the means whereby monks and laity are brought together and reminded of their mutual obligations and of their duty towards the whole mighty spiritual movement which is Buddhism.

Notwithstanding the extensive and enthusiastic participation of the laity, the Kaṭhina is at the same time a monastic observance and, as such, a part of the Vinaya or monastic code. The Kaṭhina also constitutes, therefore, a reminder of the immense importance of the Vinaya within the system of Buddhism. It is like the steel frame without which a lofty building would collapse into a chaos of cement and stone. The sangha receives the support of the laity only to the extent that it enjoys their respect, and it enjoys their respect only to the extent that it observes the Vinaya in the widest sense – not in that of pettifogging rules, but of a strict moral discipline that braces and sustains the whole spiritual endeavour.

More than once in these columns we have had occasion to draw the attention of our readers to the imperative necessity of strengthening the Buddhist movement in India by means of faithful adherence to the Vinaya. In this connection we have repeatedly pointed out the need for screening candidates for monastic ordination, whether *pravrajya* or *upasampadā*.[247] If quality is preferable to quantity, then it is far better to err on the side of strictness rather than on that of leniency. Recently there has come to our notice a most regrettable case, in which a person who was, under the Vinaya rules, disqualified from receiving the higher ordination, struck a bargain with a lay Buddhist worker to make the necessary arrangements without disclosing the facts of his case in return for a large sum of money. Fortunately the fraud was detected in time. Incidents of this type serve to underline the need for vigilance, so that the sangha may not be infiltrated and subverted by elements not really Buddhist. The Kaṭhina ceremony, with its emphasis on the need for the monk to be a good monk, and the layman a good layman, is an excellent opportunity, not only for stressing the importance of the Vinaya, but for putting us on our guard against any lowering or even relaxation of standards.

October 1962

THE PRESENT EMERGENCY

Neither the Society as such nor its journal has any connection with politics. Nevertheless, whenever politics impinges violently on religion, or in times of grave national emergency, it is impossible for us to remain unconcerned and uninvolved. We are not only Buddhists, but also Indians, and there is incumbent upon us a double duty: towards our religion and towards our country.

Ever since her achievement of independence, India has adopted and consistently followed a policy of peace and friendship towards all other countries and peoples. This policy, or rather principle, based on her age-old heritage of spiritual culture from the time of the Buddha downwards, besides constituting a solid and important contribution to the cause of world peace and stability won for her the abiding respect and admiration of a large section of responsible world opinion. In particular was India concerned with establishing friendly relations with the neighbouring Asian states, above all with Communist China, which after the invasion and subjugation of Tibet had a common frontier with India. Communist China, so it appeared, reciprocated India's friendship. Compliments flowed back and forth. Everything in the garden seemed lovely. The few warning voices that were raised pointing to the ghastly fate of Tibet went unheeded or were dismissed as those of warmongers.

Now the terrible day of awakening and reckoning has come. Deliberately, coldly, calculatingly, and perfidiously, Communist China has occupied by force of arms several thousand square miles of what is indisputably Indian territory.[248] The occupation of Tibet, it seems, was carried out partly with a view to establishing a base from which to launch an attack on India. The protestations of eternal friendship which flowed so abundantly from the lips of Chinese Communist leaders were meant to lull India into a state of total unpreparedness. Communists and fellow travellers inside the country also played their part.[249] Now the veil has been lowered, all pretence has been cast aside, and the Red Dragon emerges not as the friend of India but as her rival for the leadership of Asia, as her enemy and her aggressor.

There is no doubt that, though caught off their guard, the Government and people of India will know how to meet this unexpected threat to the integrity of their frontiers, and even to independence itself. The response has already been magnificent. Blood and money have come pouring in. The world will soon see that a democratic nation, united in defence of its liberties, is more than a match for any totalitarian juggernaut. In the present emergency there is no doubt that the Indian Buddhists – whether Bengalis, Maharashtrians, or of Himalayan origin – will give their wholehearted support to the Government. Indian Buddhists should, in fact, try to make their fellow-Buddhists abroad understand not only that China is a threat to India but that Communism itself is a menace to Buddhism.

In this connection it is to be regretted that, in certain circles both inside and outside India, there has been a great deal of loose thinking. Buddhist dignitaries, overwhelmed by the red-carpet treatment they received during their carefully supervised visits to the land of Mao Tse-tung, have been loud in their praises of the Communist regime.[250] Prominent *bhikkhus* have even declared that there is not much difference between Buddhism and Communism. All this has suited the Chinese Communists very well. The latter have, indeed, tried to lull not only India but the whole of Asia into a state of unpreparedness. In Buddhist lands one of the forms their strategy takes is that of pretending to support Buddhism. Sacred relics are sent back and forth. Delegations of monks and lay people are exchanged. Publications of Buddhist historical interest are widely distributed. In these and in numerous other ways Communist China is still trying to convince the Buddhists of Asia, devoted as they are to the Dharma, that Buddhism has nothing to fear from Communism. The Buddhist countries, forgetful of the grim tragedy of Tibet, where thousands of monks were tortured to death, monasteries reduced to heaps of rubble, and images and sacred books desecrated and destroyed, are still, even now, falling into the trap so cunningly spread for them.

Warned by recent events, the Government and people of India have started weeding out all those Communists and fellow-travellers who, by vociferously stressing China's undying friendship for India, have helped lull this country into a state of unpreparedness and thus pave the way for Chinese aggression. The Buddhists would do well to do likewise within their own ranks. Those so-called Buddhists who have, or who have had, any connection with Communism cannot be regarded as true followers of the Buddha. Rather are they using the sacred name of Buddhism as a cloak for their subversive and anti-national activities. However outwardly praiseworthy their work may be, from now onwards they must be carefully watched. In Communism both India and Buddhism have an implacable and unscrupulous foe, to resist whom will demand the utmost of our intelligence, our strength, and our devotion. We have been warned.[251]

November 1962

1963

COMING EVENTS

Regardless of the particular calendar observed, the occurrence of the new year has always been considered as possessing a particular significance. Besides the traditional celebrations, which may range in type from the religious to the very secular, not to say profane, such phenomena as the making of what are termed 'good resolutions' are also of regular occurrence. The new year is moreover a time for the casting up of accounts, not only financial but moral and psychological too, of assessing the losses and gains of the old year now dead, and endeavouring to anticipate those which may accrue in the course of the year but newly born.

So far as our Society is concerned, however, January 1963 is not so much a time of looking back as a time of looking forward. On 17 September 1964, we shall be celebrating the birth centenary of our illustrious founder, the late Ven. Anagarika Dharmapala. This means that the present year according to the Gregorian calendar, corresponding to the Buddhist Era 2506–7, is the last whole year remaining to us for making the preparations that will enable the anniversary to be celebrated with a dignity commensurate with the unique significance of the occasion. Coming events, it is said, cast their shadow before. In this case, however, it is not a shadow but a radiance – a radiance reflected from the bodhisattava-like life and achievements of Anagarika

Dharmapala. In this radiance we shall be working during the coming year. There is much to be done, and, as usual, all too few heads and hearts and hands to do it. Programmes have to be planned, functions organized, and publications arranged, so that 17 September 1964 will not be just one more celebration, however successful, but a definite milestone in the India-wide, even the world-wide, propagation of the Dharma, to which the noble Anagarika dedicated his whole life, and for the sake of which he sacrificed time, money, and health.

The coming year will, we hope, therefore be one of increased cooperation. The name of Anagarika Dharmapala is revered in circles far wider than the actual membership of the Society, extensive though that is. Hence we look forward to receiving, during the next twelve months, offers of help not only from old and tried friends but also from many other admirers of the Anagarika and his work who, for various reasons, might so far have had no personal contact with the movement he initiated. With this confidence we face the new year, invoking upon our subscribers, readers, and friends the blessings of the Buddha we take as our ideal, the Dharma we endeavour to practise, and the Sangha we aspire to serve.

January 1963

LOWERING OF STANDARDS

Without the constant intervention of spiritual forces, human affairs tend to deteriorate rather than to improve. These forces come, however, not from outside us, but from the wisdom and compassion of the enlightened human heart itself. Without their purifying and ennobling influence, ideals become tarnished, principles rust, and religion itself decays. In other words, we have constantly to be on our guard against a general lowering of standards. As the best is invariably the most difficult, our natural tendency is to settle down at ever lower levels where, as it becomes progressively easier to live, the quality of life progressively worsens.

These facts are attested by the history of Buddhism no less than by anything else. As spiritual vision becomes scholasticism, practice is replaced by speculation. Ecclesiastical pomp and show oust ascetic simplicity. Instead of a strenuous effort to come to grips with the truth, there is a comfortable acquiescence in ceremonial routine. Monks become as deeply attached to their cloisters as the laity to their homes.

The laity, likewise, begin to feel that as 'born Buddhists' Buddhism is their birthright and that no neglect of, or indifference to, its teachings, can deprive them of the title. Even those who are converts to the Dharma from other religions often compromise the integrity of their original commitment, and allow the blaze of their first enthusiasm to subside into the dull and smoky glow of mere half-interest.

Coming from generalities to particular instances, we find widespread laxity in respect of the observance of the five precepts. No Buddhist, when questioned, would ever seriously deny that these rules of ethical behaviour are of fundamental importance and binding upon even the humblest lay follower of the Enlightened One. Yet in practice concessions are made, loopholes taken advantage of, until before we know what has happened the whole structure of our moral life lies in ruins. The fifth precept requires us to abstain from intoxicating drinks and drugs. In many parts of the Buddhist world, however, drinking is as much an accepted part of social life as in the Christian West. Few are concerned by such a state of affairs; no one protests, or, if anyone does, it is regarded as an eccentricity or as a breach of good manners.

Anagarika Dharmapala was one of those rare spirits who can tolerate no lowering of standards either in themselves or in others. As his birth centenary draws near, let us resolve that, following his shining example, we shall not allow ourselves to be guilty of this commonest and most fatal of all vices.

May 1963

TRAGEDY IN VIETNAM

It is well known that the Dharma taught by the Buddha constitutes a Middle Way between various extremes, ethical, psychological, and metaphysical. As such, it has frequently had to meet criticism and repel attacks from diametrically opposite quarters, whether those of hedonism and extreme asceticism or those of dogmatic materialism and no less dogmatic pseudo-spiritualism. In modern times, the greatest threat to Buddhism, both ideologically and institutionally, comes on the one hand from militant Marxism and on the other from no less militant Christianity, especially in its Roman Catholic form. These rival totalitarianisms, while seeking to destroy each other, are simultaneously bent on the destruction of the object of their common hatred: Buddhism. With what inhumanity Buddhism has been rooted out of the cloisters and the hearths of Tibet is too well known to need particularization. Now comes news of an attack in another land and from the opposite quarter.

While other parts of the Buddhist world celebrated Buddha Jayanti happily and peacefully, the devoted Buddhists of Vietnam were the victims of brutal persecution and repression. According to a telegram received from the Supreme Patriarch of the All-Vietnam Sangha and Society, in the midst of the Vaiśākha Pūrṇimā celebrations on 8 May, the Vietnamese government troops opened fire on a peaceful Buddhist demonstration against the unjust and arbitrary ban on the hoisting of the Buddhist flag during the celebrations. Eight persons were killed, and many wounded and arrested. Buddhists all over the world, as well as lovers of religious freedom everywhere, will be shocked and horrified by this crime perpetrated against the Vietnamese Buddhists during their most sacred festival, the Buddha Jayanti, at their most sacred place, a Buddhist temple, and against one of their most sacred objects of veneration, a Buddhist flag, which symbolizes the unity and fraternity of all followers of the Enlightened One.

Those unacquainted with conditions in Vietnam will wonder how such a tragedy could have occurred. The reason is not far to seek. Vietnam is a Buddhist country. Five per cent of the population is, however, Roman Catholic. For reasons which it is not our business to elucidate, the government of the country is almost exclusively in the hands of members of the minority religious group, and it has been known for some time past that the Buddhists, who constitute the overwhelming majority of the population, have to face in the exercise of their religious rights difficulties that at times amount to actual persecution. So far, hoping that the situation might improve, the Buddhists of Vietnam have not drawn the attention of the outside world to their plight. Instead, patiently enduring all sufferings, they have simply sought to strengthen the Dharma in Vietnam by means of quiet preaching and teaching work, as well as by the celebration of Buddhist festivals. Now, however, as the news of the cold-blooded murder of eight innocent persons flashes round the globe, the intolerable conditions under which the Vietnamese Buddhists have to live can no longer remain unknown.

We salute the memory of the eight martyrs who have been called upon to sacrifice their lives for Buddhism. We call upon Buddhists all over the world, as well as lovers of religious liberty everywhere, to bring moral pressure to bear on the Government of Vietnam so that the Buddhists of that country may enjoy the full and unfettered exercise of their elementary right of freedom of worship. We appeal to His Holiness the Pope, who recently told twenty-eight Japanese Buddhist monks that both Roman Catholicism and Buddhism 'worked for the peace and good of mankind',[252] to see to it that his representatives in Vietnam implement this policy. Finally, we ask all Buddhist countries that harbour in their midst a Roman Catholic minority to watch and to beware.

June 1963

ENEMIES WITHOUT AND WITHIN

In previous issues the attention of our readers has been drawn to the shocking and shameful manner in which the Roman Catholic oligarchy in Vietnam is not only systematically denying to the Buddhists of that country, who constitute the overwhelming majority of the population, the freedom to practise their religion, but also brutally repressing their peaceful attempts to secure this fundamental right. Despite the heroic self-immolation of an aged monk in support of the five demands of the Buddhists (see July number),[253] and the intervention of the governments of several Buddhist countries, the attitude of the powers-that-be in Vietnam seems to have hardened, and the situation has, therefore, deteriorated rather than improved. By the time these words appear in print it will, in all likelihood, have deteriorated still further.

When even Roman Catholic presidents have been putting in an oar, some may wonder why no word of condemnation, or at least of disapproval, has come from the Vatican. In the headquarters of the Roman Catholic Empire they have, of course, been busy burying one pope and crowning another, both at considerable expense, and what with all the fuss and excitement of these events there might not have been time to consider the misdeeds of President Diệm and his crew. One has the feeling, though, that if it had been the other way round, and if, by some inconceivable stretch of the imagination, it had been the Buddhists who had shot, blister-gassed, and beaten up Roman Catholics, the thunders of the Vatican would have started rolling soon enough, coronation or no coronation. Besides, both the late Pope John and the reigning Pope Paul are known to the newspapers as 'liberal' popes.

Within the context of the Roman Catholic Church and the papacy, however, 'liberal' has a meaning of its own, which certainly does not extend to protecting Buddhists from the 'apostolic blows and knocks' of militant Catholics. Pope Pius IX (1846–1878) was, no doubt, a very 'liberal' pope, as popes go. This did not prevent him, however, from *condemning* the 'error' that 'Every man is free to embrace that religion which, guided by the light of reason, he shall consider true,' as well as the 'error' that 'the Church has not the power of using force' (*Syllabus of Errors* 15 and 24). All those who value freedom of religion, whether Buddhists or non-Buddhists, should realize that President Diệm's behaviour towards the Buddhists of Vietnam, far from being an unfortunate aberration, represents the *settled and declared policy of the Roman Catholic Church* from the earliest times down to the present day. In the eyes of that Church, the Buddhists have *no right* to follow Buddhism, whereas the Church – whether in Vietnam or anywhere else – *has* the God-given right and duty to *force* non-Catholics to give up their own religion and embrace Catholicism. Far from being reprimanded, President Diệm will probably be made a Knight of the Golden Spur during his lifetime, and canonized, or at least beatified, after his death.

In these circumstances, when they are confronted not by just a single fanatical individual but by the armed might of the most highly organized and ruthless religion in the world, the Buddhists of Asia should consider very seriously what is to be done. The President of the World Fellowship of Buddhists has already issued an Appeal to all WFB centres and all Buddhist organizations 'to help our long-suffering Buddhist brethren in South Vietnam'. But appeals, however stirring, are not enough. We suggest that the World Fellowship of Buddhists should at once convene, preferably in Ceylon, a special session which will not merely pass resolutions condemning the atrocities in Vietnam but also devise ways and means of bringing them to an end and inducing the authorities there to grant full religious freedom to the Buddhists of that country. During the last few years there has been much criticism of the World Fellowship of Buddhists. To be blunt, ever since its headquarters were shifted from Ceylon it has been an ineffective, almost an extinct, organization. If those who are at the helm of its affairs can, however, pull themselves together, and take up the cause of the persecuted Vietnamese Buddhists in a vigorous and effective manner, it may even now be able to make up for lost time and occupy in the economy of world Buddhism the position which its friends and well-wishers would like to see it occupying.

At the same time, while guarding the front door against attack we must be careful not to leave the back door undefended. According to All India Radio news bulletin, Bakshi Ghulam Mohammed, Prime Minister of Kashmir, declared recently at a public meeting in Srinagar that Communism was infiltrating into Kashmir through Buddhism. Kushok Bakula, Minister of State for Ladakh Affairs, seconded his remarks so far as Ladakh was concerned. Whether these disturbing statements from highly placed and responsible persons arose out of any particular incident, or had reference to any particular person, is not known. Buddhists everywhere, but particularly Indian Buddhists, would in any case be well advised not to ignore these grave warnings. Indeed, firm action should be taken whenever necessary. Those who use the sacred name of Buddhism as a cloak for non-Buddhist and even anti-Buddhist activities are even more dangerous than those who, like President Diệm, attack it openly. Such persons should be exposed whenever detected, and true Buddhists should have nothing whatever to do with them or with their activities. Only if we remove the enemies within our ranks shall we be strong enough to resist the enemies without.

August 1963

FROM BAD TO WORSE

Last month we wrote that, even before our editorial appeared in print, the tragic situation in South Vietnam would have deteriorated still further. That prediction has, unfortunately, been amply fulfilled. During the last month the Roman Catholic ruling clique has, apparently, decided that the Buddhists' demand for religious freedom must be crushed at all costs. Hundreds of Buddhist monks and nuns have accordingly been arrested, as well as thousands of students, and will, it is reported, be tried by military tribunals 'for sabotage'. Pagodas have been sacked and desecrated, images of the Buddha smashed to pieces. In the resultant fighting, many have been killed, including several hundred monks and nuns. Small wonder, therefore, the leading Calcutta daily newspaper should have headed an editorial on the subject 'After Tibet, South Vietnam'.

The flagrant disregard of President Diệm and his clique of all canons of civilized behaviour, and their open recourse to violence in its most hideous form, has by no means passed unchallenged. The Indian press has unanimously condemned the atrocities that have been committed, as well as the spirit of ferocious bigotry by which they were inspired, and a good deal of space has been devoted to describing the sufferings of the innocent Buddhists. With a few exceptions, the world press has responded with what could be described as sympathy tempered with indignation – sympathy for the unfortunate victims of religious persecution, indignation against the ruthless fanatics responsible. Public opinion has also been stirred. Protest meetings have been held in many parts of India and resolutions condemning the action of the South Vietnam Government passed. At least one prominent Hindu organization has taken up the cudgels on behalf of the oppressed Buddhists, while the secretary of the Indian National Congress Working Committee has officially described the persecution as 'diabolical'.

Others who might be expected to take an active interest in the matter have been either silent or ineffectively vocal. The Pope, for instance, has appealed for the Catholics and Buddhists of South Vietnam for a peaceful solution of their differences, and professes to be 'painfully concerned'. Apart from the hypocrisy of appealing to *the Buddhists* at all, the fact is that the Pope could, if he wished, put a stop to the reign of terror in five minutes simply by threatening to excommunicate the Diệm-Nhu ruling clique. Deprived of her 'moral vitamins', as she calls the sacraments, Mme Nhu would doubtless capitulate immediately. That His Holiness does not take any such action – does not, indeed, express the slightest disapproval of his followers' actions – can only mean, in a monolithic power-structure like the Roman Catholic Church, that he thoroughly approves of them. We should never forget that Francis Xavier, who converted thousands of Hindus to Roman Catholicism by means of brute force, is still fervently venerated by that Church as a saint of outstanding holiness.

Moral responsibility also rests on the shoulders of the people in government in the United States, especially on those of its first Roman Catholic president.[254] We are confident that the vast majority of American citizens heartily abominate President Diệm and all his works, but the fact remains that the Buddhists of South Vietnam are being killed with American weapons, with American troops standing by in support of the regime that is doing the killing. The Buddhist world cannot be blamed if it takes note of these facts and draws its own conclusions.

Meanwhile, the Buddhists of South Vietnam continue to bleed. The Prime Minister of Ceylon is making praiseworthy efforts to convene an international Buddhist meeting to consider the situation; there is talk of raising the matter in the UN: and Cambodia has set a good example by breaking off diplomatic relations. While all these are steps in the right direction, we should not delude ourselves into thinking that the militant Catholicism of the Saigon oligarchy will listen to appeals, however eloquent, or to arguments, however convincing. Roman Catholicism understands only the language of force. At the same time, as Buddhists we cannot appeal to violence even in defence of Buddhism. We can only hope, therefore, that the forces which are maintaining President Diệm in power will, in the interests of peace and justice, withdraw their support from his regime. Otherwise, the situation in South Vietnam will go not only from bad to worse but from worse to worst; for there is no doubt that, even though thousands have to die, the heroic Buddhists of that country will never rescind their demand for religious freedom.[255]

September 1963

THE NEED FOR VIGILANCE

A number of events have occurred in the course of the last few months, even the last few weeks, which spotlight the need for increased vigilance on the part of the Buddhists if they are to preserve intact for future generations the precious heritage of the Dharma.

To begin with, there are the tragic happenings in South Vietnam, from which it is clear that, as at all periods of its sanguineous history, the Roman Catholic Church is ready to oppress and persecute the followers of other faiths whenever it feels sufficiently powerful to be able to do so. All Buddhist countries that harbour a Roman Catholic minority would, therefore, be well advised to beware, and to keep a sharp eye on the attempts which, in at least one country, the followers of this militant religion are making to secure for themselves a predominance in the armed forces, in the police, and in the civil service.

Nearer home, Christian missionaries are making a determined effort to pervert the Tibetan refugees from their traditional faith and culture by means of food, clothing, medical treatment, education, and other material inducements. Only a few weeks ago a woman missionary gleefully told a Buddhist acquaintance how, at an institution run by the Canadian Mission at Jhansi, thirty Tibetan Buddhist children had been forcibly converted to Christianity. 'We took away their *chubas* (i.e. Tibetan gowns)', she chortled, 'and dressed them all in pretty little frocks, and now they pray to Jesus every day.' Surely the Government of India should intervene and put a stop to this illegal proselytization of minors by agencies which are taking a despicable advantage of the economic hardships of the Tibetans who are no longer able to maintain their children and who can therefore be induced to hand them over to the tender mercies of the missionaries.

At the same time, it must not be forgotten that Buddhism has its internal no less than its external foes. In a neighbouring Buddhist country, an Indian *mahāthera*, who works as a professor in one of the Buddhist universities there, has written a pamphlet in which he states that because Buddhism and Marxism both deny the existence of God and of an immortal soul, they are one and the same; that Marxism teaches that there is no rebirth after death and since Buddhists do not wish to be reborn they should be the first to embrace Marxism; that the Communist countries, Russia and China, are heavens on earth and so correspond to the Buddhist idea of '*loka-nibbāna*'; and finally that the relationship between the two systems is that Buddhism is the elder brother, while Communism is the younger. This pamphlet is published by a Communist organization for distribution among the ignorant peasantry. Surely this type of propaganda is even more subversive of Buddhism than all President Diệm's bullets and blister gas and all the machinations of Christian missionaries. In a democratic country anyone who wants to be a Communist is, of course, free to be one; but to be carrying on what is, in effect, anti-Buddhist propaganda while still pretending to be a *bhikkhu* and enjoying all the respect that appertains to the yellow robe would appear to be an unforgivable offence. In our opinion the Marxist *mahāthera* should be dismissed from his professorship and disrobed. However well known or learned they may be, such imposters can bring only shame and disgrace to the sangha.

In India, we are glad to see, a well-known Communist who for several years has been working behind a screen of Buddhist activities has at last been exposed. We refer to the long and informative front page article by D. F. Karaka which appears in the 'current' *Weekly* dated 28 September 1963, under the banner headlines, 'On Govt. of India notepaper… Noted Communist appeals to unwary Americans for funds for Young Lamas.' All Buddhists who are in any way concerned to protect the Buddhist movement against attacks from without and infiltration from within should carefully study this illuminating article.

In all parts of the Buddhist world, the need for vigilance continues.

October 1963

1964

A GREAT LOSS

The death of Pandit Jawaharlal Nehru, Prime Minister of India, on 27 May, came as a great shock to all Buddhists. Only the day before, Buddha Jayanti had been celebrated amidst great rejoicings all over India, and the celebrations were, in fact, still continuing in many places when the tragic news was received. Rejoicing at once changed to mourning, and meetings which had been convened in celebration of the thrice-sacred day ended on a sadder and more solemn note with the passing of resolutions expressive of a sense of the irreparable loss which the nation had sustained.

Pandit Nehru's association with Buddhism in general, and with our Society in particular, goes back many years. In 1931 he was present at the opening ceremony of the Mulagandhakuti Vihara, Sarnath, the construction of which was the last act of our late founder, the Ven. Anagarika Dharmapala. He also took the trouble of coming to Benares and welcoming His Eminence Taixu the great Chinese Buddhist leader when, in 1946, the latter came on pilgrimage to India.[256] Pandit Nehru had a particularly close connection with the Sacred Relics of the *arahants* Sāriputta and Moggallāna, the two chief disciples of the Buddha, which after spending ninety years in the Victoria and Albert Museum, were restored to the people of India due to the initiative of the Maha Bodhi Society. Not only did he come specially to Calcutta to receive them on their arrival from Ceylon in December 1949, but when, in November 1952, they were re-enshrined at Sanchi, he attended the opening ceremony of the Chaityagiri Vihara, which had been specially built to receive them, and delivered a memorable speech.[257] This was by no means all. To Pandit Nehru, more than to anyone else, is due the credit for the fact that, in India, the 2500th Buddha Jayanti celebrations were sponsored by the Government, with the result that they assumed national, indeed international, significance.

In the political sphere, Pandit Nehru's admiration for Buddhism found concrete expression in his insistence that the *dharmacakra* of the Buddha should occupy the centre of the national flag, ousting even the *charkha* or spinning-wheel favoured by the Father of the Nation, Mahatma Gandhi. His also was the decision that the state seal and emblem of India should be the lion pillar of the Buddha's great disciple Aśoka, whose ideal of the *dharma-vijaya* or 'victory through righteousness' he took as the inspiration of his foreign policy.

That a man like Pandit Nehru should have been attracted by Buddhism is not surprising. Though avowedly an agnostic, he had a feeling for humanity that verged on the mystical, and a passion for truth and righteousness that at times imparted to his utterances an authority that was almost religious. As in the case of most mortals, it was not given him to be exempt from error, but the purity of his intentions and his absolute honesty were never in doubt. With his passing from the scene where, for so many years, he played so conspicuous a part, India has lost one of the greatest of her sons, and the Buddhist movement in India one of its staunchest supporters and sincerest well-wishers.

June 1964

FURTHER *MAHA BODHI* CONTRIBUTIONS

WANTED: A NEW TYPE OF *BHIKKHU*

Change is the law of life. New conditions call for new approaches. This applies to the sangha as much as to any other institution. The report of the Buddha Sāsana Commission has highlighted the need for reforms – a need by no means confined to the Island of Ceylon, though it seems the Buddhists of that country are the first with enough courage to focus attention on the problem.[258] If Buddhism is to survive and spread what we really need, however, is a new type of *bhikkhu*. Below I have tried to give some of his qualifications. Readers may like to send the writer their comments on this list.

1. The new type of *bhikkhu* will never commit the mistake of thinking that the wearing of the yellow robe makes him a monk.
2. He will be one whose whole life is dedicated to the attainment of Enlightenment for the benefit of all.
3. He will see the Buddhist tradition as a whole.
4. He will make meditation an integral part of his daily life, not regard it as the preserve of a few specialists.
5. He will be strict without being narrow, and tolerant without being lax.
6. He will not cultivate the company of the rich, the powerful, and the famous.
7. He will be ready to serve rather than expect to be served.
8. He will not be afraid of manual work.

9. He will be totally indifferent to worldly honours and make no attempt to gain academic degrees.
10. He will not expect to be provided with all the comforts and conveniences of life in a vihara because he has 'renounced' the household life.
11. He will not wear as the badge of a *bhikkhu's* poverty robes more expensive than the dress of a layman.
12. He will not permit himself to enjoy a standard of living above that of the laity.
13. He will attach more importance to moderation in diet than to gobbling down huge quantities of food before a particular time.
14. He will be a vegetarian.
15. He will be free from racial, national, and linguistic prejudices and think, speak, and act as a citizen of the world.
16. He will disregard completely differences of *nikāya*.[259]
17. He will not condemn as unorthodox *bhikkhus* whose traditional pattern of external observances is slightly different from his own.
18. He will regard all other *bhikkhus* as his brothers.
19. If a *thera*,[260] he will not ordain novices whom he is unable or unwilling to train properly.
20. However great the respect and consideration shown him, he will not consider himself spiritually superior to others.
21. He will not demand a show of outward respect from the laity on the grounds that 'respect is shown to the robe, not to the wearer of the robe'.
22. He will in any case remember that it is more important for him to show respect for the yellow robe by his own conduct than for the laity to show respect for it by theirs.
23. While strictly adhering to the fundamentals of the Vinaya he will not attach exaggerated importance to the observance of minor precepts.
24. He will not conceal his neglect of the spirit of the Vinaya behind a rigid observance of the letter.
25. He will do in secret nothing that he would be ashamed or afraid of doing openly.
26. He will not act the hypocrite, pretending to be holier than he is, on the plea of 'keeping up the faith of the laity'.

27. He will not exploit the laity by preaching to them, for his personal advantage, doctrines that he does not himself believe.
28. He will not deceive both himself and the lay devotees by accepting luxuries from their hands in order to 'make merit' for them.
29. He will not allow the laity, out of mistaken piety, to present him with articles a *bhikkhu* ought not to possess.
30. He will not seek to excuse bad habits such as smoking and going to the cinema on the grounds that they are not specifically mentioned in the Vinaya.
31. On the pretext of propagating the Dharma he will not enjoy pleasure trips and foreign tours at the expense of the laity.
32. He will not go to see indecent films, or listen to dance music on the radio, on the pretext of improving his knowledge of English.
33. He will not create his own circle of friends and admirers and allow himself to settle down in the enjoyment of their adulation.
34. He will not hesitate to reprove the laity for wrongdoing out of fear that they might withdraw their support from him.
35. He will divide the major part of his time equally between study, meditation, and teaching.
36. He will attach more importance to understanding the meaning of the Dharma than to being able to recite the words of the scriptures by heart.
37. He will never think that he has finished studying the Dharma.
38. He will be well versed in the teachings of all schools of Buddhism.
39. He will have sufficient knowledge of science and the humanities to enable him to preach the Dharma in a convincing manner to educated men and women.
40. In particular, he will be a student of psychology and of comparative religion.
41. While preferring silence to speech, and solitude to company, he will never refuse an invitation to preach the Dharma.
42. He will not present as 'Buddhism' what is in fact the tradition of a single school.
43. He will consider no hardship too great if by undergoing it he can propagate the Dharma.
44. He will accept no payment for religious services.

45. While taking no part in politics, he will exert a healthy moral influence on public life.
46. He will always be active.
47. He will never seek to excuse a life of idleness and inactivity by saying that he is meditating. He will show no special preference for his former relations, nor use his influence as a *bhikkhu* for their benefit and gain.
49. He will feel grateful because he receives so much rather than resentful because he receives so little.
50. He will not waste anything.
51. He will bear in mind that it is better to be a good layman that a bad monk.
52. He will remember that the *bhikkhu's* life, well lived, is the best; badly lived, the worst.
53. He will never forget that he has not yet attained Enlightenment.
54. If he is tempted to feel angry after reading the above, he will remember that the new *bhikkhu* is the old one adapted to modern conditions.

October 1961

WANTED: A NEW TYPE OF *UPĀSAKA*[261]

The Buddhist community is a whole in which *bhikkhus* and *bhikkhunīs*, *upāsakas* and *upāsikās*, are mutually dependent. It is impossible for a really effective sangha to coexist with an indifferent laity, and vice versa. Encouraged by the success of my previous article 'Wanted: A New Type of *Bhikkhu*', regarding which several letters of appreciation have been received, I offer a corresponding list of suggestions for the consideration of all lay devotees. As in law, the masculine includes the feminine gender.

1. The new type of *upāsaka* will never commit the mistake of thinking that it is really possible for anyone to be 'a born Buddhist'.
2. He will not recite the *triśaraṇa* and *pañca śīla* mechanically on *uposatha* days without making any effort to embody them in his daily life.[262]
3. He will not think the practice of the Dharma is the duty of the *bhikkhu*, but not of the *upāsaka*.
4. He will keep the household shrine clean and beautiful and regularly make the traditional offerings.
5. He will be regular in his observance of the *uposatha* days, and encourage others to follow his example.
6. However deeply engaged in secular affairs, he will find or make time for the regular study of the Dharma.
7. If he is a follower of any meditative tradition he will never be tempted to underestimate the importance of *śīla*.

8. He will not indulge in intoxicants on the plea that the Buddha did not require total abstinence of his lay followers but meant them to follow a Middle Way between teetotalism and drunkenness.
9. He will not seek to excuse the eating of meat by disclaiming personal responsibility for the slaughter of the animals concerned.
10. He will not patronize circuses nor condone any other form of cruelty to animals.
11. If the editor of a newspaper or magazine he will not accept advertisements for alcoholic beverages or non-vegetarian food products.
12. He will not act as though he thought the best way of celebrating Vaiśākha and other festivals was by over-indulgence in eating and drinking.
13. If a follower of the Vajrayāna tradition, he will not seek to excuse personal shortcomings by appealing to apparently antinomian incidents in the symbolic lives of ancient teachers.
14. He will not patronize indecent or un-Buddhistic films.
15. He will not, out of sloth and greed, seek to acquire wealth quickly and easily by investing in football pools, lotteries, sweepstakes, or any other form of legalized gambling.
16. He will not earn money by any means incompatible with the principle of right livelihood.
17. He will neither misappropriate nor misuse property dedicated to the Triratna.
18. He will not utilize viharas, temples, or other buildings dedicated to the Triratna for secular purposes, neither will he smoke, talk loudly, or otherwise misbehave therein.
19. He will not disfigure the walls of his home with vulgar, untraditional oleographs of the Buddha.
20. He will encourage and actively patronize the traditional Buddhist arts and crafts.
21. He will keep up the traditional Buddhist manners, customs, and observances, but only to the extent that these do not conflict with the teaching.
22. He will not conform to un-Buddhistic social usages. In particular, he will actively discourage the pernicious Hindu institution of caste.

23. If marrying into a non-Buddhist family he/she will not succumb to any proselytizing pressure that may be exerted. On the contrary such a one will, by force of personal example, create in the minds of the non-Buddhist relatives a favourable impression of Buddhism.
24. He will treat his wife as an equal and will, if she is less educated than himself, help her in acquiring a knowledge of the basic principles of Buddhism.
25. He will give his children only Buddhist names.
26. He will teach his children simple Buddhist observances, such as the taking of the *trisaraṇa* and *pañca śīla* and the Buddha Puja, and instruct them in the meaning thereof.
27. Wherever possible, he will send his children to Buddhist schools. In any case he will not, for reasons of social prestige, send them to Christian missionary institutions, thus sacrificing their Buddhist birthright for a mess of pedagogical pottage.
28. He will encourage his children to attend the Dharma classes held at the local vihara.
29. He will never dedicate to the sangha a child who is too young to understand the significance of the monastic life.
30. He will not imagine that it is possible for any form of Buddhism to flourish without a strong and active sangha.
31. He will not, out of laziness or indifference, fail to support the *bhikkhus*, and then criticize them for earning money.
32. He will realize that it is impossible for *bhikkhus* to observe the Vinaya without the full, close, and active cooperation of the laity.
33. He will not ask *bhikkhus* to cast horoscopes, tell fortunes, or practise any of the other 'low and lying arts' condemned by the Buddha.
34. He will not invite *bhikkhus* to recite the scriptures for his benefit in the belief that such a recital will release magical forces capable of contributing to his worldly prosperity without further exertion on his part.
35. He will not neglect the *bhikkhus* for the greater part of the month, thus reducing them to near starvation, yet regale them on special occasions so sumptuously that, sloth and torpor overcoming them, they are put out of action for the rest of the day.

36. He will not encourage *bhikkhus* to eat meat so as to provide himself with a justification for his own weakness for flesh diet.
37. He will not give to *bhikkhus* motor cars, television sets, radios, gold watches, and expensive fountain pens on the pretext that '*bhikkhus* must have the best'.
38. He will not be so concerned with minor points of a *bhikkhu's* conduct and appearance that he overlooks major violations of the Vinaya.
39. He will not show outward respect to *bhikkhus* towards whom he feels no devotion merely because they are wealthy or influential.
40. He will not refuse, out of pride or for any other unworthy reason, to pay to the members of the sangha and to teachers and elders the courtesies traditionally due.
41. He will show the same respect to all *bhikkhus*, regardless of the particular school of Buddhism to which they belong, and teach his children to do likewise.
42. He will not, out of false respect for the yellow robe, hesitate to reprove a *bhikkhu* for flagrant misconduct.
43. He will help the *bhikkhu* avoid improper contact with members of the opposite sex. The *upāsikā*, for her part, will not offer to shake hands or otherwise come into bodily contact with a *bhikkhu*, or visit the vihara at unseemly hours, or wear a dress of the same colour as a *bhikkhu's* robes. She will frequent the vihara or temple dressed in a simple, sober, and decent manner.
44. He will never attempt to mobilize the influence of the sangha for selfish political ends.
45. He will not adopt the attitude that Buddhism, having already lasted 2,500 years, will automatically continue to exist in the world even in the absence of any support from Buddhists.
46. He will set aside a fixed percentage of his income for religious and charitable purposes.
47. He will be a regular subscriber to at least one Buddhist magazine.
48. Whatever money he has set aside for religious purposes he will spend in a constructive manner instead of lavishing it exclusively on the gilding of pagodas, the burning of butter-lamps, or the performance of after-death ceremonies.
49. He will support all movements as genuinely seek to promote peace and international understanding and good will.

50. He will make every effort to conduct, in the spirit of Buddhism, various humanitarian and welfare services.

March–April 1962

STATEMENT ISSUED BY THE SANGHA SABHA (COUNCIL OF BUDDHIST MONKS) OF GREAT BRITAIN

An important step in the development of the Buddhist movement in this country was taken on Sunday 20 September when the first general meeting of Buddhist monks was held at the London Buddhist Vihara, Chiswick, under the chairmanship of the Venerable Chao Kun Rajasiddhimuni of Thailand. The meeting was called by the Venerable Sthavira Sangharakshita, head of the English sangha, 'in order to take stock of the present situation, as well as to discuss ways and means of ensuring the continuance and expansion of the *śāsana* in Great Britain on a firm foundation'. The following venerable *theras* and *bhikkhus*, all of whom are resident in Great Britain, participated in the proceedings: (1) the Venerable Chao Kun Rajasiddhimuni (Thailand); (2) the Venerable Maha Thera M. Sumangala (Ceylon); (3) The Venerable Maha Thera H. Ratanasara (Ceylon); (4) the Venerable Sthavira Sangharakshita (England); (5) the Venerable Bhikkhu Maha Vichitr (Thailand); (6) the Venerable Bhikkhu Vimalo (Germany); and (7) the Venerable Bhikkhu Mangalo (England). The Venerable Sayadaw U Thittila (Burma) and the Venerable Bhikkhu Ananda Bodhi (Canada) sent messages regretting their inability to attend the meeting and expressing their appreciation of the desirability of such a meeting.

In the course of a comprehensive discussion of the progress of the Buddhist movement in this country, all present expressed their deep appreciation of the important contribution made by the Venerable

Maha Thera Dr H. Saddhatissa and hoped for his speedy return from Ceylon. The Venerable Maha Thera H. Ratanasara then proposed that, in accordance with the traditional democratic procedures of Buddhism, those present should constitute themselves into an organization known as the Sangha Sabha or Council of Buddhist Monks of Great Britain and that this body should be responsible for maintaining the internal discipline of the Order, for directing all activities of the Order, and for giving proper spiritual guidance to the community of lay Buddhists. This proposal was adopted unanimously and the Venerable Sayadaw U Thittila elected as first president and the Venerable Sthavira Sangharakshita as the first secretary of the newly formed Sabha. For the present the remaining monks will all be members of the Council, which will meet regularly.

Other important decisions were also taken, among which mention may be made of the following. The attention of the members having been drawn to reports appearing in the press regarding the formation of a Western Chapter of the Order, the Sangha Sabha expressed its satisfaction at the growing number of Western *bhikkhus* in this country and decided that it should support, foster, and guide the new Chapter. The Sangha Sabha also decided that the Venerable Sthavira Sangharakshita should be recognized as Head of the English sangha and was, moreover, of the opinion that, inasmuch as the Venerable Sthavira Sangharakshita is the seniormost Western-born *bhikkhu* in this country, with long experience of Buddhist work, he should also be recognized as the Incumbent of the Hampstead Buddhist Vihara. The meeting also highly commended the establishment, by the Buddhist Studies Trust, of the London Buddhist College, and resolved to extend its wholehearted support to this project. The question of the proper training of candidates for ordination being discussed, the Venerable Maha Thera H. Ratanasara and the Venerable Sthavira Sangharakshita were directed by the Sabha to prepare suitable *sāmaṇeras* (novices) now in this country for the higher ordination (*upasampadā*) in the near future as well as to make arrangements for their monastic and educational training. Finally, the secretary of the Sangha Sabha was directed to inform the appropriate sangha headquarters of the Buddhist countries of Asia of the establishment of the Sangha Sabha or Council of Buddhist Monks of Great Britain so as to ensure mutual support and cooperation.

Sangharakshita
Secretary
Council of Buddhist Monks of Great Britain

March 1967

PART III
BOOK REVIEWS 1952–2002

ARYAN PATH BOOK REVIEWS

AN ACHIEVEMENT WITHOUT PARALLEL

Edward Conze, with a preface by Arthur Waley, *Buddhism: Its Essence and Development,* Bruno Cassirer Ltd., Oxford 1951, pp. 212. Received through the courtesy of the British Council.

Buddhism has suffered perhaps more than any other of the great religions from the misrepresentations of those whose temperament and training rendered them quite unfit to enter into the spirit of the Dharma, even in spite of the enormous erudition which some of them undoubtedly possessed. It is therefore a most novel and welcome experience to encounter a book which sets out to describe not what the author thinks Buddhism ought to have been, but what it actually is; and which surveys the subject not from a Christian missionary, agnostic, humanistic, rationalistic or any other basically foreign point of view, but simply and solely from a Buddhist point of view. Dr Conze writes:

> In this book I set out to describe the living tradition of Buddhism throughout the centuries, and I confess that I do not know what the 'original gospel' of Buddhism was. To regard all later Buddhist history as a record of the 'degeneration' of an 'original' gospel is like regarding an oak tree as a degeneration of an acorn. In this book I assume that the doctrine of the Buddha, conceived in its

full breadth, width, majesty and grandeur, comprises all those teachings which are linked to the original teaching by historical continuity, and which work out methods leading to the extinction of individuality by eliminating the belief in it.

The result of such an attitude and such a method is that successive phases in the development of Buddhist thought have been described in such a way as to exhibit more and more clearly the essence of the Dharma considered as a timeless and partless whole, as above all else an experience – the experience of Enlightenment – the inherent dynamism of which has carried forward the entire vast movement of Buddhist history. More than any other work with which we are acquainted, does this one succeed in giving us the *feel* of Buddhism; the author takes our hand and places it where we can feel for ourselves the mighty beating heart of the Dharma. This, combined with his sometimes quite extraordinary power of psychological penetration, makes the reading of the book not so much an addition to our information about the subject as a spiritual experience which can hardly help effecting a subtle but radical change in our outlook upon life.

A further indication of the extent to which the writer has succeeded in assimilating the deep Buddhist thoughts is the refreshing simplicity with which he has expounded them. Forbidding technical terms have been almost wholly avoided, and important Sanskrit and Pāli words have not so much been translated into English as re-created in it. The result of all this is an achievement without parallel in the field of literature in English about Buddhism. It is undoubtedly the very best introduction to the Dharma at present available and will probably remain so for some time to come. We recommend the book to all those who are interested in learning about Buddhism from the Buddhist point of view which is, after all, the most correct and valid one possible.

The Aryan Path, vol. xxiii, 1952, no. 7. A new edition of Conze's book was published by Windhorse Publications in 2001.

KNOWING THE MIND AND SEEING THE REALITY

The Tibetan Book of the Great Liberation or the Method of Realizing Nirvāna Through Knowing the Mind. Preceded by 'An Epitome of Padma-Sambhava's Biography' and followed by 'Guru Phadampa

Sangay's Teachings', according to English renderings by Sardar Bahadur S. W. Laden La, CBE, FRGS and by the Lamas Karma Sumdhon Paul, Lobzang Mingyur Dorje, and Kazi Dawa-Samdup. Introductions, annotations, and editing by W. Y. Evans-Wentz, D.LITT, DSC. With 'Psychological Commentary' by Dr C. G. Jung, Geoffrey Cumberlege, Oxford University Press, London 1954, pp. lxiv + 261.

Those who have found in *The Tibetan Book of the Dead*, *Tibetan Yoga and Secret Doctrines*, and *Tibet's Great Yogi Milarepa*, inspiring glimpses of that wisdom whereof another tradition says that its price is above rubies, will certainly welcome the addition of a fourth volume to Dr Evans-Wentz's Tibetan Series. Even more richly varied in content than its predecessors, *The Tibetan Book of the Great Liberation* comprises five main sections: 'Psychological Commentary' by C. G. Jung; 'General Introduction' by the editor; 'An Epitome of the Life and Teachings of Tibet's Great *Guru* Padma-Sambhava'; an English rendering of 'The [Yoga of] Knowing the Mind, the Seeing of Reality, called Self-Liberation'; and an English rendering of 'The Last Testamentary Teachings of the *Guru* Phadampa Sangay'. Confronted by the necessity of tackling such a mass of material, much of which must appear not only unfamiliar but bafflingly strange to the modern mentality, most readers will no doubt feel inclined to follow the method adopted by the reviewer and start with the 'General Introduction'.

This, like the introductions to previous volumes in the series, is divided into a number of sections which lead the reader step by step into the very heart of the teachings set forth in the book. Not unnaturally, the longest and – in the opinion of the editor himself – most important section is that on 'Good and Evil', for the life of Padmasambhava, as tradition represents it to have been, is replete with incidents that challenge in the most violent way the ethical codes and conventions that nowadays obtain, or to which lip service is paid, in most parts of the world. Concerning Tantric Buddhism, with which the next section deals, Evans-Wentz wisely remarks that it is 'as yet too little investigated to make possible, at this time, incontrovertible or exhaustive statements concerning its origin, which, however, seems to have been exceedingly complex'. He therefore devotes most of the section to a description of Tantricism which, though of use to the general reader, adds nothing to the knowledge of a student of Buddhism.

We are told that the original text from which the Epitome of Padmasambhava's biography has been made comprises 794 large pages. The Epitome itself comprises less than one hundred pages, including annotations; but the marvels and miracles contained even in this short abridgment would be enough to set up in business several dozen ordinary wonder-workers. As a friend of the reviewer's wrote in a recent letter: 'From the various books which are ascribed to Padmasambhava I get a vastly different impression of him, namely, of a very sane and profound thinker, a great saint, and a powerful personality: who impressed the people around him so deeply that in their urge to convey his greatness to posterity, they had to take resort to the superhuman and to the miraculous.' While the present Epitome is of very great anthropological interest, one cannot help regretting that it was not possible for the first comprehensive account in English of the great guru's career to have presented him in a more balanced and, we think, in a truer way as a thinker and saint rather than as a 'Culture Hero' and thaumaturgist. Though the text translated in the next section does enable us to gain a more complete picture of his personality, those who have been fascinated by the spiritual authenticity of the life of Milarepa will, we are afraid, be deeply disappointed by the Epitome of Padmasambhava's biography.

Even in its English dress 'The [Yoga of] Knowing the Mind, the Seeing of Reality, called Self-Liberation' is beyond all praise, and the only comment we shall offer is that it is another reminder to the Western world of the untold hidden riches of Tibetan Buddhist literature. Jung's 'Psychological Commentary' on this text is further evidence of the extraordinary breadth of mind of this great psychologist and of his sympathetic insight into the spiritual life of the East. Here, however, is no hasty assimilation of radically divergent points of view, nor superficial smoothing over of genuine difficulties, and though one may question whether the Buddhist attitude is in reality so one-sidedly introverted as Dr. Jung seems to think, few will disagree with him when he says:

> If we snatch these things [spiritual methods] directly from the East, we have merely indulged our Western acquisitiveness, confirming yet again that 'everything good is outside', whence it has to be fetched and pumped into our barren souls. It seems to me that we

> have really learned something from the East when we understand that the psyche contains riches enough without having to be primed from outside, and feel capable of evolving out of ourselves with or without divine grace. (p. xxxvii)

Much more controversial is his identification of the One Mind of the text with the Unconscious of modern psychology. The crux of the difficulty seems to be whether consciousness can exist without an ego. Jung thinks not. According to him, mental states 'lose their consciousness to exactly the same degree that they transcend consciousness.' The Wisdom of the East thinks otherwise: the One Mind is consciousness devoid of ego. Perhaps the difficulty to some extent resolves itself into one of terminology. What do we mean, for instance, by consciousness? At any rate, that the illustrious psychologist is not without misgivings about the position he has adopted is indicated by the fact that, towards the end of his Commentary, he remarks:

> It is a curious paradox that the approach to a region which seems to us the way into utter darkness should yield the light of illumination as its fruit. (p. lxiv)

On the whole the Psychological Commentary is a brilliant suggestive and spiritually stimulating piece of work which should go a long way towards creating in the West an understanding of the mental and spiritual attitudes of the East.

The concluding section of the book consists of 'The Last Testamentary Teachings of the *Guru* Phadampa Sangay' to the people of Tingri in Tibet. Couched in simple language and aphoristic style, these teachings are of great practical help to all followers of the Path.

Though the editor's elaborate annotations are often extremely valuable, one cannot help feeling that some of his assimilations of Buddhist and Hindu of [sic] spiritual investigation, with the One Mind would certainly not be acceptable to the Gurus of Tibet, either past or present, or, for the matter of that to the spiritual masters of any Buddhist land.

Produced in the same sumptuous manner as its predecessors, *The Tibetan Book of the Great Liberation* is an accession of outstanding value to that collection of translated texts wherefrom the peoples of the

West are beginning to learn something of that spiritual wisdom of which tradition has always represented the East as being the custodian. The gratitude of all students of Buddhism is due to those who have helped to make possible this exceptionally important publication.

The Aryan Path, vol. xxiv, 1954, no. 7.

2500 YEARS OF BUDDHISM

P. V. Bapat (ed.), *2500 Years of Buddhism*, pp. 503; *Buddhist Sculptures and Monuments*. Twenty Plates; *Places of Buddhist Interest*, Publications Division, Ministry of Information and Broadcasting, New Delhi 1956, pp. 52; Sir Edwin Arnold, *The Light of Asia*, Published for the Buddha Jayanti Celebrations, Bombay Committee, by International Book House Private Ltd., Bombay 1956, pp. 157.

In *2500 Years of Buddhism* twenty-seven scholars, mostly Indian, attempt to survey and assess the Buddha's teaching throughout its history, in its more important ramifications and developments. The increasing recognition that Buddhism means the *whole* of Buddhism is contributing to the unification of the Buddhist world. All-inclusiveness is, however, no guarantee of proper distribution of emphasis. It was natural that India should occupy the central position, but the Buddhism of the Far East, so rich in doctrinal and cultural developments, could fittingly have been given more than a meagre dozen pages. We have very readable accounts of 'Buddhist Art' and 'Buddhist Education', as well as chapters on 'Places of Buddhist Interest', 'Buddhist Studies in Recent Times', and 'Buddhism in Modern Times'.

The perspective is rather narrowly historical; no attempt has been made to penetrate into the spirit of the *Dharma*. The usual scholarly nonsense is talked about Buddhism becoming 'a theistic religion' because the Buddha's relics were worshipped and about the 'deification of the Buddha and the Bodhisattva in Mahayana'. In chapter 2, 'Origin of Buddhism', we are treated to a long account of the non-Vedic schools of the Buddha's time. The writer seems to entertain no suspicion that the origin of Buddhism might have something to do with the Buddha's Enlightenment. In the foreword Dr S. Radhakrishnan overstates his case for the Buddha being a Hindu and Buddhism part of Hinduism.

Well-planned and comprehensive though it may be, *2500 Years of*

Buddhism will be of use chiefly as a work of historical reference: to know what Buddhism is we must look elsewhere.

Buddhist Sculptures and Monuments is an album of quite attractive plates of some of the best-known examples of Buddhist art. *Places of Buddhist Interest*, though well written and informative, is marred by curiously miscellaneous illustrations, some obviously the work of amateur hands. About the reprint of *The Light of Asia*, probably the most popular English book on Buddhism, nothing need be said except that it is in all likelihood the cheapest on the market.

The Aryan Path, vol. xxvii, 1957, no. 11

CLEAR AND SUCCINCT

Alexandra David-Néel and Lama Yongden, *The Secret Oral Teachings in Tibetan Buddhist Sects*, translated from French by H. N. M. Hardy. Maha Bodhi Society of India, Calcutta 1957, pp. 128.

Lovers of the 'occult' and 'mysterious' are likely to be disappointed by this little book. At the very outset the authoress emphasizes that, in the words of her own guru, 'It is not on the Master that the "secret" depends but on the hearer.' But more serious students of Tibetan Buddhism are likely to be perhaps even more disappointed. The teachings transcribed by Madame David-Néel, far from being either 'secret', in any sense of the term, or 'oral', are well known and easily accessible even to those who have never visited Tibet or sat at the feet of a lama. The book indeed is little more than a rather sketchy résumé of quite elementary Abhidharma, Mādhyamika, and Yogācāra doctrines – all of which are systematically studied in the great monastic colleges of Lhasa. Madame David-Néel emphasizes that her exposition makes no concession to sentiment. Instead it makes heavy concessions to Cartesian rationalism. Despite such drawbacks, however, the authoress has achieved a clear and succinct account of some of the fundamentals of the Dharma which deserves a wide circulation. The Maha Bodhi Society of India is to be congratulated on publishing a book so obviously written from the Mahāyāna point of view.

The Aryan Path, vol. xxix, 1958

Paul Levy, *Buddhism: A Mystery Religion?* University of London, Athlone Press, London 1957, pp. 111.

In this book (the Louis H. Jordan Lectures for 1953) the author tries to show that the question posed in its title should be answered in the affirmative, yet for a definition of the term 'mystery religion' we have to wait until the last chapter, where we are told, 'They owe their generic name to the fact that their principal rites and revelations are intended to be kept secret', and where the author at last exposes his ethnological bias. Till then he tacitly assumes a connection between the rites of initiation performed at puberty in primitive communities and the ceremonies connected with the ordination of Buddhist monks.

The first three chapters therefore consist of an unsystematic account, based for the most part on second-hand and third-hand sources, of ordination in the Theravādin communities and among the Northern Buddhists. The author seems to believe that because in Cambodia, for example, ordination is accompanied by certain admittedly primitive practices (not mentioned in the *Vinaya* texts) which are also a feature of tribal initiations, Buddhism can be classified as a 'mystery religion'. Surely this is not unlike the assertion that since some accounts of the Buddha's life contain elements which can be explained in terms of solar myth the Buddha himself is to be regarded not as a historical person but as a celestial phenomenon. Chapter 4, which deals with the proceedings of the First Council as a variation of the initiation theme, is hardly more convincing. Chapter 5 deals in the same way with the lives of Kāśyapa and Gavāmpati. Both contain false analogies of an astonishingly naive kind. Still, despite incidental errors and wrong basic assumptions, the book is interesting and not without value. Properly understood, it certainly makes us realize that the Buddhist ritual of ordination is richer in significance than is generally supposed. But that significance cannot be reduced to terms of ethnology. A transcendental residue remains which exalts Buddhism far above all 'mystery religions' so conceived and eludes all studies of this kind.

The Aryan Path, vol. xxix, 1958

Helmut Hoffmann, *The Religions of Tibet*, trans. Edward Fitzgerald, George Allen and Unwin Ltd, London 1961, pp. 199.

For more than a century Tibet, the Land of Snows, has aroused greater interest and curiosity among those in the West than almost any other country. This interest has been reflected, especially during the last decade, by a constantly increasing flow of publications, not all of them of unquestionable authenticity. Gradually, however, as more and more material becomes available, old misunderstandings are being corrected and new insights incorporated into the steadily growing body of reliable, scientifically documented knowledge about this fascinating but no longer mysterious land and its people.

The present book is characteristic of this process. Unlike India, Tibet, especially Buddhist Tibet, possesses a vast wealth of historical records of all kinds, and from such of them as are now accessible to modern scholarship Professor Hoffmann, a specialist in the Bön tradition, has given a historical survey of religious developments from the earliest known times down practically to the present day.

First, of course, comes an account of 'The Old Bön Religion', that is to say, of what the author characterizes (pp. 14–15) as:

> the national Tibetan form of that old animist-shamanist religion which at one time was widespread not only in Siberia but throughout the whole of Inner Asia, East and West Turkestan, Mongolia, Manchuria, the Tibetan plateaux and even China.

Then follows a brief account of 'The Development of Buddhism in India and Its Penetration into Tibet'. In this chapter the strong resistance with which Buddhism, despite royal patronage, at first met, is well brought out. As Padmasambhava, along with Śāntarakṣita (whom the author always calls Shantirakshita), was the first effective Indian missionary to Tibet, this leads to an interesting excursus on 'Padmasambhava and Padmaism' or, in other words, on the so-called unreformed Buddhism of those who became known as the Nyingmapas or 'Old-Style Ones'. 'The Religious Struggles of the Eighth and Ninth Centuries' graphically describes the grim tussle for ascendancy between the Bön and Buddhism which eventually brought about the collapse of the monarchy and the political and cultural disintegration of the whole country. At one stage the victorious Bönists 'took a malicious pleasure in forcing the ex-monks to perform humiliating and unsuitable tasks, making them slaughtermen for example and sending them out with bows, arrows, and dogs to hunt.' (p. 82) – a type of persecution which has its parallels in Tibet today.

In 'The Systematized Bön Religion' the author clearly depicts the desperate and ultimately unsuccessful efforts of the old faith to establish itself as the national religion with the help of lavish borrowings from its hated rival, the borrowings ranging from the biography of the Buddha to the doctrine of the Void.

The remaining chapters, dealing respectively with 'The Rebirth of Buddhism', 'The Rise of the Lamaist Sects', and 'The Tsongkhapa Reformation and the Priest-State of the Dalai Lamas', exhibit a process of consolidation, efflorescence, and expansion which continued with only minor setbacks until the rude irruption of Red China in 1950. This is the greater period, to which belong such figures as Atīśa and Milarepa, Tsongkhapa and the Fifth Dalai Lama.

Throughout the chequered fortunes of Buddhism in Tibet two factors constantly recur and seem to have been of special importance. One concerns the relation of Buddhism to the secular power; the other, the place to be allotted in the economy of Tibetan Buddhism to the 'unreformed' doctrines and practices stemming from Padmasambhava. Much of the history of the religion, in its outer vicissitudes and inner development, would seem to be ultimately traceable to the necessity of settling these two issues.

As the general character of the book is admittedly historical, one cannot fairly complain of a deficiency of general spiritual and doctrinal interest. Nevertheless the latter cannot be entirely excluded, if for no other reason than that a doctrinal misunderstanding may result in a distortion of historical perspective. Thus the author treats what, following certain Continental scholars, he terms 'Padmaism' as an independent religion on the ground that Padmasambhava taught the people of the countries he visited in terms of the beliefs already current among them.

> This method [he rightly says] is strikingly reminiscent of that adopted by Manichaeism, which, without changing the core of its

> own teachings, nevertheless took the local religious concepts and the names of local gods to present its own great mythos. (p. 59)

But surely it is no less reminiscent of Buddhism, especially in its Mahāyāna form? The same type of misunderstanding causes the author to speak of 'Lamaism' itself as a special religion produced by an 'amalgamation with native religious elements' (p. 28). There are also several other doctrinal misunderstandings, though some may be merely infelicities of expression. Karma is defined as 'the law of retaliation' (p. 29), and 'emptiness' or 'voidness' is characterized as 'purely negative' (p. 32). The *krodha* or wrathful form of Avalokiteśvara is wrongly described as 'the evil Avalokiteshvara' (p. 59). Rahonuśāsaka is not 'Teacher of Secrets' (p. 113) but a 'privy instructor': he is the monk responsible for questioning the candidate for ordination regarding various disabilities. Moreover, Kazi Dawasamdup was not a Tibetan (p. 62) but a Sikkimese; and a *rkang-gling* is a horn made not from a human skull (p. 62) but from a human thigh-bone.

Though best utilized in conjunction with works dealing with the more spiritual side of Tibetan religious life, Professor Hoffmann's book is a most valuable accession to our understanding of a field wherein speculation and fancy have only too often usurped the place of knowledge.

The Aryan Path, vol. xxxiii, no. 9, September 1962

HIMALAYAN PILGRIMAGE

David Snellgrove, *Himalayan Pilgrimage: A Study of Tibetan Religion by a Traveller through Western Nepal*, Bruno Cassirer, Oxford 1961, pp. xvi+304.

This well-written and pleasantly illustrated book tells the story of the author's seven-month journey through the remote Tibetan regions of western Nepal. As he writes in the preface, 'Nepal is a country of such wonderful variety that even the Nepalese themselves have not yet had time to explore the richness of their own heritage' (p. xi). Accompanied by his faithful Sherpa, Passang, and cook, Takki Babu, and such porterage as he could muster en route, Dr Snellgrove explored – on foot – areas where few Europeans or none had penetrated before him, crossing in order to do so some fifteen major passes at heights between 17,000 and 20,000 feet.

His main intention was to learn something of the different regions and peoples and to study in particular the types of Tibetan religion practised in those remote lands. How far this intention was fulfilled only the author can say, but there is no doubt that the reader who, in imagination, accompanies him on his travels learns much. A fastidious but sympathetic observer, Snellgrove describes flora, fauna, ethnic types, architecture, religions, and secular life (less sharply distinguished here than in the West today), and rugged mountain scenery with equal gusto and the same minute fidelity. Some of his word pictures are of an austere and delicate beauty.

Those who, like the reviewer, are admirers of *Himalayan Buddhism*, his previous book, will be particularly interested in his account of religious life in the areas he visited. Though the Land of Dolpo, of which he may claim to be almost the discoverer, is an exception, Buddhism seems to have declined since the Gurkha conquest. There were frequently more temples than monks, and only too often splendid images stood covered with dust. But this was by no means the whole story. Throughout western Nepal the author heard about, and repeatedly saw evidence of, the activities of the Lama of Shang, a saintly Tibetan monk whose work for Buddhism in these regions deserves to be more widely known and whom he eventually met. Despite the inroads, here and there, of modern materialism, Snellgrove is therefore not without hope for the future.

The Aryan Path, vol. xxxiv, no. 6, June 1963

MAHA BODHI BOOK REVIEWS

OUT OF HARMONY

W. Douglas P. Hill
The Holy Lake of the Acts of Rama
An English translation of Tulasi Das's *Rāmacaritamānasa*
Oxford University Press, 1952
pp. xxxvii+538.

Three-quarters of a century have passed since the first complete English translation of Tulsidas's celebrated poem was made by F. S. Growse, and there is no doubt that the need of a new translation, based on the latest editions of the Hindi text, has long been felt by students of Indian literature who are unable to read the original.

This need has now been well supplied by Mr Hill, who has given not only a careful translation of the text but a long and informative Introduction on the life, works, and theological opinions of Tulsidas, besides an extremely useful Appendix of proper names wherein the numerous mythological allusions of the poem are explained.

Though the *Rāmacaritamānasa* of Tulsidas ranks high in Indian literature, and though it has wielded for centuries an enormous influence over the Hindu masses of Northern India, one cannot help wondering whether that influence was entirely a good one. Passages of great artistic merit the poem undoubtedly does contain, but the work as a whole is sadly marred by sectarian bias, devotional extravagance carried almost to the point of frenzy, and socal orthodoxy in its most repulsive form.

With regard to the last particular, the translator remarks in his Introduction:

> For ordinary social purposes, Tulsidas, if not as exclusive as Rāmānuja and his disciples of the south, was as strict as the more liberal Rāmānanda. His first homage, after that due to his guru, is paid to the Brahmans (B.C.2), whom he is never tired of exalting as 'gods on earth' (*bhusara*: A.C.129). The greatest sin Kākabuśuṇḍi could commit was disrespect to a Brahman (U.D.106ff.). 'A Brahman is to be reverenced,' says Rama to Kabandha, 'even though he curse you and beat you and use harsh words – so say the saints. A Brahman must be revered though he be devoid of goodness or virtue; but a Śūdra never, however virtuous and learned' (Ar.C.32) (p. xxxvi)

One cannot help contrasting this pernicious teaching with the sublime doctrine of the Buddha, who declared, 'By deeds one becomes a Brahman, by deeds an outcaste,'[263] and it is not surprising that a thin vein of hostility to Buddhism runs through the whole poem. Magadha, where the Lord Buddha preached, is contrasted with Benares, the citadel of Brahminical orthodoxy, as evil with good. The River Phalgu, on whose banks the Lord attained Enlightenment, is given the name Karmanāśā – 'destroyer of good deeds' – and contrasted in a similar manner with the Ganges.

Instances of this kind may appear to non-Indian readers as relics of bygone medieval bigotry; but Indian readers will know that they represent an orthodoxy which is by no means dead and which still has to be combated. We feel that this new translation of a classic of pseudo-religious orthodoxy and social reaction is completely out of harmony with modern trends of thought in India, and that it may find but little favour in the eyes of more progressive-minded readers.

December 1953

Bhikkhu U Dhammaratana
Buddha and Caste System
Sarnath Publications, Sarnath 1955

The system of hereditary caste is a topic which for the last few decades has increasingly troubled the conscience of progressive India. The present book, in which the author, a learned Sinhalese monk who has resided in India for more than twenty years, examines the question from the Buddhist point of view, will be of great interest and value to all who are concerned with this aspect of social reform. As the writer points out, in the Buddha is embodied not only *mahāprajñā*, the supreme wisdom, but also *mahākaruṇā*, the great compassion; he is not only the teacher of Nirvāṇa, but also the one who alleviates miseries, and opposes injustice and oppression, in whatever sphere of life they may be found. It is therefore but natural that during his earthly career he should have turned upon the institution of caste the cold clear light of reason.

After an introductory chapter on 'An Institution Peculiar to India', the author expounds the Buddha's own attitude in three thoughtful and well written essays: 'Buddha and the Caste System', 'Psychological Aspect of the Problem', and 'Practical Measures Adopted by the Buddha'. It is worth pointing out that, with truly Buddhist fair-mindedness, the author nowhere condemns the Brahmin community as a whole; in fact he points out that some of the best recruits to Buddhism were drawn from this class: it is what he terms the *purohitas* who upheld caste and attacked Buddhism.

The remaining three chapters of the book are largely historical and all make extremely interesting reading. In 'Decline of Buddhism and Revival of Caste System' and 'Reason for anti-Buddhist Propaganda in Brahminical Literature' the learned *bhikkhu* has clearly shown that it was not on philosophical or religious, so much as purely social grounds, that the *purohitas* denounced and defamed the Buddha and his teaching. The author consequently does not agree that Śaṅkara was responsible for the downfall of Buddhism in India. As he points out, the Dharma continued to flourish long after the advent of the great Vedānta teacher. One is shocked, however, to learn of the virulent bigotry of Kumārila Bhaṭṭa, who in his *Tantravārttika* could write:

> How could that Buddha be depended upon to teach the right path to others, who, himself being a Kṣatriya, went against the duty of the ruling caste by taking to teaching and living by alms.... Therefore such noble doctrines as *ahiṃsā*, taught by the Buddha, are impure, unacceptable and unreliable as the milk put in a case made of the skin of the dog. (p. 70)

That this is the view of a reactionary minority even today seems evident from the fact that a certain South Indian journal is going out of its way to perform the double task of upholding casteism and vilifying the Buddhist movement in India. The two things cannot but go together. In the last chapter, 'Caste System in Buddhist Countries', the author shows how the baneful shadow of caste has fallen on Buddhist society in Nepal and Ceylon.

Bhikkhu Dhammaratana's work may be warmly recommended to our readers as a clear, readable, scholarly, and impartial account of a very thorny topic. The publishers might, however, have taken greater pains over the production of the book.

March 1956

A CLEAR AND RACY EXPOSITION

Bhikkhu Mahinda (English Buddhist monk)
The Blue Print of Happiness: An Outline of the Buddha's Teaching
The International Buddhist Centre, Bangkok

Concomitant with the present remarkable increase of interest in Buddhism, unprecedented in modern times, there is a great, indeed a growing, demand for popular literature that will provide the average layman with a brief and intelligible, yet at the same time reliable, introduction to the fundamental principles of the Dharma. Such literature a number of organizations, among them the Maha Bodhi Society of India, have for the last few decades been supplying. But it must be confessed that the booklets and pamphlets produced in this way were not unoften scarcely a credit to the cause they represented. Ill written and badly printed as they frequently were, they were hardly the best means of attracting the prospective student to the study of the Dharma. Fortunately, times are changing, and one of the signs of the change is the well written and neatly printed booklet now before us. Bhikkhu Mahinda is an English monk who, having settled in Thailand, now directs the International Buddhist Centre in Bangkok. Though as far as we know this is his first publication, he seems already to have achieved considerable mastery of his subject, the contents of the booklet including practically all the most important aspects of the Buddha's teaching as recorded in the Pāli canon. What impressed us even more, however, than the author's undoubted grasp of doctrinal fundamentals, was his delightful gift of clear and racy exposition. All too often are our expositions of the Dharma, even those meant for children and beginners, dull and ponderous in the extreme. But Bhikkhu Mahinda commits no such mistakes. He knows that to be a good Buddhist one does not have to forget how to smile, and manages to drive his points home with some very entertaining anecdotes. One complaint only we have to make, and that concerns the picture on the cover. Why, in a country with a centuries-old tradition of truly Buddhist art, was it necessary to inflict on the reader a glossy pseudo-naturalistic monstrosity of dubious Western origin? This, however is a comparatively minor blemish on an otherwise admirable production, and we congratulate not only Bhikkhu Mahinda but also the band of Thai *dāyakas* whose generosity made the publication – apparently printed for free distribution – possible. May we have many more books and pamphlets from the same source.

April 1956

A DISTINCT UNITY OF IMPRESSION

G. F. Allen (ed.)
Buddhist Wisdom for the West
The Buddha Study Association, Asalha-July 1956, pp. 32

It is one of the canons of criticism that before estimating the value of a work of literature or art one should ascertain what the author's (or artist's) aims were in producing it and whether he has succeeded in fulfilling those aims. The aim of the present compilation is sufficiently indicated by its title: it is an attempt to present the wisdom which is Buddhism – or, more correctly, the Dharma – to those in the West who, presumably, have no previous acquaintance with it. Whether or not the editor has been able to achieve his modest objective will depend partly on his knowledge of the fundamentals of Buddhism and partly on his understanding of Western mentality. At any rate, the editor being himself both a scholarly Buddhist and a westerner the result is bound to be interesting.[264]

After a rendition of the *Paramaṭṭhaka Sutta* of the *Sutta-Nipāta*, one of the main scriptural sources of the rather austere type of Buddhism favoured by Mr Allen, we have an introductory essay on 'The Buddhist Philosophy of Life' in which he contrasts Buddhism with Brahmanism, succinctly summarizes its main tenets, and distinguishes between the Mahāyāna and the Theravāda. This is followed by 'Buddhism: the Path to Wisdom', by the Ven. U Thittila, a very simple survey of the Dharma from the Theravāda point of view, after which we have 'The Buddha and His Modern Disciples', an extremely vigorous and 'Protestant' piece of writing by Madame A. David-Néel. Next comes a very short and cryptic essay on 'What is Zen?' by D. T. Suzuki. Thinking – no doubt correctly – that the Japanese scholar's paradoxes would have bewildered rather than enlightened the average Western reader, the editor follows it up with 'Zen and the West', an extremely sound and sober study by J. Evola. From Zen we pass to 'Time and Space, and the Problem of Free Will' by Lama A. Govinda, concerning which, when it was first published in the *Maha Bodhi*,[265] more than one friend wrote to me saying that it was the finest article on Buddhism he had ever read. 'Buddhism and Worship' by G. P. Malalasekera deals with its subject from a liberal Theravāda standpoint. Then, since Mr Allen is on the lookout for teachings which, while not directly Buddhist, have an affinity with Buddhism, we are treated to an extract entitled 'The Soul', from the talks of J. Krishnamurti. The last article, 'Buddha and History', by R. J. Jackson, though it does not maintain the standard of its predecessors, reminds us that the Buddha was a historical personage – rather a comforting thought after so much metaphysics. Finally, we have 'Excursions Into Freedom', a well-known but nonetheless acceptable excerpt from the *Zhuangzi* book.

Does this collection of reprinted articles and extracts from articles adequately present Buddhist wisdom to the West? Making due allowance for obvious limitations of space, I think it does. Though in a sense 'fundamentalist' it is by no means narrow. Moreover, despite their heterogeneity the articles which make up this compilation achieve a distinct unity of impression. Whether that unity has been imparted by the personality of the editor, or by the principles on which the articles were selected, or by both combined, it would be difficult to say. Perhaps we should be contented with a presentation of Buddhist wisdom to the West which, for authenticity of material and competence of arrangement, leaves very little to be desired.

September 1956

INTRUSIONS OF THE CLOVEN HOOF

Kenneth W. Morgan (ed.)[266]
The Path of the Buddha: Buddhism Interpreted by Buddhists
The Ronald Press Company, New York 1956, pp. 432

Gone, it seems – or at least on their way out – are the days when non-Buddhists, not without a touch of condescension, explained to Buddhists what the Buddha 'really' taught and what the Buddhists 'really' believed. At last we have a book, edited by a Christian minister (not a Roman Catholic, of course!) and brought out by an American publishing house, in which Buddhists themselves have actually been permitted to tell us about Buddhism. Not that non-Buddhist and non-oriental influences have been held entirely in abeyance. The 'ground plan' of the book is, of course, the work of the editor, who moreover sent to each of his contributors a list of the topics on which he thought they should expatiate. Then what are we to make of the fact that whereas more than half (seven out of twelve) contributors are from Japan, not one is from China? The explanations offered by the editor in this connection in the preface would not appear wholly convincing. Again, why is there no acknowledgement of the fact that the Path of the Buddha is now being followed by an increasingly large number of people in Western countries? It is almost as though the non-Buddhist occidental reader (for whom, of course, the book is mainly intended) was being told that Buddhism is an excellent religion – for orientals.

Despite such intrusions of the cloven hoof, however, the book as a whole does succeed in achieving a very high degree of authenticity and accuracy, and this achievement is no doubt due almost as much to the detached sympathy of the editor as to the learning and devotion of the contributors. The book falls into two main sections, one on the Theravāda, the other on the Mahāyāna, and the devices employed by the editor to prevent them from drifting too much apart are of great interest. Prefacing the first main section is a very able chapter entitled 'Origin and Expansion of Buddhism' by J. Kashyap. Then succeeding the first main section, which consists of two chapters, one on 'The Fundamental Principles of Theravāda Buddhism' and one on 'Buddhism in Theravāda Countries', comes by way of a link with the second main section the chapter 'Development of Mahāyāna Buddhist Beliefs'. Finally, rounding off the second main section, which comprises chapters on Buddhism in China and Korea, in Tibet, and in Japan, there is one on 'Unity and Diversity in Buddhism'. Thus the book achieves a degree of cohesion not always met with in works of this kind.

In addition to the general excellence of the book as a whole there are, in almost every chapter, individual excellencies of which due notice should be taken. J. Kashyap gives a striking picture of the personality of the Buddha. U Thittila in 'The Fundamentals of Theravāda Buddhism' achieves a remarkably clear and thorough exposition of dependent origination, karma, and rebirth. B. Ananda Maitreya Nayaka Thera's 'Buddhism in Theravāda Countries' is so written as to let us see that the Dharma as it prevails in Ceylon, Burma, and Siam is not quite so 'pure' as is generally represented. Susumu Yamaguchi, who the editor says 'was recommended again and again as one of the great masters of Mahāyāna thought' gives, in 'Development of Mahāyāna Beliefs', an exposition of the Madhyamaka and Yogācāra schools, and their mutual relations, which is easily the profoundest and most brilliant piece of writing in the entire book. In 'Buddhism in China and Korea' Zenryu Tsukamoto deals succinctly with a vast subject. Lobsang Phuntsok Lhalungpa, in a chapter which will probably have the greatest general appeal, has written what is undoubtedly the most authentic and reliable account of 'Buddhism in Tibet' yet to appear in any modern language. Shinshō Hanayama deals competently with 'Buddhism in Japan', to which chapter Mitsuyuki Ishida contributes a separate section on Shin and Jōdo Buddhism, Reiho Masunaga on Zen Buddhism, and Shobun Kubota on Nichiren Buddhism. Lastly, in 'Unity and Diversity in Buddhism', Hajime Nakamura very fairly discusses the factors that either divide or unite the various schools within a Buddhist community. Not unnaturally, one feels, after reading this chapter, that the uniting factors are both more numerous and more important than those which divide.

Perfection being beyond the reach of any human work, one need not be surprised to find, in four hundred pages, some small matter for disagreement, or even criticism. U Thittila, for instance, seems to regard Buddhist literature as synonymous with Pāli literature, naively saying of the latter that it no doubt represents 'the true teaching of the Buddha as he originally gave it' (p. 71). Then with the exception of Lhalungpa, none of the contributors, not even Yamaguchi, seems to have had even the vaguest idea of what Tantric Buddhism really was – most of them being content to mouth old Waddellian claptrap about Shaivite Hindu influence, magic, Shaktism, etc.[267]

Such blemishes apart, however, *The Path of the Buddha* on the whole really does give us Buddhism as interpreted by a fairly representative group of Buddhists, and we therefore hope that, despite its rather high price, it will have a wide circulation in both East and West.

December 1956

SCHOPENHAUER AND BUDDHISM

Charles Muses
East-West Fire: Schopenhauer's Optimism and the Laṅkāvatāra Sūtra: An Excursion Toward the Common Ground between Oriental and Western Religions
John M. Watkins, 21 Cecil Court, London 1955, pp. 67

It has long been acknowledged that through the writings of Schopenhauer oriental, particularly Buddhist, influences entered into the mainstream of Western thought. A systematic study of the relations between Schopenhauer and Buddhism was therefore long overdue; hence Dr Muses' preparatory exploration of the common ground between the German philosopher's *magnum opus*, *Die Welt als Wille und Vorstellung*, and the *Laṅkāvatāra Sūtra*, one of the great scriptures of Mahāyāna Buddhism, is to be welcomed. Though Schopenhauer was no pessimist, as the author rightly insists, his description of what happens when the will to live is negated is not sufficiently full and clear. Here, Dr Muses believes, the *Laṅkāvatāra* can help: its teachings set as it were a capstone upon the truncated pyramid left us by Schopenhauer. Though one would have thought that this idea, which constitutes the main thesis of Dr Muses' little book, was sufficiently obvious, the author has no doubt performed a service in reminding us of it. One feels, however, that the subject could have been given a much more extended treatment. The rather pretentious style of writing adopted in the book might then have seemed a trifle less absurd.

January 1957

A MAGNIFICENT VINDICATION

Rabindranath Tagore
Buddhadeva
Visva-Bharati, Santiniketan, pp. 28

Rabindranath, as the publishers of this booklet remind us, regarded the Buddha as 'the greatest man ever born on this earth'. It is only fitting, therefore, that they should have brought out, on the occasion of the 2500th Buddha Jayanti, the present selection from his writings. The longest prose piece, the translation of a speech delivered on 18 May 1935 at a Vaiśākha function organized by the Maha Bodhi Society, is a magnificent vindication of the Buddha as a manifestation of the Universal Man – a favourite conception of the poet's. With one or two of the ideas expressed in other prose excerpts few Buddhists will agree. That the Buddha's teaching was not derived from earlier Indian traditions does not mean that it was an accident: it had its source in his Enlightenment, in his practice of the ten *pāramitās* as a bodhisattva. With the poems, of course, disagreement is hardly possible. Several of them are very well known. But whether Rabindranath expresses himself in prose or verse, and whether one agrees or disagrees with his views, one cannot but be carried away by that combined nobility of thought and magnificence of utterance which is uniquely his.

January 1957

AN INSPIRING GLIMPSE

Buddhist Sculptures and Monuments
Ministry of Information and Broadcasting, Government of India, 1956

This brochure, which has been printed on art paper with an attractive cover showing the Maha Bodhi temple, Bodh Gaya, in full colour, consists of twenty-one plates of different Buddhist sculptures and monuments. Though some of the finest Buddhist works of art are represented, selection and arrangement would appear to have been quite arbitrary. One cannot help wondering whether the Ajanta fresco and the Tibetan thangka are to be classified as sculptures or as monuments. Moreover, the former has been very badly reproduced. On the whole, however, the publication presents not only an interesting but an inspiring glimpse of Indian Buddhist art through the ages.

January 1957

A VERY MIXED BAG

Buddha's Life by Modern Indian Painters
Ministry of Information and Broadcasting, Government of India, ten pictures

This is a very mixed bag. First of all we have some well known pieces by Nandalal Bose and Abanindranath Tagore which have done really yeoman service this Buddha Jayanti year and should now be decently retired on pension. Then there is Jamini Roy's version of a Tibetan thangka, which will strike art lovers as odd and orthodox Buddhists as blasphemous. Next we are treated to a rather attractive picture, in a folk-arty sort of style, of 'The Archery Contest' by Ishwar Singh and quite a striking rendering of 'The First Sermon' by Ishwar Das – perhaps the most rewarding part of the contents of this bright yellow folder. Among the rest are two pictures which exhibit the Bengal School at its worst and weakest. Buddhist art, we have been told, is a support for meditation. One cannot help wondering how far one could get by concentrating on some of these pictures.

January 1957

A TOLERABLE LITERARY STANDARD

Saddharma, No. 1, The Commemorative Volume of the 2500th Anniversary of Buddha Parinirvana
Japan Sangha of India, Calcutta, pp. 37

We are happy to see that our Japanese friends have launched a magazine of their own in English. Besides a contribution from Sri D. Valisinha, the articles, which are of a tolerable literary standard, include 'Atomic

Energy and the Future of Mankind', 'Buddhism and Human Society', and 'Tathāgata-Garbha' – the last, perhaps, being of the greatest interest. There is a Hindi article on 'Lord Buddha and World Peace'. The medley of Buddhism and politics which appears in the leading article will no doubt astonish Indian readers. Before bringing out further issues the editor would do well to give careful thought to the policy of 'Saddharma' in this connection.

January 1957

VERY NEATLY PRODUCED

Notes and News: a Quarterly, Vol. 1 No. 1, 1 July 1956
The Indian Institute of Culture, Bangalore, pp. 18

The *raison d'être* of this little magazine lies, we are told, in 'the desirability of a more intimate link with distant members of the Institute, a fuller and more timely sharing with them of its notes and news'. Each issue will summarize some outstanding activities of the Institute during the previous three months. This first issue accordingly features the Institute's Buddha Jayanti celebrations, which took the form of a special Buddha Jayanti week from 17 to 24 May. The rest of the issue, which like all Institute publications is very neatly produced, bears witness to the extremely wide range of the Institute's interests and activities.

January 1957

AN ENGAGING PRESENTATION

T. L. Vaswani
In the Footsteps of the Buddha
Gita Publishing House, Poona 1956, pp. 66

Sitting by the seashore at Karachi watching the sunset, many years ago, Sadhu T. L. Vaswani tells us, he happened to read in a journal the following 'words of wondrous beauty':

> May I be for all beings
> The healer of pain!

May I be to all who ail
The doctor and the nurse!
May I give food and drink to all
Who suffer from pangs of hunger and thirst!
May I be to the poor
A treasure untold!
May I be the defender of those
Who forsaken lie on the roadside!
May I be for those who long for the Other Shore
The boat and the bridge!
May I be the lamp that holds the light
To those who lose the way![268]

These words of Śāntideva – taken, of course, from his celebrated poem the *Bodhicaryāvatāra* – haunted him, he relates, with the result that he eventually gives us, in the latest of his numerous booklets, an extremely moving and musical résumé of the life and teachings of the poet-prince who left his throne to devote himself to the practice of the bodhisattva ideal. Of rather topical interest is the way in which, in the chapter 'An Ancient University', the writer contrasts the lofty educational ideals which inspired Nālandā, where Śāntideva was for some time a teacher, with the much lower aims that motivate our present-day institutions. In 'The Teacher' he gives an engaging presentation of the gist of Śāntideva's teaching in question-and-answer form. No one can read this very attractively produced little book without feeling that the life of the bodhisattva is the sublimest that can be lived upon earth.

February 1957

OF PERMANENT INTEREST AND VALUE

The March of India: Buddha Jayanti Special Number, November 1956
Ministry of Information and Broadcasting, Delhi, pp. 64

There seems to be no end to the Buddha Jayanti Special Numbers which are being brought out during the current Buddhist year. The rather sumptuous publication now before us, which is a well-known Government of India monthly's contribution to the solemnity of the 2500th *parinirvāṇa* anniversary celebration, was apparently published synchronously with the Jayanti functions that took place in New Delhi last November. Though somewhat late in the field, it has nothing to fear from comparison with its predecessors. Some of the best-known Indian scholars, such as Radhakumud Mookerji, Bharat Singh Upadhyaya, and R. C. Majumdar, have collaborated in its production, and one is therefore not surprised to find that the literary and intellectual standard of this Special Number is rather above average. The publication is moreover adorned by a number of fine photographs, some in full colour. The cover design, with its irreverently loose handling of the most sacred Buddhist motifs, could however have been improved upon. Unlike most souvenirs, this Special Number of *The March of India* is of permanent interest and value.

March 1957

THE SLAUGHTER OF INNOCENT ANIMALS

A. S. R. Chari
Veganism And Why?
Bangalore 1956, pp. 35

In this booklet the author has advanced a number of arguments, both scientific and religious, to prove the superiority of the vegetarian way of life. Himself a Buddhist for many years, Sri Chari is convinced that veganism is fully in accordance with the compassionate teachings of Lord Buddha, and it therefore rather pains him to find so many Buddhists, including even *bhikkhus*, apparently quite indifferent to the slaughter of innocent animals for food. Towards the end of his essay Sri Chari gives an interesting account of his own experiments in the field of vegetarian living. Veganism, he claims, has made him hale and hearty at the age of 76. We recommend the booklet to all interested in the application of Buddhist principles to daily life.

March 1957

LITERARY PASTICHE

W. J. Gabb
The Goose is Out
The Buddhist Society, London 1956, pp. 121

On page 29 the author relates how a verse of his, published in a Buddhist periodical over the pseudonym 'Tokuzan', was mistaken by Dr E. Graham Howe for the effusion of a real Zen master in perhaps the Tang dynasty. Your reviewer remembers reading, many years ago, some of the 'Tales of Tokuzan' published in the same periodical; but unlike Dr Howe he at once felt that they were not the genuine article: there was something in them which to him rang false. This early impression is deepened by the present volume, in which have been collected the author's lectures and essays on Zen Buddhism, originally published as *Beyond the Intellect* and *The Tales of Tokuzan*, which likewise has already appeared in pamphlet form. Though the style of writing is so virile and pointed as to be a joy to read, and though Mr Gabb is clearly a man of forceful and original personality, it would appear that the essence of his thought is much closer to the Vedānta than to Buddhism. Chapter 6, on 'Self-Realization', contains repeated references to 'the Self' (with a capital). And what are Buddhists expected to make of a statement such as 'All religions and all men and things ... are seen for what they are, aspects of the One, and the One is resolved into a universe of thought in which alone, I AM' (pp. 69–70)? In *The Tales of Tokuzan* occur several curious references to 'lay monks'. One would like to know the Chinese original of this strange expression. But perhaps it would be unreasonable to ask for the original of that which, like the *Tales* themselves, obviously has its source in Mr Gabb's fertile imagination. The book on the whole would seem to provide evidence for the regrettable fact that in certain Western Buddhist circles Zen Buddhism is in danger of becoming a kind of highbrow parlour game. Though Mr Gabb has assimilated modes of expression peculiar to one form of Zen there is nothing to show that he has penetrated its spirit. The *Tales* themselves are literary pastiche. Far from belonging to the ranks of the Zen masters, Mr Gabb's comparatively humble place is at the feet of Lewis Carroll and Edward Lear. The goose is *not* out.

April 1957

HARDLY ADEQUATE TO THE TASK

Rev. Yung His
The Commentary on the 'Formless Gatha'
Translated by Dr Chou Hsiang-Kuang
Indo-Chinese Literature Publication, Allahabad 1956, pp. 92

This book on Zen Buddhism is the antithesis of the one reviewed above. No one can doubt its authenticity. It is a commentary by a modern Chinese Zen (perhaps we should say Chan) master on the 'Formless Gatha'. The *Sūtra of Huineng*, famous as the only *sūtra* spoken by a native of China, is divided into ten chapters. Of these the most important is the chapter on wisdom, and the most important part of this chapter is the 'Formless Gatha'. In the present publication each line of Chinese text is printed separately in Roman characters, followed by its English translation. Then follow Rev. Yung Hsi's comments, which are plentifully loaded with quotations from the Mahāyāna *sūtras* and Zen anecdotes. Unfortunately Dr Chou's English is hardly adequate to the task which he has set himself. What is the reader to make, for example, of a sentence such as 'Whether your any attempt of mind look upon the good or evil things are false thoughts' (p. 44)? Or of 'If one try to enrich one's merit and soon will turn up into ignorant' (ibid.)? Nevertheless, though much is obscure much is crystal clear and the careful reader will no doubt be able to glean from these rather poorly printed pages not a little real spiritual benefit.

April 1957

THE EXTREME OF ETERNALISM

Ernest Shinkaku Hunt
An Outline of Buddhism, The Religion of Wisdom and Compassion
BM/Dharma, London 1955, pp. 28

This is the second, revised, edition of a simple and instructive pamphlet by a veteran Buddhist worker who, we believe, has laboured for well nigh fifty years in the service of the Dharma. Writing as he does for beginners, Mr Hunt naturally confines himself to what may be termed basic Buddhism, achieving a short and on the whole clear summary of the four noble truths and related teachings. We are all the more sorry, therefore, to find him speaking of the 'Oneness of all Life' (pp. 15, 21) in a sense in which no one with even an elementary knowledge of Buddhist 'philosophy' could accept. To say that all living things are interrelated is Buddhism; but to say that they are different modifications of one stuff, be it matter or spirit, is *śāśvatavāda*, the extreme of eternalism. This basic error vitiates what would otherwise have been a reliable little introduction to the Dharma.

May 1957

A RARE BLEND

East And West, Year vii, no. 4, January 1957
Istituto Italiano per il Medio ed Estremo Oriente, Roma, pp. 207–394

Though among the last, this is undoubtedly one of the best Buddha Jayanti special numbers to have been brought out in connection with the 2500th anniversary of the *parinirvāṇa* of the Lord Buddha. If one were to be asked what that special quality was that sets it apart from, even above, the majority of such productions, one would perhaps not be very far wrong in saying that it consisted in a rare blend of scholarship and imagination. This blend, though by no means absent from some of the other contributions, is particularly conspicuous in the article 'Buddha Jayanti' by the director of the Institute, Giuseppe Tucci, which prefaces and in a way determines the tone of the whole number.

August 1957

A VERY WORTHY CONTRIBUTION

The Buddhist, 2501 Jayanti Special
YMBA, Colombo, May 1957, pp. 106

As usual, the special Vaiśākha number of *The Buddhist*, one of the best known and most virile of English Buddhist periodicals, contains well written articles on different aspects of the Dharma. It is noteworthy that a number of writers feel the need of ascertaining the relations between Buddhist and other departments of life – social service, religion, the arts, literature, etc. Thus we have an impression of realism, of an attempt to get to grips with things, which is not always to be found in Buddhist publications. But then *The Buddhist* is the organ of an association of young Buddhists. We salute them for their very worthy contribution to this year's Vaiśākha Pūrṇimā literature.

August 1957

AN INSPIRING PICTURE

Dr Chou Hsiang Kuang
T'ai Hsu, His Life and Teachings
Indo-Chinese Literature Publications, Allahabad 1957, pp. 74

Along with Anagarika Dharmapala, with whose Maha Bodhi Society he was on very friendly terms, the late Abbot T'ai Hsu (Taixu) of China dominated the international Buddhist scene during the first four decades of the century. His origins were very humble. Born in Chang'an in 1890, he lost his father, a bricklayer, when only one year old and was brought up by his 'grandmother-in-law' as Dr Chou calls her. For a few years he worked as a salesman in a provisions store, but it was not long before his innate spiritual genius asserted itself, and at the age of eighteen he entered a monastery. Years passed in intensive study and meditation, and then, at an age when most young monks are just beginning to understand Buddhism, Mahāśūnyatā, as his name would be in Sanskrit, launched forth on his career as teacher, writer, reformer, and organizer. Reading the account of Taixu's activities given by Dr Chou, a personal disciple of the abbot, one wonders how one man could do so much. Besides establishing numerous temples, monastic schools, and colleges, founding journals, and making extensive tours in China and abroad, the indefatigable abbot found time to write 7,000,000 words, mainly on Buddhism, which his followers have lovingly collected under the title *The Pitaka of Bodhisattva T'ai Hsu*. We are grateful to Dr Chou for his inspiring picture of the life and teachings of one of the greatest Buddhists of modern times.

August 1957

A BRAVE OLD CHINESE PILGRIM

Fa-hsien
A Record of Buddhist Countries
Translated from the Chinese by Li Yung-hsi
Foreword by Ho Chang-chun
Chinese Buddhist Association, Peking 1957, pp. 93

This is the second English version of the well-known *Travels of Fa-hsien* to appear during the 2500th Buddha Jayanti year. The first (a reprint of the 1923 revised edition of the Giles translation) was reviewed in this year's Vaiśākha number (pp. 216–17) and little need therefore now be said about the brave old Chinese pilgrim and his book. The Chinese Buddhist Association is to be congratulated on its enterprise in bringing out this new translation which, the title page tells us, has been made by the San Shih Buddhist Institute, Peking, to commemorate the 2500th anniversary of the Buddha's *parinirvāṇa*.

August 1957

POWERS AND VIRTUES

The All-Sided One: the 24th Chapter of the Saddharma Puṇḍarīka from the 'Sacred Books of the East', XXI
Translated from Sanskrit by H. Kern, pp. 18 +16

This booklet, which strangely enough has no title page, so that we do not know for certain where and by whom it has been published, consists of a reprint of Kern's translation of the well-known 'Avalokiteśvara Chapter' of the *Saddharma Puṇḍarīka Sūtra*, wherein are extolled the powers and virtues of the bodhisattva Avalokiteśvara or Guanyin, together with the text of Kumārajīva's Chinese translation and a Romanized version of the same in the Hokkien (thus the foreword) or in Amoy (thus in the body of the booklet) dialect.

August 1957

BETTER THAN EVER

The Middle Way, vol. xxxii, no. 1. May 1957
The Buddhist Society, London, pp. 40

'Better than ever' would be a fair verdict on the Vaiśākha number of the Western world's oldest and most influential Buddhist periodical. In addition to the leading article 'Why Are We Afraid?' by the president of the Society, Christmas Humphreys, we have the usual scholarly contributions from Dr Conze and Miss I. B. Horner, the two vice-presidents. The sangha is ably represented by Dr W. Rahula, from whom we have a transcription of his Buddha Jayanti address in London last year, and by the Ven. Piyadassi Thera, who contributes an article on

'The Doctrine of An-Atta – Soullessness'. There is the usual complement of news items, book reviews, and announcements. Last but not least, there are eight glorious pages of photographs taken in Nepal and India by three members of the Buddhist Society's delegation to the World Fellowship of Buddhists conference in Kathmandu, Nepal, and the subsequent Delhi symposium.

August 1957

A CAREFUL AND LOVING PRODUCTION

The Bosat, Vesak Number, 2501/1957
Vajirarama, Vajira Road, Colombo, Ceylon, pp. 80

Of all the English Buddhist journals *The Bosat*, though in a sense the smallest, shows most clearly the signs of careful and loving production. This year it has surpassed itself.

August 1957

RATHER NARROWLY HISTORICAL

Prof. P. V. Bapat (ed.)[269]
2,500 Years of Buddhism
Foreword by S. Radhakrishnan
Ministry of Information and Broadcasting, Government of India, 24 May 1956, pp. 503

That on the 2,500th anniversary of the *parinirvāṇa* of the Buddha stock should be taken of Buddhism's achievements during its five-and-twenty centuries of history was but natural, and that this should be done under the auspices of the Government of India only what one would have expected. In *2,500 Years of Buddhism* twenty-seven scholars, mostly Indian, have attempted a survey and, to some extent, an assessment of the Buddha's teaching during the whole course of its history and in all its more important ramifications and developments. In judging such an attempt one should obviously concentrate less on matters of factual detail than on the broad general principles upon which, whether consciously or unconsciously, the presentation and interpretation of facts appear to have been based.

Perhaps the most striking feature of the book is its all-inclusiveness. This has, in fact, been a feature of all the major Buddha Jayanti publications, both in India and abroad. On their way out, it seems, are the days when 'Buddhism' meant one's own sectarian version of the Dharma thickly coated with local traditions and nationalistic sentiments. Buddhism, it is now being more and more generally recognized, means the *whole* of Buddhism, and this recognition is not only accentuating the unity but contributing to the unification of the entire Buddhist world.

All-inclusiveness is, however, no guarantee of proper distribution of emphasis among the materials included. While it was but natural and right that India, as the venue of the first proclamation of the Dharma, should occupy the central position, would it not have been more fitting if the Buddhism of the Far East, so rich in doctrinal and cultural developments, could have been given more than a meagre dozen pages? Again, while in chapter 9, 'Some Great Buddhists After Aśoka', appear such figures as Nāgasena and Buddhapālita, no mention is made of Tsongkhapa and Milarepa, Tibet being represented by Atiśa!

On the other hand, we have as it were for good measure very readable accounts of Buddhist art and Buddhist education, as well as chapters on places of Buddhist interest, Buddhist studies in recent times, and Buddhism in modern times – more than one could hope for from the average scholarly publication.

Much more serious, however, than any question of distribution of space among the various sections of the field surveyed, is that of the perspective in which the whole prospect of Buddhist history has been viewed. The perspective in this case is rather narrowly historical. Only three or four contributors seem to have felt that Buddhism was something more than a subject for scholarly research and academic dissertation, and consequently no attempt has been made to penetrate into the spirit of the Dharma. Except on pp. 447–8, there is hardly anything that might pass as an attempt to define the nature of Buddhism.

This disturbingly external and superficial, not to say materialistic, approach to the subject produces curious distortions. The usual scholarly nonsense is talked about Buddhism becoming 'a theistic religion' because the Buddha's relics were worshipped (p. 61) and about the 'deification of the Buddha and the Bodhisattva in Mahāyāna' (p. 119). More serious still, in chapter 2, 'Origin of Buddhism', on the assumption that 'philosophical ideas and doctrines do not spring up unexpectedly, but grow out of old ideas' (p. 11), we are treated to a long account of the non-Vedic schools of the Buddha's time. The writer seems to entertain no suspicion that the origin of Buddhism might have something to do with the Buddha's Enlightenment. In short we are presented with the history of Buddhism with Buddhism left out – *Hamlet* without the Prince of Denmark.

The foreword reveals bias of a different kind. So much does Dr Radhakrishnan overstate his case of the Buddha being a Hindu and Buddhism part of Hinduism that one doubts if he really believes his own thesis. One is reminded of the marginal note in the manuscript of the parson's Sunday sermon: 'Argument weak: shout here.'

Well-planned and comprehensive though it may be, *2,500 Years of Buddhism* will be of use chiefly as a work of historical reference: to know what Buddhism is we must look elsewhere.

September 1957

A FRESH AND LIVING THING

Martin Wickramasinghe[270]
Oldest Short Stories of India and *The Buddhist Jātaka Stories and the Russian Novel*
Associated Newspapers of Ceylon Ltd., Colombo 1956, pp. 173

So much is being written about Buddhism from an exclusively religious and philosophical point of view that the general reader may well welcome a more literary approach to the subject. The two principal essays of the present volume, by one of the leading writers of Ceylon, deal respectively with 'Oldest Short Stories of India' and 'The Jātaka Stories and the Russian Novel'. In the first of these Mr Wickramasinghe has no difficulty in showing that the best of the *Jātaka* stories, especially the 'Stories of the Past', are not just folklore but definitely literature, and he aptly applies to them the term 'folk-novel'. Several of these stories the author retells in a vivid and engaging style, adding his own very illuminating psychological comments. Two or three of the stories related indicate that whoever was responsible for the compilation of the *Jātaka* stories had an intuitive understanding of the workings of the subconscious mind. In the *Nanda Jātaka* (*Jātaka* no. 39) we actually find the Bodhisattva functioning in exactly the same way as a modern psychoanalyst!

The Jātaka Stories and the Russian Novel is an even more fascinating study. Brilliantly and convincingly, with extensive cross-references to ancient thought and modern literature, the author shows that the conception of man as a dual creature, capable of reaching the heights of spirituality as well as of sinking into the lowest depths of sadism and bestiality, is common to the *Jātaka* stories and Dostoyevsky. As André Gide originally pointed out, the great Russian novelist's conception of the spiritual life is Eastern rather than Western, not Christian but Buddhist. Mr Wickramasinghe, going a step further, considers that Alyosha and Father Zosima, Myshkin and Kirilov, have definite affinities with the figure of the Bodhisattva. It is certainly strange to find Kirilov quoted as saying, 'He who conquers pain and fear will himself be a god, and that other God will not be' (p. 100).

The remaining nine short studies, some of which appear to have been written as reviews, are of minor importance. Among them are 'Hunting for Dwarfs', 'An Easy Approach to Indian Sculpture', and 'Moonstones'.

This well written and extremely interesting collection of studies helps us realize Buddhist literature as a fresh and living thing, full of relevance to contemporary life and literature. We hope it meets with a reception that will encourage Mr Wickramasinghe to further achievements in the same field.

December 1957

THE VERY HEART OF THE DHARMA

Nyanatiloka Mahathera
The Buddha's Teaching of Egolessness – Anattā, an Essay, with extracts from the Saṃyutta Nikāya
The Word of the Buddha Publishing Committee, Colombo 1957, pp. 18

Of all the Buddhist doctrines none has given rise, in modern times, to so much controversy as the doctrine of *anātman*, egolessness. During the last few decades, however, scholars engaged in sifting the enormous mass of canonical literature extant in Pāli, Sanskrit, Tibetan, and Chinese, as well as fragments in minor languages hitherto unknown, have shown a marked tendency to confirm the universal Buddhist tradition that the *anātman* doctrine lies at the very heart of the Dharma.

Among those who stoutly upheld the orthodox tradition the name of the late Nyanatiloka Mahathera occupies an honoured place. Scholar, translator, and practising Buddhist, all his original works comment, directly or indirectly, on this supremely important topic. It is therefore most fitting that so soon after his death the booklet now before us should have been brought out in his memory.

The work consists of two parts: a short essay on egolessness, and a collection of thirty-one extracts from the *Saṃyutta Nikāya* all bearing on the same vital subject. In the first of these the author, without going into philosophical subtleties, has given a trenchant exposition of the Buddhist point of view. Though himself a strict Theravādin, he is fair-minded enough to point out that the doctrine of *anātman* forms 'a most essential part' of the teaching of the Mahāyāna schools. Indeed, the venerable author vigorously defends the Mahāyāna from the misinterpretations of 'some would-be Buddhists in the West who are attached to an imaginary Great Self, and who hold that the Buddha did in no way reject the view of an 'eternal Ātman' ... and who believe that the Mahāyāna texts teach such a doctrine'.

Though small in size, this booklet is not unworthy of its learned and pious author. We recommend it to all who are still in doubt whether the Buddha taught '*ātman*' or '*anātman*',

December 1957

EXTREMELY READABLE

J. N. Ganhar and P. N. Ganhar[271]
Buddhism in Kashmir and Ladakh
Shri P. N. Ganhar, New Delhi, pp. 245

As the years pass our picture of the history of Buddhism becomes more and more complete. One of the most interesting of recent contributions to this field is the book now before us, the work of two brothers, members of the learned and liberal-minded Pandit community of Kashmir to which belongs, incidentally, the prime minister, Sri Jawaharlal Nehru. Though this is a compilation rather than a work of original research, the authors have utilized their sources – chiefly the *Rājataraṃgiṇī,* the accounts of Chinese pilgrims, and the reports of modern archaeologists and anthropologists – with considerable skill, and the picture which they present of Buddhism's more than twenty centuries of history in Kashmir and Ladakh is indeed an enthralling one.

The book is divided into four parts. In the first and shortest we are given a sketch of 'The Buddha and His Gospel'. Despite their obvious goodwill towards the Dharma of the Enlightened One the authors make several rather questionable statements. We are told, for instance, that the Buddha 'attained to godhead' (p. 1) and that 'Buddhism was not a revolt against Hinduism' (p. 3). Part 2, which takes up the greater part of the volume, tells the story of 'Buddhism in Kashmir'. Despite temporary setbacks, Buddhism steadily grew from its humble beginnings under Surendra to the zenith of its glory under Aśoka and Kaniṣka, whose vast dominions embraced the Happy Valley, as well as under a succession of indigenous rulers, both Buddhist and Hindu. The authors have shown in a convincing manner the important part played by Kashmir in the propagation of the Dharma in Tibet and China. Indeed, for a while Kashmir seems to have been the centre of the Buddhist world, attracting the greatest saints and sages of the time. All the more sad, therefore, do we feel to see the slow decline which set in after the eighth century CE, due partly, it seems, to the iconoclastic zeal of invading Islam – although Muslim rulers sympathetic to Buddhism are not unknown – and partly to the growing prestige of Shaivism. The whole of this fascinating story the authors tell with scrupulous impartiality. But their sources occasionally lead them astray. For instance, quoting Evans-Wentz, they identify the *śakti* with the feminine or negative aspect of life (p. 106), whereas in the Buddhist Tantra the exact opposite is the case. Part 3 consists of a delightful and up-to-date account of 'Ladakh and its People', which fortunately are still Buddhist. In Part 4 the authors survey 'The Present Position', which after the visit of the Sacred Relics of the *arahants* Sāriputta and Moggallāna in 1950 and the statewide celebration of the 2500th Buddha Jayanti seems by no means without hope for the future.

An exhaustive index and bibliography add to the usefulness of this extremely readable volume.

March 1958

A NATION IN THE MAKING

Burma, Volume VIII, No. 2, January 1958 (Tenth Anniversary Number)
Rangoon, pp. 291

Published on the occasion of the tenth anniversary of Burma's independence, this substantial and well illustrated volume gives an impressive picture of the country's achievements during the last decade. Of special interest to the Buddhist reader are the sections on 'The Union of Burma Buddha Sāsana Council' and 'International Institute for Advanced Buddhistic Studies'. In Burma, at least, social reform and economic reorganization do not involve repudiation of traditional values. An inspiring picture of a nation in the making.

April 1958

A HANDSOME VOLUME

Diamond Jubilee Number
G. A. Natesan and Co., Madras 1957, pp. 193

Since its establishment sixty years ago the firm of G. A. Natesan and Co. has come to be regarded almost as a public institution. Its numerous publications, among them Anagarika Dharmapala's *Buddha*, have done much to create and educate public opinion on practically all topics of national interest, from religion and philosophy to politics and economics. Among the contributors to the present handsome volume are some of the most distinguished names of our times.

April 1958

THE SPIRIT OF THE MAHATMA

Gandhi Marg. A Quarterly Journal of Gandhian Thought, vol. 2, no. 1
Gandhi Smarak Nidhi, Bombay, pp. 110

The wide variety of articles contained in this publication shows that the spirit of the Mahatma is by no means dead, though the amount of space devoted to Vinoba Bhave and his Budhan movement is significant. The highlight of this number is an adaptation of an address on 'A Divided

Inheritance' by Dr S. Radhakrishnan, who alone among the contributors makes reference to Buddhism.

April 1958

FOUR BOOKLETS

Piyadassi Thera
The Seven Factors of Enlightenment (Sata Bojjhanga)
1957, pp. 28

Prof. H. Von Glasenapp
Vedānta and Buddhism
pp. 12

K. N. Jayatilleka, Robert F. Spencer and Wu Shu
Buddhism and Science – Collected Essays
1958, pp. 30

Nyanaponika Thera
The Four Sublime States: Brahma-Vihara
1958, pp. 16

These four booklets, all published for free distribution in the Wheel series by the Buddhist Publication Society, Forest Hermitage, Kandy, Ceylon, are evidence of a welcome improvement in the standard of popular Buddhist literature as regards both format and reading matter.

The first, which deals with the seven *bojjhaṅgas*, or factors of Enlightenment, is a scholarly study in an important subject by a learned Sinhalese monk who has compressed into a few pages a great deal of material drawn from canonical and extra-canonical sources.

Vedānta and Buddhism, by one of the greatest living Indologists, demonstrates in a thoroughly convincing manner that, in his own words, 'The denial of an imperishable *ātman* is common ground for all systems of Hīnayāna as well as Mahāyāna, and there is, therefore, no reason for the assumption that Buddhist tradition, unanimous on that point, has deviated from the original doctrine of the Buddha' (p. 10).

In *Buddhism and Science*, a Sinhalese, an American, and a Chinese Buddhist, all of whom seem to be as well versed in the Dharma as in scientific subjects, consider, from various points of view, the nature of the relation between Buddhism and modern science. Unlike certain other writers, they do not commit the mistake of trying to recommend Buddhism on the grounds that it is 'scientific'. In the words of the author of the first essay, a very well written and intelligent contribution to the subject, 'I have brought out these similarities [between Buddhism and science] not with the intention of showing that Buddhism teaches modern science but that the scientific revolution does not have the same adverse effect on Buddhism as it has had on another religious tradition' (pp. 3–4) – an important distinction.

Love, compassion, sympathetic joy, and equanimity are collectively known as the four sublime states (*brahma vihāras*). In explaining them, Ven. Nyanaponika Thera, in the last of these four booklets, has wisely eschewed psychological analysis and adopted, instead, a semi-poetic manner which is both attractive and inspiring.

It is extremely encouraging to mark the appearance of this timely series, evidently planned with intelligence and executed with devotion, and we trust that the high standard already achieved by the booklets here reviewed will be maintained by many dozens of successors.

September 1958

A SMALL COMPENDIUM

Dr R. L. Soni
Life's Highest Blessing
The World Institute of Buddhist Culture, Mandalay 1956, pp. 146

It is well known that the more deeply we penetrate into the words of the Buddha, the more meaningful we find them. This fact is exemplified by the present work, which consists entirely of an attempt to expound the meaning of the twelve short verses of the *Maṅgala Sutta* of the *Khuddaka Nikāya*.

Chapter 1, which is introductory, explains among other things the value of the *sutta*, its location in the scriptures, and the purpose of the present work. Chapter 2 contains the Pāli text of the *sutta* together with a word-for-word translation and free English rendering. In chapter 3, the most substantial portion of the volume, we find Dr Soni's own very pertinent and perceptive notes and comments not only on each verse but on every important word. Chapter 4 shows two ways in which the thirty-eight different blessings enumerated in the *sutta* can be distributed under the headings of *sīla*, *samādhi*, and *paññā*. In chapter 5 the author concludes by emphasizing the usefulness of the *Maṅgala Sutta*, which he correctly describes as 'The Hope of the World'.

Despite printing errors, it is obvious that a great deal of devotion and learning has gone into the production of this small compendium, which the lay reader is sure to find of great help in understanding and practising the Dharma. It is, we feel, a work particularly suitable for students, and we trust that special efforts will be made by the publishers to ensure that it has a wide circulation in schools and colleges.

October 1958

INDISPENSABLE TO ALL SERIOUS STUDENTS

Venerable Bhikkhu Buddharakkhita (trans.)
Dhammapada: A Practical Guide to Right Living
Maha Bodhi Society, Bangalore 1959, pp. 150

Regular readers of the *Maha Bodhi* will be aware of the fact that several of the early Buddhist schools compiled *Dharmapadas*, and that, though sharing large blocks of common material, they also exhibit interesting differences, both as regards the complete chapters and verses included and the variations found in the common material.

Though the non-Pāli *Dharmapadas* are now much better known than they were a few decades ago, the prestige and popularity of the Pāli version continues undiminished. Indeed, hardly a year passes without either new translations or reprints of old ones being brought out in several Eastern and Western languages.

The latest English translation by Bhikkhu Buddharakkhita is in many respects an improvement on its predecessors. The learned translator himself remarks, 'While consulting the English editions it was observed that many of the renderings were either too free or too pedantic.' A new translation therefore seemed desirable.

Besides achieving a greater accuracy in his rendering of these simple but profound verses, Bhikkhu Buddharakkhita, in a number of instances, has been able to elicit the deeper meaning of a saying by interpreting it in the light of the Abhidhamma tradition. As far as we know this feature of his translation is unique, and together with its thirty-seven pages of notes makes the volume indispensable to all serious students of the Dhamma.

August 1959

A CONSIDERABLE ACHIEVEMENT

Selected Sayings from the Perfection of Wisdom
Chosen, arranged, and translated by Edward Conze[272]
Buddhist Society, London 1955, pp. 133

Vajracchedikā Prajñāpāramitā
Edited and translated with introduction and glossary by Edward Conze
Is, M.E.O., Rome 1957, pp. 113

Buddhist Wisdom Books: containing the Diamond Sūtra and Heart Sūtra
Translated and explained by Edward Conze
George Allen and Unwin Ltd., London 1958, pp. 110

Dr Conze's *Buddhism: Its Essence and Development* (1951) and *Buddhist Texts Through the Ages* (1954), both of which achieved immediate success, revealed his formidable scholarship, both scientific and traditional, as well as his unique gift for lucid exposition and significant ordering of material. The present publications show the depth of his devotion to the Prajñāpāramitā or 'Perfection of Wisdom' literature which, he rightly maintains, is vital to an understanding of the Mahāyāna.

As the title suggests, *Selected Sayings* consists of excerpts from the whole vast literature, systematically arranged under three main headings: Sangha, Dharma, and Buddha – the advantages gained by this reversal of the customary order appear as we go along. Dr Conze says in the foreword that he has 'tried to cover the whole ground, and no important aspect of the teaching has been omitted' (p. 25). This is in itself a considerable achievement. The literatures of Perfect Wisdom, the teaching of Prajñāpāramitā, and the doctrine of emptiness, are extremely helpful for understanding not only the excerpts themselves but the nature of the Perfection of Wisdom literature and the movement to which it belongs.

Having given us a bird's-eye view of the whole field, Dr Conze proceeds to concentrate on particular items of importance, and it is not astonishing that he begins with the *Diamond* and *Heart Sūtras*, long regarded in the Far East as containing the quintessence of the whole teaching.

The *Vajracchedikā Prajñāpāramitā* consists of a scrupulously careful edition of the Sanskrit text in Roman characters, with all the variant readings, a scholarly introduction, a literal English translation, and a glossary. The bibliography contains forty-six items and is still not complete! This alone attests the enormous popularity of the work, which in fact has the distinction of being the oldest printed book known to us (11 May 868 CE).[273]

Buddhist Wisdom Books, which seems intended for a wider audience, contains more idiomatic translations of the *Diamond Sūtra* and the *Heart Sūtra*. As Dr Conze points out, 'for the last 120 years the *Diamond Sūtra* could be read in European translations, and during all that time we have been without the means which would have enabled us to solve its riddles' (p. 17). But the situation has suddenly changed. Three Sanskrit commentaries, together with a great deal of other material, are now available, and Dr Conze has utilized all these sources in preparing his own exhaustive commentaries on the two texts. The result is one of the most important works on Buddhism ever to appear in English. No one who reads it can help feeling that his previous notions about the Mahāyāna were dim and confused.

September 1959

FRESH AND FASCINATING

Buddhist Scriptures
Selected and translated by Edward Conze
Penguin Books, Harmondsworth 1959, pp. 250

There have appeared in English alone, Dr Conze tells us in the introduction, no fewer than seventeen anthologies of selections from the Buddhist scriptures, one of them being his own *Buddhist Texts Through the Ages* (1954), but so vast is the bulk of available material that, in his own words, 'there is room for many more'. Certainly there is room for one of such interest and originality as this.

Where *Buddhist Texts* is arranged according to schools, the present selection, by contrast, 'concentrates on the central tradition of Buddhism, at the expense of the more peripheral developments, on that which is common rather than that which separates. It contains very little that any Buddhist, of whichever school, would be prepared to reject.' There are three parts. Part 1 deals with 'The Teacher', part 2 with 'Doctrines', and part 3 with 'Other Worlds and Future Times'. In each of these Dr Conze is concerned to represent Buddhism as it is – 'warts and all' – not as somebody thinks it ought to be. Thus in Part 1 three *Jātaka* stories, dealing with episodes from the Buddha's previous lives, together with an outline of the Bodhisattva's progress, quite properly precede an abridged translation of Aśvaghoṣa's *Buddhacarita*. In part 2, chapters 1, 2, and 3 deal with the traditional 'groups' morality, meditation, and wisdom; chapter 4 with doctrinal formulas; and chapter 5 with doctrinal disputes. Under meditation is included a lengthy extract from Aśvaghoṣa's *Saundārananda*, entitled by Dr Conze 'The progressive steps in meditation', which is perhaps the clearest and completest, as well as the simplest, account of the subject available to the general reader.

In making these selections Dr Conze has borne in mind the needs of the average buyer of Penguin books. Nothing has been included which is not 'readily intelligible' and he has generally 'preferred texts intended for laymen to those addressed to monks'. Though this might have occasioned some sacrifice of profundity, the loss must be balanced against the great gain in comprehensibility. In any case, those who crave stronger meat can always turn to *Buddhist Texts*.

A list of sources and a glossary of technical terms enhances the usefulness of this exceptionally fresh and fascinating selection from the vast wealth of the Buddhist scriptures.

November 1959

STRIKINGLY SUCCESSFUL

Alan W. Watts[274]
The Way of Zen
Pantheon Books Inc., New York, pp. 236

During the last twenty years interest in Zen Buddhism has grown enormously in Western countries, and the output of literature on the subject has been considerable. The results of this interest have not always been quite happy, however. One of the reasons for such a state of affairs may be that, as pointed out by the author in the preface, no one – not even Professor Suzuki – has yet given the Western reader 'a comprehensive account of the subject which includes its historical background and its relation to Chinese and Indian ways of thought'. In the present work, which presents a view of Zen based on a careful study of the more important of the early Chinese records and a first-hand acquaintance with the Zen way of life, Mr Watts has done his best to remedy this deficiency. The result is the most adequate presentation of the subject as yet available in English.

The work is divided into two parts, the first of which consists of four chapters on 'Background and History'. Instead of at once plunging us into a briar-bush of Zen conundrums, like some sterner authors, Mr Watts first leads us gently through chapters on 'The Philosophy of the Tao', 'The Origins of Buddhism', and 'Mahāyāna Buddhism', and it is only in the fourth chapter, 'The Rise and Development of Zen', that we are permitted, after careful preparation, to hear a koan. Chapters 2 and 3, which are written with more than usual sympathy and understanding, are deserving of careful study even by students of Buddhism who are not particularly interested in Zen. One cannot help wondering, though, whether the idea that Taoism 'combined' with Indian Mahāyāna Buddhism to 'produce' Zen is not a little too artificial. If Zen *satori* does not differ in essence from the *bodhi* attained by Gautama surely Taoism's contribution was limited to certain modes of expression. One also feels that the author is not sufficiently aware of certain affinities between the methods of the Chinese Dhyāna school and those employed in some Indo-Tibetan Vajrayāna traditions.

Part Two deals with 'Principles and Practice', and here, especially in the first two chapters, 'Empty and Marvellous' and 'Sitting Quietly, Doing Nothing', we reach the heart of the matter, and Mr Watts' clear style and quick, intuitive intelligence show themselves to greatest advantage. At times his words seem to be not merely about Zen but the product of direct Zen experience. There is also a timely warning that 'Zen might be a very dangerous medicine in a social context where convention is weak, or ... where there is a spirit of open revolt against convention ready to exploit Zen for destructive purposes' (p. 143). 'Zazen and the Koan' is of interest mainly as disclosing certain differences of emphasis as between the Sōtō and the Rinzai schools and as helping to correct the widely prevalent idea that sweating at koan is an essential part of Zen training. 'Zen in the Arts' indicates how the spirit of Zen finds expression in painting, poetry, landscape gardening, fencing, flower arrangement, the tea ceremony, and in the other lovely arts and crafts of traditional China and Japan.

There is no doubt that in this wise and well-written book Mr Watts has not only shown us *The Way of Zen* but brought into perspective the relation between Zen and the total Buddhist tradition in a strikingly successful manner.

January 1960

HANDY AND ATTRACTIVE

Christmas Humphreys (ed.)
A Buddhist Students' Manual
The Buddhist Society, London 1956, pp. 279

Published, as the dedication tells us, 'with Funds provided by the members of the Buddhist Society in Commemoration of the Thirtieth Anniversary of the Society's Foundation', this handy and attractive volume, in part a revised and enlarged edition of several earlier publications, is of interest mainly as bearing witness to the extraordinary progress which Buddhism has made in England during recent years. This progress is, in fact, the theme of the first part of the book, beginning with the publication of Spence Hardy's *Manual of Buddhism* in 1850 and Edwin Arnold's *Light of Asia* in 1879, through many vicissitudes down to 'the expansion of 1954'. Though many individuals and organizations are naturally seen coming and going, there is a most satisfying overall impression of steady progress of which the Buddhist Society itself seems more and more to be the focal point. The remainder of the volume contains such useful material as a brief glossary of Buddhist terms, analyses of the Pāli canon and the Mahāyāna scriptures (the latter very much less detailed than the former) and an analysed bibliography of books on Buddhism. There is no doubt that this work, upon which has evidently been lavished much scholarship and even more devotion, will be of great use for reference purposes to students of Buddhism the world over.

1960 (month unknown)

OUTSTANDING CLARITY OF EXPOSITION

Lama A. Govinda[275]
Foundations of Tibetan Mysticism
Rider and Co., London 1959

Only sixty-five years ago Waddell's *The Buddhism of Tibet or Lamaism*, which many writers persist in regarding as the chief authority on the subject, could characterize Tibetan Tantrism as 'Saivite idolatry; Sakti worship and demonology ... meaningless gibberish ... silly mummery', but now the wheel has turned full circle, and with the publication of the present work Buddhism begins at last to come into its own.

Far from being a degeneration, Tantric Buddhism represents a thoroughgoing renewal, almost a rejuvenation, of the entire Buddhist tradition, a renewal wherein meditation techniques based on a profound knowledge of both the heights and the depths of the human mind bring the realization of the non-dual Reality *in this life* within the reach of the qualified aspirant.

As the fully initiated disciple of a well-known Tibetan lama, the German-born author (who like his gifted Indian wife Li Gotami is an artist of repute) brings to the task of expounding the true meaning of certain aspects of the Tantric Buddhist tradition of Tibet not only knowledge, but love, devotion, and deep intuitive understanding. Appropriately enough, he chooses to present his material in the form of a series of meditations on the significance of *oṃ maṇi padme hūṃ*, the great mantra of the bodhisattva Avalokiteśvara, the patron of Tibet, four of the five parts into which the book is divided corresponding each to one word of the mantra and one to the mantra as a whole. This arrangement by no means produces an effect of artificiality. On the contrary, the reader is conscious of the inner hidden meaning of the sacred syllable as it were slowly unfolding and flowering before his eyes. So strong is this impression, indeed, that he willingly forgets to enquire to what extent the author's interpretations accord with the Tibet tradition. Such outstanding clarity of exposition is self-authenticating.

So deeply does Lama Govinda succeed in penetrating into his subject that in exposing the foundations of Tibetan Mysticism he simultaneously lays bare those of Buddhism itself.

August 1960

SMALL BUT INTERESTING

I. B. Horner
Ten Jātaka Stories
Luzac and Company Ltd., London 1957, pp. 92

Though slight in comparison with her formidable labours on the Vinaya Piṭaka and the *Majjhima Nikāya*, this small but interesting and useful volume bears all the marks of Miss Horner's ripe scholarship. From the 547 *Jātakas*, which for the Buddhist stand in no need of introduction, she has selected ten short and attractive stories

> designed to illustrate how, in various of his anterior lives, the Great Being practised each of the ten perfections or 'goings beyond'... until he had gained the complete supremacy in them all necessary for the attainment of Buddhahood.' (p. x)

Thus we have *Sasajātaka*, the birth story of the hare, to illustrate *dāna* or giving; *Khantivādi Jātaka*, the birth story of the examplar of forbearance, to illustrate the virtue of that name, and so on. The romanized Pāli text of each birth story appears on the left hand side of the page, and the English translation opposite it on the right hand side. This is a great help to students of Pāli, who are not often provided with such aids. In her introduction, which within the limits of twenty-three pages could hardly be more informative, the author gives a general account of the birth stories, states the purpose of the present work, and adds on each of the ten selected *Jātakas* in turn a series of notes which constitute by no means the least valuable part of the book. Though her main object is 'to provide those learning Pāli with reading matter that is palatable and comparatively easy but which at the same time ... uses a large number of words' (pp. x–xi) the appeal of the stories themselves is all that is needed to ensure the book a public much wider than that for which it is primarily intended. As Miss Horner observes:

> The Stories seek to inculcate good manners, good sense and good behaviour, all of which usually reap an appropriate reward owing to the working of *kamma* by which the result of a volitional act, of body, speech or thought, is suited to the nature of that act. They contain much of cruelty and savagery, treachery and ingratitude, much of courtesy and chivalry, love and friendship, loyalty and devotion, quick-wittedness and ingenuity, self-sacrifice, endurance, patience, and care and affection for others: wife and husband, children, parents and friends. (p. ix)

Miss Horner has given us a book from which none are too big to learn.

September 1960

A FINELY PRODUCED VOLUME

Report of the Fifth General Conference of the World Fellowship of Buddhists
Bangkok, Thailand 24–30 November 2501 BE (1958)
The Buddhist Association of Thailand, Bangkok 1960, pp. 171

For those who attended the Fifth General Conference of the WFB this informative, lavishly illustrated, and finely produced volume will undoubtedly be a source of pleasant memories, while for those who could not be present it provides a full but succinct account of the proceedings. The conference was attended by 199 delegates, visitors, and observers from eighteen countries including Thailand, the host country. There were five plenary sessions, five business meetings, one for each subject committee, and an executive council meeting, besides a wide variety of religious, educational, and social engagements. Despite the criticism which has been so often levelled against the practice, the plenary sessions were as in previous years mainly occupied with the reading out of messages. The committees all passed a number of praiseworthy resolutions but without making any concrete suggestion as to how they could be implemented. As with the reports of the previous General Conferences, the reader is apt to get the impression of a week of hectic sightseeing by representatives of various Buddhist organizations or of none followed by two years of complete inactivity. The present report, for instance, comes out two years after the conclusion of the Conference.

The WFB, which claims to be the global organization of the Buddhists, has been in existence for ten years. Apart from its excellent magazine *World Buddhism*, published from Ceylon, it appears to have no permanent achievement to its credit. Work on the *Buddhist Encyclopaedia*, we understand, has practically come to a standstill. This reviewer suggests that if there is still enough life in the WFB to hold the Sixth General Conference – due to meet next month, though the venue is not yet known – all concerned would be well advised to give most serious thought to the future of the organization.

October 1960

A CATHOLICITY OF OUTLOOK

Christmas Humphreys
The Wisdom of Buddhism
Michael Joseph, London 1960, pp. 280

Christmas Humphreys, the lawyer who for thirty-five years has headed the fast-growing English Buddhist movement, is now one of the best-known figures in the Buddhist world.[276] Though already having a number of publications to his credit, the latest of them, an anthology of Buddhist scriptures entitled *The Wisdom of Buddhism*, probably represents his predilections and special approach more clearly than any.

Like most Western Buddhists, far from identifying himself exclusively with any one school, he not only accepts but rejoices in the total Buddhist tradition in all its marvellous richness, complexity, and diversity. For him, therefore, the Buddhist scriptures are not synonymous with a single fixed and closed canon but a

> vast collection of writings in a dozen languages having this in common, that they stem from the Buddha's Enlightenment as expressed through the medium of his own or lesser minds, and that they have the same basis of Teaching which is herein given as the Four Noble Truths.

With such a catholicity of outlook it is not surprising that he is able to range from the Old Wisdom schools to the New, from the Theravāda on the one hand to the Mahāyāna in India, in China and Japan, and in Tibet, on the other, as well as to encompass not only Tantric *dohās* and Zen koans but an extract from *The Mahatma Letters* and a quotation from Dr Suzuki. The central group of five chapters among which these riches are distributed are preceded by one dealing with the Buddha as Cosmic Principle, as the Buddha-principle within, and as a human being and followed by three more concerned respectively with Concentration and Meditation, the Buddhist Order (Sangha), and Nirvāṇa. Each chapter is headed by a short but very helpful prefatory note which, together with the lucid and informative Introduction to the volume, unobtrusively keeps the reader on the right track.

If Christmas Humphreys chooses to give just a little more space to Zen, and a little less to the Tantra, than some of us would have done, who will be so ungrateful as to complain? The theoretical and the practical, intellectual and devotional elements are so beautifully balanced in the book, and the whole is pervaded by so pleasing a mellowness, that the reader hardly needs to be reminded that the editor has dedicated more than forty years to studying, practising, and disseminating the wisdom of Buddhism. As a product of the full maturity of a noted English Buddhist, the work will not only serve as an indication of the growing strength of Buddhism in the West, but also act as one of the means of its further extension wherever the English language is known.

August 1961

NEED NOT HAVE BEEN WRITTEN

Hans-Ulrich Rieker[277]
Beggar Among the Dead
Translated from the German by Edward Fitzgerald
Rider and Company, London 1960, pp. 224

Ten or more years ago a German Buddhist monk, disillusioned with Western civilization, came to India in search of a guru who would show him the way to Enlightenment. After spending a few days in Bombay, he travelled to Calcutta, stayed there a few months, then walked up to Kalimpong. After an unspecified but short interval, he returned to his own country. Out of this unpromising material the author has had to make a book that was readable and would sell. If he at all succeeds it is mainly because of a gift for powerful and brilliant writing. The Indian scene is painted in meticulous, vivid detail; we can see it, hear it, and even smell it. Particularly memorable is the account of the long train journey across the subcontinent from Bombay to Calcutta, the whole of which bears the stamp of authenticity.

However, the author seems to have felt that this was not enough. After all, he had come to India not to describe beggars and sacred cows, however picturesque, but to find his guru – though why, as a Buddhist, he did not look for a guru in Ceylon or in Japan, for example, is nowhere explained. As finding his guru he is therefore determined to depict himself. At what appear to be regular fortnightly intervals he encounters figures which the psychologist will at once recognize as projections of that well-known archetype, the Wise Old Man. The Hindu yogi, complete with tiger skin and human skulls, in the Malabar Hill temple; the Punjabi in the train; the monk Ananda; the old Chinese; the leper saint; another yogi; the Tibetan 'lama'. Whether he really met any of them, or merely introduces them as mouthpieces of his own developing ideas is not clear. The latter is the more likely alternative, for more than one such figure fails to carry conviction. The Tibetan 'lama', for instance, is described as wearing the turquoise ear-pendant of a government official, which is quite out of character, and as speaking as never yet Eastern Buddhist spoke, least of all a Tibetan. Moreover these figures are in the habit of giving the author extraordinary psychic experiences. Here, I am afraid, we reach the most dubious part of the narrative; for the elaborate descriptions of these experiences are of the type usually met with in second-rate pseudo-occult literature, and do not ring true. Most of them centre about the awakening of the *kuṇḍalinī*. One can sympathize with the author's disappointment with Buddhist monasticism (overlooking the fact that he encountered it only in Bombay and Calcutta pilgrim centres, misleadingly styled 'monasteries', and equipped with 'cells' and 'abbots'), but is Hindu psychism the only alternative? Despite vague references to books and manuscripts, there is nothing to show that the author has seriously studied Buddhism. On p. 86 he speaks of Chenrezig, instead of Jambyang, as severing the mountain of Nepal with his sword. Besides revealing ignorance of the distinction between *dhammas* and *saṅkhāras*, his version of *Dhammapada* verses 277–9 informs us that 'nothing which has become is the true self' (p. 103). One cannot even be sure whether he is a monk or a layman. As a monk he indeed speaks of himself throughout, and he seems to have worn the yellow robe. But on p. 161 he says: 'I recalled the moment of my ordination: *kāmesu micchācārā veramaṇī sikkhāpadaṃ samādiyāmi*.' This, as every Buddhist knows, is the third precept of the layman.

Despite the rich and powerful descriptions of the Indian scene which are its most rewarding features, the book as a whole is one which need not have been written.

August 1961

BEAUTIFUL AND INSTRUCTIVE

David Marshall Lang[278]
The Wisdom of Balahvar – A Christian Legend of the Buddha
George Allen and Unwin, London 1957, pp. 135

It has been well known for some time that Saint Josaphat, one of the most popular saints of the Middle Ages, was in fact not a Christian at all but the Buddha, or rather the Bodhisattva. The story of how this astonishing transmogrification took place is for the first time told in full in Part One of this book, no. 20 in the Ethical and Religious Classics of East and West series, and makes quite as fascinating reading as a piece of good detective fiction. The story begins in India, with a biography akin to the *Buddhacarita* of Aśvaghoṣa. This, apparently, underwent some sort of editing at the hands of the Manichaeans of Central Asia, where Buddhism and Manichaeism overlapped. About 800 CE there appeared in Baghdad an Arabic version of the legend of Barlaam (as the Bodhisattva's teacher is called) and Josaphat, from which there proceeded not only four more Arabic recensions but one version in Georgian and another in Hebrew. From the Georgian the story was translated into Greek and attributed to St John Damascene (c.676–749), to whom it was supposed to have been related by Indian holy men. From Greek it was rendered into Latin and other languages. According to Joseph Jacobs there are over eighty versions of the original Indian Buddhist tale in the principal languages of Europe, the Christian Orient, and even Africa.

Part Two consists of a translation of *The Wisdom of Balahvar*, a second and shorter Georgian version of the legend about half as long as the first, from which it was taken. The birth of Josaphat (or Iodasaph, as he is called in the Georgian versions), the predictions of the wise men concerning his future career, his confinement in the palace by his father, and his going forth on an excursion and seeing, successively, an old man, a sick man, and a corpse, all quite faithfully reflect the legend's Buddhist originals. The fourth sight, that of the recluse, is however considerably expanded, not without effect. Balahvar, who comes secretly to see the prince, is a former minister who had been exiled for professing Christianity, to which the king was violently opposed. He instructs Josaphat in a series of parables, and the prince is converted. Eventually, after various dramatic incidents, Josaphat's father is also converted, Christianity is re-established in India, and Balahvar and Iodasaph die in the odour of sanctity. As Monsieur Lang observes, 'Despite the composite, indeed disparate, elements of which the Christian legend of Barlaam and Iodasaph is composed, it manages to retain a surprisingly large element of the authentic teaching of Gautama Buddha' (p. 17). Moreover, the account of the two worthies is even now quite readable as a story; the parables, most of which are drawn from Indian rather than specifically Buddhist sources, are beautiful and instructive. On the whole the book provides evidence of the wide, if very thinly spread, influence of Buddhism on medieval Christian Europe, and is of exceptional interest to all who are interested in the history of the interrelations between the two great religions.[279]

October 1961

ENTERTAINING, IF RATHER SUPERFICIAL

Ny Lobzang Jivaka
An English Buddhist in a Tibetan Monastery
Routledge and Kegan Paul, London 1962, pp. 210

In search of Truth, an English doctor finds himself in a Buddhist monastery in remote Ladakh (*not* Tibet), where he spends three months. This is not a very long time, but the author manages to give an entertaining, if rather superficial, account of the Tibetan type of monastic life as he saw it there during this period. Standards do not seem to have been very exacting, and though the Lhasa-trained abbot was evidently a man of learning and character, the dozen or so inmates over whom he exercised authority seem to have been quite mediocre. Owing no doubt to lack of material the author sometimes resorts to 'padding', as in the chapter on 'The King of Kashmir'. Since Marco Pallis covers much the same ground in part 1 of the classic *Peaks and Lamas* comparisons between this celebrated work and the present performance are inevitably provoked. In sensitivity, understanding, and descriptive power, Lobzang Jivaka is far inferior. As the work of a comparative newcomer to Buddhism, however, the book is commendable, and had the author lived it might well have been followed by a more substantial contribution to our knowledge of Tibetan monasticism.[280]

June 1962

A WIDE RANGE OF THOUGHTFUL ARTICLES

C. D. S. Siriwardane
The Buddhist, Vesak Number
Colombo, May 2506/1962, pp. 70

With its red, white, and gold cover, and wide range of thoughtful articles, this year's Vesak number of Ceylon's oldest English Buddhist journal worthily maintains the high standard of previous years. One cannot make mention of all the subjects dealt with by the contributors, several of whom are Western Buddhists, but 'Buddhism and Contemporary Western Philosophy' by K. N. Jayatilleke and 'The Peace Concept of Buddhism' by Dr Hajime Nakamura certainly should not be overlooked.

Several articles are controversial. Thus Chas. F. Knight castigates Neo-Zen, and H. A. C. Wickremaratne indignantly exposes the anomaly of Sinhalese Buddhists being compelled to go on living under marriage and divorce laws of dogmatic Christian origin. Other features of this artistically produced and highly readable Vesak offering are a deeply thoughtful editorial on 'The Future of Buddhism' and a book review.

June 1962

G. P. Malalasekera (ed.)
Encyclopaedia of Buddhism, Fascicle: A–ACA
Government of Ceylon, 1961, pp. 152

The compilation of an Encyclopaedia of Buddhism in English was one of the several undertakings of the Laṅkā Bauddha Maṇḍalaya (Buddhist Council of Ceylon) which was set up by the Government of Ceylon in 1955 in connection with the 2500th Buddha Jayanti celebrations. The Maṇḍalaya appointed a subcommittee, which in turn appointed as its chairman and editor-in-chief Ceylon's internationally renowned scholar diplomat Dr G. P. Malalasekera. When in 1956 the Government of Ceylon created a Ministry of Cultural Affairs, the administration of the *Encyclopaedia* was transferred to that ministry, while Dr Malalasekera continued to be chairman and editor-in-chief. In May 1957 a specimen fascicule of the *Encyclopaedia* was produced containing a few articles representing a cross-section of the kind of information the *Encyclopaedia* hoped to provide and the method it proposed to follow. This foretaste of what was to come met with an encouraging response, and many criticisms and suggestions were received. Finally, last year, appeared the eagerly expected first fascicle of this historic publication.

As the editor-in-chief points out in his preface, 'The Encyclopaedia aims at giving a comprehensive account of the origins of this world religion and of the developments that have taken place during a period of twenty-five centuries.' He moreover emphasizes the fact that the *Encyclopaedia* will contain information both on the Mahāyāna and the Theravāda and that such information will be so presented as to make it useful not only to the scholar and the expert but to the general reader as well. After much consideration, the alphabetical method of treatment of topics has been adopted, Hasting's *Encyclopaedia of Religion and Ethics* serving in many ways as a model. In some instances, more than one article is published on the same topic by different contributors, while in others more than one contributor cooperates in the production of a single article. The more specialized articles are signed. The length of the articles has been left to the discretion of the contributors, emphasis being laid on the requirement that no vital information should be omitted and that all information should be given as concisely as possible.

As might have been anticipated, the present fascicule is rich and varied, but not equal, in content. Articles vary in length from notices a few lines long to lengthy monographs, and as regards their topics range from Ababa, the name of a hell, to Abhayagiri, that of a famous monastery in ancient Ceylon, and from Abortion to Absolute. Besides the expected contributions on various Pāli and Sanskrit technical terms, titles of canonical and non-canonical works, and geographical and historical proper names, articles on English renderings of Buddhist terms and general philosophical and religious topics, together with names of modern Buddhist scholars and Buddhist publications, have also been included. Some of the articles, such as that on *ābhā*, are extremely curious, and contain information not elsewhere available, one imagines, in English. But the fascicule is really dominated by the splendid series of articles on the history, contents, and literature of the Abhidharma, in both its Pāli and Sanskrit forms, which cover between them one third of the fascicule and provide it with a very substantial background. The fascicule would in fact be worth possessing for the sake of these articles alone, which most intelligently collate information for which one would otherwise have to ransack scores of volumes in at least half a dozen languages.

Though the editorial board has not succeeded in imposing, and perhaps has not sought to impose, uniformity of style upon its diverse and at times highly individual contributors, it has certainly achieved real unity of spirit. Respect for tradition, though naturally prominent, has not been allowed to blur scientific clarity of treatment or distort historical perspective. One is astonished, however, to find that, with the possible exception of some of the Far Eastern contributors, who may be scholar-priests (but in the case of Japan at least, not *bhikṣus*), there is not a single contributor from the sangha. Are laymen now outdistancing monks in the field of Buddhist scholarship?

With so vast a range of subject matter, so many controversial issues, and so many opportunities for error, it will be impossible to satisfy everybody, and every reader, certainly every reviewer, will no doubt find occasion for criticism. My own particular complaint is that with at least four specialists in Tibetan Buddhism and the Vajrayāna on the board of honorary editors, the important topic of *abhiṣeka* should have been treated entirely, and at most adequately, from Sino-Japanese sources. One or two contributors have also been rather careless in their use of 'orthodox' and 'heterodox' and allied terms. Perhaps a note could be made and these matters rectified in the next edition.

On the whole, the first fascicule of the *Encyclopaedia of Buddhism* is a work of which the Buddhist world has no reason to be ashamed. Besides admirably fulfilling its declared objectives, it represents a partial laying down of the foundations of that grand edifice of World Buddhism whereof some of us dream. As such it ought to find a place in every Buddhist library and, if possible, in every Buddhist home – to say nothing of every vihara. All concerned in the production of this monumental work – its sponsors, the Government of Ceylon, its distinguished editor-in-chief and his devoted colleagues, its invariably learned and occasionally lively contributors, and its impeccable printers – deserve our heartiest congratulations and unfailing future support. May those of us who are young enough live to see, during the next decade, the regular publication of the remaining 99 fascicules of what we are happy and proud to think is *our* encyclopaedia.

July 1962

A SPLENDID FOLIO VOLUME

Rgyan-Drug Mchog-Gnyis
Namgyal Institute of Tibetology, Gangtok, Sikkim 1962, pp. 53, with seven plates[281]

The Namgyal Institute of Tibetology, opened by Sri Jawaharlal Nehru in 1958, already has several publications to its credit. The splendid folio volume now before us is likely, however, to prove of the greatest general interest and value. It is devoted to a set of five seventeenth-century Tibetan thangkas or painted scrolls depicting the Buddha and eight great spiritual masters of the Buddhist tradition, the Buddha himself occupying one thangka and one pair of spiritual masters each of the remaining four. Besides an introduction by the Maharajakumar of Sikkim, the president of the Institute, the work is divided into two parts. There is also an appendix. Part 1, 'Description of the Thangkas', has evidently been written bearing in mind not only the special interest of that formidable person, the Tibetologist, but also those of the simple art-lover. Besides elucidating the symbolism, and explaining the historical and doctrinal associations of the thangkas, the letter-press therefore indulges in some interesting and subtly perceptive art criticism which assists the reader to a deeper appreciation of the unique spiritual quality of these paintings. This is all the more necessary inasmuch as they are not merely examples of traditional iconography but works of art in their own right. Moreover the artist, the sixth Karmapa hierarch, no more hesitates to deviate, when necessary, from tradition, than he does to 'distort' perspective. The thangkas belong, in fact, to an earlier and less stereotyped period of Tibetan religious art. Part 2, 'Lives and Thoughts of the Eight Masters', after dealing briefly with the Buddha and Buddhism, gives a biographical sketch of each of the eight masters, as well as an appraisal of the significance of their distinctive contributions to Buddhist philosophy and religious life. The masters comprise two groups. The first, consisting of Nāgārjuna and Āryadeva, Asaṅga and Vasubandhu, and Dignāga and Dharmakīrti, are known as the *ṣaḍalaṃkārah* or 'six ornaments' of Buddhism. The second group consists of Guṇaprabha and Śākyaprabha, who are known as the *uttamapuruṣadvayaṃ* or 'two great men'. The second group is said to have been added to the first by Tsongkhapa in order to emphasize the importance of the Vinaya, Guṇaprabha and Śākyaprabha being authorities on that subject. In Tibetan, the names of the two groups are Rgyan-drug Mchog-gnyis – hence the title of the book. The appendix contains a useful Sanskrit–Tibetan glossary, some place names, original sources, traditions, and a bibliography. The five plates in colour give a not inadequate idea of the glories of the original paintings, enabling one at least to appreciate the artist's mastery of composition and the sensitiveness of his colour combinations. No pains seem, in fact, to have been spared in the production of this volume, which, with its judicious balance of scholarly and popular, scientific and aesthetic appeal, should find a wide public among lovers of Buddhism and lovers of art in general, and in particular among the growing band of devotees of Tibetan Buddhism.

August 1962

ALTERNATIVE TRADITIONS

DEDICATION

To the memory of Edward Conze (1904–1979)
Despite whose reminders I did not review
Memoirs of a Modern Gnostic

PREFACE

To a greater extent than ever before in history, those who feel drawn to the spiritual life are in a position to decide which of the various spiritual traditions of mankind they wish to follow. Previously this was by no means the case. For one born in almost any part of western Europe, for example, there was no choice except to follow Christianity in its Roman Catholic form, any attempt at deviation from the dominant socio-religious orthodoxy being ruthlessly suppressed. With the coming of the Renaissance and the Reformation, however, a great change took place. The individual found himself free to choose not only between Catholicism and Protestantism but increasingly between this or that form of Protestantism, whether Lutheran, Calvinist, Anabaptist, and so on. He even found himself free to choose between Christianity itself and the various alternative traditions which had either survived 'underground' in an attenuated form or been reconstituted from their literary remains as these happened to become available. Eventually, as contact was established with hitherto unknown parts of the world and as their spiritual traditions too gradually became known, the individual's scope for choice among the spiritual traditions of mankind became virtually unlimited.

Now we have a situation in which representatives of all the major religions can be found in practically every larger city of the Western world, from Buenos Aires to Vancouver and from Dublin to Istanbul. Where such representatives are not found their corresponding literature, at least, is readily available. Whether reliable or unreliable, popular or scholarly, books on both Western and Eastern (i.e. Asian), Christian and non-Christian spiritual traditions are obtainable not only from libraries but from bookshops and railway bookstalls everywhere. One of the biggest surprises of my life occurred when, touring Greece with a friend in the summer of 1966, I found copies of Lobsang Rampa's *The Third Eye* (purportedly the autobiography of a Tibetan Buddhist lama) on display in the kiosks of even the remoter towns and villages through which we passed. Though one could have wished to see this notorious work replaced by a more authentic version of Tibetan Buddhism, it was significant that even a distant and distorted echo of the Buddha's teaching should have penetrated so far.

Buddhism in its various sectarian forms is, in fact, established as widely and as securely in western Europe and the Americas as any of the Eastern, non-Christian spiritual traditions. Sri Lankan viharas, Vietnamese pagodas, and Tibetan *gompas* – even Japanese stupas – are rapidly becoming an accepted part of the urban landscape. In the same way, Buddhist classics such as the *Dhammapada*, the *Diamond Sūtra*, and the *Tibetan Book of the Dead* now regularly feature on the shelves of those having the remotest pretensions to spiritual literacy. Indeed, since the 1950s the amount of shelf space occupied by such works has increased tenfold and twentyfold. Publishers in the major Western languages, particularly English, have vied with one another in bringing out not only translations of classic Buddhist texts, both canonical and non-canonical, but also original works on every conceivable aspect of Buddhist philosophy, ethics, meditation, art, literature, history, economics, anthropology, and sociology.

As a result, books on Buddhism are now available in comparatively large numbers – even if, in some cases, at a price only the rich can afford. These books fall into a number of categories. There are books written (or translated) by Buddhists, whether Eastern or Western, and books written by non-Buddhists. There are popular books and scholarly books, books written from an ecumenical and books written from a sectarian point of view, books based on a profound and books based on a superficial knowledge of Buddhism. Above all, perhaps, there are reliable and unreliable books on Buddhism, that is to say, books in which the fundamentals of Buddhism are reflected with comparative fidelity and those in which they suffer more or less serious distortion.

In these circumstances it becomes necessary to discriminate. As the number of books issuing from the publishing houses of the Western world increases with every year that goes by, we have to view them with a more and more genuinely critical eye. Gone are the days – days which personally I can well remember – when a new book on Buddhism was a phenomenon of such rarity that, on its appearance, it could be hailed with delight and read with avidity almost regardless of its merits. Whether a casual or a serious, an old or a new, student of Buddhism, we now have to separate the wheat from the chaff or, in more Buddhistic phrase, the sound from the rotten timber. We have to distinguish between what truly belongs, and what does not belong, to that great raft on which untold thousands of sentient beings have been, are being, and will be ferried across the ocean of birth-and-death to the Other Shore of Nirvāṇa or Perfect Enlightenment.

This is what I have tried to do in the following pages, both for my own benefit and for the benefit of others. As each new book on Buddhism appeared (and hundreds must have arrived on my desk in the course of the last decade) I sought to ascertain to what extent it was a product of a genuine understanding of the spirit and the letter of the Buddha's teaching and what bearing it had on the actual practice of the Dharma, especially here in the West. From time to time, as I came across errors that needed to be exposed, or insights that it seemed desirable to underline, or simply as I felt that a certain book was deserving of a wider circle of readers, I committed my thoughts to paper in the form of a review article.

These reviews (and I would have written more of them if I had had more time), together with a much smaller number of reviews of books which, though not dealing with Buddhism, were of interest from a (Western) Buddhist point of view, made their appearance in the quarterly *FWBO Newsletter* between the years 1974 and 1980. In preparing them for publication in their present form it was originally my intention to arrange them in chronological order. On second thoughts, however, I decided to organize them into three main groups, according to whether the works of which they were reviews dealt with the Theravāda, with Chan or Zen, or with Tibetan Buddhism, which between them represent the three principal phases in the historical development of Indian Buddhism, i.e. the Hīnayāna, the Mahāyāna, and the Vajrayāna. Before the first of these groups I placed the reviews of those works which related to the general spiritual situation in the West, or to the background of Indian philosophy and religion against which Buddhism itself arose, while after the last group I placed a review and an article in which the life and work of two of the greatest English writers are examined from a Buddhist point of view.

Thus the book begins by plunging into the alternative traditions of the West. In a review whose heading gives its title to the whole work, I take a quick look at the history of communes and intentional communities in the West, from the earliest times down to the present century, as well as at the 'heresy' of the Cathars or Albigenses, and at Gnosticism. This gives me an opportunity of stressing the difference between the commune and the intentional community (or between the 'positive group' and the spiritual community, as we say in the FWBO), as well as of correcting a dangerous misunderstanding with regard to the nature of Buddhist meditation. I then consider the theses of two representatives of Christian socio-religious orthodoxy, one of whom tries to meet the challenge of the various alternative Eastern traditions by arguing that a 'passing over' into another religion is followed by an equal and opposite 'coming back' to one's 'own' religion. Having pointed out that some of Christianity's 'prodigal sons' have in fact gone for good, I turn to a highly idiosyncratic cross-cultural critique of modern 'mystical movements' and, in 'Hedonism and the Spiritual Life', attempt a Buddhist critique of that critique. This involves a discussion of such topics as the nature of the mystical experience, the place of the pleasure-principle in the spiritual life, the difference between *śamatha* or calm and *vipaśyanā* or insight, and the difference between puritanism and asceticism. Since the discussion is conducted in both Buddhist and Hindu terms we have, in effect, passed from the alternative traditions of the West not only to what, from the Western point of view, are the alternative traditions of the East, but also to the philosophical and religious background of Buddhism. This introductory group of reviews therefore concludes with an examination of the different Indian traditions of *ahiṃsā* or non-violence, both Vedic and non-Vedic, and an inquiry into the relation between the practice of yoga – in the broader sense – and the study of Indian philosophy. I also take exception to an implied disparagement of poetry.

During the time that I was writing the reviews that make up the present volume, not many books on the Theravāda appeared. The first main group of reviews therefore consists of only a single item, though this review is one of the longest in the book and deals, moreover, with a subject of considerable theoretical and practical importance. That subject is the development of Sinhalese religio-nationalism. It was a development that began early. Commenting chapter by chapter on a work written by a Sinhalese 'political *bhikkhu*' turned scholar, I see how from the third century BCE Buddhism gradually degenerated from a universal into an ethnic religion and the sangha from a spiritual community into a cultural elite. In the course of this process Buddhism becomes (in the ex-political *bhikkhu's* own words) 'an institution of the Sinhalese monarchy', Sri Lanka (Ceylon) becomes the Buddha's own country, the killing of non-Buddhists is declared to be no sin, and monks, having decided that scholarship is more important than spiritual practice, proceed to acquire wealth and political power. It is indeed a shameful and shocking story, and the quondam political *bhikkhu* tells it with a complacency, and even pride, on which I more than once remark. I also try to clear up his confused and muddled thinking on such topics as Buddhism and social service, the 'renunciation' of Nirvāṇa, the bodhisattva ideal, the condition of the people of India at the time of the Buddha, and what makes one a Buddhist. Rereading this review after an interval of eleven years, in the light of the tragic events that have now brought the people of Sri Lanka to the brink of civil war, it is more obvious to me than ever where the origins of that increasingly bloody conflict are to be found. I earnestly hope that the political *bhikkhus* of Sri Lanka and their lay supporters will see the error of their ways before it is too late.

From Sinhalese religio-nationalism I turn with relief to Mahāyāna Buddhism and, in particular, to Chan or Zen. After welcoming the appearance of the first volume of an important new translation of the *White Lotus Sūtra* (and incidentally laying down four conditions that must be fulfilled before this *sūtra* can be fully known and appreciated in the West), in the second main group of reviews I direct my attention to seven works on what was, for a number of years, the most popular form of Buddhism in the West. Some of these works are translations of classics that have moulded the spiritual life of generations of Far-Eastern Buddhists, while others are original productions by modern 'authorities' on Zen, both oriental and occidental. In the case of the former I find myself able to do little more than utter cries of admiration, so great are the spiritual riches to which the worthy translators have given us access. In the case of the latter, however, the cries are more often cries of outrage than of admiration, and I am obliged to devote much of my space to pointing out that Zen anecdotes should not be read out of context, that 'Daily Life Practice' is not the same thing as acceptance of the status quo, that words and concepts must be distinguished from realities, that mouth Zen is not heart Zen, that Zen practice does have something to do with Buddhist philosophy, and so on.

Tibetan Buddhism being probably the richest form of Buddhism, it is not surprising that the eight works with which I concern myself in the third main group of reviews should between them cover a wider field than those on Chan or Zen. Like the latter they comprise both translations of classics and original works by authorities in whose case quotation marks are definitely not required. I begin by taking a fairly close look at three translations, one from Tibetan, one from Sanskrit via Tibetan, and one from Tibetan but of a text closely modelled on Sanskrit sources – a fact that indicates the complexity of modern Buddhist studies. In doing so I draw attention to the importance Tibetan Buddhism attaches to the power of reasoning, even in the case of special meditation practices of the Highest Yoga (*anuttara-yoga*) of the Tantrayāna, and dwell on the strictly practical nature of the Abhidharma tradition of psychological analysis. I also deplore a Western Buddhist scholar's immersion in his own self-contained world of idiosyncratic renderings of standard Buddhist terms. Having done this, I direct my attention to an important new overview of the Tibetan religious world and to a short account of the spread of 'Lamaism' in Mongolia, both of which stress the importance of political and economic factors. In between, I glance at the autobiography of a contemporary Gelugpa monk, the nobility and disinterestedness of whose life greatly impresses me, but whom I strongly suspect of having been the victim of intellectual cramming. The third main group of reviews concludes with an appreciation of the marvellous life of the great Guru Padmasambhava, the virtual founder of Tibetan Buddhism, as described in the beautifully produced translation of one of the most vivid and colourful products of the Tibetan imagination, and a much shorter appreciation of an anthology of translations from Tibetan Buddhist literature.

The last group of reviews is of a rather miscellaneous character. After pointing out, in connection with two small but useful publications, that just as Buddhist art is visual Dharma so Buddhist instrumental music and chanting is, in reality, aural Dharma, I examine two collections of essays by one of the most distinguished Buddhist scholars of our day (since deceased). This brings me to a review of an illustrated biography of one great English writer and an article on the life and work of another. In the first I confine myself to a single topic, that of the failure of a celebrated modern attempt to establish a spiritual community, and try to identify the causes of that failure in the light of our own experience of spiritual community within the FWBO. This leads me to enumerate four basic principles. In the article which concludes this group of reviews, and thus marks the end of the present collection, I am concerned not with a single topic but with the whole life and work of my second great English writer insofar as this already communicates something of the spirit of Buddhism in the language of Western culture. Bringing Buddhism into contact with writers of this sort will, I aver, hasten its acquisition of that language and thus facilitate the spread of Buddhism in the West.

Thus the wheel comes full circle. From the alternative traditions of the West we have passed to the alternative traditions of the East, as represented especially by Buddhism, and from a Buddhism communicated in the language – or languages – of Eastern culture to the possibility, at least, of a Buddhism communicated in the language of Western culture. As I have done this, and as I have cast a critical but not unfriendly eye over a small but fairly comprehensive selection of books on Buddhism and on topics of interest to Western Buddhists, I hope I have been able to discriminate between what is in conformity with the Dharma and what is not, thereby contributing to the establishment not only of Western Buddhism, but of a purified and renascent Buddhism throughout the world.

ALTERNATIVE TRADITIONS

Kenneth Rexroth
Communalism: From its Origins to the Twentieth Century
Peter Owen, London 1975

Arthur Guirdham
The Great Heresy
Neville Spearman, Jersey 1977

Jacques Lacarrière
The Gnostics
Foreword by Lawrence Durrell, translated from the French by Nina Rootes
Peter Owen, London 1977

Many people, dissatisfied with the present state of Western civilization and their own way of life, are looking for a viable alternative. Some turn to the philosophies and spiritual traditions of the East, hoping that they may find what they are looking for there. Others explore Western civilization itself, taking a second look at the various philosophies and spiritual traditions which from time to time threatened the dominant socio-religious 'orthodoxy' and were either completely destroyed by it or survived only in peripheral or subterranean forms. Kenneth Rexroth, Arthur Guirdham, and Jacques Lacarrière all look for their alternative in the West, though Rexroth's interest in Zen is well known, and it is no coincidence, perhaps, that their books should all come to our notice at the same time. It is no coincidence either, perhaps, that although based on wide reading all three books should be popular rather than scholarly in character – one, indeed, a best-seller in the original French. Although concerned with what is broadly the same field, the field of 'alternative traditions' of the West, the American poet-critic, the English psychiatrist, and the French poet and wanderer, are all concerned with it in different ways, or at different levels. Kenneth Rexroth explores alternative forms of socio-economic organization, Arthur Guirdham what was once virtually an alternative religion, and Jacques Lacarrière an alternative philosophy. Even for those who, like ourselves, look to the East rather than to the West for our basic inspiration, all three books are of considerable interest and value.

By communalism Kenneth Rexroth means the theory of those who believe in libertarian communism and who are members of intentional communities, usually but by no means always religious in inspiration. Like all 'communists', such people want to abolish the state and return society to an organic community of non-coercive human relations. *Communalism* tells how successful, or how unsuccessful, some of them were in doing this. It is a study of the history of communes and intentional communities, mainly Western, from their known beginnings to the twentieth century. Leaving aside palaeolithic hunting groups and the neolithic village, as well as the Essenes and similar groups, the communities described fall mainly into three categories. First, there are the monastic and semi-monastic communities of the Dark Ages and the Middle Ages, whether 'orthodox' like the Benedictines and the Cistercians, or 'heterodox' like the Waldenses, the Brethren of the Free Spirit, and the Taborites. Next, there are the various radical Reformation groups, some pacifist as well as communist, the most important being the Central European Anabaptists, Mennonites, and Hutterites, and the English Diggers. Finally there are the American communes and intentional communities, beginning with groups of European origin like the Ephratans, the Harmonists or Rappists, and the Separatists, and eventually including not only Amana and the Shakers, but secular communities like New Harmony and the Fourierist phalansteries, as well as experiments like Brook Farm and Oneida, and the transplanted, and immensely successful, Hutterites.

As one goes through this enthralling study, following the fortunes of communalism over a period of more than a thousand years, one is struck not only by the abundance and diversity of the groups and movements involved, but also by the amount of human energy that went into the search for an alternative form of socio-economic organization. The picture that presents itself is of wave after wave surging up from the depths of Western society and dashing against the bastions of the established order. Sometimes a breach is made, and the waters pour in, flooding the low-lying areas and forming here and there little pools that may last for centuries. More often, the wave is repulsed, and falls back baffled into the sea. Since early man went through a long stage of primitive communism, it is as though people had an inbuilt tendency to revert to a communal way of living whenever possible, particularly in times of crisis. 'Whenever the power structure falters, the general tendency is to replace it with free communism' (p. xviii). This applies to power structures of every kind, 'communist' as well as capitalist. One is also struck, going through this study, by the extreme adaptability of human nature. There seems to be no limit to the extent to which quite ordinary people are prepared to give up long-cherished attitudes and accept major changes in every aspect of their lives. Order or disorder, austerity or self-indulgence, strict celibacy or complete promiscuity – all are equally welcome provided they result in an ultimately more satisfying life for those concerned. What perhaps strikes one most in the history of communalism, however, is the violent hostility with which groups and movements of a communalist nature were regarded by the official Church, Lutheran as well as Catholic. Originally, of course, groups and movements of this sort, many of which had the avowed aim of reviving the communalism of primitive Christianity, could be incorporated within the existing order in the form of monastic communities. Rexroth in fact seems to think that monasticism was the Church's way of 'containing' libertarian communism and preventing it spreading through the rest of society. Be that as it may, when it could no longer be contained in this manner, and when communalist groups and movements started attacking the existing order of things, denouncing the Church for its manifold corruptions and denying the efficacy of the sacraments when administered by unworthy hands – even denying that sacraments and priests are necessary to salvation at all, thus striking at the very root of the Church's power – then the

Church fell upon them with fire and sword and exterminated them without mercy wherever it found them.

From a study of this kind there is clearly much to be learned, and in the epilogue Kenneth Rexroth helps us by drawing a few conclusions of his own. Secular communes, he assures us, have almost always failed in very short order. 'A simple belief that all men are brothers is not sufficiently well defined to inspire a strong commitment' (p. 295). The longest-lived colonies owed their cohesion and commitment to supernatural sanctions, besides being governed by individuals of powerful charisma. In more Buddhistic terms, the longest-lived colonies were spiritual communities, and recognized some kind of spiritual hierarchy, in however rudimentary a form. Ceremonies and the practice of confession are also factors making for cohesion, as well as a certain degree of interpersonal tension. Communism as such does not seem to have been a factor in the failure of most colonies, though many of those that fail, perhaps the majority, do so for economic reasons. On the contrary, 'Wherever there existed powerful forces for commitment and cohesion, a carefully screened membership, and intelligent leaders with wide practical experience, communism proved to be, economically, extremely successful' (p. 297). Rexroth also emphasizes that communal living (he is referring, of course, to 'mixed' communities) is in theory very advantageous to women, for most of the work of a housewife or mother can then be divided and distributed, so that each woman has considerable leisure. Summing up, he says that in all the many books which have been written about the communalist movement in America in the nineteenth century, there is little disagreement as to the factors that make for success. They are: 'A religion, or at least a powerful ideology which all the members of the group accept, which should include the belief that the dominant society fails to provide sufficient value for a happy life, and is sick, or doomed, or dying, or, nowadays, already dead, and that the commune is a saving remnant plucked from burning' (p. 301). In addition the community needs a leader with powerful charisma, the ability to persuade people, equanimity, and a wide range of talents. There should also be an accepted method of assigning and rotating tasks, with both sexes sharing the boring jobs and housekeeping. On the negative side, a community cannot survive as such with a completely 'open gate' policy. 'Selectivity is the first law of communalism.... The communes that are most successful today either do not allow visitors at all, or do not allow them to stay more than overnight, and prospective members are subjected to a searching novitiate' (p. 304).

In all this there is very little from which a Buddhist need dissent. The conclusions Kenneth Rexroth draws undoubtedly do follow from the histories of the groups he surveys, and to the extent of their applicability are valid for communes and intentional communities of all kinds. This is not to say that his study does not have its limitations, especially on the theoretical side. The most serious of these is that he does not make sufficiently clear the distinction between commune and intentional community, or as we would say, between the 'positive group' and the spiritual community. This is because he does not recognize the importance of the principle of individuality, or see that whereas the group is of a collective and corporate nature a spiritual community is a free association of true individuals, i.e. of those who have developed self-awareness and emancipated themselves at least from the cruder forms of group conditioning.[282] Because he fails to recognize the importance of individuality, and therefore to distinguish commune from intentional community, he tends, at times, to see the spread of communalism in terms of a sort of mass movement. To the extent that communalism means communes, i.e. the positive group, the spread of communalism may indeed be a mass movement (some chapters of his study demonstrate as much), but to speak of the spread of intentional communities in this way involves a contradiction in terms. Failure to appreciate the importance of individuality has other consequences. As we have already noted, Rexroth tends to see communalism as a reversion to the primitive communism of early man, in other words as a sort of sociological throwback. Again, this may well be true of libertarian communism as such, but it is not true of the spiritual community. The latter may indeed incorporate elements from an earlier form of social organization, but inasmuch as it consists of a free association of true individuals it is essentially not a regression but a higher 'evolutionary' development. There are also limitations that relate to monasticism. Besides seeing organized monasticism as 'a method of quarantining the Christian life' (p. 30), and celibacy as a device for preventing (lay) monasticism from becoming a counter-culture, Kenneth Rexroth gives the impression that monasticism dropped out of the picture somewhere about the time of the Reformation, whereas the truth of the matter is that, both in East and West, the longest lived of all intentional communities are monastic communities. Indeed, the monastic community has claims to be considered the spiritual community *par excellence*. Despite its limitations, however, which are limitations of perspective and interpretation rather than of informational content, and as such easily remedied, *Communalism* is required reading for all who are engaged in the creation of a truly alternative society. Though there are specialist studies of a number of the groups that Kenneth Rexroth describes, I doubt if there is any other book that discusses so many of them in such detail, or that paints such a vivid and inspiring picture of a movement which, despite all the setbacks it has experienced, remains the only real hope of mankind.

The 'heresy' of Dr Guirdham's title is that of the Cathars or Albigenses, who are only briefly mentioned by Kenneth Rexroth (pp. 36–7). Strictly speaking, Catharism was not so much a heresy as the latest manifestation of an entirely different religious and philosophical tradition, a tradition which tended to assume a Christian form in Europe, just as it tended to assume a Zoroastrian form in Persia and a Buddhistic form in Central Asia and China. The Cathars indeed considered themselves the true Christians, and their church the true church, and to the extent that Christianity itself was of Gnostic rather than Judaic origin they may well have been right. To the people of Languedoc they were simply the *Bonshommes* (good men). The ancient tradition of which Catharism was the latest manifestation was that of Dualism. According to Arthur Guirdham, its basic tenets were threefold. It believed that forces of good and evil existed in the universe from the beginning and would do so to the end; that the world was created not by God but by the Devil, who was identical with the Old Testament Jehovah, and that man was a spiritual being distinct from matter who in course of successive 'reincarnations' purified himself by leading a moral and spiritual life until he was reunited with the Light. The Cathars denied the efficacy of the sacraments. They refused to believe that sins could be wiped out by means of divine grace, or that this grace could be dispensed through the official sacramental channels by the priests of the established (Catholic) Church solely by virtue of their ordination, regardless of their moral and spiritual character. The Cathar community comprised two kinds of followers. There were the Perfect, or Cathars proper, and the Believers. The Perfect, both men and women, practised absolute non-violence and chastity, and abstained from the eating of meat. The Believers, who formed the majority, while fully accepting the basic tenets of Catharism, were less rigorous in practice. Catharism spread to Western Europe probably from what is now part of Yugoslavia and Bulgaria. It appeared in southern France at least as early as the beginning of the eleventh century, and towards the end of the twelfth century was well established there, being particularly strong in Languedoc and the county of Provence, which then formed one of the most prosperous and highly civilized areas in the whole of Europe. In Languedoc it was indeed the dominant religion, being supported by all classes of people. (It was from Albi, a town in Languedoc, that the Cathars received the name by which they are best known. The term Cathar itself means 'Pure'.) The established Church became thoroughly alarmed. Earlier attempts to suppress Catharism having failed, in 1207 Pope Innocent III launched what has become infamous in history as the Albigensian Crusade. The loot-hungry nobles of northern France were called upon to crush the heresy by force of arms, and offered remission of all their sins for doing so. The crusade lasted off and on for forty years. Hundreds of towns and villages were laid waste, and many tens of thousands of men, women, and children were massacred. The civilization of Languedoc was destroyed, and the whole area so badly devastated that the effects persist, it is said, down to the present day. Upwards of a thousand Perfect were burned at the stake. Catharism never recovered from the blow. In the wake of the horrors of the crusade came the terrors of the Inquisition, and by the middle of the fourteenth century Catharism as such had ceased to exist.

Not content with exterminating Catharism physically, for the last seven hundred years the Catholic Church has systematically vilified and misrepresented it. An abridged edition of M. L. Cozens's *A Handbook of Heresies*, published by Sheed and Ward in its popular 'Prayer and Practice' series as late as 1974, describes Catharism as 'poison' and accuses the Cathars of 'endeavouring by force of arms to uproot Christianity in southern France'!! (p. 63). But now the tide is turning. The literature devoted to Catharism has increased enormously during the last thirty years, and the truth about the Cathars is beginning to be known. Most of this literature is in French, and Dr Guirdham's publishers rightly claim that a book in English on the Cathars is long overdue. Part One of *The Great Heresy* deals with Catharism as it is known to historians, theologians, and philosophers. Packing a great deal of information into fourteen short chapters, Dr Guirdham describes the origins of Catharism, its brief flowering, and its terrible end, and gives a clear, fair-minded, and sensible account of its beliefs and practices. In so doing he not only 'reveals truth' but 'exposes error'. He is particularly good, in fact, at showing the complete falsity of such charges as that Catharism was pessimistic, that it advocated mass suicide, that its attitude to sex 'was at its worst perverted and at its best so ascetic as to amount to psychological self-mutilation' (p. 28), and that its followers were the enemies of society. Such misrepresentations, glibly repeated by generation after generation of historians, both Catholic and Protestant, were often based (he reminds us) on isolated statements obtained from ordinary Believers under torture. To rely for solid unbiased information about the Cathars on the registers of the Inquisition is indeed 'comparable to insisting that the Gestapo is the best authority to enlighten us as to the nature and practice of Jewry' (p. 24). The parallel between the Catholic Inquisition and the Nazi Gestapo is quite striking. 'Heretics were often condemned to wear a yellow cross, the dimensions of which were carefully stipulated, sewn on to the garments of the victim. The Nazis adopted an identical measure against the Jews' (p. 72). On balance, however, the worse of the two was the Inquisition, which

> 'developed into a systemized instrument of terror unequalled in human history. Over a huge area those innocent of heresy were as liable to suffer as those addicted to it. What it aimed at was the creation of an atmosphere in which Catharism simply could not live. That the latter lasted even as long as it did is proof of the toughness of its adherents. It is undeniable that the havoc wrought by the Inquisition far exceeds that achieved by the Ogpu and the Gestapo. The Jews and Poles were not wholly exterminated either actually or politically. In just short of a century Catharism, which had threatened the very existence of Catholicism in the Midi, had been reduced to a handful of clandestine activists. When one considers that Hitler had at his command all the devices for the dissemination of information and defamatory propaganda, the achievements of the Inquisition are truly impressive. (p. 75)

If society had any enemies in the thirteenth century it was not the Cathars. The Cathars, far from being the anti-human monsters that they were made out to be, were in fact friends and benefactors of humanity. In particular, they sought to remove from people the insidious, soul-destroying fear of hell that, then as now, the Catholic Church so sedulously inculcated. This, Arthur Guirdham says, was perhaps the Cathars' 'most significant contribution to the welfare of the common man' (p. 23). As for their being against marriage – in Catholic eyes a most heinous offence – they were hostile to it not as an institution but as a sacrament. 'They did not believe that sexual conduct was sinful and taboo until the hour of wedlock and that afterwards what was illicit and sordid became in some way sanctified' (p. 26). Had Catharism indeed been against the institution of marriage and (according to the Catholic Church) therefore against the family and society, it is difficult to see how it could have enjoyed the strong support of the Languedoc aristocracy. As Dr Guirdham remarks, 'It is not in the nature of ruling classes to plan their own destruction in full, waking consciousness' (p. 29). In view of these and other considerations he therefore concludes that Catharism was not only 'a comprehensive and lucid philosophy' (p. 26) but also 'sane and evolutionary' and even – for what the compliment is worth – 'contemporary'.

Part Two of the book deals not with Catharism as it is known to historians, theologians, and philosophers, but with its deeper teachings as revealed to the author by a group of discarnate entities, all but one of whom were alive in the twentieth century. Basing himself on these teachings, Arthur Guirdham deals, in the course of seven short chapters, with such topics as the transmigration of souls, auras, the Creation, jewels, the sun and the moon, mechanism of evil, and alchemy. Even those who believe in life after death and in 'reincarnation' would probably prefer, pending further investigation, to consider the material contained in this section of *The Great Heresy* strictly on its own merits. One idea that I personally found very appealing – and quite in accordance with Buddhist teaching – was that flowers develop a 'soul' as a result of the attention paid to them by human beings, and that colour and perfume are the means by which they attract this attention.

Himself a spiritist as well as a believer in reincarnation, Dr Guirdham tends to regard Catharism as having its roots in primitive Christianity – which he describes as 'a markedly spiritist religion' (p. 102) – and Christianity itself as 'an episode in the history of Dualism' (p. 103).

No one reading *The Great Heresy* with even a smattering of Buddhist knowledge could fail to notice a resemblance between Catharism and Buddhism or to wonder, perhaps, if Catharism had roots in Buddhism too. Dr Guirdham is not unaware of this. He acknowledges that the likeness between the practice of Catharism and Buddhism must attract attention, and that vegetarianism and non-violence are common to both. At the same time, he is unable to agree with the late Maurice Magre, a devotee of Catharism, that the Cathars are 'the Buddhists of Europe'. According to him this is a completely erroneous over-simplification. The philosophy of Catharism, he says, is quite distinct from that of Buddhism. Whether this is indeed the case can be decided only when we have a better knowledge of Catharist philosophy – as well, perhaps, as a better knowledge of Buddhist philosophy. (It is interesting that Dr Guirdham tells us, earlier on (p. 48), that the Cathars believed, as much as the oriental philosophers who provided the bedrock of Hinduism and Buddhism, in 'the necessity of ultimately transcending the world of irreconcilable opposites'.) Meanwhile, M. Magre's statement can be taken as true, at least sociologically. After all, what he said was that the Cathars were the Buddhists of Europe, i.e. that they occupied analogous positions in their respective socio-religious contexts, not that the philosophies of Catharism and Buddhism were identical. Within their widely differing timescales, the fortunes of the Cathars of southern France and the Buddhists of India, at least, were in some respects remarkably similar. One must also join issue with Arthur Guirdham on the subject of meditation. He appears to think that meditation involves emptying the mind, and that, when this is done too precipitately, it results in the mind being invaded by lower entities (p. 46). This is certainly not true of Buddhist meditation. Far from involving any emptying of the mind, Buddhist meditation involves the intensive development of skilful mental states. Nevertheless, despite misunderstandings of this sort, from what Dr Guirdham has to tell us about them in *The Great Heresy* it is clear that the beliefs and practices of the Cathars are highly relevant to Western Buddhists. (Those concerned with what the FWBO calls 'team-based right livelihood' will be interested to learn that the Cathars were 'ferocious workers' and that they had workshops in which men were trained in various cottage industries.) Even more relevant than the beliefs and practices of the Cathars is their history. At a time when, in this country, non-Christians have been suddenly made aware that they do not have quite as much freedom as they had thought, it would be well for English Buddhists at least to remind themselves that the ghosts of Pope Innocent III and the Inquisitors are still very much abroad and that it is still possible for a religion to be destroyed.

Gnosticism is not an alternative tradition of the West in quite the same way as communalism, or even Catharism. Flourishing as it did throughout the second and third centuries in the lands all round the eastern end of the Mediterranean, it was an alternative tradition once, at least in places like Rome and Marseilles, but ceased to be such as soon as Christianity became the official religion of the Roman Empire in the fourth century. Thereafter it was subject to intense persecution and except as an underground influence survived, in the West, only in remote corners of the Balkans, where for the rest of the millennium it gathered strength for its journey to north Italy and southern France in the form of Catharism. For fifteen hundred years the West had no knowledge of groups like the Ophites and the Carpocratians, or thinkers like Basilides and Valentinus, other than what could be derived from the meagre scraps of information contained in the writings of such Fathers of the Church as Hippolytus, Irenaeus, and Eusebius, all of whom were of course interested in showing Gnosticism in the worst possible light. The position with regard to Gnosticism was, in fact, remarkably similar to that with regard to Catharism, our knowledge of which was dependent for five hundred years on the records of the Inquisition. Only with the discovery of the Askew Codex (containing the 'Pistis Sophia') towards the end of the eighteenth and of the Bruce and Berlin Codices towards the end of the nineteenth century, and above all the discovery of a complete Gnostic library at Nag Hamadi in Egypt (the ancient Chenaboskion) in about 1945, has the situation changed – and changed radically. For the first time in fifteen hundred years we know enough about Gnosticism for it to be a genuine option for some at least of those people in the West who are looking for an alternative philosophy, and the appearance of Jacques Lacarrière's 'strange and original essay', as Lawrence Durrell calls *The Gnostics*, is one of the signs of this changed state of affairs. All the more is it such a sign, indeed, for being – as Durrell goes on to say – 'more a work of literature than of scholarship' and 'as convincing a reconstruction of the way the Gnostics lived and thought as D. H. Lawrence's intuitive recreation of the vanished Etruscans' (p. 7).

Despite the fact that it was not a genuine option for so many centuries, Gnosticism is in principle the alternative philosophy – and religion – *par excellence*. An alternative philosophy, or an alternative way of life, is such only to the extent that it is an alternative to something else which it rejects. Gnosticism parallels Buddhism in being alternative not just to some other philosophy or religion existing beside it in the world but to 'the world' or 'conditioned existence' itself. As the irredeemable product of primeval error the world is radically evil, and man – who does not really belong to the world – should have nothing to do with it. Man is in his essence an alternative being, and for an alternative being the only appropriate philosophy – the only appropriate way of life – is one which is likewise 'alternative'. Being an alternative philosophy – an alternative wisdom, a counter-wisdom – *in principle*, and not simply by reason of its forcible suppression by official Christianity, Gnosticism was an alternative philosophy from the very beginning. Describing the doctrine of Simon Magus, Lacarrière says that here in 'the very first years of our era' we find set out the fundamental certitudes of Gnosticism, which are that

> the world we live in was not created by the true God, it is the work of an imposter, and man's task will consist in rejecting the swindle of the world, together with the Biblical and Christian teaching which claims to uphold it and all the institutions through which it is perpetuated. Thus, from the start [he concludes] the Gnostic identifies himself as a marginal creature, forced (by the historical evolution of society as well as by his own inclinations) to form alternative and secret communities which will transmit the teaching. (pp. 49–50)

Consequent on Gnosticism's certitude about the world is its certitude about man. Because his task is to reject the world, and because he is a marginal creature, 'man is called upon, in this struggle against the generalized oppressiveness of the real, *to create a soul for himself*, or if you prefer, to nourish, fortify, and enrich the luminous spark he carries in his inmost being' (p. 50). There are different ways of doing this. One is by means of what Lacarrière calls an '*inversion of values and symbols*' – italicizing the words to emphasize the importance of the process. This process of inversion, or 'mechanism' as he terms it, which was an aspect of the counter-life led by the Gnostics, tended to favour, to invest with power, light, and efficacy all those whom the orthodox tradition looks upon as the damned: Seth, the Serpent, Cain. It is these first rebels in the history of the world whom the Gnostics were to raise to the highest dignity, to claim as the authors of their esoteric books. Their *mythical history thus transmutes itself into a counter-history which places the great rebels in the foreground* (p. 85).

Inversion of values and symbols is of course a form of deconditioning, and without deconditioning there is no creation of a soul. 'As I write this word, deconditioning,' Jacques Lacarrière says, 'I perceive that I am reaching the very heart of Gnostic doctrine. No knowledge, no serious contemplation, no valid choice is possible until man has shaken himself free of everything that effects [sic] his conditioning, at every level of his existence' (p. 97).

The Gnostic techniques for deconditioning oneself are of both the ascetic and the licentious type, some groups favouring the one and some the other. (Those who are not concerned with team-based right livelihood may be interested to find Bishop Timothy saying of the Enchites or Messalians, one of the licentious groups, sometimes called the Lazy Men, 'They spend their time doing nothing and sleeping'.) Whether ascetic or licentious, the 'single, solitary purpose' of all techniques, of all these 'violations of all the rules and conventions', was 'to be the brutal and radical means of stripping man of his mental and bodily habits, awakening in him his sleeping being and shaking off the alienating torpor of the soul' (p. 98). Adding that he finds it strange that all the books written about Gnosticism leave their authors untouched (one could say the same thing of many books written about Buddhism), and that he is well aware that one never writes a book that is not about oneself, Jacques Lacarrière wonders why he is particularly attached to those that are known as the licentious Gnostics, that after all represent only one sect among others. 'Am I the unwitting victim of a phenomenon born in my own time,' he asks, 'one which leads us to interrogate ourselves more deeply than ever before on sexual questions?' (p. 98). Or are there other explanations? He finds it difficult to make up his mind. There is little doubt, though, that Lacarrière is a product of the century of Artaud and Sartre, and that his reading of Gnosticism is the result, to some extent, of his French literary inheritance. He sees the general

Gnostic attitude towards the world as one of 'decadence', and although, formally speaking, his definition of decadence is unexceptionable, the word cannot but carry with it a *fin de siècle* flavour hardly in keeping with what Durrell calls 'the grand poetic challenge of the Gnostics' (p. 7). He also indulges in occasional outbursts of lyricism on the subject of woman, her body, and her indispensability to salvation (i.e. men's salvation). His particular conditioning shows itself most clearly, perhaps, in his failure to appreciate the importance of schools and communities, the formation of which he sees as somehow contrary to the spirit of Gnosticism. He appreciates that man is 'a stranger here'. Indeed, he devotes a whole chapter to the topic. With considerable eloquence he speaks of the Gnostics as 'the autochthons of another world', and describes 'their feeling of having fallen onto our earth like inhabitants from a distant planet, of having strayed into the wrong galaxy, and their longing to regain their true cosmic homeland, the luminous hyper-world that shimmers beyond the great nocturnal barrier' (p. 30). That 'I am in the world but not of the world', he says, is the most basic Gnostic formula. What he does not appreciate is that when one stranger, one foreigner, one Gnostic, happens to meet another he experiences not only a great relief but a great joy, and that it is out of this joy that the spiritual community is born. Because he fails to appreciate the significance of the spiritual community – indeed, seems not to believe in communities at all, or in the oriental religions and philosophies to which, he says, those who reject the world in its modern form almost always have correlative recourse – Lacarrière seeks to discover what he calls a New Gnosticism in the pages of contemporary writers like Emile Coiran, whose works, he believes, 'match the loftiest flashes of Gnostic thought' (p. 127). But flashes, however lofty, are not enough. Literary attitudes, however striking, literary reconstructions, however convincing, are not enough. We need not only an alternative philosophy but an alternative religion and an alternative way of life: we need an alternative form of social organization. Perhaps Jacques Lacarrière should read Kenneth Rexroth and Arthur Guirdham – and vice versa. Perhaps all three should pay greater attention to the spiritual traditions of the East.

CALLING HOME THE PRODIGAL SON

Daniel Jenkins
The British: Their Identity and Their Religion
SCM, London 1975

John S. Dunne
The Way of All The Earth: An Encounter with Eastern Religions
Sheldon, London 1973

Both these books are written by Christian academics, and both have a thesis to propound. Indeed, despite their origin on different sides of the Atlantic the non-Christian critic may be forgiven for seeing both of them as part of a defensive-offensive rearguard action waged by a traditional Christianity uneasily surviving in a post-Christian society.

Daniel Jenkins is a British, more specifically a Welsh, Presbyterian, and was until recently Chaplain and Reader at the University of Sussex and Visiting Professor at the University of London. His thesis is that the malaise of communal life in modern Britain calls for a fresh look at ourselves and our institutions, and that such a look reveals that our national consciousness and our religious heritage are more closely related than it has been customary to suppose. This is true not only of Britain as a whole, but also, more particularly, of the constituent nations of Britain, i.e. the English, the Scots, and the Welsh. Any attempt to restore the vision of Britain must therefore take into account the fact that church loyalty and national loyalty are closely linked, and that the problems of national identity in relation to Christian faith cannot be honestly faced in English terms alone. This leads the author into a survey of the 'Matter' of Britain, of Scotland, and of Wales, followed by a much lengthier study of 'The English and Their Churches', in the course of which he appeals for the recognition of a distinctively Scottish and a distinctively Welsh national identity in a way that deserves consideration not only by English Christians but by English Buddhists as well.

Committed English, Scottish, and Welsh Buddhists alike, however, will hardly agree with what he has to say about Eastern religion, very briefly discussed in the concluding paragraph of a section on 'Other religious groups in England'. Indeed, they may well find his attitude towards them no less patronizing than he finds the attitude of the English towards the Scots and the Welsh. One would have thought that Professor Jenkins would have known what it was like to be a member of a religious minority! He observes,

> It is fashionable at present among some self-conscious people to say that Western tradition is bankrupt and that the inherited values of England, those of her religion and patriotic loyalty and family life, must be repudiated. This carries with it a new interest (it can hardly be much more than that at present) in Eastern religion, notably some forms of Buddhism, and in the view of the world associated with it. One could not look to such an attitude for a renewal of the English vision, since part of its point would be to deny the validity of such a vision. (p. 122)

What this English vision is the author does not tell us, though since he is at pains to distinguish England from Britain we must assume that it is not quite the same thing as the British ideal, which in a chapter on 'The Community of Britain' he finds to consist in a tension between the 'Cavalier' and 'Roundhead' elements in our tradition, as well as in the qualities of respect for privacy, modesty, fair play, and moderation – an ideal that plainly has its limitations, as he himself admits.

We must also assume, no doubt, that the vision is a Christian vision. But if this is the case, then surely the (absolute) validity of the English vision is denied not only by the self-conscious people who are 'interested' in Buddhism and other Eastern faiths but by hundreds of thousands, perhaps millions, of people in these islands who have not even heard of Buddhism! Professor Jenkins rebukes John Cowper Powys for invoking the ancient pre-Christian Brythonic God instead of 'the Christian God, who is the Father of us all' (p. 53). What he fails to realize is how many there are to whom the Christian God is as unreal and as remote as the Brythonic God is to him. However much we are all agreed that Britain is spiritually sick, and that a national renewal is possible only on the basis of a religious renewal, it by no means follows that the renewal has to be – or even can be – a Christian one. The fact is that the majority of people in Britain are no longer Christian. They do not believe in the Christian God. Indeed, in his concluding chapter, 'Jerusalem and Albion: The Christian Community', Professor Jenkins admits that 'the chief reason why the British churches are weak today is that they do not believe enough in the Christian God whom they profess to serve' (p. 18). Those who do not believe that religious renewal is possible on the basis of Christianity because they do not believe in Christianity are therefore faced with two alternatives. They must either give up all hope of any renewal or they must look for the vision that will bring it about *outside Christianity*. To Professor Jenkins, of course, the second alternative is unthinkable. For him, all the viable options are within the Christian faith. The reason for this shortsightedness is to be found partly in the fact that his original point of departure is communal life in modern Britain rather than the individual in modern Britain. It is in fact the main weakness of Professor Jenkins' book that his thesis assumes too much. Our national consciousness and our religious – i.e. Christian – heritage may indeed have been closely linked in the past, but before considering how the churches can help bring about a renewal of the communal life of Britain we must surely ask ourselves how acceptable Christianity itself still is to the individual Briton.

John S. Dunne is currently Professor of Religious Studies at Yale University, and has been hailed (by *Newsweek*) as 'the only foreseeable successor to Paul Tillich'. As benefits one who has studied at Notre Dame University in America and at the Gregorian University in Rome, he has written a subtler and more scholarly book than Professor Jenkins and one that is seemingly more liberal. His thesis is that what seems to be occurring in our time is a 'passing over' from one culture to another, from one way of life to another, from one religion to another, and that this 'passing over' is followed by an equal and opposite process of 'coming back', coming back with new insight to one's own culture, one's own way of life, one's own religion. The holy man of our time is not a man who could found a new religion, but a figure like Gandhi, a man who passes over by sympathetic understanding from his own religion to other religions and comes back again with new insights to his own. According to Professor Dunne this passing over and coming back is the spiritual adventure of our time, and it is an odyssey that takes one not only through the wonderland of other religions back into the homeland of one's own religion, but also through the lives of prophets and divine incarnations back into one's own life. After beginning his odyssey by passing over into the life of Gandhi, and his renunciation of sexuality and violence, he therefore goes on to pass over into, and come back from, the lives of the Buddha, Krishna, Jesus, and Mohammed.

In all this there is much that the Western Buddhist, whether American or British, will find acceptable. 'Passing over' is in fact something that is very well understood in Buddhism, especially, perhaps, in Mahāyāna Buddhism. Indeed, Śāntideva's great teaching of *parātma-parivarta* or 'Transference of the Other and the Self' can well be regarded as the classic, and most radical, statement of this process in all spiritual literature.[283] Whether Professor Dunne himself really succeeds in passing over into the lives of prophets and divine incarnations is however doubtful. In the case of the Buddha he certainly does not succeed very well. Though seeing clearly that 'The remarkable thing about Gotama the Buddha was that he walked alone, without a friend, even without a God' (p. 29) he is still able to ignore the testimony of the Pāli texts and say, 'Gotama did not deny the existence of God or the existence of the soul (although his refusal to talk about the soul has ordinarily been interpreted in this way); he simply refused to offer any teaching on them' (p. 30). We are therefore not surprised when, some pages later, he finds that 'In our effort to re-enact the life of Gotama we have found it necessary to try passing over to a standpoint of providence or universal care,' and triumphantly concludes, 'We might have suspected that God would figure somehow' (p. 60). Indeed we might! For all his protestations, Professor Dunne does not really pass over from his own religion at all, but in fact carries his theistic assumptions with him into non-theistic Buddhism. He even finds the Buddha's description of the Middle Way in terms of the Noble Eightfold Path 'unhelpful', having apparently not 'passed over' into the Buddhist scriptures sufficiently to discover the meaning of right view, right resolve, and the rest of its constituent factors. Despite some illuminating comments on the four sights, and on the Buddha's 'four confidences' one is therefore left with the overall impression that in reality there has been no passing over at all, not even in thought, and that Professor Dunne has been engaged in the performance of an elaborate exercise – not to say a skilful piece of play-acting, or even a conjuring trick – the purpose of which is to return the Western reader safely to his Christian base after a carefully conducted tour of world religions. That this is not just a construction arbitrarily imposed upon the book by the ill-natured non-Christian critic is borne out by what another Christian academic, Geoffrey Parrinder, writes in the introduction. 'It is often thought that acquaintance with other religions will weaken our own. One of the chief merits of Professor Dunne's book is his evidence that the opposite can happen. Far from faith being undermined, it can be enlarged and strengthened by wider studies and by looking at our own religion from other angles.' As a general principle few Western Buddhists would wish to dispute this. What they would strenuously deny is that, as all three Christian academics seem to assume, one's 'own' religion is necessarily the religion that one was born into. Such an assumption gives far too much importance to cultural factors. Neither Professor Jenkins nor Professor Dunne faces up to the fact that times have changed, and that an individual westerner now may, in all seriousness, commit himself to a religion other than the one into which he was born and which forms part of his national heritage. For this reason Professor Jenkins is unable to envisage a spiritual renewal for Britain except on the basis of Christianity. Similarly, Professor Dunne is unable to imagine anyone passing over from Christianity into another religion *and staying there*. Professor Jenkins indeed goes so far as to say, 'Those who know the love and power of the Father can be confident that, in due time, the prodigals will come to themselves and want to return' (p. 195). What both Christian academics fail to realize – what academics in general fail to realize – is that some of the prodigals, at least, have gone for good, and that whether in peremptory or in dulcet tones it is no longer any use trying to call them home.

HEDONISM AND THE SPIRITUAL LIFE

Agehananda Bharati
The Light at The Center: Context and Pretext of Modern Mysticism
Ross Erikson, Santa Barbara 1976

This is one of those entertaining and instructive essays in cultural anthropology that, over the last two or three decades, we have learned to expect from the campuses of North America. In his preface the author tells us that the book aims at showing up the common base of 'the trimmings of transcendental meditation, the Hare Krishna gymnastics, the dilated smiles of Jesus freaks, and the now defunct hippydom of the sixties' through their common errors, and that 'as such it aims to be a perennial critique of mystical movements and of utopia in general' (p. 10). Agehananda Bharati is well equipped for the task. Born and brought up in Vienna, where he began studying Sanskrit and other Indian languages while still a boy, he served during the Second World War as an interpreter in Hitler's 'Free India' legion and then, after two years of Indology and philosophy, in 1949 he made his way to India. In India he stayed for seven years, during which time he became a Hindu monk, taught at universities, and upset orthodox Hindus with his 'cultural criticism'. He left India rather under a cloud, as I remember from newspaper reports published at the time. After surfacing in Thailand and in Japan, he eventually reappeared in the New World, where from the late fifties onwards he has taught classes, criticized, and copulated on the spacious campuses of North America. In 1961 he published *The Ochre Robe*, a provocative melange of autobiography and cultural criticism. This was followed by *A Functional Analysis of Indian Thought and its Social Margins* (1964), which I have not seen, and *The Tantric Tradition* (1965), an important study mainly from Hindu Sanskrit sources.

According to the publishers *The Light at the Center*, his latest book, is an investigation of mysticism in the tradition of Butler, Underhill, and Zaehner. This it certainly is not. The author's approach is synchronistic rather than historical, and despite much preliminary flourishing of ethnoscientific and ethnosemantic tools – now *de rigueur* in the religious field, it would seem – the work is on the whole belletristic rather than scholarly. *Time* magazine goes so far as to say 'Bharati unscrews the inscrutable with the precision tools of language, philosophy, and behavioural sciences.' He does not quite do that, but evidently it is what he sees himself as doing. Despite his efforts the inscrutable is not unscrewed, and though light is thrown on a variety of topics no generally acceptable definition of mysticism emerges. This is hardly surprising. 'Mysticism' is one those protean words that elude precise definition, and for this reason I personally prefer not to use it. Instead of arguing whether Agehananda Bharati's definition is correct, and whether mysticism is 'really' what he says it is, I shall therefore take his definition at its face value and try to see whether what he calls mysticism corresponds to anything with which we are familiar within the context of Buddhism.

As defined by him, mysticism is the '*intuition of numerical oneness with the cosmic absolute, with the universal matrix, or with any essence stipulated by the various theological and speculative systems of the world*' (p. 25, author's italics). A mystic is a person who has experienced this numerical oneness, or seeks to experience it, and who, when questioned about his most important pursuit, consistently says 'I am a mystic' in the *etic* sense rather than in an emic sense (i.e. in the generally accepted meaning of the term, not in the meaning which it has for a particular coterie). Agehananda Bharati himself is a mystic, as are the Buddha, Ramakrishna, Ramana Maharshi, Arthur Koestler, Timothy Leary, Alan Watts, Allen Ginsberg, and Aldous Huxley. All have had the zero-experience, as Bharati also terms the intuition of numerical oneness with the absolute, although in Huxley's case there appears to be some doubt about it. A mystic is also a person who, in seeking numerical unity with the absolute, does so by espousing psycho-experimental methods which are hedonic rather than non-hedonic. Among these methods are sexual and aesthetic experience and the use of psychedelic drugs. For Bharati the achievement of pleasure, euphoria, ecstasy, is central to the mystic quest, and with this we come to the real crux of his whole discussion of the subject matter of the book – whether called mysticism or any other name. As he sees it, mysticism is that form of religious life or religious experience in which the pleasure-principle reigns supreme. This is not to say that he denies that the zero-experience can be triggered off with the help of non-hedonic, ascetic psycho-experimental methods: it is simply that the possibility does not interest him, and he therefore does not concern himself with it. In his own words, 'Rejection of euphoria does not disqualify a person from the mystic title: but he falls into a somewhat marginal category' (p. 27). Yet despite its supremacy in its own sphere, the pleasure-principle affords us no access to the domain of the reality-principle. Bharati makes it quite clear that while mysticism is the intuition of numerical oneness with the absolute it does not follow from this that the absolute actually exists. The zero-experience does not confer ontological status on its own content. What really happens is that a thought chain occurs which is felt by the mystic as meaning that he has achieved oneness with the absolute (p. 11). From this it follows that the zero-experience does not entail a specific theology or ideology, or any specific type of action or inaction (p. 69). Similarly, the zero-experience does not change the mystic in any respect, though it may alter his self-image and, in this way, bring about a change in his environment by changing people's attitudes towards him. In particular, the zero-experience does not make the mystic a better man. The stinker remains a stinker. Indeed, as if rubbing it in, Bharati assures us that 'some of the best mystics were the greatest stinkers among men' (p. 91) and that 'mystics can be saints, they can be vicious tyrants, or anything else' (p. 124). He does, however, concede that the mystic arranges his deeds and thoughts in a hierarchy with the zero-experience at the top and the rest in a descending scale of importance below (p. 102) – a concession which has the effect of undermining his whole position. Bharati also believes that it is unimportant how the mystic comes by the experience (p. 112) – a view that separates means and end, that it is 'in one category perhaps with totally consummated erotic experiences, or with artistic and similar peak sensations' (p. 75), and that, if a person who has had the experience 'dislikes' it, he can 'of course' have it analysed – i.e. psychoanalysed – out of him (p. 143). The mystical experience is what it is. It is to be sought not because it is noble, but simply because it is a skill which confers delight, and because it 'inures the practitioner against the vicissitudes of life, against boredom and despair' (p. 78). This is an arid message, Agehananda Bharati admits, to 'those who have expected to find the ultimate panacea of the religious and the secular life in the mystical' (p. 75), but there's nothing he can do about it: the zero-experience is really all there is.

Arid though the message may be, there is nothing arid about the way in which the author delivers it. He delivers it, in fact, not only with refreshing candour but with panache. Not that his candour is likely to be appreciated in the quarters where it is most needed. Some of his harsher strictures may indeed be found deeply offensive by the 'sanctimonious little men who impress the gullible by their accent, their smell, their robe' (p. 174), i.e. by the urban, middle-class, English-educated swamis of the Hindu Renaissance who, in this book as in *The Ochre Robe*, are the favourite targets of Bharati's cultural criticism. To the extent that they have the wit to perceive that it applies to them too, it will also be found deeply offensive by the swami's opposite numbers in Buddhism, i.e. the globe-trotting *bhikkhus* of South-east Asia who flit from capital to capital purveying the corresponding brand of 'pietistic talk' (p. 35). Those who are genuinely interested in the 'Wisdom of the East', and who are tired, perhaps, of the pseudo-spiritual claptrap of the pompous gurus and the 'stink of occidental adulation' that surrounds them, will welcome Agehananda Bharati's straightforwardness. They will be glad to hear him denouncing the 'glib and quite dangerous guru mania' (p. 200), as well as the warning against the 'pathological eclecticism' that permeates the entire counter-culture (p. 37) and the 'latent Hindu fascism which, fortunately for the world, has no power except in India' (p. 199). Swami Vivekananda and the Ramakrishna Mission come in for especially severe handling. Bharati is 'certain that Vivekananda has done more harm than good to the seekers of mystical knowledge' (p. 154). As for the Ramakrishna Mission, its dozen or so centres in Europe and America are well established and stagnant, and their clientèle has not changed in twenty years. The swamis in charge as well as their flock are against experimentation of any sort; the 'patently mystical directive' of their official monism is watered down to a respectable Sunday sermon, and the swamis 'vie with each other in giving establishmentarian, ecclesiastic advice, very much like the most average protestant ministers in the cities until thirty years ago' (p. 34). Once again, Bharati's criticism applies beyond its immediate context: we have our Ramakrishna Missions in Buddhism too.

Among the things for which Bharati most strongly criticizes both the swamis of the Hindu Renaissance and their 'grassroots' Indian counterparts is what he regards as their 'puritanical' attitude towards pleasure. Puritanism is in fact his *bête noir*, and although the word does not appear as often in *The Light at the Center* as it does in *The Ochre Robe*, and is not listed in the index, the earlier anathemas are still clearly in force. Whether a term of such distinctly Anglo-American provenance as 'puritanism' can really be applied in this naively uncritical fashion to Indian religious life is more than doubtful, but we perhaps should not be over rigorous. By puritanism Bharati appears to mean any disposition to check the totally uninhibited enjoyment of the fullest possible (hetero-) sexual pleasure. As an example of modern Hindu puritanism he cites the attitude of scholars and others to the *ānanda-mīmāṃsā* or 'pleasure scale' of the *Taittirīya Upaniṣad*, which according to him they reject. Prof. J. L. Mehta, for instance, 'got furious' when he quoted it (p. 63). To the best of my recollection, far from rejecting the *ānanda-mīmāṃsā*, or 'beatific calculus' as some of them call it, modern Hindu scholars and swamis – even the etiolated swamis of the Ramakrishna Mission – refer to it and expatiate on it *ad nauseum*. Indeed, I sometimes used to think that there was far too much bliss talk in Hindu religious circles. Bharati's discussion of the subject is not very clear. According to the *ānanda-mīmāṃsā*, a hundred measures of human bliss, i.e. the bliss experienced by a healthy well-educated young man in possession of the riches of the whole world, equal one measure of bliss on the scale of the human *gandharvas*; a hundred measures of bliss on the scale of the human *gandharvas* equal one measure of bliss on the scale of the divine *gandharvas*, and so on from the divine *gandharvas* to the ancestors and the ancestors to the gods by birth, etc., right up to a hundred measures of bliss on Prajāpati's scale, which equal one measure of bliss on the scale of Brahman or 100,000,000,000,000,000,000,000 times the measure of human bliss. The general principle involved, that of the existence of a whole hierarchy of blissful experiences, from the grossest bodily to the most refined spiritual, is perfectly clear, and is accepted not only by all Hindus but also by all Buddhists and, probably, by all Christians as well. They also accept, as the practical corollary of this, that in order to pass from a lower to a higher degree of bliss it is necessary to detach oneself from, or grow out of, or transcend – the vocabularies vary – the lower degree of bliss. This is why the *Taittirīya Upaniṣad* as it enumerates each level of bliss, declares it to be equal not only to a hundred measures on the preceding scale but also to the measure of bliss 'of the man well versed in scripture *who is not smitten by desire*', i.e. desire for the lower degree of bliss. As the *Dhammapada* says, 'If by renouncing limited bliss (*mattāsukha*) one can experience abundant bliss (*vipulaṃ sukhaṃ*), let the wise man renounce the limited bliss for the sake of abundant bliss'.[284] Herein hedonism and asceticism coincide. What Mehta and others who think like him reject is – so it appears – not the euphoric content of the mystical experience, as Bharati alleges, but the suggestion that a lower degree of bliss (e.g. sexual pleasure) is *qua* bliss identical with a higher degree of bliss (e.g. the bliss of Brahman), so that there is no question of one being better or nobler than the other and no question, therefore, of detaching oneself from the lower degree of bliss in order to experience the higher degree, i.e. no question of asceticism. Bharati himself – in *The Ochre Robe* at least – takes the quantitative language of the *Taittirīya Upaniṣad* quite literally, denying that the quantitative changes of the pleasure scale ever change into qualitative ones. But in a sense he does not take it literally enough. So concerned is he to insist that sex and Brahman are equally bliss that he forgets that they are not equally blissful, thus depriving himself of all motivation for passing from the one to the other. But it is time for us to see whether what Bharati calls mysticism corresponds to anything with which we are familiar within the context of Buddhism – and time to look at his references to Buddhism.

One of the most basic distinctions in all Buddhism – basic to thought and spiritual practice alike – is the distinction between *śamatha* or 'calm' and *vipaśyanā* or 'insight', the one representing the entire range of dhyānic or superconscious experience, from the lowest discursive to the highest non-discursive, the other the direct, intuitive, wordless, and conceptless confrontation with the ultimate reality of things. It does not take much reflection to see that the type of religious experience that Agehananda Bharati terms mystical coincides roughly with the lower levels of *śamatha* experience, which are hedonic and non-sensuous, plus the more intensely hedonic forms of sensuous experience. (On the higher levels of *śamatha* experience bliss is not present as a separate, distinguishable factor.) In terms of Buddhist psychology, the range of the mystical extends from the higher reaches of desire-world consciousness (*kāmāvacaracitta*) through all the levels of form-world consciousness (*rūpavacaracitta*) up to, and not including, the formless-world consciousness (*arūpavacaracitta*), while in 'mythological' terms it extends from the heaven of the Four Great Kings and the heavens of the other gods of the desire-world up through the heavens of the Brahma gods, of the gods of limited, unlimited, and sonant light, of the gods of limited, unlimited, and wondrous beauty, and of the 'unconscious' gods as far as the gods of the 'pure abodes' (*suddhāvāsa*). In terms of the stages of the Path the mystical extends from the satisfaction and delight (*prāmodya*) that arises in dependence on faith (*śraddhā*), through interest, enthusiasm, joy, rapture (*prīti*), and calmness, repose, tranquillity, serenity (*praśrabdhi*), up to bliss (*sukha*), and total psychical integration (*samādhi*) – these being, of course, the third to the seventh in the series of 'positive' *nidānas*.[285] All these levels of *śamatha* – whether interpreted as states of consciousness, heavens, or stages of the Path – are characterized by euphoria, which gradually increases in intensity, though inasmuch as it is the concomitant of psychical integration the more intense it becomes the less it is possible to speak of it as a separate mental factor. *Śamatha bhāvanā*, the cultivation or development (lit. 'making to become') of 'calm,' – one of the two most basic forms of Buddhist meditation, is therefore a cultivation or development of bliss. The meditative life is the blissful life. As the Buddha exclaims in the *Dhammapada*: 'blissfully indeed we live, we that regard nothing as our own. Enjoyers of ecstasy shall we be, like the Gods of Sonant Light'.[286]

But although bliss – mysticism – is almost the whole of *śamatha* it is not the whole of the spiritual life – taking the spiritual to include the transcendental. It is not the whole of Buddhism. *Śamatha* has its limitations – limitations which make clearer still the extent to which mysticism in general and the zero-experience in particular, coincides with *śamatha*. They are: (1) *Śamatha* experiences are mundane (*laukika*), not transcendental (*lokuttara*, lit. world transcending); they belong to the realm of the compounded or conditioned (*saṃskṛta-dhātu*), not to the realm of the uncompounded or absolute (*asaṃskṛta-dhātu*). In dependence on conditions they arise, and in the absence of those conditions cease. Pictorially speaking, they form part of the wheel of life, and revolve as it revolves – even though, towards the outermost edge of the wheel, each revolution may take – or seem to take – hundreds of aeons. All *śamatha* experiences being equally mundane, regardless of whether they are 'lower' or 'higher', Bharati is from the Buddhist point of view technically right in refusing to recognize any more than a quantitive difference between the successive degrees of mystical euphoria. (2) *Śamatha* experiences have no ontological content; that is to say, they do not in themselves constitute an experience of ultimate reality, and it is not possible for us to draw from them any conclusions about the nature of ultimate reality. The nature of ultimate reality is revealed only to insight (*vipaśyanā*) or wisdom (*prajñā*). Although *śamatha* experiences, as such, are devoid of ontological content, they are important – even necessary – from the spiritual point of view in that they provide a basis for the development of *vipaśyanā* and thereby contribute, indirectly, to the attainment of Enlightenment. *Śamatha* as transfigured by, and inseparably united with, the insight for whose development it provided the basis, is what is known as *samādhi* in the more Mahāyānistic usage of the term. (3) In the absence of *vipaśyanā*, *śamatha* experiences can – and often do – become the basis for the construction of various pseudo-ontologies or 'views' (*dṛṣṭi*) which, although they may purport to reveal the nature of ultimate reality have, in fact, no genuine ontological content. Buddhism traditionally regards all forms of theism, for example, as originating in this way. (4) *Śamatha* experiences do not, of themselves, bring about any permanent or radical change in the person enjoying them. Temporary and superficial changes may, indeed, occur, but these are doomed to pass away as soon as the *śamatha* state itself comes to an end. Like a stretched-out piece of elastic, the mind reverts to its original position as soon as the expanding agency is removed. Only insight into the nature of ultimate reality is able to bring about permanent and radical change, by exposing the baselessness of the assumption that there exists, as the subject of *śamatha* or any other experiences, a separate, unchanging, independent ego identity. Yes, *śamatha* does have its limitations, and these limitations do indeed make clear the extent to which *śamatha* coincides with mysticism or zero-experience as defined by Bharati. Both are blissful, both are unable to confer ontological status on their own content, and both are powerless to bring about any change in the meditator/mystic. Whether *both* can be analysed away remains to be seen. Bharati, Koestler, & Co. are indeed mystics – as are some, at least, of the swamis of the Hindu Renaissance. We need not, as Buddhists, dispute the fact. By one means or another – or by no means – they have indeed enjoyed what in Buddhism are known as *śamatha* experiences – experiences which were euphoric, without ontological significance, and which left them exactly as they were. But beyond *śamatha* there is *vipaśyanā*. Beyond euphoria there is ultimate reality. Beyond Bharati, Koestler & Co. – beyond the swamis – there is the Buddha.

That Bharati brackets himself and his fellow modern mystics with the Buddha almost as a matter of course is due neither to simple effrontery nor to megalomania, but to the fact that he is unable to distinguish between *śamatha* and *vipaśyanā*, calm and insight. Because he is unable to distinguish between calm and insight he has no means of telling a mystic from a spiritually enlightened being. He has, also, no means of access to the 'ontological dimension': no means of access to ultimate reality. (The mystic's intuition of numerical oneness is only a *feeling*.) Brahmin teachers like Vasiṣṭha, Patañjali, and Śrīharṣa, he tells us, taught that the sources of information about 'the ontological status of divinity, or reality, of the cosmos', is 'the infallible word of the Veda' (p. 85), a view which he as a Hindu apparently accepts. More than once, however, he refers to the rishis, the 'seers' of the mantra, the Vedic word, as mystics, and to 'canonical passages' as being 'statements made by people who have had the zero-experience' (p. 77). If the rishis are mystics the Vedas cannot be sources of ontological information, i.e. information about ultimate reality. Or is the ontological status conferred on the content of the rishi's experience by some means extraneous to the experience itself? Bharati does not say. Buddhism does not, of course, accept the Vedas as sources of ontological information, i.e. it does not accept their 'infallibility'. For Buddhism too the rishis are mystics. That is why the Buddha – or rather the Bodhisattva – left Ārāḍa Kālāma and Udraka Rāmaputra: they could teach him *śamatha*, but not *vipaśyanā*; they could not show him the way of Supreme Enlightenment. Bharati's references to ontology are not, in fact, very clear, and seem to be based on metaphysical assumptions of the 'common sense' order.

According to Buddhist teaching, in ultimate reality there is no distinction of subject and object, and *vipaśyanā* or insight 'intuits' or 'reflects' this non-distinction. For Buddhism, therefore, there is no question, in the ultimate sense, of an ontology as distinct from an epistemology: *vipaśyanā* does not reveal an object – even a transcendental object – as distinct from a subject, but it 'reveals' an ultimate reality which, when made the object of thought and speech – when brought within the dualistic framework of the subject-object relation – can be regarded only as object as opposed to subject. In the Mahāyāna this ultimate reality is known as *śūnyatā*. '*Śūnyatā*' is not an object but a pseudo-object. As a term in spiritual discourse – in spiritual communication – it 'points out' or 'indicates' not a real ontological object but an ultimate reality that transcends the duality of subject and object, ontology and epistemology. In the same way, Buddhist ontology is a pseudo-ontology, or rather, a symbolical ontology – in the mathematical rather than the Jungian sense. Just as '*śūnyatā*' does not indicate a real ontological object, even though the exigencies of language compel us to say of it that it is neither existent nor non-existent, so the conceptual constructions of Buddhist 'ontology' (a term I use only because Bharati uses it) do not purport to mediate a world of really existing metaphysical objects to a really existing epistemological subject but have, instead, the function of 'pointing out' a condition of ultimate reality in which the distinction of subject and object does not obtain, and of providing, moreover, a practical support for the development of insight or wisdom (*prajñā*). Bharati does not, it seems, understand this. Though he correctly says that Nāgārjuna, as a Buddhist, 'denied ontological status to any experience', i.e. to any mystical (=*śamatha*) experience, and that 'he did not feel that the zero-experience could add anything to the experiencing person's knowledge about the world' (pp. 82–3), this does not mean, as he seems to think it does, that for Nāgārjuna there is no ultimate reality beyond the zero-experience. *As a Buddhist*, Nāgārjuna affirmed the 'existence' of such an ultimate reality, which he termed *śūnyatā*, and which was to be realized by wisdom, or rather by the perfection of wisdom (*prajñāpāramitā*).

Though Buddhism plays only a very minor part in Bharati's book (Zen does not interest him – p. 185), it is apparent from his occasional references to it that his knowledge of it is neither wide nor deep. He shows no acquaintance with primary sources, on the importance of which he places great emphasis in the case of Yoga and Vedānta, and seems, in fact, to rely for much of his information on the Buddhist equivalent of the Hindu Renaissance type of pamphlet literature which he so heartily despises. In one place he gives us (p. 135), without references, a greatly expanded – not to say 'spiced up' – and entirely apocryphal version of the Buddha's well-known reply to Ānanda's question as to how monks are to comport themselves with regard to women.[287] In another, he tells us that, 'every single one' of the Buddha's speeches, 'starts with *bhikkhave*, "ye begging monks"; he never addressed anyone who wanted to stay out' (p. 133). Such slovenliness in someone who makes such a parade of scholarship as Agehananda Bharati does is quite breath-taking. Even a quick look at the middle fifty discourses of the *Majjhima Nikāya*, the 'Collection of Middle Length Discourses', for example, would have shown him, out of a total of fifty discourses, ten addressed to householders (*gahapati*), ten to non-Buddhist wanderers (*paribbājaka*), ten mainly to or about royalty, ten to brahmins, and only ten to the *bhikkhus* or begging monks. In any case, did not the Buddha exhort his first sixty spiritually enlightened disciples to journey forth for the welfare and happiness of many people (*bahujana*) and proclaim the Dharma?[288] There is no question of his message being addressed only to monks, even though these might have formed the largest and most important section of his community.

Bharati's most serious misunderstanding, however, is in connection with Buddhist meditation, about which he has some quite odd ideas. 'In the Pure Land School of Northern Buddhism', he says, 'the Buddha is the giver of grace to those who worship him faithfully, with very little attention to the highly individualistic, speculative, and affect-less meditations which go with the Theravāda and with many Mahāyāna schools' (p. 123). What these 'speculative' meditations are we can only guess, while as for them being 'affect-less', this is surely almost a contradiction in terms. As we have already seen, *śamatha* involves elements of delight, rapture, ecstasy, and bliss: the meditative life is the blissful life. There is also the example of the four *brahma vihāras*, one of the most popular meditations with the Theravāda and the Mahāyāna schools alike. Surely Bharati does not seriously mean to describe the meditative development of friendliness (*maitrī*), compassion (*karuṇā*), sympathetic joy (*muditā*), and equanimity (*upekṣā*), as being 'highly individualistic, speculative, and affect-less'. Some of the more extreme representatives of the modern so-called 'vipassanā meditation' (not to be confused with the traditional *vipaśyanā bhāvanā* common to practically all forms of Buddhism) do, of course, believe that it is possible to develop *sukkha-vipassanā* or 'dry insight', i.e. insight that has not been 'moistened' by the blissful experiences of the *dhyāna* states, and of this some rumour may have reached Bharati, but in general meditation teachers do not see the development of 'dry insight' as a practicable possibility. The whole notion of *sukkha-vipassanā* would appear to rest on a confusion between two radically different things: (1) actual insight into ultimate reality, and (2) recollection of the doctrinal categories of the Abhidhamma. What may be termed the standard or classic formulation of the Buddhist spiritual path, the Buddhist spiritual life, sees it as progressing from ethical observance through ever higher levels of psychical integration and euphoria to insight and wisdom and, from these, eventually to Enlightenment. The experience of dhyānic bliss, though itself mundane, is the means of transition from the mundane to the transcendental. Hedonism – the higher hedonism that coincides with asceticism – is an integral part of spiritual life. Enlightenment itself, indeed, can be thought of not in exclusively noetic terms but, rather, as the inseparable unity of ineffable Bliss and transcendental Awareness.

Despite its title, *The Light at the Center* conveys no inkling of this unity. On the contrary, there runs through the book a psychical cleavage that affects not only the author's whole approach to his subject but also the style with which he writes, e.g. mysticism is 'a highly structured pursuit of experiential maximization' (p. 91). Bharati is not unaware of the cleavage. 'I have long maintained,' he says, 'that the mystic who happens to be a scholar must live and think in a manner which psychiatrists call schizophrenic' (p. 82). This is to understate the matter. Bharati's 'schizophrenia' does not consist just in his being a mystic who 'happens' also to be a scholar. After all, what makes one a mystic – apart, of course, from saying that one is a mystic – is the zero-experience, and this, as he makes quite clear, is of very rare occurrence. The schizophrenia consists in the fact that, in the absence of *vipaśyanā* – and in the absence of any form of asceticism – Bharati is left not with mysticism and scholarship but with sexual and aesthetic euphoria and scholarship. Indeed, he is left with rather less than that. The gap between sense and intellect, the emotions and reason, can be bridged with the help of the fine arts, and the enjoyment of natural beauty, all of which have a unifying effect on the psyche. With the exception of classical and baroque music (played as he drives to work and while copulating) Bharati seems to be no more interested in these things, however, than he is in Zen. At any rate, there is no mention anywhere in his book of poetry, or of the visual arts, or of nature, nor anything to show that he is so much as aware of their existence. In the absence of the fine arts, therefore, and the enjoyment of natural beauty, he is left not with sexual and aesthetic euphoria and scholarship, even, but simply with sex and scholarship, or sex and academic research. If Gerald Scarfe[289] was ever to caricature Agehananda Bharati, it would probably be as a pair of outsized genital organs hanging from an enormously overdeveloped brain – an image that might do equally well for some of his counterparts in the field of Buddhist studies.

Bharati's greatest mistake, perhaps, has been to ignore the part played by asceticism in the religious life and in religious experience. He knows that there is such a thing as asceticism, of course, but he brushes it aside or tries to forget about it – or confuses it with puritanism. Occasionally, however, the truth will out. 'The professional mystics in India,' he has to admit, 'are almost all monastics – they have obtained ordination in orders which enjoin celibacy' (p. 171). That seems clear enough. Later on, however, he says, 'The fact that most methods now taught for supreme religious consummation are of the ascetic order, is a complex series of historical accidents which I cannot go into' (p. 209). What these accidents are it would be interesting to know. Perhaps Bharati will be able to particularize them in another book. Meanwhile, we have this book, which despite serious limitations does do a number of useful things. It provides us with a highly individual critique – not to say exposé – of the India-originated religious movements, insists on the dysfunctional nature of eclecticism, and stresses the need for the would-be mystic to follow a genuine tradition. Above all, perhaps, it reminds us that pleasure is not something to be feared, and that the hedonistic element is an essential part of the quest of seekers in the West. Even though we still have to remember that hedonism – ecstasy – mysticism – *śamatha* – is only part of the spiritual life, not the whole of it, for ex-Christian Hindus and ex-Christian Buddhists alike, the reminder is still, no doubt, a salutary one.

PATTERNS OF NON-VIOLENCE

Unto Tähtinen
Ahiṃsā: Non-violence in Indian Tradition
Rider, London 1976

The development of ethical ideas is inseparable from the development of consciousness. Nature is unconscious. Even at the level of organic existence, life is, to begin with, sentient rather than conscious, and even when, with the emergence of animal life, sentience develops into consciousness, it is simple consciousness that develops, not the reflexive consciousness that is the distinctive characteristic of human beings. Since nature is unconscious it is either 'mechanical' or instinctual rather than intelligent, and in each of its forms operates without regard for – because without (real) awareness of – any of its other forms. Nature is therefore the 'nature red in tooth and claw' of the poet and does not so much shriek against man's creed as remain blind to the possibility of any such achievement.[290] As it is weight and mass that count on the level of inorganic existence, so it is size and strength that count on the level of organic life. Nature is governed by 'power', and man, to the extent that he remains simply a part of nature, i.e. to the extent that he has not developed reflexive consciousness – to the extent that he is not truly human – is governed by power too. It is only when, as a result of the development of reflexive consciousness, he begins to realize that others are capable of suffering just as he is, and that they would not like done to them what he would not like done to him, that ethical ideas develop. Human life then comes to be governed, to a limited extent at least, not by power, i.e. violence in the form of force or fraud, but by an entirely different principle. It comes to be governed by love, not in the sentimental sense, but rather in the sense of the Confucian *shù*, 'reciprocity' or 'altruism', or the Godwinian 'benevolence'.[291]

In Indian tradition this higher principle finds expression in the idea of *ahiṃsā* or non-violence, which although grammatically negative in form stands for an ethical ideal that is positive as well as negative in content. Non-violence is, in fact, a key concept of Indian ethics, and there are six comprehensive philosophies of non-violence in Indian thought. In *Ahiṃsā: Non-violence in Indian Tradition*, a work based on original Sanskrit, Pāli, Prakrit, and Tamil sources, the Finnish Indologist Unto Tähtinen compares, for the first time, the different meanings of *ahiṃsā* in Buddhism and Jainism, in the Hindu *Vedas*, *Dharmaśāstras*, and *Purāṇas*, and in the thought of Mahatma Gandhi and his followers. We are thus given an extremely comprehensive and detailed study which in nine short chapters covers the definition, the roots, and the nature of *ahiṃsā* (1, 3, 4), the nature of *hiṃsā* or violence (2), the relation between *ahiṃsā* and other moral norms, *ahiṃsā* and war, *ahiṃsā* and crime, *ahiṃsā* and subhuman beings (5–8), and *ahiṃsā* in contemporary Indian life and thought (9).

One does not have to read very far in this study before becoming aware of the extent to which the idea of *ahiṃsā* or non-violence permeates the Indian religious consciousness, especially in the post-Vedic period, and the thoroughness with which Buddhism and Jainism, in particular, discuss the subject. In their concern for the practice of absolute non-violence, without the slightest taint of violence, the Jains, in the person of Amitagati, enumerate 432 types of *hiṃsā*, and there are other enumerations almost as elaborate. As Dr Tähtinen observes, however, such enumerations could be carried on *ad infinitum*. 'The basic distinction appears to be that of violence in thought, word, and deed, which, in addition, may be directly committed, commissioned, or consented to. These classifications are common to all schools of thought' (p. 16). Non-violence itself is no less thoroughly discussed. Here too there is a good deal of common ground. Though the word *ahiṃsā* is often popularly understood as 'non-killing', all the philosophical schools take it in the broader sense of 'non-injury', and most of them regard this as being mental and verbal as much as, or even more than, physical. Nevertheless there are two distinct traditions of non-violence in Indian thought, the Vedic or brāhmaṇic, and the ascetic or śrāmaṇic. According to the latter, which comprises mainly Buddhism and Jainism, non-violence is a universal principle and should be practised towards all living beings without exception. 'The ascetic conception of *ahiṃsā*', says Dr Tähtinen, 'differs from the Vedic conception by not including any form of justified violence into the idea of ahiṃsā. Nor does it imply that any type of hiṃsā is morally good' (p. 8). 'Thus the ascetic ahiṃsā is extended to every living being without exception. This implies that injury to an enemy, harm done to a criminal, or to an attacking beast, are to be termed as violence. It is this ascetic concept of non-violence which is applied universally' (p. 53). According to the Vedic or brāhmaṇic tradition, on the other hand, non-violence is not a universal principle and should be practised only towards non-violent beings. 'It is not applicable to enemies in war, to criminals, wicked people, offending beasts, and animals to be sacrificed or killed for one's livelihood' (p. 52). Killing such beings as these one commits no sin: such *hiṃsā* is in fact *ahiṃsā*. Indeed, as Krishna reminds Arjuna in the *Bhagavad Gītā*, by refusing to wage righteous war a Kṣatriya or member of the warrior caste incurs sin. War is an open door to heaven, or, as the *Varāha Purāṇa* says, 'Those braves who die for the *brāhmaṇas*, their milk cows and their state go to the city of Indra, or heaven' (p. 93).

Although ascetic non-violence is universal, i.e. to be extended to all living beings without exception, this does not mean that there will not be degrees in its application. On account of the very nature of his position the layman will not be able to practise non-violence to the same extent as the monk. Nonetheless both are practising one and the same principle, the universal principle of non-violence: there is not one principle for the monk and another for the layman. 'According to the ascetic branch of thought a layman's ethics are the morality prescribed for a monk, though in a much diluted form' (p. 12). Collating various Pāli Buddhist texts the author therefore says, 'A definite distinction can be drawn between the non-violence of a monk and that of a householder. Household life is full of hindrances and it is difficult for a man who dwells at home to live the higher life in full. As free as the air, so is the life of him who has renounced all worldly things. A householder is bound to destroy other living beings, but a monk practising self-restraint protects living beings. A [lay] Buddhist should at any rate avoid the practice of tormenting others (*para-paritāpana*) and not earn his livelihood as a cattle-butcher, a pig-killer, fowler, deer-stalker, hunter, fisherman, thief, executioner, jailer, or through any other cruel occupation (*kurūrakammanta*)' (p. 29). According to Jaina sources, 'When one is engaged in complete abstention [from violence] one becomes a saint. He who is engaged in partial restraint (*ekadeśa-virati*) is only a disciple (*upāsaka*)' (p. 61). In Vedic or Brahmanic non-violence there are also degrees of application, as of the monk and the layman, but with a vitally important difference. If the general duty of *ahiṃsā*, which according to Manu is applicable to all the four castes, comes into conflict with caste-duties or specific duties, e.g. the warrior's duty to fight or the king's duty to inflict punishment, then the caste-duties have preference (p. 56). Above all, if it comes into conflict with the Vedic injunction to kill animals in sacrifice, then non-violence must give way to violence (p. 5). In the words of the *mīmāṃsā* principle as stated by Khaṇḍadeva: 'The specific rule of killing at sacrifices is stronger than the general rule of prohibiting killing' (p. 35). Animal sacrifices are, in fact, good for all, including the animals slaughtered (p. 35). Indeed Śaṅkara, the celebrated exponent of non-dualist (*advaita*) Vedānta, declares that such sacrifice 'purifies the heart of a truth-seeker and ultimately awakens the desire to know the highest truth (*brahman*)' (p. 22). According to another source, however, the killing of animals in sacrifice having been enjoined on man by the divinely authoritative Vedas, whatever merit or demerit may accrue from the performance of such sacrifices goes to God (p. 5).

Since for the ascetic schools non-violence was a universal principle they refused to agree that it must give way to caste duties or to the Vedic injunction to kill animals in sacrifice, and this led them to deny the authority of the Vedas. To them violence was violence, and any attempt to argue that killing is justified because enjoined by the infallible Vedas only made matters worse by adding to the sin of violence the no less serious sin of ignorance (*avidyā*). They therefore attacked the authority of the Vedas vigorously. In fact, it is difficult to say whether the opposition of the ascetic schools to the slaughter of animals in sacrifice, and with it their rejection of the Vedas, was the cause or the effect of their belief in non-violence. As Unto Tähtinen puts it, 'The vehement opposition against killing at sacrifices was a good cause for the protagonists of *ahiṃsā*. The extreme care of animal life might have originated in view of the fact that *ahiṃsā* flourished as a reaction against the ritual slaughter of animals. Non-violence did not come to be generally recognized so much as a reaction against injury done to men (e.g. in war) rather than as a profound opposition to the institutionalized killing of animals. The heterodox schools lived and prospered on this reaction, and their position was buttressed by the simultaneous denial of the authority of the Vedas' (pp. 37–8). This reaction against killing animals was, like the reaction against meat-eating, more the work of Jainism than Buddhism, possibly because Jainism was older than Buddhism and because at the time of Pārśva (eighth century BCE) animal sacrifice was more widespread than in the Buddha's day. 'The Buddha emphatically and persistently fought against such social maladies as robbery, strife, fear of violence, and use of intoxicants. He paid more attention to these social evils than the Jains, who were more concerned about the slaughter of animals at sacrifice. This seems to have provided a good reason for the spread of Buddha's doctrine' (p. 48). But if the Buddha's opposition to animal sacrifice and meat-eating was less emphatic than that of the Jainas he was more concerned than they were about violence against oneself. They approved of self-mortification, whereas he regarded it as an extreme to be avoided. They maintained 'that man, under specific conditions, will be morally advised to kill himself' (p. 26), whereas he did not maintain any such thing. 'According to Pāli Buddhism,' says Dr Tähtinen, 'suicide is not to be approved' (p. 24). There is, however, the curious case of the monk Godhika, whose suicide – committed after he had gained 'temporary release' for the seventh time – was apparently not disapproved of by the Buddha.[292] Moreover, in the *Saddharma Puṇḍarīka Sūtra*, also not mentioned by Dr Tähtinen, the bodhisattva Sarvasattvapriyadarśana burns his own body with the object of worshipping the Buddha and his teaching of the Dharma, and this heroic act is applauded by innumerable Buddhas.[293]

Important as the idea of non-violence undoubtedly is, it is not the only form in which the principle of love – the higher principle that emerges when man ceases to be governed solely by the principle of power – finds expression in Indian tradition. This is particularly so in the case of Buddhism. Despite the fact that *ahiṃsā* is listed in the Abhidharma as one of the positive mental events, i.e. one of the *dharmas* present in all wholesome/skilful mental states, the actual term *ahiṃsā* or non-violence does not occur nearly so frequently in Buddhism as it does in Jainism, for example. Jainism regards even sexual abstinence and truthfulness as forms of non-violence, and in fact tends to interpret the whole religious life in terms of the practice of this one all-important virtue. Buddhism does not do this. Buddhism speaks not only of non-violence but also, no less frequently, of non-cruelty (*avihiṃsā*), while the first of its five (or ten) precepts takes the form of abstention from injury to living beings (*pāṇātipātā veramaṇī*) – not abstention from killing, as Unto Tähtinen seems to think (p. 79).[294] So far as Buddhism in fact is concerned, the higher principle of love finds its richest and most characteristic expression in the twin concepts of *mettā* or universal friendliness and *karuṇā* or universal compassion. In the words of Dr Tähtinen's summary, 'In Jainism the whole ethic revolves around the concept of *ahiṃsā*, in Buddhism other terms are stressed. *Mettā* or universal friendliness is of central ethical importance in Pāli Buddhism, whereas *karuṇā* acquires this position in Sanskrit Buddhism. We may say that both *mettā* and *karuṇā* imply *ahiṃsā*' (p. 79). Both *mettā* and *karuṇā* also imply, needless to say – as does the concept of *ahiṃsā* itself – that vivid awareness of the existence of other people, that keen sensitivity to their joys and sorrows, which arises from the development of reflexive consciousness and in which true humanity consists. *Mettā* and *karuṇā* find their highest expression in the life of the bodhisattva. 'A Bodhisattva will, by his every bodily, verbal, and mental action, regard only his fellow creatures. The mighty compassion (*mahākaruṇā*) has as its object the good of all living beings. The mighty compassion is the antidote to *hiṃsā*. The Bodhisattva helps all living beings to enter the city of *nirvāṇa*. This can be facilitated by the transference of merit in the sense of eternal happiness radiated by all the *buddhas*. Compassion is extended to the limits of speculation. Non-violence assimilates and submerges into the notion of compassion' (p. 78). Since the principle of love finds its most characteristic expression in friendliness and compassion we are not surprised that 'For the Buddha non-violence seems to have been mainly mental' (p. 68) and that he 'wished to cut violence at its root rather than tackle its manifestations' (p. 69). Such an emphasis is fully in accordance with the general nature of Buddhism which, in the words of one of the contemporary interpreters cited by Dr Tähtinen, is 'essentially a mind-culture'.

In modern times the concept of non-violence is for many people associated with the name Mahatma Gandhi. Within the context of contemporary Indian thought Gandhi represents the ascetic tradition of non-violence, just as Aurobindo represents the Vedic tradition of non-violence which, says Dr Tähtinen, 'has survived to the present day, and may appeal even now to the large majority of Indians and particularly politicians' (p. 116). Gandhi, who sometimes called himself 'a practical idealist', understands non-violence as essentially mental behaviour and regards it as involving dissociation of oneself from evil activities such as economic exploitation (p. 119). For him non-violence is a common duty, not a specific one. As Dr Tähtinen says, 'Gandhi's idea of *ahiṃsā* was not based on the Vedic conception of *ahiṃsā*. He ruled out all exceptions in the application of *ahiṃsā*. He derived his *ahiṃsā* from the ascetic sources, and it was this ascetic or śrāmaṇic concept which he applied, for the first time, to politics and economics' (p. 121). More specifically, 'Gandhi pleaded to adopt non-violence in the practical life of social groups and nations. He tried to apply non-violence in every walk of life, domestic, institutional, economic, and political. He knew of no case in which non-violence would not have provided a good guiding principle of action' (p. 123). This more extended application of the concept of non-violence – of the principle of love – is of great significance today. As Dr Tähtinen reminds us in the preface to his study, the need for non-violence has become more pressing than ever before because of its manifold applications. Non-violence can be applied to the settling of colonial, racial, and other social problems, to the need for making a choice between world peace and total destruction, to the need for the control of pollution created by industrial processes and products, and to the conservation of natural resources and the non-exploitation of subhuman life. Before we can apply the principle of non-violence, however, we must understand it, and how better shall we be able to understand it than by thoroughly acquainting ourselves with the six comprehensive philosophies of non-violence that have appeared in the history of Indian thought, particularly with those connected with the ascetic schools? It is this which Unto Tähtinen's systematically organized and richly informative study enables us to do.

THE TWAIN SHALL MEET

Karel Werner
Yoga and Indian Philosophy
Motilal Barnarsidass, Delhi, Varanasi, Patna 1977

Unbelievable as it may seem, this is the first study of yoga and Indian philosophy to be published in the English language. We have, to be sure, any number of popular books on yoga, and quite a lot of learned tomes on Indian philosophy; but never before, I think, have the two topics been brought together and dealt with in comparative fashion within the compass of a single volume. The reason for this is not far to seek. In England, at least, yoga and Indian philosophy tend to be the preoccupation of two different sorts of people, even of two different circles, one of them very much larger than the other. When one thinks of yoga the picture that springs to mind is of the overweight British matron in breathless pursuit of health and beauty, whereas when one thinks of Indian philosophy the picture that presents itself is of a wizened academic poring over dusty oriental manuscripts in a remote corner of one of the less prestigious departments of one of our older seats of learning. Rarely, if ever, do the two circles overlap. The British matron pursues health and beauty with little thought of philosophy, Indian or otherwise; the academic pores over his manuscripts without ever suspecting that they might have some bearing on the conduct of his own life. At last, however, yoga and Indian philosophy come together in the person of an

Indologist who is at the same time a teacher of yoga – or of a teacher of yoga who is at the same time an Indologist. His conception of yoga goes as far beyond that of the British matron as his conception of philosophy goes beyond that of the academic. The result is not only an increase of breadth but also an increase of depth. Yoga is not just a series of physical exercises but 'a consciously adopted system of training or pattern of behaviour aiming at enlarging or deepening man's direct experience of reality rather than his ability to describe or explain it' (p. xi). Similarly, philosophy is neither the history of philosophical opinions nor linguistic analysis but 'a constant endeavour of the human mind to describe and rationally explain experienced reality in clearly defined concepts and create an overall and systematic as well as intuitively penetrative picture of the world including man which satisfies man's intellectual curiosity or urge for formulated knowledge' (p. xi).

Born in Czechoslovakia, Karel Werner studied Western philosophy and Indology, and after obtaining his PhD in 1949 became a lecturer in Sanskrit and Indian civilization in Olomouc University. In 1968 he emigrated to England, where since 1969 he has been the Spalding Lecturer in Indian Philosophy and Religion in the University of Durham. In addition to his academic work he teaches yoga and has also published articles on yoga and Buddhism in English, German, and Czech. *Yoga and Indian Philosophy* is his first book in English, and represents the fruit of more than three decades of study and personal involvement. The work consists of seven chapters. After a short introduction, in the course of which yoga and philosophy are defined in the terms already quoted, the author opens with a widely ranging chapter on 'The Existential Situation of Man' in which stress is placed on the fact that, 'unlike in Europe, philosophy in India has always been concerned with the individual, his existential situation, his destiny and salvation, i.e. with the final solution of the riddle of man's existence' (p. 14). There then follow three chapters on Indian philosophy and three on yoga. In the first group of chapters Dr Werner looks at the nature of the world, as the stage on which the drama of man's search for absolute freedom takes place, and gives us a survey of Indian cosmology. He then explores the essence and destiny of man, and reviews the various Indian conceptions of salvation. Each chapter follows the same general pattern. The Vedic and Upanishadic contribution to our understanding of the world, man, and salvation having been considered, we are given an account of the more systematic teachings of the Sāṃkhya, the Dvaita Vedānta, and Buddhism, both Theravāda and Mahāyāna, on each of these three topics. Reference is also made to the Viśiṣṭādvaita and Dvaita schools of Vedānta and to Jainism, as well as to the philosophy of Aurobindo Ghosh, which according to the author is deeply influenced by Mahāyāna Buddhism. In the second group of chapters Dr Werner deals with the origin and purpose of yoga, as well as with its relation to philosophy, with the schools of yoga, and with yoga in the modern world. The second of these chapters, on 'Schools of Yoga', contains sections on the yoga of Early Buddhism and the yoga of Patañjali, the first of these being a short but careful study of the Buddha's Noble Eightfold Path. Probably the most important chapters of the book and, with the possible exception of the last one, those of the greatest general interest, are chapters 1 and 5, on 'The Existential Situation of Man as Reflected in European and Indian Thought' and 'Yoga, its Origin, Purpose, and Relation to Philosophy', and these will therefore be considered at slightly greater length.

Western philosophy begins with the cosmological speculations of the Milesian school, and it is here – according to Dr Werner – that we find the start of extraverted investigation of the world and, therefore, of that objective approach to reality, including man, that is so characteristic of European thought. Strengthened by the work of Plato and Aristotle, this 'objectivist' tendency eventually led to the birth of science and its domination over our lives and thought. Until quite recently Western philosophy did not really concern itself with the existential situation of the individual. Even though objective values exist only when experienced by individual subjects, in the quest for objectivity of values – for universally valid general ideas – the experiencing individual was finally lost sight of and, despite his rediscovery by the modern existentialists, 'is still missing in the structure of our scientifically oriented, objectivist civilization' (p. 2). In India the situation is very different. For Indian philosophy the important and central problem of investigation has always been 'the nature of man and the means of transcending his present limited situation' (p. 14). Apart from not going to the extreme of totally objectifying reality and divorcing it from intelligent consciousness, Indian philosophy has always enjoyed a 'dialectical' relation to religion, neither becoming subservient to religious dogma, nor having the results of its investigations ignored by religious thought. Above all, it has been kept in touch with actual human experience through its relation with yoga, which 'has always been used in India on the one hand as a means of confirming or testing the results of philosophical investigation and speculation on transcendence and on the other as a source of inspiration and a stimulus for philosophical thinking' (p. 15). From all this, as well as on account of its 'phenomenological' method and its humanism, it is obvious that Indian philosophy has much in common with modern existentialism. Like existentialism, it is concerned with despair or dread, with death, and with freedom. For Indian philosophy, however, freedom is no mere theoretical concept or philosophical problem. Freedom is an experience. It consists in one's actually rising above the limitations of the existential situation, i.e. in the experience of 'transcendence', and 'the only way to the achievement of the experience of transcendence is individual yoga practice of some kind' (p. 21). While recognizing that yoga in the broad sense of the term is not confined to India (p. 96), Dr Werner clearly believes that (Indian) yoga has a part to play in the West. There is, for instance, 'the possibility of resorting to yoga methods, or of deriving help from them when the philosophical quest has reached its utmost limit in conceptual analysis' (p. 98). At the same time, he sounds a note of warning. Owing to the separation of the two circles already mentioned, 'the popularization' of yoga and its practice in the West is in the hands either of Eastern gurus with little or no understanding of the Western psyche and tradition or of Western amateurs with varying degrees of competence' (p. 99). Experimental research into yoga is therefore necessary.

Though by no means a big book, *Yoga and Indian Philosophy* covers quite a lot of ground, and inevitably there are a number of topics which one wishes the author could have discussed more fully. Querying the applicability of Western evolutionary thinking to the history of yoga, for instance, Dr Werner rightly points out that at a later stage of its history a religious tradition cannot ever be regarded as spiritually higher than it was at the beginning. The point would have been made clearer, perhaps, if he explained that, in this kind of context, evolution is a term which strictly speaking applies to the *individual* rather than to the religious tradition to which the individual is regarded as belonging. This would have involved defining the 'individual', as well as distinguishing him from the 'group' and the group from the 'spiritual community'. There are also topics in connection with which the Buddhist might find himself disagreeing with the author. Is the state of deep sleep really one of 'unification with the essence' (p. 54) or with 'the Universal Self' (p. 75) as Dr Werner, following the Upanishadic teaching, seems to think? Was it in fact the 'storehouse consciousness' (*ālaya vijñāna*) which was 'newly recognized' by C. G. Jung and by him called the 'collective unconscious'? (p. 50). Is traditional Buddhism really just 'silent' on the problem of what is the essence of man, and is the five *khandha* analysis of the Pāli canon 'purely an analysis of the empirical constituents of the human personality as accessible to his present experience'? (p. 61). My own difference with Dr Werner relates to his implied disparagement of poetry. Speaking of the *Rig Veda*, which he describes as an extensive collection of hymns comprising 'the reactions of the Indian mind to its encounters with experienced reality, both external and internal', he objects to the view of Western scholars like Macdonell that the Vedas are 'imaginative creations of poets' (p. 23). But is that view really so very far from the truth? According to Shelley a poem is 'the very image of life expressed in its eternal truth', poetry 'the record of the best and happiest moments of the happiest and best minds', and poets themselves 'the hierophants of an unapprehended inspiration'.[295] If this indeed be so, then surely there could be no greater praise for the Vedas than to say of them that they were the imaginative creations of poets – especially when one considers what the word imagination meant not only to Shelley but also to Blake and Coleridge. After all, poetry is much more than versified fancies. Apart from whatever might be said on such topics such as these, however, there is little in Dr Werner's book to which either scholar or yogi could reasonably object. Mature and balanced in its approach, this pioneering exploration of an important field is clearly the product not only of the study of Indian philosophy but also of the practice of yoga, and as such merits our respectful attention.

RELIGIO-NATIONALISM IN SRI LANKA

Walpola Rahula
The Heritage of the Bhikkhu
Grove Press, New York 1974

When I met Walpola Rahula in 1945, in Ceylon (now Sri Lanka), he was probably the best known – certainly the most notorious – monk in the whole island. His thesis that the Buddhist monk had the right to take an active part in politics had split the entire sangha into two factions, one enthusiastically supporting, the other violently condemning, the stand he had taken. It was not until some years later, however, when I was myself a monk, that I really came to know anything about him. Sinhalese *bhikkhus* whom I met in Calcutta in the fifties, on my periodic visits to the Maha Bodhi Society's headquarters, gave me a vivid account of the disturbing effect he had had on the socio-religious life of Buddhist Ceylon. (By that time he was living in virtual exile in Paris.) One of them, with whom I was on particularly friendly terms, took the trouble of giving me a general idea of the contents of Rahula's famous book *Bhikṣuvagē Urumaya* or *The Heritage of the Bhikkhu*, published in 1946. There matters rested for a number of years. I met Walpola Rahula for the second time in 1965 or '66, when he was on a visit to London, and in the course of a conversation we had at the Ceylon Vihara it became evident that despite a scholarly preoccupation with Mahāyāna thought his ideas were as 'radical' as ever. Now, twenty-nine years after the publication of the original Sinhalese edition, comes an English translation of *Bhikṣuvagē Urumaya*, so that we are at last able to see for ourselves what the fuss was all about. To Western Buddhists the whole subject is, indeed, of special interest, inasmuch as the author has recently aired his views on 'The Future of the Sangha in the West' in two articles in *The Middle Way* (June and August, 1974). I shall therefore go through the whole book chapter by chapter, commenting on anything that seems deserving of special notice. In this way we shall be able to see what sort of heritage we in the West may expect to take over from the sangha in the East – or at least from a section of the sangha in Ceylon.

1. BUDDHISM AND SOCIAL SERVICE

On the whole this chapter draws attention to an aspect of Buddhism which is often overlooked, i.e. its concern for the material as well as for the spiritual well-being of man, and the author rightly draws attention to passages in the Pāli canonical texts which represent the Buddha as advising people on their economic, social, and political affairs. Unfortunately, the chapter opens with the sentence 'Buddhism is based on service to others'. Such ambiguity as this can spring only from extreme confusion of thought, and we are therefore not surprised when, after referring to the Buddha's renunciation of Nirvāṇa in his previous life as Sumedha the hermit, the author goes on to conclude the first paragraph of this chapter with the statement 'A true Buddhist should have the strength to sacrifice his own nirvana for the sake of others' – it being assumed, apparently, that to such a true Buddhist Nirvāṇa is as 'accessible' as it was to Sumedha. With the help of a truncated reference to the Buddha's well-known exhortation to his first sixty *Enlightened* disciples to wander from village to village preaching to people for their good and well-being (nothing is said about him exhorting them to proclaim the Dharma, and to make clear the perfectly pure *brahmacarya* or holy life),[296] as well as by means of the plethora of references to the Buddha's advice on purely secular subjects already referred to, the impression is created that 'a true Buddhist' is concerned with the promotion exclusively of the material well-being of humanity. In other words, having in effect dismissed Nirvāṇa as a sort of antisocial selfishness, the bodhisattva ideal is equated with the secular concept of social service. Could the degradation of a sublime spiritual ideal be carried further than this? Despite his extensive scholarship, the author seems totally unaware of the true significance either of the 'transcendental' state of Nirvāṇa, the goal of the Theravāda, or of the transcendental 'career' of the bodhisattva, the ideal of the Mahāyāna schools.

Besides degrading the Dharma, Walpola Rahula denigrates the people to whom it was preached by the Buddha and his disciples as they travelled from place to place. 'Generally' he says, 'the villagers were poor, illiterate, not very clean, and not healthy.' What evidence there is for the greater part of the population of northern India being poor (by what standard?), dirty, and unhealthy in the Buddha's time we are not told. Even quite a cursory reading of the Sutta and Vinaya Piṭakas conveys quite a contrary impression. Indeed, if the villagers had not been prosperous, in the sense of having sufficient food, clothing, and shelter, how would they have been able to support so large a number of monks, both Buddhist and non-Buddhist? As for their being illiterate, *of course they were*. With the possible exception of a few traders, who may have used writing for purposes of business correspondence, everybody in that society was 'illiterate' – including the Buddha and his disciples. Religion and culture were transmitted exclusively by oral means. To be illiterate did not imply any lack of education or culture – or even of Enlightenment. One cannot help thinking that Walpola Rahula has fallen victim to what a distinguished fellow-countryman of his called 'the bugbear of literacy'.[297]

2. THE EVOLUTION OF THE LIFE OF THE *BHIKKHU*

Quite a few Buddhists, even in the West, seem to be under the impression that the Buddha drew up, once and for all, a code of discipline for his monks to which the 'orthodox' among them have adhered ever since. The author shows that this was not so, and that even during the lifetime of the Buddha 'the Rules of Discipline were introduced and changed and modified in accordance with changing economic and social conditions to suit times and places' (p. 11). He therefore rightly concludes that 'The Vinaya (the Code of Disciplinary Rules for the Sangha) is not an absolute truth; it is only a convention agreed upon for the orderly and smooth life of a social organization. As it should be conducted according to the social and economic changes to suit the place and the time, the

Buddha laid down appropriate rules and also changed and modified them' (pp. 11–12). One would have thought, however, that if the Vinaya could be modified according to changed social and economic conditions, it could with even greater reason be modified in accordance with changed psychological and spiritual needs, but on this aspect of the subject the author has – perhaps characteristically – nothing whatever to say. His concern seems to be exclusively with the social and the economic. There is also a certain amount of semantic confusion in connection with the word 'democracy'. Democracy means a form of government in which the 'governed' govern themselves, whether directly or through their elected representatives. It is therefore inapposite to say that 'the Buddha's system of controlling *bhikkhus* was purely democratic' (p. 11). If he really 'controlled' them surely the system was not democratic, and if it had really been democratic, the *bhikkhus* would have *elected* him as their 'undisputed master' – which is surely unthinkable. The dilemma illustrates the confusion that is created when popular concepts are used without too close attention to their meaning.

3. THE COUNCILS

These are the councils of Rājagṛha, Vaiśālī, and Pāṭaliputra, and the author's very brief summary follows the traditional Theravādin accounts. He brings them in, apparently, simply in order to make the point that the differences of opinion about the Rules of Discipline which had sprung up among the *bhikkhus* by the time of the Second Council, were all due to the fact that 'A hundred years after the death of the Buddha the economic and social structure as well as the outlook of the people must have undergone changes' (p. 13). Once again we hear nothing of any spiritual changes. However, the author agrees with Dr B. M. Barua, who in turn agrees with Dr Nalinaksha Dutt, that the rise of schools and sects within the sangha during this period was a sign of health rather than of decay.

4. INTRODUCTION OF BUDDHISM TO CEYLON: THE NATIONAL RELIGION OF THE SINHALA PEOPLE

According to Sinhalese tradition, Buddhism was introduced into Ceylon in the third century BCE by the *arahant* Mahinda, son of the Emperor

Aśoka. In reply to a query by the king of Ceylon, Mahinda is said to have declared that Buddhism could not be considered to have taken firm root in Ceylon unless and until a Ceylonese, born in Ceylon and of Ceylonese parents, ordained in Ceylon, learned and recited the Vinaya in Ceylon. In other words, Buddhism would not be established in Ceylon unless the sangha there was completely autonomous, i.e. not dependent on the parent body in India – an attitude fully in accordance with the spirit of Buddhism. However, Walpola Rahula takes Mahinda's statement to mean much more than that. 'Mahinda's desire' he says, 'was to make Buddhism the national religion of the Sinhalese people. And so it happened.... Buddhism became the state religion' (p. 17). For 2,200 years legal possession of the throne was the right only of Buddhists. In the tenth century a king declared that only bodhisattvas should become kings of Ceylon! (Presumably those who became kings were bodhisattvas.) In the thirteenth century the *Pujavaliya* declares that the island of Lanka (Ceylon) belongs to the Buddha himself. Religio-nationalism seems to have run wild. As if that was not bad enough, however, we are told that 'Historical evidence clearly shows that Buddhism existed as an institution of the Sinhalese monarchy' (p. 18). In other words, Buddhism has been subordinated to the state. By the time we come to the end of the chapter, therefore, we are not surprised to find the author concluding 'Thus, because of the unity of the religion, nation, and state, *bhikkhus* began to participate in many ways in public affairs and in the freedom and protection of the nation' (p. 19). What this 'participation' involved we shall see in the next chapter.

5. RELIGIO-NATIONALISM AND THE NATIONAL CULTURE

'From the time of King Dutugamunu ... religious and national fervour of both the laity and the Sangha began to grow intensely' (p. 20). The Sinhalese from the south, we are told, mounted a 'crusade' to liberate the nation and the religion from the foreign yoke (the capital had been occupied by a South-Indian king), and Dutugamunu, 'the greatest of national heroes', after proclaiming that he was warring not for the pleasures of kingship but for the re-establishment of Buddhism, marched at the head of his advancing army carrying a spear *with a sacred relic of the Buddha enshrined in it*. Western Buddhists will no doubt wonder where they have heard all this before. But the story is not yet finished.

‘In this decisive battle for the liberation of Buddhism and the Sinhalese,’ Walpola Rahula relates, ‘the *bhikkhus*, headed by their great Elders, did not remain in their cells’ (p. 20). One *bhikkhu*, ‘who was about to become an *arahant*,’ disrobed and joined the army, a large number of the others accompanied the army into battle, and ‘blessed and inspired by the presence of *bhikkhus*, the warriors fought with great courage and determination’ (p. 21). In these circumstances we are not surprised to learn that ‘From this time the patriotism and the religion of the Sinhalese became inseparably linked. The religio-patriotism at that time assumed such overpowering proportions that both *bhikkhus* and laymen considered that even killing people in order to liberate the religion and the country was not a heinous crime’ (p. 21). Indeed, when the victorious king one day became remorseful when he thought of the destruction of thousands of beings in battle, eight *arahant bhikkhus*, i.e. monks who had attained Nirvāṇa, came to the king and assured him that he had committed no sin. Non-Buddhists, they declared, were no better than beasts! Once again, we cannot help wondering where we have heard all this before.

At this point, feeling perhaps that he has been rather carried away by his enthusiasm for religio-nationalism, Walpola Rahula seems to check himself. He has the grace to admit that the statement of the eight *arahants*, as recorded by the *Mahāvaṃsa* or Great Chronicle of Ceylon, is diametrically opposed to the teaching of the Buddha. Yet he is clearly unwilling to condemn it outright. ‘It is difficult for us today either to affirm or to deny whether the *arahants* who lived in the second century BCE did ever make such a statement’ (p. 22). (Apparently they *could* have made it, then.) However, being concerned with precedents rather than principles, he does not allow the problem to bother him for very long. By the fifth century CE, when the *Mahāvaṃsa* was written, monks and laity alike had clearly recognized that working for the freedom and uplift of the religion and country was so important and noble that *arahants* themselves, they believed, had accepted the idea that the destruction of human beings for this purpose was not a very grave crime – and this is all the author really wants to know. ‘It is evident’, he says, ‘that the *bhikkhus* of that time considered it their sacred duty to engage themselves in the service of their country as much as in the service of their religion’ (p. 22). He then gives examples illustrating the national and cultural activities in which the *bhikkhus* engaged. Some of the activities are innocent enough. In the reign of King Dutugamunu we find *arahants* functioning as architects and *bhikkhus* rendering manual labour by supplying the masons with bricks and mortar. Later on, however, the monks play a leading part in politics and even decide who should occupy the throne. Walpola Rahula is therefore able to conclude, very much to his own satisfaction, that 'from the earliest period of Ceylon history to the recent past, it is abundantly clear that in addition to participating in numerous other responsibilities, the *bhikkhus* played a leading role even in the highly responsible political function of selecting a suitable king to rule the country' (p. 23).

6. FUNDAMENTAL INNOVATIONS

The most important of these innovations was the writing down of the Tipiṭaka. Hitherto, of course, it had been preserved exclusively by oral means, but in the last century BCE – in the reign of King Valagamba (Vattagamani-Abhaya), an invasion from South India, internal dissensions, and above all, the most disastrous famine in Ceylon history, between them brought about such unsettled conditions in the country that the elder monks, fearful for the future of the religion, decided to commit the Buddha's teaching to writing. This was a courageous and far-sighted decision, and we cannot be sufficiently grateful to the ancient worthies who, at such a time, preserved the 'Pāli' recension of the sacred tradition not only for the Buddhists of Ceylon but for the world. Unfortunately, however, besides committing the Tipiṭaka to writing they resolved that doctrinal study was more important than the practice of ethics and meditation. As Walpola Rahula points out, this was directly contrary to the original teaching of the Buddha, according to which the practice of virtues and the realization of Nirvāṇa were more important than the mere study of the Dharma. Not that this was not realized at the time. There was a lengthy debate between the *paṃsukūlika* or ascetic 'rag-robed' *bhikkhus* and the *dhammakathika* or 'Dharma expounding' *bhikkhus*, but in the end the latter, who seem to have been in the majority, carried the day.[298] As a result, a fundamental change took place in the character of Buddhism and the way of life of the monks. Scholarship came to be considered more important than spiritual practice. Monks who were good scholars came to be more highly esteemed than those who devoted themselves to meditation. As Rahula puts it, 'The solitude-loving meditator lives in seclusion away from society, doing no service to society. The scholar is engaged in service which is necessary for society, and valued by it' (p. 27). From the first century BCE, therefore, it is the scholar monk who dominates the scene in Ceylon. The 'rag-robed' monk disappears into the forest, where he exercises less and less influence, and at times even partially adapts himself to the new trends. Eventually, though this the author does not tell us – perhaps because he does not consider the matter important enough – the practical knowledge of meditation virtually died out in Ceylon and had to be reintroduced from Burma and Thailand in the twentieth century.

7. STUDY AND MEDITATION: ACADEMIC DEVELOPMENTS

Scholarship having come to be considered more important than spiritual practice, two separate and mutually exclusive monastic vocations came into existence. A monk could be either a scholar or a meditator, but he could not be both. More extraordinary still, meditation was considered suited to the weak and incapable. 'Able and intelligent *bhikkhus* who were strong in body and mind followed the vocation of scholarship, while *bhikkhus* of weaker intelligence, feeble in body and mind – particularly those who had entered the order in their old age – followed the vocation of meditation (*vipassanā-dhura*)' (p. 30). By the time of King Mahinda IV, in the tenth century CE, the salary paid to the teacher of the Abhidhamma Piṭaka, which was 'conducive to the advancement of knowledge', was equal to that of the two teachers of the Vinaya and Sutta Piṭakas, which were traditionally held to deal with monastic discipline and meditation respectively. With incentives of this sort being offered them, it is not astonishing that monks who took up the vocation of scholarship should have widened their scope to include the various branches of secular knowledge. In this way the whole field of secular education came into the hands of these monks, who enjoyed a comfortable and lucrative existence. They even took up medicine and law. At the end of the chapter Rahula is able to record with satisfaction that as early as the first century CE an elder monk held a post equal to that of Chief Justice of Ceylon. The scholarly monks had clearly become what Coleridge called a *clerisy*, and a Buddhist clerisy is no more the Sangha than a Christian clerisy is the Church.

8. MONASTERIES: THEIR ADMINISTRATION AND MAINTENANCE

As a result of the educational and other services rendered by the monks to the nation, the monasteries became extremely wealthy. So much so, indeed, that special departments of state had to be created to administer the monasteries and their landed estates, which often included whole villages. The possession of such wealth was not without its disadvantages. Whenever law and order broke down the monasteries had to pay to robbers and bandit chiefs what can only be described as protection money, a practice that eventually came to be regarded with approval. The monasteries also owned large numbers of slaves, both male and female. As Walpola Rahula frankly admits, all this constituted a radical departure from the way of life prescribed for the monks by the Buddha, so much so, indeed, that what he disingenuously calls 'a new monastic way of life' (p. 39) developed in Ceylon. Not that the change seems to bother him particularly. As he says, 'It was the natural result of the inevitable changing political, economic, and social conditions of the country from time to time' (p. 39). The chapter concludes on a curious note. The author finds it difficult to believe that the monks were given so large a portion of the national wealth solely for religious reasons. They were treated so generously, he believes, because they 'worked for the common welfare of the people and the cultural advancement of their country' (p. 39).

9. ARTS, CRAFTS, AND LITERATURE

This chapter strikes a happier note. From the fourth century CE onwards the monks of Ceylon not only greatly encouraged the visual arts but themselves sometimes practised them, particularly painting and sculpture. Monks also played an important part in the development of secular literature. Mahānāma, in the fifth century CE, composed the *Mahāvaṃsa* or 'Great Chronicle', our principal source for the early history of the island. This work consists mainly of stories about kings, ministers, bandits, wars and rebellions, towns, cities, and countries, all of which are subjects that the Buddha had said it was improper for monks to discuss.[299] Mahānāma gets round the difficulty in a highly ingenious manner. By concluding with a reference to death and impermanence, to which even kings are subject, he could claim that each chapter had been converted from a description of worldly affairs into a meditation on the sublime truths of the Dharma. The use of such a device, though innocent in itself, well illustrates the ingenuity with which the Ceylon monk often sought to combine extreme unfaithfulness to the spirit of the Buddha's teaching with scrupulous regard for its letter.

10. NATIONAL FREEDOM AND THE PROTECTION OF PEACE

Here we see the monks of Ceylon busy with all kinds of political activities. From the fifth to the eighteenth century they depose and enthrone kings, approve declarations of war, settle feuds, answer questions on the constitution, and negotiate trade pacts. Apart from allowing King Parakramabahu the Great to send an army to India to spread 'the Right Faith', they used their vast influence in a humane and moderate manner, and seem to have well deserved the tribute which Rahula pays them for their zeal and prudence.

11. THE PORTUGUESE PERIOD

The Portuguese arrived in Ceylon in 1505, at a time of political disintegration, and ruled the maritime provinces from then until 1658. Throughout the territories under their control Roman Catholicism was propagated with fire and sword, and many people embraced the new faith. In the kingdom of Kandy, still ruled by a Sinhalese monarch, the situation was if anything even worse. King Rajasimha I not only gave up Buddhism for Hinduism but behaved with great brutality, killing many *bhikkhus* and burning a large number of religious books. So great was the havoc that the monastic order ceased to exist, and had to be reintroduced from Arakan at the beginning of the following century. Despite the uninterrupted patronage it had received for centuries, it seems to have collapsed with remarkable ease.

12. THE DUTCH PERIOD

The Dutch ruled the maritime provinces from 1658 to 1796. Though there was sixty years of peace at the beginning of this period, on the whole the presence of the Dutch was as disastrous to the political, economic, and cultural life of the country as that of the Portuguese had been. So far as the unfortunate inhabitants of the occupied territories were concerned, the only difference was that instead of being forcibly converted to Roman Catholicism they were now forcibly converted to Protestantism. Twice the monastic order died out and twice it had to be reintroduced, once – for the second time – from Arakan, and once from Siam (Thailand). On each occasion the reintroduction seems to have consisted in little more than the restoration of the technically correct tradition of *bhikkhu* ordination. Despite the noble personality of Saranankara, who eventually became head of the revived sangha, there was no question of spiritual renewal. The clerisy re-formed its scattered ranks, and clung on to whatever patronage was still available.

13. BRITISH RULE

In 1796 the British conquered the maritime provinces from the Dutch, and in 1815 they gained control of the kingdom of Kandy, thus becoming 'the first and the only foreign power in history to occupy the whole of Ceylon' (p. 64). The author relates a story to show how, on the sad day when the Kandyan Convention was signed, 'the honour and prestige of the Sinhalese and their religion was saved and protected by a *bhikkhu*' (p. 64). This enables him to conclude that 'On every occasion when both the nation and the religion were in danger, Buddhist monks came forward to protect them' (p. 65). However, though otherwise meticulous in citing sources, he gives no authority for his story.

14. STRUGGLE FOR FREEDOM: REBELLIONS

In this chapter we find Buddhist monks assisting, and even leading, armed rebellions against British rule. One elder monk was, indeed, shot on suspicion of complicity in one of these rebellions. 'In the nineteenth century, as in the past, patriotic Sinhalese laymen and the clergy fought together, sacrificing their lives in the cause of freedom and religion' (p. 67).

15. THE STRENGTH OF THE *BHIKKHUS*: LAY–CLERGY UNITY
16. BRITISH TACTICS: DISRUPTION OF THE LAY–CLERGY UNITY
17. BRITISH TACTICS: CONFUSION OF MONASTIC ADMINISTRATION
18. BRITISH TACTICS: INTRIGUES TO DESTROY BUDDHISM (CHRISTIAN EDUCATION)

In this group of chapters the author describes the way in which the British disrupted the unity and solidarity of the *bhikkhus* and the laity, won over some of the most prominent elder monks, severed the government's connection with the administration of Buddhist temporalities, and spread Christianity and Christian culture throughout the country. Article 5 of the Kandyan Convention had declared that 'The Religion of Boodhoo ... is declared inviolable, and its Rights, Ministers, and Places of Worship are to be maintained and protected,' but this was not observed in the spirit, and hardly in the letter. Indeed, in 1816, the year after the signing of the Convention, we find Governor Sir Robert Brownrigg, in a letter to William Wilberforce, protesting against the suspicion that the word 'inviolable' was being understood in an 'anti-Christian' sense in Ceylon, and assuring his correspondent that the chief object of his government had been the religious and moral improvement of people, and the propagation of the Gospel (p. 87). For some years the salaries of all Christian missionaries were paid out of the civil list, which meant that Sinhalese Buddhists were having to finance the cost of their own conversion to Christianity! Measures of this sort, which were aimed at the destruction of Buddhism and the enfeeblement of the Sinhalese nation, understandably arouse Walpola Rahula's indignation – an honest indignation that will be shared by all who cherish the ideals of national self-determination and religious tolerance. His harshest strictures, however, are reserved for the chief high priests of the Malwatta and Asgiriya Chapters, who on appointment to office undertook to be 'loyal and faithful' to the government, as well as to report any subversive activities that came to their notice. Such conduct might not have been very heroic, but the author adduces no evidence to show that they necessarily acted from unworthy motives. Perhaps he does not consider it necessary to do so, religio-national patriotism being for him obviously the highest of all virtues.

With the spread of Christianity and Western education Sinhalese Buddhist culture came to be neglected and despised, even by the Sinhalese Buddhists themselves. The position of the *bhikkhus* deteriorated. As they 'could not adapt themselves to suit the changed political, economic, and social situation, they were rendered useless to society' and 'laymen had nothing to learn from them' (p. 91). Worse still, the Buddhist monk was 'driven to limit his activities to the recitation of the *suttas* (*pirit* chanting), preaching a sermon, attendance at funeral rites and almsgiving in memory of the departed, and to an idle, cloistered life in the temple' (p. 91). Some Buddhists would probably feel that such activities as chanting and preaching were not altogether unworthy of a Buddhist monk, but Ven. Rahula seems to think that for someone who had been used to enthroning and deposing kings they represent a great comedown in the world, and he speaks bitterly of the 'melancholy and abject situation' of such a monk. More extraordinary still, he refers with approval to the ancient Sinhalese idea that a Sinhalese had to be a Buddhist! This is surely a complete denial of the individual's freedom to follow the religion of his own choice, and as such a complete negation of both the spirit and the letter of the Buddha's teaching. One cannot be a Buddhist unless one is free not to be a Buddhist – unless one is free to be a Christian, or a Muslim, or a tree-worshipper, or anything else one wants to be. What Walpola Rahula in effect does is to turn Buddhism from a universal religion into an ethnic religion, surely the worst of all betrayals, the worst of all perversions, of a teaching that stressed above all others the responsibility of the individual for his own development. Indeed, had Walpola Rahula been around at the time of Mahinda's arrival in Ceylon, he probably would have objected to the introduction of the new faith on the grounds that it was of Indian origin, and would have exhorted the Sinhalese people to remain true to their own traditions. At the end of the chapter he says that 'what the Sinhalese Buddhists opposed was not the religious teaching of Jesus of Nazareth, but a religion together with an alien civilization propagated by the imperialists as a mode of destroying patriotism and national culture, and re-establishing foreign rule in Ceylon' (p. 92). But this does not really help him very much. It was undoubtedly right for the Ceylon Buddhists to resist the forces of Christian religio-imperialism, but what if a Sinhalese wanted to adopt, of his own free will, 'the religious teaching of Jesus of Nazareth'? According to Ven. Rahula, he is not free to do so. He is a Sinhalese and he must be a Buddhist. Moreover, if the Christian missionaries did not represent 'the religious teaching of Jesus of Nazareth' neither did the *bhikkhus* of Ceylon – at least those with whom Rahula is concerned – represent the religious teaching of Gautama of Kapilavastu. Rahula does not understand this. He does not understand that what really happened during the period of British rule, if it had not happened even earlier, was that the Christian clerisy, as represented by the missionaries, to a large extent superseded the Buddhist clerisy as represented by the monks. The more powerful 'medicine' of the West virtually ousted the weaker 'medicine' of the East. Quoting Rahula's own words in an earlier chapter one might say that this was an example, on an even wider and historically more important scale, of 'the inevitable changing political, economic, and social conditions' in the world. In fact, what took place was not so much a clash between Buddhism and Christianity, or even a clash between Buddhism and the forces of religio-imperialism, but a clash between two rival clerisies. Buddhism as a living spiritual tradition had disappeared from Ceylon long before the British came. What collapsed under the combined impact of Christianity and Western education was the clerisy, and it is degeneration in this sense that Rahula is really lamenting in this chapter.

20. THE REVIVAL

Just as degeneration was the degeneration of the clerisy, so revival was the revival of the clerisy. From 1841 onwards *pirivenas* or Buddhist monastic institutes for the study of the traditional learning and culture were established, Buddhist schools were opened, and Buddhist societies founded. However, reading between the lines of Rahula's account, it is clear that 'revival' tended to mean two quite different things. In the first place it meant the revival of the traditional learning and culture. In the second it meant the teaching of Western arts and sciences under 'Buddhist' auspices. Thus there were, in fact, now two clerisies, one consisting of those Buddhist monks who had been educated at the *pirivenas*, and one consisting of those laymen – and monks too, eventually – who had received a Western education. As a result of this, the conflict between the 'Christian' clerisy and the 'Buddhist' clerisy was reproduced within the Sinhalese Buddhist community itself. One interesting development of this conflict was that many of the wealthy, Western-educated Sinhalese Buddhists not only sent their children to Christian missionary schools (presumably because they believed Western 'medicine' to be superior to Eastern medicine) but believed that *bhikkhus* 'ought to confine themselves to purely religious activities and' in Rahula's own words, 'live a life limited to the four walls of their temples' (p. 95). Rahula believes that such wealthy laymen wanted to keep the *bhikkhus* out of politics for purely selfish reasons, and with regard to some of them he is undoubtedly right. At the same time it ought to be considered that some laymen of this class, being themselves members of the dominant clerisy, looked to the members of the monastic order for something more than just learning and culture – for a higher, 'spiritual' something that neither the Christian missionaries nor the 'political' *bhikkhus* possessed. Where a need of this sort is concerned, however, Rahula seems quite unsympathetic, even uncomprehending. *Bhikkhus* ignorant of the modern world and its problems he dismisses as 'a set of meaningless ancients' (p. 96). His ideal is represented by the knowledgeable and energetic *bhikkhus* of the present generation who, he declares, have no wish to chant *pirit*, perform funeral rites, or deliver 'the usual sermons'. Such *bhikkhus* have 'considered it their duty and heritage once again to liberate their country, nation, and religion' and this, according to him, is 'the inevitable course of history which cannot be stopped' (p. 97).

On this stirring note *The Heritage of the Bhikkhu* ends. Since its original appearance in Sinhalese in 1946, however, a great deal has happened in Sri Lanka, and Walpola Rahula has therefore added to this English edition of his famous book a postscript which brings the story down to 1971, the year of the great insurgency. In 1948 Ceylon became independent. Those who had assumed that the end of foreign rule would mean automatic reversion to full-fledged religio-nationalism were, however, soon disappointed. Whether or not the process of history cannot be stopped, Rahula and his friends had certainly miscalculated its direction. Nevertheless, such was the enthusiasm for national, cultural, and religious revival that, in the first decade after independence, it seemed as though a veritable renaissance was taking place. A World Fellowship of Buddhists was inaugurated, a Buddhist council held, a Buddhist Committee of Inquiry appointed, and the 2500th Buddha

Jayanti celebrated on a grand scale throughout the country. At the same time, the *bhikkhus* became more deeply involved in social reform and welfare activities of various kinds, while among both monks and laymen there was a growing demand for the implementation of the recommendations of the Buddhist Committee of Inquiry, which had proposed widespread changes, and the declaration of Sinhalese as the national language. This demand was spearheaded by the 'political' *bhikkhus*, and with their support the Sri Lanka Freedom Party, which had promised to implement the Committee's proposals, won the General Election of 1956. For a while it seemed as though the wildest dreams of religio-nationalism were about to become a reality. Then in 1958 the prime minister, Mr S. R. W. D. Bandaranaike, was assassinated by a Buddhist monk. I was in India at the time and I well remember the sensation the news created. 'Generally speaking', Rahula tells us, 'the *bhikkhus* could not face the public for several years' (p. 109). In the light of what Rahula has told us about the *bhikkhu* 'in educational, cultural, social, and political life' throughout the centuries it now seems, in retrospect, that sooner or later a tragedy of this sort was bound to take place. Indeed assassination, or attempted assassination, was part of the heritage of the *bhikkhu* in Ceylon. In a curious footnote, Rahula tells us that in the first century CE about sixty *bhikkhus* who had attempted to assassinate the king were executed by being thrown off a high rock (p. 161). When the *bhikkhus* again 'faced the public' and appeared on the political scene, at the time of the 1965 General Election, their forces were divided. Some supported the United National Party, which carried the day, and some the Sri Lanka Freedom Party which went back into opposition. 'Thus,' Rahula concludes with satisfaction, '*bhikkhus* on both sides were again in the forefront' (p. 109).

Again in the forefront! These words contain a clue to much that is muddled in Rahula's thinking, and much, indeed, that is ambiguous in his own position. To him it does not matter, apparently, if *bhikkhus* campaign for rival political parties – and from what I remember from newspaper reports at the time the campaigning was not conducted in a very gentlemanly fashion. What matters is that they should take a prominent part in whatever happens to be going on. In other words, the *bhikkhu* – or rather the 'political' *bhikkhu* – like his 'socially' oriented counterpart in the modern 'Christian' West is in fact *looking for a role*. Two thousand years ago he lost faith in Buddhism as a path of individual spiritual development and gave up being a monk in the original, more 'spiritual' sense of the term to become a member of the Buddhist clerisy. This gave him both influence and prestige and for some centuries he was satisfied. Now, however, the 'Buddhist' clerisy has been superseded by a secular, modern clerisy to whom he has forfeited much of his former position in society and with whom he is increasingly compelled to compete on equal terms. The results of this are to be seen in the second decade after independence. Losing all contact with Buddhism as a path of individual development, the 'political' *bhikkhus* lose their separate identity and become submerged in the mainstream of secular political life. Eventually, in the mass insurgency that followed the failure of the United Left Front to honour its election promises, 'hundreds of *bhikkhus* were arrested, humiliated, tortured, or killed' (p. 117).

Going through Ven. Rahula's celebrated essay (based, he tells us, on a speech given in Kandy in 1946), it should not be forgotten that his reading of the history of Buddhism in Ceylon is a somewhat selective one, and that even in Ceylon the heritage of the *bhikkhu* is not so exclusively political and cultural as he would have us believe. 'Rag-robed', forest-dwelling monks seem to have existed at all periods, and in recent times there has even been a revival of interest in meditation. Nevertheless, there is no doubt that the account that he gives is substantially correct, and that religio-nationalism is the dominant feature of the Buddhism of Ceylon. There is no doubt, either, that Rahula himself is deeply committed to this trend. Indeed, one of the most remarkable features of the whole book is his entire unconsciousness of the more spiritual, transcendental aspects of the Dharma. For Rahula these simply do not exist. He knows about them as a scholar, of course, but it is clear that for him they are only ideas, only words, and mean nothing to him personally. With the spiritual life a closed book, and religio-nationalism in a state of collapse, he is indeed in a strange position, being left with the purely scholarly work for which he is, of course, now best known.

In an interesting appendix, Rahula argues that patriotism is not necessarily the last refuge of a scoundrel, and that politics, understood as disinterested participation in public life, is not incompatible with the religious life – indeed, may even be an expression of it. Even though they may agree with this in principle, however, most Western Buddhists will put the book down with an overwhelming impression that the heritage of the *bhikkhu*, as described by Rahula, is a heritage of shame. With its record of almost continuous betrayal of the spirit of the Buddha's teaching it provides us with a saddening and sickening example of what happens when ultimate spiritual objectives are replaced by secondary cultural and political ones – when a universal religion is transmogrified into an ethnic one and the spiritual community becomes a cultural elite. It is therefore a heritage with which I for one want as little as possible to do. What our *real* heritage is, in both East and West, is for me sufficiently indicated by the Buddha, when he declared, 'O monks, ye are mine own true sons, born of my mouth, born of the Dharma. Therefore, O monks, be ye heirs of the Dharma, not heirs of worldly things'.[300]

THE *WHITE LOTUS SŪTRA* IN THE WEST

Tripitaka Master Tu Lun
The Essentials of the Dharma Blossom Sūtra, volume 1
Translated by Bhikṣu Heng Ch'ien, Buddhist Text Translation Society, San Francisco 1974

The *Saddharma Puṇḍarīka* or 'White Lotus-flower of the True Doctrine' *Sūtra* is one of the oldest and most important of the Mahāyāna *sūtras*. Cited by the Indian master Nāgārjuna, who flourished towards the end of the first century CE, as a literary composition it belongs essentially to the first century BCE and thus is contemporaneous with the Pāli Tipiṭaka, which was also committed to writing at about this time. The *sūtra* is important for a number of reasons. Doctrinally speaking, it is important mainly on account of its two fundamental teachings, both of which, after being distinctly enunciated for the first time in this *sūtra*, became an integral part of the basic structure of Mahāyāna thought and practice. According to the first of these teachings, there is ultimately only one *yāna*, the Buddhayāna, which leads to Buddhahood. The Buddha speaks of two *yānas*, or three *yānas*, simply as an expedient device in order to help those of lesser spiritual attainments who, for the time being at least, are aiming at inferior goals. Eventually, all beings will come into the One Way and all will attain Buddhahood. According to the second of these two teachings, the Buddha's span of life is infinite. He is in truth neither born nor passes away into final Nirvāṇa, both of these acts being only appearances, only expedient devices for the benefit of the less spiritually developed. The *sūtra* is also important for its literary form. Unlike some Mahāyāna *sūtras*, it has a definite structure, almost dramatic in character, which remains more or less intact despite the apparent incorporation, at a later date, of extraneous, or at least not very directly related, material. But the great glory of the *White Lotus Sūtra* are its parables. These include the parables of the Burning House, the Raincloud, the 'Prodigal Son', the Magic City, and many others. Closely connected with the *sūtra's* importance as literature is its importance for art. In China and Japan particularly, scenes from the *sūtra* – like that in which Śākyamuni, having opened the miraculously-appearing stupa and revealed the 'extinct' Buddha Prabhūtaratna, takes his seat on one half of the latter's lion-throne – were frequently depicted in both painting and sculpture, as a result of which the message of the *sūtra* became more and more widely known, even outside specifically Buddhist circles. Historically speaking, the *White Lotus Sūtra* is important because of the high esteem in which it was held by the eclectic and philosophical Tiantai school, which, with the possible exception of the Huayan or Avataṃsaka school, is probably the most representative and influential school of Chinese Buddhism. According to this school, the *White Lotus Sūtra* is the Buddha's ultimate teaching, delivered during the last phase of his earthly career, and it has been the subject of profound and systematic study by the third patriarch and virtual founder of the school, Zhiyi, as well as by numerous other masters of the Tiantai lineage.

In modern times, the *Saddharma Puṇḍarīka* was one of the first Buddhist scriptures to be translated into a European language. The Sanskrit text having been brought from Nepal earlier in the century, it was translated into French by Eugene Burnouf as early as 1852. Some years later, in 1884, came the first English translation. This appeared as Volume 21 in the famous 'Sacred Books of the East' series, edited by F. Max Müller, and was the work of the Dutch orientalist Hendrik Kern. Bearing in mind that in those days there was little sympathy in the world of oriental scholarship for Buddhism as a spiritual teaching, and that its technical vocabulary was hardly understood at all, Kern's translation is a good pioneer attempt, even though its pages are frequently marred by footnotes in which he tries to prove that the Buddha was a solar myth. Perhaps unfortunately, Kern's translation is even now the one in which the *White Lotus Sūtra* is most widely known in the English-speaking world, it having been reprinted several times. After Kern came W. E. Soothill, who in collaboration with the Japanese scholar Bunnō Katō produced an English version of the *sūtra* based on Kumārajīva's Chinese translation, made in 406 CE. Soothill's version, which was published in an abridged form in 1930 as *The Sūtra of the Lotus of the Wonderful Law*, is much easier reading than Kern's, being in fact altogether more poetic and inspiring. Though an ex-missionary, and a professor at Oxford, Soothill was highly appreciative of the religious and 'apocalyptic' elements in the *sūtra*, and did his best to do full justice to these, though the profounder, more 'philosophical' content of the *sūtra* tends to escape him. After Soothill little happened for forty years to make the *White Lotus Sūtra* more accessible to the English-speaking world. In 1962 there appeared Conze's translation of the Sanskrit text of chapter 5, 'On Plants', and that was all. English and American Buddhists and students of Buddhism, who meanwhile had greatly increased in number, especially since the end of the war, remained dependent for their knowledge of one of the greatest and most important of all Buddhist scriptures either on Kern's unattractive and sometimes misleading translation or on Soothill's more readable but incomplete version. Since the beginning of the present decade the situation has changed, and due to the efforts of Chinese, Japanese, and American Buddhists, it is now possible for us to have a better understanding of the *Sūtra* in the West. In 1970 the Kosei Publishing Company, Tokyo, brought out a revised version of the complete Soothill/Katō translation, while in 1975 this version reappeared under the Weatherill/Kosei imprint together with translations of 'The Sūtra of Innumerable Meanings', and 'The Sūtra of Meditation on the Bodhisattva Universal Virtue' as *The Threefold Lotus Sūtra*. Both volumes were meticulously edited and beautifully produced. A year earlier, in 1974, the Buddhist Text Translation Society, San Francisco, had brought out *The Essentials of the Dharma Blossom Sūtra*, volume 1, by the Chinese Tripiṭaka Master Tu Lun, and it is with this that we are now concerned.

According to the Short Biography of the Master which is appended to the volume, Ven. Tu Lun was born in north-eastern China in 1908. Becoming a *śrāmaṇera* or novice monk at the age of 19, after his mother's death, he lived in solitude for a while and practised meditation. After the Second World War he was ordained as a *bhikṣu* or full monk, and travelled south to pay his respects to the Venerable Master Xuyun, then

109 years old. In 1950 he left for Hong Kong, where for the benefit of refugee monks from the mainland he helped establish monasteries and temples throughout the island. In 1962 he arrived in San Francisco, and there from 1968 to 1970 delivered the lectures on which *The Essentials of the Dharma Blossom Sūtra* is based. This work, which has been edited and translated by the Master's American disciple Bhikṣu Heng Ch'ien (David Fox), will be complete in three volumes, the second and third of which are yet to come. The work is of special importance for three reasons: (1) It is the first English translation of the *White Lotus Sūtra* to be made entirely by believing and practising Buddhists working in the traditional manner; (2) It is the first English translation of the *sūtra* to be accompanied by a commentary in which the *sūtra* is explained according to the traditional interpretation of the text, in this case that of the Tiantai school; and (3) It is the first English translation of the *sūtra* to be made as a result of close collaboration between Eastern and Western Buddhists, especially Tripiṭaka Master Tu Lun and his disciple Bhikṣu Heng Ch'ien.

The present volume consists of the first two chapters of the *sūtra*, which contains in all twenty-seven or twenty-eight chapters, together with the Master's commentary on each chapter in turn. The text of the *sūtra* has been translated from Kumārajīva's Chinese version, which is the one generally used in China, and for the convenience of the reader each chapter is printed twice, first in its entirety before the commentary, and again in sections in the body of the commentary. Text and commentary are preceded by a lengthy introduction, as well as by a biography of Kumārajīva. The introduction, which serves to introduce the commentary to the entire *sūtra*, takes the form of an exposition of the Tiantai school's fivefold discussion of the recondite principles of the *sūtra*, viz. explanation of the title, clarification of the substance, elucidation of the doctrine, discussion of the function, and determination of the teaching. This part of the work gives us a better insight into the teachings of the Tiantai school, and its approach to the *White Lotus Sūtra*, than anything that has yet appeared in English. One stands amazed at the profundity of thought of Zhiyi and the other Tiantai masters, and feels deeply grateful to Ven. Tu Lun and Bhikṣu Heng Ch'ien for making this thought accessible to us. The commentary itself follows the detailed and highly analytical outline of the *sūtra* made by the Ming dynasty Dharma master Ouyi Zhixu. Like the introduction, the commentary is rich and varied in content, giving us not only treasures of Tiantai thought but expositions of standard Buddhist teachings, biographies of eminent disciples of the Buddha, pithy sayings, poems, anecdotes from the Master's own experience, and even specimens of Chinese Buddhist folklore. Particularly noteworthy are the Master's exposition of the portent of shaking the earth (pp. 199–201), his discussion of the eight *vimokṣas* or 'liberations', here called the eight renunciations (pp. 337–40), as well as the whole of the introduction to chapter 1, 'Expedient Devices', in which the Master explains the interdependency of the provisional and actual teachings and points out how, in the context of this chapter, 'expedient device' has the specific meaning of opening up the provisional teaching to reveal the actual. On a somewhat different level, there is an interesting reference to the Buddha's age on leaving home and on gaining Enlightenment. Following a well-known Pāli verse, in which the Buddha himself is represented as speaking, one usually says that the Buddha left home at the age of 29 and gained Enlightenment six years later at the age of 35. Ven. Tu Lun, however, presumably following ancient Indian traditions translated from Sanskrit into Chinese, says of the Buddha, 'He left the palace and all its pleasures at the age of nineteen to cultivate the Way and realized Buddhahood at the age of thirty' (p. 108). This would seem to agree with texts like the *Pabbajjā Sutta* of the *Sutta-Nipāta*, one of the more ancient 'books' of the Pāli canon, which give the definite impression that the future Buddha must have left home at a considerably earlier age than 29. There is also the curious story of the delayed birth of the Buddha's son Rāhula. Again presumably following ancient Indian tradition, Ven. Tu Lun tells us that on his father's demanding a grandson from him before he would permit him to leave the home-life, 'Śākyamuni Buddha merely pointed a finger at the belly of his wife, Yaśodharā, and told her that in six years time she would bear a son' (p. 154). The master goes on to remark that this may seem rather incredible, but that in the Buddhadharma there are a great many mysteries more profound. No doubt there are, but is it not possible that the story of Rāhula's delayed birth arose in order to reconcile the fact that he had been born after the Buddha's departure from home with the 'fact' that, according to the accepted account, the Buddha's departure had taken place some years later than it actually had done? The whole question awaits further investigation, and the key to its solution may well be found in the traditions on which Ven. Tu Lun has drawn. Meanwhile, we had best keep an open mind on the subject, and perhaps accustom ourselves to the idea of a quite youthful Buddha.

Though there is much else in this invaluable work that invites comment, in a short review it is hardly possible to do justice to the wealth of material that Ven. Tu Lun and Bhikṣu Heng Ch'ien have placed at our disposal. Enough has been said, I hope, to show that the publication of *The Essentials of the Dharma Blossom Sūtra* marks the beginning of a new era in the study and appreciation of this *Sūtra* in the West. Even when the two remaining volumes have been brought out, however, much will still remain to be done. The *White Lotus Sūtra* will be fully known and appreciated in the West only when four conditions have been fulfilled: (1) There must be a new English translation of the Sanskrit text of the *Sūtra*. This should be both accurate and inspiring, doing full justice to the doctrinal terminology and poetic imagery alike. Dr Conze's rendering of chapter 5, 'On Plants', is a step in the right direction, and it is to be hoped that either Dr Conze himself or a scholar of equal ability will soon provide us with a comparable version of the remainder of the *Sūtra*. Bhikṣu Heng Ch'ien's version of the *gātha* (verse) portion of the *Sūtra* is in the same short, breathless lines as Soothill's, only more regularly stressed, and though on the whole admirably clear, direct, and vigorous its language is not only less polished than Soothill's but even, at times, quite rough and clumsy. (2) We must have at our disposal all the traditional interpretations of the *White Lotus Sūtra*. Though the Indian master Vasubandhu is said to have written a commentary on the *Sūtra*, this appears to have been lost, and we therefore have to rely mainly on the expositions of Chinese and Japanese masters, especially those of the Tiantai School. (3) The *Sūtra* must be studied directly, in the light of what we know about the historical development of Buddhism, as well as studied in the light of traditional expositions, and the real nature of its teaching ascertained. It will also be necessary to examine the relation between that teaching and (a) the total Buddhist tradition, and (b) Western thought. Ven. Tu Lun's approach to the *Sūtra* is 'fundamentalist', but for the Western Buddhist, aware as he usually is that the tradition represented by Ven. Tu Lun is not the only one in the Buddhist world, such an attitude is not possible – or possible only at the sacrifice of some of the very qualities on which the pursuit of the spiritual life itself depends. But not to be fundamentalist is not to be untraditional, much less still un-Buddhistic. We have to adopt towards the vast mass of material that has poured into the West from all over the Buddhist world the same approach that Zhiyi, in the fifth century CE, adopted towards the material that had flooded into China from India and Central Asia. What we need is a new, updated Tiantai school! (4) The teaching of the *Sūtra* must be related to the concrete spiritual needs of Western Buddhists. However sublime a teaching may be, it is virtually meaningless unless it is able to bring about a radical transformation in the lives of individual human beings.

These four conditions will probably not be fulfilled for some time to come. Meanwhile, in *The Essentials of the Dharma Blossom Sūtra* we have a major contribution to the fulfilment of at least the second of them, and the appearance of the second and third volumes of the work will therefore be eagerly awaited.

ZEN PAST AND PRESENT

The Blue Cliff Record, volume 1
Translated from the Chinese *Pi Yen Lu* by Thomas and J. C. Cleary. Foreword by Taizan Maezumi Roshi Shambhala Publications, Boulder & London 1977

Irmgard Schloegl
The Zen Way
Sheldon, London 1977

Thomas Merton on Zen
Sheldon, London 1976

Bhagwan Shree Rajneesh
No Water No Moon: Reflections on Zen
Sheldon, London 1977

Trevor Leggett
The Tiger's Cave: Translations of Japanese Zen Texts
Routledge & Kegan Paul, London & Henley 1977

According to tradition, Zen began when the Buddha held up a golden flower in the midst of the assembly. No one understood the meaning of his action except Mahākāśyapa, who smiled. The Buddha thereupon declared, 'This is the profound and mysterious principle of Enlightenment, which I now transmit to you, O Mahākāśyapa!' In this way the Dharma was transmitted to Mahākāśyapa, who thereupon became the first Zen patriarch. It was transmitted not through the medium of words, nor even through the medium of thoughts, but directly, from mind to mind, or from heart to heart, by a process of what may be called transcendental telepathy. Emphasizing this aspect of Zen, a traditional Chinese verse speaks of it as 'A special transmission outside the scriptures; No dependence on words and letters'. Nonetheless, despite its claim to be a 'wordless', purely spiritual transmission of the Buddha's 'teaching', and its apparent aversion to scriptural studies, in the course of more than a thousand years of recognizable historical existence the Zen school produced an enormous quantity of literature, much of it of great literary and spiritual significance, and including works which came to be regarded as being in effect scriptures in their own right. This literature was produced, of course, mainly in Chinese and Japanese. In recent decades a small portion of it has been translated into various European languages, and in this way has come to influence the spiritual lives of a number of people in the West. Besides such translations of the Zen classics, as they may be called, books 'about' Zen have been written by Buddhists and non-Buddhists, easterners and westerners, of widely varying degrees of authority and experience. A fairly representative batch of such publications is now before us. It might be useful to look first at the translation of a Zen classic of exceptional importance and then, using this as a sort of touchstone, at the modern works.

The Zen classic in question is the *Biyan Lu* or *Blue Cliff Record*, an eleventh-century Chinese compilation in one hundred chapters, the first thirty-five of which have now been translated by two American scholars. To review a work of this kind is almost as much out of the question as reviewing a *sūtra*. One could, of course, shout 'Mu!' or threaten the translators and their publishers with thirty blows. Or one could even leave these columns blank by way of registering one's protest against being expected to 'add flowers to brocade' in this way. But much as connoisseurs of Zen might relish such behaviour, it would not be of much help to the ordinary reader. Let us therefore approach the work by way of its literary structure. Essentially it is a collection of one hundred anecdotes of the sayings and doings of the Chinese Chan masters and disciples of the eighth to the tenth centuries CE, a period which may be regarded as the Golden Age of Chan. These anecdotes were compiled from traditional sources by the Chan master Xuedou Chongxian (980–1052 CE), who also composed a poem on each anecdote. About sixty years after Xuedou's death another Chan master, Yuanwu Keqin (1063–1135 CE) gave a series of talks elucidating the anecdotes and the poems. Each chapter of *The Blue Cliff Record* (so called from the name of the temple where Yuanwu gave his talks) therefore consists of six parts: (1) Yuanwu's introduction (missing in some cases); (2) the anecdote, taken from Chan tradition or Buddhist scripture; (3) remarks by Yuanwu on certain points in the anecdote; (4) commentary on the anecdote by Yuanwu; (5) the poem by Xuedou, interspersed with remarks by Yuanwu, and (6) commentary by Yuanwu on the poem and its relation to the anecdote.

The nucleus of each chapter is thus the anecdote, to which poem, remark, and commentary were gradually added in a manner resembling the process of accretion that forms a pearl, and it is worth enquiring why this should be so. As noted already, Zen claims to be 'A special transmission outside the scriptures'. In its own terminology, it was the 'school of the patriarchs', that is to say, the school of the living exemplars of Enlightenment, as distinct from the Tiantai and Huayan schools, for example, which were 'doctrinal schools', or schools specializing in the systematic study of a certain *sūtra* or group of *sūtras*. This being so, it was hardly possible for the Zen masters to base their teaching on systematic expositions of the scriptures. They therefore developed the practice of taking as their starting point something that an earlier Zen master (or other ancient Buddhist worthy) had said or done. Since the master was Enlightened, his words or actions would be an expression of the Enlightenment-experience, and therefore able to give the Zen disciple some clue as to what it was all about. They would serve as a spiritual precedent, as it were, by which the validity of his own attainment could be tested. In this way originated the *gong an* (Chinese) or *kōan* (Japanese), as the anecdotes which were used in this way came to be called. Literally the term *kung an* means a 'public case' or 'public record', that is to say, a legal case which can be cited as a precedent for the settlement of new cases. *The Blue Cliff Record* is therefore essentially a collection of koans, complete with examples of the way in which these were used by, and the kind of effect they had on, subsequent generations of masters and disciples of the most spiritually vital and creative period in Chan history – which is to say, one of the most spiritually vital and creative periods in the entire history of Buddhism. The purpose of the koans was to function as catalysts of Enlightenment. As Yuanwu says, 'Whenever the Ancients handed down a word or half a phrase, it was like sparks struck from flint, like a flash of lightning, directly opening up a single straight path' (p. 47).

The rather complex literary structure of the *Biyan Lu* made possible the creation of a work of extraordinary richness, variety, and beauty, and in his foreword to the translation Taizan Maezumi Roshi rightly describes it as 'one of the most wonderful dharma-treasures of the world's Eastern heritage' (p. ix). Its hundred 'cases' are, he tells us, equivalent to all the *dharmas* preached by Śākyamuni Buddha, and each 'case' contains innumerable *dharmas*. The work is, in fact, a whole world in itself – a world in which, or in even a corner of which, one could well spend one's whole life and hardly notice that the time had passed. In this world – which is the world of Tang and Song dynasty China and yet, at the same time, our own world – we encounter all sorts of wonderful and extraordinary figures, some of whom are already known to Western students of Zen. Apart from semi-legendary figures like Bodhidharma, there is Huangbo, who was seven feet tall, had a lump in his forehead like a round pearl, and who 'understood Chan by nature'; Baizhang, who compiled the so-called 'pure standards' for Zen monasteries, and who first thundered in the scandalized ears of an eleemosynary generation, 'A day of no working is a day of no eating'; the nun Iron Grindstone Liu, who had studied for a long time, and whose active edge was 'sharp and dangerous'; and Yunmen, to whose lineage belonged both Xuedou and Yuanwu. Yunmen liked to teach three word Chan. He also taught one word Chan. In ordinary situations, even, he would revile people. 'When he uttered a phrase it was like an iron spike' (p. 39). Xianglin Chengyuan, one of the 'Four Sages', served as Yunmen's attendant for eighteen years. Whenever Yunmen dealt with him, he would just call out, 'Attendant Yuan!' Xianglin would answer 'Yes?' Yunmen would say, 'What is it?' It went on like this for eighteen years, when one day Xianglin finally awakened. We also meet Master Juzhi, who whenever anything was asked would just raise one finger; Mazu, famous for polishing a rock in order to make it into a mirror; and Zhaozhou, who awakened to the way when he was nearly 60, settled down at a temple at 80, and taught until his death at 120. He was also known for his asceticism. 'When one leg of his rope chair broke, he tied on a leftover piece of firewood with rope to support it. There were repeated requests to make a new leg for it, but the master would not allow it' (p. 228). We hear, too, Dongshan's celebrated 'three pounds of hemp', see the hermit of Lotus Flower Peak holding up his staff, and listen to the dialogue between Mañjuśrī and Wuzhuo.

The world of *The Blue Cliff Record* is in fact a world in which we encounter no one except masters and disciples, all of whom are concerned with nothing except Enlightenment. 'When the ancients travelled on foot to visit the monasteries everywhere', says Yuanwu, 'they only had this matter on their minds; they wanted to discern whether the old teacher on the carved wooden seat possessed eyes or did not possess eyes' (p. 195). For 'patch-robed monks' of this kind, who spent the greater part of their lives trudging the roads of China or meditating on remote mountain peaks, Zen was not a matter of 'the witty word among the teacups' (as a correspondent once described the London based Zen of the 1950s) but literally a matter of life and death. Yunmen went to see Muzhou.

> As soon as he opened the door a little, [Yunmen] immediately bounded in; Mu Chou [Muzhou] held him fast and said, 'Speak! Speak!' Yun Men hesitated, and was pushed out; he still had one foot inside when Mu Chou slammed the door, breaking Yun Men's leg. As Yun Men cried out in pain, he was suddenly greatly enlightened. (pp. 37–8)

In a word, the world of *The Blue Cliff Record* is a world in which *Buddhism matters* – is the only thing that matters – and in which people are prepared to go to any lengths in order to attain – and transmit – 'the profound and mysterious principle of Enlightenment'.

In introducing us to this world, so strange and yet so familiar, the translators of the *Biyan Lu* have widened our spiritual horizons immeasurably, and given us access to an inexhaustible treasure. As they state in their introduction, 'The publication of *The Blue Cliff Record* in English will help open new vistas in the study of Buddhism in the West' – even though it is true that this is, in their own modest words, 'only part of a larger task' (p. xxiii). What effect these new vistas will have on the spiritual lives of American and English Buddhists, and on the course of Western Buddhism, it is impossible to predict. There is little doubt, however, that this classic of Zen literature will not be used in quite the same way as in ancient China or modern Japan, and that its influence will not be confined to 'official' Zen circles. There is also little doubt that, when the two remaining volumes are published, this version of *The Blue Cliff Record* will take its place with Rhys Davids's *Dialogues of the Buddha* and Conze's *Perfection of Wisdom* as a major contribution to our knowledge of the primary sources of Buddhist tradition.

From the Zen classic of the eleventh century CE to the modern works 'about' Zen is nearly a thousand years, and it would not be strange if something of the spirit of Zen had evaporated in the interim. The author of *The Zen Way*, Irmgard Schloegl, has at least spent twelve years in Japan undergoing traditional Zen training, and her chapter on 'Training in a Japanese Zen Monastery', a fascinating account of the whole cycle of the monastic year, will certainly dispel a few illusions. Though life in a Zen monastery is hard, and discipline strict, Dr Schloegl is at pains to show that the human element is not lacking, and that even head monks have hearts of gold. Valuable as this chapter is, however, the real substance of the book is to be found in the short introduction and the chapters entitled 'Fundamentals' and 'Application'. For Dr Schloegl, the Zen way is above all a way of training that has as its object the genuine transformation – not merely the sublimation – of primitive emotional energy. It is this energy which is traditionally spoken of as the 'heart' (not 'mind', she insists) of man, and which is symbolized by the 'splendid, tremendously strong, powerful, wild, and quite ungovernable bull' of the well-known bull-herding pictures. In dealing with the practical side of the transformation process, clearly her central concern, Dr Schloegl rightly emphasizes that primitive emotions should be neither repressed nor expressed, and well shows how the disciplined life of the Zen monastery helps the monk to achieve the middle way in this respect. She is also alive to the danger of what she terms 'seizure', which occurs when a man is carried away by untransformed emotional energy, as well as to the related danger of regression, when the unleashed energy turns destructive. In dealing with the theoretical implications of the transformation process she is less reliable. Her grasp of Buddhist doctrine is, in fact, at times distinctly shaky. Yet even though her active edge may not be as sharp and dangerous as Iron Grindstone Liu's it is certainly formidable enough to deal with anything she is likely to find in the neighbourhood of Eccleston Square.

I have only one real criticism. In the absence of temples and training monasteries Dr Schloegl suggests that we in the West should take our ordinary daily life (i.e. job, housework) as our training discipline. This is, of course, something that could well be done – indeed, in principle should be done. In making the suggestion, however, Dr Schloegl appears to overlook two things: (1) the extent to which modern economic life violates the principles of right livelihood; and (2) the possibility of our going away 'on retreat' from time to time and benefiting from the positively structured routine of a quasi-monastic environment *for a limited period* – as frequently happens in the FWBO. If the routine of ordinary life was sufficient as a training discipline the Buddha would not have founded a monastic order, the masters and disciples of *The Blue Cliff Record* would not have all been monks, and there would have been no Zen monastery for Dr Schloegl herself to stay at when she went to Japan. 'Daily Life Practice' is not the same thing as the acceptance of the status quo.

Thomas Merton was a Roman Catholic monk of the Cistercian Order of Strict Observance (the Trappists) who wrote a great deal about Eastern mysticism, especially Zen. The essays collected in *Thomas Merton on Zen* are a selection from what the publishers call his 'prodigious output'. Some are chapters taken from books which he himself published as such, while others are prefaces to books by other people. In view of the miscellaneous nature of its origin, it would not be fair to review the present collection as though it was a book in the strict sense of the term. Nevertheless it does have a certain unity which allows us to treat it in this way to some extent. This unity is not due to the fact that all the essays are about Zen, or have some bearing on it, nor even to the fact that the author always approaches his subject from the same point of view. It stems, rather, from the nature of the author's own mental makeup as revealed in all these pieces. Thomas Merton is clearly a well read, well informed man of great mental agility and verbal fluency who is ready to define Zen – or anything else – at the drop of a biretta. On page 4 he tells us that 'It is a product of the combination of Mahāyāna Buddhism with Chinese Taoism which was later transported to Japan and further refined there'. Though what may be called the Mrs Beeton theory of the origin of Zen[301] has enjoyed the support of people who should have known better, even a cursory glance at the first volume of *The Blue Cliff Record* will show us no sign of Mahāyāna Buddhism in process of being 'combined' with Taoism in this way. One will be lucky if one finds very much 'Mahāyāna Buddhism'. All one finds is people concerned, either as masters or disciples, with 'this matter'. On page 52 Father Merton returns to the attack. 'Zen is, in fact,' he assures us, 'an Asian form of religious existentialism'. He is equally ready to define – and compare – Zen enlightenment and Rilke's 'nowhere without no'.

> Zen enlightenment is an insight into being in all its existential reality and actualization. It is a fully alert and superconscious act of being which transcends time and space. Such is the attainment of the 'Buddha mind' or 'Buddhahood'. (Compare the Christian expressions 'having the mind of Christ', [1 Corinthians 2:16] being 'of one spirit with Christ', 'He who is united to the Lord is one spirit', [1 Corinthians 6:17] though the Buddhist idea [sic] takes no account of any supernatural order in the Thomist sense.) (p. 6)
>
> That 'Nowhere without no' (a mysterious expression) is the void of *śūnyatā* [Thanks for telling us!] and the emptiness of Eckhart's 'Ground' or, perhaps more properly, Boehme's 'Un-ground' (Ungrund). 'God' says Boehme, 'is called the seeing and finding of the Nothing. And it is therefore called a Nothing (though it is God Himself) because it is inconceivable and inexpressible.' This is more theological than Rilke.... (p. 78)

etc., etc., blah, blah, blah. Thomas Merton is quite capable of going on like this for pages together. In a famous phrase, he is 'intoxicated with the exuberance of his own verbosity'.[302] Or as Yuanwu puts it, 'Because later students become attached to their words and more and more give rise to intellectual interpretations, therefore they do not see the Ancients' message.' (*The Blue Cliff Record*, p. 57)

This is not to say that there are not good things to be found in these essays. Despite his weakness for 'intellectual interpretations', Father Merton's facility of expression at times enables him to hit the nail firmly and squarely on the head. Speaking of the results of koan study and the identity of 'individuality' and 'desire', for instance, he says, 'It is not as if the "individual" were a hard, substantial, ontological core from which desires proceed, but rather that desires themselves form a kind of knot of psychic energies which seek to remain firmly tied as the autonomous "self"' (p. 74). This could hardly be better put. Nonetheless, the overall impression remains that in these essays Thomas Merton is preoccupied not with Zen so much as with what others have thought and said about Zen. This is not because he was never in Japan. It is not even because he never actually practised Zen Buddhism. Rather, it is because he was so highly skilled in the manipulation of words and concepts, and became so deeply absorbed in the exercise of that skill, that he was unable to distinguish words and concepts from realities, and when he was playing elaborate games with the one thought he was dealing meaningfully with the other. It is surprising, therefore, to find Irmgard Schloegl, in her introduction to the volume, saying of Father Merton's comments that they 'belong to the best that a westerner has produced' (p. x). This could, of course, be taken as an example of damning with faint praise, especially when one thinks of the worst that westerners have done in this line. But Dr Schloegl's judgement appears to be made in good faith. Being herself a practical, down-to-earth kind of person she is, I suspect, over-impressed by the agility with which Father Merton performs on the intellectual tightrope and, with true grandmotherly kindness, concludes that he must have a pair of spiritual wings somewhere that prevent him from falling.

After going through *No Water No Moon* one might be tempted to conclude that hot air rather than wings was the sustaining factor. Whether or not Shree Rajneesh ('Bhagwan' to you!) is 'one of the most highly regarded and admired teachers in India' (back cover blurb) he certainly does have what seems to be increasingly regarded as one of the most indispensable qualifications of a teacher nowadays – the gift of the spiritual gab. Thomas Merton's output of words may have been prodigious but Shree Rajneesh's is spectacular. This is because instead of having the trouble of writing it all out he just talks. In *No Water No Moon* he talks about Zen. Or rather, he talks at length about ten traditional Zen stories, and two admiring female disciples have compiled and edited his comments for our benefit. Let me say at once that Shree Rajneesh talks brilliantly and amusingly – for a few chapters. He also talks excellent sense – on half a dozen pages. Unfortunately, he has the same weakness for intellectual interpretations as Thomas Merton, and really believes that he has explained exactly what each story means. Talking about 'Gutei's Finger', he says, 'Oneness is needed – when the other is not a constant fight. This is why Gutei used to raise one finger whenever he was explaining Zen. He was saying, "Be one! – and all your problems will be solved"' (p. 113). It is interesting to compare this 'explanation' with Yuanwu's commentary on 'Juzhi's One Finger Chan' in *The Blue Cliff Record*, where the koan on which the story is based originally appeared. 'If you understand at the finger, then you turn your back on Chu Ti [Juzhi]; if you don't go to the finger to understand, then it's like cast iron. Whether you understand or not, Chu Ti still goes on this way; whether you're high or low, he still goes on this way; whether you're right or wrong, he still goes on this way' (*The Blue Cliff Record*, pp. 123–4). Shree Rajneesh certainly understands a lot about Zen. In the end we become tired of the constant stream of dogmatic assertions, misleading half truths, and sweeping generalizations – not to mention undigested gobbets of Shree Rajneesh's reading, from the Bible to the *Reader's Digest*, which are also borne along on the stream. 'Monks are repressed people' (p. 18), 'Rituals are repeated by idiots' (p. 21), 'All temples are inventions of the clever people to exploit the stupid' (p. 4), and 'Enlightened persons are always inconsistent' (p. 143), are good examples of some of his wilder generalizations, and tell us, perhaps, more about himself than about Zen.

Like some other modern teachers, Shree Rajneesh is concerned to invoke the authority of the Buddha, Jesus, etc. for some of his own assertions, and if a suitable quotation is not available he does not hesitate to manufacture one. Thus we learn that 'Buddha never answered questions' (p. 134) and 'Buddha used to say, "Don't ask if you want to be answered. When you don't ask, I will answer. If you ask, the door is closed"' (p. 134). Also, 'Buddha used to insist with newcomers: "For one year remain with me without asking anything. If you ask, you cannot be allowed to live with me, you will have to move. For one year simply be silent"' (p. 134). The purpose of these fabrications – not to use a stronger term – seems to be to make out Bhagavan Buddha to have been very much like 'Bhagwan' Rajneesh, for then 'Bhagwan' Rajneesh would be very much like Bhagavan Buddha. At one point in the talks – given at his ashram in the fashionable quarter of Poona – Shree Rajneesh even says, 'A Buddha comes – I am here,' (p. 128) as though the two were identical. He would do well to take to heart his own excellent advice: 'It is good to sit in a Buddha posture; but remember you are not Buddha' (p. 21).

The back cover blurb tells us, 'This is not the Zen that has been intellectually adopted in the West; it is the Zen of the heart.' I cannot agree. Whatever the Zen that has been adopted in the West may or may not be, there is little doubt that the Zen that has been adopted in these talks resembles mouth Zen rather than heart Zen. Entertaining and instructive though they often are, Shree Rajneesh's thinking is at times so muddled that they will increase rather than decrease the confusion that surrounds the word Zen, and thus in all likelihood do more harm than good. At a time when it has become more necessary than ever to clarify the fundamentals of the spiritual life this is a pity.

The first edition of *The Tiger's Cave* appeared in 1964. Besides talks on the *Heart Sūtra* by Abbot Obora of the Sōtō Zen sect (contemporary), these translations of Japanese Zen texts include *Yasenkanna*, an autobiographical narrative by Zen master Hakuin (eighteenth century), and various shorter pieces. In the past thirteen years I have frequently recommended this book, as well as its predecessor *A First Zen Reader*, as one of the very few really good books on Zen, and although many other works on the subject have appeared since it was originally published I find, on reading it again in this new edition, no reason to revise that judgement.

THE WISDOM OF THE ZEN MASTERS

The Wisdom of the Zen Masters
Translated by Irmgard Schloegl, Foreword by Christmas Humphreys
Sheldon Press, London 1975

In the course of the last two or three decades there have been published, in English and other European languages, an enormous number of books on Buddhism, some of them translations of ancient Buddhist texts, others original works, both scholarly and popular, by writers with varying degrees of understanding of the true nature of the Dharma. So great has been the output, indeed, that the Western student is often embarrassed by the riches now placed at his disposal. For such a one, the safest course is for him to confine himself to authentic material which nourishes his own spiritual life and to study that material intensively with a spiritual teacher or, should this be impossible, in the company of like-minded fellow students.

Of the various special forms of Buddhism, few have attracted more attention in recent years than Chan or Zen, and though the tide of its popularity now seems to have turned, books on the subject continue to appear. One of the latest of these is *The Wisdom of the Zen Masters*, a collection of stories and sayings with an introduction by the translator, an Austrian Buddhist who spent twelve years in Japan undergoing traditional Zen training, and a foreword by that veteran popularizer of literature on Zen Buddhism, Christmas Humphreys. Among the stories and sayings included are both old favourites like the one about the monk who carried a pretty girl across the river and then put her down on the other side, while his more strait-laced companion continued to carry her in his mind; and ones which to me at least are quite new, like Master Rinzai's 'Do not offer your poem to a man who is not a poet' (p. 55). Though the stories and sayings themselves cover only forty-five pages, Dr Schloegl's harvest is a rich one, and Western Buddhists will find in it much that is both inspiring and instructive, while her introductory essay provides the necessary minimum of background information, as well as several useful reminders, such as that 'Zen is firmly based on the fundamental Buddhist teachings' (p. 3) and that 'There is no specific "body of teaching" in Zen' (p. 38), and some down-to-earth practical advice. Sticklers for precision of doctrinal statement might however question her seeming identification of the Buddha Nature, or Heart Ground, or Heart, with the 'divinity immanent in creation' of 'Eastern religions' (p. 5).

Quite a number of the stories and sayings, including some of the very best in the collection – such as the three belittling supernatural powers ('supernormal' would have been a better rendering) (pp. 42–3), and my own favourites, the one about the game of chess (p. 61) and the one about Master Kendo, who secretly cooked and ate the scraps which the young monks had wasted (p. 66), are Buddhist rather than specifically Zen, and illustrate the wisdom not so much of Zen masters as such as of all truly wise and compassionate Buddhists. Indeed, Master Kyogen's statement, 'The painted picture of a dumpling does not take one's hunger away' (p. 59) in one form or another is the common property not only of all forms of Buddhism but of all the spiritual traditions of the world. I for one cannot help thinking that, so far as actual practice and experience of the Dharma is concerned at least, it would be better if we spoke in terms of Buddhism rather than in terms of Zen – or, in fact, in terms of any particular school of Buddhism at all.

At the same time, Dr Schloegl's little collection does contain a few anecdotes of the kind which, rightly or wrongly, have come to regarded in the West as typically 'Zen' or 'Zennish' – fashionable usages which the author herself deplores (p. 3). Master Takuan, in reply to a question, says that he does not recite the Amida Buddha invocation for fear it might sully his mouth (p. 49). Master Chokei, asked what is meant by the True Dharma Eye, curtly replies 'Don't just sling dirt about' (p. 59).

Master Tanka, to the horror of the temple incumbent, burns a wooden statue of the Buddha for fuel (p. 77). The trouble with anecdotes of this type, of which Dr D. T. Suzuki has given us so many, is that the ordinary Western reader, on the basis of a purely mental understanding of what the master says or does, tends to identify himself with the Enlightened master of the anecdote rather than with the unenlightened disciple, which encourages the development of a quite unjustified sense of spiritual superiority. Identifying themselves with 'the master' in this way, some such people have even been known to produce, out of their purely mental understanding, lengthy expositions of Zen, when what they ought to have done was to learn to recite the Amida Buddha invocation, or to cultivate the desire to know what was meant by the True Dharma Eye or the kind of devotion that could be shocked by the destruction of a sacred image. Like their counterparts in the Tibetan tradition, the Zen stories and sayings are essentially *precepts*, that is to say, they are personal teachings directly relating to the individual spiritual needs of the disciple concerned, and should not be read out of context, or taken as applying to people whose spiritual needs may, indeed, be the exact opposite of those of the disciples for whom the teachings were originally meant. Unless this is borne in mind, armchair followers of 'Zen' in the West will continue to regard themselves as having transcended the traditional Buddhist virtues when they have, in fact, yet to develop them. I hope that, despite its small size, Dr Schloegl's attractively produced volume will on the whole tend to discourage aberrations of this kind and help promote the actual practice of the Dharma.

THE GATELESS GATE

The Gateless Gate
Newly translated with commentary by Zen master Koun Yamada
Center Publications, Los Angeles 1979

'We use words to get free from words until we reach the pure wordless Essence.'[303] This quotation from *The Awakening of Faith in the Mahāyāna* sums up the position of Buddhism with regard to the true function of the various conceptual-cum-verbal formulations which make up what, in the West, is usually referred to as Buddhist philosophy. Far from being an attempt to interrogate the nature of reality by rational means, 'Buddhist philosophy' is a communication by such means of a reality already experienced, i.e. it is a communication from the Enlightened to the unenlightened mind – a communication that makes use of conceptual symbols. In the course of time, however, the conceptual-cum-verbal formulations that made up Buddhist philosophy became so elaborate that their true function was for all practical purposes lost sight of, with the result that in at least some Buddhist circles the study of Buddhist philosophy became, in effect, an end in itself. Thus conceptual symbols came to stand *between* the unenlightened mind and reality. Intellectual understanding of the conceptual-cum-verbal formulations by means of which the Enlightened mind communicated its experience of reality was mistaken for the experience – even for the reality – itself. A way had therefore to be found of bypassing conceptual symbols – of bypassing the intellect – and communicating the nature of experienced reality by non-conceptual means.

The Chan School of China did this mainly with the help of the *gong-an* (Japanese *kōan*). A *gong-an* (literally, 'public document') is the record of a brief encounter between master and disciple, the master's response to the disciple's question being a word or phrase – even an action – that points to ultimate reality without being susceptible to logical interpretation. Collections of koans (the Japanese form has now been naturalized in English, and is therefore to be preferred) were made from the tenth century CE onwards, with verses and comments being added to each koan. Probably the best known and most influential collections are the *Biyan Lu* or 'Blue Cliff Record' and the *Mumonkan*, variously translated as 'Gateless Gate' or 'Gateless Barrier'. The latter was compiled and arranged by the thirteenth-century Chan master Wumen (Japanese: Mumon), and consists of forty-eight koans, together with Wumen's own comments and verses, nearly all of which are quite short. The collection opens with the most famous of all koans, Jōshū's 'Mu!' Jōshū (Chinese: Zhaozhou), the ninth-century Chan master, was once asked by a monk, 'Has a dog Buddha nature?' The master replied 'Mu!' ('No' or 'Not'). Practitioners of Chan/Zen in China, Japan and, more recently, the West, have been cudgelling their brains about the 'meaning' of this enigmatic reply ever since. Apart from the Buddha himself, Maitreya, Ānanda, Kāśyapa, Bodhidharma, and the Sixth Patriarch (Huineng), the worthies who appear in the koans are all enlightened Chan masters of the period from the eighth to the twelfth centuries CE, with most of them being found nearer the beginning than the end of the period. This period, sometimes called the golden age of Chan, was the era of the 'latter patriarchs' and their successors, and coincided with the early Tang dynasty, the golden age of Chinese civilization.

As one of the outstanding products of the richest and most creative periods of Chinese Chan, the *Mumonkan* played an important part in the development of Japanese Zen, being commented on by an uninterrupted series of Zen masters down to the present day. *Gateless Gate* is a new translation of this basic koan collection by Yamada Roshi, a contemporary Japanese Zen master (at least three translations have already appeared in English), together with a collection of *teisho*, or 'commentaries' on the koans, delivered by him to Western practitioners of Zen. The work is not for casual reading. In a sense, it is not for reading at all, and one cannot but admire the attitude of the twelfth century Chan master who, on finding that Chan students had become infatuated with *The Blue Cliff Record*, destroyed the wood blocks of the book and dealt with the koans in a different way. Koans in fact are not material for a good quiet read so much as instruments of meditation – though one does not meditate on them in order to discover their 'meaning'. In other words, their true significance and value emerges only within the context of intensive spiritual practice. The same holds good of the *teisho*, which are not commentaries in the intellectual sense but 'encouragement talks' addressed to actual practitioners of Zen, usually on the occasion of an intensive meditation retreat. Though the work is not for casual reading, studies in a receptive spirit of *Gateless Gate* may however act as a catalyst of spiritual development, and it is for this reason, no doubt, that the book has been made available. Even the casual reader may well be caught unawares! The usefulness of the work is enhanced by a very informative introduction by Thomas Cleary, one of the translators of *The Blue Cliff Record*, as well as by Taizan Maezumi Roshi's foreword, in which we are given very clear explanations of both the koan and the *teisho* as 'basic instructional tools used in traditional Zen training'.

One feels much less happy with the preface by Rev. H. M. Enomiya-Lassalle, S. J., which for some reason or other it has been thought necessary to add to all the other preliminary matter. It contains some very questionable statements. According to this Jesuit admirer of Zen, 'Christians have found and are continuing to find that they can attempt yoga and Zen without jeopardizing their own religion' (p. xiii). When the practice of Zen jeopardizes Buddhism itself, one wonders what sort of Zen the Christians referred to could have 'attempted' if it leaves their own religion intact. (Perhaps there is an ambiguity in the use of the word 'religion' here.) In the same ecumenical spirit, Father Enomiya-Lassalle also tells us that 'the end, whether called "God" or "Absolute" is after all ONE'. What would he make of a koan that does not appear in the *Mumonkan*, which asks, 'If all things are reduced to the One, to what will you reduce the One?' Perhaps his most questionable statement is that 'Zen practice has nothing to do with Buddhist philosophy.' If by this he means that Zen does not regard Buddhist philosophy as an end in itself he is giving expression to a truism. If on the other hand he means (as he appears to mean) that Zen has no more to do with Buddhist philosophy – and presumably no more to do with Buddhism – than with the philosophy of Aristotle or St Thomas Aquinas, his statement is both false and misleading. What it does, in effect, is to reduce Patriarchal Chan to Tathāgata Chan, i.e. it reduces the practice of Zen to a matter of concentration and concentration techniques, which of course do not, in themselves, jeopardize any religion, and can be combined with any philosophy. By reducing Zen in this way liberal Catholic thinkers like Father Enomiya-Lassalle hope to 'contain' Zen and thus neutralize its influence. That they should want to do this is not surprising. What is surprising is that a Buddhist organization like the Zen Center of Los Angeles should appear to countenance the attempt.

THE WISDOM OF TIBET

Tenzin Gyatso, the Fourteenth Dalai Lama
The Buddhism of Tibet and the Key to the Middle Way
Translated in the main by Jeffrey Hopkins and Lati Rimpoche
George Allen & Unwin, London 1975

Nāgārjuna and the Seventh Dalai Lama
The Precious Garland and The Song of The Four Mindfulnesses
Translated and edited by Jeffrey Hopkins and Lati Rimpoche with Anne Klein
Foreword by His Holiness Tenzin Gyatso, the Fourteenth Dalai Lama
George Allen & Unwin, London 1975

Mind in Buddhist Psychology
Translated from the Tibetan by Herbert V. Guenther and Leslie Kawamura
Dharma Publishing, Emeryville 1975

Speaking in terms of cultural geography, there are at present three major historical forms of Buddhism extant in the world. These are South-east Asian Buddhism, which is found in Sri Lanka, Burma, and Thailand, as well as in Cambodia and Laos; Sino-Japanese Buddhism, which exists not only in China and Japan but also in Korea and Vietnam; and Tibetan Buddhism, which from the Land of Snows spreads into

Mongolia, Sikkim, Bhutan, and Ladakh. In terms of the three *yānas* South-east Asian Buddhism belongs to the Hīnayāna; Sino-Japanese Buddhism to the combined Hīnayāna and Mahāyāna, with the latter predominating, especially in Japan; while Tibetan Buddhism belongs equally to the Hīnayāna, the Mahāyāna, and the Vajrayāna, with each succeeding *yāna* providing the orientation for the preceding one. As for the specific traditions by which they are represented, South-east Asian Buddhism is represented by the Theravāda; Sino-Japanese Buddhism on the practical side mainly by Chan/Zen and Jōdo Shinshū and on the theoretical side by the Tiantai and Huayan (Avataṃsaka) schools; and Tibetan Buddhism by the Nyingma, Kagyu, Sakya, and Gelug schools.

All three forms of Buddhism are continuations of Indian Buddhism as it existed at a certain historical stage of its development. This is particularly true of Tibetan Buddhism. Though elements from Central Asia may have enriched the final synthesis, and though outstanding Tibetan Buddhist personalities like Milarepa and Tsongkhapa undoubtedly made original contributions of great value, Tibetan Buddhism is essentially the brilliant and complex Buddhism of the Pala dynasty in north-eastern India transported as it were bodily from the subtropical plains and forests of Bengal and Bihar across the mighty barrier of the Himalayas into the icy, windswept tablelands of Tibet. This transportation was not like the transferral of an artefact from one place to another, but rather resembled the translation of living bodies which, while continuing faithfully to transmit their ancestral lineaments, at the same time adapted themselves to their new environment and propagated there a strong and vigorous new generation of their kind. In matters of monastic organization and general doctrinal teaching Tibetan Buddhism perpetuates the Sarvāstivāda. In 'philosophy' it is the true successor of the twin schools of the Madhyamaka and the Yogācāra, the 'profound' and the 'sublime'. As regards Tantric spiritual practice, it keeps alive the symbolic rituals and esoteric meditations of a hundred different lineages of Indian yogis and adepts.

Now the old Tibet is gone, and some of its most distinguished representatives are scattered to the four corners of the earth. The loss, appalling though it is, has been compensated for to a small extent by the increase of interest in Tibetan Buddhism which has occurred in many parts of Western Europe and the North American continent – an interest which, so far as the English language at least is concerned, finds both expression and powerful reinforcement in an ever-growing body of new books on Tibetan Buddhism. With the appearance of these publications, which include translations of classics of Tibetan Buddhist literature as well as works of modern Western scholarship, the true nature of Tibetan Buddhism is gradually becoming better known – so far as it can be known in this way.

Some of these new publications, like the first two volumes of the Wisdom of Tibet Series, 'Published under the aegis of the Library of Tibetan Works and Archives with the authority of His Holiness the Dalai Lama as revealing oral tradition', bear witness to the fidelity with which the Buddhists of Tibet have preserved the teachings committed to them by their Indian masters. The first volume of the series, *The Buddhism of Tibet and the Key to the Middle Way*, is by the Dalai Lama himself, and as the title indicates consists of two separate works. The first of these is a revised version of the appendix called 'An Outline of Buddhism in Tibet' in the Dalai Lama's book of memoirs *My Land and My People*. It consists of a series of short sections on such fundamental topics as the four noble truths, liberation, Hīnayāna, Mahāyāna, Tantrayāna, the Two Truths, training in higher meditative stabilization, and the Mind of Enlightenment. As one would have expected, the Dalai Lama's approach to his subject is 'orthodox' in the true sense of the term, being firmly based on traditional sources, both literary and oral. No concessions are made to contemporary *mithyā-dṛṣṭis*, however fashionable. Barring the occasional obscurity due to extreme conciseness of expression, the exposition is very clear, and it is evident to how great an extent Tibetan Buddhism coincides with the two other major cultural-geographical expressions of the Dharma. The second work in the volume is more advanced. In it the Dalai Lama – who won his degree as a *geshe* or 'Doctor of Buddhist Philosophy' the hard way after years of study with the best teachers and a gruelling public *vive voce* – gives a résumé of the doctrine of the Middle Way as expounded by the great teachers of the Prāsaṅgika-Madhyamaka school. According to this school, the Middle Way is much more than a golden mean between the extremes of hedonistic self-indulgence and ascetic self-mortification. Its significance is essentially 'metaphysical', consisting in the fact that dependently-arising phenomena abide in a 'middle way', being neither truly and inherently existent nor utterly non-existent, and that this 'middle wayness' of phenomena is identical with their voidness and emptiness. Voidness and emptiness is the object of true cognition, which is not the cognition of the non-existence in phenomena of an existent object, not even of an object called 'emptiness', but simply the cognition of the absence in phenomena of their own inherent existence. Such cognition is also cognition of the non-existence, in the ultimate sense, of the 'I-ness' which is the basis for the arising of craving, hatred, and so on. For this reason it is of the greatest practical importance. It is the cognition of emptiness which makes the difference between worldly life and spiritual life, suffering and happiness, bondage and liberation, and on this point the Dalai Lama insists with great earnestness.

Like the classic Indian treatises on which it is based, and from which it profusely quotes, *The Key to the Middle Way* approaches its great subject in a way that, despite the unfortunate devaluation that the word has undergone in recent years, can only be described as 'intellectual', and its method of treatment is scholastic. At intervals, an imaginary opponent raises objections, which are conscientiously shown to be without foundation. We are reminded of Aquinas rather than of Schopenhauer or Nietzsche. Indeed, the Dalai Lama has a faith in reason, and a willingness to use it to the limit of its capacity, which nowadays is not often encountered in 'religious' circles, least of all in those devoted to 'the Wisdom of the East'. Commenting on the last of Maitreya's 'four reliances', he says, 'With respect to a non-conceptual wisdom that apprehends a profound emptiness, one first cultivates a conceptual consciousness that apprehends the emptiness, and when a clear perception of the object of meditation arises, this becomes a non-conceptual wisdom. *Moreover, the initial generation of that conceptual consciousness must depend solely on a correct reasoning*' (pp. 55–6. My italics). Even when speaking, in the first work in the volume, of the special meditation practices of the Highest Yoga (*Anuttara-Yoga*) of the Tantrayāna, he is careful to add, 'Although there are definitely instances of achievements among these paths through the power of belief, these powers are mostly achieved through the power of reasoning' (p. 30). To those for whom Tibetan Buddhism is all magic and mystery, who see it through a thick haze of pseudo-occult 'romance', or a fog of sentiment, the sunlit rationality of the Dalai Lama's approach may well come as a shock.

The second volume in the Wisdom of Tibet Series also contains two works, the second of which is a translation of the Tibetan version of the *Ratnamālā* (otherwise known as the *Ratnāvalī*) or 'Precious Garland' of Nāgārjuna – the second- and/or third-century 'popularizer' of the Perfection of Wisdom *sūtras*, inaugurator of the Mādhyamika tradition, and perhaps the greatest name in Indian Mahāyāna Buddhism. Not that we are, in reality, as far removed from the original text as we might think. Sanskrit Buddhist manuscripts, where they exist at all, are very corrupt, and Tibetan translations are very faithful. An English version of the Tibetan translation, made with the help of a Tibetan teacher 'in the lineage', may well get us closer to the original Indian author's real meaning than would a translation made from the actual Sanskrit text by a Western scholar who had no access to the oral explanations of the text which are – or were – transmitted in Tibet as part of the total tradition. The work is addressed to an unnamed king, supposedly one belonging to the South Indian Sātavāhana dynasty, and consists of five chapters each containing one hundred verses. Two of the chapters are here translated for the first time, the remaining three having been translated by G. Tucci and published in 1934–6. In chapter 1, 'High Status and Definite Goodness', a short account of the practices conducive to high status, i.e. rebirth in a state of happiness as a man or god, is followed by a longer and more detailed description of the wisdom by means of which one achieves definite goodness, i.e. liberation and omniscience. For Nāgārjuna, of course, this wisdom is the cognition of the emptiness expounded by the Buddha in the Perfection of Wisdom *sūtras*. Chapter 2 is 'An Interwoven Explanation of Definite Goodness and High Status' and includes, among other teachings, a further explanation of the truth of emptiness, an exhortation to reflect on the foulness of a woman's body as an antidote to lust, and a description of the particular virtuous deeds which lead to the acquisition of each of the thirty-two major marks of a Buddha. Chapter 3 is devoted to 'The Collections for Enlightenment', the collections being, of course, those of merit and wisdom. (For some reason the translators fail to distinguish between *prajñā/sherab* and *jñāna/yeshe*, rendering both as 'wisdom'.) Among other things, the king is advised to provide for the propagation of the Dharma, to maintain a wide variety of social services, to provide food for ants, and to eliminate high taxes. Chapter 4 is entitled 'Royal Policy' and contains Nāgārjuna's advice to the king as king. After exhorting him to govern not only with justice but with compassion (prisoners are to be made comfortable so long as they are not freed, while murderers are simply to be banished), he urges him to renounce attachment to the senses, which in any case are not truly real. This leads to another discussion of wisdom, which by way of a reference to the merits and wisdom of the bodhisattva in turn leads to a vigorous defence of the Mahāyāna as the veritable word of the Buddha. Interestingly enough, Nāgārjuna makes no criticism of the Hīnayāna, clearly regarding the two teachings as being in essence identical. The Mahāyāna is the fuller explanation of what is taught in brief in the Hīnayāna – particularly as regards the actual practice of the bodhisattva ideal. Despite the excellence of the advice he has given him, Nāgārjuna realizes that it might be hard for him to rule religiously in an unrighteous world. In that case, the right thing for the king to do is to become a monk. Chapter 5, 'Bodhisattva Deeds', describes the various practices in which he should then engage. First, there are more than fifty-seven faults to be given up, after which the perfections are to be cultivated. These are briefly described, as are the ten stages of a bodhisattva's progress and their fruits. In order to develop his faith in the limitlessness of the Buddha's qualities the king is advised to recite twenty stanzas three times a day in front of an image or reliquary. These twenty stanzas are a version of the Sevenfold Puja, with a particularly extensive Rejoicing in Merits.

As the translators observe in their introduction, the *Precious Garland of Advice to the King* (*Rājaparikathā-ratnamālā*), to give it its full title, is renowned among the works of Nāgārjuna for its comprehensive description of the two inseparable aspects of the bodhisattva's life, his realization, through wisdom, of the profound emptiness, and his fulfilment, through compassion, of the extensive deeds. The *Ratnamālā* is thus a *vade mecum* of the Mahāyāna from both the 'theoretical' and the practical points of view, and as such it has ever been highly esteemed by Tibetan Buddhists. As such, I hope, it will come to be esteemed by Western Buddhists too. Its inclusion in the present volume makes available to us in full one of the masterpieces of Indian Mahāyāna expository literature – succinct, comprehensive, and inspiring. It also enables us to appreciate the kind of material that has been preserved by the lamas of Tibet, and that contributed to the creation of that many-splendoured thing known to us in the West as Tibetan Buddhism. The remaining work in the volume is entitled *Instructions for Meditation on the View of Emptiness, The Song of the Four Mindfulnesses, Causing the Rain of Achievements to Fall*, by the Seventh Dalai Lama (1708–1757 CE). Though very much shorter than the *Ratnamālā*, being only two pages long, its spiritual value is no less. The four mindfulnesses are not those which are included in the thirty-seven helps to Enlightenment,[304] but a special Tantric set, consisting of mindfulness of the teacher, of the altruistic aspiration to the Highest Enlightenment (*bodhicitta*), of your body as a divine body, and of the view of Emptiness. The inclusion of this little work, based on a personal revelation to Tsongkhapa by the bodhisattva Mañjuśrī, illustrates the importance of the Tantrayāna in the spiritual life of Tibet, besides providing us with a fine example of an original Tibetan contribution to Buddhist literature. The extreme shortness of the work can be taken, perhaps, as hinting at the fact that specifically Tantric teachings cannot be made available so easily, or indeed in the same way, as those of the two other *yānas*.[305]

One of the most important developments of Indian Buddhism to be introduced into Tibet was the Abhidharma. For five hundred years, from the time of Aśoka to the time of Nāgārjuna, it dominated the field to such an extent that it has recently been suggested that this period, generally known as the Hīnayāna period, should be called instead the Age of Abhidharma. Even at the time of the introduction of Buddhism into Tibet, from the seventh to the twelfth century CE, it was still influential. Basically, the Abhidharma was an attempt to clarify and systematize the Buddha's teachings as contained in the *sūtras*. As such it may be described as a form of scholasticism, though with the proviso that it is concerned not so much with metaphysics as with psychology. There were three distinct, though not dissimilar, Abhidharma traditions: those of the Sarvāstivāda, the Theravāda, and the Yogācāra. Only the first and third of these were introduced into Tibet.

Mind in Buddhist Psychology is a translation of *The Necklace of Clear Understanding: An Elucidation of the Working of Mind and Mental Events* by Yeshe Gyaltsen, an eighteenth-century Tibetan lama of the Gelug school, and the work represents a continuation, on Tibetan soil, of the Indian Yogācāra Abhidharma tradition. In form it is an auto-commentary of the author's own verse text, which explains the mind and its 51 mental events in 177 four-lined stanzas. As the translators point out, Yeshe Gyaltsen's presentation of his subject is closely modelled on the *Abhidharma-samuccaya* or 'Compendium of Abhidharma' of Asaṅga, the originator on earth of the Yogācāra tradition, helped out by plentiful quotations from the *Lamrim Chenmo* or 'Great Stages of the Path' by Tsongkhapa, the founder of the Gelug school. Not counting the 'Verses of Veneration and Intention', with which it opens, the work falls into five sections, the third of which deals with 'Mind' and the fourth with 'Mental Events'. The author's purpose in discussing the subject is, of course, strictly practical. We all experience frustration. This frustration has a cause, which is the power of karma and the emotions, i.e. our own mind. Moreover, it is the mind, the positive mind, that gives rise to all spiritual qualities and attainments. Mind is the root of both *saṃsāra* and *nirvāṇa*. Consequently, it is essential to know what is meant by mind and mental events, and to be able to distinguish positive mental events from negative ones, so that the former can be cultivated and the latter rejected. For Yeshe Gyaltsen, as for the Abhidharma tradition generally, psychological analysis is undertaken not as an end in itself but for the sake of gaining from it an understanding that can be transformed into a living experience – an experience that culminates in Enlightenment.

Following his Indian authorities, the author defines mind as the awareness of the factual presence of a particular object, and mental events as the becoming involved with this object by way of other specific functions. Between mind as the primary factor and the mental events as its 'entourage' there exist five functional co-relations, of which two partly differing accounts are given, one deriving from the Sarvāstivāda, the other from the Yogācāra. Mental events are said to be altogether fifty-one in number. Five are omnipresent, i.e. operate in the wake of every mind situation; five are object-determining; eleven are of a positive nature; six are basic emotions, and are of a negative nature; twenty are proximate emotions and also negative; and four are variables, being so called because they become positive, or negative, or indeterminate, according to the level and quality of the mental situation. All these mental events are described in detail, with the result that this section of *The Necklace of Clear Understanding* is not only the longest but also the most interesting and useful of the whole work. We find, for instance, that what Guenther terms 'directionality of mind' (*sems-pa*), one of the five omnipresent mental events, is the most important of all mental events whatever. It is what propels forward the mind and its corresponding mental events and causes them to settle on an object. We also find that faith (or confidence, as the translators prefer to call it) comes first in the list of eleven positive mental events which are essential to spiritual development, and that it is described as consisting of a *lucid faith* that realizes the value of the Three Jewels, a *trusting faith* that sees the connection between one's action and its consequences, and a *longing faith* that moves one to aspire to the realization of the four noble truths by one's own efforts (p. 39). Though in his discussion of the different kinds of mental events Yeshe Gyaltsen relies on the *Abhidharma-samuccaya* and the *Lamrim Chenmo*, he does at the same time have something original to contribute. Indeed, we are throughout very much aware of the venerable author's presence as, with great kindliness and patience, and with deep feeling for his subject, he guides us through the complexities of what may be considered the central theme of the Abhidharma. What a wonderful teacher he must have been!

Even in the old Tibet, however, things were not always as they should have been. Yeshe Gyaltsen has to lament that 'Those who realize the works of the Sages and sublime persons of India as the very foundation of instructions are like the stars in daytime' (p. 40) and that, in words that have a familiar ring, 'young people nowadays do not consider this division between good and evil as very important' (p. 62). Probably the truth of the matter is that, however favourable outward conditions may be, there will always be some who do not care to devote themselves to the study of the Dharma. Similarly, however unfavourable such conditions may be, some will always be found who, for the sake of obtaining the gift of the Dharma, are prepared to undergo any hardship, to make any sacrifice. At the present day, even in the West, there are many who will welcome such a book as *Mind in Buddhist Psychology*. Though writers on Buddhism often sing the praises of Buddhist psychology, telling us how profound it is, and how far in advance of its modern Western counterparts, we are very rarely given any concrete information about it. One of the merits of the present work is that it consists of nothing but concrete information, clearly and systematically presented. Indeed, it is the best traditional exposition of the mysteries of the Abhidharma available to the English-speaking Western reader – the best modern exposition is Dr Guenther's *Philosophy and Psychology in the Abhidharma* (1956)

– and I recommend it as highly suitable for adoption as a text book for study courses in the Abhidharma.[306]

The work would have been still more useful if the translators had given us the original Sanskrit of the numerous psychological terms, as well as their Tibetan equivalents. Perhaps they would argue that in the course of centuries the Tibetan equivalents acquired subtle connotations of their own, but even so it seems strange that the Sanskrit terms should not be given even in the numerous quotations from Indian works – more especially as the work is liberally peppered with Dr Guenther's highly individual, not to say idiosyncratic, renderings of standard Buddhist terms. Thus, in the absence of the Sanskrit, how is the uninformed reader to know that 'inspection' corresponds to 'mindfulness', or that 'analytical-appreciative understanding', which is Dr Guenther's translation of *prajñā/sherab*, corresponds to what less brilliant scholars uniformly render as 'wisdom'? Perhaps Dr Guenther wants his writings and translations to constitute a self-contained world of their own, without signposts to other worlds. If so, it is a pity, for it is a world well worth exploring. It also seems strange that, whereas the names of the two translators appear on the title page, the name of the author does not. *Pūjā ca pūjanīyānaṃ*.[307] No doubt the omission, which must have been due to an oversight, will be rectified in a further edition, which I hope will soon be called for.

THE RELIGIONS OF TIBET AND MONGOLIA

Giuseppe Tucci
The Religions of Tibet
Translated from the German and Italian by Geoffrey Samuel
Routledge & Kegan Paul, London & Henley 1980

The Life and Teaching of Geshe Rabten: A Tibetan Lama's Search for Truth
Translated and edited by B. Alan Wallace (Gelong Jhampa Kelsang)
George Allen & Unwin, London 1980

Walther Heissig
The Religions of Mongolia
Translated from the German edition by Geoffrey Samuel
Routledge and Kegan Paul, London and Henley 1980

Every year the number of books on Buddhism published in English is increasing, and more and more of them are showing signs of a deeper understanding of the Dharma than was often the case even twenty years ago. It is no longer a question of having to distinguish the partly reliable from the totally unreliable so much as a question of having to distinguish the partly unreliable from the almost totally reliable. It is also a question – so far as the FWBO is concerned – of having to distinguish what is relevant to the needs of the Buddhist spiritual community in twentieth-century England, New Zealand, Finland, and India (to begin with) from what is not relevant to those needs. Many of the books now appearing are of sufficient importance to demand full length review articles. All that can be offered, on the present occasion, are short notices of a random but not unrepresentative selection of the books already received for review this year.

According to the publisher, Giuseppe Tucci's *The Religions of Tibet* is the first comprehensive account of Tibetan Buddhism to be published in English since Waddell's *Buddhism of Tibet* appeared in 1894. This does not take into account Hoffmann's *The Religions of Tibet* (1961), but there is no doubt that this rich and readable book by 'one of the greatest scholars whom Buddhist studies has so far produced' (E. Conze) is far and away the best 'overview of the Tibetan Buddhist world' (p. ix) that we have yet been given. Despite its comprehensiveness, it is no mere historical survey of religious developments *ab extra* but a sensitive exploration of the depths of the Tibetan religious spirit. After summarizing the diffusion of Buddhism in Tibet in two admirably concise chapters, Professor Tucci plunges into the heart of his subject with three masterly chapters on the general characteristics of Lamaism, the doctrines of the most important schools, and monkhood, monastery life, the religious calendar, and festivals. These chapters, which form the central part of the book, probably bring us closer to the real nature of Tibetan Buddhism than all the previous lucubrations on the subject put together. There are also chapters on the folk religion of Tibet and the Bön religion. Throughout the book Professor Tucci draws on an extensive knowledge of Tibetan texts, as well as on personal observation and research in Western and Central Tibet. In order to illustrate a point, he is even able to refer to his own experience when he obtained the consecration of *Kye rdo rje* in *Sa skya* (p. 82). Yet great as his learning is he is never overwhelmed by it. At every turn we are impressed by his easy mastery of his complex material, his capacity for lucid exposition, and his great power of expression. Whether expounding the views of the different Buddhist schools on the nature of the relation between light and mind (*'od gsel* and *sems*), describing the economic structure of the monasteries, or explaining the origins of the new year's festival, he is invariably well informed, penetrating, and judicious.

With much of the book representing the results of previously unpublished research, a number of things not clear before are clarified, while things that were already clear receive further clarification. We are made aware of the extent to which political motives were involved in the introduction of Buddhism into Tibet (p. 6), as well as of the fact that the monastic communities were institutions of economic power, and therefore decisive factors in Tibetan history (p. 25). Indeed, we are told that the secular power of the religious communities released 'a militant attitude which aspired to hegemony in the temporal world as well as in the spiritual' (p. 27). Emphasis is laid on the experience of pure, undifferentiated light as the common fundamental trait of the entire course of the religious experience of Tibetan man, and on the fact that 'the magical and gnostic foundations of Tantrism lend their unmistakable imprint to the whole Lamaist way of thinking and practice' (p. 93). In connection with this latter point Professor Tucci finds it necessary to stress the importance of soteriological goals for Tibetan Buddhism. 'It would be a great error, and reveal an insufficient understanding of the special nature of Tibetan Buddhism,' he says, perhaps with some of his more 'academic' colleagues in mind, 'if one were to disregard the soteriological goals permeating and dominating it. It is not a question here of a purely intellectual process, not of the acquisition of theoretical knowledge, but rather of the alignment of the entire cognitive activity towards the goal of salvation. All along the line intellectual understanding remains subordinate to lived experience' (p. 93). This could hardly be better expressed. Soteriological goals may, however, be obscured by the magical and exorcistic preoccupations of the folk religion. In speaking of the 'particular psychic disposition of the Tibetan' Professor Tucci more than once reminds us that the Tibetan 'lives in a permanent state of anxious uneasiness' (pp. 172–3), and that 'the entire spiritual life of the Tibetan is defined by a permanent attitude of defence, by a constant effort to appease and propitiate the powers whom he fears' (p. 187). He also draws attention to the fact that a remarkable characteristic of Tibetan religiosity is 'its striking lack of social compassion' (p. 210). Though the bodhisattva vow is recited daily, 'the teachings enshrined in the vow rarely receive more than a vague theoretical assertion' (p. 211).

One of the most interesting features of Professor Tucci's book is the way in which he regularly describes the Buddhism of Tibet as 'Lamaism'. For most scholars this term, first apparently used by Kopen (1859), and presumably coined by him, is now obsolete. As long ago as 1914 Waddell himself, writing in Hastings' *Encyclopaedia of Religion and*

Ethics (vol. 7, p. 784), characterized it as 'in many ways misleading, inappropriate, and undesirable', adding that it was 'rightly dropping out of use'. Rightly or wrongly, Professor Tucci has now revived the term. This is not so surprising as it might seem. One of the facts that emerges most strongly from his whole 'overview' is the extent to which Tibetan Buddhism is the product of creative interaction between Indian Buddhism on the one hand and, on the other, the 'pre-Buddhist beliefs, myths, rituals, and invocatory formulae of Tibet' (p. 30). For so distinctive a synthesis a distinctive term is needed, and it may well be that the old term 'Lamaism' is the most appropriate. The use of such a term is not without its advantages for Western Buddhists. It reminds us that Tibetan Buddhism is quite as much Tibetan as Buddhist, and that inasmuch as it is, in part, the product of a culture very different from our own, there can be no question of the whole system being transported bodily from Tibet to the West.

In *The Religions of Tibet* the life of the monastic communities is one subject among many, and we hear about it from a sympathetic observer. In *The Life and Teachings of Geshe Rabten* it is virtually the only subject, and we hear about it from one who, for more than twenty years, experienced it for himself. Though he tells us little that we cannot learn from Professor Tucci (the Professor, indeed, tells us much that we do not learn from the Geshe), he gives us an incomparably more vivid and fascinating picture of daily life in a great Tibetan monastic establishment than we could possibly obtain from any second-hand account, however informative. Born in Kham (Eastern Tibet) in 1921, of farming stock, the young Tadin Rabten grew up more familiar with horses, dogs, and guns than with books. When he was 15 he noticed how 'simple, pure, and efficient' the lives of the monks were, and at 17 decided to join one of the monastic universities. Two years later, having made the three-month journey to Lhasa, he was admitted to Sera Monastery, the second largest in Tibet. From then onwards his days – and sometimes his nights as well – were devoted to study and religious practices. Only in 1959, at the time of the Lhasa uprising, was he affected by the presence of the Chinese. By that time he had decided to take the *geshe* examination, which he eventually passed in India, as a refugee, after twenty-four years of hard work. In order to qualify he had to pass through fifteen classes, familiarizing himself with such subjects as Logic and Epistemology,

Abhidharma, Vinaya, the Perfection of Wisdom, and Madhyamaka. The first subject he was taught, however, was the relationship between the four primary and eight secondary colours. Besides engaging in doctrinal studies he memorized thousands of pages of texts, participated in endless formal debates, practised meditation, recited prayers and mantras, and rose before dawn to perform prostrations. Such was his zeal that he was content with a minimum of food and clothing, often going hungry for days on end and wearing nothing but rags held together with bits of wire. Not surprisingly, when he visited his old home after six years of monastic life he found that his outlook had changed. 'Even when I looked up at the pastures where I had loved to roam as a child, I felt no attraction. The same was true of my home. Nothing interested me. It was all rather depressing. I found that my way of thinking had changed entirely' (p. 74).

Despite the hardships, life at Sera Monastery suited Geshe Rabten very well. Study and meditation brought their own rewards, while the kindness with which the monks treated one another – older monks making personal sacrifices in order to assist younger monks and newcomers – helped to create an atmosphere of warmth and spiritual friendship. His strongest emotional ties were with his teachers, for whom he felt boundless reverence and devotion – a devotion that finds heartfelt utterance in a letter written to his principal guru, Geshe Jampa Khedup, which appears in the first part of the book, containing the story of his life. Devotion is, in fact, the keynote of Geshe Rabten's character. Combined with deep understanding and wide learning, it is very much in evidence not only in the first, but also in the second part of the book, containing his teachings. In this part the Geshe deals mainly with the 'three principles of the path', i.e. with renunciation, 'an awakening mind' (i.e. the *bodhicitta*), and the ideal view. He also gives us an introduction to the Buddhadharma, an explanation of the (Tantric) preliminary practices, and instruction in 'mental quiescence' (i.e. *śamatha*). Reading these clear and practical teachings, one cannot but conclude that they represent the noble fruit of a noble life.

Such is the nobility and disinterestedness of Geshe Rabten's life, indeed, that one is reluctant to make even the smallest criticism of the system that produced him. Criticism based on modern, secular notions of education would be irrelevant in any case. As the Geshe himself points out, a monastic university like Sera differs from a Western university in that only the Buddhadharma is studied, and in that because the field of training is the Dharma, the mind experiences greater and greater happiness, regardless of physical hardships. Nonetheless it must be said that, reading the story of Geshe Rabten's life, one gets the impression that under the Gelugpa system of monastic training there was a distinct overemphasis on doctrinal and scholastic studies. The Gelugpa system in fact seems to have favoured intellectual cramming. It is not without significance, perhaps, that Geshe Rabten more than once has recourse to the image of the factory. Speaking of his early years at Sera, for example, he says, 'Many people working in a factory have nothing to occupy their attention but their daily routine. Similarly in the monastery throughout the day and night, I had nothing to think of but the Dharma' (p. 53). Some Western Buddhists might find the idea of a monastery being a *factory* less than appealing. They might wonder whether it was *really* the function of a monastery to produce *geshes* – even *geshes* as devout and learned as Geshe Rabten. They might even wonder whether an exhaustive study of all the different schools of 'Buddhist philosophy' was really necessary to the attainment of Enlightenment. Considerations of this sort become all the more pressing when, towards the end of his career, we find Geshe Rabten receiving from six to ten 'empowerments' (i.e. *abhiṣekas*, or 'consecrations' as Tucci calls them) every day for weeks on end. Significantly, he says of the daily recitations of the corresponding rituals that they never took so much time that his studies were impaired (p. 111). It would seem that much as Geshe Rabten gained for his twenty-four years of intensive study, something was also lost.

Both geographically and culturally, the step from Tibet to Mongolia is not a very great one. Walther Heissig's *The Religions of Mongolia* is the companion volume to Giuseppe Tucci's *The Religions of Tibet*, the two having been first published together in German as parts of a single work. It is, however, a very different kind of book. Not only is it much shorter, but it devotes far more space to the shamanistic folk religion of the Mongols than it does to Mongolian Buddhism. There are two reasons for this. In the first place, judging by the twenty-nine items listed under his name in the bibliography, Professor Heissig is more interested in Mongolian shamanism than in Mongolian Buddhism, having personally collected from the libraries of Europe seventy-eight manuscripts containing prayers, invocations, and so on. The part of the book dealing with the non-Buddhist folk religion of the Mongols is in fact firmly based on original sources. In the second place, 'the forms of Northern Buddhism in Mongolia correspond to those of Tibet from which they originated' (p. ix), and there was no point in Professor Heissig describing what Professor Tucci had already described.

> Although numerous Mongolian lamas made substantial contributions to Lamaist theology [sic], which were significantly all composed in Tibetan, the church [sic] language of Lamaism, the Mongolian theological schools, developed no divergent doctrinal interpretations. Only in those cases where ... the Mongolian folk religion was incorporated in a syncretic fashion into the doctrinal edifice of Lamaism, did there take place any truly local development. (p. 34)

This about sums up the matter. Professor Heissig is therefore left free to concentrate on the 'beliefs and concepts which belong to the non-Buddhist folk religion of the Mongols' (p. ix), such as those relating to the mythical 'Cinggis Khan' (Genghis Khan), the deity of fire, and the 'White Old Man', giving us only a short description of the spread of Lamaism in Mongolia, though there are also chapters on the relation between Lamaism and the folk religion and the Lamaist suppression of shamanism. (In case anyone should raise the cry of 'intolerance' against Buddhism on this account, let it be noted that the suppression consisted in the abolition of human and animal sacrifice and the burning of the felt Ongghot dolls.)

Even the short description that Professor Heissig gives us of the spread of Lamaism in Mongolia is not without significance for Western Buddhists. As with the dissemination of Buddhism in Tibet, political as well as spiritual factors played an important part. Chinese emperors favoured the spread of Lamaism into Mongolia from China, where it had flourished since the Yuan dynasty, mainly as a means of pacifying the warlike Mongols, while Mongol princes saw in it a means of boosting their political prestige. 'Conversion' tended to take place 'from above'. In 1578, on the occasion of his first meeting with the Third Dalai Lama, Altan Khan had a number of noblemen, princes among them, 'enter the priestly state [sic]' (p. 29). As Professor Heissig observes, 'It is difficult to avoid the impression that part of the conversion consisted in acts of the government' (p. 29). Earlier on, there were the usual misunderstandings about 'Tantrism', i.e. the Vajrayāna. Tantric ritual was understood as a more efficacious form of worldly magic than shamanism, while Tantric sexual symbolism was taken quite literally, with disastrous results. Eventually, Lamaism was established throughout Mongolia, retaining its influence until the middle of the twentieth century. According to Professor Heissig, the downfall began with the decay of Manchu power, and when 'the divergence between preaching and reality [on the part of the monks] was no longer to be bridged' (p. 35).

PADMASAMBHAVA COMES TO THE WEST

The Life and Liberation of Padmasambhava (*Padma bKa'i Thang*)
Recorded by Yeshe Tsogyal, rediscovered by Terchen Urgyan Lingpa, translated into French as *Le Dict de Padma* by Gustave-Charles Toussaint, translated into English by Kenneth Douglas and Gwendolyn Bays, corrected with the original Tibetan manuscripts and with an introduction by Tarthang Tulku
Dharma Publishing, Emeryville, California 1978

With his lotus cap, his red cloak, and trident resting in the crook of his left arm, the figure of Padmasambhava is one of the most striking and distinctive in the whole range of Buddhism. Well do I remember the tremendous impression it made upon me when, in the early fifties, I encountered it for the first time in the gloom of a temple in the foothills of the Eastern Himalayas. In English very little information about Guru Rimpoche, or the Precious Master, as the Tibetans generally call Padmasambhava, has been available. We had 'An Epitome of the Life and Teachings of Tibet's great guru Padmasambhava' in Evans-Wentz's *The Tibetan Book of the Great Liberation* (1954), and a chapter on Padmasambhava and Padmaism in Hoffmann's *The Religions of Tibet* (1961), as well as various short summaries of his career in books about Tibet and histories of Buddhism, and that was about all. Now under the title of *The Life and Liberation of Padmasambhava*, Tarthang Tulku has brought out, in two bulky volumes, an English version of the French translation of the *Padma bKa'i Thang*, so that at last we are able to follow in detail the career of the extraordinary being who was mainly responsible for introducing Buddhism into Tibet and whose magical personality has dominated the spiritual lives, and fired the imaginations, of a large section of the Tibetan people ever since.

The *Padma bKa'i Thang* is a *terma* or 'treasure' text which we are told was taken from the heart of the fierce deity guarding the door of the Crystal Rock Cave by Urgyan Lingpa, its preordained revealer, in 1326, after it had lain concealed within the image for more than five centuries. The original authorship of the text is attributed to Yeshe Tsogyal, one of the twenty-five principal disciples of Padmasambhava. The work is divided into 108 cantos, as the English translator calls them, the first fifty-three of which have been assigned to Part 1 of this edition under the heading 'India' and the remaining fifty-five to Part 2 under 'Tibet'. According to the English translator's preface, 'In many respects this work in two volumes is comparable to the Germanic sagas or the Greek and Roman epics' (p. xx). So far as the Greek and Roman epics are concerned, the comparison is not really valid. Though the storyline is reasonably clear and continuous the *Padma bKa'i Thang* is a somewhat chaotic work and rather lacking in formal literary structure of the more classical type. If it is comparable to anything within the Western epic genre it is, perhaps, rather to the Italian romantic epics and the Arthurian romances. At times, however, particularly in Part 1, the Tibetan work seems to resemble nothing in Western literature so much as Blake's later 'Prophetic Books'. There is the same brilliant visual imagery, more Tibetan than Indian (the French translator, Gustave-Charles Toussaint, does not believe that there was a Sanskrit original for the work as claimed), the same visionary atmosphere, and the same ability to project the 'collective archetypes of the collective unconscious', both the terrible and the fascinating, in forms of hallucinatory vividness. Prosodically speaking the text consists mainly of long sequences of nine-syllable lines, with both longer and shorter lines also sometimes occurring. Changes of pace and mood are frequent. In the vigorous words of the French translator, 'Various tones follow each other in the incantation. It passes and repasses from dithyramb to macabre nightmare, from evocatory vertigo to objurgation, from a vehement and sombre realism to didactic dryness, but also to fervour, to the epic, to prophecy' (p. xxv).

The central event in Padmasambhava's life is his visit to Tibet, where he performed the celebrated feat of subduing the local gods and demons and participated in the consecration of the great temple-monastery of Samye. This historic visit took place in the reign of King Trisong Detsen (755–797 CE) and modern scholarship therefore regards Padmasambhava's career as being confined within the limits of the eighth century. The *Padma bKa'i Thang* takes a different view. While giving a full description of Padmasambhava's activities in Tibet, it sees the Precious Master's career as extending both forward into the distant future and backward into the remote past and as covering a period of altogether nearly three thousand years. The story begins in the land of Uḍḍiyāna. Amitābha, the Buddha of Boundless Light, emanates a ray of crimson radiance that falls upon a lotus in the Dhanakośa Lake, whereupon there appears seated on the calyx of the flower an 8-year-old child. This miraculous child, who is Padmasambhava, is adopted by Indrabhūti, the childless king of Uḍḍiyāna, and brought up as heir to the throne. Though married to a beautiful and virtuous princess he is mindful of his spiritual mission and wishing to renounce the kingdom gets himself exiled and, like the Buddha, leaves the palace on horseback. After performing austerities and mastering all manner of arts and sciences he receives ordination as a monk from Ānanda, the disciple of the Buddha and his constant companion during the last years of his life. Ānanda tells Padmasambhava of the Buddha's predictions, from which we learn that Padmasambhava was born forty-two years after the *parinirvāṇa*. Chronology is further dislocated by the fact that, according to Tibetan tradition, the Buddha was born not in 563 BCE (the generally accepted date) but several centuries earlier. Having received ordination Padmasambhava visits Kashmir, Nepal, Zahor, Khotan, and other places and stays in the eight great cremation grounds expounding the Dharma to the *ḍākinīs*. He then goes to China, and learns astrological calculations from Mañjuśrī, the Bodhisattva of Wisdom. In Zahor he meets the spiritually-minded princess Mandāravā and accepts her as his disciple, whereupon her father, angry that the princess has consorted with a man, tries to burn him alive. *Ḍākinīs* extinguish the flames of the pyre, and after seven days it is transformed into a lake of water and Padmasambhava appears in the form of an 8-year-old boy seated on a lotus and converts the king – an incident that is repeated, with variations, two or three times later in the story.

Centuries passing, the Precious Master establishes the Dharma in Baiddha, Nepal, Serling (Sumatra?), Assam, Tukhara, and Persia, and his career becomes interwoven with the lives of such celebrated personages of Buddhist history as King Aśoka – at whose prayer the genies build ten million stupas in a single night – and the teachers Nāgārjuna and Āryadeva. There are also references, apparently anachronistic, to the persecution of Buddhists in Bengal and to the destruction of the great monastery of Vikramaśīla by the Hulagu Khan of Persia and of the shrines of Bodh Gaya by the *tīrthikas* or non-Buddhists under King Nāgaviṣṇu. Eventually, Padmasambhava receives King Trisong Detsen's invitation and travels to Tibet via Nepal, subduing the gods and demons as he goes, and forcing them to surrender their life-principle and swear an oath to protect the Dharma.

According to the *Padma bKa'i Thang*'s reckoning Padmasambhava spent 111 years in Tibet. Samye being completed he and the 'Bodhisattva Abbot' Śāntarakṣita perform the consecration ceremony to the accompaniment of many marvels, the king promulgates the code of laws which henceforth governs the social and religious life of Tibet, and the work of translating the Buddhist scriptures into the Tibetan language begins. Young Tibetans are trained as translators and, in the case of the most intrepid, go to India to study the Dharma. Indian monk-scholars are invited to Tibet. The most celebrated names in this connection are those of Vairotsana, who studies with twenty-five great Indian pandits, and Vimalamitra, who on his arrival in Tibet shows wonders, the story of each of them being related at some length over a number of cantos. Trisong Detsen having abolished the sanguinary Bön rites, the work of translation is brought to a successful conclusion, and despite strong opposition from the Bönists – due to whose machinations Vairotsana is banished and Vimalamitra slandered – the Dharma is at last established in Tibet. Secular works are also translated. The establishment of the Dharma is followed by the revision of the translations of the scriptures, after which the king recognizes the services of the translators and pandits with lavish gifts and most of them go home. In connection with these latter events, as well as with the death of Princess Pale Lotus, the king's daughter, Padmasambhava predicts the destruction of the monasteries and the slaughter of the monks and describes how, over a period of five thousand years, the teaching of the Buddha will grow and decline until the coming of the next Buddha, Maitreya. He also describes whereabouts in Tibet the *termas* or 'treasures' of texts and other objects which he has hidden for the benefit of future generations will be found, as well as the 'signs of the earth' and the times when these treasures will appear and who will discover them. The predictions having been made, King Trisong Detsen dies and Padmasambhava thinks of leaving Tibet but is persuaded to stay for three more years and makes more predictions and gives many teachings. In particular he addresses to the new king and to all the people of Tibet a lengthy exhortation which takes the form of an appallingly realistic description of the sufferings of the six realms of existence and of birth, old age, disease, and death. His mission in Tibet accomplished, the Precious Master mounts a marvellous winged horse, blue in colour, and accompanied by 'heroes of the four orders' and enveloped in rainbow-hued light leaves through the heavens for the land of the Rākṣasas or cannibal demons – where, enthroned on the Copper-Coloured Mountain, he is still living and teaching.

No bare summary of the *Padma bKa'i Thang* can possibly do justice to the richness and diversity of its contents. Interwoven with the life of Padmasambhava, which of course is the principal theme, there are biographies of subordinate characters, descriptions of non-human beings, summaries of medical and astrological lore (in the latter the twelve *nidānas* and the months of the years are correlated with the Twelve Actions of the Buddha!), sublime spiritual teachings, ecstatic songs of praise, a guide book to Samye, catalogues of texts translated, and much else besides. As Tarthang Tulku writes in his Introduction, the *Padma bKa'i Thang* 'is indeed a treasure, having the complexity and brilliance of a finely cut crystal, its facets the 108 cantos' (p. xxviii). Not that the crystal is perfectly symmetrical in shape, or that its facets are all equally well cut or of the same degree of brilliance! Nevertheless there is no doubt that, like the rainbow light that plays within the crystal, it is the magical figure of Padmasambhava that dominates the entire work, especially the central group of cantos, and it is the events described in these cantos, i.e. his visit to Tibet and his subjugation of the local gods and demons, that set the tone of the whole extraordinary narrative. In the earlier, Indian part of his three-thousand-year career Padmasambhava converts *ḍākinīs*, kings, butchers, black magicians, and *tīrthikas*, while one of the last things he does before leaving Tibet is to make a contract with the great demon king, King Pekar. Reading *The Life and Liberation of Padmasambhava* one gets the impression not only of a vivid and powerful spiritual 'personality' heroically battling with the forces of evil but also of a stream of impersonal spiritual energy which is coterminous with historical Buddhism itself and which, intervening in the course of events age after age, and assuming a variety of forms, brings under its control all the swirling emotional-psychic energies which at one or another level of mundane existence obstruct the liberating influence of the Dharma. This impression is heightened by the fact that Padmasambhava is actually involved in some of the most important events of Buddhist history, as well as by the fact that, at various stages of his career, he is known by different names. He has, we are told, eight secret names, eight borrowed names, eight present names, twenty magic names 'which vary at will', and so on. One indeed gets the impression that, perhaps extrapolating from Padmasambhava's exploits in Tibet, the text sees not only the history of Buddhism but the whole course of mundane existence in terms of a conflict between the forces of light and the forces of darkness – a conflict in which the forces of light are concerned not simply to conquer but to transmute and transform.

The most striking illustration of this almost Gnostic world-view occurs towards the beginning of the *Padma bKa'i Thang*, in the cantos describing the series of the births of the Rudra Tarpa Nagpo, or Black Salvation, and his subjugation by the Horse and the Swine, i.e. by the teacher Tubka Shunukyuwa, himself a form of Padmasambhava, and his disciple Den Pag, in the form of the horse-faced Vajrasattva and the swine-faced Vajrapāṇi. The Rudra is a fallen monk, once a disciple of Tubka, who after myriads of existences in various evil and hideous forms is eventually reborn as a monster with three heads, six hands, four feet, two wings, and nine eyes. Feeding on the corpse of his mother, a prostitute who had been impregnated by three demons, he grows to enormous size and becomes the ruler of the demon kings who have seized control of the earth. Mad with pride, he fancies that there is none greater than he. The Horse and the Swine subjugate him by penetrating him through the rectum and the urethra and coming out of the top of his head, where they join each other. Tarpa Nagpo becomes the Dharma protector Mahākāla, and is predicted to Buddhahood. He reappears later in the work, towards the end of the canto on 'The discourse on the Council of the Treasure, of the Law of the Treasure, of the Revealer of the Treasure' (canto 53) where it is said, 'Although subdued, Rudra Tarpa Nagpo rises up again', as though he represented, in his unregenerate form, a force which has to be subdued over and over again. In a remarkable passage the *termas* or 'treasures' are described as being hidden in various parts of his cosmic body, as if to suggest that the antidote to egotism is to be found in egotism itself – *bodhi* in the defilements, the Unconditioned in the conditioned. There is even a suggestion, elsewhere in the work, that the forces of light are actually strengthened by their conflict with the forces of darkness, and that one should therefore seek to learn from painful situations rather than run away from them. 'Hell is the lama of all the Buddhas' declares the Precious Master, when asked by Prince Lhaje to exert his mercy and cut off the whole misery of the cycle of transmigration for himself and his parents.

Like much Tibetan Buddhist literature, the *Padma bKa'i Thang* is pervaded by a keen sense of the impermanence of all worldly things and a strong 'yearning faith' in the Three Jewels, commitment to which makes it possible for one not only to transcend the human predicament but also to become a stream of 'impersonal' spiritual energy working for the emancipation of all living beings. In addition to its vivid portrayal of Padmasambhava himself, and its powerful dramatization of the conflict between the forces of light and the forces of darkness, the work also contains many important spiritual teachings, some of them being of a highly esoteric nature. Partly because they are not always explained in full, partly because of the literary rather than scholarly nature of the French translation, these are often difficult, even impossible, to understand. The general import of the work is nonetheless in no doubt whatever. Reading *The Life and Liberation of Padmasambhava* is a major imaginative and spiritual experience. This is due, principally, to the fact that 'the poetic beauty and symbolic strength of the Tibetan original' have been carried over from the French into the English translation, so that we can read this great work of literature in its present version not only for information but also for inspiration. Enjoyment and inspiration are alike enhanced by the reproductions of thangkas which illustrate the material within the text, as well as by the care and devotion with which Tarthang Tulku and his co-workers at Dharma Publishing have produced these two splendid volumes. Holding them in our hands, we cannot but agree with Tarthang Tulku that Padmasambhava's teachings have now come to the West. We cannot but feel that Padmasambhava himself has now come to the West.

THE DOOR OF LIBERATION

Geshe Wangyal
The Door of Liberation
Prefatory note by H. H. the Dalai Lama
Maurice Girodias Associates, New York 1973

Geshe Wangyal is a Mongolian lama who studied at Drepung Monastery, near Lhasa, one of the three great Gelugpa monastic centres of Tibet. When I met him in Kalimpong in the early fifties, through the good offices of Marco Pallis, he was already proficient in English, having in fact spent some time in England before the war. In 1955 Geshe-la went to America, where he eventually founded Labsum Shedrup Ling (Lamaist Buddhist Monastery of America), the first Tibetan Buddhist monastery in that country. By the time I visited him there in 1970, when I was teaching at Yale, he had gathered around him a small band of serious-minded lay students of the Dharma who evidently valued the opportunity of sitting at the feet of a representative of the Tibetan Buddhist tradition who combined, to an unusual degree, profound learning, fervent devotion, and extreme simplicity of life.

The present volume is the outcome of Geshe Wangyal's work with these students. As an introductory note informs us, the translations of which it consists 'were taught to various disciples on different occasions, and over the years English versions of most were written down a number of times; this work was the foundation from which the present volume was prepared' (p. 10). In other words *The Door of Liberation* consists of *precepts*, i.e. of material selected by Geshe Wangyal from the vast mass of Tibetan Buddhist literature, canonical and non-canonical, in accordance with the spiritual needs of those who were studying with him. As such, it exemplifies the well-known dictum of Atīśa, in his reply to a question put to him on his arrival in Tibet: 'The precept of the Lama is more important than the scriptures and commentaries' (p. 121).

All the precepts thus selected have been taken, moreover, from works handed down in, or originating with, the spiritual lineage to which the translator himself belongs, i.e. the lineage of Atīśa's chief disciple Geshe Dromtön, founder of the Kadam school, and of Tsongkhapa, the founder of its continuation, the Gelug school. Apart from the introduction, the work falls into two main parts. In the first part we have a short history of the lineage of the teaching, with accounts of Ānanda, Upagupta, Nāgārjuna, Āryadeva, Asaṅga, and other masters in the succession, together with stories illustrating workings of the law of karma. The first of these stories is a highly colourful account of the miraculous deeds of Śākyamuni Buddha, by means of which he gained victory over the Six Pandits; the second the romantic story of his previous life as Prince Gedun; and the third the unbelievably disastrous history of the nun Utpaladok. All these stories are paralleled in Pāli canonical literature, and elsewhere.

The second part of the work consists entirely of material originating in Tibet. First comes a complete translation of the *Kadamthorbu*, or 'Precepts Collected from Here and There'. These precepts, which, as the collector Tsunba Jegom reminds us, are 'the heartfelt speech of many holy beings', begin with short dialogues between Atīśa and his closest disciples and are followed by the teachings of Dromtön and his later successors. Some of the precepts are very striking indeed. For example Yerbay Shangtsun tells us, 'If you do not meditate on impermanence in the early morning, by midday you will have many desires.' Next we have a group of four works by Tsongkhapa. The first is an ecstatic hymn of praise to the Buddha, as teacher of dependent origination, composed after a profound spiritual experience in which he had seen the true meaning of the Madhyamaka teaching and obtained final insight into the nature of existence. The three other works are brief but systematic expositions of the Path from different points of view. The best known of the three is *The Three Chief Paths*, an English version of which I produced some years ago with the help of John Driver and Mr Trethong at the special request of the Dalai Lama.[308] Here it is accompanied by a commentary written by the Fourth Panchen Lama which firmly places the work within a context of spiritual practice in general and meditation practice in particular. All three works emphasize the importance of a total disengagement from conditioned existence, the development of the Will to Enlightenment, and the realization of Voidness through insight into the true meaning of dependent origination.

As one goes through the volume, one feels pervading every page a deep reverence for the Three Jewels, for the spiritual life, and the spiritual tradition. The actual production of the book, moreover, has evidently been carried out in the same spirit. Geshe Wangyal and his associates are deserving of our deepest gratitude for this gift of the Dharma, which places us in direct contact with one of the outstanding spiritual lineages of Tibetan Buddhism.

VISUAL DHARMA AND AURAL DHARMA

Chögyam Trungpa, Rinpoche
Visual Dharma: The Buddhist Art of Tibet
Shambhala Publications, Berkeley & London 1975

Piyadassi Thera
The Book of Protection
Mrs H. M. Gunasekera Trust, Colombo 1975

Buddhist art has been known in the West almost as long as Buddhism, but it is only quite recently that its true nature, i.e. the nature of its relation to Buddhism and its place in the spiritual life, has begun to be understood. Formerly the function of Buddhist art was considered to be decorative, or at best illustrative. Buddhism (so it was thought) was essentially a system of abstract ideas, and these ideas were to be apprehended by the rational mind. The function of Buddhist art was to render the ideas more palatable, or to make them more easily comprehensible to the dull-witted. Buddhist art was thus of the nature of a concession, and in a better world would not have been necessary. Recently, however, a change has taken place, both in our understanding of Buddhism and our attitude towards Buddhist art. Indeed, the two are interrelated. Buddhism is now seen not as a system of abstract ideas, i.e. not just as a 'philosophy', but rather as a concrete spiritual experience. The abstract ideas are only the medium through which the experience is communicated. As for Buddhist art, it too is seen as a medium of communication – in its own right. Its function is not to illustrate the ideas in terms of which Buddhism, as a spiritual experience, is communicated to the rational mind, but rather to act as an alternative means of communication altogether. Buddhist art communicates spiritual experience to the imagination through the medium of form and colour. It is visual Dharma. This more traditional attitude towards Buddhist art is exemplified in Chögyam Trungpa's book. *Visual Dharma: The Buddhist Art of Tibet*, which is the catalogue of an exhibition of thangkas and images (mostly thangkas) held at the Massachusetts Institute of Technology, gives us not only a series of fifty-four plates, three of them in colour, but also descriptive notes on all the exhibits and an introductory essay that begins with the uncompromising statement 'The art of Tibet is entirely based on the spirituality of Buddhism.' Thus we get both a glimpse into the transcendental wonderland of Tibetan Buddhist art and a guide to its true significance. The introductory essay is divided into three parts: 'Background and History', 'Elements of Iconography', and 'Five Buddha Families'. In the second of these, which is of particular interest and value, the Rimpoche tells us that thangkas and other forms of Tibetan art express the vision of Tantric Buddhism and that they fall, according to their subject matter, into six general categories: (1) Enlightened beings (i.e. Buddhas, gurus, and bodhisattvas), (2) *yidams*, (3) *dharmapālas*, (4) mandalas and stupas, (5) illustrations of the teaching, and (6) *yantras*. Accounts are given of all of these, the greatest amount of space being devoted to the *yidams* or personal deities. 'A practitioner's yidam represents his particular characteristic expression of Buddha-nature. Identifying with his yidam, therefore, means identifying with his own basic nature, free from its distorted aspects' (p. 20). Many of the illustrations depict *yidams*, and this tells us a great deal not only about the Tantra but about the Buddhist art of Tibet.

As visual Dharma, Buddhist art directs itself to the sense of sight, for it is sight that perceives form and colour, the medium through which Buddhist art communicates with the imagination. In addition to the sense of sight, however, there is another highly developed sense, that of hearing. Buddhist art therefore communicates not only through the medium of form and colour but through the medium of sound. In addition to visual Dharma there is aural Dharma. This aural Dharma consists in instrumental music (such as that which accompanies many Tibetan ceremonies) and chanting. When it consists of chanting there must, of course, be something chanted. What is this? In Sri Lanka at least, the answer would be, more often then not, that it is the *Pirith Potha* or '*The Book of Protection*', and it is this which Piyadassi Thera has translated from the original Pāli with an introductory essay and explanatory notes. Originally compiled for the use of novice monks, the work is, the translator tells us, the most widely known Pāli book in Sri Lanka (Ceylon), and can be called the Buddhist Bible(!) It consists for the most part of twenty-four short texts selected from the Sutta Piṭaka of the Pāli canon, and the nature of the selection tells us a good deal about the general character of traditional Sinhalese Buddhism. Besides the well-known *Maṅgala, Ratana*, and *Karaṇīyamettā Suttas*, there are spiritual instructions like the three discourses on the factors of Enlightenment (*bojjhaṅga*); practical advice like the ten verses on the Advantages of Friendship; ancient legends like the Discourse at Isigili; 'magical' and 'mythical' material like the *Mahāsamaya* or 'Great Assembly' Discourse; social comment like the Discourse on Outcastes; and profound 'philosophical' expositions like the Discourse on the Analysis of the (Four Noble) Truths (*sacca-vibhaṅga*). With one or two exceptions all these discourses were traditionally ascribed to the Buddha. In the present context, however, we are concerned not so much with the contents of the texts as with the use that is made of them. Piyadassi Thera tells us that it is the practice, in Buddhist lands, to listen to the recital of the Dhamma or doctrine of the Buddha 'in order to avert illness or danger, to ward off the influence of malignant beings, to obtain protection and deliverance from evil, and to promote health, prosperity, welfare, and well-being' (p. 11). How the recital is able to do this he explains partly with the help of modern tradition and partly with the help of modern discoveries in the field of parapsychology. He also gives us a description of the way in which the *paritta* – or in Sinhalese *pirith* – ceremony is performed in Sri Lanka. It is clear, however, that the true significance of *paritta* transcends any purely rationalistic explanation, and that it is most effective when, with concentrated mind, the devotee makes himself completely receptive to the spiritual reality which is behind the words as recited. *Paritta* thus becomes aural Dharma.

Should a further edition of *The Book of Protection* be called for, the author may consider it worth his while to include the Pāli texts of the *suttas* in Roman characters. As he himself points out, 'the habit of listening to the recital of *paritta suttas* among westerners is growing' (p. 18), and it would be helpful if material of this kind was more widely available.

THIRTY YEARS OF BUDDHIST STUDIES

Edward Conze
Thirty Years of Buddhist Studies: Selected Essays
Bruno Cassirer, Oxford 1967

The name of Dr Edward Conze requires no introduction to any English-knowing person with an interest in Buddhism. Since 1951 he has given us a steady stream of original works on Buddhism and translations of Buddhist texts, the majority of them marked by thoroughness of scholarship, distinction of thought and style, wide range of literary and philosophical reference, an agreeable tartness of expression, and an all-pervading spiritual concern. The present volume, his seventeenth dealing with Buddhism according to my reckoning, garners some of the chips from his workshop over the last three decades.

As might have been expected, the essays comprising *Thirty Years of Buddhist Studies* (a slightly misleading title, perhaps) reflect most of the author's major interests. Seven of them deal, in one way or another, with the Prajñāpāramitā or 'Perfection of Wisdom' tradition, one of them consisting of a translation of *The Perfection of Wisdom in Seven Hundred Lines* hitherto available only in typescript and duplicated form. Others deal with Mahāyāna Buddhism, with recent progress in Buddhist studies, and with Buddhist philosophy and its European parallels, both genuine and spurious. For good measure, there is one on the meditation on death as well as a translation of chapter 5 of the

Saddharma Puṇḍarīka which makes us very much wish that Dr Conze would give us (as I suggested to him some years ago) a complete version of this important *sūtra*. Surely he is not going to leave us indefinitely to the tender mercies of Kern and Soothill!

Despite the severely intellectual and technical nature of much of the material with which he deals, Dr Conze's concern for Buddhism as a living spiritual tradition breaks through whenever it finds an opportunity. Some of his comments are particularly relevant to the Western Buddhist scene. Speaking of Prof. T. R. V. Murti's *The Central Philosophy of Buddhism* he says, 'Its title is a challenge to Western Buddhists which so far they show little sign of heeding, with the result that their faulty perspective vitiates both their theory and practice. The central tradition is that of Emptiness, represented by the Sarvāstivādins, Mādyamikas, and Tibetan lamas. By contrast, Theravādins and Zen, which alone have caught on so far, are peripheral' (pp. 20–1). Even more acidly, 'Zen was designed to operate within emptiness. When coming West it transferred into a vacuum' (p. 29). Himself an intellectual, he is deeply aware of the limitations of a purely theoretical approach to Buddhism, and reminds us, 'It is up to us to see to it that the rain which has descended so abundantly from the Rain-cloud of the Dharma actually nourishes our spiritual faculties, and does not just go down the drain of mere intellectual curiosity' (p. 32). Finally there is a word of advice to would-be bodhisattvas. 'A very high degree of sanctity is necessary to do good to others without harming or irritating them' (p. 58). The volume would be well worth buying simply for the sake of aperçus such as these.

FORTY YEARS IN THE WORKSHOP

Edward Conze
Further Buddhist Studies: Selected Essays
Bruno Cassirer, Oxford 1975

More than thirty-five years ago I carried home from a second-hand bookshop in south London the four stout volumes of Max Müller's *Chips from a German Workshop*, and I can still remember the thrill of pleasure they gave me. It is with no less pleasure, and even greater profit, that I explored the second volume of 'chips' from the good German workshop which Dr Conze set up on British soil in 1933 with, as he tells us, no other capital than 'a fairly large work on *Der Satz vom Widerspruch* which, modelling myself a bit on Arthur Schopenhauer, I was inclined to regard as my *Hauptwerk*' (p. ix).

Like his great predecessor Dr Conze writes a fluent and readable English of some literary distinction, and we are reminded that English is not his native tongue by little more than the fact that he writes it more correctly than the educated Englishman normally would do. In the extent of his range, too, he resembles Max Müller, and if there is less philology, and more psychology, in the *Studies* than in the *Chips*, the general reader, at least, will not complain. Like Max Müller, too, Dr Conze has been occupied for the greater part of his working life with a single major literary project. In Max Müller's case this was, of course, the editing and translating of the *Rig Veda*, and many of the ‘chips’ in my four stout volumes were, I found, the by-products of this great undertaking. Similarly, Dr Conze has for thirty years and more devoted himself to editing, translating, and elucidating the corpus of Mahāyāna *sūtras*, approximately three dozen in number, which deal with Prajñāpāramitā or Perfect Wisdom, and which together constitute, as he has more than once reminded us, one of the greatest outbursts of spiritual creativity in the history of mankind. Both in *Further Buddhist Studies* and in its predecessor *Thirty Years of Buddhist Studies* some of Dr Conze’s biggest and most important chips are a by-product of his heroic labours at this colossal task, labours which have resulted in what is, with the possible exception of the Pāli Text Society’s translations of the Sutta and Vinaya Piṭakas of the Pāli canon, probably the biggest single contribution to the English-speaking world’s knowledge of the Buddhist scriptures.

The essays brought together in the present volume are distributed under four headings: (1) Longer Articles, (2) The Philosophical Background, (3) Shorter Articles, and (4) Reviews; and they range backwards and forwards over the fields of philosophy, psychology, logic, comparative religion, sociology, history, and the fine arts. Now Dr Conze is examining an eleventh-century Sanskrit manuscript, now exploring the social origins of nominalism, now casting doubt on the ability of ‘analytical psychology’ to do justice to the higher ranges of the spiritual life. Out of the riches thus placed at our disposal, probably it is the three longer articles that will have the greatest appeal to the English-speaking Western Buddhist, particularly the third, ‘Love, Compassion, and Sympathetic Joy’, in which we see Dr Conze at his most caustic and most acute. To me the most interesting of the essays, in many ways, is the second of the longer articles, ‘Buddhism and Gnosis’. In this essay, originally a paper read at a learned congress on ‘The Origins of Gnosticism’, Dr Conze describes what he thinks are the eight basic similarities between Near-eastern Gnosis and Indian Mahāyāna Buddhism. Though I have long felt that there was some connection, not necessarily a historical one, between Buddhism and Gnosticism, on the whole I find Dr Conze’s similarities not very convincing – possibly because the discussion is not exhaustive enough to be conclusive. In particular, the discussion of Wisdom as a feminine deity seems to require, in the case of Mahāyāna Buddhism at least, rather more than the rash application of the vague and uncritical distinction between ‘matriarchal’ and 'patriarchal' religions. Most uncharacteristically, Dr Conze would seem to have fallen victim here to the methods of 'analytical psychology'.

The three articles that make up 'The Philosophical Background' are the product of Dr Conze's Marxist studies, having been decanted into English, as he tells us in the foreword, from the original German of *Der Satz vom Widerspruch*. Not very surprisingly, they all foreshadow to some extent certain of his later preoccupations in the field of Buddhist thought. Consideration of the objective validity of that bedrock of formal logic the principle of contradiction, for instance, leads him from the dialectics of Heraclitus, Nicholas of Cusa, and Hegel straight into the transcendental domain of Perfect Wisdom, wherein all the laws of thought are suspended, and so to thirty years of work on the Prajñāpāramitā *sūtras*. Despite early ascetical and mystical leanings, Dr Conze must sometimes have asked himself how the author of a Schopenhauerian *Hauptwerk* could ever have ended up in this way.

The atmosphere of the 'Shorter Articles' is on the whole much less rarefied, and in most of them we find ourselves on what is, conventionally speaking, firmer ground. Indeed, in 'The Present State and Future Prospects of Buddhism in Asia' Dr Conze brings us back to earth with a nasty bump. How many Western Buddhists, I wonder, realize how great has been the damage suffered by Buddhist institutions in Asia, and the extent to which the pressure of modern life affects monastic institutions, doctrinal integrity, and cooperation between monks and laity? Dr Conze indeed goes so far as to speak of 'the deadly and irreconcilable conflict between Buddhist traditions and the main forces of the modern age' (p. 126), and I do not think he exaggerates.

In the 'Reviews', where we are given a mere 31 out of a total of 143 actually written and published, we are very much in the workshop, and the chips fly thick and fast as Dr Conze, axe in hand, gives a keen and workmanlike appraisal of the products of other workshops, these latter being largely in the form of editions and translations of Sanskrit Buddhist texts and expositions of the Dharma both scholarly and popular. Sometimes the sparks fly too, for Dr Conze finds some of the products extremely shoddy. Arthur Koestler's *The Lotus and the Robot* is shown to be 'a mere travesty of the facts', while the author of *Philosophy of the Buddha*, A. J. Bahm, is convicted of total ignorance of his subject. Where praise is due, however, Dr Conze can be both warm and generous, and in the fairly numerous instances where the workmanship is of uneven quality, or the product only partly satisfactory, he deals out praise and blame with judicial impartiality.

In this volume, which jointly with its predecessor the publishers rightly describe as representing 'an almost inexhaustible source for all serious students of Buddhism', Dr Conze throughout shows himself very much the scholar, indeed, very much the German scholar – thorough, conscientious, and painstaking, and in all that concerns his chosen field of study well-informed to the point of virtual omniscience. At the same time he reveals himself to be very much a Buddhist. In the foreword where he has, so he rather engagingly confesses, at the prompting of friends let his hair down 'quite a bit', he tells us that during the war he devoted himself to the practice of meditation first in a wood in Hampshire, then in a caravan in Oxfordshire. In the eyes of some scholars so 'unscientific' an approach totally disqualifies him from writing on Buddhism, and it is clear that, in Dr Conze's own words, some of his views stick in the gullets of his academic contemporaries. Indeed, his acceptance of magic induced the then president of the Aristotlean Society, who was also the first female professor of logic in modern history, to absent herself from the meeting where she should have chaired his paper on 'Dharma as a Spiritual, Social, and Cosmic Force'. Having had my own experience of the workings of this kind of logic, I feel I can share Dr Conze's amusement. Quite recently a translation of one of my books was refused by a European-language publisher on the grounds that the author was a Buddhist and could not, therefore, be objective about Buddhism. Eventually he decided to publish, instead, a translation of a book by Alan Watts. So far as Western Buddhists are concerned – so far as Buddhists everywhere are concerned – whether the author be a scholar who has meditated or a monk who tries not to be unscholarly, a book on Buddhism is none the worse for having been written by someone who actually believes in the Dharma. Indeed, they will rejoice that a scholar of Dr Conze's standing should say such things as 'there is no greater menace than a mere grammarian let loose on a sacred text' (p. 138), not to mention aperçus like 'a religion's unworldliness is its greatest asset' (p. 179) and 'It is foolish to expect too much advance information about spiritual states' (p. 149).

Apart from the fact that it is written by one who is both *paṇḍita* and *upāsaka*, scholar and devotee, one of the strongest impressions that one gets from this book is that of continuity and completeness of development. From the Teutonic lucubrations of *Der Satz vom Widerspruch* to the genial asperity of the latest book reviews, the themes with which Dr Conze is preoccupied remain constant. Nor is this all. Despite the difficulties with which he has had to contend, he has had the satisfaction not only of having throughout his career

> ... wrought
> Upon the plan that pleased his boyish thought[309]

but also of being able to carry to a successful conclusion one of the most important literary undertakings in the history of Western Buddhism. Indeed, now that he has given us *The Larger Sūtra of Perfect Wisdom* (1976), it would appear that (apart from the unfinished translation of the *Saddharma Puṇḍarīka*?) Dr Conze's *biographia literaria* has no loose ends left, and it is perhaps significant that he rounds off *Further Buddhist Studies* with a bibliography. After forty years in the workshop, who will blame him if he wishes to lay down his tools at last and retire, if not to the wood in Hampshire or the caravan in Oxfordshire, at least to some quiet retreat in the depths of rural Dorset, there to adopt again, perhaps, the more direct approach to the great truths which he has served so faithfully and so long.

D. H. LAWRENCE AND THE SPIRITUAL COMMUNITY

Keith Sagar
The Life of D. H. Lawrence: An Illustrated Biography
Eyre Methuen, London 1980

D. H. Lawrence died in Vence, in the south of France, on 2 March 1930, at the age of 44. In the course of twenty years of writing life he had produced a substantial body of work that comprised fiction, poetry, travel-writing, essays, criticism, history, reminiscence, letters, reviews, and plays, as well as paintings. A considerable portion of this output occupies an important place in twentieth-century English literature, and some of it – mainly fiction and poetry, undoubtedly ranks as a permanent part of our literary heritage. In the decade following his death Lawrence's reputation as a writer declined, but in more recent years it has steadily increased and he is now widely regarded as the outstanding creative force of his generation. It was therefore to be expected that the fiftieth anniversary of his death should be marked by the production of radio and television versions of his novels, revivals of his plays, and, of course, the publication of books on the man himself, his life, and his work.

Among the books that have so far appeared is this illustrated biography by Keith Sagar, already well known as the editor of Lawrence's *Selected Poems* in the Penguin Poets series. Glossy, large, and lavishly illustrated as it is, it would be easy to dismiss *The Life of*

D. H. Lawrence as yet another 'coffee table' volume; but the book is in fact much more than that. As any biography of Lawrence must, it of course takes us from the township in the semi-rural, semi-industrialized Midlands where 'Young Bert' grew up, to the villa on the Côte D'Azur where, 'The Longest Journey' ended, the famous – perhaps notorious – author died of tuberculosis. In between we are taken to London and Cornwall, Germany and Italy, New Mexico, Ceylon, and Australia. We meet intellectuals and aristocrats, writers and artists, peasants and peons, bohemians and bankers.

But although we are taken on the usual biographical conducted tour, we are not taken on it in quite the usual way. What Mr Sagar has done is both novel and interesting. He has told the story of Lawrence's life mainly by means of extracts from Lawrence's own writings, especially the letters, as well as from the letters, diaries, and reminiscences of his friends. Mr Sagar himself provides the connecting narrative. In this way we are given a sort of running commentary on the events of Lawrence's life more or less as they actually happen, and given it, for the most part, in Lawrence's own words and the words of those who, for a longer or a shorter period, were in personal contact with him and who were themselves a part of his life. The result of this method is a tremendous immediacy of impact. We seem to be living *with* Lawrence rather than reading about him long afterwards. The impression of immediacy is heightened by the fact that the text is accompanied throughout by 150 pictures, many of them not previously published, which are almost as essential to the book as the text itself. These pictures enable us to see the places in which Lawrence lived, and the people with whom he associated. They enable us to see the physical changes that took place in him over the years. It is indeed with something like a shock that we see the handsome, healthy young man of 23 slowly turning into the haggard, shrunken figure of 44. Sixteen of the pictures are in colour, eight of them being reproductions of Lawrence's own paintings. The colours of the paintings tell us something about Lawrence that we could not, perhaps, have learned in any other way.

By permitting Lawrence's life to speak, virtually, for itself, Keith Sagar enables us to see a number of things that might otherwise have remained obscure. I for one am convinced that what killed Lawrence was not so much tuberculosis as the war. Keith Sagar himself seems to believe as much. In the introduction to his *Penguin Selected Poems* he says, 'The horrors of the war, the moral debacle at home, the suppression of his splendid novel, *The Rainbow*, persecution, ill-health, and poverty, all combined to destroy in Lawrence, during the war, his faith in humanity and a human future'. As early as 1915 Lawrence stated bluntly, 'The War finished me: it was the spear through the side of all sorrows and hopes' (p. 75), while towards the end of his life he told Trigant Burrow that his illness was nothing but chagrin caused by 'the absolute frustration of my primeval societal instinct' (p. 218) and Witter Bynner that his sickness was 'a sort of rage' (p. 242). The war was, indeed, a kind of watershed in his life. Between the pre-war and the post-war Lawrence there is a whole world of difference. The first was the man of whom Jessie Chambers wrote, 'Lawrence seemed so happy that merely to be alive and walking about was an adventure, and his gift for creating an atmosphere of good fellowship a joy' (p. 26); the second the man who, at 30, described himself as being 'mad with misery and hostility and rage' (p. 85), and who wrote, 'Sometimes I wish I could let go and be really wicked – kill and murder – but kill chiefly. I do want to kill. But I want to select whom I shall kill. Then I shall enjoy it' and, 'I am hostile, hostile, hostile to all that is, in our public and national life. I want to destroy it' (p. 86). The first Lawrence did not, of course, die completely – in a sense he even outlived the second Lawrence – and in the end attained a kind of wan resurrection. Mr Sagar is not quite correct, however, in saying that, during the war, Lawrence's faith in humanity and a human future was destroyed. What happened was that his faith took a more specialized, a more desperate, form. It took a form that was, in effect, a response to the challenge of the war. It took the form of what Lawrence called Rananim and what Buddhists call sangha or spiritual community.

This is not to say that there is much in Mr Sagar's biography that is of direct Buddhist interest, though there is much that is of indirect Buddhist interest, as least so far as Western Buddhists are concerned. Lawrence's references to Buddhism are few, and most of them are uncomplimentary. To Earl and Achsah Brewster, Americans, vegetarians, and 'budding Buddhists' as Richard Aldington called them, whom he had met in Capri in 1921 and with whom he joined up in Ceylon for a few weeks the following year, on his way to Australia, Lawrence wrote 'The American Indian, the Aztec, old Mexico – all that fascinates me and has fascinated me for years. *There* is glamour and magic for me.

Not Buddha. Buddha is so finished and perfected and fulfilled and *vollendet*, and without any new possibilities – to me I mean' (pp. 128–9). In Ceylon itself, where Earl Brewster was studying Pāli, his impressions of Buddhism were even less favourable, though he enjoyed the Kandy Perahera, which was 'wonderful, gorgeous and barbaric with all its elephants and flames and devil dances in the night'. Not without insight, in view of the fact that it is the Theravāda Buddhism of Ceylon on which he is commenting, he continues, 'One realizes how barbaric the substratum of Buddhism is. I shrewdly suspect that the high-flownness of Buddhism altogether exists mostly on paper: and that its denial of the soul makes it always rather barren, even if philosophically, etc., it is more perfect'. He concludes, 'In short, after a slight contact, I draw back and don't like it' (p. 130). He certainly did not like what, writing to another friend, he described as 'the nasty faces and yellow robes of the Buddhist monks, the little vulgar dens of the temples' (p. 130), but then the heat that year was exceptional even for Ceylon, Lawrence was ill all the time he was there, and when he wrote he was evidently in a bad mood. Later, from Australia, he wrote to Earl Brewster, 'How I *hated* a great deal of my time in Ceylon: never felt so sick in my life. Yet now it is a very precious memory, invaluable. Not wild horses would drag me back. But neither time nor eternity will take away what I have of it: Ceylon and the East' (pp. 130–1). It is interesting to speculate what might have been the result had Lawrence come into contact with a form of Buddhism more spiritually alive than the Theravāda Buddhism of Ceylon. What would he have made of Zen, for instance, or of Tibetan Buddhism, had they been more accessible in his day? What would he have thought of our own Movement, had he lived long enough to see it? Despite his unfavourable opinion of Buddhism, or what purported to be Buddhism, there is little doubt that some of the questions with which he was most deeply concerned were questions on which Buddhism had something of special value to say to him. It is therefore important that Buddhists, especially Western Buddhists, should not be misled by Lawrence's bad-tempered snarlings at monks and temples but try to understand what he meant by Rananim and why his efforts to establish it were unsuccessful.

'*Ra'annanim*' is a Hebrew word meaning 'green, fresh, and flourishing', and Keith Sagar tells us that 'Rananim was to be a monastic community secluded from the sick world, of some twenty righteous or at least like-minded people dedicated to fostering 'new shoots of life' within themselves, and subsequently to seeding the sterile ruins of Western civilization' (p. 75). The similarity to our own conception of spiritual community is obvious. At one time Lawrence referred to Rananim as the 'island' idea, adding, 'But they say, the island shall be England, that we shall start our new community in the midst of the old one, as a seed falls among the roots of the parent' (p. 83). (There are overtones here of Blake's building Jerusalem in England's green and pleasant land, but Lawrence seems to be unconscious of them.) At another time it was 'the colony', and it was to be in Florida – or Cornwall (p. 94). Once the idea took the still more tenuous form of founding a publishing company 'that publishes for the sake of truth' (p. 97). According to Keith Sagar, Lawrence had long been fascinated by the monastic life. 'Despite his allegiance to the body, he led a very simple, slightly ascetic life, and his hatred of the human [as distinct from the animal and vegetable] world led him to explore various forms of withdrawal from it. He often spoke of Rananim as a "monastic community"' (p. 117). (Buddhist 'monasticism' is not, of course, based on hatred of the human world.) On at least one occasion, towards the end of his life, when he had given up hope of being able to establish Rananim, he advised the young Rolf Gardiner to found what – using an interesting expression – he called 'flexible monasteries' (p. 206). In one form or another, the idea of Rananim was, according to Keith Sagar, 'always Lawrence's last resort. All his other ideas about human relationships were put to the test, if not in reality, then in his fiction. But he never dared follow through, imaginatively, the Rananim idea; it was too precious to put at risk. When he writes of it in his letters, his language lapses into Arcadian or Prelapsarian' (p. 104).

Reluctant as he may have been to follow the Rananim idea through imaginatively, in his fiction (as Goethe, for instance, had done, with a similar idea, in *Wilhelm Meister's Travels*) Lawrence certainly strove to bring it into existence as a concrete social reality, at least during the decade from 1914 to 1924, and at least intermittently. In 1915 he was doing his best to co-opt such Cambridge-Bloomsbury figures as E. M. Forster and Bertrand Russell, as well as John Middleton Murry and the young Aldous Huxley. In 1925 came the famous party at the Café Royal when, a few days after his return from America, Lawrence asked his seven special friends, one by one, if they would go with him (and Frieda Lawrence) back to New Mexico and start a new life, and when only the deaf artist Dorothy Brett – accompanied by Toby, her ear trumpet – actually did so. In between, he and Murry started up a little monthly paper and organized weekly meetings, both of which soon fizzled out, he and Murry swore blood brotherhood (or at least Lawrence did), and the Lawrences and the Murrys tried to live together in Cornwall. Perhaps the nearest Lawrence ever came to realizing his idea of Rananim was when, in 1922, he and Frieda lived for four months in New Mexico very close to the two itinerant young Danish artists, Knud Merrild and Kai Gotzsche. 'The Lawrences and the Danes made no demands on each other,' says Keith Sagar, 'and an easy friendship developed spontaneously' (p. 146). In the end Lawrence was reduced to projecting his idea of Rananim onto the lives of the ancient Etruscans who, provided one did not look too closely, could be regarded as having created a perfect human society – a society that had been destroyed by the brutal militaristic Romans.

Seeing how desperately Lawrence believed in the idea of Rananim – *needed* to believe if he was to retain any faith in humanity and a human future – the question that confronts us is: Why was Lawrence unable to give concrete, social embodiment to his idea? Why was he unable to establish Rananim as a living reality? After all, besides being, as a writer, the outstanding creative force of his generation, as a man he was, by all accounts, an exceptionally charming and stimulating companion. Yet towards the end of 1916, looking back over what was to have been the Year One of the New World, he could write to Koteliansky, from whose chanting of Hebrew music he had taken the word Rananim, 'I tell you Rananim, my Florida idea, was the true one. Only the *people* were wrong. But to go to Rananim *without* the people is right.' On which Keith Sagar wryly comments, 'a colony without people. A sad conclusion' (p. 100). A sad conclusion indeed! A colony, a Rananim, a spiritual community, consisting, in effect, of just Lawrence and Frieda! What had gone wrong? What was it that *continued* to go wrong, and continued to go wrong until, even though he so passionately believed that 'Men are free when they belong to a living, organic, *believing* community, active in fulfilling some unfulfilled, perhaps unrealized purpose' (p. 145) – even though he complained so bitterly of the frustration of his primeval societal instinct ('societal' perhaps in a deeper sense that he knew) – Rananim in the end became no more than a dream and Lawrence could write to Ralph Gardiner, resignedly now, but still sadly, 'As far as *anything* matters, I have always been very much alone, and regretted it'? (p. 206).

What had gone wrong was not one thing, but a number of things, all interrelated. In the light of our own experience of spiritual community within the FWBO, it may be possible for us not only to identify the principal factors leading to the failure of Lawrence's idea of Rananim but also to make it clear how, given those factors, the idea was doomed to failure from the start. We can best do this, perhaps, by first reminding ourselves of some basic principles – principles that, as a result of our own efforts to put the Buddhist ideal of spiritual community into practice in the West, we have found to be true – and then applying those principles to the idea of Rananim as Lawrence actually sought to carry it out. Enumerated more or less at random, the principles in question are: (1) The spiritual community consists of individuals. (2) The 'couple' is the enemy of the spiritual community. (3) The spiritual community is not a group. (4) The spiritual community must have a common ideal and a common method of practice. Though enumerated at random, these four principles will provide us with a framework for a brief discussion of Lawrence's failure to give concrete, social embodiment to his idea of Rananim and, at the same time, enable us to see the limitations of the idea of Rananim itself – limitations that were obvious to at least some of Lawrence's friends, even though they were not all obvious to all of them, or even to Lawrence himself.

1. THE SPIRITUAL COMMUNITY CONSISTS OF INDIVIDUALS

The significance of this statement is not so obvious as it might, at first sight, appear to be. What do we mean by 'individuals', and in what way does a spiritual community consist of them? At least so far as the establishing of Rananim was concerned, Lawrence himself, it seems, did not have a clearly defined concept of 'the individual' – perhaps would not have wanted to have one – although when he told Koteliansky 'only the *people* were wrong,' what he may have meant was that they were not individuals, i.e. not true individuals. From the Buddhist point of view, the (true) individual is one who is self-conscious or self-aware (though not in the alienated way that Lawrence so rightly condemned), able to think for himself, emotionally positive, creative rather than reactive in his attitude towards life, spontaneous, sensitive, and responsible. The spiritual community consists of (true) individuals in the sense that it is a free association of – the sum total of the non-exploitive, non-addictive relationships between – a number of people who are individuals in the sense defined. Lawrence perhaps had an inkling of what this sort of community was like when, towards the end of his life, he wrote that 'the new relationship will be some sort of tenderness, sensitive, between men and men and men and women, and not the one up one down, lead on I follow, *ich dien* sort of business' (p. 207).

2. THE 'COUPLE' IS THE ENEMY OF THE SPIRITUAL COMMUNITY.

By the couple, in this context, one means two people, usually of the opposite sex, who are neurotically dependent on each other and whose relationship, therefore, is one of mutual exploitation and mutual addiction. A couple consists, in fact, of two half-people, each of whom unconsciously invests part of his or her total being in the other: each is dependent on the other for the kind of psychological security that can be found, ultimately, only within oneself. Two such half-people, uneasily conjoined as a couple, can no more be part of a spiritual community than Siamese twins can be part of the *corps de ballet*. Their 'presence' within the spiritual community can only have a disruptive effect. The couple is therefore the enemy of the spiritual community. Lawrence, however, did not see this. Perhaps, because of his personal history, and the pervasive influence of our culturally-conditioned notion of 'romantic love' between the sexes, he *could* not see it. As is well known, for him the man–woman relationship was at the very centre of things, even though balanced, to some extent, by the man–man relationship. This meant, in effect, that the couple was at the centre of things. Rananim was to be made up of married couples: a contradiction in terms. Among all Lawrence's friends, the only person who seems to have spotted the contradiction was E. M. Forster. Writing at the beginning of 1915, after Lawrence had scolded him so much on his visits to Greatham that, as Keith Sagar says, 'at last the worm turned', he began his letter, 'Dear Lawrences,' and continued, significantly, 'Until you think it worthwhile to function separately, I'd better address you as one' (p. 82). Because Lawrence did not think it 'worthwhile' to function separately it was not really possible for him to relate to others *as an individual* – certainly not to the extent that is required in the spiritual community – and because he could not relate to others as an individual he was unable to bring Rananim into existence. He could not have his wedding cake and eat it too, although, like most of us, he wanted to.

3. THE SPIRITUAL COMMUNITY IS NOT A GROUP

It is not a group because a group, unlike a spiritual community, does not consist of individuals but of those who have yet to become individuals. Before one can distinguish the spiritual community from the group, therefore, one must be able to distinguish the individual from the proto-individual or 'group member', and in order to do that one must be an individual oneself, for only an individual can recognize another individual. From this it follows that if one is not an individual, and therefore unable to distinguish individual from proto-individual, one will tend to bring into existence not a spiritual community but, at best, a 'positive group'. This is what happened with Lawrence. Moreover, if one is not able to relate to others as an individual one will tend to relate to them in some other way. Lawrence was not able to relate to others as an individual: he had to be their leader; he had to ask them to follow him. Most of his friends did not want to do this, much as they loved and admired him, and some of them were honest enough to say so. 'I like you Lawrence,' said Mary Cannan, when *she* was asked if she would go with him back to New Mexico, 'but not so much as all that, and I think you are asking what no human being has a right to ask another' (pp. 168–9). Eventually, Lawrence himself repudiated the idea of leadership, as we have seen, declaring, 'the leader of men is a back number' (p. 207). He had seen that Rananim could not be a group; but he had not really seen how it could be a spiritual community. He could not 'link up with the social unconscious,' i.e. could not be simply a member of the group; at the same time, not being a true individual, he was unable to enter into a free association with other individuals, even had he been able to find them. Consequently, 'One has no real human relations – that is so devastating' (p. 218).

4. THE SPIRITUAL COMMUNITY MUST HAVE A COMMON IDEAL AND A COMMON METHOD OF PRACTICE

As we have seen, the spiritual community consists of individuals. But individuals, i.e. true individuals, do not come ready made: they have to be created; they have to create themselves. A spiritual community, therefore, cannot be established in the sort of way that a group can be established. It comes into existence only when a number of people work on themselves – and on one another – in such a way that they actually become individuals and are able to relate to one another as individuals. But how does one work on oneself? How does one actually become an individual? In order to become an individual one needs a definite method of practice, by which is meant not a mere technique of bringing about 'results' irrespective of one's mental attitude but an effective means of radical self-transformation. In Buddhism the principal method of practice is meditation, in which one works directly on the mind itself, transforming self-consciousness into transcendental consciousness and so on. Lawrence wanted to establish Rananim. But he and his friends were not individuals to start with, though Lawrence himself, at least, had some of the characteristics of the true individual, nor were they able to work on themselves and become individuals. They were unable to work on themselves because they had no common method of practice. All that Lawrence was able to offer them was the prospect of somehow reverting to the pre-conscious state of the infant, in which self-consciousness does not exist and one feels at one with the whole of existence – thus implying that the pre-conscious state is higher than the conscious state. Moreover, a definite method of practice presupposes a definite ideal, for a method is a method only in relation to a certain end. Since Lawrence had no clearly defined concept of the individual it was not really possible for him to have the individual as his ideal, and because he did not have the individual as his ideal it was not possible for him and his friends to become individuals, or even to have a means of becoming such. In Buddhism the end in relation to which meditation is the principal means is true individuality. The ultimate ideal of Buddhism is the ideal of human Enlightenment, which is not an ideal imposed upon man from without (the kind of pseudo-ideal against which Lawrence protested) but one which is implicit in his own nature and which represents the fulfilment of his nature in the deepest and truest sense.

Lawrence's idea of Rananim was much more than one sensitive, creative person's response to the challenge of war. In reality it represented the proto-individual's response to the challenge of the group as such, whether in peace or war, a response that in Lawrence's case took the form of an attempt – a blind, almost instinctive attempt – to rise from the level of the group to a higher level of human development, both individual and collective, by establishing the kind of new society that Buddhists call sangha or spiritual community. Unfortunately, for the reasons that have been given, Lawrence's attempt to give concrete, social embodiment to his idea of Rananim was a failure. For us that failure is not without its uses, especially at a time like the present, when the brute mass of corporate existence by which we are surrounded – in which we live embedded – poses a greater threat, and presents a greater challenge, than it ever did in Lawrence's time. Among other things, Lawrence's failure serves to remind us that the spiritual community is something that has to be striven for. The fact that the ideal of sangha or spiritual community is an integral part of Buddhism does not mean that spiritual community comes to us on a plate. It is not something that, as 'Buddhists', we automatically have. On the contrary, it is something we bring into existence from moment to moment by virtue of our free association one with another as individuals. Lawrence failed to bring Rananim into existence because he did not have the 'blueprint' of the spiritual community. We have the blueprint, but we shall no more be able to bring the spiritual community into existence than he was unless we can become true individuals and can relate to one another as such. Even though we make the effort that this involves, we shall make it all the more successfully if we have even a little of the sensitivity and creativity of the Lawrence who lives so vividly in the pages of Mr Sagar's biography.

BUDDHISM AND WILLIAM BLAKE

Buddhism is a universal teaching. It speaks to all men. It speaks to them, moreover, not as belonging to any particular social group, e.g. clan, tribe, caste, race, nation, but as individual human beings. What it tells each one of them is that he can grow – that he can grow from manhood into Buddhahood, or from unenlightened humanity into Enlightened humanity. It also tells him how he can do this. When Buddhism speaks to men in this way it of course has to speak to them in a language which they can understand. This means much more than speaking to them in their own vernacular. It means communicating with them through the medium of their own ideas, their own culture. Since Buddhism originated in ancient India it at first had to speak – the Buddha had to speak – the language of ancient Indian culture. In fact it had to speak the language of two cultures, the śrāmaṇic and the brāhmaṇic. Later, when Buddhism spread outside India, it had to speak the language of other cultures, in particular those of South-east Asia, China, Japan, and Tibet. (Sometimes, when the indigenous 'linguistic' resources were inadequate, it had to take Indian culture along with it, but that is another story.) Since Buddhism did not spread beyond Asia, all the cultures with which it came into contact, and through which it had to communicate, were Asian cultures. Although it is in reality a universal teaching, when identified with its medium of communication Buddhism tends to appear as a phenomenon of the cultural history of the East. It tends to appear as an Eastern religion.

During the last century Buddhism has begun to spread beyond Asia. It has begun to make contact with Western culture. As yet, however, it has not really begun to communicate through the medium of that culture. Western Buddhists, and those interested in Buddhism, therefore have to study it in a foreign language, as it were, i.e. through the medium of one or another Asian culture. The situation is made more difficult by the fact that what Asian Buddhist teachers bring to the West is, only too often, not so much Buddhism as the cultural forms with which, for them, it is associated, even identified. Buddhism will not really spread in the West until it speaks the language of Western culture. This will take time. One of the ways in which we can hasten the process is by bringing Buddhism into contact with those Western poets, thinkers, and mystics in whose life or work, or both, there is a reflection, however faint, of the supra-historical splendours of the principial Dharma and who, therefore, already communicate to us something of the spirit of Buddhism in the language of Western culture. One of the greatest of these winged spirits is the English poet, prophet, and visionary William Blake.

Blake was born in London on 28 November 1757, and died there on 12 August 1827. His life thus coincided with one of the most momentous periods in English – indeed in modern Western – history. As a young man he saw and welcomed the American and French Revolutions, while in middle life he was witness to the tremendous upheavals of the Napoleonic wars. He also lived through the Industrial Revolution, with all the changes that this brought about in the social, economic, and political life of the nation. Although he lived in such eventful times, Blake's outward life at least was uneventful. He attended a drawing school for a few years (the only formal education he received), and when he was 15 his father, a hosier, apprenticed him to an engraver, with whom he spent the customary seven years learning his trade. Thereafter Blake supported himself by his own labour, but since the skill of the engraver was less in demand than previously he had often to fight a losing battle with poverty and want – a battle that ended only with his death. In 1782 he married the daughter of a market gardener, and though childless the union was a happy one. From 1782 to 1827 only two events occurred to interrupt the even tenor of Blake's existence in a succession of London lodgings and his work as engraver, poet, painter, and printer of his own illuminated books. The first of these was when, at the invitation of his would-be patron Hayley, he and his wife left

London for Felpham, a village on the coast of West Sussex, where they lived – not very happily – for three years (1801–1803). The second occurred shortly after this period of exile when, as a result of an incident with a drunken soldier which had taken place the previous summer, at Felpham, Blake was accused of seditious libel and tried for the capital crime of high treason. Apart from these two events, both of which made a deep impression on him, the history of the greater part of Blake's life is the history of his spiritual realizations and his creative work.

This truer history begins quite early, for Blake's extraordinary qualities quickly revealed themselves. When only 4 years old he saw God looking in at the window, which set him screaming, and thereafter visionary experiences of this sort were not uncommon. Indeed, they became part of his ordinary waking life. His literary and artistic development was no less rapid. It has been said of him that he 'became an artist at the age of 10, and a poet at the age of 12'. More remarkable still, his tastes and preferences were very decided, and he showed striking independence of judgement. As he wrote long afterwards, 'I saw and knew immediately the difference between Raffaelle and Rubens'.[310] This was not a difference that was apparent to everybody at the time, but neither then nor in later life did Blake ever hesitate to differ from – or to denounce – even the most respected authorities. Both as a man and as an artist he thought and felt and spoke for himself, without fear and without favour. Independence and originality were in fact among his most outstanding characteristics, together with sturdy self-confidence, honesty, openness, and extreme vehemence of expression. But much as his independence and originality contributed to the ultimate greatness of his achievement, they tended to isolate him from his contemporaries. Some people thought him mad. Although he is generally included among the older generation of the romantic poets, along with Wordsworth, Coleridge, and Southey, and his life and work accounted part of the Romantic Movement, his personal contact with them was of the slightest, and they knew hardly anything of his work. Southey, indeed, was among those who thought him mad. Yet despite isolation, and even neglect, Blake's life was a happy one, and towards the end of it he had the satisfaction of gathering around him a small group of young artists who loved and venerated him. When death came he was ready. 'His countenance became fair, his eyes brightened, and he burst out singing of the things he saw in heaven.'[311]

Being so much an individual himself, it was only natural that Blake should uphold the importance of the general principle of individuality. Indeed, he regarded it as the indispensable basis of true morality and true religion. For him the individual was sacred and inviolable. He therefore believed that it was the duty of each man to be himself, to develop his own potentialities to the utmost, and to allow others to do likewise. 'The Worship of God,' he wrote in one of his finest passages, 'is honouring his gifts in other men; & loving the greatest men best, each according to his Genius: which is the Holy Ghost in man.'[312] Blake meant this quite literally: for him God is man, and there is no other God. In another passage he insists that vice is not so much giving expression to one's own energies as hindering the energies of others. Man cannot develop his potentialities unless he is free. The corollary of the principle of individuality is the principle of liberty. As a young man Blake was a revolutionary, and he therefore saw liberty in primarily social and political terms, as freedom from the tyranny of kings and priests. Later his ideas changed, or rather they developed as he developed, and he saw it first psychologically, as the liberation of the instinctual and emotional energies from the bondage of reason, and then as the liberation of the whole man from the internal divisions into which he had fallen, including the division between reason and emotion. True liberty was to exercise 'the Divine Arts of Imagination'. It was to expand one's consciousness, exploring 'inward into the Worlds of Thought'. It was to enter, or rather re-enter, Eternity.

Blake's enlarged conception of liberty corresponds to an enlarged conception of man. Man is not twofold but fourfold, consisting of the body and its instincts, reason, the emotions, and imagination. This obviously anticipates Jung's four basic functions of sensation, thought, feeling, and intuition. There is also some resemblance to the first four of the five spiritual faculties of Buddhist tradition, i.e. to (in matching order) vigour (*vīrya*), wisdom (*prajñā*), faith and devotion (*śraddhā*), and concentration (*samādhi*), although the fact that these are accompanied by a fifth spiritual faculty, that of mindfulness (*smṛti*), which balances faith and wisdom, and vigour and concentration, means that all four are raised to a higher level and enabled to work together for the attainment of Enlightenment. For Blake man is fourfold both in his divided and in his undivided state. In his fallen and divided state the body and its instincts are present as his Shadow, by which Blake meant suppressed desires, the emotions as his (fallen) Emanation, or split-off feminine counterpart, while reason is present as his Spectre, which is also the self-centred Selfhood with which the fallen man now identifies himself. Imagination, or his Humanity, is absent, or rather is in abeyance, sunk 'in deadly sleep'. Within the context of this enlarged conception of man the individual develops his potentialities when his Humanity awakes. When his Humanity awakes, i.e. when he identifies himself with his Imagination, he can enter his Shadow, absorb his Emanation, and cast out (and also love) his Spectre.

In man's unfallen and undivided state, or in Eternity, the four basic functions appear in their 'archetypal' forms as what Blake calls the Four Zoas. These are Tharmas, 'the mildest son of heaven', the Zoa of sense; Urizen, the Prince of Light, the Zoa of reason; Luvah, the Prince of Love, the Zoa of the emotions; and Urthona, 'the keeper of the gates of heaven', the Zoa of Imagination. There is thus a correspondence, in the hermetic sense, not only between the four basic functions and the four Zoas, but also between Shadow, (fallen) Emanation, Spectre, and sleeping Humanity and the four Zoas, in other words between the fallen and divided and the unfallen and undivided states of the four basic functions. This is not unlike the general correspondence, in the Mahāyāna and Vajrayāna forms of Buddhism, between *saṃsāra* and Nirvāṇa, *kleśa* (defilement), and *bodhi* (Enlightenment), or, more specifically, between the five poisons of delusion, hatred, pride, craving, and jealousy, and the mandala of the five Jinas or five Buddhas, i.e. (in matching order), Vairocana, Akṣobhya, Ratnasambhava, Amitābha, and Amoghasiddhi. There is, however, one important difference. In Buddhism there is no doctrine concerning the absolute beginning of things, which is said to be imperceptible. *Saṃsāra* does not originate from Nirvāṇa; *bodhi* never becomes the *kleśas*. In Blake's system the four Zoas divide one from another and fall from Eternity into time, from Truth into error. They fall in anticlockwise order. Tharmas, whose compass point is west, enters time first, followed by Urizen (south), Luvah (east), and Urthona (north). The story of how the Zoas fell, and what terrible conflicts took place between them and their Emanations, as well as the story of how they were all delivered and restored to unity, constitutes Blake's great myth. It is this myth which, in various stages of development, forms the subject matter of the major 'prophetic books', especially the second longest of them, the central but unfinished *Vala*, or *The Four Zoas*.

The correspondence between psychic functions and Zoas, and poisons and Buddhas, is not the only one. Both Blake and Vajrayāna Buddhism see the whole of existence as one vast and complex system of correspondences. Both use the hermetic principle, as it may be termed, as a principle of order, as a means of organizing the more prominent features of our experience into a beautiful and meaningful pattern, i.e. into a mandala, and in this way achieve integration. Both Blake and Vajrayāna Buddhism are therefore concerned to establish sets of correlations, some of them natural and obvious, others apparently quite arbitrary. Blake correlates the four Zoas not only with the four basic psychic functions, but also with various other sets of four, such as the four points of the compass, the four worlds, the four occupations, the four metals, the four continents, the four arts, the four quarters of the British Isles, the four cities, and the four senses. Thus Tharmas, the Zoa of sense, is associated with the western direction, the world of generation, the occupation of shepherd, the metal brass, the continent of America, the art of painting, Ireland, the city of York, and the tongue or sense of taste. Some of the correlations are quite elaborate (though not without minor discrepancies), such as those between the counties of Great Britain and the Sons of Israel, and the counties of England and the Sons of Albion. Blake's system of correspondences is most fully worked out in *Jerusalem, the Emanation of the Giant Albion*, the longest of the prophetic books and the last. In much the same way Vajrayāna Buddhism correlates the five Jinas or five Buddhas not only with the five poisons but with the five wisdoms (*jñānas*), the five colours, the five directions, the five elements, the five *mudrās* or hand-gestures, the five emblems, the five vehicles or mounts, and the five aggregates (*skandhas*). (The Vajrayāna deals in pentads rather than tetrads inasmuch as the central Buddha Vairocana and his absolute wisdom represent the unity of the other four – though according to an early Buddhist Tantric tradition 'everything goes in fours'.) Thus the Buddha Akṣobhya, the 'Imperturbable', is associated with the mirror-like wisdom, the colour blue, the eastern direction, the element water, the earth-touching *mudrā*, the emblem of the vajra or 'mystic thunderbolt', the elephant vehicle, and the aggregate of form (*rūpa*). There are, of course, many other sets of correlations. Both Blake and Vajrayāna Buddhism see a correspondence between the order in which the Four Zoas, or the Four Buddhas (i.e. the Five Buddhas minus Vairocana, the

Buddha of the centre) are distributed round the four quarters of the mandala and the successive stages by which the individual develops his potentialities. Beginning with Tharmas in the west, the four Zoas enter into time in anticlockwise order, which is the order in which their corresponding psychic functions develop in the individual. In Buddhism, of course, there is no original cosmic fall, but when the four Buddhas, beginning with Amoghasiddhi in the north, are enumerated in anticlockwise order this corresponds to the order in which, upon the occurrence of the profound spiritual experience of 'turning about' (*parāvṛtti*), the five sense-consciousnesses, the mind-consciousness, the soiled-mind-consciousness, and the (relative) store-consciousness, are transformed into the corresponding four Buddha-wisdoms.[313] It also corresponds to the clockwise order in which the five Buddhas appear to the consciousness of the deceased person in *The Tibetan Book of the Dead* (where, so far as the individual is concerned, a 'fall' may indeed occur), as well as to the order in which they are depicted as constituent parts of the visualized seed-syllable *hūṃ* in the yoga of the long *hūṃ*.[314]

Blake's emphasis on the importance of individuality connects not only with his conception of man and his system of correspondences but also with his deep insight into the true nature of the individual. Man is in reality not a natural but a spiritual being, and his essence is eternal. Nature has, indeed, no existence apart from man, and like man is fundamentally spiritual, being simply 'a portion of soul [i.e. the emotions] discerned by the five senses, the chief inlets of soul in this age'. Nature appears as a separate entity from man only after the fall, when the individual's senses are turned inside out, so that he perceives what is internal as external, and when, forgetting his true existence, he passes through various states or worlds. These states are quite different from the individual who passes through them, and it is important that the two should be distinguished. States can change, and be annihilated, but individuals cannot. States may be judged and condemned, but individuals can only be forgiven. This is Blake's great doctrine of the forgiveness of sins, and since the forgiveness of sins is mutual it is the basis of the brotherhood of man. The way in which fallen man passes, like a traveller, through various states or worlds, is not unlike the way in which, according to Buddhist tradition, the ever-changing stream of consciousness wanders as a result of spiritual ignorance (*avidyā*) from one to another of the five (or six) realms of conditioned existence, appearing now as a god, now as an animal, and now as a man, and so on, through a whole series of lives until, with the cessation of craving and the attainment of Nirvāṇa, the process of compulsory rebirth comes to an end. In keeping with its refusal to recognize a causal nexus between phenomenal existence and the Absolute, Buddhism does not, of course, speak of a fallen Buddha who wanders through the five (or six) realms of conditioned existence for a while and then gains, or regains, Enlightenment. Yet there is a parallel between Blake and Buddhism at least so far as the origin of the states or worlds is concerned. According to Blake the states are created by the imagination, or by Jesus (for him it amounts to the same thing), as a means of defining the errors into which man has fallen and thus delivering him from them. In Buddhism, at least in its Tibetan form, Shinje, the Lord of the Dead, who judges people after their death and assigns them a place in the other world according with their deeds, is in reality a form of Avalokiteśvara, the Bodhisattva of Compassion.

The fact that the states are created by the imagination makes it clear that, as Blake insists, 'The Imagination is not a State: it is the Human Existence itself . . .'[315] Since the imagination is also identified with Jesus, and since Jesus is God, the true man is not only the imagination, or poetic genius, but also God. Blake in fact explicitly equates God and man. 'Thou art a Man, God is no more, / Thy own humanity learn to adore . . .'[316] This does not mean that man in his fallen state, or man as a purely animal and rational being, can be set up in the place formerly occupied by God, as so often happens in the case of secular humanism. It means that instead of submitting to the arbitrary commands of an angry God who dwells high above him in an external heaven man should develop his own imagination, his own divine humanity, and become what, in the depths of his being, he truly is. Blake's humanism is a spiritual humanism, and as such is akin to the transcendental humanism of Buddhism, which acknowledges no form of existence higher than a Buddha or perfectly Enlightened human being. Blake not only equates God and man but also, with equal explicitness, rejects deism. His position is, in fact, not just non-deistic but even, in effect, non-theistic, and so to that extent not really Christian, at least not in the traditional sense of that term. His name for the 'angry God' is Nobodaddy (i.e. 'nobody's daddy'), and he identifies him with the jealous God of the Old Testament, with Satan the Accuser, and with the fallen Urizen. It is this false God, the God of this world, that is worshipped by the worldly. Blake's position here is broadly that of Gnosticism. He also rejects the religion of this God, which is that of punishment for sin, as well as the dogmas of the Virgin Birth, the Vicarious Atonement, a personal Devil, and an everlasting Hell. He rejects, in fact, the whole structure of orthodox Christian belief, and although he considers himself a Christian his version of Christianity – if it can be called that – is not only different from, but diametrically opposed to, the more popular 'Urizenic' version. Blake is fully aware of this opposition. In a well-known couplet he declares, 'The vision of Christ that thou dost see, / Is my vision's greatest enemy.'[317] At times he seems to reject not just 'orthodox' Christianity but religion itself, as when he speaks of Jesus sending his seventy-two disciples 'against religion and government'. One modern commentator in fact says that Blake often used 'religion' as a smear word, and it is true that at his best and most characteristic he speaks in terms of artistic inspiration rather than in terms of religious belief. Even when he does use the language of belief he uses it in his own way, i.e. not literally and dogmatically but metaphorically and symbolically. According to him this is in fact the right way to use it, for all religion is 'decayed poetry' and to understand it poetically is to understand it as it was originally meant to be understood.[318] Then as now, it is the poetic genius, the man of imagination, who is the truly religious man.

A whole century before Buddhism was really known in the West Blake offers us the unique example of a non-theistic imaginative vision of rare intensity and integrity. That he could do this was due in the first place to his own extraordinary creative powers – powers which manifested early, and of which he remained in unimpaired possession to the end of his days, he being faithful to them, and they being faithful to him. It was also due to the fact that in addition to the Bible and the major English poets Chaucer, Spenser, Shakespeare, and Milton (and, of course, the works of Michelangelo and the monuments in Westminster Abbey) Blake was able to draw inspiration – indeed, to derive certain elements of his own system – from the 'alternative tradition' of Agrippa and Paracelsus, Boehme and Swedenborg. He was also indebted to some of his more unorthodox contemporaries, such as the freethinker and radical Thomas Paine, the Swiss poet and theologian Gaspar Lavater, Thomas Taylor the Platonist, and the mythologogue William Stukeley. But important though all these were for his development, Blake's combative and fiery genius probably owed as much to his spiritual enemies as to his spiritual friends, for it was largely in opposition to their mistaken beliefs that he formulated his own system. The most distinguished and influential of these enemies – the enemies of Blake's 'Divine Vision' – were Bacon, Newton, and Locke, whose mechanistic science, mechanistic natural philosophy, and mechanistic psychology left no room for imaginative truth or spiritual values. In setting himself in opposition to them – a David against three Goliaths – Blake set himself against the master current of the age, and in this lies the true measure of his greatness. Indeed, through his life and his creative work Blake accomplishes in his own person what he calls a Last Judgement, which is not a condemnation of sinners to everlasting hell-fire but a final casting out of error from the bosom of the Eternal Man or the imagination. What Blake therefore offers us is not only a non-theistic imaginative vision – not only something of the spirit of Buddhism in the language of Western culture – but an example of the kind of radical revaluation of Western religion and culture that Buddhism, in the person of the Western Buddhist, may soon be called upon to undertake.

BOOK REVIEW FROM *GOLDEN DRUM*

Martin Willson
Rebirth and the Western Buddhist
Wisdom Publications, London 1984

Western Buddhists with even a passing interest in the subject of rebirth are strongly advised to read Martin Willson's *Rebirth and the Western Buddhist*. Indeed, the fact that there are so many Western Buddhists with but a passing interest in this important subject bears ample testimony to the timeliness of this excellent essay.

There is no scriptural doubt that the Buddha revealed and taught a doctrine of rebirth. All accounts agree that he often spoke about his own previous lives and those of others; they also agree that, as an aspect of his Enlightenment, he gained insight into the moral principles affecting the rebirth process. Despite their diversity, all the schools and sects of Buddhism – including those whose stated ideals may occasionally strike a somewhat prosaic and limited note – are unanimous in declaring that the goal of Buddhist practice is release, not merely from the dissatisfaction inherent in this our present life, but from all the sufferings and frustrations of numberless lives; in other words, from an endless round of rebirth.

Excepting those who turn eagerly to the rebirth doctrine for purposes of self-aggrandizement or for psychological reassurance in the face of death, many Western Buddhists prefer – and feel free to prefer – to keep their minds passively open on the question. Disillusioned by the dogmas and superstitions of Christianity and other forms of theism, many are attracted to Buddhism precisely because of its 'rational', even 'scientific' qualities. Few are in a hurry to embrace a rather complex doctrine of rebirth, no matter how central it may seem, while it remains 'unproven' by respectable, scientific evidence. If the Dharma is 'whatever helps one to develop', as it is sometimes minimally put, who can be blamed for wanting to pick and choose a little between the teachings, not least when some of them look disturbingly like the accretions of oriental superstition? Rebirth doctrine can be to some extent interpreted in down to earth, psychological terms, 'Is there any point,' the sceptics ask, 'in taking things further than that?'

Martin Willson says that there is. He says so, moreover, neither as a crank nor as a coldly detached scholar, but as a clearly committed Buddhist who sees in the refusal to give this doctrine serious consideration at least a failure of receptivity and devotion. He further questions, with telling perception, how anyone might mobilize the commitment and supreme effort required to practise Buddhism, even for their own sake, unless motivated by a response to the implications of rebirth. We have much to lose by failing to take this teaching as seriously as we could.

Willson approaches his theme from several important angles. He begins with a brief survey of the rapidly mounting observational evidence for rebirth, passing tantalizingly, if necessarily quickly, through the researches and writings of Francis Story, Joan Grant, Edgar Cayce, Ian Stevenson, Arthur Guirdham, et al. Here, as elsewhere in the work, he demonstrates the impressive amount of research that he has devoted to his subject, and presents his findings in a way that will stimulate many readers to follow in his tracks.

In two rather dense sections he investigates the 'logical proofs' for rebirth according to traditional Buddhist philosophy, and the limitations of the materialistic, 'scientistic' world-view which have given rise to so much scepticism in this area. What is notable about both these chapters is the even-handedness and honesty of Willson's thinking, his impressive grasp of his subject matter, and his refreshing freedom from a partisan desire to champion one cause at the expense of the other. For example, when examining the seemingly opposing claims of heredity and karma as psychophysical determinants, he alights on a genuinely 'synthetic' approach which not only allows each perspective its due, but which throws stimulating shafts of light on both. In the last major segment of the work, Willson deals with some specific and problematic aspects of his theme. How are we to approach teachings that offer us the daunting prospect of non-human rebirths? What are we to make of those insistent 'reminders' that every being has been at some time our mother? After death, can we expect an instant rebirth, or a period in some kind of intermediate state? Moving with impressive ease from anecdote to science and from philosophy to logic, Willson proposes a few excesses in need of pruning, and offers some modified interpretations. It is not his intention to convince or to present the reader with a fully developed 'theory'. Rebirth, he believes, will become increasingly widely accepted whether Buddhists participate in the research process or not.

He does, however, believe that Western Buddhists have much to gain from actively working towards this synthesis – if only in the recesses of their own Western conditioned minds. He strongly urges us neither to 'ignore Science nor beat a headlong retreat before it, but work towards a new synthesis ... (for) it cannot be claimed that the Dharma has been established in the West until it is possible for anyone to accept the Buddhist teachings without feeling that they conflict with scientific truth' (p. 77).

All in all, this is a well-written, conscientiously researched, and clearly presented piece of work. It is rather strange that Wisdom Publications, who normally lavish great care on their productions, have seen fit to give this one such a scrappy finish. Let us hope that the next edition (the first being already out of print) will be better produced. Such a significant essay – one which could make a significant impact on the Western Buddhist world – deserves not only congratulations but the best treatment.

This review first appeared in Golden Drum *no. 1, April–June 1986, p. 19.*

BOOK REVIEWS FROM
A MOSELEY MISCELLANY
1997–2002

BUDDHISM WITHOUT BELIEFS?

Stephen Batchelor
Buddhism Without Beliefs: A Contemporary Guide to Awakening
Riverhead Books, New York 1997, pp. 127

Why does one write book reviews? This was the question that occurred to me recently, when I resumed writing them after an interval of several years.

On reflection I concluded that one engaged in this minor form of literary activity principally for four reasons. In the first place, through a review one can draw attention to a book that might otherwise be undeservedly neglected. Then one can point out particular beauties in a work, especially if it is a work of imagination, in this way not only delighting in those beauties oneself but perhaps being the cause of others delighting in them too. Again, reviewing a book enables one to correct factual inaccuracies, expose muddled thinking, and challenge one-sided views. Finally, by obliging one to engage closely with the product of another mind, writing a review helps one to clarify and refine, even to modify, one's own ideas.

Most of these reasons entered into my decision to review *Buddhism Without Beliefs*, of whose appearance on the scene I was made aware through excerpts published in the Spring 1997 issue of *Tricycle*, the American Buddhist review. As I later discovered, these excerpts were taken from three sections of the book, sections headed, respectively,

Agnosticism, Imagination, and Culture, the lengthiest being taken from the first section. With certain elements in Batchelor's thinking I found myself very much in agreement, for instance his insistence on the importance of the agnostic imperative in Buddhism and his contention that Dharma practice was more akin to artistic creation than technical problem-solving. I therefore procured a copy of the book from which the *Tricycle* excerpts had been taken. Unfortunately, *Buddhism Without Beliefs* proved to be something of a disappointment. To begin with, it was a slim volume of 127 pages including ten pages of Sources and Notes, whereas I had expected a more substantial work. That it was only a slim volume was no accident, as I afterwards realized. Moreover, the author.... But to give reasons for my disappointment is in effect to start reviewing the book, and since it is best to proceed systematically, I shall look at (1) those points in it that are acceptable and (2) those that are unacceptable, (3) examine Batchelor's idea of a belief-free, agnostic Buddhism in detail, (4) offer a few general observations, and (5) ask myself what I have learned from the exercise.

The work consists of fifteen short essays divided into three groups. The first group, collectively entitled 'Ground', contains essays on, respectively, awakening, agnosticism, anguish, death, rebirth, resolve, integrity, and friendship; in the second, entitled 'Path', essays on awareness, becoming, emptiness, and compassion; while the third, entitled 'Fruition', contains essays on freedom, imagination, and culture. In looking both at the points that can be accepted and those that are unacceptable, rejoicing in the former and deploring the latter, I shall deal with them in the order in which they occur in the book. Obviously I shall not be able to deal with all such points, or even to deal with each essay individually. I shall try, however, to cover all the points that to me seem important.

1. Batchelor begins at the beginning, going back to Siddhārtha Gautama's awakening (as he calls it, instead of the more usual Enlightenment) and to his giving, as the Buddha, his first discourse, delivered to his five former ascetic companions in the Deer Park at Sarnath, near Benares. This is where many expositions of Buddhism begin; but Batchelor, in addition to summarizing the discourse, draws attention to the fact that each of the four ennobling truths (as he calls them) of anguish, its origins, its cessation, and the path leading to its cessation, which together form

the core of the discourse, requires being acted upon in its own particular way. Anguish has to be *understood*, its origins have to be *let go of*, its cessation has to be *realized*, and the path leading to its cessation has to be *cultivated*. Thus 'Buddhism' (the quotation marks being Batchelor's) suggests a course of action; the four truths are challenges to act. Though more Buddhists may be aware of the distinction between the first discourse's four ways of action than our author thinks, his emphasis on the importance of action certainly deserves to be taken seriously by all Buddhists. As Professor Richard F. Gombrich has recently pointed out, albeit from within a different perspective, karma or 'action', in the word's primary sense of morally relevant action, lies at the heart of the Buddha's world-view; such action being, as he goes on to point out, not only physical and vocal but also mental.[319] Though Batchelor nowhere mentions Going for Refuge, Going for Refuge to the Buddha, the Dharma, and the Sangha is likewise an action – the central, definitive act of the Buddhist life, by virtue of which one is a follower of the Buddha. It is in fact as a direct consequence of our Going for Refuge, after 'hearing' the Buddha-word, that we seek to understand, to let go of, to realize, and to cultivate. Thus karma in the sense of morally relevant action, and the act of Going for Refuge, can in truth no more be separated from the first discourse's four actions than these can be separated from one another. Together they form 'an interwoven complex of truths' (p. 4) even richer than the one envisaged by Batchelor.

As I have noted, Batchelor speaks of the four *ennobling* truths rather than of the four *noble* truths (the usual translation of *ārya-satya*.) This enables him to speak of the Buddha's experience of these truths as ennobling, so that 'awakening' granted to his life a natural dignity, integrity, and authority, and this in its turn enables him to distinguish between authority which is natural and non-coercive and that which consists in imposing our will on others 'either through manipulation and intimidation or by appealing to the opinions of those more powerful than ourselves' (p. 6). The distinction is an important one, and in view of the widespread modern habit of lumping true authority together with false and rejecting both he could well have said more about it. Though unfortunately he does not do this, at least he recognizes that there are degrees of awakening, thereby implicitly also recognizing that there are degrees of ennoblement and, therefore, degrees of true authority. In other words, there is a spiritual *hierarchy* – a hierarchy of degrees of awakening or ennoblement or true authority – and this hierarchy is a true hierarchy, as opposed to the false or at least conventional hierarchy based on earthly power and worldly position. Batchelor appears not to see this, though it follows from the distinction he himself draws between the two kinds of authority, for on the page immediately preceding the one where he speaks of degrees of awakening he uses the word 'hierarchy' in a pejorative sense that suggests he lumps true hierarchy together with false hierarchy in the same simplistic manner that people lump together true and false authority (pp. 11–12).

Awakening is an individual matter, and Buddhism declined as fewer and fewer Buddhists succeeded in achieving this state. Batchelor in effect attributes the decline to increased monasticization, and he may well be right, at least to an extent. He is certainly right when he points out that the traditional explanation for the decay of the religion relies on the Indian idea of the 'degeneration of time', as he calls it, a notion that regards the course of history as a process of inexorable decline. 'According to this notion, those who lived at the time of the Buddha were simply less degenerate, more "spiritual", than the corrupted mass of humanity today' (p. 12). Batchelor does not enlarge on the topic, but in its Buddhistic form as the doctrine of the three periods of the Dharma – the period of the true Dharma, the period of the image (or counterfeit) Dharma, and the period of the destruction of the Dharma, in which we are now living – the idea of the 'degeneration of time' influenced the course of the Far Eastern Buddhism profoundly.[320] Yet though the consciousness of living in the Dark Age of Buddhism precipitated doctrinal and spiritual developments of enormous importance, in my view there can be little doubt that the notion of an *inevitable* decline of Buddhism is inconsistent with both the spirit and the letter of the Buddha's teaching. Social and political conditions admittedly may be less (or more) supportive of the practice of the Dharma at one period, or in one place, than another, but *intrinsically* it is no more difficult to practise it now than it was in the past. The idea of the 'degeneration of time', and therewith the doctrine of the three periods of the Dharma, is one that can have no place in Western Buddhism. Likewise there can be no place in Western Buddhism for the inverted form of the idea, according to one popular version of which, humanity having entered the Age of Aquarius, spiritual progress will henceforth be collective and automatic.

Since Batchelor's idea of a belief-free, agnostic Buddhism will be examined later, I shall not look now at those points in his essay on agnosticism that I find acceptable. The next two essays, on anguish (the term Batchelor uses when referring to *duḥkha* as personal experience of the kind of suffering caused by self-centred craving) and on death, do not require much in the way of comment. Both strike a meditative note. In the first he takes the reader through a simple exercise in respiration-mindfulness and in the second through a meditation on death. The guidance he offers here is obviously based on personal experience and moreover is framed, in both cases, by heartfelt reflections that from time to time crystallize into aphorisms that are themselves appropriate subjects for reflective meditation. Not only do we try to forget the idea that the only certainty in life is that it will end, but 'Everyone collaborates in everyone else's forgetting' (p. 22). Similarly, 'Evasion of the unadorned immediacy of life is as deep-seated as it is relentless', so that 'Even with the ardent desire to be aware and alert in the present moment, the mind flings us into tawdry and tiresome elaborations of past and future' (p. 25). Batchelor also reminds us, in connection with Siddhārtha's encounter with the four sights, that when the questioner realizes that he himself is the question, such a question is a mystery, not a problem, and that 'It cannot be "solved" by meditation techniques, through the authority of a text, upon submission to the will of a guru' (pp. 26–7). Other aphorisms are 'Reflective meditation is a way of translating thoughts into the language of feeling' and 'How extraordinary it is to be here at all' (p. 32), the second of which put me in mind of Spinoza's wonderment at the fact that there should be anything rather than nothing.[321] Less aphoristic, but equally true and no less worthy of reflective meditation, is a sentence that comes towards the end of the essay on death: 'To meditate on the certainty of death and the uncertainty of its time helps transform the experience of another's death from an awkward discomfiture into an awesome and tragic conclusion to the transience that lies at the heart of all life' (p. 33).

The essay on rebirth opens with the declaration 'Religions are united not by belief in God but by belief in life after death' (p. 34). Buddhism, of course, teaches rebirth, and Batchelor recognizes that the Buddha himself accepted the idea and found this 'prevailing Indian view' (p. 35) sufficient as a basis for his ethical and liberating teaching. Although he taught Dharma practice to be meaningful whether or not we believe in rebirth (a quotation to this effect from the Pāli canon prefaces the essay), the evidence does not suggest that he held an agnostic view on the matter. Is it then true that, as often claimed, you cannot be a Buddhist if you do not accept the doctrine of rebirth? Batchelor is aware that, from a traditional point of view, it is indeed problematic to suspend belief in the idea of rebirth, since many basic notions then have to be rethought, 'But if we follow the Buddha's injunction not to accept things blindly, then orthodoxy should not stand in the way of forming our own understanding' (p. 36). Orthodoxy and blind belief, it would seem, are synonymous! Not that the idea of rebirth presents no difficulties. Unfortunately Batchelor drags across the trail the old red herring of the alleged incompatibility of the idea of rebirth and the central Buddhist idea that there is no eternal self. However, he is right when he points out that the mere fact of rebirth does not entail any ethical linkage between one existence and the next. He is also right in pointing out that 'While the Buddha accepted the idea of karma as he accepted that of rebirth, when questioned on the issue he tended to emphasize its psychological rather than its cosmological implications. "Karma", he often said, "is intention": i.e., a movement of the mind that occurs each time we think, speak, or act' (p. 37). Though Batchelor does not actually tell us this, the fact that karma is *cetanā* implies that skilful actions are to be performed not so much because they will result in a good rebirth (the cosmological reason) as because they will help us understand, let go of, realize, and cultivate (the psychological reason). What he does however tell us, and very rightly, is that the Buddha 'denied that karma alone was sufficient to explain the origin of individual experience' (p. 37).

The point is an extremely important one; so important I wish Batchelor had enlarged upon it, the more especially as he makes it clear that the Buddha's denial that karma alone suffices to explain the origin of individual experience is in contrast to 'the view often taught by religious Buddhists' (p. 37). Who these religious Buddhists are he does not say (in his vocabulary 'religious Buddhists' means, apparently, those Buddhists who are not agnostic Buddhists), but they certainly include those Tibetan lamas and their disciples who, as I know from personal experience, not only teach but strongly, even vehemently, insist that karma alone is sufficient to explain the origin of individual experience. In the words of an eminent Gelugpa lama, '*All* happiness and suffering is the *exclusive* result of our *individual* karmic deeds created through *past* lives' (my italics).[322] He could hardly have expressed himself more clearly. The Buddha was no less clear. There are at least three passages in the Sutta Piṭaka of the Pāli canon in which he speaks of the various *non*-karmic factors in human experience, and in one of these, addressing the wanderer Sīvaka of the Top-Knot (Moḷiyasīvaka), he explicitly rejects the view of those recluses and brahmins who, like the Tibetan lamas and their disciples, hold that 'whatsoever pleasure or pain or mental state a human being experiences, all that is due to a previous act'. Holding such a view, he declares, they go beyond 'what is known by personal experience and what is generally acknowledged by the world as true – in both they go too far. Wherefore I declare those recluses and brahmins to be in the wrong.'[323]

Though it might seem that there are only two options, either to believe in rebirth or not, Batchelor is convinced there is a third: to acknowledge, in all honesty, *I do not know*. If it is a question of either knowing or not knowing *in the absolute sense* then, clearly, we do not know and should admit it. Such acknowledgement is not incompatible with a *provisional* belief in rebirth as the more reasonable of the two options (or of the three, if we include the Christian and Muslim option of post-mortem but not pre-natal existence). Nonetheless Batchelor's emphasis on the desirability of agnosticism in connection with the question of rebirth is a welcome one, especially when one considers the kind of fantasies in which some religious Buddhists, as he calls them, have indulged in this regard.

Also welcome is his emphasis, in the essays on 'Resolve and Integrity', on the fact that Dharma practice can embrace a range of purposes (all subordinate to the supreme purpose, awakening) and on the fact that ethical integrity is rooted in empathy. Thus at times we may concentrate on 'creating a livelihood that is in accord with our deepest values and aspirations. At times we may retreat: disentangling ourselves from social and psychological pressures in order to reconsider our life in a quiet and supportive setting. At times we may engage with the world: responding empathetically and creatively to the anguish of others' (p. 42). Though Batchelor himself does not draw the conclusion, such a position tends to undermine the monk–layman dichotomy: at one time in our Buddhist life we may be living more as a monk, at another more as a layman. More specifically, at different times, and for longer or shorter periods, we may be working in a team-based right livelihood business, enjoying a solitary retreat, raising funds for a third-world social project, teaching meditation, or writing a book on the Dharma. As for his emphasis on the fact that integrity is rooted in empathy, Batchelor reminds us that it requires courage and intelligence as well, because every significant ethical choice entails risk, since we cannot know in advance the consequences of the choices we make and have to learn from concrete mistakes. He also reminds us that ethical enquiry is not the same thing as moral certainty and that 'While moral conditioning may be necessary for social stability, it is inadequate as a paradigm for integrity' (p. 48).

But welcome as his emphases on resolve and integrity are, still more welcome is Batchelor's assertion that Dharma practice is embodied in friendship, and that 'Our practice is nourished, sustained, and challenged through ongoing contact with friends and mentors who seek to realize the dharma in their own lives' (p. 49). Despite the fact that the Buddha stressed the importance of spiritual friendship (*kalyāṇa mitratā*), even declaring it to be the whole of the holy life (*brahmacarya*),[324] books on Buddhism rarely mention the subject, and it is therefore all the more heartening to find Batchelor devoting an entire essay to it. Besides singing the praises of friendship, and emphasizing its significance and value, he points out that the forms of Buddhist friendship have changed over history and that today a new model may be needed. He is very much alive to the fact that true friendship can be compromised by issues of power, and warns, 'We should be wary of being seduced by charismatic purveyors of Enlightenment.' Our true friends 'seek not to coerce us, even gently and reasonably, into believing what we are unsure of. These friends are like midwives, who draw forth what is waiting to be born' (pp. 50–1).

Like the essays on anguish and death, those on awareness, becoming, and emptiness strike a meditative note, as Batchelor leads us through an exercise in the expansion of awareness, a reflection on the five primary factors of mental life, and a contemplation of the fact that things are devoid of intrinsic, separate being. In the course of so doing he reminds us that 'To meditate is not to empty the mind and gape at things in a trance-like stupor' (apparently a point that still needs to be made) and that 'emptiness', which he admits is a confusing term, although used as an abstract noun 'does not in any way denote an abstract thing or state' (pp. 64–5, 81). The essay on compassion introduces us to a variant of the *mettā bhāvanā* or 'development of (universal) loving-kindness' practice which Batchelor rightly sees not just as a separate exercise but also as a means to developing mindfulness and loosening the grip of self-centredness. 'Insight into emptiness and compassion for the world', he reminds us, 'are two sides of the same coin' (p. 88). But there are dangers. The exaggeratedly altruistic person may come to think of himself as the saviour of others, thus risking messianic and narcissistic inflation.

Freedom – spiritual freedom, the freedom of awareness – is of the essence of Buddhism, and it is not surprising that Batchelor should devote space to the subject. His essay on freedom is not so much an essay on it as a paean to it, and we are left with a sense of exhilaration at the prospect of our being free *from* confusion and craving, free to realize our creative potential, and free to be *for* others. What perhaps *is* surprising is that the last two essays in *Buddhism Without Beliefs* should be devoted to imagination and culture. Studies of the Buddhist, or at least the Buddhistic, culture of this or that 'Buddhist' country are not unknown, but to devote an entire section of a book on Buddhism to the subject of imagination is to my knowledge unprecedented – and very welcome. Batchelor sees imagination as the faculty through which authentic vision finds expression in concrete and vivid forms. For him, therefore, 'dharma practice is more akin to artistic creation than technical problem solving' (p. 103), as I noted at the beginning. 'The technical dimension of dharma practice (such as training to be more mindful and focused) is comparable to the technical skills a potter must learn in order to become proficient in his craft. Both may require many years of discipline and hard work' (p. 103). The potter's raw material is clay. Similarly, 'The raw material of dharma practice is ourself and our world, which are to be understood and transformed according to the vision and values of the dharma itself' (p. 103). Moreover, as soon as imagination is activated in the process of awakening, the natural beauty of the world is vividly enhanced and our appreciation of the arts enriched. Great works of art in fact succeed in capturing both the pathos of anguish and a vision of its resolution, while the Buddha's four ennobling truths themselves provide us with 'not only a paradigm of cognitive and affective freedom but a template for aesthetic vision' (pp. 105–6). Batchelor does not go so far as to describe the Buddha himself as an artist (though he might well have done), but he does say of him that his genius lay in his imagination:

> He succeeded in translating his vision not only into the language of his time but into terms sufficiently universal to inspire future generations in India and beyond. His ideas have survived in much the same way as great works of art. While we may find certain stylistic elements of his teaching alien, his central ideas speak to us in a way that goes beyond their reference to a particular time or place. But unlike ancient statues from Egypt or Gandhara, the wheel of dharma set in motion by the Buddha continued to turn after his death, generating ever new and startling cultures of awakening. (p. 107)

Such a culture of awakening is forged, according to Batchelor, from the tension between an indebtedness to the past and a responsibility to the future. We have to distinguish between what is central in the Buddhist tradition and what peripheral, between elements vital for the survival of Dharma practice and alien artefacts that might obstruct that survival. Nor can a culture of awakening exist independently of the specific social, religious, artistic, and ethnic cultures in which it is embedded. Resisting creative interaction with those cultures, Dharma practice today could end up as a marginalized subculture, a beautifully preserved relic. On the other hand, through losing its inner integrity and critical edge it could end being swallowed up by something else, such as psychotherapy or contemplative Christianity. In any case, a culture of awakening – a culture in which the Buddha's Eightfold Path is cultivated – is always an expression of a community. 'Community is the living link between individuation and social engagement. A culture of awakening simply cannot occur without being rooted in a coherent and vital sense of community, for a matrix of friendships is the very soil in which dharma practice is cultivated' (p. 114). At this point I started wondering where I had heard it all before, and just where I had seen the idea of a culture of awakening being translated into action. But that is another story. Like the essays on agnosticism, friendship, and imagination, that on culture is something of a departure and therefore deserves, like them, to be given serious consideration by Western Buddhists.

2. Being able to agree with a respected fellow Buddhist is pleasant, but having to disagree with him is painful. When one has looked at those points in *Buddhism Without Beliefs* that are acceptable, and rejoiced

in them, it is with reluctance that one turns to those points that are unacceptable and that have, therefore, to be deplored and rejected. For this reason I shall touch on only some of the more significant of these latter points which, fortunately, are few in number. In any case, my principal disagreement with Batchelor is in connection with his advocacy of a belief-free, agnostic Buddhism, and with this I shall deal separately later.

If it is true that 'Religions are united not by belief in God but by belief in life after death' (p. 34), then it follows that they are united by the belief that consciousness – for want of a better term – is separate from the physical body and can exist independently of it. Similarly, if consciousness exists independently of the body, it follows that it cannot be explained in terms of brain function. To believe that it can be so explained is materialism, just as to believe the contrary is idealism or at least immaterialism. Batchelor appears to believe that consciousness *can* be explained in terms of brain function. At least he dismisses the notion that consciousness cannot be explained in terms of brain function as an 'article of faith' adopted on account of 'ancient Indian metaphysical theories' (p. 37). It is odd, he thinks, that a practice concerned with anguish and the ending of anguish should be obliged to accept these ancient theories and, along with them, the article of faith in question. But if the belief that consciousness cannot be explained in terms of brain function is an article of faith, the belief that it *can* be so explained is no less so, inasmuch as the brain of which consciousness is supposedly an epiphenomenon is 'material' and belief in the existence of 'matter' is as much an article of faith as belief in the existence of 'spirit'. Since Batchelor dismisses the notion that consciousness cannot be explained in terms of brain function, it is not surprising to find him rejecting 'a transcendent absolute in which ultimate meaning is secured' and insisting 'Dharma practice starts not with a belief in a transcendent reality but through embracing the anguish experienced in an uncertain world' (p. 40). Dharma practice may indeed begin in this way (though how one 'embraces' anguish is not clear), but this does not mean that it cannot begin in any other way. *Logically* speaking it begins with the 'existence' of what may be described as a transcendent Absolute, for as the Buddha declares in the *Udāna*, 'There is, monks, an unborn, unbecome, unmade, uncompounded; if there were not, there would be known no escape here from the born, become, made, compounded' (i.e. there would be no ending of anguish).[325] Batchelor also insists that 'Dharma practice can never be in contradiction with science', since the former's concern 'lies entirely with the nature of existential experience' (p. 37). But if consciousness can be explained in terms of brain function, and if the physical organism is indeed 'capable of consciousness' when in the course of evolution it reaches a certain degree of complexity (p. 29), then it would seem that inasmuch as existential experience is unthinkable apart from consciousness such experience is, like consciousness itself, the concern of science rather than religion, so that there is nothing left for Dharma practice to concern itself with. Here Buddhism is subsumed under science, and 'dharma practice' becomes no more than an applied science. Probably Batchelor would not agree that such was the case, but nonetheless it is what appears to follow from certain of his assumptions. Moreover, he is convinced that 'One of the great realizations of the [eighteenth-century] Enlightenment was that an atheist materialist could be just as moral a person as a believer – even more so' (p. 35). But if an atheistic materialist can be moral, then on the basis of his reasoning it should be possible for a materialist scientist – one who by definition shares Batchelor's rejection of a transcendent Absolute – not only to practise what in effect is the Dharma but to practise it without ceasing to be a materialist.

When discussing friendship Batchelor rightly points out that our true friends do not seek to coerce us, and that it is possible for friendship to be compromised by issues of power (pp. 50–1, 53). In other words true friends do not seek to exercise power over us, and perhaps do not even consider themselves as being morally possessed of such power. Here power is equated with coercion or the exercise of force or authority without regard to the wishes or desires of the person or persons who are its object. This is the sense in which I use the term when I speak of the power mode as contrasted with the love mode, as I call them, and maintain that power has no place within the sangha or spiritual community and that members of the sangha or spiritual community relate to one another solely in accordance with the love mode. So far all is clear and there would seem to be no disagreement between Batchelor and me. However, towards the end of the essay on Friendship he speaks of the possibility of imagining a community of friendships in which diversity is celebrated rather than censured, smallness of scale regarded as success rather than failure, and in which 'power is shared by all rather than invested in a minority of experts' (p. 54). Here power is clearly power in the sense of coercion. That this is the case is indicated by the fact that only a few lines back he says 'true friendship has tended to be compromised by issues of power' and before that 'true friends seek not to coerce us' – thus equating power and coercion. In speaking of the possibility of a community of friendships in which 'power is shared by all rather than invested in a minority of experts' he is therefore speaking of the possibility of one in which force or authority is exercised not by a few over the rest but by everybody over everybody, which is absurd, unless it is to be exercised not internally but externally, i.e. over a person or persons not belonging to the community. Batchelor has in fact imposed on his community of friendships a 'democratic' constitution, complete with equal rights for all, without considering whether this form of constitution is the appropriate one for a spiritual community. He has also failed to see that the idea of power being shared by all is inconsistent with his earlier recognition that there are degrees of awakening and ennoblement, and therefore of authority, for if there are degrees of authority (whether coercive or non-coercive) there are, correspondingly, also degrees of power, and if some have more power than others then power cannot be said to be shared, i.e. equally shared, by all. The difficulty is partly due to the fact that Batchelor nowhere defines power, or tells us in what sense (or senses) he uses the term, thus ignoring a contemporary philosopher's warning that 'it is disastrous to talk of power without first engaging in an analytical exercise of some complexity'.[326]

Two of the points on which I disagree with Batchelor relate to the Path, disagreements regarding which are a serious matter, pertaining as they do to the very means by which Enlightenment or Nirvāṇa is to be achieved. Both these points arise in connection with the cultivation of awareness. Having spoken of awareness, in the sense of stopping and paying attention to what is happening in the moment, as 'a reasonable definition of meditation', Batchelor goes on to describe it as 'a process of deepening self-acceptance' (p. 59). The first point is by far the more unacceptable of the two and hence the more decisively to be rejected, ignoring as it does all higher spiritual experience. Stopping and paying attention to what is happening in the moment may be a reasonable definition of mindfulness or awareness (*smṛti*, Pāli *sati*), which is indeed an important practice, but is totally inadequate as a definition of meditation (*samādhi*), which besides mindfulness or awareness includes the eight *vimokṣas* or 'emancipations' and the nine *samāpattis* or 'attainments'. Without a full experience of these higher states awakening is incomplete, though of course there can be degrees of meditative experience even as there can be degrees of awakening. That such is the case is clear from what the Buddha, speaking to Ānanda, says of his own attainment of Enlightenment:

> And so long, Ānanda, as I attained not to, emerged not from these nine attainments of gradual abidings, both forwards and backwards, I realized not completely, as one wholly awakened, the full perfect awakening, unsurpassed in the world with its gods, Māras and Brahmās, on earth with its recluses, godly men, devas and men; but when I attained to and emerged from these abidings suchwise, then, wholly awakened, I realized completely the full perfect awakening unsurpassed....[327]

In reducing meditation to stopping and paying attention to what is happening in the moment Batchelor is in effect precluding the possibility of Enlightenment. Such reductionism is not uncommon in Buddhist circles today and was not unknown in the past. As Professor Richard F. Gombrich has recently shown in *How Buddhism Began*, in a fascinating chapter entitled 'Retracing an Ancient Debate: How Insight Worsted Concentration in the Pāli Canon', the ambiguity of the term *prajñā* or insight led to a differentiation between release by both insight *and* meditation (the kind of release exemplified and taught by the Buddha) and release by insight alone. This led to the development of the idea that Enlightenment could be attained without meditation (i.e. without any experience of the *samāpattis*), simply by means of *prajñā* in the sense of a process of intellectual analysis.[328] Batchelor's affinities would seem to lie with the modern representatives of this kind of development. Just as they emphasize *vipaśyanā* or insight in the intellectual sense at the expense of *śamatha* or calm, similarly he reduces meditation to stopping and paying attention to what is happening in the moment. The result in both cases is the elimination of meditation in the normative Buddhist sense.

'Self-acceptance' is one of the catchphrases of Californian psychobabble, and it is a pity to see a respected Buddhist like Batchelor falling victim to this usage and to its underlying ideology. Not only is awareness 'a process of deepening self-acceptance' (p. 59) but 'There is nothing unworthy of acceptance' (p. 59). Indeed, awareness 'embraces' whatever it observes, though Batchelor at least warns us, rather confusingly, that to embrace a mental state like hatred does not mean to indulge it but to accept it for what it is (p. 60). The root of the confusion, and thus of the wrong view and wrong practice which that confusion entails, is a misuse of the word 'accept', which means: 'To take with pleasure; to receive kindly; to admit with approbation' (*Johnson*); 'To receive with favour; to approve' (*Webster*); 'To tolerate or accommodate oneself to ... to receive with approval' (*Collins*); 'regard with favour' (*Concise Oxford*). Johnson in fact, after giving his definition of 'accept', makes the precise meaning of the word perfectly clear by adding, with his usual perspicacity, 'It is distinguished from *receive*, as *specific* from *general*; noting a particular manner of receiving.' Thus it is obvious that there can be no question of a Buddhist, least of all a Buddhist meditator, ever regarding the unskilful mental state of hatred (to take Batchelor's example) with pleasure, or approval, or toleration, or favour. For Buddhism it is axiomatic that hatred, like all other unskilful mental states, is to be rejected, even though in most cases the rejection will admittedly be a gradual process rather than instantaneous. So axiomatic is it that actual quotations from the scriptures are hardly needed, and it is perhaps sufficient simply to refer to the *Dhammapada*'s 'Kodhavagga' or Chapter on Anger[329] and to the references and citations in the Pali Text's Society's *Pāli–English Dictionary* under '*kodha*'. The proper attitude to unskilful mental states, as well as to unskilful speech and unskilful bodily action, is not acceptance but awareness in the sense of recognition (i.e. recognition of the fact of their unskilfulness), followed by the taking of measures to rid oneself of those states. In the case of skilful mental states, speech, and bodily action, awareness will be followed by measures to cultivate and develop them. All this is clear from the Buddha's teaching of right effort (*samyag-vyāyāma*), the sixth factor of the Eightfold Path, which is fourfold, consisting in the effort to prevent the arising of unarisen unskilful qualities, to suppress arisen unskilful qualities, to develop unarisen skilful qualities, and to maintain arisen skilful qualities. Here there is no talk of the unskilful being 'accepted' or 'embraced'. Dharma practice involves not a weak, and probably indulgent, 'self-acceptance', but an unflinching self-knowledge that recognizes both one's strengths and one's weaknesses and which, while accepting and encouraging the former, no more hesitates to reject the latter than a man who, in the traditional comparison, finding a snake round his neck hesitates to fling it off.

My remaining points of disagreement with Batchelor, apart from those connected with his advocacy of a belief-free agnostic Buddhism, are two in number, and since they relate to topics on which he touches only lightly I shall deal with them briefly, even though each of them represents the tip of an ideological iceberg of enormous dimensions. Concluding his essay on compassion, which he rightly describes as the heart and soul of awakening, Batchelor says: 'It becomes abundantly clear that we cannot attain awakening for ourselves: we can only participate in the awakening of life' (p. 90). With the first half of the sentence I have no quarrel, but what is this *awakening of life*? The phrase suggests a *collective* attainment of Enlightenment, in which the individual participates by virtue of the fact that 'life', as represented by humanity as a whole, has reached a higher stage of evolution. Here Batchelor appears to have fallen victim, at least momentarily, to that particular strain of New Age thinking according to which the Age of Aquarius is upon us and we shall all ride to Enlightenment on the crest of an evolutionary wave. Such thinking is inconsistent with his own rejection, in the essay on awakening, of the Indian idea of the 'degeneration of time', an idea of which the New Age notion of automatic spiritual progress for everyone is the 'positive' counterpart. The second of these two remaining points of disagreement is not dissimilar to the first. In the essay on freedom Batchelor speaks of awakening as 'that awesome freedom into which we were born but for which we have substituted the pseudo-independence of a separate self' (p. 99). Into which *we were born*? The phrase suggests either that freedom is our *destiny* (cf. 'the man born to be king'), in which case it is redolent of New Age ideology, or that we as infants are born free and awake and only later, when we have learned to speak and say 'I', develop a separate self, in which case the phrase is suggestive of a Rousseauistic, or a Wordsworthian, idealization of infancy as a state of innocence and purity and the child as not only 'best Philosopher' but 'best Buddhist'.[330]

3. Eastern Buddhists, and Western Buddhists to the extent that they are followers of this or that form of Eastern Buddhism, often give their

assent to propositions for which there is no proof. They assent to such propositions either because they are to be found in the scriptures or because they encounter them in the teachings of their own lama or guru. Some are of a 'scientific' nature, relating as they do to such areas of modern knowledge as history, geography, and astronomy, and of these propositions some, again, have not only not been proved true but have been shown to be demonstrably false. We now know that the Buddha was not born in 1030 BCE, that the Earth is not flat, and that the sun and moon do not revolve round Mount Meru. Batchelor's 'agnostic Buddhist' is therefore perfectly right in not regarding the Dharma as a source of 'answers' to what are really scientific questions and right in seeking such knowledge 'in the appropriate domains' (p. 18). This is no more than what all Buddhists should do. At the same time, we must be careful just where we draw the line between the respective spheres of Buddhism, correctly understood, and the different sciences. Batchelor says of the agnostic Buddhist that he is not a 'believer' with claims to 'revealed information about supernatural or paranormal phenomena' (p. 18). This is rather too sweeping, for we must be open to the possibility of there being phenomena which are inexplicable in scientific terms, though some scientists may, of course, *believe* that science will be in a position to explain them one day.

Batchelor's agnostic Buddhist is also perfectly right in founding his agnostic stance on 'a passionate recognition that *I do not know*' (p. 19). This is a recognition that is badly needed in many parts of the Buddhist world, where only too often 'infallible' lamas and 'omniscient' gurus think they know when in fact they merely believe, and therefore I hope that agnosticism *in this healthy sense* will blow like a refreshing breeze through *gompas*, viharas, *zendōs*, meditation centres, and international Buddhist conference halls everywhere, scattering to the four winds of heaven whatever pseudo-answers, dogmatic assertions, and exaggerated claims prevail in those places. There is much that we do not know, whether regarding the world, regarding Buddhism, or regarding ourselves. In every field of knowledge, what we know is infinitesimal compared with what we do not know. Nowhere is this more true than in the case of Buddhism. In speaking about the Dharma we ought, therefore, always to distinguish between what we know from direct personal experience (e.g. that respiration-mindfulness can lead to the attainment of the *dhyānas*), what seems reasonable to us according to the evidence at our disposal (e.g. that people are reborn after death), and what we accept on the testimony of the scriptures (e.g. that the Buddha was Enlightened). These categories are illustrative rather than definitive, and we must in any case always bear in mind that with regard to the second and third of them, at least, considerations of a more general philosophical nature cannot be excluded.

The breeze of a healthy agnosticism has of course blown, from time to time, through the corridors of Western thought. According to Batchelor, the methodological principle that T. H. Huxley expressed positively as 'Follow your reason as far as it will take you' and negatively as 'Do not pretend that conclusions are certain which are not demonstrated or demonstrable' runs through the Western tradition, from Socrates, via the Reformation and the (eighteenth-century) Enlightenment, to the axioms of modern science. This is what Huxley, who coined the term 'agnosticism' in 1869, called the 'agnostic faith',[331] and Batchelor believes that the Buddha shared this faith, for he, too, followed his reason as far as it would take him and did not pretend that any conclusion was certain unless it was demonstrable (p. 17). There are several points to be made here. In view of the fact that for a thousand years the Western tradition was a Christian tradition one cannot really say of Huxley's agnostic principle that it 'runs through' that tradition. It is also doubtful if Socrates was an agnostic, for while he regularly exposed the pretensions of those who, though they claimed to know, in fact merely believed, he also asserted the immortality of the soul, accepted the pronouncement of the Delphic oracle regarding himself, and maintained that there was a daimon who at times directed him to refrain from a certain course of action. It is even more doubtful to what extent the agnostic principle runs through the Protestant Reformation, for did not Martin Luther, its great inaugurator, not only preach salvation by faith rather than works but go so far as to call reason a whore?[332] There is no doubt that the principle runs through the (eighteenth-century) Enlightenment. At the time of the French Revolution the breeze in fact became a hurricane that blew down, at least for the time being, all manner of ancient idols. Unfortunately it also set up an idol of its own in their place, an idol called Reason, which in the form of a young woman from the Opera was taken in procession to the cathedral of Notre Dame, set on the high altar, and worshipped with the singing of hymns.[333] Batchelor does not set up any idols, not even an idol called Agnosticism, but he certainly believes that 'Buddhists' (to borrow his own quotation marks) do something very much like this in relation to Buddhism, and to this aspect of his thinking I must now turn. But first there is a final point to be made in connection with his claims on behalf of Huxley's 'agnostic faith'. The Buddha definitely believed that you should 'follow your reason as far as it will take you', but this does not mean that there is not in man a higher faculty capable of taking him beyond reason. The Dharma is explicitly stated to be *atakkāvacara*, 'beyond reason' or 'inaccessible to logic'.[334] This was why the Buddha initially hesitated to communicate his discovery of it to the world.[335]

According to Batchelor, Buddhists make the mistake of turning 'four ennobling truths to be acted upon' into 'four propositions of fact to be believed' (p. 5). They do this because 'the crucial distinction that *each truth requires being acted upon in its own particular way* (*understanding* anguish, *letting go of* its origins, *realizing* its cessation, and *cultivating* the path) has been relegated to the margins of specialist doctrinal knowledge' (p. 4). I have already questioned Batchelor's assertion that 'Few Buddhists today are probably even aware of the distinction' between these four kinds of action (p. 4), and it is still more questionable whether the four truths were, in fact, turned into four propositions on account of a failure to make this admittedly important distinction. Batchelor does not tell us exactly when the 'mistake' was originally committed, or just who committed it, but he appears to believe that it was committed shortly after the Buddha's death, perhaps even before it, and that it was subsequently committed by all Buddhists except for a handful of iconoclastic Indian Tantric sages and others who were, presumably, the forerunners of his belief-free, agnostic Buddhism. He does, however, tell us into just what propositions the truths were – and are – turned. 'The first truth becomes: "Life Is Suffering"; the second: "The Cause of Suffering Is Craving"' – and so on. (p. 5). But if we turn to the *locus classicus* of the Buddha's teaching of the four truths, the *Dhammacakkappavattana Sutta* or 'Discourse setting in motion the Wheel of the Doctrine', what do we find? We find the Buddha telling the five ascetics:

> Now this, monks, is the noble truth of pain [or suffering, *dukkha*]: birth is painful, old age is painful, sickness is painful, death is painful, sorrow, lamentation, dejection, and despair are painful.

Contact with unpleasant things is painful, not getting what one wishes is painful. In short the five groups of grasping are painful.

Now this, monks, is the noble truth of the cause of pain: the craving, which tends to rebirth, combined with pleasure and lust, finding pleasure here and there, namely the craving for passion, the craving for existence, the craving for non-existence.[336]

And so on. Here we obviously have a number of *propositions*. In particular we have the proposition 'The five groups of grasping (*pañcupādānakkhandhā*) are suffering' and the proposition 'The cause of pain is craving'. Having affirmed these and the other two propositions (i.e. those relating to the cessation of suffering and the way thereto), the Buddha goes on to declare that he has, respectively, understood, let go of, cultivated, and realized them. Here there is no question of four ennobling truths to be acted upon being 'neatly turned', in Batchelor's phrase (p. 5), into four truths to be believed (or if there is, it is the Buddha himself who is responsible for the transformation), much less still is there any question of the turning being due to a failure to make the crucial distinction that '*each truth requires being acted upon in its own particular way*' (p. 4). Believing in a proposition of fact is *not* incompatible with acting upon it. Indeed, action presupposes belief, whether explicit or implicit. It was only because the five ascetics had come to *believe* that their erstwhile companion had in fact attained Enlightenment (they did not *know* this) that they were able to *believe* the four noble truths and act upon them. This is not to say that belief may not sometimes be blind; Batchelor equips with initial capital letters the words making up the propositions into which, he alleges, the first two truths were 'turned'. This would appear to signal his conviction – I had almost said his belief – that belief is blind almost by definition. For him therefore, action, i.e. acting upon the four truths, and belief, i.e. believing in the four truths as propositions of fact, are not only distinct but separate, not only separate but mutually exclusive. Nor is this all. Action and belief being mutually exclusive, for Batchelor it follows that Dharma practice consists in acting upon the four truths to the exclusion of all beliefs, and although he *might* argue that he believed in the four truths, but not as propositions, the fact of the matter is that a belief is necessarily expressed in propositional form. It is his advocacy of this belief-free Dharma practice that characterizes the agnostic Buddhist and distinguishes him from those Buddhists who, by turning the four truths into propositions to be believed and thus the Buddha's teaching into a 'religion' (for Batchelor a pejorative term), make it possible for 'Buddhist [to be] distinguished from Christians, Muslims, and Hindus, who believe different sets of propositions' and for 'The four ennobling truths [to] become principal dogmas of the belief system known as "Buddhism"' (p. 5).

We have seen that for the Buddha, in the *Dhammacakkappavattana Sutta* (and elsewhere), belief in a proposition of fact is not incompatible with acting upon such a proposition. It remains for us to see what consequences flow from this position, as well as what consequences flow from the contrary position adopted by Batchelor, namely, that in the case of the four truths, at least, action and belief are incompatible, even mutually exclusive.

Belief in the four truths as propositions of fact is not incompatible with action upon them because neither the belief nor the acting is ever absolute. There are *degrees* of such belief and *degrees* of such acting, the latter being usually commensurate with the former. We have no hesitation in setting out on a journey to Rome, for example, because we really do believe that such a place exists and that if we take the right road we will sooner or later arrive there. On the other hand, there are occasions when we are not sure – perhaps cannot be sure – either that the goal on which we have set our heart exists or that, assuming it really does exist, that we have adopted the right means for its achievement. Nonetheless, believing that it exists and that the means we have adopted are the right ones, we go on employing those means until such time as experience confirms both our belief in the existence of the one and our belief in the rightness of the other – or does *not* confirm them. Belief of this kind is relative, not absolute; qualified, not unqualified; provisional, not final; and tentative, not certain. It is on account of this *provisional* belief – as for the sake of convenience it may be termed – that we accept the four truths as propositions of fact and act upon them in the particular way each requires and according to the degree of our belief. Actual *knowledge* of the four truths comes only with the attainment of the transcendental path.[337] Not that provisional belief is ever mere belief. It is belief that enjoys the support of evidence and arguments which, though they may not be conclusive, are yet sufficiently strong for us to be willing to take the risk of acting upon the belief. Provisional belief is therefore also rational belief. In the case of the five ascetics, they were initially unimpressed by the Buddha's claim to be Enlightened and refused to listen to his teaching. Only when he had convinced them with an argument ('Have you ever known me to speak like this before?') did his declaration ('The Tathāgata is an Accomplished One, a Fully Enlightened One') become for them a proposition of fact to be (provisionally) believed. Similarly, it was only on account of their provisional, rational belief in the four truths he subsequently taught them that they were able to act upon those truths and, by so doing, come to know them for themselves and attain Nirvāṇa.[338] Here there is a progression from ignorance and scepticism to actual knowledge (or transcendental knowledge, as *pace* Batchelor I prefer to call it), via the successive stages of a provisional belief which, as it is confirmed by experience, becomes less and less provisional and provides an increasingly firm basis for further action. The path is thus a graduated path in which, as the Buddha said when comparing the Dharma and Vinaya to the Great Ocean, 'there are progressive trainings, progressive obligations, progressive practices, there being no sudden penetrations of supreme Knowledge.'[339]

Since the path is a graduated path instruction must be methodical, beginning at the beginning, and not introducing more advanced teachings until the disciple has mastered the more elementary ones. We find the Buddha adopting this approach on a number of occasions. He adopted it with Anāthapiṇḍika, the wealthy merchant who was to be one of his principal supporters:

> Then did the Exalted One discourse unto Anāthapiṇḍika, the housefather, with talk that led gradually on, thus: of charity and righteousness and the heaven-world; of the danger, uselessness, and defilement of the passions, and of the profit of giving up the world. And when the Exalted One saw that the heart of Anāthapiṇḍika, the housefather, was made pliable and soft without obstruction, uplifted and calmed, then did he set forth the Dharma teaching of the Buddhas, proclaimed the most excellent, that is, suffering, the arising of suffering, the ceasing of suffering, and the way leading to the cessation of suffering.[340]

A discourse of this kind is known (in Pāli) as an *ānupubbi-kathā* or 'graduated discourse', dealing as it does with the ever higher values of charity (*dāna*), righteousness (*sīla*), the heaven-world (*sagga*), and the path (*magga*). It was to provide, in the centuries that followed, the pattern for discourses and systematic expositions of the Dharma throughout the Buddhist world, in the case of the Mahāyāna being associated with the concept of *upāya kauśalya* or 'skilful means'. In twelfth-century Tibet, for example, we find 'Teacher' Dromtön, Atīśa's chief disciple, leading a pious, but perhaps simple-minded, layman to a deeper understanding of the meaning of Dharma practice in the following manner:

> One day an old gentleman was circumambulating the Radreng monastery. Geshe Dromtön said to him, 'Sir, I am happy to see you circumambulating, but wouldn't you rather be practicing the Dharma?'
>
> Thinking this over, the old gentleman felt it might be better to read Mahāyāna sūtras. While he was reading in the temple courtyard, Geshe Dromtön said, 'I am happy to see you reciting sūtras, but wouldn't you rather be practicing the Dharma?'
>
> At this, the old gentleman thought that perhaps he should meditate. He sat cross-legged on a cushion, with his eyes half-closed. The teacher Dromtön said again, 'I am so happy to see you meditating, but wouldn't it be better to practice the Dharma?'
>
> Now totally confused, the old gentleman asked, 'Geshe-la, please tell me what I should do to practice the Dharma?'
>
> The teacher Drom replied, 'Renounce attraction to this life. Renounce it now. For if you do not renounce attraction to this life, whatever you do will not be the practice of Dharma, as you have not passed beyond the eight worldly concerns. Once you have renounced this life's habitual thoughts and are no longer distracted by the eight worldly concerns, whatever you do will advance you on the path of liberation.'[341]

Strange to say, this anecdote from the *Kadamthorbu* or 'Precepts Collected from Here and There' features as the epigraph to the second part of *Buddhism Without Beliefs*, on the Path, though Batchelor appears to have mistaken its meaning. He appears to believe that practices such as circumambulating monasteries, reading *sūtras*, and even meditation as practised by the old gentleman, are a complete waste of time. They are a waste of time because they form part of *religion*, along with exotic names, robes, and insignia of office. Buddhism became a 'religion' when the four ennobling truths to be acted upon were turned into four propositions of fact to be *believed*. Authentic Dharma practice therefore has nothing to do with practices and observances of a 'religious' nature. For Batchelor, as we have already seen, acting upon the four truths and believing them as propositions of fact are incompatible, even mutually exclusive. Curiously enough, in his 'reworking' of Geshe Wangyal's translation of the anecdote from the *Kadamthorbu* he substitutes for Dromtön's final reply, which is sufficiently plain, straightforward, and practical, a version 'heard from Tibetan lamas' (p. 122). 'When you practise', Dromtön is made to say, 'there is no distinction between the Dharma and your own mind' (p. 55) – a gnomic utterance that could well have left the old gentleman feeling more confused than ever.

Batchelor illustrates his thesis that the four truths are simply injunctions to act, and have nothing to do with belief or with religious practices and observances, by referring to a passage in *Alice's Adventures in Wonderland*. In this passage Alice enters a room to find a bottle marked with the label 'DRINK ME'. As Batchelor points out, the label does not tell Alice what is inside the bottle but tells her what to do with it. Similarly, 'When the Buddha presented his four truths, he first described what each referred to, then enjoined his listeners to act upon them' (p. 7). For reasons I have never quite understood, Lewis Carroll's classic children's story has always been popular with a certain type of British Buddhist (the late Christmas Humphreys was fond of describing the work as 'pure Zen'), and it is interesting to find Batchelor citing it in this connection. Apparently all we have to do is act upon the four truths without asking any questions, just as Alice drank the contents of the little bottle simply because the label told her to do so. Not that the 'wise little Alice' of the story was going to do such a thing in a hurry. Though Batchelor does not mention the fact, she decides to look first and see whether or not the bottle is marked 'poison',

> for she had read several nice little histories about children who had got burnt, and eaten up by wild beasts, and many other unpleasant things, all because they *would* not remember the simple rules their friends had taught them such as, that a red-hot poker will burn you if you hold it too long; and that, if you cut your

> finger *very* deeply with a knife, it usually bleeds; and she had never forgotten that, if you drink much from a bottle marked 'poison', it is almost certain to disagree with you sooner or later.[342]

Apparently Batchelor has not read any such nice little histories, for he evidently thinks we should be less wise than Alice and drink the contents of the bottle without first seeing whether they will disagree with us or not. In Alice's case there was only one bottle, it was not marked 'poison', and drinking its contents only made her grow smaller. Today anyone who follows the White Rabbit down the rabbit-hole into the Wonderland of the spiritual supermarket will find themselves confronted not by one bottle but hundreds, of all shapes, sizes, and colours, and all marked 'DRINK me' – some of them in very large letters indeed. Among the bottles there is one, usually also marked 'BUDDHISM', that contains the four truths. Why should we drink the contents of this bottle rather than the contents of one – or more – of the various other bottles? All bear the same injunction: 'DRINK me'. Admittedly, the label on the yellow 'BUDDHISM' bottle tells us what ingredients its particular contents contain. As Batchelor says, when the Buddha presented his four truths, he first described what each referred to. But the labels on all the other bottles also describe what their respective bottles contain, some of them at great length and in very forcible terms. Some, indeed, describe not only the advantages to be gained from drinking the contents of their particular bottle but the terrible things that will happen to one if one does *not* drink them. One might argue (if argument was permitted) that the contents of the Buddhist bottle are described by the Buddha; it is the Buddha who enjoins us to act upon the four truths, and since he is the Buddha, having himself understood anguish, let go of its origins, realized its cessation, and cultivated the path, we have no alternative but to comply. But how do we know that the Buddha is what he is said to be, i.e. Enlightened? Like the five ascetics, we need to be convinced of the fact, and it is only evidence and argument that will convince us. Once convinced, we are in a position to develop the degree of rational faith sufficient to enable us to start acting as he enjoins. We may also need to be convinced that 'anguish' is, in fact, caused by craving, that craving really can be made to cease, and that there is a path leading to its cessation. There are people who doubt all these things, and who are no more prepared to comply with an injunction to act upon the four truths than they are prepared to observe the ten commandments. Batchelor's assertion that action and belief are incompatible not only rules out 'the dogmas of the belief system known as "Buddhism"' (p. 5) but precludes both the possibility of developing a rational belief and the following of a graduated path. Authentic Buddhist practice consists in acting upon the four truths, to the total exclusion of practices and observances of a religious nature ('religion' is equivalent to belief), and we act upon them simply because we are so enjoined. Strictly speaking, indeed, there is no question of any 'because'. We are told to act upon them, and we act, just as Alice was told 'DRINK ME' and she drank – except that in our case we are not, it seems, allowed to harbour any doubts. Buddhist agnosticism thus turns out to be a form of authoritarianism. The Buddha speaks – or Batchelor speaks in his name – and we have no option but to obey.

4. That '*le style est l'homme même*' and that 'the medium is the message' may well be clichés, but there is still a good deal of truth in them. An author's choice of words, as well as the way in which he actually uses those words, can often reveal something of his conscious and unconscious intentions. In the preface to *Buddhism Without Beliefs* Batchelor tells us that he has tried to write a book on Buddhism in ordinary English that avoids the use of foreign words, technical terms, lists, and jargon. This is obviously a laudable aim. But he also tells us, 'The one exception is the word "dharma", for which I can find no English equivalent' (p. xi), which is really rather ingenuous, suggesting as it does that he has found English equivalents for all the other Buddhist terms. The reader is thus lulled into a false sense of security and into an uncritical acceptance, therefore, of words such as 'awakening', 'freedom', 'awareness', and 'meditation' as being the actual equivalents of traditional Buddhist terms and as providing us with a vocabulary adequate to the discussion of important aspects of the Dharma. It is also noteworthy that although he professes to write in ordinary English there is a whole class of words that Batchelor repeatedly employs not in accordance with standard usage but only pejoratively. Such are the words 'religion', 'belief', 'spiritual', 'mystical', 'transcendental', 'holiness', 'hierarchy', 'ritual', and 'institution'. Even 'Buddhism', within quotation marks, is employed in this way. All these words, in their pejorative sense, Batchelor associates with what he terms 'religious Buddhism' (also pejorative). Words such as 'freedom', 'democratic', 'secular', and 'pluralist', together with the

fashionable 'vulnerability' and 'empowerment', he on the contrary associates with belief-free, agnostic Buddhism. Moreover, Batchelor is not above occasionally playing to the populist gallery, as when, speaking of the challenging of certain views, he declares, in ringing tones as it were, 'The doors of awakening were thrown open to those barred from it by the strictures and dogmas of a privileged elite. Laity, women, the uneducated – the disempowered – were invited to taste the freedom of the dharma for themselves' (p. 13).

Batchelor indeed is stronger in rhetoric than in argument, in assertion than in demonstration. There is in fact very little in the way of actual argument in his book, which is probably why it is such a slender production. Reading it, I was reminded of the occasion when, nearly thirty years ago, I heard a solemn-voiced Norman O. Brown slowly and deliberately reading extracts from his forthcoming book *Love's Body* to an audience of some three hundred American undergraduates. The reading was received in complete silence. There were no questions afterwards. No questions were expected. The oracle had spoken.[343] *Buddhism Without Beliefs* will certainly not be received in silence. Questions will certainly be asked (they are being asked already), despite the fact that much of the book is written in an oracular, categorical style that gives one the impression that Batchelor is speaking *ex cathedra*. This impression is heightened by his noticeable fondness for the imperative mood, sentences in which mood are scattered throughout the book. None of this is surprising. Reliance on rhetoric rather than argument, an oracular, categorical style, an *ex cathedra* delivery, and a fondness for the imperative, are all characteristics of the language of authoritarianism.

This is not to say that Batchelor himself necessarily has an authoritarian personality. The authoritarianism is inherent in his intellectual position, according to which acting upon the four truths and belief in them are incompatible, so that authentic Dharma practice consists in our acting upon those truths simply because we have been enjoined to do so, anything of the nature of ('religious') belief, even rational belief, being entirely excluded. Nor is it to say that Batchelor's reliance on rhetoric is a matter of personal choice. This too is inherent in his intellectual position, for if one is convinced that Dharmic practice consists simply in compliance with, or obedience to, an injunction, not much room will be left for argument. Batchelor is in fact not unaware of the danger of 'falling prey to the bewitchment of language' (p. 40), and if he does fall prey to that bewitchment himself to an extent, it is due as much to the logic of his position as to inadvertence. Similarly, if there is a trace of messianism in his attitude, this is not because he is unaware of 'the danger of messianic and narcissistic inflation' (p. 90), much less still because he has any messianic pretensions, but rather because he is genuinely convinced that he, perhaps alone in his generation, has discovered what the Buddha *really* taught and how it can be made relevant to Western culture.

Disagreement with a respected fellow Buddhist is painful, as I observed earlier, even as agreement is pleasant. Though there is much in Batchelor's book that I find unacceptable and which I deplore, fortunately there is also much that is acceptable to me and in which I can rejoice. Similarly, though I am obliged to reject his basic thesis as illogical and as a serious misrepresentation of the Dharma I can, at the same time, not only appreciate his sincerity of purpose but sympathize with his position. It is not easy to be a Western Buddhist. Inheritors as we are of an enormously rich and complex spiritual tradition that does not always speak with a single voice and comes to us embedded in a variety of colourful alien cultures, it is not easy for us to separate the essential from the non-essential, to decide what is relevant to our spiritual needs and what is not, or to determine the exact nature of the relationship between Buddhism on the one hand and Western culture on the other. If some of us, in our struggle to make sense of Buddhism for ourselves and others, should happen to overestimate the importance of this or that aspect of the Dharma, or allow ourselves to be carried to extremes of affirmation and denial, as Batchelor does with his advocacy of a belief-free, agnostic Buddhism, this is understandable and forgivable. Extremism will always find a following, and *Buddhism Without Beliefs* will no doubt find many appreciative readers. This need not dismay us. People come into contact with the Dharma in a variety of ways. Many, I know, have come in contact with it through reading Lobsang Rampa's *The Third Eye* or Christmas Humphreys' *Buddhism*, or as a result of seeing a Bruce Lee film, and I am confident that at least some of those in whom an interest in Buddhism is awakened by *Buddhism Without Beliefs* will sooner or later find their way to more adequate sources of information. The end of the golden string now being in their hand, they have only to wind it into a ball.

5. What, then, have I learned from writing this review? I must confess I have not learned anything I did not know before, though the exercise has certainly helped clarify some of my perceptions and this is always useful. It is clearer to me than ever that the Dharma is an ocean, and that its depths are not to be plumbed by reason alone, that the human mind is capable of mingling truth and falsehood to such an extent that in some cases 'A Hair perhaps divides the False and True'[344] and it is difficult to separate them, that ideologically speaking Buddhism's near enemies can be more dangerous than its distant ones, that language must be looked at no less clearly than its content, and that for one seeking to understand and explain the Dharma sincerity is not enough. Finally, it is clearer to me that while the writing of reviews may be a minor form of literary activity, so long as new books on Buddhism continue to be published it is possible for it to perform a useful, even a necessary, function.

This review was first published in the Western Buddhist Review, *vol. 2, August 1997.*

ASIAN COMMITMENT

David Snellgrove
Asian Commitment: Travels and Studies in the Indian Sub-Continent and South-East Asia
Orchid Press, Bangkok 2000, pp. 635

David Snellgrove's first exposure to Asia took place during the war, and after demobilization he had looked forward to a career in the ICS, a career in which a life of practical good works in the Indian subcontinent would be combined with local scholarly researches. The achievement of political independence by India and Pakistan put paid to that youthful dream, and Snellgrove, who had already developed 'a consuming interest' in Tibetan Buddhism, was faced by the prospect of a life of scholarly research for its own sake. Scholarship, however, proved to be only tolerable when combined with new ventures in foreign lands, and *Asian Commitment* is the very readable – and lavishly illustrated – record of how, over a period of more than fifty years, the author sought to live simultaneously in the two worlds, the world of scholarship and the world of travel. Not that any of his experiences during the war years were wasted. During that period, he tells us, he learned resourcefulness in travel of all kinds and in dealing with superior authorities and difficult bureaucracies. He met for the first time men and women of very different cultural and religious backgrounds, and learned later, when he lived as one of them, to accept their ways almost as though they had become his own.

Asian Commitment is divided into two parts. Part 1 covers the period 1943–1982, in the course of which the author made ten journeys to India and the surrounding region, including Nepal, Sikkim, Bhutan, and Ceylon (he refuses to call it Sri Lanka), besides making a number of journeys to places of Buddhist interest within India itself. The stories of these travels are told, to a great extent, through the medium of letters, often very lengthy, which Snellgrove wrote at the time to his parents, his sister, and various academic colleagues. This introduces a directly personal element into a narrative that might otherwise have been a dry account of distances traversed, places visited, and ancient manuscripts and paintings discovered. Thus we learn about his dealings with the School of Oriental and African Studies; about his being snowed up in a 14-foot-square room in Dolpo, a remote frontier region of Nepal, with the local lama and six other persons; and about his grief when a favourite horse has to be put down. We also learn about the various companions of his travels, especially Pasang, the young Sherpa who became a lifelong friend and who ended his days as a producer of peach brandy in his native Nepal, and in memory of whom *Asian Commitment* has been written. Snellgrove evidently is a man with a gift for friendship, so much so that his book, like his life, might be described as being dedicated not only to scholarship and travel but also to friendship.

In 1967, during his seventh visit to India, Snellgrove started to feel a sense of disillusion with India and Nepal, a sense that was later to take possession of him. 'For me everything changes here for the worse,' he writes from the Nepal Valley to a friend. 'Temples and stupas are in ever greater decay. Even the great Bodnath stupa is filthy and covered with green mould. There are more and more foreigners, and Tibetan books, paintings and *objets d'art* command such fantastic prices that I am out of the market.' Eleven years later, writing from the same place, he complains that the valley had been rendered even more hideous by 'development projects' and even more filthy due to the increasing population and the absence of sanitation. Nor were these the only changes for the worse. The ending of all cultural relations with Tibet, combined with the pressure of 'Nepal-style' education was gradually undermining what remained of Tibetan civilization and culture in the northern frontier areas. It seemed that there would be even fewer Tibetan-speaking areas in Nepal where scholars like him could study

Tibetan Buddhism, and in 1979–80 and 1982 he made his last two journeys to the subcontinent.

The next five years were spent working on *Indo-Tibetan Buddhism*, probably his most important book, and it was not until 1987 that he was able to resume his Asian travels. This time they were in South-east Asia, where between 1987 and 1999 he made fifteen journeys. These journeys are chronicled in Part 2 of *Asian Commitment*, and they took him to the Malay archipelago and Funan, to the Hindu-Buddhist states of Java, Sumatra, and Bali, and to Cambodia, where he bought a house and became the adoptive father of several young Cambodians orphaned by the Khmer Rouge. Like Part 1, the much shorter Part 2 is rich in information about the history, culture, and religion of the areas visited by the author and monuments are, as usual, described meticulously. Partly because the narrative is not diversified by the inclusion of letters, Part 2 is academically denser than Part 1, and dealing as it does with a different geographical region could well have been published as a separate book.

Asian Commitment concludes with an epilogue in which, after a few general observations on religion as both a cohesive and a divisive element in human affairs, Snellgrove offers us his reflections on Buddhism and Hinduism, on Christianity, on Dualism and the Manichean 'heresy', on Islam, and on personal religion and experience. The fruit of a lifetime of study, these reflections – the reflections of a Roman Catholic scholar who does not believe in converting Tibetan Buddhists to Christianity – will be of no less interest to students of comparative religion than the book, as a whole, will be of interest to 'Tibetan religion enthusiasts', lovers of the Himalayas, and all devotees of tales of travel and adventure in distant lands.

This review was first published in the Times Higher Education Supplement, *25 April 2002.*

PATHS THAT CROSS IN THE EAST

Brian Carr and Indira Mahalingam (editors)
Companion Encyclopedia of Asian Philosophy
Routledge, London 1997, pp. 1136

What is philosophy? What is Asian philosophy? The definitions given by the editors of the *Companion Encyclopedia of Asian Philosophy* in answer to these questions are in both cases broad rather than narrow. Compiled 'with the intention of doing justice to the arguments, ideas, and presuppositions of philosophers working largely outside the confines of western philosophical traditions,' their collection of forty-eight scholarly essays covers a period of some 3,000 years, from the beginning of the first millennium BCE to the present day, and discusses the life and work of thinkers from regions as far apart as Spain and Japan.

The work is divided into six parts, each of which covers a specific tradition within Asian philosophy: Persian, Indian, Buddhist, Chinese, Japanese, and Islamic. All six parts begin with a chapter on the origins of the tradition in question, and end with one sketching the contemporary philosophical preoccupations of the descendants of that tradition. Each part also includes a chapter on the philosophy's view of morals and society, and the parts covering Indian, Buddhist, Chinese, and Islamic philosophy contain chapters on logic and language and on knowledge and reality, some of these being among the most important – and most rigorous – chapters in the entire volume.

Not surprisingly, the editors have not always been able to distribute their material strictly in accordance with the headings of the six parts into which the work is divided. Buddhist philosophy not only has a sixth of the volume to itself, it also figures prominently in connection with Indian, Chinese, and Japanese philosophy. There is even a degree of overlap between Asian and Western philosophical traditions. The major period of Islamic philosophy occurred when, in the ninth to the twelfth centuries of the Common Era, Islamic ideas met those of ancient Greece, while in Japan the Meiji restoration brought with it an enthusiasm for Comte and Mill. Contemporary Asian philosophy, in all six geographical areas, is probably unthinkable apart from the influence of Kant, Schopenhauer, Marx, Russell, Whitehead, and Wittgenstein.

Besides allowing them to take account of this overlap, Brian Carr and Indira Mahalingam's broad definition of philosophy enables the contributors to the volume to write from a number of different perspectives. For Philip G. Kreyenbroek, writing on morals and society in Zoroastrianism, the latter could be said to be a strongly philosophical religion even though in the extant tradition only a few texts of a predominantly philosophical nature are preserved. While A. Roy believes that most Indian philosophical thought depends for its main source of knowledge on the ancient thought of the Vedas, Upanishads, and Vedānta, Hajime Nakamura believes that the doctrine of the Buddha is not a system of philosophy in the Western sense, but a path, and Chung-yin Cheng that philosophy is developed primarily to conceptualize the ideal aspirations of a people at a certain stage or under certain specific circumstances of cultural development. Some of the Asian philosophers discussed had their own perspectives on philosophy. For example it is probable, according to Ian Richard Netton, that in the mind of al-Kindi, the 'father of Arab philosophy', there was no rigid division between philosophy and theology.

Comprehensiveness is no guarantee of completeness, and despite its wealth of material the *Companion* is not guiltless of omissions. The most serious of these is in connection with aesthetics, on which there is not a single chapter in the entire volume. Apart from ten perfunctory lines on Buddhism and aesthetics in the chapter on contemporary Buddhist philosophy the subject is not even mentioned, and there is no reference to it in the index. The omission is particularly glaring in the case of Indian philosophy, which boasts a remarkably rich tradition of thought on aesthetics to which a succession of Hindu, Buddhist, and Jain thinkers made valuable contributions. Similarly in the eleven chapters of part two, covering Indian philosophy, there is no mention of the important Trika system of Kashmir Shaivism. Nor are these the only omissions in this part. Sarasvati Chennakesavan and K. Vasudeva Reddy's rather sanitized account of the caste system, in the chapter on morals and society in Indian philosophy, makes no mention of untouchability, while A. Roy, writing on contemporary Indian philosophy, fails to mention either M. N. Roy, India's leading Marxist thinker, or her most radical reformer, B. R. Ambedkar, whose social and political ideals have affected the lives of millions of his countrymen. Roy also fails to mention Tagore, even though Sarvepalli Radhakrishnan, to whom four pages are devoted, has written a book with the title *The Philosophy of Rabindranath Tagore*. Admittedly Tagore was not a systematic thinker, but then neither were Vivekananda or Gandhi, to both of whom space is devoted in this chapter.

M. N. Roy, Ambedkar, and Tagore are not the only ones who fail to receive their due. Francis Soo, writing on contemporary Chinese philosophy, mentions the names of Ouyang Jingwu and Master Taixu, the most notable of the Chinese philosophers who have devoted their efforts to the development of Chinese Buddhism this century, but he does not discuss their work, on the grounds that Indian and Chinese Buddhism are dealt with in chapters 17 and 28 of the encyclopedia. Perhaps due to an editorial oversight, not only are the two philosophers not discussed in these chapters, they are not even mentioned there, nor do their names appear in the index. There are other inconsistencies, as well as a few misprints. Although *anattā* (Sanskrit *anātman*) is correctly defined in the glossary, as 'the doctrine that there exists no permanent, independent partless self underlying impermanent phenomena', the editors choose to render the term, in their introduction to Part 2 of the encyclopedia, as 'no consciousness', which is patently absurd. They have also chosen to adhere to the convention BC and AD for all dates. In a work devoted to Asian philosophy BCE and CE would surely have been more appropriate.

According to the publishers, the volume is crucial for students and scholars working in philosophy, theology, and a variety of area studies, including Asian, Indian, and Middle East studies. Probably they do not exaggerate. Many of the volume's users will no doubt be content to dip into it occasionally, whether in connection with their own academic work or simply to extend their knowledge, and indeed the encyclopedia is designed, in the words of the editors, as a reference volume for students, scholars, and others who require more than just a simple sketch of 'oriental' ideas. But perhaps the best use of the work, if one had time and the intellectual stamina, would be to read it from cover to cover, to provide a superb education in Asian philosophy. One would not only encounter many different philosophies (indeed, many different conceptions of the nature of philosophy), but also all the major religions of Asia, as well as seeing the different ways in which the philosophies and religions have interacted over the centuries. It might even be argued that the process of interaction, in Asia, between these two great areas of human experience that in the West are designated 'philosophy' and 'religion' forms the encyclopedia's major unifying theme.

Be that as it may, there is little doubt that philosophers in Europe and the Americas are beginning to take a serious interest in Asian philosophy, even as their counterparts in Asia have for a century or more taken a serious interest in the philosophy of the West. The appearance of the *Companion Encyclopedia of Asian Philosophy* is thus a sign of the times. Together with the Oxford academic *Journal of Asian Philosophy*, also co-edited by Carr and Mahalingam, and the same scholars' European society for Asian philosophy, as well as the research centre for Asian philosophy at the University of Nottingham, it will be a means of contributing to the further growth of an interest of which it is itself a manifestation. The day will soon come, I hope, when it will no more be possible for the European student of philosophy to ignore Nāgārjuna, Śaṅkarācārya, or Avicenna than it is possible to ignore Plato, Kant, or Schopenhauer.

This review was first published in the Times Higher Education Supplement, *10 October 1997.*

PROPHET AND LOSS ACCOUNT

Mick Brown
The Spiritual Tourist: A Personal Odyssey Through the Outer Reaches of Belief
Bloomsbury, London 1998, pp. 309.

'Spiritual Tourism' is really a contradiction in terms, and journalist and self-styled spiritual tourist Mick Brown seems to suspect as much. Probably this is why he has given *The Spiritual Tourist* a subtitle that characterizes this story of his encounters with prophets and divine incarnations in three continents as a spiritual odyssey, as though to invest it thereby with an aura of mythic significance.

The Neoplatonist commentators on *The Odyssey* certainly saw Homer's epic as a symbolic narrative, and even gave detailed philosophical interpretations of some of its more important episodes. One therefore wonders if Brown intends us to see a parallel between the extraordinary characters he meets in the course of his travels and any of the beings, human and non-human, encountered by the wandering Odysseus. Is Mother Meera a kind of mystic Circe whose magic deprives men of their reason? Are the Western denizens of Puttaparthi and Dharamsala the Lotus Eaters?

Our spiritual tourist more than once finds himself struggling to steer a middle course between the Scylla of credulity and the Charybdis of scepticism. When a woman he meets at a dinner party tells him that he is too much the journalist, and should stop asking questions and open his heart, he reflects, 'It was what people kept telling me. I felt as I always did at such times, stranded between reason and a craving for faith, uncomfortable in the knowledge that while a spiritual life may lead you to believe in anything, a materialist outlook on life will lead you to believe in nothing.'

A spiritual life may indeed lead one to believe anything. The woman at the dinner party no more doubts that Sai Baba himself, the miracle-working *avatāra* of Puttaparthi, is divine, than does Sai Baba himself, who in 1968 told a world conference of devotees in Bombay, 'In this human form of Sai, every divine entity, every divine principle, that is to say, all the names and forms ascribed to God by man are manifest.'

His faith having been exercised by *avatāras* and talk of living goddesses, Brown finds it comparatively easy to believe that a ten-year-old Spanish boy might be the reincarnation of a Tibetan teacher who died in the West. He is also open to the possibility that the Dalai Lama, with whom he discusses the subject of reincarnation, may have a special connection with previous Dalai Lamas – though he reflects that identifying reincarnations seems an inexact science.

Reason is, in fact, called for from time to time and even scepticism is justified. The Crosses of Light that miraculously appear in the windows of a small church in Tennessee, and which have attracted tens of thousands of visitors, turn out to be due to natural causes. Not that it would change anything for the pastor of the church if somebody said they could prove this to him. The belief that they were witnessing a miracle had changed people's lives, and the fact that for the last year he kept the doors of his church open to them means that he became the guardian of their faith.

Our spiritual tourist has a similar attitude. He may even see the writing of *The Spiritual Tourist* as constituting him a guardian of such faith. However it may be, his account of life on the highways and back roads of spiritual tourism is both entertaining and informative. Vignettes of people and places alternate with potted histories of, for example, Tibetan Buddhism and Madame Blavatsky and theosophy. Who the book is meant for is unclear, but the professional student of contemporary religious trends and the armchair spiritual tourist can both be sure of a good read.

This review was first published in the Times Higher Education Supplement, *20 April 1998.*

QUIET LIVES HIT TROUBLED TIMES

Damien Keown (editor)
Contemporary Buddhist Ethics
Curzon, Richmond 2000, pp. 217

His Holiness the XIV Dalai Lama
Transforming the Mind
Thorsons, London 2000, pp. 208

Religion is undergoing an *aggiornamento*. Christianity has perforce led the way, and other religions are increasingly obliged to follow. As a very old religion, Buddhism is probably as much in need of an update as any other, especially as it continues to spread in the West and as its views on contemporary issues are increasingly sought.

Updating is not easy. Many of the problems we face today are the result of modern social, economic, and technological developments that could scarcely have been imagined in ancient times, and to which there is no reference in the Buddhist scriptures.

Moreover, historically the Buddhist order of monks has been the backbone of the religion, and in traditional Buddhist societies the view that the monk should not be concerned with the problems of civil society and family life was and is influential.

This view cannot survive in the modern West. In his introduction to *Contemporary Buddhist Ethics*, Damien Keown points out that one of the prominent features of contemporary Western Buddhism is an increased emphasis on lay organization and lay participation. As the momentum of modernization gathers pace, it is difficult to hope that the problems of modernity will go away and allow the monk to resume 'an untroubled medieval pace of life'.

In this innovative volume, seven scholars examine a range of contemporary moral issues from a Buddhist perspective. They address specific issues in applied ethics: human rights, animal rights, ecology, abortion, euthanasia, and business practice. Two chapters explore the sources, nature, and proper classification of Buddhist ethics, and trace its ethical teachings back to their ancient roots to discover the appropriate foundations for Buddhist ethics in the modern world. The articles will be of interest to anyone with an interest in Buddhism, comparative ethics, or contemporary moral issues.

James Whitehill conjectures that Buddhism is most likely to succeed in the West if Buddhist ethics are grafted to and enriched by the character-based 'ethics of virtue' tradition that goes back to Socrates and Aristotle. He is critical of the kind of ontological dismissal of morality preached by Robert Aitken, a contemporary interpreter of Zen who is enmeshed, according to Whitehill, in D. T. Suzuki's vigorous antirationalism and antinomianism. Robert Florida concludes that, traditionally, Buddhists have understood that the human begins at the instant of conception, when sperm, egg, and *vijñāna* or 'intermediate being' come together. There is no qualitative difference between an unborn foetus and a born individual. Abortion is thus taking a life – a violation of the first precept.

Yet in Thailand, one of the most devout Theravāda Buddhist countries, the abortion rate is high, possibly in the range of 300,000 a year. In Japan, which may have the highest abortion rate in the world, many Buddhist temples conduct memorial services for aborted foetuses – a bizarre practice that has been adopted by some North American Buddhists.

Potentially the most controversial chapters of the book are those on Buddhism and human rights and Buddhism and animal rights, by Damien Keown and Paul Waldau respectively. Waldau shows that although the first precept prohibits intentionally killing or causing harm to animals as well as to humans, in many respects the general view of animals in Buddhism may be characterized as negative. Buddhist tradition appears to accept the instrumental use of 'other animals' such as elephants, the training of whom involved great cruelty. Waldau believes, nonetheless, that the tradition has great potential for a contribution to environmental ethics and to the benefit that increased environmental awareness entails for other animals' lives. He does not examine the notion of rights as such or ask what place, if any, it has in contemporary Buddhist discussion of ethical issues.

This is done by Keown who explores some of the issues that must be addressed if a Buddhist philosophy of human rights is to develop. While admitting that there is no word in Sanskrit or Pāli that conveys the idea of 'rights', understood as a subjective entitlement, he believes that the concept of rights is not alien to Buddhist thought. Buddhism recognizes duties, and because these duties are reciprocal and complementary, as between husband and wife, he argues that the fact that one of the parties has duties implies that the other has corresponding rights. For Buddhism, however, duties imply not corresponding rights but corresponding duties. It does not follow that one party's duty implies the other party's right. Buddhist ethics cannot be grounded on the concept of rights.

For the Dalai Lama, Buddhist ethics are grounded on compassion. His *Transforming the Mind: Teachings on Generating Compassion* consist mainly of the teachings he gave in London in 1999 on *The Eight Verses on Transforming the Mind*, a short but important text written by the eleventh-century Tibetan master Langri Thangpa. The book is divided into four chapters. The first three are 'The basis of transformation', 'Transforming through altruism', and 'Transforming through insight'. The fourth is a verse-by-verse commentary on Thangpa's text.

Because the basis of transformation is meditation, the teachings in chapter 1 deal with such topics as meditation as a discipline, the obstacles to meditation, and the nature of consciousness, as well as discussing the 'four seals', a set of doctrinal axioms common to all schools of Buddhism, and the epistemological question of how the validity of the path is to be ascertained.

Generating compassion is dealt with in chapter 2, which is as much the heart of the book as altruism is the heart of the Dalai Lama's own Mahāyāna Buddhism. The *bodhicitta* or 'altruistic intention' (an unavoidably weak translation) is the aspiration to attain full Enlightenment for the benefit of all sentient beings. This involves both the development of compassion for sentient beings and the wish to attain Enlightenment. According to an ancient authority, the practice of *bodhicitta* surpasses all ethical practices, so that, the Dalai Lama believes, 'the practice of generating and cultivating the altruistic intention is so comprehensive that it contains the essential elements of all other spiritual practices'. But compassion must be combined with the complementary factors of wisdom and insight. This is dealt with in chapter 3, which contains a succinct account of the subtle and obscure Mind Only school that will be of particular interest to students of Buddhist philosophy.

This review was first published in the Times Higher Education Supplement, *8 December 2000.*

SEARCHING FOR ME, ME*, OR I?

Shaun Gallagher and Jonathan Shear (editors)
Models of the Self
Thorverton Imprint Academic, Exeter 1999, pp. 524

As one who is an author of three volumes of memoirs, and who is currently engaged in adding a fourth to the series, I have sometimes stopped and asked myself who this 'I', whose history I have been recalling and recording, really is. Did the self that I experienced as the subject of those memoirs in fact exist, and if it did, what was its nature? Was it permanent or impermanent, simple or composite, physical or mental, or both, or neither?

Questions such as these have been mooted from ancient times. While for Aristotle 'who I am' is closely tied to embodied existence and yet transcends it, for Plato and Augustine the animal elements are excluded from the human essence. In the modern era Descartes' thesis that the self is a single, simple, continuing, and unproblematically accessible mental substance came to dominate European thought, providing a background for Locke's discussion of the problem of personal identity and Hume's reduction of the so-called self to a stream of particular perceptions.

Yet, Hume's analysis notwithstanding, we continue to experience a sense of self, and contemporary responses, in part, have been attempts to explain how this is possible. If the self is not an Aristotelian soul or psyche or a Descartian substance, why do we still believe we have a certain identity over time? The responses to the problem vary immensely. They include the assertions that there is no self, that it is a fiction, a matter of brain processes, a sociological locus, a centre of narratives (as in the case of my memoirs, for instance), or that it belongs to an ineffable category all its own. Thus there is no consensus, and both our commonsensical and philosophical notions of self have been rendered utterly problematic. This lack of consensus suggests that, like consciousness itself, the problem of the self is a complex and multidimensional phenomenon, and no one discipline on its own will be able to capture it in an adequate way. A cross-disciplinary approach is obviously the answer. In *Models of the Self*, Shaun Gallagher and Jonathan Shear have brought together 28 essays by 31 writers (three are co-authors). They develop divergent models of the self, grouped under six sectional headings and representative of their respective approaches, whether philosophical, psychological, or neuroscientific, addressing such questions as what is meant by the self, whether it consists of an enduring thing or function, whether there are aspects of the self that are not reducible to such things as brain functions, linguistic and social phenomena, or consciousness, or all of them collectively.

With questions concerning the existence and nature of the self having first been debated by philosophers, it is fitting that a contemporary discussion should be inaugurated by a philosopher. *Models of the Self* opens with an essay on 'The Self' by Galen Strawson, which the editors diplomatically characterize as 'intriguing'. Most of the other authors make reference to this chapter, and Strawson responds to their comments and criticisms at the end of the volume.

For Strawson, the problem of the self arises not from an unnatural use of language but from a prior and independent sense that there is such a thing as the self. It is therefore a real problem and requires, he thinks, a metaphysical approach; but he also thinks that metaphysics must wait on phenomenology. 'One must have well-developed answers to phenomenological questions about the experience of the self before one can begin to answer metaphysical questions about the self.'

Starting, then, with the phenomenological fact of the ordinary, human sense of the self, Strawson proposes that people experience themselves as being: a thing, in some robust sense; a mental thing, in some sense; a single thing that is both synchronically considered and diachronically considered; ontically distinct from all other things; a subject of experience, a conscious feeler and thinker; an agent; and a thing that has a certain character or personality. Though admitting that most of these properties can be contested, and that the list may contain redundancy, Strawson believes that it provides a framework for discussion, and that nothing essential to a genuine sense of the mental self has been omitted. Keeping to this framework he argues for a mental self, of which the apparent necessary unity is only synchronic, not diachronic, so that each one of us is properly understandable as a sequence of many selves, existing and following each other one at a time, like a string of pearls. 'The basic form of our consciousness is that of a gappy series of eruptions of consciousness from a substrate of apparent non-consciousness.' Strawson suggests that each short-lived 'pearl' is an individual physical thing, namely a set of neurons in a certain state of activation. He also states his belief that 'the Buddhists have the truth when they deny the existence of a persisting mental self in the human case' and makes a fascinating and potentially fruitful distinction between thinking of oneself in terms of I and thinking of oneself, more fundamentally and existentially, in terms of what he characterizes as Me*.

The authors of the four essays that make up the opening section of the volume are largely critical of Strawson's approach. Kathleen V. Wilkes disagrees with his idea that 'the self', being synchronic, needs to have little or nothing to do with time-related plans and emotions; John Pickering, for whom the self is a semiotic process, takes him to task for excluding the experience of being a social self from the meaning of 'the self' in a stricter ontological sense; and Eric T. Olson, while not actually referring to Strawson, in effect undercuts his position by arguing that there is no problem of the self, discussions under the heading of 'self' being really about other things. Only Andrew Brooks is 'in complete sympathy' with Strawson's conclusions, though he wants to look at certain aspects of the framework of argument and observation used to reach them. In the section on 'Developmental and phenomenological constraints', Dan Zahavi takes issue with Strawson's understanding of phenomenology, arguing that only a phenomenology guided in a methodological fashion, of the sort initiated by Edmund Husserl, would be adequate to discover a genuine sense of self.

For me, some of the most interesting responses to Strawson's essay are found in the section 'Meditation-based approaches'. Here Steven

Laycock, looking at Sartre's notion of the transparency of consciousness from a Buddhist point of view, argues that since consciousness itself is unidentifiable, and cannot be distinguished from the objective contents of one's awareness, the 'I' necessarily remains hopelessly anonymous. None of Strawson's 'pearls' can succeed in representing the self, even the self of a moment. Jeremy Hayward presents a Dzogchen (Tibetan Buddhist) interpretation of the sense of self. This model of self/non-self, which is grounded in the disciplined method *śamatha-vipaśyanā* meditation, agrees with Strawson's analysis as far as the discontinuity of the self, but elaborates the momentary self not as any kind of thing, but as an energy process having both particle-like and field-like aspects. The moment-by-moment appearance of a sense of self arises in stages over a finite duration from a background of non-dual intelligence and energy.

In the final essay, Strawson responds at length and mounts what the editors think is a convincing defence of his position, though not without strengthening his argument in certain respects and modifying it in others. Having thanked those who commented on his paper, he begins by characterizing the result as 'a festival of misunderstanding' – adding, optimistically, 'misunderstanding is one of the engines of progress'. In similar vein, he concludes by observing: 'Interdisciplinary discussion throws up a chaos of uses, but this turns out to be part of its value.' The layperson may be forgiven for thinking that the chaos thus thrown up is not so different from the dust that, according to Berkeley, philosophers raise and then complain they cannot see.

In principle, *Models of the Self* should be of interest to all thinking human beings, but I suspect that, covering as it does such a wide range of disciplines, most readers will be content to sample the volume in accordance with their particular specialist concerns. For my part, I have found many of the contributions stimulating, and in places illuminating, but I shall return to the writing of my memoirs very little wiser about the existence and nature of the self that is the subject of my narrative.

This review was first published in the Times Higher Education Supplement, *17 March 2000.*

THE SEARCH FOR NIRVĀṆA

Richard F. Gombrich
How Buddhism Began: The Conditioned Genesis of the Early Teachings
Athlone Press, London 1996, pp. 180

Buddhism has recently been described as Europe's fastest-growing religion. Popular as well as scholarly interest in the Buddha and his teaching has certainly increased enormously during the past few decades, finding expression in the creation of Buddhist centres and communities and the carrying on of scientific research into the history, doctrines, and institutions of Buddhism. A good deal of literature has also been produced, both popular and academic.

How Buddhism Began by Richard Gombrich, the Boden Professor of Sanskrit at Oxford, belongs to this latter category, though certain of his conclusions have a definite bearing on the actual practice of the Buddha's teaching and are therefore of special interest to those wishing to take that teaching seriously. Given as lectures in 1994 at the School of Oriental and African Studies, the work will be of interest to students of comparative religion and, in fact, to anyone seeking to achieve a better understanding of some of the factors conditioning the genesis of one of the world's great religions.

A Popperian nominalist by conviction rather than an essentialist, Gombrich sees Buddhism not as an inert object but as a chain of events.

Such a way of seeing it is, he points out, in the spirit of the Buddha's own teaching of conditioned genesis (*pratītya-samutpāda*), according to which things, including living beings, exist not as adamantine essences but as causally determined dynamic processes. The beginning of the chain is, however, involved in obscurity, an obscurity Gombrich seeks to dispel, at least to an extent, by a critical study of the 'earliest texts', the texts of the Pāli canon, which happen to have received far less critical attention than the text of the Bible.

In studying these ancient records he follows a middle way between the extreme of deadly over-simplification and the extreme of the deconstruction fashionable among social scientists who refuse all generalization, ignore the possibilities of reasonable extrapolation – and usually leave us unenlightened.

His first point is that most of our physical evidence for the Pāli canon is astonishingly recent, far more recent than our physical evidence for the Western classical and biblical texts. Hardly any Pāli manuscripts are more than about 500 years old, and the majority are less than 300 years old. Gombrich thinks we can apply our critical intelligence, and at least point out where they seem to be incoherent and therefore perhaps corrupt. We may even be able to suggest an emendation, even one that has no manuscript support.

As for the relation between these texts and what the Buddha taught, Gombrich insists that there are divergencies and incoherencies of significance within the *Nikāyas* (the five collections of the Buddha's sermons), that doctrinal developments during the period of oral transmission were not minimal, and that his main purpose is not to stratify the texts but to trace the evolution of some of the ideas in the Buddha's teachings as reported in the Pāli texts, to get a clearer idea of what they say.

The processes and mechanisms of that evolution include debate, 'skill in means', metaphor, allegory, satire, and literalism, and it is to a discussion of these that the greater part of *How Buddhism Began* is devoted. Though the Buddha's experience of Enlightenment was private and beyond language, the truths to which he had 'awakened' had to be expressed in language – not so much in the narrow literal sense, such as Sanskrit or Pāli, as in that of the set of categories and concepts that language embodies. The Dharma or teaching of the Buddha is, in fact, the product of argument and debate, the debate going on in the oral culture of renouncers and Brahmins (*samaṇa-brāhmaṇa*), as the texts' recurrent phrase has it, in the upper Ganges plain in the fifth century BCE.

The Buddha's teaching of karma or 'action' is a case in point. According to Gombrich it developed as a reaction to Brahminism. For Brahminism, 'action' (*karman*) is ritual action in accordance with the prescriptions of the Vedas, the typical action being a sacrifice, which is normally positive. By means of sacrifice a man obtains rebirth in higher forms of life on earth and in heaven(s). For the Buddha, action is primarily ethical action, and what makes action ethical is intention. In redefining 'action' as 'intention' – a use of language which Gombrich characterizes as audacious – the Buddha turned the Brahmin ideology upside down and ethicized the universe. 'I do not see how one could exaggerate the importance of the Buddha's ethicization of the world, which I regard as a turning point in the history of civilization', writes Gombrich.

Though a kind thought is good, purifying karma, it does not come naturally to call it 'action', as Gombrich admits. Yet action it undoubtedly is, karma or action being not only physical and vocal but also mental. Karma is good and bad, skilful (*kuśala*) and unskilful (*akuśala*), according to the nature of its motivation. The bad motivations for karma are greed, hatred, and delusion, while the good motivations include the aspect of non-greed.

At the higher stages of spiritual progress, as when one is mainly living the life of the mind in meditation, one's karma tends to be purely mental and purely skilful. Gombrich's appreciation of this fact enables him to see, not only that the practice of pervading every direction with thoughts of kindness, compassion, sympathetic joy, and equanimity (a well-known Buddhist 'meditation') constitutes mental action, but also to see that these four qualities, when cultivated to the uttermost, actually bring Enlightenment or escape from the cycle of rebirth. According to the older Upanishads, such escape was to be achieved by realizing the unchanging essence of man and the universe, an essence which is 'being' as opposed to 'becoming'. Ontology is merged, even confused, with epistemology.

For the Buddha, of course, there was no common, unchanging essence of man and the universe: there was no self (*anātman*). He was not an essentialist, and Gombrich sees his teaching of conditioned genesis as his answer to Upanishadic ontology. Just as 'being' lies at the heart of Upanishadic world-view, so 'action' or karma, in the word's primary sense of morally relevant action, lies at the heart of the Buddha's. The Buddha was concerned not so much with *what*, as with *how*.

Forgetful of the Buddha's wisdom in bypassing ontology, an important pre-Mahāyāna intellectual tradition reified the concept of karma, so that good karma was turned into something that could be possessed, accumulated, and even transferred from one person to another. Whereas in early Buddhism the Buddha was a saviour only in the sense that he taught the way to salvation, in the Mahāyāna both Buddha and bodhisattvas saved more directly, by transferring merit. Gombrich sees this transfer of a reified karma as being what is crucial in turning Buddhism into a religion in which one could be saved by others.

In extreme cases, as when such karma is distributed to the wicked, it results in the original doctrine of karma being stood on its head. Reification is the child of literalism. While the Buddha himself seems to have had a lively awareness of the dangers of literalism, and even designated the literalist (*pada-parama*) as a distinct type of person,[345] his followers did not always share that awareness. Unintentional literalism, Gombrich argues, was a major force for change in the early doctrinal history of Buddhism. He sees in some doctrinal developments what he calls scholastic literalism – which is 'the tendency to take the words and phrases of earlier texts (maybe the Buddha's own words) in such a way as to read in distinctions which they were never intended to make'.

Examples of this tendency are the Vaibhāṣikas' separation of act from the intention to act (for the Buddha the two were virtually synonymous), and the Mahāyāna's separation of Nirvāṇa from *bodhi*, or 'awakening'. More controversial still, Gombrich makes literalism responsible for the creation of Buddhist cosmology.

Scientific research of this kind is not of merely theoretical interest; it has, in some cases, a practical significance. In a fascinating chapter headed 'Retracing an Ancient Debate: How Insight Worsted Concentration in the Pāli Canon', Gombrich shows how scholastic literalism played a leading role in the development of the idea that Enlightenment can be attained without meditation, by a process of intellectual analysis (technically known as *pañña*, or insight) alone. This change in the soteriology took place, he believes, within at least sixty-five years of the Buddha's death, when the *suttas* and other texts were still being transmitted orally.

In a lengthy piece of brilliant scholarly detective work, Gombrich traces back the Theravāda's sevenfold classification of moral and spiritual types to a jockeying for position among the three faculties of faith, concentration, and insight; this back to the devaluation of concentration (and faith); and this back to the differentiation between release by insight and meditation and release by insight alone, a differentiation made possible by the ambiguity of the term *paññā*.

In another piece of scholarly detective work Gombrich tries to show that the famous mass murderer Aṅgulimāla, whom the Buddha converted by means of a significant play upon words, was actually a long-standing worshipper of the god Shiva and thus a Tantric. The evidence for such an identification rests upon Gombrich's emendations to the text of two canonical Pāli verses. But though they make excellent sense, and resolve several difficulties, in the end one has to say of them that like a celebrated emendation of the dying Falstaff's 'table of green fields', they are brilliant but not wholly convincing.[346]

Despite the book's rather catchpenny title, Gombrich does not really tell us how Buddhism began. Indeed, he professes to be more concerned with formulating problems and raising questions than with providing answers. Many of his conclusions, he assures us, are tentative. Nonetheless he manages to shed a good deal of light on some of the factors conditioning the genesis of the early teachings of Buddhism, so giving us an idea of the way in which the religion (as he does not hesitate to call it) arose and developed.

On certain points his thinking is in need of clarification. In one place he says of the Dharma that it is 'a set of truths, and as such is abstract and eternal, like all truths – think for example of the truths of mathematics. The truths exist whether anyone is aware of them or not'. Yet elsewhere he speaks of the Dharma as having 'emerged from debate'.

Similarly, though rightly pointing out that summaries of the Buddha's teachings 'rarely convey how much use he made of simile and metaphor', he speaks at the same time of the 'language' in which the Buddha had to express his experience of Enlightenment as embodying a set only of 'categories and concepts'. That the Buddha might also have had recourse to myth and symbol is a possibility he fails to consider. These and other shortcomings do not in any way detract from the overall merits of a work in which genial scholarship is skilfully and imaginatively deployed. There can be little doubt that we have in *How Buddhism Began* as readable an introduction to a difficult and thorny subject as we are likely to find.

This review was first published in the Times Higher Education Supplement, *4 July 1997.*

WAYS OF ALL BUDDHISTS

Rupert Gethin
The Foundations of Buddhism
Oxford University Press, Oxford 1998, pp. 333

Of the making of many books on Buddhism there is no end. Here is yet another one. Fortunately Rupert Gethin's very readable introductory volume is a book on Buddhism with a difference. It is not a survey-type work that attempts, whether sketchily or in a more systematic manner, to cover the whole field of Buddhism and to devote the same amount of space to all the philosophical schools and popular movements that have arisen within it in the course of the past 2,500 years. Instead, Gethin seeks to identify and focus on those fundamental ideas and practices that constitute 'something of a common heritage shared by the different traditions of Buddhism that exist in the world today'.

Thus there are separate chapters on the story of the Buddha; a textual and scriptural tradition; the framework of the four noble truths; the monastic and lay ways of life; a cosmology based around karma and rebirth; the teaching of 'no self' and 'dependent arising'; a progressive path of practice leading on from good conduct and devotion through stages of meditation to a higher understanding; the theoretical systems of either the Abhidharma or the Madhyamaka and Yogācāra; and the path of the bodhisattva. There is also a concluding chapter on what the author calls the evolving traditions of Buddhism, i.e. those that appear in South-east Asia, the Far East, Tibet, and the West, subsequent to Buddhism's rise and expansion in the Indian subcontinent, its original home.

One of the great merits of Gethin's approach is that it calls into question the view that tends to see the history of Buddhism in terms of a division into two major 'sects': the Hīnayāna/Theravāda and the Mahāyāna. As he is at pains to point out, many elements of Buddhist thought and practice that were once believed to be characteristic of the emerging Mahāyāna were simply developments within mainstream Buddhism. Although the Mahāyāna certainly criticized aspects of mainstream Buddhist thought and practice, much more was taken as said and done, and carried over.

Though the ideas and practices outlined by Gethin are fundamental, in that all are in some way assumed by and known to all Buddhists, some are less fundamental than others. For the Jōdo Shinshū, the monk–layman dichotomy has no significance, while Zen has no time for Abhidharma studies. Nonetheless Gethin's discussion of all nine of his 'foundations' is on the whole well informed as regards ancient tradition and modern scholarship. He also has a talent for clear and succinct exposition that makes *The Foundations of Buddhism* a joy to read – a talent honed, it would seem, by his experience as a teacher of introductory courses on Buddhism at a university.

This talent is very much in evidence in the chapters on the four truths, the Buddhist cosmos, and the teaching of 'no self' and 'dependent arising', where it might be thought to be needed. But whereas the four truths and the teaching of 'no self' and 'dependent arising' have been the subject of a good deal of scholarly discussion, the subject of the Buddhist cosmos – with its 'thrice-thousandfold world-system', its hierarchy of worlds and gods, its five realms of sentient existence, and its great world mountain – have generally been passed over in embarrassed silence, especially by modern Buddhists anxious to demonstrate that Buddhism is a 'scientific' religion.

Gethin, however, succeeds in showing that the traditional Buddhist cosmology is not to be regarded as only of quaint and historical interest. On the contrary, it forms an important and significant part of the common Buddhist heritage, while the world-view it embodies still exerts considerable influence on traditional Buddhist societies. The key to the understanding of the Buddhist cosmological scheme lies in the principle of the equivalence of cosmology and psychology, Buddhist cosmology being at once a map of the different realms of existence and a description of all possible experiences. Gethin explains in some detail the way in which cosmology is in essence a reflection of psychology and vice versa, and how in Buddhism cosmology and psychology, on the one hand, and the teaching about karma and rebirth on the other, dovetail into each other.

Combining as it does readability and exact scholarship, elegance and erudition, this new Oxford University Press series volume provides the novice with a solid foundation for his studies, and his elders food for reflection.

This review was first published in the Times Higher Education Supplement, *2 April 1999.*

WHO'S WHO OF GURUS

Andrew Rawlinson
The Book of Enlightened Masters: Western Teachers in Eastern Traditions
Open Court, Chicago 1997, pp. 650

One day in the late 1950s, when I was living in India, I received a visit from a 40-year-old English doctor, a disciple of the notorious Lobsang Rampa of *Third Eye* fame. He had come to my monastery hoping I would agree to teach him how to levitate, to read people's thoughts, and to see what was happening at a distance. Naturally I wanted to know why he was so keen to learn those things, to which he replied, 'They will be useful to me in my work.' When I enquired as to the nature of that work, he would only say darkly, 'You will be told that later.' Subsequently it transpired that he 'knew' that he was a Teacher 'with a capital T'. 'In that case you will need something to teach,' I pointed out, with a touch of irony that was lost on him. 'I suppose I will,' he replied. 'I hadn't thought of that.' At my suggestion, he embarked on the study of Buddhism. Within a month or two, he was an authority on the subject and writing books and articles. Had he lived (he died a few years later) he would probably have become a successful guru with an international following and might well have found a place in Andrew Rawlinson's *The Book of Enlightened Masters*.[347]

Rawlinson's 150 enlightened masters (or spiritual teachers, as he also calls them) are a mixed bunch. Not all of them claim to be enlightened, and even among the enlightened there are some who are more enlightened than others. A few were born enlightened, and two are enlightened not as individuals but as a couple. Most of them come from America, and there are more men than women teachers – though one would not suspect this from the book's politically correct front cover.

In terms of traditions, Western teachers have encountered more or less all forms of Buddhism, Hinduism and Sufism. Besides moving from one tradition to another or entering more than one tradition, they may have established a western offshoot of a tradition or abandoned traditions altogether and continued as independent teachers. They may even have created completely new 'traditions'.

The phenomenon with which Rawlinson has to deal is extraordinarily rich and complex, and although the manner in which he has presented 'the entire western pantheon of gurus, bodhisattvas, swamis, scoundrels, roshis, and self-proclaimed mystics' may not enable the reader to separate the wheat from the chaff quite so easily as one of his back cover sponsors thinks, he does manage to introduce a certain amount of order into the confusion.

He does this in two ways. In Part 2, 'A directory of spiritual teachers', which makes up the greater part of the book, he explains who the masters are, who influenced them, what they teach, what their personalities and personal lives are like, and the strange adventures many of them have experienced. (At this point I had better declare an interest as I am one of the teachers listed.)

In 'How to understand Western teachers', Rawlinson explains what westerners are doing in all the Eastern traditions. He also tells the story of how westerners have become spiritual teachers and discusses the meaning and significance of the phenomenon.

Westerners have become spiritual teachers in four stages. In the initial phase (1875–1916), the first westerners entered Eastern traditions, some becoming teachers. That was followed by a consolidation of westerners in Eastern traditions (1917–1945), a stage of propagation (1946–1962), when westerners became firmly established as spiritual teachers, and, finally, a stage (1963 to the present) when westerners 'do *everything*', so that 'the phenomenon of western teachers and masters is now in full bloom'.

Rawlinson believes that these people are changing Western culture by making available a view of the human condition that is new to the West. According to this view, human beings are best understood in terms of *consciousness* and its modifications: consciousness can be transformed by spiritual *practice*, and there are *gurus/masters/teachers* who have done this and who can help others to do the same by some form of *transmission*. Of course, methods will vary.

Despite the links with Eastern traditions, this 'spiritual psychology' is a *Western* phenomenon. It has come into existence because all the Eastern traditions now exist in one place: the West. Because they all exist in one place, these traditions can interact, new questions can be asked, and distinctively Western forms of Buddhism/Hinduism/Sufism created. These questions cross traditional boundaries because Western participation in Eastern traditions is trans-traditional. Rawlinson believes that the era of self-contained traditions is over and that we need something broader and more accommodating to understand the import of Western teachers.

He puts forward a fascinating model of experiential comparative religion, the starting point of which is two pairs of polar concepts: *hot* and *cool*, and *structured* and *unstructured*. These can overlap, can be combined, and can be used to highlight the four categories that are fundamental to all traditions in some form or other: ontology, cosmology, anthropology, and soteriology. The model can also be applied to a particular tradition or sub-tradition, Eastern or Western, as well as to individual teachers and their organizations. This gives rise to a whole range of permutations too complex to be summarized but made clear with the aid of diagrams.

Diagrams, tables, lineage trees, and photographic displays, together with a chronology of spiritual teaching in the West and thirty mini-biographies of figures of historical significance, are useful features of the work.

Rawlinson, a retired academic who remains a researcher and writer, emerges as a friendly and reliable guide to the multifaceted phenomenon that he claims is changing Western culture. His approach is balanced without being bland, sympathetic without being uncritical. He is not above letting the reader know when his information is incomplete or when, as in the case of an intra-sectarian dispute, he has heard only one side of the story.

Though we may have reservations about the value of the author's model of experiential comparative religion, there can be little doubt that this veritable encyclopedia of Western gurus and their teachings is both useful and timely. Students of sociology and of comparative religion will find it a mine of information. Would-be disciples in search of a guru will be happy to browse through its pages.

As for the enlightened masters themselves, using Rawlinson's diagrams and tables they will be able to see just where they stand in relation to one another and to their own traditions.

This review was first published in the Times Higher Education Supplement, *12 December 1997.*

APPENDIX 1

What Was the *Maha Bodhi* Journal?

by Kalyanaprabha

This was originally part of the introduction to Beating the Drum *(published in 2012). It has been slightly adapted for this* Complete Works *volume to give a picture of the* Maha Bodhi *journal at the time of Sangharakshita's editorship.*

THE FOUNDING OF THE *MAHA BODHI* JOURNAL

In 1891 Anagarika Dharmapala founded the Maha Bodhi Society in support of his campaign to restore the fortunes of the holy site where the Buddha gained Enlightenment. Early in 1892 the Society established offices in Calcutta, and in May, Dharmapala began the *Maha Bodhi* journal in order to facilitate the interchange of news between Buddhist countries. The first issue of the magazine consisted of eight closely-printed quarto pages, and bore as its motto the Buddha's great exhortation to his first sixty disciples:

> Go ye, O Bhikkhus, and wander forth for the gain of the many, the welfare of the many, in compassion for the world, for the good, for the gain, for the welfare of gods and men. Proclaim, O Bhikkhus, the doctrine glorious. Preach ye a life of holiness, perfect and pure.[348]

The journal was edited by Dharmapala, and his two articles on 'A United Buddhist World' and 'The Mahāyāna School of Buddhism' were the first of the hundreds of articles which he was to write for its pages. It is interesting to find him controverting Sir Monier-Williams' opinion that the Southern School of Buddhism belongs to the Hīnayāna, maintaining instead that 'the Buddhism of Ceylon belongs to the oldest school of the Mahāyāna', and asserting that only 'the eighteen schismatic schools, offshoots of the Theravāda school, because they taught the incomplete doctrines, were included in the Hīnayāna'. As well as an article by Col. Olcott entitled 'The Sweet Spirit of Buddhism', the magazine contained historical notes by Dharmapala, correspondence, news of Buddhist activities in Japan and Burma, and a reproduction of a significant article from the *Indian Mirror*, which contains the statement 'India dates her misfortunes since the day of the disappearance of Buddhism', indicating the extent to which educated Indian opinion was in agreement with Dharmapala's views. Translations from the Buddhist scriptures and papers on Buddhist philosophy, as well as articles on Buddhism by writers both oriental and occidental, were included in subsequent issues, and before many months had passed the journal had attained a fairly wide circulation not only in Asia but in Europe and America as well. Progress was by no means either smooth or easy, however; funds were often lacking and frequently the Society's sole worker had to choose between buying stamps for posting the journal and food for his evening meal. But the sacrifice was made joyfully, with the reflection that since there was no self, there was no sacrifice either.

SANGHARAKSHITA BECOMES EDITOR

Almost sixty years later, embarking on his own work for the good of Buddhism in the Himalayan town of Kalimpong in 1950, the young Sangharakshita also had an idea, which hovered over his head 'like a beautiful iridescent ball', as he described it in his memoirs. The idea was for a Himalayan journal of religion, culture, and education. Sangharakshita invited the ball to descend and *Stepping-Stones* was born. In a financially arid climate, the journal survived only seventeen months, but though its life was brief, it was a remarkable achievement that in some ways prepared the ground for editing the *Maha Bodhi*. Though the journal was new and the editor an unknown English monk without any academic qualifications (he left school at 15), he managed to attract as contributors some of the foremost writers of the time: Edward Conze, Lama Govinda, Herbert Guenther, Marco Pallis, Alexandra David-Néel, and so on. It is the more remarkable when one recalls that Sangharakshita was only 24 years old when the first issue of *Stepping-Stones* appeared.

Not long after the demise of *Stepping-Stones*, its editor received the invitation to write his biographical sketch of Dharmapala and thus he came within the orbit of the Maha Bodhi Society. He spent some time in the Calcutta offices of the Society as he researched and wrote his biography of the *anagārika*, who became, as Sangharakshita wrote later, the object of his fervent admiration. Thereafter, Sangharakshita began to write a regular column in the journal under the pseudonym Himavantavasi. In the autumn of 1953, Devapriya Valisinha wrote him another letter. Would Sangharakshita be willing to relieve him of the burden of editing the Society's journal? Had the request come even eighteen months earlier, perhaps it would have been refused. But Sangharakshita had in the meantime discovered Dharmapala, and a deeply-felt resonance with his life and work. Mindful of his resolve to help Dharmapala's organization in whatever way he could, and surely mindful of the journal's potential for reviving the spiritual tradition inaugurated by the Buddha and for propagating the Buddha's teaching throughout the English-speaking world, his reply was in the affirmative. Though he did not wish to move to Calcutta (as Valisinha had suggested), he was willing to go there to bring out his first two numbers.

So it was that in December 1953, with his friend Sachin for companion, he travelled once more to Calcutta, there to take up the editorial chair of the leading Buddhist English-language journal of the time, the journal founded by Dharmapala just sixty years previously, the journal through whose pages he hoped to further his work for the good of Buddhism.

Stepping-Stones had perhaps been a sort of prototype for a Buddhist journal, even the ideal Buddhist journal, at least from Sangharakshita's point of view. It was natural, then, that as far as he could he took with him to the *Maha Bodhi* elements that could be transposed into the very different world of the Maha Bodhi Society. He took with him some of his contributors, and also the idea for a monthly editorial.

THE EDITORIAL BOARD

Before taking a closer look at the journal itself, it is worth getting into view the organizational context in which it was produced. In theory at least, the journal was brought out by an editorial board, under the direction of the Maha Bodhi Society (India)'s Governing Body. What sort of a body that was may be something of a surprise.

If we turn to the inside cover of the January 1954 issue of the *Maha Bodhi*, the first issue which Sangharakshita brought out, we find its name, the *Maha Bodhi*, standing proudly at the top of the page and beneath a subtitle, a description, devised no doubt by the founder, Dharmapala. The *Maha Bodhi*, we learn, is 'a monthly Journal of International Buddhist Brotherhood'. Beneath this information are listed members of the editorial board, which naturally we imagine to be the embodiment of that international Buddhist brotherhood for which the journal stands. The chairman, we learn, is Dr Kalidas Nag, and then come the names of three members who are apparently without portfolio: Bhikṣu Sangharakshita, Bhikkhu Dhammaratana, and Bhikkhu Silabhadra, followed by N. Jinaratana Thera, who is 'Managing Editor', and Sri D. Valisinha, who is simply 'Secretary'.

Over the decade of Sangharakshita's editorship the editorial board changed little. There was a notable addition in July 1954 when Dr Nalinaksha Dutt appears for the first time – not only his name but also a full list of his academic and other credentials. As if to keep up, Dr Nag now also has a string of letters after *his* name, and even Bhikkhu Dhammaratana and Sri D. Valisinha are awarded B.A. Only Bhikkhu Silabhadra and Bhikṣu Sangharakshita are there with neither portfolio nor academic qualifications, the editor (I cannot help imagining) quietly amused at all this bother about status.

Silabhadra died in 1955, being listed for the last time in the July issue (an obituary appears in August). He was not replaced. From June 1956 there was, however, an important addition to the otherwise masculine bastion of the board: Mrs A. A. G. Bennett of 9 Portland Square Mansions, London, joins as 'Editorial Representative in Europe and the Americas'.

You may be interested to know something of these board members, so a few words follow about each:

- Dr Kalidas Nag, M.A., D. Litt., M.P., (chairman) was a professor at the University of Calcutta, known as a writer on Indian history. He was arrested and interrogated along with Devapriya Valisinha during the war. Sangharakshita describes him as 'silver-tongued': he charmed the people of Kalimpong when he visited on a tour to promote the Buddha Jayanti celebrations at Maha Bodhi centres. He was good enough to present the journal's editor with a verbal bouquet at the editorial board meeting in late March 1955.
- Bhikkhu Dhammaratana was quiet and studious and seemed to prefer smiling to speaking. He had been a novice monk for twenty years when Sangharakshita came to know him, but for some reason he refused to take higher ordination. He lived at the Sri Dharmarajika Vihara in Calcutta. His article, 'The Reason for Anti-Buddhist Propaganda in Brahminical Literature', was published in the *Maha Bodhi* in November 1954. Writing under the pseudonym Himavantavasi, in January 1955 Sangharakshita refers to it as a 'fine and vigorous' piece of writing. Dhammaratana's contribution as editorial board member consisted of sometimes helping with proof-reading.
- Bhikkhu Silabhadra was born in 1883 into a Bengali brahmin family and trained as a lawyer in Burma, where he came across the Dharma. In 1934 he returned to India and became a *bhikkhu*. He, too, was now based at the Sri Dharmarajika Vihara. He gave talks and translated scriptures into Bengali. Sangharakshita, on making his acquaintance, was struck that there was somehow 'more of the lawyer about him than the *bhikkhu*'. He sometimes contributed book reviews or short pieces for the News and Notes section of the journal.
- Dr Nalinaksha Dutt, M.A., PhD., D.Litt., P.R.S., B.L., M.P, was head of the department of Pāli at the University of Calcutta and wrote widely on Buddhism. His scholarly *Aspects of Mahāyāna Buddhism in its Relation to the Hīnayāna* was a work Sangharakshita knew and valued. It was Dr Dutt who compiled the invaluable 'The Maha Bodhi Society, its History and Influence' for the Maha Bodhi's *Diamond Jubilee Souvenir*.
- N. Jinaratana Thera (managing editor) was joint-secretary of Maha Bodhi Society (India) along with Sangharatana of Sarnath. He had run the Society during the war years and after, when Valisinha had been in Ceylon. Since the General Secretary's return, he had been seeking ways to get that coveted position for himself. As managing editor

of the journal he was responsible for subscriptions, advertisements, dispatch, and distribution. To work with someone for whom he could feel neither liking nor respect and whom he in fact regarded as 'a bad monk, a bad Buddhist, and even, in some respects, a bad man' was not the easiest of matters, but Sangharakshita tried to foster the best working relations he could without compromising or giving the impression that he condoned aspects of Jinaratana's behaviour that were in fact to him unacceptable.

- Sri D. Valisinha (secretary) was brought up by Dharmapala's mother, and studied in Calcutta and at Santiniketan, Tagore's educational establishment in Bengal. As a result he not only spoke Bengali fluently but dressed and even acted as a man of Bengal. Throughout his life he was a faithful disciple of Dharmapala, supporting his work during the *anagārika*'s life and after his death doing all he could to further the work of the Maha Bodhi Society. His life's achievements were considerable, most notably securing the Sacred Relics of Śāriputra and Maudgalyāyana for re-enshrinement in India, as well as his contribution to resolving the Bodh Gaya issue and the building of the Mulagandhakuti Vihara.
- Mrs A. A. G. Bennett had been librarian of the Buddhist Society, London, and for a short time (1951–2) editor of its magazine, the *Middle Way*. She is best known as a translator of and commentator on Pāli texts. Sangharakshita created the position of 'editorial representative in Europe and the Americas', working with her successfully via correspondence. They met for the first time only in 1964. She made a valuable contribution to the *Maha Bodhi*, writing articles and book reviews, and translating French and German contributions into English. Sangharakshita drew on her translation of the Sanskrit *Bodhicaryāvatāra* of Śāntideva when he compiled a puja for the new Buddhist movement he went on to found.

The initial difficulty Sangharakshita encountered in working with the *Maha Bodhi* editorial board is illustrated by what happened during his absence from Calcutta between March 1954, when he was there editing the Vaiśākha number, and the end of July, when he returned to do more editorial work. While he was away, a meeting of the editorial board had been held and decisions were made that were clearly meant to put a brake on his work as editor. The prime mover, it seems, was Silabhadra.

Sangharakshita was new to the editorial board, a junior monk, and by far the youngest person on the board, being at that time twenty-eight years old. What was he to do? Looking back on his younger self, perhaps with a little amusement, Sangharakshita remarked that the action he took was rather high-handed. Perhaps it was. What he did, as he recounts in his memoirs, was to tell Silabhadra that he proposed to take no notice whatsoever of the board's decision. He asked Jinaratana to call a special meeting of the board, and then got on with making up the August issue of the journal without bothering to try to obtain the approval of the board as he was now supposed to do. His discovery that Jinaratana and Silabhadra had tried to intercept his letters to the Governing Body probably only made him still more determined not to let injustice go unchecked. The special meeting duly took place – it was rather stormy – but, with what he describes as the 'rather lukewarm support' of Dr Kalidas Nag and Dr Nalinaksha Dutt, the young editor managed to get the decisions taken by the editorial board in his absence rescinded.

But what was the whole affair about? In relating this I hope the reader will come to see how Sangharakshita, in trying to propagate the living spirit of Buddhism in India in the 1950s, in working for the revival of the Buddha's teaching in the land of its birth, not only had to battle with antagonistic forces from Hinduism but also with those from within the Buddhist world itself.

It all began with a letter from one Joseph Alles, editor of the *Buddhist World*, a fortnightly paper published in Colombo, who wrote to the *Maha Bodhi* complaining that the journal was publishing articles by Mahāyāna Buddhists.

But before following the chain of events set off by that letter, we need to gain some understanding of the broader context in which it was written. The *Buddhist World* of which Mr Alles was editor had already published vitriolic attacks on the new editor of the *Maha Bodhi*, strongly criticizing his appointment, on the basis that he was a Mahāyānist. The writer of these critical articles (who, it turned out, was the wife of the paper's founder) believed, as did Alles, that the Maha Bodhi was a Theravādin society and assumed that Dharmapala – perhaps because he came from Ceylon – like them, associated the Theravāda and the Theravāda only with the 'pure Dhamma'. Rather than entering into courteous and reasoned debate, as the Buddha exhorted his followers to do, attacks were made in the following manner:

> The *Mahabodhi*, vol. 62, no. 2 announces an improvement to its editorial board consequent on the appointment of a Mahayanist Bhikshu (not Bhikkhu) as one of its senior members.... What improvement, we are entitled to ask, could be expected from association with one having vetulyan ideas?[349] Is it not an insult to the memory of its revered Founder and the numerous Theravādins who have supported and maintained this journal?...

The suggestion was made that unless the 'Rakshita' was made to 'change his spots' i.e. cease to be editor, the journal's future would be in jeopardy.

This, then, was in the background when Alles' letter arrived at the Maha Bodhi headquarters. It seems that his letter was opened by Silabhadra who informed the Governing Body that a letter of complaint had been received *about the editorials*. Without the members of the Governing Body actually reading the letter, a resolution was passed upholding Alles' complaint and by implication criticizing the editor. On the basis of this, Silabhadra then persuaded the editorial board to pass a resolution to restrict the editor in his work. This is what Sangharakshita discovered when he returned to Calcutta in July 1954, and it was in response to this that he took action.

At the special meeting of the editorial board that Sangharakshita had asked Jinaratana to arrange, the journal's editor confronted Silabhadra with the deception he had practised on both the Governing Body and the editorial board, taking him 'severely to task' for his behaviour. Silabhadra did not want the editorial board to change its position and seemed to share Alles' view that the *Maha Bodhi* was – or should be – a Theravādin publication, but in the end, as we have seen, the resolution Silabhadra had recommended was rescinded.

As for the Governing Body, Sangharakshita went to speak to its vice-president, Keshub Chandra Gupta, who had chaired the meeting that had upheld Alles' complaint. He put all the facts to him. Gupta was a lawyer and Sangharakshita did not find it difficult to marshal the evidence that showed that the Governing Body had acted wrongly. Since Alles' letter had not been a complaint about the editorials but about the fact that the journal published articles by Mahāyāna Buddhists, what the Governing Body actually needed to decide was whether publishing articles by Mahāyāna Buddhists did or did not contravene the Society's own policies. Gupta promised to raise the matter at the next meeting of the Governing Body.

In the News and Notes section of the August issue of the journal there appears a short article by Dr Nalinaksha Dutt who, though he had given Sangharakshita rather lukewarm support at the special editorial meeting, in private had shown himself to be rather more warmly inclined to the editor's outlook. Now in his article he cited Dharmapala's own words defining the ethos of the Maha Bodhi Society:

> The Society, representing Buddhism in general, not only single aspects of it, shall preserve absolute neutrality with respect to the doctrines and dogmas taught by sections and sects among the Buddhists.… It will be equally ready to publish expositions of all Buddhist sects.

The editor was fully vindicated.[350] Attacks such as these no doubt only served to strengthen Sangharakshita's determination to maintain the journal's ecumenical editorial stance. While it did, of course, publish articles by Buddhists of Theravādin background, it also published articles by Buddhists of other persuasions. Perhaps it was the wish to dissociate himself from this kind of Theravādin fundamentalism that led to Sangharakshita's appearing in the *Maha Bodhi* journal with the Sanskrit title 'Bhikṣu' rather than the Pāli (or Theravādin) 'Bhikkhu' before his name, even though his own ordination was Theravādin.

All this raged in late July and early August, but Sangharakshita was one step ahead. He had already published his thoughts on debate and discussion in the March 1954 editorial which was called simply 'Controversy'.

TAKING A LOOK: THE JANUARY 1954 ISSUE

But perhaps by now we are eager to get out of the political world that was part of the context in which the editor was obliged to operate. Perhaps it is time to make a closer acquaintance with the *Maha Bodhi* journal itself by picking up the first issue edited by Sangharakshita and taking a look. We find a 40-page volume measuring 15cm x 23cm (a little larger than A5). The cover, printed with a rich dark blue ink, displays appropriately enough a sketch of the Maha Bodhi Temple showing white through rough brush strokes of blue that form the background. Below this sketch is the journal's title, *The Maha Bodhi*, and beneath that the information that it is an 'international Buddhist monthly'. Right at the bottom we discover that the year is 2497 BCE (on the left) and 1954 CE (on the right) and that the volume number is 62 (on the left), number 1 (on the right). In between we read that the month is January. In the top left-hand corner in the white margin is the Society's circular stamp, again in blue, about 3cm across. Around the circle's rim is written 'Buddha Dharma Sangha' above and 'Maha Bodhi Society' below. In the middle is the Nālandā crest with its two deer flanking the Wheel of the Dharma. Above it are what look like two deities.

The contents list appears on the inside cover. The journal begins, we discover, with a quotation from the *Saṃyutta Nikāya*, and is followed by a poem, 'Nagarjunikonda' by Bhikṣu Sangharakshita. Then comes a five-page article, 'Hate, Love and Perfect Wisdom', by the well-known scholar Edward Conze. After that, one Ñāṇavīra Bhikkhu has a nine-page piece on 'Anattā and Nibbāna' with many scholarly quotations from the Pāli. This is followed by the very personal 'Diary Leaves of the Late Ven. Anagarika Dharmapala' edited by Sri D. Valisinha. Then comes a short article by one P. P. Sirivardhana about the third president of the Maha Bodhi Society, who has recently died, in the course of which he warmly congratulates his successor, the Maharaj Kumar of Sikkim. (The innocent reader would be astonished if someone told him or her that the election of the new president of the Maha Bodhi Society had been little short of a struggle for power between Buddhists and Hindus.) The next piece is quite different. 'In the Light of the Dhamma' is written by the mysterious Himavantavasi. Though living in some remote place cut off from the world, the postman seems to get through, so that the hermit is able to keep up with current religious journals. Recently Himavantavasi's frosty breath has been quite taken away by the unabashed impudence with which the Buddha's teachings have been travestied in one of these publications. He issues a ringing challenge to the shoddy editor of the transgressing journal to produce the evidence, whether Pāli, Sanskrit, Chinese, or Tibetan, to prove that what he has published really is *Buddhavacana*. Himavantavasi's piece is followed directly by the more sober and weighty voice of the *Maha Bodhi*'s editor in an editorial. This is a new departure for the *Maha Bodhi* and is in fact the first of what will be at least 96 individual editorials to be written over the next decade. The topics on which the editor speaks this time are (1) Nagarjunikonda, an 'Ancient Buddhist Site in Danger', and (2) 'Vaiśākha Pūrṇimā as a Public Holiday'. But who the editor is, the leading English-language Buddhist journal does not disclose.

The final entry in the list of contents is the 'News and Notes' section, the news and notes that appear being as follows: Bhikṣu Sangharakshita and Bhikkhu Silabhadra appointed members of the editorial board, Suggestions to Contributors, Calcutta Lectures on Buddhism, Anniversary Celebrations at Sarnath, Darjeeling Lectures, Kalimpong Activities, 'Buddhism and Art', Kalyani Congress, and Bhadanta Ananda Kausalyayan's Visit to Thailand. The Calcutta and Darjeeling lectures, the Kalimpong Activities, and 'Buddhism and Art' feature Sangharakshita's vigorous work to spread the Dharma. They stand as an example and a challenge to his fellow Buddhists, a challenge to be active, a challenge to heed the words of the Buddha, that exhortation that Dharmapala chose to stand as masthead at the beginning of every issue of the journal: 'Go ye, O Bhikkhus, and wander forth for the gain of the many, for the welfare of the many … for the welfare of gods and men. Proclaim, O Bhikkhus, the Doctrine glorious, preach ye a life of holiness, perfect and pure.' That challenge would sound again and again in the editorials and in the News and Notes as the new editor of the *Maha Bodhi* began to beat the drum.

THE COVER

The January 1954 issue of the *Maha Bodhi* is the first of eleven issues that appeared that year (there is a double issue for May–June, a special Vaiśākha number). Apart from that special issue, the same Maha Bodhi Temple design appears on all the covers that year, although the colour of the background varies from one issue to the next: green, yellow, lilac, brown, and so on. In 1955 the year's design was a bodhi leaf within patterned concentric circles. In 1956, being the special Buddha Jayanti year, the cover shows a great bell-like stupa, with *harmikā* and conical spire, blazing with light and worshipped by two robed figures, one kneeling and one standing. In 1957 the cover depicts an elephant bearing a lotus in its trunk. The 1958 cover features a *dharmacakra* wheel and in 1959 there are scenes from the Buddha's Enlightenment, a design that is used again in 1961. In 1960 the design is a bodhi tree, used again in 1962.

SANGHARAKSHITA'S FIRST VAIŚĀKHA ISSUE: MAY–JUNE 1954

Every year the Vaiśākha number, coinciding with the celebrations of the Buddha's Enlightenment, was a special issue. The first Vaiśākha number that Sangharakshita brought out (a double issue, May–June 1954) has a three-colour cover (yellow, orange, and green). The motif is a vigorous bodhi tree growing out of a monk's begging-bowl. The inside cover bears a message of greeting from Commonwealth Jewellers of Calcutta. (No doubt they made a handsome donation for this place of honour.) On the very first page is a rather more stirring message from no less a person than Pandit Nehru, Prime Minister of India, in which he contrasts the teaching of the Buddha with the violence of the contemporary world and concludes with a salutation: 'To the memory of this greatest of the sons of India, I offer my deep homage.' Only after the usual contents page, a photograph of the Mathura Buddha, and a poem, 'The Conquest of Māra' by Bhikṣu Sangharakshita, do other messages follow: from Dr S. Radhakrishnan, Vice-President of India, from the Prime Minister of Ceylon, and from the Maharaj Kumar of Sikkim, the newly-appointed president of the Maha Bodhi Society. Publishing such messages of support from people in high office in the Vaiśākha number had become something of a tradition with the *Maha Bodhi*. In the same way it would publish photographs of distinguished men and women visiting Buddhist sites or meeting Devapriya Valisinha or other members of the Maha Bodhi Society. Sangharakshita would have preferred to do away with all that for he did not look to the support and influence of politicians and the like to further spiritual aims. However, he did not press his point, seeing that Valisinha was keen to continue, deeming it a useful way to further the influence of the Maha Bodhi Society.

The line-up of contributors is impressive. Devapriya Valisinha must surely have felt some delight at such developments occurring within only a few months of his handing on the editorship. The 1954 Vaiśākha edition of the *Maha Bodhi* includes articles from:

B. L. Broughton, M.A. (Oxon.), who helped Dharmapala establish the Maha Bodhi Society in London: 'The Enlightenment'

E. J. Thomas, M.A., D.Litt., writer and translator: 'New Year Resolutions'

Lama A. Govinda: 'The Buddha as the Ideal of the Perfect Man and the Embodiment of the Dharma'

Dr Edward Conze, German-born Sanskrit scholar and translator: 'Conditions and the Unconditioned'

G. Constant Loundsberry, BSc, American-born founder and president of the French *Les Amis du Bouddhisme*: 'Differences and Difficulties'

HRH Prince Peter of Greece and Denmark: 'Buddhism and the Japanese Character'

Alexandra David-Néel, French traveller and writer: 'On Anicca'

D. T. Davendra of the archaeological department, Ceylon: 'Where a Hero King was Born'

Dr Ankul Chandra Banerjee, M.A., LLB., PhD., Lecturer in Pāli and Sanskrit, University of Arts, Calcutta: 'Dasadhyayavinaya'

Marco Pallis, Greek-born author of *Peaks and Lamas*: 'Some Aspects of a Buddhist Education'

W. Pachow, PhD., Chinese and Pāli scholar at the University of Ceylon: 'India and Buddhist Culture'

Christmas Humphreys, President of the Buddhist Society, London: 'The Menace of Belief'

George Roerich, leading Tibetologist: 'Vanaratna – the Last of the Great Panditas'

Keshab Chandra Gupta, author, litterateur and advocate, and vice-president of the Maha Bodhi Society: 'Buddhism in Dr Nehru's 'Discovery''

R. Kulkarni, Brahmin lawyer and sympathizer with Buddhism, founder of the Buddha Society of Nagpur: 'The Dhamma or Doctrine'

H. de S. Kularatne, J.P. U.M., Principal of Buddhist school in Ceylon: 'Washing away your Sins'

Neluwe Jinaratana Thera, Managing Editor of the *Maha Bodhi* journal: 'A Retrospect'

A. A. G. Bennett, British Pāli scholar: 'I Went to Them and Said'

U. Maung Maung Ji, M.A. (Cantab.), Barrister-at-Law, a Burmese disciple of Annie Besant: 'Buddhism and the Western World'

Dr Kalidas Nag, Professor at Calcutta University and chairman of the Maha Bodhi Editorial Board: '2500th Anniversary of the Maha Parinirvana'

Himavantavasi: 'In the Light of the Dhamma'[351]

The Vaiśākha number also included a book reviews section. Mrs A. A. G. Bennett writes a full-length review of *Sacred Books of the World*, a companion source book to *Comparative Religion*, while Bhikkhu Silabhadra contributes a shorter one on *Moha-Mukti* or 'Delusion's End', a religious drama in Bengali by Sridhar Chandra Barua.

The special issue consists of nearly 100 pages making it, naturally, the longest issue of the year. The January and February issues contained only 32 pages, thereafter it grew until the journal settled at an average over the year of around 40 pages per issue. Only towards the end of the 1950s did the journal become a little – though not much – thinner.

The Vaiśākha number offers the reader rather a glut of advertising – no doubt necessary to defray the cost of printing so lavish an edition. Happily the advertisements are not of the kind we know today, being simple statements in black and white within a box, and placed all together at the end, rather than breaking into the articles in the body of the journal. Singli Dyers and Cleaners of Calcutta offer a Quick Service with Moderate Charge by Chinese Experts. Barua Bakery recommends its cake which is, it assures you, highly spoken of by eminent personages of India *as well as* by Indian National Congress (members of the congress apparently not being counted among the eminent). You are warned, however, to beware of spurious imitations, for Barua cake is baked in factories with equipment imported from the United Kingdom. Most advertisements, however, have a directly Buddhist theme and most are recommending Buddhist books, especially those published by the Maha Bodhi Book Agency at 4A Bankim Chatterjee Street: *Mulagandhi Wall Paintings* is Just Out! A Great Work is available in Hindi, National Language of India: *Buddhacariya* by Pandit Rahula Sankrityayana,... and so on. The long list of 'Books on Sale' at the Maha Bodhi Book Agency gives an interesting glimpse of the contemporary world of published books on Buddhism.

This brief survey gives us a good idea of the basic look and content of the journal. Over the years there were some changes or improvements to its look: in 1957 the double-column layout was replaced by a single column, but the following year the double-column was reinstated. Black-and-white photographs were joined by coloured ones. The special Buddha Jayanti number in 1956, also 100 pages in length, has no fewer than twenty illustrations, including two in full colour. The following year's Vaiśākha edition is more modest, yet the black-and-white photograph of a stone head of the Buddha and the five simple but evocative line drawings of scenes from his life do much to convey the significance of Vaiśākha. Usually, however, the journal could not afford to publish many illustrations (sometimes there were none at all). But though not numerous, taken together they constitute a valuable historical resource about the Buddhist world of the time, the people, the places and the events. Here are a few examples:

November 1955: The Hon. Nu, Prime Minister of Burma, planting a bodhi sapling at Ashoka Vihara, Delhi
November 1956: Dr Ambedkar calls upon his followers to embrace Buddhism
December 1956: His Holiness the Dalai Lama in Gangtok
March 1957: Delegates to the Symposium on Buddhism's Contribution to Art, Letters and Philosophy, New Delhi
December 1958: Ven Narada Maha Thera with Dr Buddhadasa P. Kirthisinghe of the American Buddhist Academy, New York
May 1961: Sri D. Valisinha in conversation with HRH Queen Elizabeth II on the steps of the Mulagandhakuti Vihara at Sarnath.

Not only the photographs but also some of the articles and especially the News and Notes section are a particularly rich resource on the history of the revival of Buddhism in India, including the activities of Sangharakshita. We also find here and there articles, poems, and paintings by or referring to various characters who appear in Sangharakshita's memoirs, including Sachindra Coomar Singh who writes a poetic evocation of 'Life in the Hills', published in April 1954, and Anagarika Dharmarakshita (Miss D. Delannoy), a French Buddhist nun whose 'learned lecture' is reported in January 1954. Later there are contributions from Rev. Jack Austin and the Ven. Robert Stuart Clifton, founder of a Western Buddhist Order, from Prof. N. K. Bhagwat and Francis Story, while a poem of Sangharakshita, 'Himalayan Sages', published in the July 1954 edition, is illustrated by a rather strange painting by one Joseph E. Cann.

WHAT IS THE *MAHA BODHI*?

But what is the *Maha Bodhi*, we might find ourselves beginning to wonder. Is it a scholarly journal? A literary one? Is it for disseminating news around the Buddhist world? It was all these things under Sangharakshita's editorship – and it was more. Typically, he had asked himself the same question and answered it in depth in the December 1954 editorial, 'The Functions of a Buddhist Journal' which he summarizes as (1) To reflect the unchanging light of Truth in the mirror of contemporary attitudes and aspirations. Articles may include presentations of different aspects of Buddhism in relation to specific modern problems, interests, and needs. There is also a place for literary pieces to encourage those with literary gifts to devote their talents to the service of the Dharma. (2) To furnish news of Buddhist activities so that the individual Buddhist is inspired by 'the magnificent spectacle of the mighty forward movement of the whole Buddhist world', and at the same time is enabled to appreciate his own small part in that movement, in consequence of which 'his determination is strengthened and the torch of his enthusiasm kept brightly burning'. (3) To foster a sense of community between both individual Buddhists and Buddhist groups in different parts of the globe. The editor notes that allegiance to an ideal is of greater value than formal membership of a society and it is this that really holds Buddhists together as a community. A Buddhist journal has a valuable part to play. He imagines readers in distant places receiving the journal through the post. 'As they remove the wrapper and turn over its pages their sense of being isolated in the midst of a hostile, or at least alien, religious environment, suddenly leaves them; they feel like a child who has just been gathered to his mother's breast; a sensation of warmth and kinship possesses them; they feel they belong.'

For the twelve or so years in which Sangharakshita was its editor, the *Maha Bodhi* flourished, becoming the most widely-read and influential English-language Buddhist journal of the time. Through its articles contemporary issues of the Buddhist world were discussed and new discoveries in academic research were published, however horrified Theravādin fundamentalists might be at some of the findings. During that pivotal decade the journal tracked the movement of the revival of Buddhism in India and the East and its growth in the West so that groups and individuals did indeed come to know of one another's existence and thereby, I am sure, gained inspiration to carry on their own work. Whether the journal was able to foster that sense of kinship Sangharakshita mentions as the third function of a Buddhist journal, I wonder. Perhaps for that feeling of belonging to a community of Buddhist practitioners, something quite different needed to come into being.

WHAT HAPPENED TO THE EDITOR?

For fourteen years Sangharakshita beat the drum in India, delivering hundreds of lectures all over the subcontinent, writing articles and editing and contributing to the *Maha Bodhi*. He worked for the *revival* of Buddhism, participating in the renewal that had been inaugurated by Dharmapala and which was magnificently taken forward by Dr Ambedkar, and he worked for the *reform* of Buddhism where the living spirit of the Dharma was dying or even dead. Then, in 1962, he received the letter that became the impetus for a complete change in the outer course of his life. At the invitation of a small Buddhist group in England, he returned to the West to deliver lectures in the land of his birth and decided to stay on there. In the West it was not a worker for revival that was needed, nor was there much to reform. What was needed was something new. The Dharma, of course, was not new, it was *sanātana*, that is, its truths about life and existence are unchanging. But there had to be a new start, a new initiative, a new impetus, even a new vehicle for expressing those unchanging truths, one that avoided the pitfalls of aspects of Eastern Buddhism, one that could speak directly to men and women whose cultural background was a modern Western one. He sought to establish something new by returning to the roots of Buddhism, to its most basic principles. And so it was that from revivalist and reformist, Sangharakshita turned radical, some might even say revolutionary. He set up a Buddhist order that includes men and women, both eastern and western, northern and southern, and which from early on included Buddhists from Dr Ambedkar's revolution in India. But that, as they say, is another story.

APPENDIX 2

Triyana Vardhana Vihara Kalimpong Report 1957–1962

THE PRELIMINARY WORK: 1950–1956

The Triyana Vardhana Vihara, Kalimpong, was established in May 1957 after seven years of preliminary work. The founder, Bhadanta Bhikṣu Sangharakshita (Sthavira) came to this colourful and cosmopolitan township on a short visit in March 1950. At the suggestion of Bhadanta Bhikṣu Jagdish Kashyap (Maha Sthavira), his teacher in Pāli and Abhidharma, he decided to make the place his headquarters and to inaugurate there various religious activities.

With the cooperation of Nepali, Tibetan, and Sikkimese Buddhists, as well as of persons of many nationalities interested in Buddhism, he accordingly established the Young Men's Buddhist Association in May that year and began publishing the monthly magazine *Stepping-Stones* in June. The YMBA, which functioned in a succession of rented premises, celebrated Vaiśākha Pūrṇimā (Buddha Jayanti) and other Buddhist festivals, arranged lectures, conducted tutorial classes for school and college students, and maintained a shrine, a free reading room and library, and a games room. *Stepping-Stones*, which specialized in articles on Tibetan Buddhism, continued for twenty numbers and achieved a modest celebrity. Contributors included Lama Anagarika Govinda, Mme Alexandra David-Néel, Marco Pallis, H. R. H. Prince Peter of Greece and Denmark, Dr George Roerich, Dr H. V. Guenther, and Dr R. Nebesky de Wojkowitz.

At the end of March 1951, an impetus was given to the work of the YMBA by the arrival in Kalimpong of the Sacred Relics of the *arhants* Śāriputra and Maudgalyāyana, which had already toured many parts of the Buddhist world. Arrangements for their reception and exposition were made by Bhikṣu Sangharakshita, who also accompanied them to Gangtok and Darjeeling and (towards the end of the year) to Nepal, where he delivered numerous lectures. In 1952 he wrote for the Maha Bodhi Society of India's *Diamond Jubilee Souvenir* a Biographical Sketch of Anagarika Dharmapala, participated in the opening ceremony of the Chetiyagiri Vihara, Sanchi, where the relics of the two *arhants* were eventually re-enshrined, and joined the editorial board of the *Maha Bodhi* journal. As a result of these contacts, it was decided to affiliate the YMBA to the Maha Bodhi Society of India, and to change the name of the organization accordingly.

During this period, as well as every year thereafter, Bhikshu Sangharakshita lectured regularly in Kalimpong and the neighbouring towns, especially in Gangtok, the capital of Sikkim. He also undertook extensive preaching tours to different parts of India, including places as far afield as Calcutta, Bombay, and Madras. At the invitation of the Indian Institute of World Culture, Bangalore, he delivered in July 1954 a series of lectures under the general title of 'A Survey of Buddhism'. The same year saw the publication of *Messengers From Tibet*, a collection of poems.

From May 1956 to May 1957 the Buddhist countries of Asia, not excluding India, as well as Buddhist groups all over the world, celebrated the 2,500th anniversary of the Buddha's *parinirvāṇa*, the occasion being one not only of great rejoicing but of a tremendous resurgence of the Dharma. In Kalimpong, where a representative committee was set up, with Rani Chuni Dorje as president and Bhikṣu Sangharakshita as general secretary, the celebrations were the biggest and most colourful the town had ever witnessed. Towards the end of the year, with fifty-six other distinguished Buddhists from the Border Areas, the Bhikṣu toured the sacred places at the invitation of the Government of India and attended the 2,500th Buddha Jayanti celebrations in New Delhi, where he met their Holinesses the Dalai and Panchen Lamas, as well as the President, Vice-President, and Prime Minister of India. He also contributed to the Government of India publication *2,500 Years of Buddhism*. Simultaneously the Indian Institute of World Culture brought out in book form *A Survey of Buddhism*,[352] which met with an immediate success, one Buddhist periodical hailing it as the chief event of the Buddha Jayanti year.

Returning from New Delhi to Kalimpong via Bombay, Bhikṣu Sangharakshita received at Nagpur news of the sudden death of Dr B. R. Ambedkar, whom he had known and advised since 1950. The first historic mass conversion to Buddhism having taken place at Nagpur only just under eight weeks previously, Baba Saheb's followers were smitten with dismay by the dreadful tidings, and for a time the whole conversion movement seemed about to collapse. Tens of thousands of people flocked for consolation to the Bhikṣu who, realizing the critical nature of the situation, remained in Nagpur for four days, addressing thirty-five mass meetings (one of them more than 100,000 strong) and receiving 60,000 more new converts into the fold of Buddhism.[353]

Only when satisfied that the movement was no longer in danger did he depart. Owing to his having stood by them in those dark days, when suddenly they found themselves leaderless, the Buddhists of central and western India developed great confidence in Bhikṣu Sangharakshita, and reinforced by later preaching tours his influence with them steadily increased.

On 27 January 1957 the efforts of almost seven years were blessed, and an impetus given to fresh developments on a larger scale, by a visit from His Holiness the Dalai Lama, then in Kalimpong, who as a token of his appreciation was pleased to present a beautiful image of Amitābha Buddha, two volumes of scriptures in Tibetan, and an autographed picture of himself.

By this time experience had shown that without a material basis more permanent than that provided by a rented building, consolidation and further expansion of the *dharmadūta* activities was impossible. After discussing the matter with friends and supporters, Bhikṣu Sangharakshita decided to establish in Kalimpong a vihara that would serve both as his personal headquarters and as a centre of living Buddhism. In 1957 a property was acquired for 19,000 rupees, the donors being Marco Pallis Esq., Richard Nicholson Esq., and the Sikkim Durbar, all of whom, but especially the first, had encouraged and supported the Bhikṣu's work since the time of his arrival in Kalimpong.

Aims and Objects

Buddhism has entered upon a new phase. After being static, if not actually on the wane, for several centuries, it is at present, in many parts of the world, undergoing a remarkable transformation. Though the extent of the revival and expansion now in progress can be exaggerated, and though gains must always be balanced against losses, it is nevertheless true that knowledge of Buddhism is more widespread, and its followers more active, than was the case a century ago. In the West it has begun to enter the mainstream of modern thought, and centres dedicated to its advancement yearly multiply. At home, in the Buddhist countries of Asia, there has begun a great process of reorganization and reappraisal, while in India, its long-forsaken original home, millions have recently taken refuge in the Three Jewels. The foundation of the Triyana Vardhana Vihara in Kalimpong, a predominantly Buddhist part of India, by a *bhikṣu* of English birth, with the help of European and Asian friends, is therefore no isolated event but part of a movement of worldwide significance.

Though much has been done, much remains to be done. One of the greatest needs of the Buddhist world today is unity. Not, indeed, unity in the sense of uniformity, much less still in that of centralization of authority, but in the sense of a deeper and more effective recognition of the basic fact that despite differences, even divergences, of doctrine and method, all Buddhist traditions have for their ultimate goal that state of *bodhi* or Enlightenment whence the very name of their religion derives. The Triyana Vardhana Vihara has therefore been dedicated by its founder to the study, practice, and dissemination *of the total Buddhist tradition*. With Dr Edward Conze, perhaps the most illustrious of Western Buddhist scholars, it holds that

> the doctrine of the Buddha, conceived in its full breadth, width, majesty, and grandeur, comprises all those teachings that are linked to the original teaching by historical continuity, and which work out methods leading to the extinction of individuality by eliminating the belief in it.[354]

As its name indicates, the vihara is therefore a place where the three *yānas*, or major historical developments of Buddhism, all flourish. These are the Hīnayāna, the Mahāyāna, and the Vajrayāna, these designations being used merely in a descriptive sense and being understood as covering both the theoretical and the practical aspects, as well as including developments such as the Theravāda and Zen. The name of the vihara was given, in a mood of high spiritual inspiration, by the Venerable Chattrul Sangye Dorje ('Without Concerns' Buddhavajra), a celebrated lama of the Nyingma school who, predicting its foundation at a time when this seemed impossible, addressed to Bhikṣu Sangharakshita the Tibetan original of the following stanzas:

In the sky devoid of limits, the teaching of the Muni is
The sun, spreading the thousand rays of the three *śikṣās* [i.e. morality, meditation, and wisdom];
Continually shining in the radiance of the impartial disciples,
May this Jambudvīpa region of the Triyāna be fair!
In accordance with his request, [made] in the Fire-Monkey Year
On the ninth day of the first month by the Mahā Sthavira Sangharakshita,
This was written by the *Śākya-upāsaka*, the Vidyādhara Bodhivajra: [may there be] happiness and blessings!

More specifically, the vihara aims to function in a threefold capacity:

1. As a centre for the systematic study of Buddhism in all its aspects, for research, and for the production of Buddhist literature, both original and translated, in English, Nepali, Tibetan, Hindi, Marathi, and other languages;

2. As a meditation centre, where both monks and laymen will be provided with all the facilities for the practice of *dhyāna* according to the traditional methods and where arrangements can be made for longer and shorter periods of spiritual retreat; and

3. As a centre of the ordination and training of *bhikṣus*, *śrāmaṇeras*, and lay *dharmadūta* workers, in order to meet the growing need for dedicated workers now being felt both in the hill areas and the plains as a result of the movement of Buddhist revival.

Description

The vihara is located two miles out of town, and comprises four acres of terraced hillside land. The main building, or vihara proper, is perched on a rocky spur about 4,000 feet above sea level. Consisting of four rooms and a spacious veranda, it faces due west, and commands a magnificent panoramic view of the foothills rising on either side of the River Rangit, which separates India from Sikkim, of Mount Kanchenjunga and other snow-peaks of the eastern Himalayan Range, and, on clear days, of the passes debouching into the Tibetan plateau. The central room of the building is the shrine, which with its rhythm of regular puja and meditation functions as the spiritual heart of the entire establishment. As the sun sets behind the blue Darjeeling hills, its last rays, slanting down across the valley and in at the shrine door, set ablaze the silver and brass altar utensils and softly light up the smiling gilded face of the standing Buddha image occupying the place of honour on the topmost tier.

In addition to the main building, which had to be renovated to serve its present purpose, the property included at the time of its acquisition a four-roomed wooden outhouse and servants' quarters. To these were added, in 1958, a four-roomed thatched guest house of the local Nepalese type of construction. Other improvements to the property include the installation of a piped water supply and the building of several hundred feet of support walls, mostly below the main building, to guard against the possibility of landslides. Various maintenance and repair works were also carried out from time to time.

As much of the vihara land as possible is kept under cultivation. Rice, maize, millet, and buckwheat are grown every year, but though good the crop is insufficient to meet the needs of all the inmates. As regards vegetables, however, the vihara is usually self-supporting, allotments having been laid out for this purpose. There is an orange orchard, from the produce of which a small annual income is derived, as well as plums and pears. Last year four dozen orange saplings were planted to take the place of trees grown old or diseased. In addition there are plantations of bamboo which provide not only building material and fuel, but shade for outdoor meditation. Timber is relatively scarce, the local population being greatly addicted, unfortunately, to the destruction of trees, none of which are ever replaced. The vihara garden, cultivated for its own sake as well as to provide flowers for the shrine, ranges from English roses to Himalayan orchids, and from African gerberas to South American cacti.

Organization

The vihara is organized along traditional lines, the founder and first *adhipati* being vested with sole and complete authority, both spiritual and secular. It is, therefore, an independent institution, and is not part of, nor affiliated to, nor in any way legally connected with, any other institution or organization. As the practice is in most Buddhist lands, it relies for support on the devotion of its lay followers, some of whom live in Kalimpong, some in other parts of India, and some abroad. Though independent, it nevertheless maintains, through correspondence at least, frequent and friendly contact with individual Buddhists as well as with Buddhist groups and movements, all over the world, and is ever ready to cooperate with them in whatever way it can.

Relations with the Maha Bodhi Society of India are particularly close and cordial. In the account of the Preliminary Work reference has been made to the affiliation of the YMBA to the Society in 1952. After the founding of the vihara, the Kalimpong branch of the Society gratefully accepted an offer of free accommodation within the vihara premises. Bhikṣu Sangharakshita, while continuing to be the *bhikṣu*-in-charge of this branch, simultaneously acts as the Society's representative in the area and in general looks after its interests. The branch receives from the Calcutta headquarters a monthly subsidy. Vaiśākha Pūrṇimā celebrations and other public functions are conducted in the joint names of the Triyana Vardhana Vihara and the Maha Bodhi Society of India, Kalimpong Branch. As a member of the editorial board of the *Maha Bodhi* journal, Bhikṣu Sangharakshita also utilizes the vihara for the fulfilment of his share of the editorial work.

Ordinations and Initiations

The Buddha has said that the greatest miracle is the miracle of conversion.[355] This may be either from the lay to the monastic state or from a religion other than Buddhism, or from no religion at all, to the Truth and Way taught by the Buddha. Though conversion, whether in the form of ordination or initiation, is essentially an inner and spiritual event, for institutional purposes there is also in each case a simple ceremony. We are happy to report that during the period under review several such ceremonies were performed at the vihara. Though few in number, their significance is great.

In 1957 Bhikṣu Sangharakshita conferred the lower ordination (*pravrajya*) on Mr Donald Miller, of the USA, who had been studying Buddhism with him for over a year, and gave him the name of Dharmadhara. After he had spent another year with his *upādhyāya* arrangements were made for the new *śrāmaṇera* to pursue his studies in Thailand. On 20 July 1958, the Bhikṣu ordained Rigdzin Wangpo, a Lhasa-born Tibetan who, some years previously, had studied Pāli in Ceylon, besides working for two years at the School of Oriental Languages in London. Śrāmaṇera Prajnaloka (in Tibetan Getsul Sherab Nangwa), as he is now known, is a gifted poet and writer, and has proved a great asset to the vihara. Since his ordination he has been occupied mainly with translation and teaching work, and has rendered a number of Pāli texts into Tibetan (see below, Publications). While out on tour in the plains Bhikṣu Sangharakshita also participated in the *upasampadā* or higher ordination of two *śrāmaṇeras* in Bangalore, besides acting as *ācārya* when Jivaka Kumara was given the lower ordination in Sarnath.

On 3 May 1958, the Bhikṣu formally initiated into Buddhism Kazini Elisa-Maria Dorji-Khangsarpa of Chakhung, the Scottish-born wife of a Sikkimese nobleman. A well-known journalist and educationist, the Kazini Sahiba regularly assists the vihara with legal advice and in numerous other ways. Shri Krishna Bahadur Rai of Darjeeling was similarly initiated at the beginning of 1962 and spent, in all, nearly a year at the vihara studying Buddhism and assisting with office work. In the course of his preaching tours among the followers of the late Dr B. R. Ambedkar Bhikṣu Sangharakshita initiated into Buddhism and personally instructed not less than 100,000 men and women (see below: Preaching Tours).[356]

Many *bhikṣus*, *śrāmaṇeras*, and *upāsakas* have also spent longer or shorter periods of time at the vihara either studying Buddhism or learning English or both, as well as assisting Bhikṣu Sangharakshita in various ways. Bhikṣus Khemasiri of Thailand and Sugatapriya of Assam stayed for more than a year each, Sāmaṇera Sujiva (afterwards Bhikkhu Khantipālo) and Jivaka Kumara for about six months, and scores of others for shorter periods. From among the newly initiated Indian Buddhists came Shri Amritlal Bechardas of Ahmedabad and Shri D. R. Maheshkar of Poona, each of whom spent a month at the vihara engaged in the intensive study of Buddhism as well as in translation work. Mr Armin Gottmann of Germany came for special training in meditation. Many students from different parts of the Buddhist world, especially from Visvabharati University, Santiniketan, and the Nalanda Pāli Institute, spent their summer vacation at the vihara as did a party of two monks and sixteen novices from various monasteries in Ladakh who were then studying at Sarnath. After the 1958 uprising in Tibet, accommodation was also provided, for a few weeks, to a dozen refugee monks.

Celebrations

In addition to the 'Tiratana Vandanā' (Worship of the Three Jewels) and meditation conducted, mainly for the benefit of inmates, daily from 6 to 7 a.m. and from 6 to 7 p.m. in the shrine, the vihara publicly celebrates various important Buddhist festivals and anniversaries. These celebrations, by means of which the Dharma is spread and consolidated among a much larger number of people, are of three kinds: monthly, annual, and occasional.

The monthly celebration is predominantly devotional in character and consists in the observance of the *pūrṇimā* or full-moon day at the vihara premises. This function is held in the shrine, on the altar of which, decorated with flowers and lighted lamps, are placed the seven traditional offerings, both symbolically and in kind. After those present have one by one offered a lighted candle and incense stick, there is a reading from the scriptures, usually a chapter of the *Dhammapada*, followed by an hour's discourse on the Dharma. Proceedings in the shrine conclude with a short period of group meditation, after which light refreshments are served.

Annual celebrations comprise Vaiśākha Pūrṇimā (Buddha Jayanti), Dharmachakra Day (the anniversary of the Buddha's first sermon at Sarnath), which are lunar festivals, and Anagarika Dharmapala's birthday on 17 September. In its observance of these days, as well as in all other functions, the vihara emphasizes the importance not only of sincere faith and devotion, but also of artistry, dignity, orderliness, and punctuality. There is no place for cheap and vulgar decorations or blaring loudspeakers. Above all, the vihara strictly eschews the practice, so common in certain quarters, of inviting as speaker or president persons who are eminent in the world for reasons other than their knowledge of, or sympathy for, the Buddha's teaching. Much less still does it follow the unfortunate practice of offering the hospitality of its platform to those who are actually hostile to Buddhism.

As was fitting, the vihara's first celebration of the Vaiśākha Pūrṇimā, on 3 May 1958, was held at its own premises, in a specially erected *shamiana*, the public meeting being presided over by H. H. Lieut.-Col. P. T. Namgyal, PB, OBE, Maharajkumar of Sikkim. Devotional songs were sung, and speeches delivered in Tibetan, English, Hindi, and Nepali by eminent incarnate lamas (*tulkus*), monks, and laymen. Among those participating were H. H. Dudjom Rimpoche, spiritual head of the Nyingma school, and the Ven. Dhardo Rimpoche, an eminent Gelug *tulku* who addressed the gathering. Colour was given to the occasion by a Tibetan-style procession, complete with Buddha image, banners, and trumpets, and a full set of scriptures (in more than 300 huge xylograph volumes), which arrived from Durpindhara, three miles away, shortly before the meeting began. This procession, consisting of about 400 monks and laymen, was organized by the Tsechu Offering Association, the members of which are devout followers of Guru Padmasambhava. Apart from the fact that they were held in the Kalimpong town hall and in the 'Dharma Hall' of the Kumudini Homes School respectively, the Vaiśākha Pūrṇimā celebrations of 1959 and 1962 followed the same general pattern. In 1960 and 1961, when Bhikṣu Sangharakshita was out on tour, celebrations on a smaller scale were organized by Śrāmaṇera Prajnaloka.

Dharmachakra Day follows two months after the Vaiśākha Pūrṇimā. This is also celebrated with a programme of worship of the Three Jewels, devotional songs, and religious discourses. In 1961 the occasion was celebrated in the town hall, Kalimpong, under the presidentship of Shri S. R. Das, Vice-Chancellor of Visvabharati University and ex-Chief Justice of India. In other years a function was held at the vihara in conjunction with the usual full-moon day observances. Anagarika Dharmapala's birthday was celebrated every year with a memorial service and a special lecture, usually by Bhikṣu Sangharakshita, on the significance of his life and work.

Outstanding among the occasional functions was the celebration, on 2 and 3 December 1961, of the 542nd death anniversary of Jetsun Tsongkhapa, the reformer of Tibetan Buddhism and founder of the Gelug school. On the first day a famous golden image of the great teacher, lent for the occasion, was brought in a mile-long colourful procession from the Tharpa Choling Gompa, Tirpai, to the town hall, and a public meeting held. Chief speaker was Ven. Tijang Rimpoche, teacher of H. H. the Dalai Lama. Also present on the platform were H. H. Dudjom Rimpoche and Ven. Mindroling Doong Rimpoche, representing the Nyingmapas. Ven. Khamtul Rimpoche, an eminent Kagyupa lama, and Ven. Dhardo Rimpoche, Ven. Tomo Geshe Rimpoche, Ven. Pabongkhapa Rimpoche, and the Ven. Abbot, Tharpa Choling Gompa, from the Gelugpa side. Most of these lamas addressed the gathering on the life and work of Tsongkhapa, as did Bhikṣu Sangharakshita, Śrāmaṇera Prajnaloka, and Shri Parasmani Pradhan. In the course of his speech, Ven. Tijang Rimpoche remarked that even in Tibet a celebration of this kind had not been possible. It was, in fact, the first time that Jetsun Tsongkhapa's death anniversary had been publicly celebrated in India, and the significance of the occasion was marked by a truly record attendance. So great was the crush that a thousand people, unable to gain admittance, had to listen to the speeches over the loudspeaker system from outside the hall. On the following day, the image having been reverentially kept all night in the town hall, it was taken in procession back to the Tharpa Choling Gompa, where a small function was held. The vihara subsequently received a letter of congratulation from H. H. the Dalai Lama.

Publications

With the extension of literacy, the diffusion of the Dharma through the medium of the written word has assumed even greater significance than it possessed in the past. The vihara therefore attaches considerable importance to this type of activity. Soon after he arrived in Kalimpong, Bhikṣu Sangharakshita was astonished to find that apart from a dramatic version of the life of the Buddha published many years ago by Shri Parasmani Pradhan there existed not a single book on Buddhism in Nepali, the lingua franca of the area, despite the fact that this language was the mother tongue of tens of thousands of Buddhists. This discovery led to the publication of Nepali translations of Bhikkhu Silachara's

Buddhism for Beginners (1953), the *Dhammapada* (1956), and the *Khuddakapāṭha* (1956), the last two being printed together with the original Pāli text. All these translations were made at the request of Bhikṣu Sangharakshita by Shri Bhaichand Pradhan, a young Nepalese writer of Kalimpong, and published in the name of the Maha Bodhi Society of India, Kalimpong Branch. The branch also brought out two booklets in English by Bhikṣu Sangharakshita: *Buddhism and Art* (1956) and *Is Buddhism For Monks Only? A Dialogue* (1957).[357]

During the period under review the vihara has sponsored only three publications. This is partly due to the fact that, as a result of the recent widespread increase of interest in Buddhism, it is now much easier to bring out Buddhist literature through the ordinary commercial publishing channels than it was previously (see below: Literary Work), as well as being much more economical. 1957 saw the publication of the second edition of the Nepali *Dhammapada*, all copies of the first having been exhausted within a year. On Dharmachakra Day, 20 July 1959, the vihara brought out its first publication in Tibetan. This was a translation of the *Maṅgala Sutta*, which as far as it has been possible to ascertain is not included in the Tibetan Kangyur. This translation was made by Śrāmaṇera Prajnaloka. One thousand copies were printed, in booklet form, and distributed free among the Tibetan-speaking monks and lay people of the area, many of whom expressed their great appreciation of the work. Śrāmaṇera Prajnaloka has also translated many other Pāli texts, including the *Khuddakapāṭha*, the *Uraga-vagga* of the *Sutta-Nipāta*, and the *Sigālovāda Sutta*, all of which will be published as soon as the necessary arrangements can be made. Finally, to commemorate the fifth anniversary of its foundation the vihara has brought out a booklet entitled *Dharma ke ho?* This is a Nepali translation by Shri Narayanmani Pradhan of a transcription by Bhikkhu Khantipālo of a talk on 'What is Dharma?' given at the vihara by Bhikṣu Sangharakshita one full-moon day earlier in the year. A Marathi translation by Shri D. R. Maheshkar of the same talk has been brought out from Poona.

Library

As ancillary to the prosecution of its first specific objective, namely the systematic study of Buddhism, the vihara maintains a library consisting, at present, of about one thousand volumes. Nearly half of these are

Buddhist texts in Pāli, Sanskrit, and Tibetan, translations in English, Hindi, and Bengali, and modern works on Buddhism. The remainder are devoted to such subjects as philosophy, religion, psychology, and literature. While a few books were presented by friends and well-wishers, the greater part of the library had to be acquired by way of purchase. All the books are available to inmates of the vihara for study and reference, but generally speaking it has not proved practicable to issue them to outsiders. The vihara also receives free from the organizations concerned about a dozen Buddhist periodicals, besides a number of other magazines. These too are available to inmates.

Literary Work

During the period under review the vihara saw the accomplishment of a considerable amount of literary work of various kinds. In the intervals in between preaching tours, Bhikṣu Sangharakshita has been engaged on two major literary undertakings, *The Heritage of Buddhism*, scheduled for publication in 1965, and an autobiography entitled *The Golden Pilgrimage*.[358] He also contributed a large number of articles to Buddhist magazines and other periodicals, the most important being *The Meaning of Orthodoxy in Buddhism: A Protest* (France-Asie, February–June 1955), and 'Ordination and Initiation in the Three Yānas' (*The Middle Way*, November 1959). Two much slighter productions: 'Wanted: A New Type of Bhikkhu' and 'Wanted: A New Type of Upāsaka',[359] both written during 1961, have been reprinted in Buddhist magazines all over the world and attracted a good deal of attention. At the special request of His Holiness the Dalai Lama, Bhikṣu Sangharakshita also prepared with the assistance of Mr John Driver and Mr T. Trethong, an English version of Tsongkhapa's work 'The Three Chief Paths'.[360] This was published, together with introduction and notes, in the November 1960 number of *The Middle Way*. In 1958 he prepared a second edition of his well known work *A Survey of Buddhism*, which appeared the following year under the imprimature of the Indian Institute of World Culture, the publishers of the first edition.[361] Other inmates of the vihara were hardly less prolific. Jivaka Kumara wrote, at Bhikṣu Sangharakshita's suggestion, *Practising the Dhammapada*, subsequently published by the Maha Bodhi Society of India, besides numerous articles on Buddhism and allied subjects. Bhikkhu Khantipālo completed two small works on *The Buddha's Middle Way* and *Tolerance: A Study from Buddhist Sources*, besides writing essays and articles. Shri Amritlal Bechardas translated the greater part of *What the Buddha Taught*, by Walpola Rahula, into Gujarati, while Shri D. R. Maheshkar rendered Bhikṣu Sangharakshita's talk on 'What is Dharma?' into Marathi. Mention should also be made of articles written about the vihara and its activities. These include 'The Ordination of Rigdzin Wangpo' (Sherab Nangwa) by Miss Julie Medlock, an American writer, and an illustrated article in Vietnamese by Ven. Thich Thien Chau.

Since 1959 Bhikṣu Sangharakshita has been editor of *The Buddhist Library*, a series of pocket-sized publications on Buddhism sponsored by a leading Indian publishing house, Chetana Ltd. of Bombay. These volumes, of which it is hoped to publish at least a hundred, are designed for the intelligent general reader rather than for the professional scholar, and will eventually cover all aspects of Buddhism. Four titles have so far been brought out. As its first, the *Library* was privileged to publish *A Short History of Buddhism*, by Dr Edward Conze. This was followed by *Crossing the Stream*, a collection of essays by Bhikṣu Sangharakshita.[362] *Long Discourses of the Buddha I–XVI*, a new translation of the greater part of the *Dīgha Nikāya* by Mrs A. A. G. Bennett, and *The Buddha's Middle Way* by Bhikkhu Khantipālo. All these have met with a favourable reception from the reading public and further titles are now under active preparation.

English Classes

From the time of his arrival in Kalimpong Bhikṣu Sangharakshita was constantly approached by persons of various nationalities, mostly Nepalese and Tibetans, who were desirous of learning English. Many of them were pupils in the various educational institutions in the town who, finding the English instruction there inadequate, were in need of special coaching. Under the auspices of the YMBA tutorial classes were therefore opened, the daily attendance at one time exceeding sixty. Individual tuition was also given, no charge being made for any of these services. After the foundation of the vihara, when Bhikṣu Sangharakshita's time began to be more and more taken up with literary and preaching work, it became necessary to reduce these activities. At no time, however, except during the periods of his absence from Kalimpong, were they wholly discontinued. It was thought desirable, though, to give preference to those students who intended to utilize their knowledge of English for the service of the Dharma. In a way, especially after the Tibetan uprising of 1958, a number of Tibetan monks who were eager to propagate Buddhism through the medium of English came to study at the vihara, some of them as inmates. These included not only ordinary *gelongs* (*bhikṣus*) and *getsuls* (*śrāmaṇeras*) but the abbot of the Tharpa Choling Monastery, Kalimpong, as well as highly respected incarnate lamas like the Ven. Rechung Rimpoche who, after studying with Bhikṣu Sangharakshita for two years joined the staff at the Namgyal Institute of Tibetology, Gangtok, and is now teaching Tibetan at the University of Leiden, Holland. At the time of writing Bhikṣu Sangharakshita has only five or six students, but as the number of Tibetan monks desirous of studying English with him has increased the formation of regular classes in now under consideration.

Distinguished Visitors

During the five years of its existence the vihara has been visited not only by thousands of local people but also by prominent Buddhists and friends of Buddhism from India and overseas. While it is obviously impossible to make mention of all the distinguished visitors that the vihara has been happy to welcome (permanent residents of Kalimpong are in any case excluded), there are some names which cannot be omitted.

Among distinguished members of the Sangha the first place belongs to the late Ven. Jamyang Khyentse Rimpoche, one of the greatest scholar-saints that Tibet has produced in recent times, who at the invitation of Bhadanta Sangharakshita visited the vihara in November 1958, and after being accorded a ceremonial reception in the shrine by the assembled inmates blessed the place by chanting verses of benediction. In November 1961, a similar function was held in honour of Ven. Tijang Rimpoche, junior teacher to His Holiness the Dalai Lama. Other members of the Tibetan sangha who paid visits to the vihara included Ven. Kachu Rimpoche, Head Lama of the Pemayangtse Gompa, western Sikkim, who paid several visits and more than once stayed for a week or ten days; the Ven. Tomo Geshe Rimpoche, whose previous *tulku* founded a number of Gelugpa monasteries in the Darjeeling area; and the youthful Ven. Pabongkhapa Rimpoche, the reincarnation of a celebrated scholar of Sera Monastery in Lhasa. The Theravāda branch of the sangha was well represented by the Ven. Dharmadhirarajamahamuni, first abbot of the Thai Monastery, Bodh Gaya; Bhadanta Ananda Kausalyayan, the noted Hindi writer and translator of Pāli texts; and the Ven. Dhirananda Maha Sthavira, of the Bengal Buddhist Association, who spent a week at the vihara shortly after its foundation. The vihara also had the opportunity of welcoming, on more than one occasion, the Ven. Thich Minh Chau, one of the most active and erudite members of the Vietnamese sangha. Though the *bhikṣuṇī* sangha is now practically extinct, it is good to be able to record the visit of at least one nun, and a Westerner at that, in the person of Sister Amita Nisatta, who by her modest and dignified demeanour impressed all with whom she came in contact.

Lay Buddhists and friends of Buddhism came in even larger numbers, and naturally presented an even greater variety of national origins. First and foremost were two out of the three founder-donors of the vihara, Mr Marco Pallis and H. H. Lieut.-Col. P. T. Namgyal, PB, OBE, Maharajkumar of Sikkim. The latter paid, indeed, a number of visits, and always evinced keen interest in the activities of the vihara. The best-known Buddhist visitor from outside India was, however, Christmas Humphreys, the dynamic president of the Buddhist Society, London, and an old friend of Bhadanta Sangharakshita, who in the course of a short visit to this corner of the Himalayas in April 1962 found time for two long visits to the vihara and much discussion. Bhadanta Sangharakshita also accompanied him to Darjeeling. From nearer home came Shri Devapriya Valisinha, the indefatigable General Secretary of the Maha Bodhi Society of India, who in June 1958 spent a quiet week at the vihara enjoying a well-earned rest. Shri Apa B. Pant, the political officer in Sikkim, who during his tenure of office had invited Bhadanta Sangharakshita to deliver several series of lectures (see below: Preaching Tours)[363] paid him a farewell visit in September 1961 prior to proceeding to Indonesia as ambassador to India. A number of well-known Buddhist scholars also came in contact with the vihara, for longer or shorter periods, and these naturally included several Tibetologists. Mr John Driver, who spent two years in Kalimpong engaged in Tibetan studies, was, with his wife, a regular visitor. Dr Leibenthal and Mr John Blofeld, both specialists in the field of Chinese Buddhism, each stayed for a couple of weeks at the vihara. Dr Tom Schmidt, the Swedish

Tibetologist, paid several visits. In conclusion, mention should be made of Dr N. C. Sinha, director of the Namgyal Institute of Tibetology, Gangtok, Mr and Mrs Simons Roof, two American students of Indian religions, and Mr Maurice Frydman of Bombay.

SOURCES

PART I: ANAGARIKA DHARMAPALA

The *Biographical Sketch* was originally published by the Maha Bodhi Society of India in 1952. A second edition was published by the Maha Bodhi Society in 1956, and a third by the Buddhist Publication Society in Kandy in 1964. This biography, together with a collection of the sayings of Anagarika Dharmapala published by the Maha Bodhi Society in 1957, was brought out again in 1980 by Triratna Grantha Mala (the publishing wing of TBMSG) under the title *Flame in Darkness: The Life and Sayings of Anagarika Dharmapala*, and a fifth edition was published in 1995. This, together with the account of the life of Mrs Mary E. Foster, Dharmapala's patron, was brought out by Ibis Publications in 2013; this version forms Part I of this volume, together with a few other pieces about Anagarika Dharmapala and Mrs Mary E. Foster originally written for and published in the *Maha Bodhi* journal.

PART II: *MAHA BODHI* WRITINGS

The first section, *In the Light of the Dhamma*, is a collection of pieces written by Sangharakshita for the *Maha Bodhi* journal in the years 1953 to 1955 under the name 'Himavantavasi', and previously included in the 2013 Ibis Publications work *Anagarika Dharmapala: A Biographical Sketch, and other Maha Bodhi Writings*.

The second section consists of editorials written for the *Maha Bodhi* journal during the period 1954 to 1964, when Sangharakshita was editor of the journal. Most of these were published in *Beating the Drum: Maha Bodhi Editorials*, published by Ibis Publications in 2012. A few more have been added to this volume, with the aim of making the complete set of editorials available. Note that some *Maha Bodhi* editorials were originally published in *Crossing the Stream*, which now appears in *Complete Works*, volume 7, and that some *Maha Bodhi* issues covered two months, and a few contained no editorial.

PART III: BOOK REVIEWS 1952–2002

The first section consists of reviews written in India for the *Maha Bodhi* journal and the *Aryan Path*. The second section includes reviews written and published in England, a collection of which was published by Windhorse Publications in 1986 under the title *Alternative Traditions*. This is followed by a review published in the FWBO's magazine *Golden Drum* and then several reviews written for the *Times Higher Education Supplement* and one written for the *Western Buddhist Review*, all of which were included in A *Moseley Miscellany*, published by Ibis Publications in 2015.

APPENDICES

Appendix 1 contains information about the *Maha Bodhi* journal originally included in Kalyanaprabha's introduction to *Beating the Drum*. Appendix 2 is the first half of Sangharakshita's report on the Triyana Vardhana Vihara, his base in Kalimpong from 1957 to 1964. (For a description of the vihara and its naming by Chattrul Sangye Dorje, see *Precious Teachers*, *Complete Works*, vol. 22, pp. 390–4.) The second half of the report, which describes Sangharakshita's preaching tours in India during that period, introduces the sections of an account of those tours in *Complete Works*, vol. 10, pp. 115–180.

NOTES AND REFERENCES

FOREWORD

1 'Mahant' is a title referring to the head of a *math* or Hindu monastery. At the end of the sixteenth or beginning of the seventeenth century a wandering Shaivite ascetic (i.e. a worshipper of the Hindu god Shiva), known as Gossiain Ghamandi Giri, arrived at Bodh Gaya and settled down there. (The Giris are one of the orders of monks established by the ninth-century Hindu reformer Śaṅkara.) Over the centuries that followed, the hermitage he established grew into a large monastery or *math*. Gossiain Ghamandi Giri's successors were the various Mahants who appear in this history.

2 *Facing Mount Kanchenjunga, Complete Works*, vol. 21, pp. 380–1.

3 Published as *Flame in Darkness*, Triratna Grantha Mala, Pune 1980.

4 *A Survey of Buddhism, Complete Works*, vol. 1, p. 394.

5 In 2015, tens of thousands of Rohingya Muslims living in the Rakhine State of Myanmar (Burma) were forcibly displaced with extreme violence by the Burmese military.

6 *In the Sign of the Golden Wheel, Complete Works*, vol. 22, p. 69.

7 The Buddha's words from the *Ariyapariyesanā Sutta, Majjhima Nikāya* 26 (i.171); see Bhikkhu Ñāṇamoli and Bhikkhu Bodhi (trans.), *The Middle Length Discourses of the Buddha*, Wisdom Publications, Boston 1995, p. 263; or I. B. Horner (trans.), *The Collection of the Middle Length Sayings*, vol. i, Pali

Text Society, London 1976, p. 215.

8 These words of the Buddha were chosen by Anagarika Dharmapala to stand as the masthead at the beginning of each issue of the *Maha Bodhi*. See Vinaya Piṭaka i.21 (*Mahāvagga* 1.11), in I. B. Horner (trans.), *The Book of the Discipline*, part 4, Pali Text Society, Oxford 1996, p. 28.

9 This review (on p. 357 below) was published in the *Maha Bodhi* in December 1953, just before Sangharakshita became editor. The review is also mentioned in *In the Sign of the Golden Wheel*, *Complete Works*, vol. 22, p. 71 and note 75 in that volume.

10 See 'Remembering Ambedkar', *Complete Works*, vol. 10, p. 5.

11 For details about the members of the editorial board, see Appendix 1, pp. 634ff.

12 Here, of course, Sangharakshita is referring to the *arhant* as understood by the Mahāyāna, not the fully Enlightened *arahants* of the Pāli canon.

13 *The Rainbow Road from Tooting Broadway to Kalimpong, Complete Works,* vol. 20, p. 85.

14 This section was written in 2012 for the introduction to *Beating the Drum,* but the reflections are no less relevant – perhaps even more so – today (2022).

15 *Abhayarājakumāra Sutta*, *Majjhima Nikāya* 58 (i.395). See Bhikkhu Ñāṇamoli and Bhikkhu Bodhi (trans.), *The Middle Length Discourses of the Buddha*, Wisdom Publications, Boston 1995, p. 500; or I. B. Horner (trans.), *The Collection of the Middle Length Sayings*, vol. ii, Pali Text Society, Oxford 1994, pp. 62–3.

16 Sangharakshita writes about his contact with Christianity – both positive and negative – in *From Genesis to the Diamond Sūtra* in *Complete Works*, vol. 13, pp. 579ff.

17 Lord Dalberg-Acton (1834–1902), Roman Catholic, liberal politician, friend of Gladstone, historian and writer, is perhaps best known for his aphorism, 'Power tends to corrupt, and absolute power corrupts absolutely.' He was writing against the move by the First Vatican Council in 1870 to declare the infallibility of the pope. In 1859 Lord Acton succeeded John Henry Newman as editor of the Catholic monthly, the *Rambler*. His views about Indian religion and culture are from the May 1862 edition, quoted in *The Betrayal of Buddhism: An abridged report of the Buddhist Committee of Inquiry*, Ceylon, 1956, p. 2.

18 *Facing Mount Kanchenjunga, Complete Works,* vol. 21, pp. 364-6.

19 Ibid., ch. 17, pp. 345ff.

20 Ibid., pp. 350–3.

21 See *Complete Works*, vol. 25, pp. 250–1.

22 *In the Sign of the Golden Wheel, Complete Works,* vol. 22, p. 59.

23 The *śāsana*, which literally means 'message', is the dispensation, doctrine, and legacy of the Buddha.

24 These longer articles were later incorporated into *The Three Jewels*, which is included in *Complete Works*, vol. 2, pp. 1ff.

25 *A Survey of Buddhism, Complete Works,* vol. 1, pp. 1ff.

26 *In the Sign of the Golden Wheel, Complete Works,* vol. 22, p. 133.

27 *Alternative Traditions* might also have found a home in vol. 13 of the *Complete Works*, whose title is *Eastern and Western Traditions.*

28 *Adhisthana Writings*, *Last Words*, *Complete Works*, vol. 26, pp. 695–8.

ANAGARIKA DHARMAPALA

29 The hymn, which begins 'From Greenland's icy mountains', was written in 1819 by the young Reginald Heber, apparently at the request of his father-in-law, Dean Shipley, who asked him to 'write something to sing at the missionary meeting tomorrow'.

30 'Cast as rubbish to the void' is from Canto 54 of Alfred, Lord Tennyson's *In Memoriam A.H.H.*, a requiem poem for his friend, Arthur Haley Hallam, completed in 1849. See also note 94 below.

31 'Hewavitarne' was Dharmapala's preferred spelling; the name is today more often rendered Hewavitharna according to standard transliteration.

32 Then a remote village, today Hikkaduwa is a popular holiday resort.

33 'Reminiscences of my Early Life', *Maha Bodhi* vol. 41, nos. 5&6, p. 152.

34 This was Sunīta, who was born into a family of scavengers and earned his living as a road-sweeper. His story is told in the *Theragāthā*; see C. A. F. Rhys Davids (trans.), *Psalms of the Brethren*, Pali Text Society, London 1980, pp. 271–5.

35 Alfred Percy Sinnett was a member of the Theosophical Society and published *The Occult World* in London in 1881; it was based mainly on his notes on the work of Madame Blavatsky and thus made her occult philosophy more widely known.

36 There are other accounts of the events which led to Madame Blavatsky's departure from Adyar. See, for example, Marion Meade in *Madame Blavatsky: the Woman Behind the Myth*, G. P. Putnam's Sons, New York 1980.

37 *Dhammapada* 29, trans. Sangharakshita (*Complete Works*, vol 15).

38 According to popular tradition, the wearing of

tortoiseshell combs by the Sinhalese began when a Malay prince was deported from Java to Ceylon in the eighteenth century; the locals adopted it and it became a 'tradition', albeit a colonial one. In a list of points for his fellow Sinhalas, Dharmapala included the exhortation: 'Don't wear the head comb like the Javanese in Batavia.' See Steven Kemper, *Rescued from the Nation: Anagarika Dharmapala and the Buddhist World*, University of Chicago Press, Chicago 2015, p. 341.

39 The *Satipaṭṭhāna Sutta* (*Majjhima Nikāya* 10) is a classic text that describes the mindfulness of breathing meditation and other mindfulness practices. The *Visuddhimagga* was written by Buddhaghosa, a fifth-century Indian scholar who went to Sri Lanka to study commentarial texts. The *Visuddhimagga* is his most famous work, in which he describes forty meditation practices (the *kammaṭṭhānas*).

40 T. S. is the Theosophical Society. E. S. its Esoteric Section.

41 Sangharakshita was writing in 1952. At the time of writing this note, seventy years later, the *Maha Bodhi* is still being produced.

42 Vinaya Piṭaka i.21 (*Mahāvagga* 1.11). See I. B. Horner (trans.), *The Book of the Discipline*, part 4, Pali Text Society, Oxford 1996, p. 28.

43 *St Louis Observer*, 21 September 1893.

44 Anāthapiṇḍika was a leading lay disciple of the Buddha. He was very wealthy and renowned for his generosity. The story of his conversion to Buddhism and his donation of the Jetavana, or Jeta Grove in Sāvatthī, is told at Vinaya Piṭaka ii.154–9 (*Cullavagga* 6.4). See I. B. Horner (trans.), *The Book of the Discipline*, part 5, Pali Text Society, London 1975, pp. 216–23. The generosity of Viśākhā, a laywoman known as 'Migāra's mother' (Migāra was in fact her husband, whom she converted to the Buddha's teaching) is told at Vinaya Piṭaka i.290–4 (*Mahāvagga* 8.15). See I. B. Horner (trans.), *The Book of the Discipline*, part 4, Pali Text Society, Oxford 1996, pp. 413–20.

45 The thirty-seven *bodhipakṣya-dharmas* ('wings of Enlightenment' or 'requisites of Enlightenment') are listed by the Buddha in, for example, the *Mahāparinibbāna Sutta*, *Dīgha Nikāya* 16 (ii.120). See M. Walshe (trans.), *The Long Discourses of the Buddha*, Wisdom Publications, Boston 1995, p. 253; or T. W. Rhys Davids (trans.), *Dialogues of the Buddha*, part 2, Pali Text Society, London 1971, p. 128.

46 Devapriya Valisinha (1904–1968) was born in Ceylon. He was adopted by Anagarika Dharmapala, and brought up

by the *anagārika*'s mother. He studied in Calcutta and at Santiniketan. He became recording secretary and treasurer of the Maha Bodhi Society in 1927 and, after the death of Anagarika Dharmapala in 1933, its general secretary, continuing the *anagārika*'s work for Buddhism and for the control of the Maha Bodhi temple. He was arrested in 1941 because of his (Buddhist) connections with the Japanese with whom the British, still rulers of India, were at war. His harsh treatment during the weeks of his arrest led to a nervous breakdown. Several years elapsed – during which time Jinaratana was acting secretary – before he could resume his work for the Society. Sangharakshita first met him in Gangtok in 1951 but their acquaintance flourished when Sangharakshita went to Calcutta in the autumn of 1952 at Devapriya Valisinha's request to write a biographical sketch of Anagarika Dharmapala. See *Facing Mount Kanchenjunga*, *Complete Works*, vol. 21, chapter 18, pp. 367–89.

47 When he was living in India, Sangharakshita got to know Sangharatana, with whom he first visited Bodh Gaya in 1949. (See *The Rainbow Road from Tooting Broadway to Kalimpong*, *Complete Works*, vol. 20, pp. 453–5.) Sangharatana invited Sangharakshita to the celebration of the anniversary of the opening of the Mulagandhakuti Vihara (*Facing Mount Kanchenjunga*, *Complete Works*, vol. 21, pp. 97–8; and was present at his ordination (ibid., p. 108). Later Sangharatana invited Sangharakshita to join him and Jagdish Kashyap as the official delegation accompanying the Sacred Relics of Śāriputra and Maudgalyāyana to Sikkim (ibid., p. 173 and chapter 11), and they met again on Sangharakshita's return visit to India in 1964; see *Moving Against the Stream*, *Complete Works*, vol. 23, p. 359.

48 'The nose of Cleopatra: if it had been shorter, the whole face of the earth would have changed.' Blaise Pascal, *Pensées* 162.

49 Vinaya Piṭaka i.39–41 (*Mahāvagga* 1.23); see I. B. Horner (trans.), *The Book of the Discipline*, part 4, Pali Text Society, Oxford 1996, pp. 52–5.

50 The reference is to the traditional story that Zen began when the Buddha held up a golden flower and his disciple Mahākāśyapa understood what he meant.

51
> And as imagination bodies forth
> The forms of things unknown, the poet's pen
> Turns them to shapes, and

gives to airy nothing
A local habitation and a name.

From Shakespeare's *A Midsummer Night's Dream*, Act V, Scene i.

52 See Vinaya Piṭaka i.21 (*Mahāvagga* 1.11), in I. B. Horner (trans.), *The Book of the Discipline*, part 4, Pali Text Society, Oxford 1996, p. 28.

53 Buddhaghosa, *Visuddhimagga* 300–1, trans. Pe Maung Tin, Pali Text Society, London 1975, p. 346.

54 *Ahaṃkāra* literally means 'I-maker' i.e. egotism. *Mamaṃ* is 'mine' so *mamaṃkāra* means 'mine-maker' i.e. possessiveness.

55 These are the opening words of the praises of the Buddha which begin the Tiratana Vandanā, the praises of the Three Jewels chanted in many parts of the Buddhist world. The text of the Tiratana Vandanā is found in several places in the Pāli canon, notably in the *Mahāparinibbāna Sutta*, *Dīgha Nikāya* 16 (ii.93). See M. Walshe (trans.), *The Long Discourses of the Buddha*, Wisdom Publications, Boston 1995, p. 241; or T. W. and C. A. F. Rhys Davids (trans.), *Dialogues of the Buddha*, part 2, Pali Text Society, London 1971, pp. 99–100.

56 *Mahāparinibbāna Sutta*, *Dīgha Nikāya* 16 (ii.81); see M. Walshe (trans.), *The Long Discourses of the Buddha*, Wisdom, Boston 1995, p. 234; or T. W. and C. A. F. Rhys Davids (trans.), *Dialogues of the Buddha*, part 2, Pali Text Society, London 1971, p. 86.

57 *Ratnagotravibhāga* 1.73, quoted in E. Conze et al (eds.), *Buddhist Texts Through the Ages*, Harper & Row 1964, p. 130.

58 The Mahāyāna formulation of the ten perfections is rather different, and a list can be found in *A Survey of Buddhism*, *Complete Works*, vol. 1, pp. 426–72.

IN THE LIGHT OF THE DHARMA

59 Matthew 7:16.

60 An editorial on this theme, 'Stars and Stupidity', appeared in the February 1962 issue of the *Maha Bodhi*. (See Sangharakshita, *Beating the Drum* p. 303 below.)

61 In the *Brahmajāla Sutta*, *Dīgha Nikāya* 1 (i.10–12) gives a long list of fortune-telling 'low arts' from which the Buddha 'holds aloof', including astrology. See M. Walshe (trans.), *The Long Discourses of the Buddha*, Wisdom Publications, Boston 1995, pp. 71–3; or T. W. Rhys Davids (trans.), *Dialogues of the Buddha*, part 1, Pali Text Society, London 1973, pp. 16–26.

62 *Lobha, dveṣa*, and *moha* are the three root poisons of

the mind: greed, hatred, and delusion. *Alobha, adveṣa*, and *amoha* indicate the absence of those poisons and characterize the Enlightened mind of contentment, love, and wisdom.

63 Giuseppe Tucci (1894–1984) co-founded the Istituto Italiano per il Medio ed Estremo Oriente (Institute for the Middle and Far East) in Rome in 1933 after returning to Italy from India, where he had studied at a number of Indian universities and at the Vishva-Bharati founded by Rabindranath Tagore. He knew an array of languages including Pāli, Sanskrit, Chinese, and Tibetan, and was one of the founders of Buddhist studies in Europe. He became especially interested in Tibet and was known as a foremost Tibetologist of his time.

64 *Abhidhammattha-Saṅgaha, An Outline of Buddhist Philosophy*, Colombo 2491, p. ii. Bhadanta Narada Thera (1898–1983) was a Theravādin *bhikkhu* known for his writings on Buddhism, his translations from the Pāli, and for the Dhamma talks which he gave all over the Buddhist world. He travelled widely to teach the Dhamma and was one of the first Ceylonese *bhikkhus* to teach in the West.

65 Dr Nalinaksha Dutt (1893–1973) was a Pāli and Sanskrit scholar. He was head of Pāli at the University of Calcutta, vice-president of the Asiatic Society, and vice-president of the Maha Bodhi Society. He wrote widely on Buddhism, including the scholarly *Aspects of Mahāyāna Buddhism in its Relation to the Hīnayāna* (1930). His article 'The Maha Bodhi Society, its History and Influence' was published in the Maha Bodhi Society's *Diamond Jubilee Souvenir* in 1952. In July 1954 he joined the journal's editorial board. His 'The Rise and Fall of Buddhism in India' was published in the *Maha Bodhi* in June 1955.

66 Robert Stuart Clifton (1903–1963) was an American whose interest in Buddhism took him to the Far East. He was ordained in Japan as a Zen priest and eventually returned to the West and began teaching, setting up a 'Western Buddhist Order' in 1951. It was to be 'an organization dedicated to interpreting the Dharma to the West' (the *Western Buddhist*). He styled himself its 'Superior-General'. According to Sangharakshita's account in *Facing Mount Kanchenjunga* (*Complete Works*, vol. 21, pp. 339–42), based on letters he received at the time from Jack Austin, Clifton ordained a number of English Buddhists during a short visit to England and then disappeared from the scene. Within a few years his Western Buddhist Order had collapsed (though Jack Austin

continued to bring out the magazine) and Clifton himself was again in the East where he received Theravādin ordination in Laos and became known as Bhikkhu Sumangalo. He went on to become the head of the Poh Ern Shih temple in Singapore. He died in Penang. When Sangharakshita came to inaugurate his own Buddhist movement in England in 1967, he called it 'The Friends of the Western Sangha'. The following year, when he ordained twelve men and women and in doing so founded a new Buddhist order, he called it the 'Western Buddhist Order' considering that the original order of that name had been defunct for more than a decade. The movement of which the new Western Buddhist Order was the heart then became known as the Friends of the Western Buddhist Order (FWBO). In 2010, by which time it was established as a worldwide movement, it was renamed the Triratna Buddhist Community, and the Order became the Triratna Buddhist Order.

67 The English novelist H. G. Wells (1866–1946) is best known for his science fiction writing, including *The War of the Worlds* (1898). Written following the catastrophic First World War, Wells' *The Outline of History* (1920) had the lofty goal of providing a historical basis for future agreement on humanity's overall purpose and mutual benefit. Professor Simon James wrote of him in 2016:

> No writer is more renowned for his ability to foresee the future than H. G. Wells. His writing can be seen to have predicted the aeroplane, the tank, space travel, the atomic bomb, satellite television and the worldwide web. His fantastic fiction imagined time travel, alien invasion, flights to the moon and human beings with the power of gods.... Yet for all these successes, the futuristic prophecy on which Wells's heart was most set – the establishment of a world state – remains unfulfilled.

68 U Nu (1907–1995) was the first prime minister of independent Burma. His first term of office was from 1947 to 1956. He was re-elected twice. A Theravādin Buddhist, in 1961 he saw through parliament the act which made Buddhism Burma's official state religion. This was revoked the following year after the *coup d'état* led by General Ne Win.

69 In one of his earliest teachings, the Buddha mentioned these three kinds of craving in describing the second of the four noble truths; see *Dhammacakkappavattana Sutta*, *Saṃyutta Nikāya* v.421–4 (56.11); see Bhikkhu Bodhi (trans.), *The Connected*

Discourses of the Buddha, Wisdom Publications, Boston 2000, p. 1844; or F. L. Woodward (trans.), *Book of the Kindred Sayings*, part 5, Pali Text Society, London 1979, p. 357.

70 For more on this topic, see p. 140 below.

71 The 'Sincere European Buddhist' was G. F. Allen, known also as Bhikkhu Y. Siri Nyana. (The 'Y' stood for 'Yeovil', his native town!) He had spent several years in Ceylon and India and was highly regarded in Theravādin circles as a scholar. He went on to contribute a number of scholarly articles to the *Maha Bodhi*.

72

> O Bhikṣus, my words should be accepted by the wise, not out of regard for me, but after due investigation – just as gold is accepted as true only after heating, cutting, and rubbing.

Ganganatha Jha (trans.), *The Tattvasaṅgraha of Shāntarakṣita*, Motilal Banarsidass, Delhi 1986, vol. ii, p. 1558, text 3588.

73 Himavantavasi's contribution to the February 1954 *Maha Bodhi* sparked off a virulent attack in the pages of the *Buddhist World*, a fortnightly paper published in Colombo. Not only did the writer complain bitterly about the suggestions made by the 'Sincere European Buddhist', but attacked the newly-appointed editor, Sangharakshita, who was suspected of being 'a Mahāyānist'. See *In the Sign of the Golden Wheel*, *Complete Works*, vol. 22, pp. 170–3.

74 Elsewhere Sangharakshita says he invented this story. See *Know Your Mind*, chapter 9, in *Complete Works*, vol. 17, p. 645. Doubtless he had in mind the character of one of his acquaintances.

75 The *Buddhist World* soon went out of circulation. Himavantavasi's dream is, of course, a parody of the auto-da-fé of the Spanish Inquisition. The portly gentleman with the military air sounds rather like the *Buddhist World*'s editor, Major-General Tun Hla Oung. (Years later Sangharakshita met him in Madras where they had an amicable exchange. Perhaps the General did not know who Sangharakshita was; or perhaps the intervening years, which had reduced him to a rather abject state, had brought about a change in his attitude to suspected Mahāyānists.)

76 Paul Carus (1852–1919) emigrated from Germany to the United States where he became managing editor of the Open Court Publishing Company and editor of two periodicals, *Open Court* and *The Monist*. He wrote books and articles on history, politics, philosophy, logic,

mathematics, anthropology, science, and social issues. He had a particular interest in comparative religion and was present at the 1893 World's Parliament of Religions in Chicago where he heard Dharmapala speak. He became friends with Zen teacher Soyen Shaku and a sponsor of the works of D. T. Suzuki. He founded the American branch of the Maha Bodhi Society and invited Anagarika Dharmapala for a return visit to America in 1886. Carus' book *The Gospel of Buddha*, the story of the Buddha's life told through parables, was published in 1894, bringing the story of the Buddha's life to the attention of many westerners for the first time. Though Carus never committed himself to any religion, he did much to make Buddhism better known in America and the West, albeit on occasion inadvertently distorting the Dharma.

77 According to Malalasekera's *Dictionary of Pāli Proper Names* (Pali Text Society, Oxford 1997, p. 1165) there is no record in the Pāli canon of the Buddha discoursing to General Sīha on the topic of war. The canonical sources show that General Sīha was originally a follower of the Nigaṇṭhas (or Jains). When Sīha met the Buddha and decided to become his follower, the Buddha instructed him to continue supporting the Nigaṇṭhas as he was one of their foremost patrons. When the General invited the Buddha and his followers to a meal, meat was served. The Nigaṇṭhas claimed an ox had been slaughtered for the Buddha and his disciples and that the Buddha had accepted. The Buddha therefore made the rule that no *bhikkhu* should eat meat if he had reason to believe an animal had been killed especially for him (Vinaya Piṭaka i.238). On another occasion General Sīha asked the Buddha if it is possible to show the visible results of giving. The Buddha demonstrated that it is (*Aṅguttara Nikāya* iii.39).

78 An 'e.a.' in the body of the work referred the reader to the Explanatory Additions at the end. The unsuspecting reader could easily assume that these additions were the words of the Buddha rather than explanatory notes created by the author.

79 This is a reference to *Dhammapada* 127.

80 U Dhammaratana was a member of the Maha Bodhi Society editorial board. A quiet, scholarly monk from Sri Lanka, he was for a while resident at the Maha Bodhi headquarters in Calcutta where Sangharakshita came to know him. His 'fine and vigorous article' was 'The Reason for Anti-Buddhist Propaganda in Brahminical Literature'.

81 *Experiments with Humility*: a satirical reference to Gandhi's autobiographical *The Story of My Experiments with Truth* (first published, in instalments, 1925–1929).

82 Vinoba Bhave (1895–1982) is commonly regarded as Gandhi's chief disciple. Through the Budhan movement which he inaugurated, wealthy landowners were persuaded to donate portions of their land to landless members of lower castes.

83 These lines by Thomas Gray are from his *Elegy Written in a Country Churchyard* (1750).

84 Henri-Frederic Amiel (1821–1881) spent most of his life in Geneva where he was a professor first of Aesthetics and later of Moral Philosophy. It was his posthumously published *Journal Intime* ('Private Journal') that brought him to the notice of the European reading public.

85 Sangharakshita wrote of Sir Thomas Browne (1605–1682) that he was

> a doctor, a scholar, an antiquarian, and a busy professional man. Above all he was the author of *Religio Medici*, a work remarkable for its beautiful, baroque style. I came across it when I was 14 and was so fascinated by its style that I strove to imitate it in an essay of my own. So far as I remember, Sir Thomas Browne was the only writer whose style I ever wanted to imitate.

The allusion here is unclear.

86 Arthur Schopenhauer (1788–1860) was a German philosopher whose most famous work, *The World as Will and Representation*, was first published in 1818.

87 Johann Gottfried von Herder (1744–1803) was a German philosopher, poet, and literary critic.

88 Matthew 10:34.

89 André Gide (1869–1951) and Romain Rolland (1866–1944): French writers whose work Sangharakshita was reading at this time. The lines quoted here are probably all from Gide's *Les Nourritures Terrestres* (published in 1897 and translated into English under the title *Fruits of the Earth*) and Rolland's most famous work, *Jean-Christoph*, published in ten volumes from 1903 to 1912.

90 Billy Graham (1918–2018) was an evangelical preacher who held mass rallies.

BEATING THE DRUM: *MAHA BODHI* EDITORIALS

91 Nagarjunikonda is 'Nāgārjuna's hill' in the Telugu language.

92 Nāgārjuna, who lived in India in the second century CE (the exact dates are uncertain), is regarded as the founder

of the Madhyamaka school. His *Mūlamadhyamakakārikā* (*Fundamental Verses of the Middle Way*) is a Sanskrit text, in part a commentary on discourses of the Buddha, which demonstrates the futility of metaphysical speculation and affirms the Middle Way the Buddha taught as a direct perception of *śūnyatā* or the 'emptiness' of all things.

93 Now known as Visakhapatnam, situated on the eastern coast of India, it is the second largest city in Andhra Pradesh.

94 This is from part 54 of Alfred, Lord Tennyson's 1833 poem 'In Memoriam A. H. H.', dedicated to his friend Arthur Hallam:

> That not one life shall be destroyed,
> Or cast as rubbish to the void …

95 Jawaharlal Nehru (1889–1964), first prime minister of independent India 1947–1964. Sangharakshita was introduced to Nehru at the Anandamayi Ashram in Dehra Dun in 1947 (see *The Rainbow Road from Tooting Broadway to Kalimpong*, *Complete Works*, vol. 20, pp. 190–1). They met again in Delhi in 1956 during the Buddha Jayanti celebrations when the group of 'eminent Buddhists from the border areas' were invited to lunch at the prime minister's residence. (*In the Sign of the Golden Wheel*, *Complete Works*, vol. 22, pp. 344–5.) A third meeting, not recorded in Sangharakshita's memoirs, took place probably in 1953 when Nehru visited Kalimpong, the township where Sangharakshita was resident. (Nehru described it to the Indian parliament as 'a nest of spies'.) Dutt-Majamdar, the Deputy Commissioner of Kalimpong, with whom Sangharakshita was on very friendly terms, organized the prime minister's visit. He was keen that Sangharakshita, too, should meet him. Having nothing special to ask the prime minister, Sangharakshita at first demurred, but in the end let himself be persuaded. The two met in the garden of a private house, Arunachal. Sangharakshita recalls,

> I thought for someone as unimportant as me, twenty minutes with the prime minister was really quite a big thing, especially as I had nothing to ask him for. But I thought I'd better say something so I told him about the YMBA and the work it was doing among the young men of the town, both Buddhists and Hindus.

Though afterwards he remembered that he had done most of the talking and could not recall Nehru having said anything, it was nevertheless a pleasant meeting. Perhaps it accounts for Nehru's invitation to Sangharakshita after their Delhi luncheon three years later to accompany him into the garden where he showed him the giant pandas.

Construction on the Nagajunasagar Dam began in 1955. Within a few years the ancient Buddhist site was submerged under the waters of a reservoir. In advance of the flooding, however, several monuments were excavated and relocated to the top of the hill where a museum was erected in 1966. Other monuments were relocated to the mainland, east of the flooded area. Sangharakshita composed a poem on this theme the previous year (1953) which appeared in the January 1954 issue of the *Maha Bodhi*. 'Nagarjunikonda' is included in *Complete Works*, vol. 25, p. 263.

96 *Pūrṇimā* means the full moon. *Vaiśākha* is the Sanskrit equivalent of the more familiar Sinhalese *Wesak*, the lunar month of April–May.

97 Robert G. Ingersoll (1833–1899) was a veteran of the American Civil War. He was known also as a satirist, orator, politician, and friend of Walt Whitman.

Swami Vivekananda (1863–1902) was the chief disciple of Ramakrishna Paramahansa and founder of the Ramakrishna Mission that brought Advaita Vedānta to the notice of America and the West. Like Anagarika Dharmapala, he attended the first World's Parliament of Religions in 1893.

98 The Brahmo Samaj was a monotheistic sect of Hinduism. The movement began through meetings of Bengalis in Calcutta in 1828, in a group known as the Brahmo Sabha. One of the leading figures was Ram Mohun Roy. In 1831, Roy visited England as a reforming ambassador and died there in 1833. Debendranath Tagore, the father of Rabindranath Tagore, was a key member of the Brahmo Sabha, and in 1843 he was involved in the creation of the Brahmo Samaj. Rabindranath Tagore's Visva Bharati University was founded in 1921 as an expression of Brahmo universalism.

99 Dr Harendra Coomar Mookerjee (1877–1956) was Governor of West Bengal from 1951 to 1956. A retired college professor rather than a politician, he was well-liked for his simple and unassuming ways. Though an Anglican, he accepted an invitation to join in the local Vaiśākha Pūrṇimā celebrations held at the Hermitage, Sangharakshita's Kalimpong headquarters in 1953. (See *In the Sign of the Golden Wheel*, *Complete Works*, vol. 22, p. 9.)

100 These are all Indian saints and mystics. Kabir (1440–1518) was an Indian poet and mystic

revered by Hindus, Muslims, and Sikhs. Guru Nanak (1469–1539) was the founder of Sikhism. Dadu Dayal (1544–1603) was a Gujerati mystic, composer of many religious verses, who inspired the formation of the Dadu Panth sect.

101 Sangharakshita met another Shankaracharya of Puri who claimed the title for himself. Having in his own possession the Shankaracharya regalia, he asserted *he* was the truly authentic one (*The Rainbow Road from Tooting Broadway to Kalimpong*, *Complete Works*, vol. 20, pp. 175, 343–4). In 1949 Sangharakshita stayed near the Sringeri Math and briefly met its Shankaracharya of whom he tells a rather sad story (ibid., pp. 369–72).

102 See Sangharakshita's account of speaking at the All-India Religions Conference in Ahmedabad in 1947 (ibid., pp. 173–4).

103 The compound *samaṇa-brāhmaṇa* appears in the Pāli scriptures referring to the wandering religious teachers collectively, both the Vedic, i.e. the *brāhmaṇa*, and the non-Vedic – even anti-Vedic – the *samaṇa* (Sanskrit *śramaṇa*). The latter included the Jains and the followers of the Buddha.

104 *Saṃyutta Nikāya* iii.11. This is F. L. Woodward's translation; see *The Book of the Kindred Sayings*, part 2, Pali Text Society, Oxford 1997, p. 13. Bhikkhu Bodhi's translation can be found in *The Connected Discourses of the Buddha*, Wisdom Publications, Boston 2000, p. 862.

105 *Spectator* no. 239, Tuesday, 4 December 1711. Joseph Addison (1672–1719), together with his friend Richard Steele, published the *Spectator* six days a week from March 1711 to December 1712. (Addison revived it for six months in 1714.) Its aim was 'to enliven Morality with Wit, and to temper Wit with Morality', and to bring philosophy 'out of Closets and Libraries, Schools and Colleges, to dwell in Clubs and Assemblies, at Tea-tables, and in Coffee-houses'. More than 3,000 copies were published daily. Addison estimated that 60,000 Londoners (one tenth of the capital's population) read the paper. While in India, Sangharakshita had received a gift of Addison's *Essays* from a Canadian friend (*In the Sign of the Golden Wheel*, *Complete Works*, vol. 22, p. 73, and note 99).

106 Pierre Bayle (1647–1706): French philosopher. His *Dictionnaire Historique et Critique (Historical and Critical Dictionary)* was one of the first encyclopedias of ideas.

107 The *Buddhist World* was a fortnightly paper published in Colombo by a Burmese

Theravādin, Major-General Tun Hla Oung. He and his wife – who contributed some of the most virulent attacks – took an extreme anti-Mahāyāna stance. In *In the Sign of the Golden Wheel*, chapter 11 (*Complete Works*, vol. 22, pp. 168ff), Sangharakshita explains the background to this editorial in some detail. See also 'The Editorial Board' in Appendix 1 (pp. 634ff in this volume).

108 Gunapala Piyasena Malalasekera (1899–1973) was a Sri Lankan professor and scholar (he compiled the *Dictionary of Pāli Proper Names*) as well as diplomat. He was president of the All-Ceylon Buddhist Congress from 1939 to 1957 and president of the World Fellowship of Buddhists from its inauguration in 1950 until 1958. In *In the Sign of the Golden Wheel* Sangharakshita refers to him as 'one of the *Buddhist World*'s principal *bêtes noires*' (*Complete Works*, vol. 22, p. 178), for though he was himself a Theravādin Buddhist, he was sympathetic to the Mahāyāna. He met Sangharakshita again in London in 1966 when Dr Malalasekera was one of the speakers at the Buddhist Society's Vaiśākha Pūrṇimā celebrations (*Moving Against the Stream*, *Complete Works*, vol. 23, p. 236).

109 'On Zeal', *Spectator* no. 185. Tuesday, 2 October 1711.

110 *Aṅguttara Nikāya* i.199. This translation is from F. L. Woodward (trans.), *Some Sayings of the Buddha*, Oxford University Press, Oxford 1973, pp. 60–1. See also F. L. Woodward (trans.), *The Book of the Gradual Sayings*, vol. i, Pali Text Society, Oxford 2000, p. 180; or Bhikkhu Bodhi (trans.), *The Numerical Discourses of the Buddha*, Wisdom Publications, Boston 2012, pp. 288–9.

111 *Śikṣā-Samuccaya* 21, in Śāntideva, *Śikṣā-Samuccaya*, trans. Cecil Bendall and W. H. D. Rouse, Motilal Banarsidass, Delhi 1971, p. 23.

112 *Dāyaka*: one who gives out of kindness (*dāya*), by implication a lay supporter of the *bhikkhus*.

113 In response to the suggestion that so much should not be spent on gilding shrines but rather in propagating the Dhamma, the editor of the *Light of the Dhamma*, official organ of the Union of Burma Buddha Sāsana Council, threatened Sangharakshita with rebirth as a dwarf, while 'the *Buddhist World* attacked me … in the most vitriolic terms' (*In the Sign of the Golden Wheel*, *Complete Works*, vol. 22, p. 171).

114 The four great pilgrimage sites are Lumbinī, where the Buddha was born, Bodh Gaya, where he gained Enlightenment, Sārnāth, where he first taught the

Dharma, and Kusinārā, where he attained *parinirvāṇa*. See p. 193 below.

115 As with all figs, the flowers of the *uḍumbara* (*ficus racemosa*) are enclosed within its fruit. Because the flower is hidden, a legend developed to explain the absence (or supposed rarity) of the visual flower, and it came to symbolize events of rare occurrence. In some Buddhist texts, the flower is said to bloom once every 3,000 years.

116 To this day the Maha Bodhi temple complex is run by a committee of whom four must be Hindus and four Buddhists, while the *ex-officio* chairman is the District Commissioner or Collector, a Hindu.

117 *Sarvodaya* (meaning 'the uplift of all') was popularized by Gandhi and later developed into a social movement by, among others, Vinoba Bhave.

118 Vinoba Bhave (1895–1982). Sangharakshita writes about Bhave's disciples who, in July 1954, the date of this article, organized a programme of lectures to commemorate Gandhi's eighty-sixth birthday at which Sangharakshita spoke on 'Buddhism'; see *In the Sign of the Golden Wheel*, *Complete Works*, vol. 22, p. 158.

119 Sarvepalli Radhakrishnan (1888–1975), scholar and statesman, was the first vice-president of India (1952–1962) and subsequently its president (1962–1967). Though a Telagu Brahmin, he was proposed as president of the Maha Bodhi Society by Hindu members of the Governing Body. In fact it was the Maharaj Kumar of Sikkim, a Buddhist, who was elected to the position (see Foreword, p. xxi). Sangharakshita and other 'eminent Buddhists' met him in Delhi during the Buddha Jayanti celebrations in 1956 (*In the Sign of the Golden Wheel*, *Complete Works*, vol. 22, p. 344).

120 Vedānta refers to all those schools of Hindu philosophy that are based on the three main authorities, i.e. the Upanishads, the Brahma Sūtras and the *Bhagavad Gītā*. Some schools of Vedānta (such as Advaita) are non-dualist, others are dualist.

121 Dr Rajendra Prasad (1884–1963), after playing a prominent role in the independence movement, became India's first president, 1950–1962. Sangharakshita met him at his official residence during the Buddha Jayanti celebrations in Delhi in 1956 when he put to Dr Prasad various requests on behalf of the Buddhists present. The president assented to all the requests. Sangharakshita thought it wisest not to raise at this meeting the vexed question of ownership of the temple at Bodh Gaya (*In the Sign of*

the Golden Wheel, *Complete Works*, vol. 22, pp. 342–4).

122 A *mahant* is the head of the Shaivite (i.e. Hindu) monastery.

123 For the background to this editorial see *In the Sign of the Golden Wheel*, *Complete Works*, vol. 22, pp. 127–8.

124 Aesop was a Greek slave and storyteller who is thought to have lived in the period 620–564 BCE, and his fables are still well known today. In the story of the quarrelsome brothers and the bundle of sticks, their father shows them that individual sticks can be broken one by one, but a bundle of sticks is much stronger – hence the moral, 'Unity is strength.'

125 In 1954, under the premiership of U Nu, Burmese Buddhist monks organized what they termed the Sixth Great Buddhist Council. It met for two years, was attended by some 2,500 – mainly Burmese – monks. It succeeded in checking the entire (Theravādin) Tipiṭaka or Pāli canon, and rendering it into the native scripts of all participating countries except India.

126 Percy Bysshe Shelley (1792–1822), from stanza 60 of his poem *Adonais*, written on the death of John Keats (1795–1821):

> He has outsoared the shadow of our night;
> Envy and calumny and hate and pain,
> And that unrest which men miscall delight,
> Can touch him not and torture not again …

127 John Milton (1608–74), *Paradise Lost*, book 5, line 87:

> So spake the Seraph Abdiel faithful found,
> Among the faithless, faithful only he….

128 Aśoka (c.304–232 BCE) expanded the Mauryan empire across almost the whole of the Indian subcontinent. The battle of Kalinga (a feudal state situated on the east coast of modern-day Orissa) took place in 262 or 261 BCE. Sangharakshita wrote a sonnet on this theme, also in 1955: 'Kalinga', see *Complete Works,* vol. 25, p. 271.

129 *Mahāparinibbāna Sutta*, *Dīgha Nikāya* 16 (ii.141). See M. Walshe (trans.), *The Long Discourses of the Buddha*, Wisdom Publications, Boston 1995, p. 264; or T. W. and C. A. F. Rhys Davids (trans.), *Dialogues of the Buddha*, part 2, Pali Text Society, London 1971, p. 154.

130 This quotes a line from Paul Valéry's poem 'The Graveyard by the Sea', first published in 1922.

131 Sangharakshita was among those who accompanied the Sacred Relics of the Buddha's two chief disciples on their journey to Nepal,

and describes that occasion in *Facing Mount Kanchenjunga*; see *Complete Works*, vol. 21, pp. 263–306.

132 Christmas Humphreys (1901–1983) was an English barrister and later a judge whose theosophical interests led him to Buddhism. The Buddhist Lodge of the Theosophical Society which Humphreys founded in 1924 was one of the first Buddhist organizations in Europe. In 1926, breaking with the Theosophical Society, it was renamed simply the Buddhist Society, with Humphreys as its president until his death. Humphreys wrote many books on Buddhism which were widely read. Sangharakshita first met Christmas Humphreys at the Buddhist Society in London in 1944. At its Vaiśākha Pūrṇimā meeting in 1944, in the middle of the London Blitz, and in the presence of Humphreys and other friends, the 18-year-old Dennis Lingwood (as he then was) 'took *pañca śīla*' from the Burmese monk U Thittila, thus formally becoming a Buddhist (see *The Rainbow Road from Tooting Broadway to Kalimpong*, *Complete Works*, vol. 20, pp. 102–3). Humphreys later became a contributor to the *Maha Bodhi* under Sangharakshita's editorship. On Sangharakshita's return to England in 1964, the two men had quite a lot to do with each other as recounted especially in *Moving Against the Stream*, *Complete Works*, vol. 23.

133 'For the race is run by one and one and never by two and two,' from Rudyard Kipling's 1891 poem 'Tomlinson'.

134 The year after this editorial was published, in October 1956, the great leader of the oppressed classes, Dr B. R. Ambedkar, formally become a Buddhist along with several hundreds of thousands of followers. Since then millions more have converted so that according to the 2011 Census, there were then 8.4 million people in India who declared themselves to be Buddhist, and the number has grown since then. However, the need for teaching and training for the Buddhists of India is as urgent as ever.

135 *Dhammapada* 100, 103, 106, 110, 113, and 114.

136 *Kakacūpama Sutta*, *Majjhima Nikāya* i.128–9. I. B. Horner (trans.), *The Collection of the Middle Length Sayings*, vol. i, Pali Text Society, London 1976, pp. 165–6; or Bhikkhu Ñāṇamoli and Bhikkhu Bodhi (trans.), *The Middle Length Discourses of the Buddha*, Wisdom Publications, Boston 1995, pp. 221–3.

137 These are the 'four right efforts'. For commentary on them, see chapter 6 of *The Buddha's Noble Eightfold Path* in *Complete Works*, vol. 1, pp. 554–64, and for

a canonical reference, see the *Mahāsatipaṭṭhāna Sutta*, *Dīgha Nikāya* 22 (ii.311); M. Walshe (trans.), *The Long Discourses of the Buddha*, Wisdom Publications, Boston 1995, p. 348; or T. W. and C. A. F. Rhys Davids, *Dialogues of the Buddha*, part 2, Pali Text Society, London 1971, p. 344.

138 Sangharakshita, commenting many years later, pointed out that what is needed is simply someone who, being experienced in meditation themselves, can introduce others to meditation practice and help them with any difficulties. He does not consider it necessary to find someone who is known as a 'meditation teacher' and who has a following on that account.

139 The six perfections were the subject of a series of talks delivered by Sangharakshita in 1969 which form the basis of three chapters of *The Bodhisattva Ideal* in *Complete Works*, vol. 4: chapters 4, 5, and 6, pp. 84–167.

140 See *A Survey of Buddhism*, *Complete Works*, vol. 1, pp. 43–56.

141 The Vaiśākha edition of the *Maha Bodhi* in which this editorial appeared and some of the difficulties that had to be overcome before it could be dispatched are described in *In the Sign of the Golden Wheel*, *Complete Works*, vol. 22, p. 230.

142 Echoes of the Anglican priest and theologian Richard Hooker (1554–1600) and his well-known evocation of the Sacraments as 'The outward and visible sign of an inward and spiritual grace'. (See the 1604 version of the *Book of Common Prayer*.)

143 The Buddhist revival inaugurated by Anagarika Dharmapala was still very small. As already noted, the following year Dr Ambedkar would convert with hundreds of thousands of followers – but Sangharakshita did not yet know of his plans.

144 Here Sangharakshita is countering Hindu claims that the Buddha's teaching is merely a development of pre-existing religious tradition as recorded in the Vedas.

145 See Sangharakshita's poem, 'Taking Refuge in the Buddha' (*Complete Works*, vol. 25, pp. 250–1), written the previous year in circumstances described in *Facing Mount Kanchenjunga*, *Complete Works*, vol. 22, p. 429.

146 Theistic religions – including Judaism, Christianity, and Islam – are based in the belief of a creator God. They, along with Hinduism, insist on the existence of an unchanging soul or self (*ātman*). Various ethnic and pagan religions hold the belief that external

acts, such as sacrifice, can bring about salvation.

147 Sangharakshita discusses in greater depth how ethical practice is inseparable from the act of Going for Refuge in *The Ten Pillars of Buddhism*, *Complete Works*, vol. 2, pp. 323–5.

148 Sangharakshita's deepening understanding of the significance of the Going for Refuge and its centrality in the Buddhist life is described in *The History of My Going for Refuge*, *Complete Works*, vol. 2, pp. 397ff.

149 *Sutta-Nipāta* 1.7, the Buddha's teaching to a Brahmin on how to lead a virtuous life. The teaching is only on the level of *śīla* or ethics, and does not extend to the higher levels of the Buddhist path.

150 Frederic Wertham, *Seduction of the Innocent*, Museum Press, London 1955.

151 *Saṃyutta Nikāya* iv.306 (42.2). See Bhikkhu Bodhi (trans.), *The Connected Discourses of the Buddha*, Wisdom Publications, Boston 2000, pp. 1333–4; or F. L. Woodward (trans.), *The Book of the Kindred Sayings*, part 4, Pali Text Society, London 1980, pp. 214–6.

152 'Honour to those worthy of honour', *Maṅgala Sutta*, *Sutta-Nipāta* 2.4, verse 2.

153 See p. 163 above.

154 *Mūlamadhyamakakārikā* xxv.10.

155 This theme is taken up in a short story, 'The Two Roses', which appeared in the September 1952 edition of the *Maha Bodhi* and was later published by Ola Leaves (1980) as one of three short stories collected together under the title *The Artist's Dream*. It now appears in *Complete Works*, vol. 25, pp. 524–32.

156 According to the International Vegetarian Union, these oft-cited words of Gandhi are from a speech on the moral basis of vegetarianism which he delivered to the London Vegetarian Society on 20 November 1931.

157 Hanuman is a Hindu deity in monkey form. Sri C. Rajagopalachari (1878–1972) was the last Governor-General of India (1948–1950) and a leader of the Indian National Congress. He was known as a proponent of disarmament and world peace.

158 See 'The Two Paths', in H. P. Blavatsky, *The Voice of the Silence*, Theosophy Trust, 2006, p. 14.

159 This is presumably the *Samantakūṭa-vaṇṇanā*, a poem written in Pāli by Vedeha Thera in the fourteenth century CE which describes the life of the Buddha and his legendary visit to Sri Lanka.

160 Edwin Arthur Burtt (1892–1989) was an American philosopher who wrote extensively on the philosophy of religion. His *The Teaching*

of the Compassionate Buddha was published in 1955.

161 Stainless in the sense that Buddhist history does not include violence and bloodshed in the name of its founder. (See 'Religion vs God', pp. 281–3 below.)

162 i.e. the Hīnayāna and the Mahāyāna.

163 Reference to this editorial can be found in *In the Sign of the Golden Wheel*, *Complete Works*, vol. 22, p. 308.

164 Reference to this editorial is in ibid., pp. 309–10. An article on 'The Path of the Inner Life' by Sangharakshita appeared in the November 1955 issue of the *Maha Bodhi*. Along with nine other essays, it was published in a booklet of the same name (*The Path of the Inner Life*, FWBO Publications, London 1975), and these ten essays were then included as the third section of *Crossing the Stream*, for which see *Complete Works*, vol. 7, pp. 355–418.

165 Vinaya Piṭaka ii.139 (*Cullavagga* 5.33); see I. B. Horner (trans.), *The Book of the Discipline*, part 5, Pali Text Society London 1975, p. 194.

166 In the dedication to his *Essays* published the year before his death, Francis Bacon (1561–1626) wrote 'of all my other works [they] have been most current; for that, it seems, they come home, to men's business, and men's bosoms' – men's 'business' being, of course, their outer activity, their 'bosoms' the inner life.

167 In his memoirs Sangharakshita describes a public meeting which took place in 1953 in the Kalimpong town hall to celebrate Vaiśākha Pūrṇimā. Lectures were given in four or five languages so that everyone could hear the Dharma in their mother tongue or a language with which they were familiar (*In the Sign of the Golden Wheel*, *Complete Works*, vol. 22, p. 10).

168 The first page of each edition of the *Maha Bodhi* included a poem or quotation from the Buddhist scriptures. This month it was 'The Holy Cuckoo's Advice to the Birds' from *The Buddha's Law Among the Birds*, translated from the Tibetan by E. Conze, Bruno Cassirer, Oxford 1955.

169 See *Facing Mount Kanchenjunga,* chapter 19, in *Complete Works*, vol. 21, pp. 390ff.

170 *Bhikkhus* were expected to accept whatever almsfood was offered to them, but the Buddha instructed them not to eat meat if they had reason to believe the animal had been killed especially for them (Vinaya Piṭaka i.238). See I. B. Horner (trans.) *The Book of the Discipline*, part 4, Pali Text Society, Oxford 1996, p. 325.

171 For more on Rabindranath Tagore (1861–1941) see

note 241. We're not sure to which poem Sangharakshita is referring here, but Tagore himself suffered many bereavements; his parents, his first wife, his daughter, and his son all died within a few years. In *My Reminiscences* he wrote: 'My acquaintance with death in my twenty-fourth year was a permanent one. Merging its pain with grief of every successive bereavement since then, it has continued to weave a long garland of tears.' But it is reported of him that 'Death itself became a loved companion – no longer the king of terrors, but altogether transformed into cherished friend.' Death is the theme of many of his poems and songs – the *Gitanjali*, for instance – and in *Stray Birds* (section 268) he wrote 'Death belongs to life as birth does. The walk is in the raising of the foot as in the laying of it down.' In his song *Achhe Dukkho Achhe Mrityu* ('Pain Exists, Death Exists'), he wrote:

There exists pain, exists death
The pain of separation burns one
And yet reigns peace, prevails happiness in eternity
Flows the ceaseless life-stream, beams the sun, moon, the stars
Spring arrives in the forest in varied hues
Waves ebb, they rise again
Flowers wilt as they bloom again
There's no destruction, no trace of misery
My soul desires to take refuge at the feet of that completeness

Translation by Ratna Dey.

172 Georg Hegel (1770–1831), in his Preface to *Phenomenology of Mind* (*Phänomenologie des Geistes*), published in 1807.

173 Reference to this editorial can be found in *In the Sign of the Golden Wheel*, *Complete Works*, vol. 22, pp. 310–1.

174 Ceylon became an independent republic on 4 February 1948.

175 Māra here represents the lower levels of conditioned existence and Brahmā the highest levels. Nothing in conditioned existence can prevent the rolling of the wheel of the Dharma. Sangharakshita wrote a poem on this theme in 1947, 'The Wheel of Dharma' which proved particularly popular and was published in all the English-language Buddhist journals of the East (see *Complete Works*, vol. 25, p. 169).

176 This was a 24-page booklet: Srimad Acharya Swami Neminath Maharaj, *Is the Republic of India Secular?*, D. L. Bardiya, Calcutta 1956. The foreword was written by Dr Naga Raja Sharma.

177 Ibid., p. 18.

178 Ibid., p. 4.

179 Ibid., p. 2.

180 Three influential Hindu philosophers: Śaṅkara (788–820), regarded as the foremost proponent of Advaita (non-dualist) Vedānta; Rāmānuja (1017–1137), leading proponent of Viśiṣṭādvaita (qualified non-dualism); and Madhvācārya (1238–1317), chief proponent of Advaita (dualist) philosophy.

181 The source of this is perhaps Spinoza's second letter to H. Oldenburg.

182 In Greek mythology, Procrustes was a robber who forced his victims to lie on an iron bed. If they were too short, he would stretch them to fit the bed, and if they were too tall, he would cut off their legs. In either case, they died. The 'Procrustean bed' has thus come to stand for arbitrarily, and perhaps cruelly, forcing someone or something to fit into an unnatural scheme or pattern.

183 According to tradition, Sumedha was a Brahmin who lived countless ages ago at the time of the Buddha Dīpaṅkara. When Sumedha lay down in the mud so that Dīpaṅkara could walk across him, Dīpaṅkara realized that Sumedha would be a Buddha in the future – and indeed he is said to have become the Buddha of our own era, Śākyamuni. For Sumedha's story, see *The Three Jewels*, *Complete Works*, vol. 2, pp. 17–18; also T. W. Rhys Davids (trans.), *Buddhist Birth-Stories*, George Routledge, London 1950, pp. 83–112.

184 This is from the poem 'A Psalm of Life' by the American poet Henry Wadsworth Longfellow, who apparently wrote it after the death of his first wife, when he was wondering how to make the best of his life. It was first published in 1838.

185 See p. 99 above.

186 Vijayadaśamī (the ten-day victory) is a Hindu festival celebrated under the lunar calendar to commemorate the victory of the god Rama over the demon Rāvaṇa. (The story is told in the great Sanskrit epic the *Rāmāyana* and is said to represent the triumph of the forces of good over the forces of evil.) On the day of that festival in c.261 BCE that greatest of Indian leaders, King Aśoka, converted to Buddhism, so that to the Buddhists of India the day is known as Ashok Vijayadaśamī. In 1956, as Sangharakshita says here, the festival fell on 14 October, the day on which Ambedkar and his followers became Buddhists.

187 Dhananjay Keer, *Dr Ambedkar: Life and Mission*, Popular Prakashan, Bombay 1981, p. 253.

188 This editorial also appears in 'The Mass Conversion and the Years After', *Complete Works*, vol. 10, pp. 93–4, and reference to it can be found

in *In the Sign of the Golden Wheel*, *Complete Works*, vol. 22, pp. 350–2.

189 'Buddhism in Tibet' by Lobsang Phuntsok Lhalungpa in Kenneth W. Morgan (ed.), *The Path of the Buddha: Buddhism Interpreted by Buddhists*, Ronald Press, New York 1956, p. 255.

190 Sangharakshita describes the Dalai Lama's visit to his residence in Kalimpong in *In The Sign of the Golden Wheel*, *Complete Works*, vol. 22, pp. 368–72.

191 Ibid., chapters 21 and 22, pp. 304ff.

192 See, for example, *Ambedkar and Buddhism*, *Complete Works*, vol. 9, chapter 7, pp. 120-35.

193 See *In the Sign of the Golden Wheel*, *Complete Works*, vol. 22, pp. 353–4, and *Dear Dinoo*, *Complete Works*, vol. 21, pp. 529–30.

194 See *In the Sign of the Golden Wheel*, *Complete Works*, vol. 22, pp. 379–80.

195 This editorial also appears in *Complete Works*, vol. 10, pp. 106–8, and reference to it can be found in *In the Sign of the Golden Wheel*, *Complete Works*, vol. 22, pp. 366–7. Sangharakshita himself played an important role in the continuation of Dr Ambedkar's work; see *Complete Works*, vols. 9 and 10.

196 The epic poem *The Light of Asia: the Great Renunciation* recounts the life of the Buddha and is based on the *Lalitavistara Sūtra*. It was written by Sir Edwin Arnold (1832–1904), an English poet and journalist, and first published in London in 1879.

197 Edward Conze, *Buddhism: Its Essence and Development*, Windhorse Publications, Birmingham 2001, p. 39.

198 This point was made by Sangharakshita himself in a talk given in the presence of (among others) the vice-president of India, Dr Radhakrishnan, who referred to Sangharakshita's remarks in the closing speech of the meeting (*Facing Mount Kanchenjunga*, *Complete Works*, vol. 21, p. 394).

199 The Centre = Central Government.

200 This hope of Indian Buddhists has yet to be fulfilled. India recognizes three national public holidays: Republic Day, Independence Day, and the birthday of Mahatma Gandhi. Other holidays are recognized by different regions and states according to local religious allegiances. Buddha Jayanti continues to be one of the Central Government's office holidays and is celebrated in about half of India's states. Although it is not an official holiday, it is notable that Christmas Day is observed nationally.

201 The *triśaraṇa* and *pañca śīla* are the Three Refuges and Five Precepts.

202 Today generally referred to as 'Dalits' or 'oppressed' classes. Those who have converted to Buddhism prefer to use the term Dalit Buddhist.

203 The threefold path – ethics, meditation, and wisdom – is the threefold division of the Noble Eightfold Path, sometimes (as here) called the threefold training. The Buddha is said to have expounded the threefold path many times during his last teaching tour; see, for example, the *Mahāparinibbāna Sutta*, *Dīgha Nikāya* 16 (ii.81): M. Walshe (trans.), *The Long Discourses of the Buddha*, Wisdom Publications, Boston 1995, p. 234; or T. W. and C. A. F. Rhys Davids (trans.), *Dialogues of the Buddha*, part 2, Pali Text Society, London 1971, pp. 85–6.

204 This was *The Third Eye: Autobiography of a Tibetan Lama*, by Lobsang Rampa (Cyril Henry Hoskins, 1910–1981). Hoskins believed himself to be 'hosting' the spirit of a Tibetan lama, Tuesday Lobsang Rampa (born on a Tuesday). The title of his book, published in England in 1956, refers to an operation which he claimed opened his third eye. He was unmasked by the British press in 1958 and went to live in Ireland. He went on to write many other books, including *Living with the Lama: 25 Years with Lobsang Rampa*, dictated to Rampa by his cat, Mrs Fifi Greywhiskers. Sangharakshita refers to the author as 'a plumber from Plympton with a vivid imagination and a racy style'; see *Precious Teachers*, *Complete Works*, vol. 22, p. 436.

205 Sangharakshita commented in 2010 that zoos can only be justified as the means to preserve a species in danger of extinction.

206 *Dhammapada* 131–2.

207 *Sutta-Nipāta* 1.3; see, for example, K. R. Norman (trans.), *The Rhinoceros Horn and Other Early Buddhist Poems*, Pali Text Society, London 1985, pp. 7–11.

208 Much of this restoration work has since been completed, but improvised shops and stalls still clutter the approach to the Maha Bodhi temple.

209 There have been wars in which Buddhists have fought, for example the civil war in Sri Lanka, in which the predominantly Buddhist Sinhalese fought against Hindu and Christian Tamils. This was, however, primarily politically rather than religiously motivated. There is nothing in Buddhism that corresponds to the Islamic notion of *jihad* or the Christian notion of a Crusade. The Dalai Lama, temporal and spiritual leader of Tibet, has shown an unprecedented stance in refusing to condone violence to end the occupation of Tibet by the Chinese.

210 Some of these themes were discussed in the Vaiśākha 1954 edition of the *Maha Bodhi* in articles by Lama Govinda and Marco Pallis (see *In the Sign of the Golden Wheel*, *Complete Works*, vol. 22, pp. 124–5). Sangharakshita takes them up in *The Religion of Art*, *Complete Works*, vol. 26, pp. 89ff.

211 'Meditation on a Flame', a poem written the same year, appears in *Complete Works*, vol. 25, p. 291.

212 'In Praise of Water', another poem of 1958, appears in *Complete Works*, vol. 25, p. 289.

213 *Dhammapada* 354.

214 In the sixty years since this editorial was first published (writing this note in 2022) there has been a huge increase in *dharmadūta* activity, bringing the Dharma to Europe, the Americas, and Australasia. Nevertheless, even in these places there is still an enormous amount of work that needs to be done, and the situations in Africa and the Muslim Middle East have hardly changed.

215 Venerable U Chandramani (1876–1972) was a Burmese *bhikkhu* based from 1904 at Kusinara. He campaigned for the restoration of Buddhist viharas and stupas not only there but in Sarnath, Lumbini, and other Buddhist holy sites. It was at Kusinara, in May 1949, that he conferred on Sangharakshita *sāmaṇera* or novice ordination (see *The Rainbow Road from Tooting Broadway to Kalimpong*, *Complete Works*, vol. 20, pp. 408–10). At a meeting in December 1955 (possibly early January 1956) Dr Ambedkar asked Sangharakshita if he would administer the Refuges and Precepts at the forthcoming conversion ceremony. Sangharakshita suggested that he ask U Chandramani instead. As the seniormost *bhikkhu* then in India, the Buddhist world might take the conversions more seriously. See 'Remembering Ambedkar', *Complete Works*, vol. 10, p. 7.

216 From John Milton's 1671 drama, *Samson Agonistes*, verse 986.

217 Today on the Diksha Bhumi there is a magnificent stupa that can accommodate more than 5,000 people. Building began in 1978 and the monument was finally completed in 2001. The site includes a Buddhist vihara and a bodhi tree as well as Buddha *rūpas*. The agricultural college is sited at Akola.

218 Early Hindu and Buddhist texts respectively.

219 In *Precious Teachers* (*Complete Works*, vol. 22, p. 459), Sangharakshita writes: 'Ascertaining of key words and their meanings was one of the things I had tried to do in *A Survey of Buddhism*,

published in 1957.' *A Survey of Buddhism* is now included in *Complete Works*, vol. 1.

220 'And what should they know of England who only England know?' is from the first stanza of Rudyard Kipling's 1891 poem *The English Flag*.

221 The Buddhist Publication Society came into being in Kandy, Ceylon on New Year's Day 1958. It was initially run by Ven. Nyanaponika, Mr Karunaratna, a lawyer, and Mr Abeyasekera, a retired teacher. More than sixty years later the BPS continues to publish tracts and books and distributes, free of charge, about a hundred copies of each new major publication to Buddhist centres, viharas, and libraries around the world. It also sends a substantial portion of its 'Wheel' publications to various centres for free distribution. In 1964 it published Sangharakshita's biographical sketch of Anagarika Dharmapala, which had first appeared in the Maha Bodhi Society's *Diamond Jubilee Souvenir*, and is now included in this volume of the *Complete Works*, pp. 1ff.

222 Ven. Nyanaponika Mahathera (1901–1994), born in Germany and ordained as a *bhikkhu* in Ceylon in 1937, was editor-in-chief of the BPS until 1984 and its president until 1988. He wrote a number of books, the best known being *The Heart of Buddhist Meditation* (1954). Among his own disciples is the renowned translator, Bhikkhu Bodhi, who succeeded Ven. Nyanaponika as president of the BPS in 1988.

223 i.e. the Maha Bodhi Society.

224 Sangharakshita commented in 2012 that while there are Sinhalese communities in parts of Africa with their own *bhikkhus*, he was not aware that they undertook any work to spread the Dharma.

225
> From today I will wander
> from village to village,
> from town to town, paying
> my respects to the Fully
> Enlightened One and to his
> perfect teaching!

Āḷavaka Sutta, *Sutta-Nipāta* 1.10, verse 12, trans. H. Saddhatissa, Curzon Press, London 1985, p. 20.

226 The Prime Minister of Ceylon, S. W. R. D. Bandaranaike (1899–1959) was shot by a Buddhist monk on 25 September 1959, an act that shook the nation and indeed the Buddhist world. In the months that followed two prime ministers were appointed (one in September directly following the assassination, the other in March 1960) but neither was able to hold the Government together.

227 Sirimavo Bandaranaike (1916–2000), widow of the assassinated leader, took up office as Ceylon's prime

minister on 21 July 1960. She remained in office until 1965, serving twice more in 1970–1977 and 1994–2000.

228 In the traditional monastic Buddhist world men and women have not been regarded equally. In the Theravāda tradition, for instance, nuns are subordinate to monks. What is more fundamental, however, is that the Buddha affirmed that both men and women can practise the Dharma and gain Enlightenment, and did not hesitate to teach women as well as men. The order that Sangharakshita founded in 1968 has one ordination which is valid equally for men and women, who have the same opportunities and the same responsibilities.

229 Arthur Schopenhauer (1788–1860). *Die Welt als Wille und Vorstellung (The World as Will and Representation)* – his best-known work – was published in 1819. In the second volume he writes:

> If I wished to take the results of my philosophy as the standard of truth, I should have to concede to Buddhism pre-eminence over the other [religions].

The World as Will and Representation, Dover Publications, New York 1966, vol. ii, p. 169.

230 See p. 5.

231 Prime Minister Sirimavo Bandaranaike's government was successful in nationalizing the schools of Ceylon.

232 Sangharakshita had himself visited the Kanheri Caves in April 1949; see *The Rainbow Road from Tooting Broadway to Kalimpong*, *Complete Works*, vol. 20, pp. 381–2.

233 *Aṅgulimāla Sutta*, *Majjhima Nikāya* 86 (ii.97–105). Bhikkhu Ñāṇamoli and Bhikkhu Bodhi (trans.), *The Middle Length Discourses of the Buddha*, Wisdom Publications, Boston 1995, pp. 710–17; or I. B. Horner (trans.), *The Collection of the Middle Length Sayings*, vol. ii, Pali Text Society, Oxford 1994, pp. 284–92.

234 Sangharakshita himself, despite his protests, was enumerated in 1951 as 'a Hindu by religion and a Buddhist by caste'. See *Facing Mount Kanchenjunga*, *Complete Works*, vol. 21, pp. 168–9.

235 Eventually the *bhikkhus* won their case but only after considerable conflict.

236 To date (2022) there has been no effective action from the Government of Maharashtra on this matter.

237 Sangharakshita writes about the World Fellowship of Buddhists in *Moving Against the Stream*, *Complete Works*, vol. 23, pp. 158–62.

238 These words were written by Ben Jonson (1572–1637) about William Shakespeare, in his poem, *To the Memory of my Beloved, the Author*

Mr William Shakespeare: And What He Hath Left Us, published in the First Folio of Shakespeare's works, 1623.

239 The front cover of this issue announced itself as the 'Rabindranath Tagore Centenary Number'. It included several of Tagore's poems, as well as articles on themes such as 'Buddha and Tagore', 'Rabindranath on Buddhism' and Devapriya Valisinha's 'Reminiscences of Gurudeva Tagore'. A photograph of the poet in his old age faced the title page.

240 See note 98.

241 Some influence of the poetry of Tagore may be discerned in Sangharakshita's poem, 'The Veil of Stars' whose stanzas, like those of Tagore's *Stray Birds*, are variations on the Japanese haiku. He describes the effect on him of *Stray Birds* in his memoir *Facing Mount Kanchenjunga* (*Complete Works*, vol. 21, p. 94). Although he arrived in India too late to meet the poet, he came to know Tagore's daughter-in-law, Mrs Pratima Devi Tagore, as she was known, who was a neighbour in Kalimpong. (Ibid., pp. 153–6.) He also made several visits to Santiniketan, the educational and cultural establishment founded by Tagore in West Bengal. There he met eminent artists and intellectuals from the East and the West and gave some lectures himself. (See *In the Sign of the Golden Wheel*, *Complete Works*, vol. 22, chapter 4 and pp. 320–2.)

242 The Mahabharata War is described in the *Mahabharata*, an ancient Indian Sanskrit epic, the oldest strands of which are thought to date back to c.400 BCE.

243 *Yajñas* are sacrifices in general; *homas* are fire sacrifices.

244 For example, the *Brahmajāla Sutta*, *Dīgha Nikāya* 1 (i.10–12) gives a long list of fortunetelling 'low arts' from which the Buddha 'holds aloof'. See M. Walshe (trans.), *The Long Discourses of the Buddha*, Wisdom Publications, Boston 1995, pp. 71–3; or T. W. Rhys Davids (trans.), *Dialogues of the Buddha*, part 1, Pali Text Society, London 1973, pp. 16–26.

245 *Dhammapada* 190–2.

246 'Militant materialism': i.e. communism in countries such as China and North Korea. 'Dogmatic spiritualism': Christianity in countries such as Vietnam and South Korea.

247 *Pravrajya* (*pabbajjā* in Pāli) is ordination as a novice. *Upasampadā* (the same spelling in Pāli) is full or higher ordination as a *bhikṣu* (Pāli *bhikkhu*).

248 This took place on 20 October 1962 when Chinese troops crossed the north-eastern border of India with Tibet,

eventually attacking along 550 miles. Although Kalimpong, where Sangharakshita was resident, lay some 500 miles away, the effects of the invasion were soon felt, as he relates in *Precious Teachers* (*Complete Works*, vol. 22), chapter 14, pp. 208–18. Years after writing this editorial, Sangharakshita discovered that the 1913 agreement to the McMahon Line as defining the boundary between north-eastern India and Tibet had never been ratified by the Chinese, who regarded the territory south of the line as theirs and viewed the northerly position of the McMahon Line as an expression of British aggression (see *Precious Teachers*, *Complete Works*, vol. 22, pp. 549–50).

249 The term 'fellow travellers' was used in the United States during the 1940s and 1950s to refer to someone who was sympathetic to Communism or to Communist states, but who was not a card-carrying member of a Communist party. In his memoirs Sangharakshita describes an event in which he was almost tricked into supporting a political meeting at which resolutions condemning America were to be proposed (*In the Sign of the Golden Wheel*, *Complete Works*, vol. 22, pp. 211–2).

250 Mao Tse-tung (Mao Zedong) (1893–1976), founding father of the People's Republic of China, was its leader from its inception in 1949 until his death.

251 'Unlike many of my generation I had no sympathy with Communism…' In his memoirs Sangharakshita explains his attitude, and also what 'China' meant to him: not 'Mao Zedong and the *Little Red Book*'. See *In the Sign of the Golden Wheel, Complete Works*, vol. 22, pp. 209–11.

252 *World Buddhism*, January 1963, p. 17.

253 The first Vietnamese monk to self-immolate in protest at the persecution of Buddhists by the Vietnamese Government led by Ngô Đình Diệm was Thích Quảng Đức. It took place on 11 June 1963 at a busy crossroads in Saigon. He was 66 years old. David Halberstam, a New York Times journalist who witnessed the event, wrote in *The Making of a Quagmire* (Random House, New York 1965): 'As he burned he never moved a muscle, never uttered a sound, his outward composure in sharp contrast to the wailing people around him.' Sangharakshita writes about the events in Vietnam in *Precious Teachers*, *Complete Works*, vol. 22, pp. 516–17, and in *From Genesis to the Diamond Sutra*, *Complete Works*, vol. 13, p. 560.

254 This was President John F. Kennedy.

255 On 2 November, following a military *coup*, Ngô Đình Diệm, the president of South Vietnam, was executed. Less than two years later, following an uprising of the communist Viet Cong, the Vietnamese war erupted between north and south, and it continued for a whole decade.

256 Ven. Taixu, 1890–1947, monk and philosopher, worked to reform the training of monks, for the promotion of social welfare and to create national and international Buddhist organizations.

257 Sangharakshita gives an account of this occasion in *Facing Mount Kanchenjunga* (*Complete Works*, vol. 21, chapter 19).

FURTHER *MAHA BODHI* CONTRIBUTIONS

258 Prime Minister S. W. R. D. Bandaranaike appointed a Buddha Sāsana Commission in 1957 to investigate the state of Buddhism in the country in view of the fact that Christian missionaries were running so many schools. A report was published in 1959.

259 *Nikāya* here refers to the different monastic orders of Theravāda Buddhism. The differences between them were not doctrinal but tended to be about etiquette, such as what sort of umbrella might be carried or over which shoulder the robe should be worn.

260 A *thera* is a *bhikkhu* who has observed ten rainy-season retreats.

261 An *upāsaka* is a layman, feminine: *upāsikā*. As Sangharakshita explains, he is here addressing all Buddhist lay people, both men and women.

262 *Uposatha* are days of observance corresponding to the new and full moon (and sometimes other days in between). For the laity in Theravādin countries, the observance includes attendance at the local temple or vihara for Dharma talks and meditation, making offerings, performing devotional acts, and so on.

MAHA BODHI BOOK REVIEWS

263 *Vasala Sutta, Sutta-Nipāta* 1.7.

264 G. F. Allen was an Englishman who 'took the Buddhist robe'. He became known as Bhikkhu Y Siri Nyana and was an occasional contributor to the *Maha Bodhi*. Allen was the 'Sincere European Buddhist' whose letter to the editor is the subject of Himavantavasi's column in February 1954 (see p. 129 above). Sangharakshita came to meet him only in the 1960s when visiting a mutual friend, Eva Faulkner, in Stroud, Gloucestershire.

265 The *Maha Bodhi*, May 1955.

266 Kenneth W. Morgan (1908–2011). As a student at the

Harvard Divinity School in the 1930s, he came into contact with the Ramakrishna Mission and went on to spend a year at a Ramakrishna ashram in India, developing an interest in world religions. After returning to the United States he taught at Colgate University and founded the Center for the Study of World Religions at Harvard. Sangharakshita met him in Kalimpong when Morgan was visiting Lobsang Phuntsok Lhalungpa to discuss Lhalungpa's contribution to *The Path of the Buddha*. This chapter, contributed under Lhalungpa's name, was in fact the result of a collaboration with Dhardo Rimpoche, who provided the basic teaching, and Sangharakshita, who helped formulate it into English (see *In the Sign of the Golden Wheel*, *Complete Works*, vol. 22, p. 265.) In his preface, Morgan refers to them as 'two scholarly lamas who [shared Lhalungpa's] concern for an accurate presentation of Tibetan Buddhism'.

267 Laurence Waddell was an early writer on Tibetan Buddhism who, according to Sangharakshita, was very well informed but didn't have much understanding. See 'Tibetan Buddhism', *Complete Works*, vol. 13, p. 68.

268 *Bodhicaryāvatāra* 3.7–9, 3.18–19.

269 P. V. Bapat, MA, AM, PhD (Harvard), was Professor of Ancient Indian Culture, Pāli, and Buddhism at Poona University and Fergusson College, Poona. In 1957, as a follow-up to the government-sponsored celebrations of 2,500 years of Buddhism, a Chair of Buddhist Studies was created at the University of Delhi. P. V. Bapat was appointed to the chair. Sangharakshita met him several times in Bombay. *2500 Years of Buddhism* includes a lengthy article by Sangharakshita: 'Buddhism in the Modern World: Cultural and Political Implications'; see 'A Sense of Direction', *Complete Works*, vol. 7, pp. 433–53.

270 Martin Wickramasinghe (1890–1976) was a Sri Lankan novelist whose books have been translated into a number of languages. His *Viragaya*, published in 1956, is sometimes considered the greatest novel in the Sinhalese language. *Bava Taranaya* (1973) was his own interpretation of the life of the Buddha.

271 J. N. and P. N. Ganhar were brothers. J. N. Ganhar also published books on the folk tales of Kashmir and the wildlife of Ladakh.

272 Edward Conze (1904–1979) was an Anglo-German scholar and academic who mastered some fourteen languages including Sanskrit. He eventually took up the study

and practice of Buddhism – one of the first Western scholars to actually practise the Dharma. In his preface to *Selected Sayings from the Perfection of Wisdom*, Conze notes that

> in 1952, in the last issue of *Stepping-Stones*, the Bhikshu Sangharakshita, of Kalimpong, began to print this collection of sayings from the Prajñāpāramitā. Funds soon gave out, and only the first instalment appeared.

(See also *Facing Mount Kanchenjunga*, *Complete Works*, vol. 21, pp. 315–6.) The association of the two men continued, with Conze submitting articles to the *Maha Bodhi*. They came to meet only after Sangharakshita's return to England in 1964; see *Moving Against the Stream*, *Complete Works*, vol. 23, pp. 55–6, where Sangharakshita expresses his appreciation of Conze and his contribution to Buddhism.

273 The copy of the *Diamond Sūtra* (in Chinese) held by the British Library is the world's earliest dated, printed book, produced on 11 May 868.

274 Alan Wilson Watts (1915–1973) joined the London Buddhist Lodge founded by Christmas Humphreys when he was only 16. He later moved to New York to receive Zen training but went on to become an Episcopal priest. He left the priesthood after five years. He joined the faculty of the American Academy of Asian Studies in California and wrote and lectured extensively. His highly popular *The Way of Zen* introduced a whole generation to Zen Buddhism. Sangharakshita met Watts in London when Christmas Humphreys issued Sangharakshita with an invitation to the Dorchester Hotel for lunch with Watts and his wife and Watts' 90-year-old father. Sangharakshita found the hale and hearty father to be in rather better shape than the son.

275 Lama Anagarika Govinda (1898–1985) was a Buddhist scholar, poet, and painter who for many years was resident in India. He founded the Arya Maitreya Mandala whose activities extended to Europe. There the AMM became one of the first Buddhist movements in the West. He was a close friend of Sangharakshita, who recalled their meetings and discussions in his memoirs (*Facing Mount Kanchenjunga, In the Sign of the Golden Wheel*, and *Moving Against the Stream*). Lama Govinda contributed many articles to the *Maha Bodhi*. Some of those writings were subsequently included in his books, including his well-known *Creative Meditation and Multi-*

Dimensional Consciousness. Lama Govinda's last years were spent in the Bay Area of San Francisco where he was associated with the San Francisco Zen Center founded by Shunryu Suzuki in 1962.

276 For Christmas Humphreys see note 132.

277 Hans-Ulrich Rieker (1920–1979). In a preface to Rieker's *The Secret of Meditation*, published in 1955, Rieker is described by the publisher's 'literary adviser' as 'a Buddhist monk of Swiss origin'. Elsewhere he is described as German. In his early adult life he worked as an actor. His interest in Buddhism led him to being ordained as a monk at the Berlin Buddhist Temple in 1950. He later trained in yoga and wrote and taught extensively on both yoga and Buddhism. In 1952 he received ordination from Lama Anagarika Govinda into the lama's newly-founded Arya Maitreya Mandala, and he went on to set up a western wing of the Order based in Berlin. Govinda contributed a preface to *Beggar Among the Dead*. Although Rieker visited Kalimpong, as recounted in the book, Sangharakshita does not recall having met him.

278 David Marshall Lang (1924–1991) was Professor of Caucasian Studies at the University of London. He was one of the most productive of British scholars specializing in Georgian, Armenian, and ancient Bulgarian history.

279 For more on the Barlaam and Josaphat legend see Sangharakshita's *From Genesis to the Diamond Sūtra*, *Complete Works*, vol. 13, pp. 653–64.

280 For a longer version of the story of Jivaka (as he was called), see *In the Sign of the Golden Wheel*, *Complete Works*, vol. 22, pp. 434–45.

281 The Namgyal Institute of Tibetology was founded by the king of Sikkim, Sir Tashi Namgyal (1893–1963), and opened in October 1958. Its aim was to sponsor and promote research on the religion, history, language, art, and culture of the Tibetan cultural area (including the then Indian Protectorate of Sikkim). Today the NIT's library holds one of the largest collections of Tibetan works in the world outside Tibet and a museum of Tibetan iconography and religious art. Sangharakshita visited Gangtok as a friend and Buddhist adviser to the Maharajkumar, Polden Thondup Namgyal, the son of Sir Tashi (see *In the Sign of the Golden Wheel*, *Complete Works*, vol. 22, chapter 16, pp. 240–9).

ALTERNATIVE TRADITIONS

282 For further elucidation see *What is the Sangha?*, *Complete*

Works, vol. 3, pp. 434–44 and pp. 467–73.

283 See, for example, *The Endlessly Fascinating Cry*, *Complete Works*, vol. 4, pp. 314 & 615.

284 *Dhammapada* 290.

285 The 'positive' *nidānas* are described in *What is the Dharma?*, *Complete Works*, vol. 3, chapter 7, pp. 258–79.

286 *Dhammapada* 200.

287 *Mahāparinibbāna Sutta*, *Dīgha Nikāya* 16 (ii.142); M. Walshe (trans.), *The Long Discourses of the Buddha*, Wisdom Publications, Boston 1995, p. 264; or T. W. and C. A. F. Rhys Davids (trans.), *Dialogues of the Buddha*, part 2, Pali Text Society, London 1971, p. 155.

288 Vinaya Piṭaka i.21 (*Mahāvagga* 1.11). See I. B. Horner (trans.) *The Book of the Discipline*, part 4, Pali Text Society, Oxford 1996, p. 28.

289 Gerald Scarfe (b. 1936) is a political cartoonist known for his grotesque caricatures of public figures in *Private Eye, Punch*, and several daily newspapers, especially during the 1960s and 1970s.

290 See section 56 of Alfred, Lord Tennyson's poem *In Memoriam A.H.H.*, completed in 1849, a requiem poem for his friend, Arthur Haley Hallam:

> Tho' Nature, red in tooth
> and claw
> With ravine, shriek'd against
> his creed.

291 William Godwin (1756–1836) was an English writer and philosopher said to have begun a trend of thought sometimes called 'philosophical anarchism'. His views on universal benevolence, which were later much criticized by Thomas Malthus and others, are set out in Book Two of his *Enquiry Concerning Political Justice*, which rapidly went through three editions, each much revised, the third being published in 1798.

292 *Saṃyutta Nikāya* i.122; see Bhikkhu Bodhi (trans.), *The Connected Discourses of the Buddha*, Wisdom Publications, Boston 2000, pp. 214–5; or C. A. F. Rhys Davids (trans.), *The Book of the Kindred Sayings*, part 1, Pali Text Society, London 1979, pp. 151–2.

293 This episode is recounted in chapter 22 or 23 of the *Saddharma Puṇḍarīka Sūtra* (*White Lotus Sūtra*) – different translations have slightly varying chapter arrangements. See, for example, Bunnō Katō and W. E. Soothill (trans.), *The Threefold Lotus Sutra*, Kosei Publishing, Tokyo 1975, p. 307, in which Sarvasattvapriyadarśana is translated 'the Bodhisattva Loveliness'.

294 But see *The Ten Pillars of Buddhism*, *Complete Works*, vol. 2, pp. 357–63.

295 These are all quotations from Percy Bysshe Shelley's essay, *A Defence of Poetry* (1821).

296 See Vināya Piṭaka i.21 (*Mahāvagga* 1.11), in I. B. Horner (trans.), *The Book of the Discipline*, part 4, Pali Text Society, Oxford 1996, p. 28.

297 This was Ananda Kentish Muthu Coomaraswamy (1877–1947). According to his biographer,

> A pioneer in the study of Indian art, the name of Coomaraswamy conjures up in our mind a world of aesthetics, religion and culture. The most versatile mind of his generation, Coomaraswamy was brilliantly polymath and his work, straddling aesthetics and literary criticism, reflects the deepest intuitions of the perennial tradition derived from Indian and European sources. His life was given to interpreting the East to the West, and often the West to itself.

Moni Bagchee, *Ananda Coomaraswamy*, Bharata Manisha, Varanasi 1960, p. xv. Coomaraswamy published his collection of essays entitled *The Bugbear of Literacy* in 1948.

298 See also 'Wisdom Before Words', *Complete Works*, vol. 10, p. 436.

299 For these examples of *tiracchāna-kathā* (low talk), see *Saṃyutta Nikāya* v.419–20 (56.10); see Bhikkhu Bodhi (trans.), *The Connected Discourses of the Buddha*, Wisdom Publications, Boston 2000, p. 1843; or F. L. Woodward (trans.), *The Book of the Kindred Sayings*, vol. v, Pali Text Society, London 1979, pp. 355–6.

300 See, for example, *Itivuttaka* 100 in John D. Ireland (trans.), *The Udāna and the Itivuttaka*, Buddhist Publication Society, Kandy 2007, p. 226.

301 Mrs Beeton was the author of a famous Victorian cookery book, so Sangharakshita is evidently decrying the idea that Zen could have been the product of the mixing together of ingredients as some people have asserted.

302 In *The Times*, 29 July 1878, the politician Benjamin Disraeli (then the prime minister of the UK) wrote of his fellow politician William Gladstone (then leader of the opposition) that he was 'a sophistical rhetorician, inebriated with the exuberance of his own verbosity'.

303 Aśvaghoṣa, *The Awakening of Faith in the Mahāyāna*. This translation is taken from Dwight Goddard (ed.), *A Buddhist Bible*, Beacon Press, Boston 1966, p. 363.

304 These are the thirty-seven *bodhipakṣya-dharmas* or 'principles conducive to

Enlightenment'. See *A Survey of Buddhism*, *Complete Works*, vol. 1, p. 423; and for a canonical reference see note 45.

305 Sangharakshita conducted a seminar on *The Precious Garland* which was published as two books, *Living Ethically* and *Living Wisely*; see *Complete Works*, vol. 17, pp. 149ff and pp. 319ff respectively.

306 Sangharakshita himself conducted a study seminar on *Mind in Buddhist Psychology*, which appeared in edited form as *Know Your Mind*; see *Complete Works*, vol. 17, pp. 429ff.

307 This expression is best known from the *Maṅgala Sutta* (*Sutta-Nipāta* 2.4) and the *Dhammacakkappavattana Sutta* (*Dīgha Nikāya* 16).

308 See *Tsongkhapa's Three Chief Paths* in *Complete Works*, vol. 17, pp. 426–8.

309 From William Wordsworth's 1815 poem 'Character of the Happy Warrior'.

310 This is one of the many notes Blake wrote in the margin of a copy of the *Works of Sir Joshua Reynolds* (now in the possession of the British Library).

311 Blake died in his rooms at Fountain Court, the Strand, London, on 12 August 1827. These words were written by George Richmond, who was a member of The Ancients, a group of Blake's followers, in a letter to the artist Samuel Palmer.

312
> Once I saw a Devil in a flame of fire, who arose before an Angel that sat on a cloud, and the Devil utter'd these words: 'The worship of God is: Honouring his gifts in other men, each according to his genius, and loving the greatest men best: those who envy or calumniate great men hate God; for there is no other God.'

These are the opening words of Blake's 1790 work *The Marriage of Heaven and Hell.*

313 For an explanation of the 'turning about', the *parāvṛtti*, see Sangharakshita, *The Meaning of Conversion in Buddhism*, chapter 4 (*Complete Works*, vol. 2, pp. 275–85).

314 For the yoga of the long *hūṃ*, see W. Y. Evans-Wentz (ed.), *Tibetan Yoga and Secret Doctrines*, Oxford University Press, London 1958, book VI, pp. 334–41.

315 These words are from a letter the 20-year-old Blake wrote in response to one from the Reverend John Trusler, who had commissioned a work from Blake but had written to him to criticize it.

316 These are lines 146 and 147 of Blake's long poem 'The Everlasting Gospel', found in fragmentary form after his death.

317 These are the first two lines of 'The Everlasting Gospel'.

318 For his comment on Blake's use of 'religion' as a smear word, see Samuel Foster Damon, *A Blake Dictionary: the Ideas and Symbols of William Blake*, Brown University Press, Providence 1965, p. 345. We haven't been able to trace the reference to 'decayed poetry'.

A MOSELEY MISCELLANY

319 Richard F. Gombrich, *How Buddhism Began*, Athlone Press 1996, pp. 48–9.

320 This doctrine arose in the context of Chinese Buddhism. The *Lotus Sūtra* mentions the 'counterfeit' Dharma (see Bunnō Katō and W. E. Soothill (trans.), *The Threefold Lotus Sūtra*, Kosei Publishing, Tokyo, 1975, p. 82 and p. 135) and Sangharakshita discusses it in his commentary on that text; see *The Drama of Cosmic Enlightenment*, *Complete Works*, vol. 16, pp. 82–3.

321 The question 'Why is there something rather than nothing?' has caused philosophers of all times, from Plato to Wittgenstein, to wonder. The Jewish Dutch philosopher Baruch Spinoza (1632–1677) wrote much about substance (for example in his *Ethics*) but the question 'Why is there something rather than nothing?' is more often associated with his contemporary, the German mathematician and philosopher Gottfried Wilhelm Leibniz (1646–1716).

322 Thrangu Rinpoche, *King of Samādhi*, Rangjung Yeshe Publications, Boulder Colorado 1994, p. 89. According to the same author, ibid., p. 47, children die of starvation in Africa due to their lack of merit.

323 *Saṃyutta Nikāya* iv.230 (36.21) in F. L. Woodward (trans.), *The Book of the Kindred Sayings*, Pali Text Society, London 1980, part 4, p. 155; see also Bhikkhu Bodhi (trans.), *The Connected Discourses of the Buddha*, Wisdom Publications, Boston 2000, p. 1279.

324 *Saṃyutta Nikāya* v.2. See F. L. Woodward (trans.), *The Book of the Kindred Sayings*, part 5, Pali Text Society, London 1979, p. 2. See also Bhikkhu Bodhi (trans.), *The Connected Discourses of the Buddha*, Wisdom Publications, Boston 2000, pp. 1524–5.

325 *Udāna* 8.3, trans. Richard F. Gombrich in *How Buddhism Began*, Athlone Press, London 1996, p. 42.

326 Peter Morris, *Power: a Philosophical Analysis*, Manchester University Press 1987, p. 4.

327 *Aṅguttara Nikāya*, iv.448. For this translation, see F. L. Woodward (trans.), *The Book of the Gradual Sayings*, vol. iv, Pali Text Society, Oxford 1995, p. 295; see also Bhikkhu

Bodhi (trans.), *The Numerical Discourses of the Buddha*, Wisdom Publications, Boston 2012, p. 1318.

328 Richard F. Gombrich in *How Buddhism Began*, Athlone Press, London 1996, p. 96 et seq.

329 *Dhammapada*, chapter 17.

330 In *Émile, or On Education* (1762) the French philosopher Jean-Jacques Rousseau not only rejects the doctrine of original sin, but maintains that children are innately innocent, only becoming corrupted through experience of the world. Forty years later, the English poet William Wordsworth echoed this view in his 'Ode: Intimations of Immortality': 'Heaven lies about us in our infancy!'

331 The English biologist Thomas Henry Huxley coined the word 'agnostic' in 1869, and said,

> It simply means that a man shall not say he knows or believes that which he has no scientific grounds for professing to know or believe.

332 Martin Luther (1483–1546) was an Augustinian monk, then priest, scholar, and chief figure of the German reformation, who challenged the Pope and Roman Catholic orthodoxy on their practice of selling so-called 'indulgences' and other corrupt practices. An oft-quoted statement is:

> Reason is a whore, the greatest enemy that faith has; it never comes to the aid of spiritual things, but more frequently than not struggles against the divine Word, treating with contempt all that emanates from God.

It isn't clear where this comes from, but it seems to be extracted from Luther's last sermon at Wittenberg, given on 17 January 1546.

333 For a colourful description of the ceremony see Thomas Carlyle, *The French Revolution*, Chapman and Hall 1871, vol. iii, pp. 193–4.

334 *Aggivacchagotta Sutta, Majjhima Nikāya* 72 (i.487). See Bhikkhu Ñāṇamoli and Bhikkhu Bodhi (trans.), *The Middle Length Discourses of the Buddha*, Wisdom Publications, Boston 1995, p. 593; or I. B. Horner (trans.), *The Collection of the Middle Length Sayings*, vol. ii, Pali Text Society, Oxford 1994, p. 165.

335 The story of how the Buddha was inclined not to teach but was persuaded by Brahmā Sahampati is told at Vinaya Piṭaka i.4–7 (*Mahāvagga* 1.4–6). See I. B. Horner (trans.), *The Book of the Discipline*, part 4, Pali Text Society, Oxford 1996, pp. 6–10. See also *Ariyapariyesanā Sutta, Majjhima Nikāya* 26 (i.167–170): Bhikkhu Ñāṇamoli and Bhikkhu Bodhi (trans.), *The*

Middle Length Discourses of the Buddha, Wisdom Publications, Boston 1995, pp. 260–2; or I. B. Horner (trans.), *The Collection of the Middle Length Sayings*, vol. i, Pali Text Society, London 1976, pp. 211–13.

336 *Saṃyutta Nikāya* v.421. This translation is from Edward J. Thomas (trans.), *Early Buddhist Scriptures*, Kegan Paul, Trench, and Trubner, 1935, p. 30. See also Bhikkhu Bodhi (trans.), *The Connected Discourses of the Buddha*, Wisdom Publications, Boston 2000, p. 1844; or F. L. Woodward (trans.), *The Book of the Kindred Sayings*, vol. v, Pali Text Society, London 1979, p. 357.

337 This is a reference to that most essential Buddhist teaching, the Noble Eightfold Path. According to the Buddha, one begins by traversing the mundane eightfold path, starting with right view, which leads to the progressive development of the remaining seven stages: right resolve, right speech, right action, right livelihood, right effort, right awareness, and right *samādhi*. In the course of spiritual practice one gradually refines each area of one's life until transcendental insight is attained. It is then that one begins to tread the transcendental eightfold path, which is divided into the Path of Vision and the Path of Transformation. The Path of Vision corresponds to the arising of Perfect Vision, the transcendental counterpart of right view, while the Path of Transformation comprises the perfection of each of the other seven stages of the path – right resolve becomes Perfect Emotion, right speech becomes Perfect Speech, and so on. When all eight stages have been perfected, full Enlightenment is attained. See chapter 1 of Sangharakshita's *The Buddha's Noble Eightfold Path*, *Complete Works*, vol. 1, pp. 469ff.

338 *Ariyapariyesanā Sutta*, *Majjhima Nikāya* 26 (i.173); see Bhikkhu Ñāṇamoli and Bhikkhu Bodhi (trans.), *The Middle Length Discourses of the Buddha*, Wisdom Publications, Boston 1995, p. 264–5; or I. B. Horner (trans.), *The Collection of the Middle Length Sayings*, vol. i, Pali Text Society, London 1976, pp. 216–7.

339 *Udāna* 5.5 in Peter Masefield (trans.), *The Udāna,* Pali Text Society, 1994, p. 97.

340 The story of the conversion of Anāthapiṇḍika is told at Vinaya Piṭaka ii.154 (*Cullavagga* 6.4). See I. B. Horner (trans.), *The Book of the Discipline*, part 5, Pali Text Society, London 1975, p. 216. This translation is from F. L. Woodward (trans.), *Some Sayings of the Buddha*, Buddhist Society,

London 1973, p. 96 (but with Woodward's 'Norm' changed to 'Dharma').

341 Geshe Wangyal, *The Door of Liberation*, Wisdom Publications, Boston 1995, p. 100.

342 Lewis Carroll, *Alice's Adventures in Wonderland* (1865), chapter 1, 'Down the Rabbit Hole'.

343 Norman O. Brown was an American professor of philosophy. *Love's Body*, published in 1966, has been described as a 'critique of contemporary culture that wove myth, religion, poetry and psychoanalysis together in collage-like effect'.

344 The quotation is from the forty-ninth stanza of the *Rubáiyát of Omar Khayyám*, translated by Edward Fitzgerald.

345 See, for example, *Aṅguttara Nikāya*, ii.135:

> Bhikkhus, there are these four kinds of persons found existing in the world. What four? One who understands quickly; one who understands through elaboration; one who needs to be guided; and one for whom the word is the maximum (*pada-paramo*).

Bhikkhu Bodhi (trans.), *The Numerical Discourses of the Buddha*, Wisdom Publications, Boston 2012, p. 515; see also F. L. Woodward (trans.), *The Book of the Gradual Sayings*, vol. ii, Pali Text Society, Oxford 1995, p. 138.

346 This is a reference to Shakespeare's *Henry V* (Act II, Scene iii), in which Mistress Quickly describes the death of Falstaff. Part of her speech read in the original folio, 'for his nose was as sharp as a pen, and a' table of greene fields'. This baffling statement was famously changed at the suggestion of the Shakespeare scholar Lewis Theobald (1688–1744) to 'for his nose was as sharp as a pen, and 'a [that is, he] babbled of green fields' – a suggestion considered so inspired that it evidently made Theobald's scholarly reputation.

347 See note 280.

APPENDIX 1

348 Vinaya Piṭaka i.21 (*Mahāvagga* 1.11), in I. B. Horner (trans.), *The Book of the Discipline*, part 4, Pali Text Society, Oxford 1996, p. 28.

349 'Vetulyan' refers to the Vetulyavāda of early Sinhalese Buddhism, regarded by orthodox Theravādins as synonymous with doctrinal error and moral depravity! For more about these attacks see *In the Sign of the Golden Wheel*, *Complete Works*, vol. 22, pp. 168–72.

350 Ibid., pp. 172–8.

351 The content of some of these articles is described in ibid., pp. 122–8.

APPENDIX 2

352 *Complete Works*, vol. 1.

353 For an account of this time, see 'The Mass Conversion and the Years After', *Complete Works*, vol. 10, pp. 95–105.

354 Edward Conze, *Buddhism: Its Essence and Development*, Windhorse Publications, Birmingham 2001, p. 16.

355 *Kevaddha Sutta*, *Dīgha Nikāya* 11 (i.214); M. Walshe (trans.), *The Long Discourses of the Buddha*, Wisdom Publications, Boston 1995, p. 176; or T. W. Rhys Davids (trans.), *Dialogues of the Buddha*, part 1, Pali Text Society, London 1973, p. 279.

356 This second part of the report is included not in this volume, but in 'The Mass Conversion and the Years After', *Complete Works*, vol. 10, pp. 115–84.

357 *Buddhism and Art* (under the title *The Meaning of Buddhism and the Value of Art*) is included in *The Religion of Art*, *Complete Works*, vol. 26, pp. 102–32. *Is Buddhism For Monks Only?* is included in 'Student in Benares', *Complete Works*, vol. 7, pp. 177–89.

358 *The Heritage of Buddhism* was subsequently published as *The Eternal Legacy*; see *Complete Works*, vol. 14, pp. 5–284. Presumably the autobiography was what later became the memoir *The Rainbow Road from Tooting Broadway to Kalimpong*, *Complete Works*, vol. 20.

359 For *The Meaning of Orthodoxy in Buddhism* and 'Ordination and Initiation in the Three Yānas' see *Complete Works*, vol. 7, pp. 471–84 and pp. 514–46. For 'Wanted: A New Type of Bhikkhu' and 'Wanted: A New Type of Upasaka', see pp. 327–35 above, in Further *Maha Bodhi* Contributions.

360 See *Complete Works*, vol. 17, pp. 421–8.

361 *Complete Works*, vol. 1.

362 See *Complete Works*, vol. 7, pp. 249–418 or pp. 249ff.

363 See note 356.

INDEX

A GUIDE TO THE COMPLETE WORKS OF SANGHARAKSHITA

Gathered together in these twenty-seven volumes are talks and stories, commentaries on the Buddhist scriptures, poems, memoirs, reviews, and other writings. The genres are many, and the subject matter covered is wide, but it all has – its whole purpose is to convey – that taste of freedom which the Buddha declared to be the hallmark of his Dharma. Another traditional description of the Buddha's Dharma is that it is *ehipassiko*, 'come and see'. Sangharakshita calls to us, his readers, to come and see how the Dharma can fundamentally change the way we see things, change the way we live for the better, and change the society we belong to, wherever in the world we live.

Sangharakshita's very first published piece, *The Unity of Buddhism* (found in volume 7 of this collection), appeared in 1944 when he was eighteen years old, and it introduced themes that continued to resound throughout his work: the basis of Buddhist ethics, the compassion of the bodhisattva, and the transcendental unity of Buddhism. Over the course of the following seven decades not only did numerous other works flow from his pen; he gave hundreds of talks (some now lost). In gathering all we could find of this vast output, we have sought to arrange it in a way that brings a sense of coherence, communicating something essential about Sangharakshita, his life and teaching. Recalling the three 'baskets' among which an early tradition divided the Buddha's teachings, we have divided Sangharakshita's creative output into six 'baskets' or groups: foundation texts; works originating in India; teachings originally given in the West; commentaries on the Buddhist scriptures; personal writings; and poetry, aphorisms, and works on the arts. The 27th volume, a concordance, brings together all the terms and themes of the whole collection. If you want to find a particular story or teaching, look at a traditional term from different points of view or in different contexts, or track down one of the thousands of canonical references to be found in these volumes, the concordance will be your guide.

1. FOUNDATION

What is the foundation of a Buddhist life? How do we understand and then follow the Buddha's path of Ethics, Meditation, and Wisdom? What is really meant by 'Going for Refuge to the Three Jewels', described by Sangharakshita as the essential act of a Buddhist life? And what is the Bodhisattva ideal, which he has called 'one of the sublimest ideals mankind has ever seen'? In the 'Foundation' group you will find teachings on all these themes. It includes the author's *magnum opus, A Survey of Buddhism*, a collection of teachings on *The Purpose and Practice of Buddhist Meditation*, and the anthology, *The Essential Sangharakshita*, an eminently helpful distillation of the entire corpus.

2. INDIA

From 1950 to 1964 Sangharakshita, based in Kalimpong in the eastern Himalayas, poured his energy into trying to revive Buddhism in the land of its birth and to revitalize and bring reform to the existing Asian Buddhist world. The articles and book reviews from this period are gathered in volumes 7 and 8, as well as his biographical sketch of the great Sinhalese Dharmaduta, Anagārika Dharmapala. In 1954 Sangharakshita took on the editing of the *Maha Bodhi*, a journal for which he wrote a monthly editorial, and which, under his editorship, published the work of many of the leading Buddhist writers of the time. It was also during these years in India that a vital connection was forged with Dr B. R. Ambedkar, renowned Indian statesman and leader of the Buddhist mass conversion of 1956. Sangharakshita became closely involved with the new Buddhists and, after Dr Ambedkar's untimely death, visited them regularly on extensive teaching tours.

From 1979, when an Indian wing of the Triratna Buddhist Community was founded (then known as TBMSG), Sangharakshita returned several times to undertake further teaching tours. The talks from these tours are collected in volumes 9 and 10 along with a unique work on Ambedkar and his life which draws out the significance of his conversion to Buddhism.

3. THE WEST

Sangharakshita founded the Triratna Buddhist Community (then called the Friends of the Western Buddhist Order) on 6 April 1967. On 7 April the following year he performed the first ordinations of men and women within the Triratna Buddhist Order (then the Western Buddhist Order). At that time Buddhism was not widely known in the West and for the following two decades or so he taught intensively, finding new ways to communicate the ancient truths of Buddhism, drawing on the whole Buddhist tradition to do so, as well as making connections with what was best in existing Western culture. Sometimes his sword flashed as he critiqued ideas and views inimical to the Dharma. It is these teachings and writings that are gathered together in this third group.

4. COMMENTARY

Throughout Sangharakshita's works are threaded references to the Buddhist canon of literature – Pāli, Mahāyāna, and Vajrayāna – from which he drew his inspiration. In the early days of the new movement he often taught by means of seminars in which, prompted by the questions of his students, he sought to pass on the inspiration and wisdom of the Buddhist tradition. Each seminar was based around a different text, the seminars were recorded and transcribed, and in due course many of the transcriptions were edited and turned into books, all carefully checked by Sangharakshita. The commentaries compiled in this way constitute the fourth group. In some ways this is the heart of the collection. Sangharakshita often told the story of how it was that, reading two *sūtras* at the age of sixteen or seventeen, he realized that he was a Buddhist, and he has never tired of showing others how they too could see and realize the value of the '*sūtra*-treasure'.

5. MEMOIRS

Who is Sangharakshita? What sort of life did he live? Whom did he meet? What did he feel? Why did he found a new Buddhist movement? In these volumes of memoirs and letters Sangharakshita shares with his readers much about himself and his life as he himself has experienced it, giving us a sense of its breadth and depth, humour and pathos.

6. POETRY, APHORISMS, AND THE ARTS

Sangharakshita describes reading *Paradise Lost* at the age of twelve as one of the greatest poetic experiences of his life. His realization of the value of the higher arts to spiritual development is one of his distinctive contributions to our understanding of what Buddhist life is, and he has expressed it in a number of essays and articles. Throughout his life he has written poetry which he says can be regarded as a kind of spiritual autobiography. It is here, perhaps, that we come closest to the heart of Sangharakshita. He has also written a few short stories and composed some startling aphorisms. Through book reviews he has engaged with the experiences, ideas, and opinions of modern writers. All these are collected in this sixth group.

In the preface to *A Survey of Buddhism* (volume 1 in this collection), Sangharakshita wrote of his approach to the Buddha's teachings:

> Why did the Buddha (or Nāgārjuna, or Buddhaghosa) teach this particular doctrine? What bearing does it have on the spiritual life? How does it help the individual Buddhist actually to follow the spiritual path?… I found myself asking such questions again and again, for only in this way, I found, could I make sense – spiritual sense – of Buddhism.

Although this collection contains so many words, they are all intent, directly or indirectly, on these same questions. And all these words are not in the end about their writer, but about his great subject, the Buddha and his teaching, and about you, the reader, for whose benefit they are solely intended. These pages are full of the reverence that Sangharakshita has always felt, which is expressed in an early poem, 'Taking Refuge in the Buddha', whose refrain is 'My place is at thy feet'. He has devoted his life to communicating the Buddha's Dharma in its depth and in its breadth, to men and women from all backgrounds and walks of life, from all countries, of all races, of all ages. These collected works are the fruit of that devotion.

We are very pleased to be able to include some previously unpublished work in this collection, but most of what appears in these volumes has been published before. We have made very few changes, though we have added extra notes where we thought they would be useful. We have had the pleasure of researching the notes in the Sangharakshita Library at 'Adhisthana', Triratna's centre in Herefordshire, UK, which houses his own collection of books. It has been of great value to be able to search among the very copies of the *suttas*, *sūtras* and commentaries that have provided the basis of his teachings over the last seventy years.

The publication of these volumes owes much to the work of transcribers, editors, indexers, designers, and publishers over many years – those who brought out the original editions of many of the works included here, and those who have contributed in all sorts of ways to this *Complete Works* project, including all those who contributed to funds given in celebration of Sangharakshita's ninetieth birthday in August 2015, and to a further outpouring of generosity after Sangharakshita's death in October 2018. All these donors have made the publication of this series possible, and we are very grateful. Many thanks to everyone who has helped; may the merit gained in our acting thus go to the alleviation of the suffering of all beings.

Vidyadevi and Kalyanaprabha
Editors

THE COMPLETE WORKS OF SANGHARAKSHITA

I FOUNDATION

VOLUME 1 A SURVEY OF BUDDHISM / THE BUDDHA'S NOBLE EIGHTFOLD PATH
A Survey of Buddhism
The Buddha's Noble Eightfold Path

2 THE THREE JEWELS I
The Three Jewels
The Meaning of Conversion in Buddhism
Going for Refuge
The Ten Pillars of Buddhism
The History of My Going for Refuge
My Relation to the Order
Extending the Hand of Fellowship
Forty-Three Years Ago
Was the Buddha a Bhikkhu?

3 THE THREE JEWELS II
Who is the Buddha?
What is the Dharma?
What is the Sangha?

4 THE BODHISATTVA IDEAL
The Bodhisattva Ideal
The Endlessly Fascinating Cry (seminar)
The Bodhisattva Principle

5 THE PURPOSE AND PRACTICE OF BUDDHIST MEDITATION
The Purpose and Practice of Buddhist Meditation

6 THE ESSENTIAL SANGHARAKSHITA
The Essential Sangharakshita

II INDIA

7 CROSSING THE STREAM: INDIA WRITINGS I
Early Writings 1944–1954
Crossing the Stream
A Sense of Direction

WINDHORSE PUBLICATIONS

Windhorse Publications is a Buddhist charitable company based in the UK. We produce books of high quality that are accessible and relevant to all those interested in Buddhism, at whatever level of interest and commitment. We are the main publisher of Sangharakshita, the founder of the Triratna Buddhist Order and Community. Our books draw on the whole range of the Buddhist tradition, including translations of traditional texts, commentaries, books that make links with contemporary culture and ways of life, biographies of Buddhists, and works on meditation.

To subscribe to the *Complete Works of Sangharakshita,* please go to: windhorsepublications.com/sangharakshita-complete-works/

THE TRIRATNA BUDDHIST COMMUNITY

Windhorse Publications is a part of the Triratna Buddhist Community, an international movement with centres in Europe, India, North and South America and Australasia. At these centres, members of the Triratna Buddhist Order offer classes in meditation and Buddhism. Activities of the Triratna Community also include retreat centres, residential spiritual communities, ethical Right Livelihood businesses, and the Karuna Trust, a UK fundraising charity that supports social welfare projects in the slums and villages of India.

Through these and other activities, Triratna is developing a unique approach to Buddhism, not simply as a philosophy and a set of techniques, but as a creatively directed way of life for all people living in the conditions of the modern world.

For more information please visit thebuddhistcentre.com

SANGHARAKSHITA.ORG

You can find out more about Sangharakshita's life, teachings, and the Buddhist movement he founded on his official website: sangharakshita.org